__THE OMAC PROJECT ◼

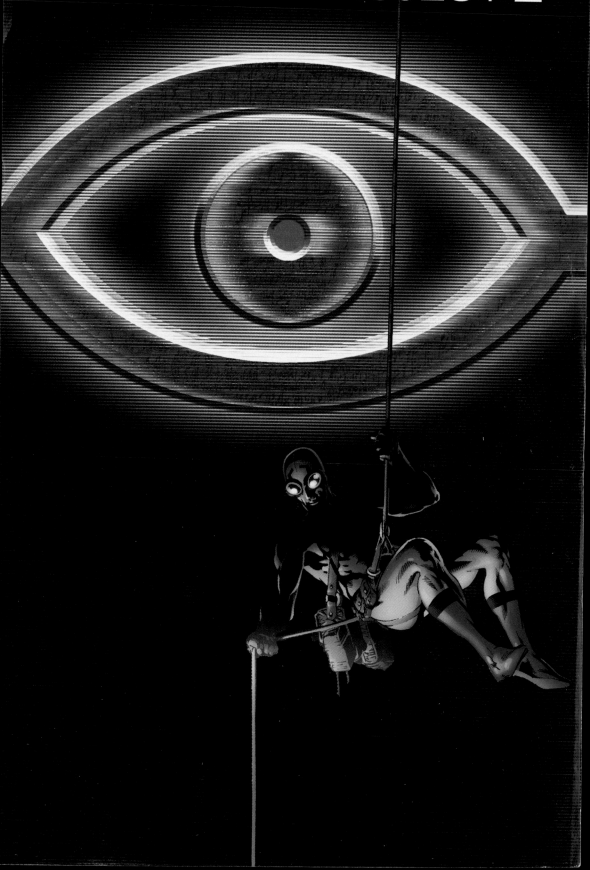

Dan DiDio VP-Executive Editor

Joan Hilty Ivan Cohen Editors-original series

Rachel Gluckstern Jann Jones Assistant Editors-original series

Robert Greenberger Senior Editor-collected edition

Robbin Brosterman Senior Art Director

Louis Prandi Art Director

Paul Levitz President & Publisher

Georg Brewer VP-Design & DC Direct Creative

Richard Bruning Senior VP-Creative Director

Patrick Caldon Senior VP-Finance & Operations

Chris Caramalis VP-Finance

Terri Cunningham VP-Managing Editor

Stephanie Fierman Senior VP-Sales & Marketing

Alison Gill VP-Manufacturing

Rich Johnson VP-Book Trade Sales

Hank Kanalz VP-General Manager, WildStorm

Lillian Laserson Senior VP & General Counsel

Jim Lee Editorial Director-WildStorm

Paula Lowitt Senior VP-Business & Legal Affairs

David McKillips VP-Advertising & Custom Publishing

John Nee VP-Business Development

Gregory Noveck Senior VP-Creative Affairs

Cheryl Rubin Senior VP-Brand Management

Jeff Trojan VP-Business Development, DC Direct

Bob Wayne VP-Sales

THE OMAC PROJECT

Published by DC Comics. Cover and compilation copyright
© 2005 DC Comics. All Rights Reserved.

Originally published in single magazine form in
COUNTDOWN TO INFINITE CRISIS, THE OMAC PROJECT 1-6,
WONDER WOMAN 219. Copyright © 2005 DC Comics.
All Rights Reserved. All characters, their distinctive
likenesses and related elements featured in this publication
are trademarks of DC Comics. The stories, characters and
incidents featured in this publication are entirely fictional.
DC Comics does not read or accept unsolicited submissions
of ideas, stories or artwork.

DC Comics, 1700 Broadway, New York, NY 10019
A Warner Bros. Entertainment Company
Printed in Canada. First Printing.
ISBN: 1-4012-0837-1
Cover art by Ladronn

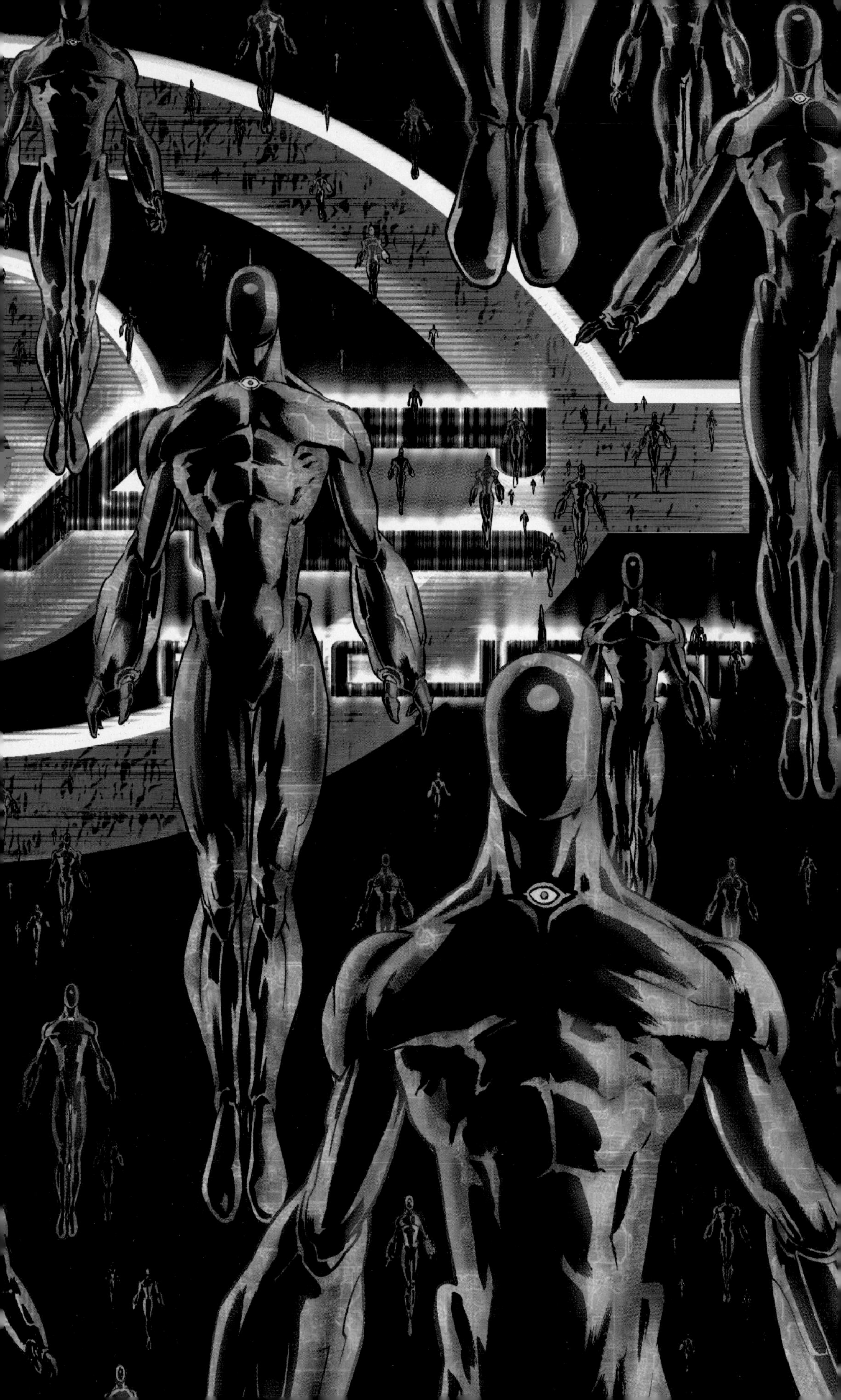

CRISIS COUNSELING

WHAT IS CHECKMATE?

Checkmate was established by Amanda Waller as an independent arm of the Federal Government's Task Force X, a bureau that also had administration over the Suicide Squad. Like the Squad, Checkmate engaged in top-secret missions vital to U.S. interests. Structured after the hierarchy of chess pieces, Checkmate is led by a Queen or King, followed by administrative Bishops, field director Rooks, armored and well-armed field agents Knights, and support-tech Pawns. In its brief existence, Checkmate has gone through numerous administrators and the identity of the King has traditionally been a closely guarded secret.

WHO IS SASHA BORDEAUX?

Millionaire Bruce Wayne needed a bodyguard in the opinion of Wayne Enterprises CEO Lucius Fox. Wayne, though, didn't need to be encumbered by such an employee, no matter how well-trained or attractive Sasha Bordeaux was. Slowly, he made Sasha aware of his Batman persona and brought her into his dark world. Later, when Wayne was framed for the murder of ex-girlfriend Vesper Fairchild, Sasha was tried and imprisoned as an accessory. After Wayne was exonerated, but before he could have Sasha freed, she seemingly died. Her death was faked by Checkmate, who decided she was their ideal type of agent. She had herself remade to create a new life and chose to break off the budding romance with Wayne in favor of a fresh start. She acquitted herself well with the team and rapidly rose to a position of trust and authority.

WHO IS MAXWELL LORD?

Little is known about the early life of Maxwell Lord IV, but he arrived in the public spotlight as a multi-millionaire and visionary. What people didn't know is that he was kidnapped by a computer that convinced Max the world needed a worldwide peacekeeping organization. The computer was a piece of Fourth World technology created by Metron, part of a grand experiment that was spoiled when Max destroyed the equipment. As a result, Max bankrolled one incarnation of the Justice League, playing on both sides since he was also a member of the Arcana, a version of the Royal Flush Gang. He's been married twice, once to Sylvia Duani and then to Claire Montgomery, who wound up competing with her ex by funding the Conglomerate, a mercenary super-team. Later, during an alien invasion of Earth, Max's latent telepathic powers were augmented, a skill he kept to himself. Only every now and then did he give his heroes a little "push" to accomplish a goal.

During his association with the League, Max was shot and critically injured during a conflict with Bialya's Queen Bee. Dreamslayer, a foe, briefly took over his body, but Max prevailed. Some time later Max found himself maneuvered out of controlling the League only to discover he was suffering from brain cancer. To avoid dying, he stole the power of the techno-organic Kilg%re and became a new being called Lord Havoc. Lord Havoc and the Arcana battled the JLA but lost, and Max disappeared. Evidence was found indicating he had not died, but exactly what became of him and the Arcana remains a mystery.

WHAT IS HAPPENING TO THE DC UNIVERSE?

Recently, Sue Dibny, wife of the Elongated Man, was killed in her own home. This sent shock waves through the super hero community and in the course of their investigation, their opposite numbers, the villains, learned that the heroes had manipulated their memories, through varying means several times over the years. The heroes rationalized this as a means of protecting their loved ones, allowing the fight for justice to continue. Dr. Light's magical "lobotomy" was undone and he vowed vengeance.

Batman sensed something was amiss among his peers and acted accordingly, building his own safety net to ensure the heroes would not undermine the trust that they had worked so hard to earn.

A mentally unbalanced Jean Loring, ex-wife of the Atom, turned out to have accidentally committed the crime in a complicated scheme to reunite with her former partner. She was remanded to Arkham Asylum, and the Atom vanished from sight. As word of what the JLA had done spread among the current heroes, the reactions have been mixed.

The very notion of what it means to be a hero has become a topic of debate as teams examined their actions. Superman, Batman, and Wonder Woman have each reacted differently to the mindwipe revelation, causing a rift among the heroic trinity. Throughout the heroic community, a sense of unease is felt from Metropolis to Gateway City, from the Teen Titans to the Outsiders.

Since this revelation, the villains have been processing information and devising a plan. Lex Luthor, the former President of the United States, has emerged from hiding to put together a new organization and has been recruiting a core council to direct the activities.

Trouble is brewing, both mortal and magical; events stirring that can only build to a crisis — a crisis that will leave no one unaffected.

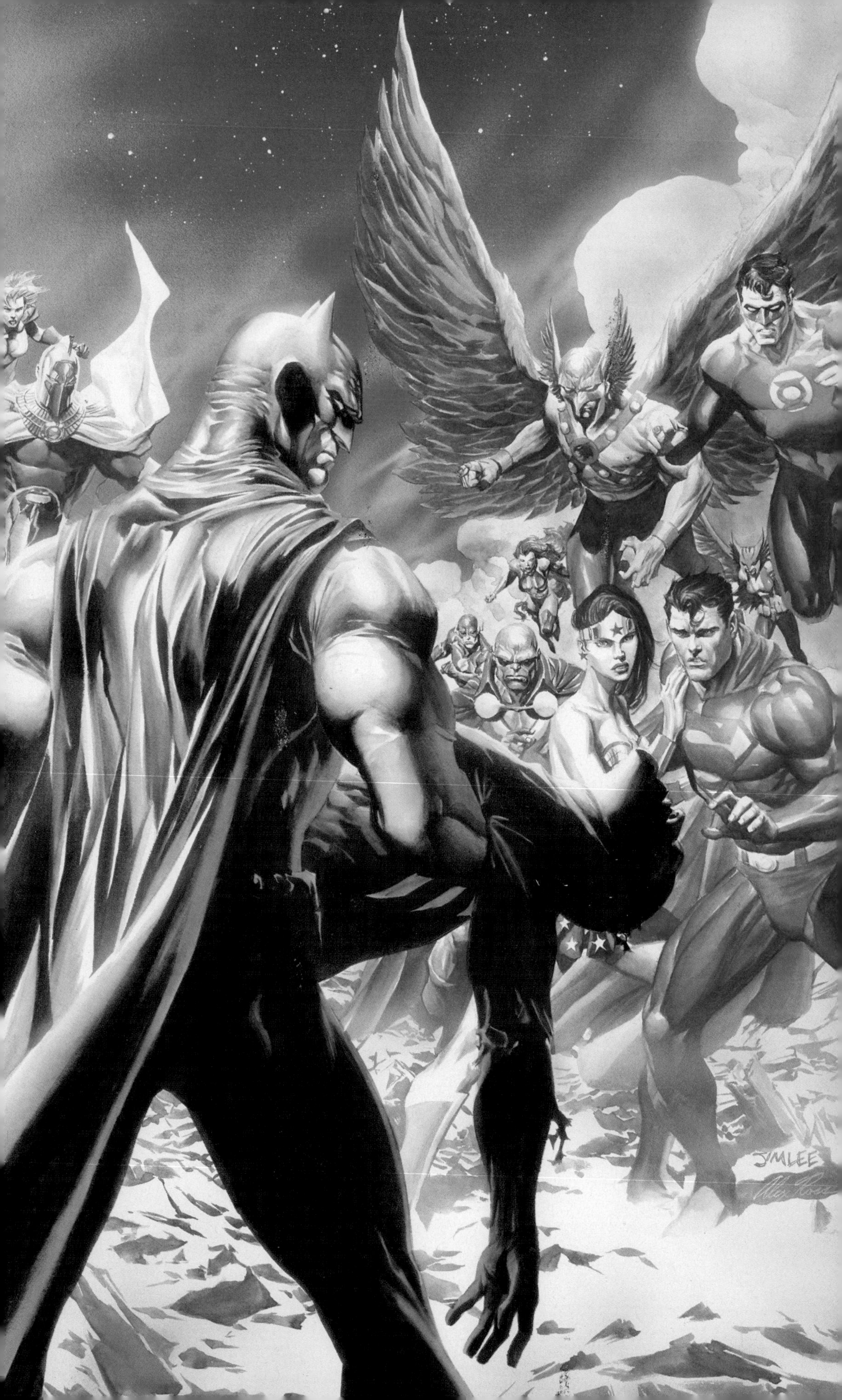
JIMLEE

Geoff Johns   Greg Rucka   Judd Winick Writers

CHAPTER ONE
Rags Morales & Michael Bair Artists   Moose Baumann Colorist

CHAPTER TWO
Ed Benes Artist   Hi-Fi Colorist

CHAPTER THREE
Jesus Saiz & Jimmy Palmiotti Artists   Paul Mounts Colorist

CHAPTER FOUR
Ivan Reis & Marc Campos Artists   Guy Major Colorist

CHAPTER FIVE
Phil Jimenez & Andy Lanning Artists   Steve Firchlow Colorist

Nick J. Napolitano Letterer

Jim Lee & Alex Ross Original covers

Special thanks to Brad Meltzer and Paul Levitz

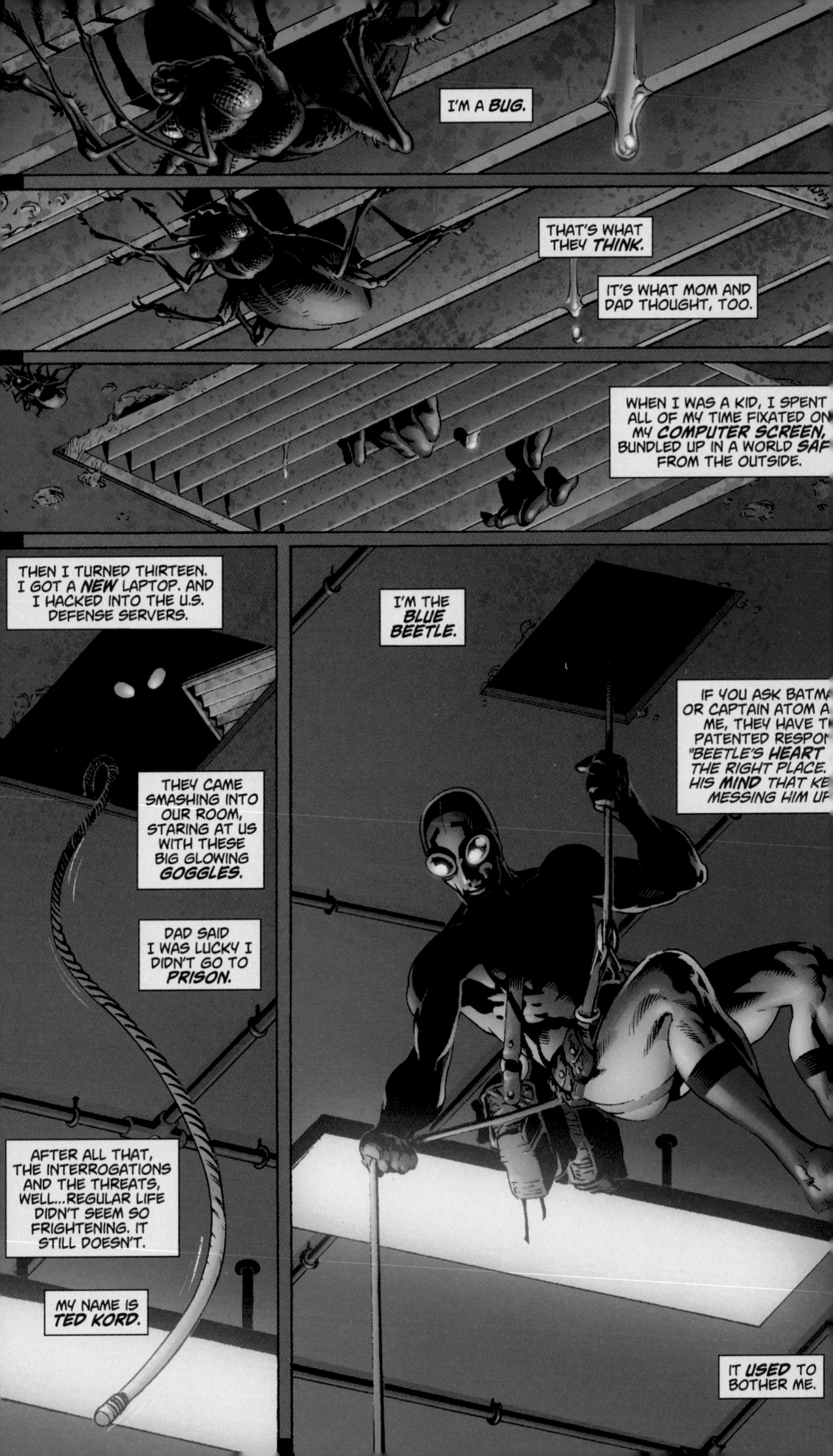
I'M A BUG.
THAT'S WHAT THEY THINK.
IT'S WHAT MOM AND DAD THOUGHT, TOO.
WHEN I WAS A KID, I SPENT ALL OF MY TIME FIXATED ON MY COMPUTER SCREEN, BUNDLED UP IN A WORLD SAF FROM THE OUTSIDE.
THEN I TURNED THIRTEEN. I GOT A NEW LAPTOP. AND I HACKED INTO THE U.S. DEFENSE SERVERS.
THEY CAME SMASHING INTO OUR ROOM, STARING AT US WITH THESE BIG GLOWING GOGGLES.
DAD SAID I WAS LUCKY I DIDN'T GO TO PRISON.
AFTER ALL THAT, THE INTERROGATIONS AND THE THREATS, WELL...REGULAR LIFE DIDN'T SEEM SO FRIGHTENING. IT STILL DOESN'T.
MY NAME IS TED KORD.
I'M THE BLUE BEETLE.
IF YOU ASK BATMA OR CAPTAIN ATOM A ME, THEY HAVE T PATENTED RESPON "BEETLE'S HEART THE RIGHT PLACE. HIS MIND THAT KE MESSING HIM UP
IT USED TO BOTHER ME.

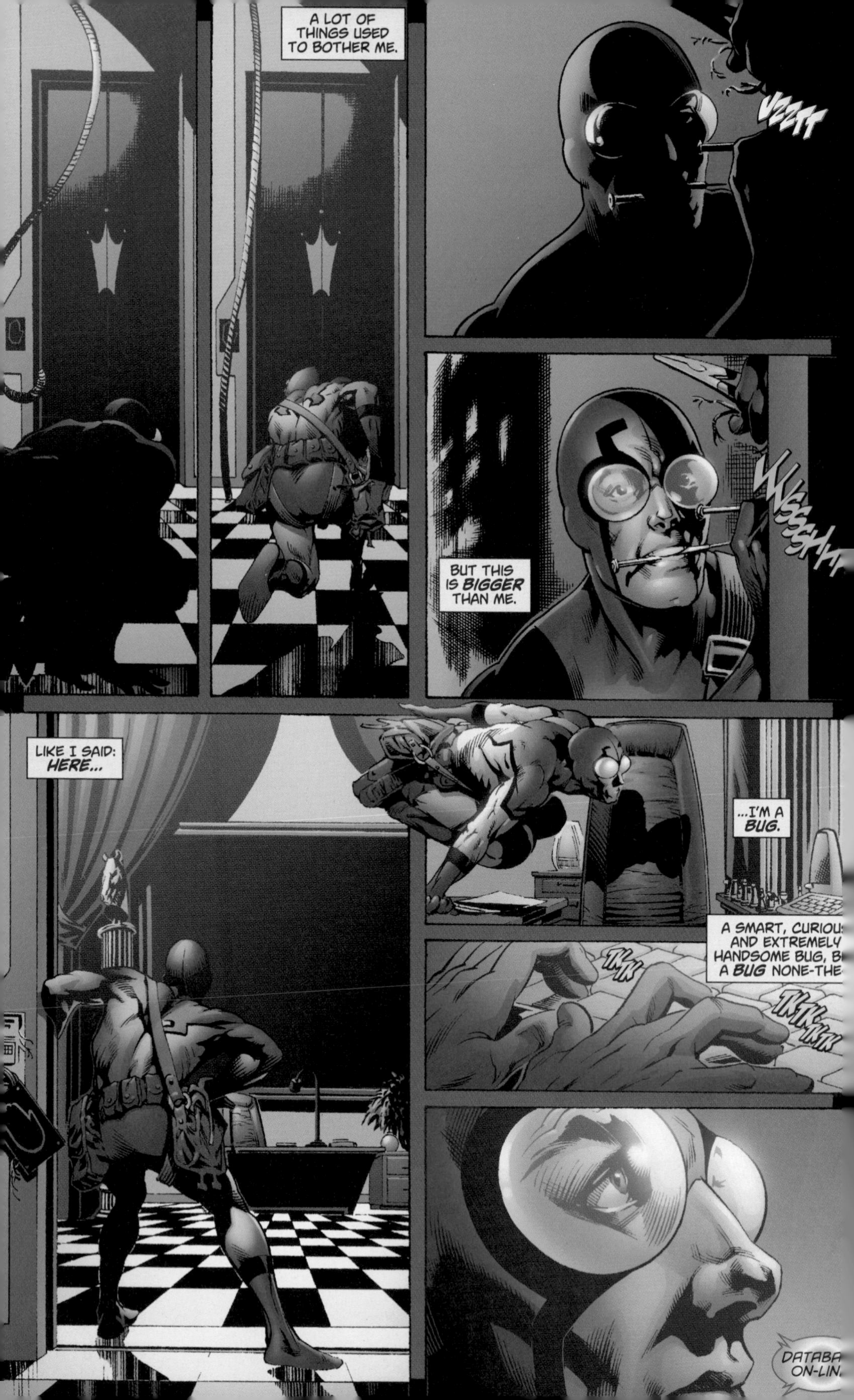
A LOT OF THINGS USED TO BOTHER ME.
VZZTT
WSSSHHH
BUT THIS IS BIGGER THAN ME.
LIKE I SAID: HERE...
...I'M A BUG.
A SMART, CURIOU
AND EXTREMELY
HANDSOME BUG, B
A BUG NONE-THE
TKTK
TKTKTKTK
DATABA
ON-LIN

DC COMICS PROUDLY PRESENTS

COUNTDOWN TO INFINITE CRISIS

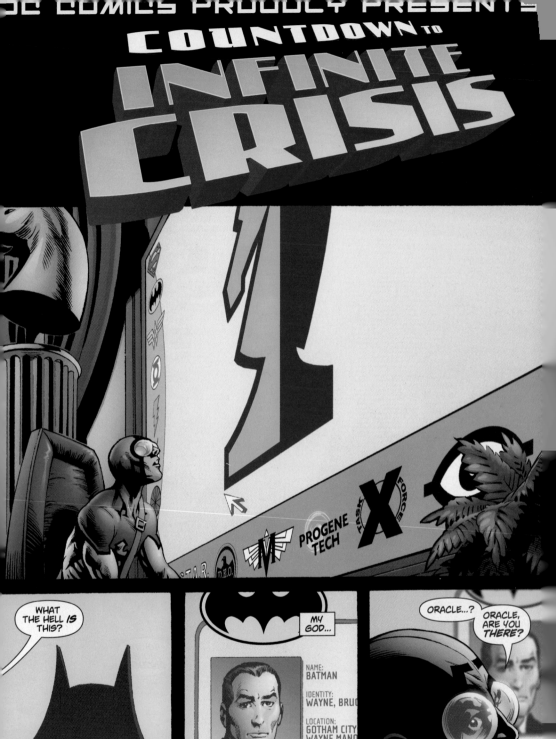

WHAT THE HELL *IS* THIS?

BEEP

MY GOD...

NAME:
BATMAN

IDENTITY:
WAYNE, BRUC

LOCATION:
GOTHAM CITY
WAYNE MANO
CREST HILL

AFFILIATION(S):
JUSTICE LEAGUE OF AMERICA, THE OUTSIDERS
(INACTIVE), WAYNE ENTERPRISES

POWERS: GENIUS

ABILITIES AND EQUIPMENT:
HAND-TO-HAND COMBAT (A1), MARTIAL ARTIST (A2
UTILITY BELT (TECH FACTOR A2)

ASSOCIATES:
• CAIN, CASSANDRA – BATGIRL
• DRAKE, TIMOTHY – ROBIN
• GORDON, BARBARA (BATGIRL I) – ORACLE
• GORDON, COMMISSIONER JAMES – RETIRED
• GRAYSON, RICHARD – NIGHTWING

ORACLE...?

ORACLE, ARE YOU *THERE?*

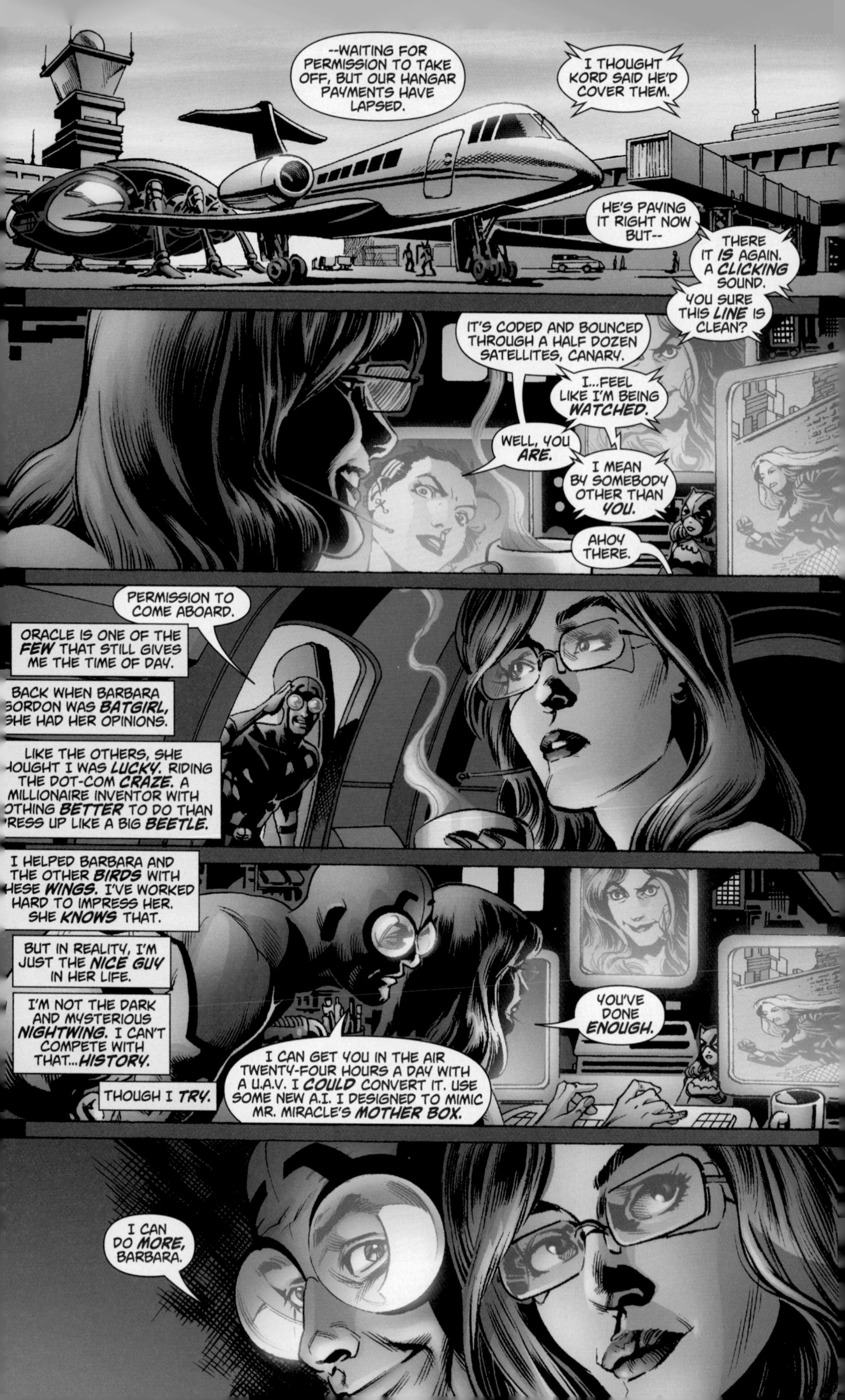
--WAITING FOR PERMISSION TO TAKE OFF, BUT OUR HANGAR PAYMENTS HAVE LAPSED.
I THOUGHT KORD SAID HE'D COVER THEM.
HE'S PAYING IT RIGHT NOW BUT--
THERE IT IS AGAIN. A CLICKING SOUND.
YOU SURE THIS LINE IS CLEAN?
IT'S CODED AND BOUNCED THROUGH A HALF DOZEN SATELLITES, CANARY.
I...FEEL LIKE I'M BEING WATCHED.
WELL, YOU ARE.
I MEAN BY SOMEBODY OTHER THAN YOU.
AHOY THERE.
PERMISSION TO COME ABOARD.
ORACLE IS ONE OF THE FEW THAT STILL GIVES ME THE TIME OF DAY.
BACK WHEN BARBARA GORDON WAS BATGIRL, SHE HAD HER OPINIONS.
LIKE THE OTHERS, SHE THOUGHT I WAS LUCKY. RIDING THE DOT-COM CRAZE. A MILLIONAIRE INVENTOR WITH NOTHING BETTER TO DO THAN DRESS UP LIKE A BIG BEETLE.
I HELPED BARBARA AND THE OTHER BIRDS WITH THESE WINGS. I'VE WORKED HARD TO IMPRESS HER. SHE KNOWS THAT.
BUT IN REALITY, I'M JUST THE NICE GUY IN HER LIFE.
I'M NOT THE DARK AND MYSTERIOUS NIGHTWING. I CAN'T COMPETE WITH THAT...HISTORY.
THOUGH I TRY.
I CAN GET YOU IN THE AIR TWENTY-FOUR HOURS A DAY WITH A U.A.V. I COULD CONVERT IT. USE SOME NEW A.I. I DESIGNED TO MIMIC MR. MIRACLE'S MOTHER BOX.
YOU'VE DONE ENOUGH.
I CAN DO MORE, BARBARA.

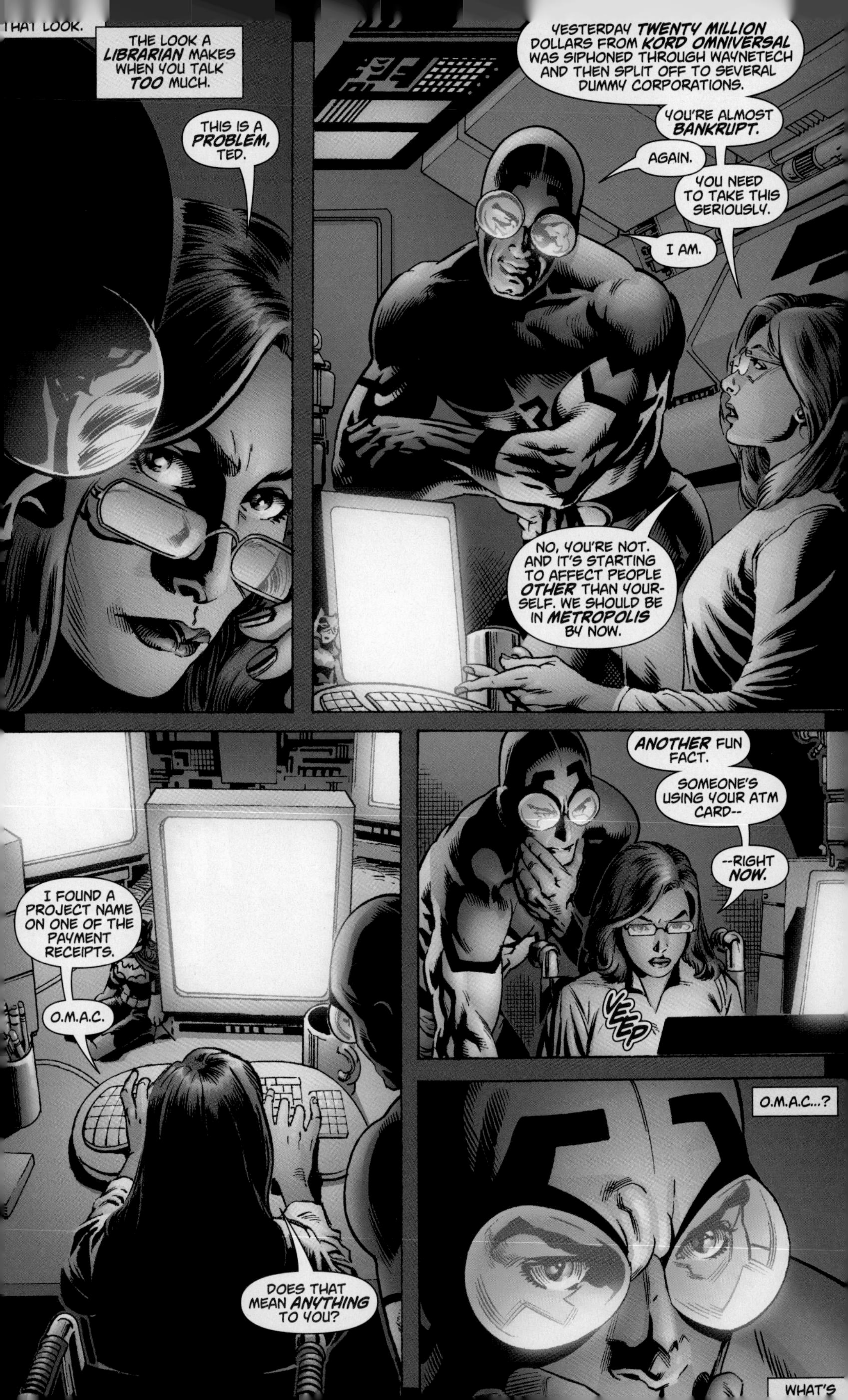
THAT LOOK.
THE LOOK A LIBRARIAN MAKES WHEN YOU TALK TOO MUCH.
THIS IS A PROBLEM, TED.
YESTERDAY TWENTY MILLION DOLLARS FROM KORD OMNIVERSAL WAS SIPHONED THROUGH WAYNETECH AND THEN SPLIT OFF TO SEVERAL DUMMY CORPORATIONS.
YOU'RE ALMOST BANKRUPT.
AGAIN.
YOU NEED TO TAKE THIS SERIOUSLY.
I AM.
NO, YOU'RE NOT. AND IT'S STARTING TO AFFECT PEOPLE OTHER THAN YOURSELF. WE SHOULD BE IN METROPOLIS BY NOW.
I FOUND A PROJECT NAME ON ONE OF THE PAYMENT RECEIPTS.
O.M.A.C.
DOES THAT MEAN ANYTHING TO YOU?
ANOTHER FUN FACT.
SOMEONE'S USING YOUR ATM CARD--
--RIGHT NOW.
VEEP
O.M.A.C...?
WHAT'S

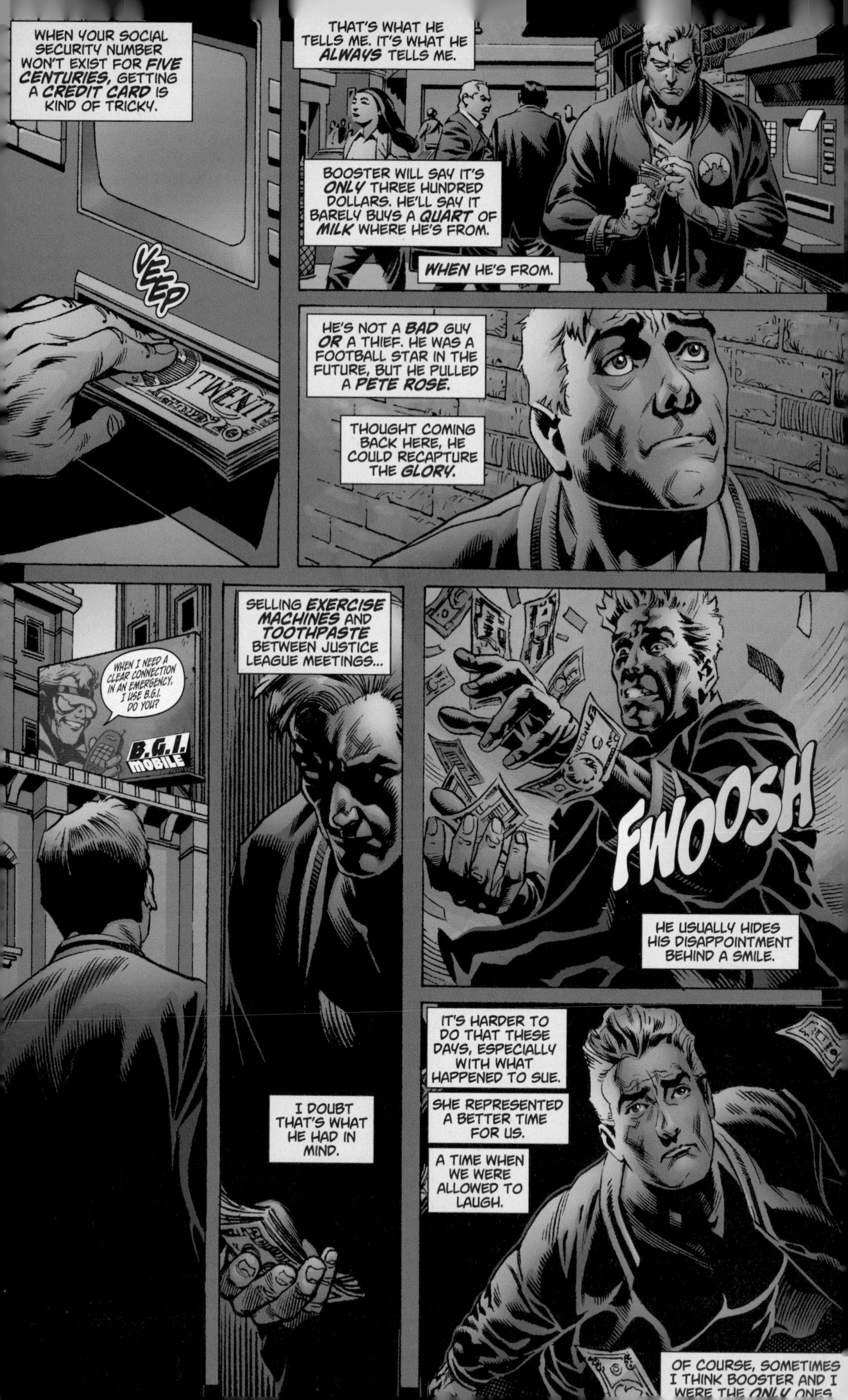
WHEN YOUR SOCIAL SECURITY NUMBER WON'T EXIST FOR FIVE CENTURIES, GETTING A CREDIT CARD IS KIND OF TRICKY.
VEEEP
TWENTY
THAT'S WHAT HE TELLS ME. IT'S WHAT HE ALWAYS TELLS ME.
BOOSTER WILL SAY IT'S ONLY THREE HUNDRED DOLLARS. HE'LL SAY IT BARELY BUYS A QUART OF MILK WHERE HE'S FROM.
WHEN HE'S FROM.
HE'S NOT A BAD GUY OR A THIEF. HE WAS A FOOTBALL STAR IN THE FUTURE, BUT HE PULLED A PETE ROSE.
THOUGHT COMING BACK HERE, HE COULD RECAPTURE THE GLORY.
WHEN I NEED A CLEAR CONNECTION IN AN EMERGENCY, I USE B.G.I. DO YOU?
B.G.I. MOBILE
SELLING EXERCISE MACHINES AND TOOTHPASTE BETWEEN JUSTICE LEAGUE MEETINGS...
I DOUBT THAT'S WHAT HE HAD IN MIND.
FWOOSH
HE USUALLY HIDES HIS DISAPPOINTMENT BEHIND A SMILE.
IT'S HARDER TO DO THAT THESE DAYS, ESPECIALLY WITH WHAT HAPPENED TO SUE.
SHE REPRESENTED A BETTER TIME FOR US.
A TIME WHEN WE WERE ALLOWED TO LAUGH.
OF COURSE, SOMETIMES I THINK BOOSTER AND I WERE THE ONLY ONES

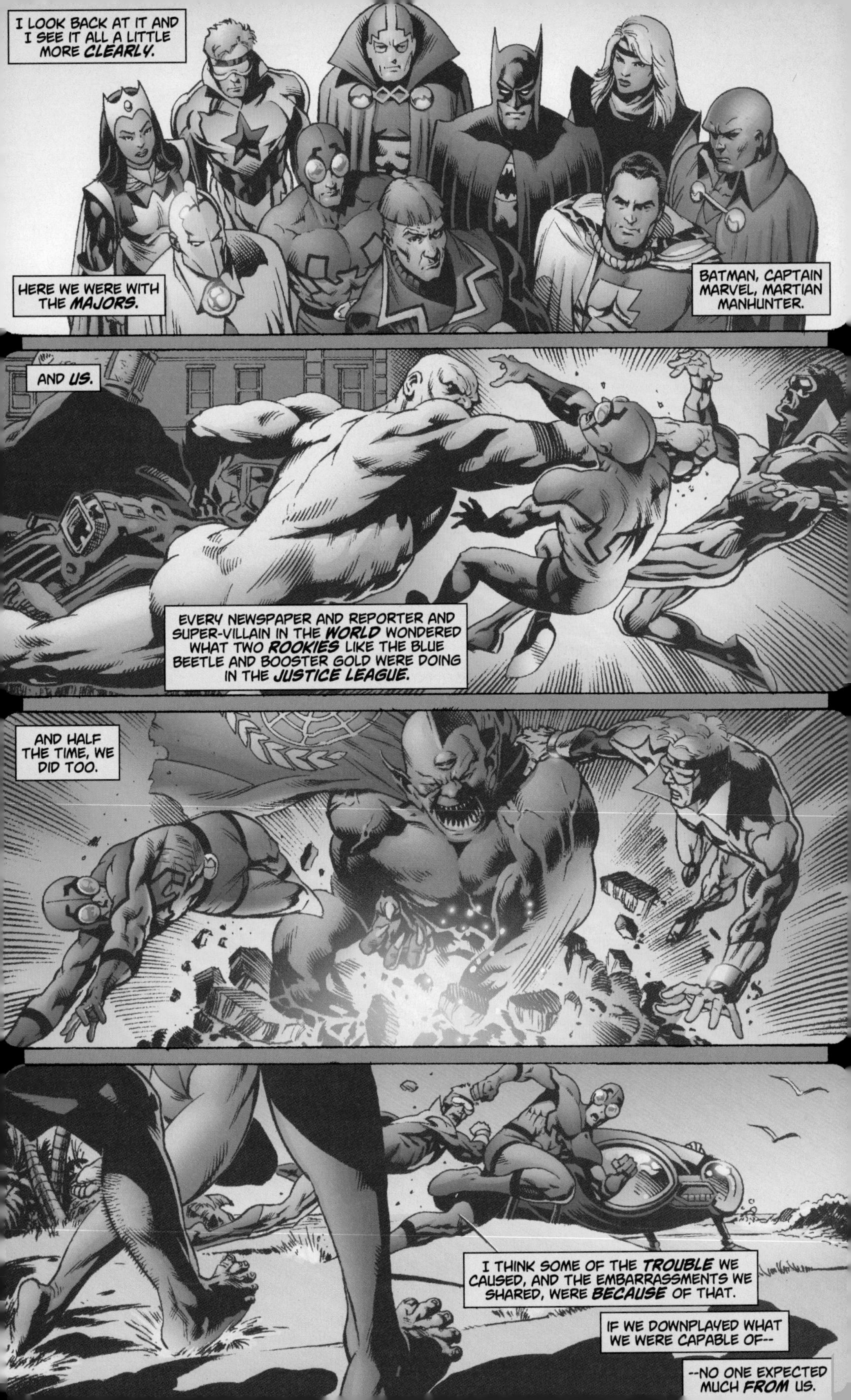
I LOOK BACK AT IT AND I SEE IT ALL A LITTLE MORE CLEARLY.
HERE WE WERE WITH THE MAJORS.
BATMAN, CAPTAIN MARVEL, MARTIAN MANHUNTER.
AND US.
EVERY NEWSPAPER AND REPORTER AND SUPER-VILLAIN IN THE WORLD WONDERED WHAT TWO ROOKIES LIKE THE BLUE BEETLE AND BOOSTER GOLD WERE DOING IN THE JUSTICE LEAGUE.
AND HALF THE TIME, WE DID TOO.
I THINK SOME OF THE TROUBLE WE CAUSED, AND THE EMBARRASSMENTS WE SHARED, WERE BECAUSE OF THAT.
IF WE DOWNPLAYED WHAT WE WERE CAPABLE OF--
--NO ONE EXPECTED MUCH FROM US.

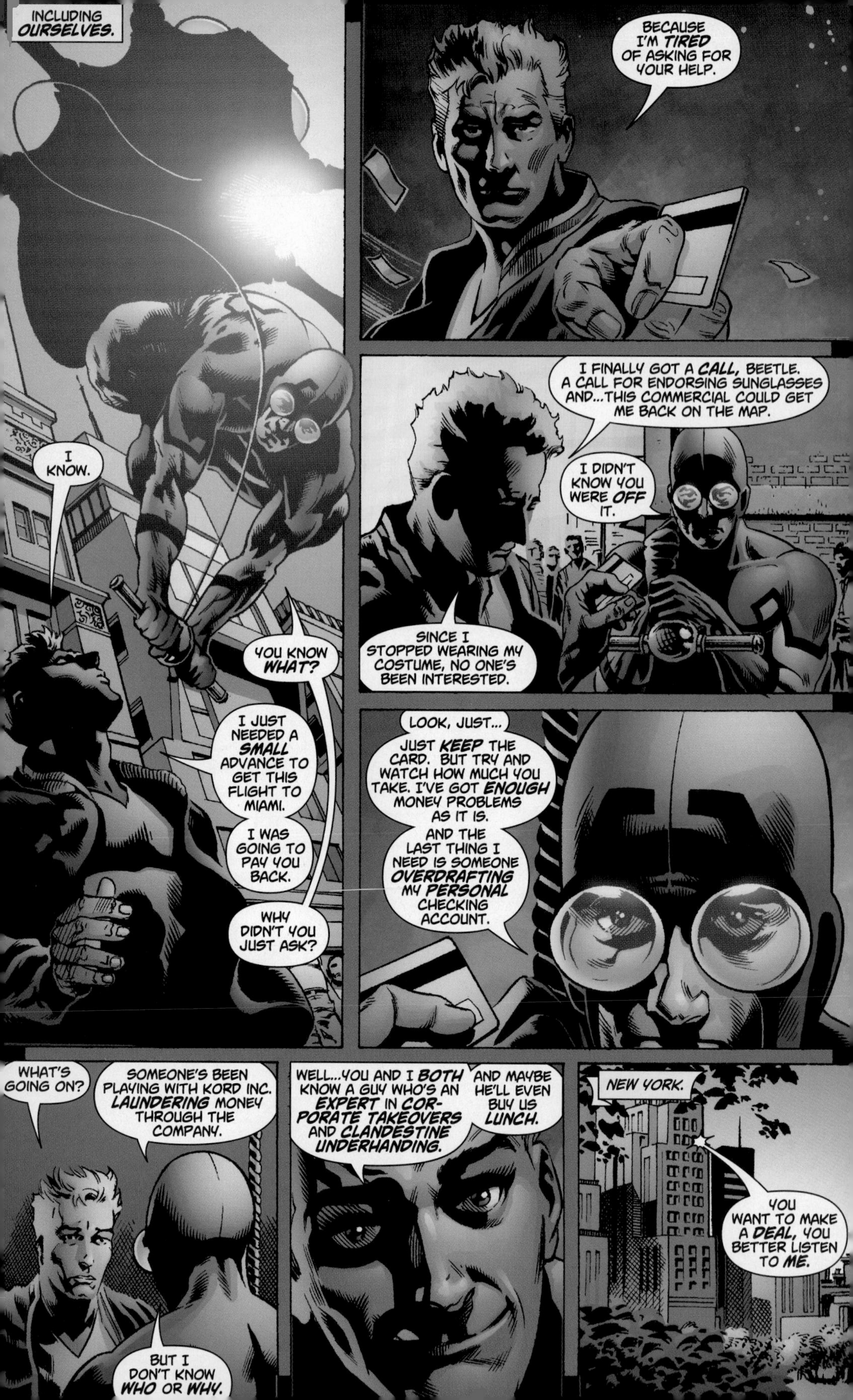
INCLUDING OURSELVES.
BECAUSE I'M TIRED OF ASKING FOR YOUR HELP.
I KNOW.
YOU KNOW WHAT?
I JUST NEEDED A SMALL ADVANCE TO GET THIS FLIGHT TO MIAMI.
I WAS GOING TO PAY YOU BACK.
WHY DIDN'T YOU JUST ASK?
I FINALLY GOT A CALL, BEETLE. A CALL FOR ENDORSING SUNGLASSES AND...THIS COMMERCIAL COULD GET ME BACK ON THE MAP.
I DIDN'T KNOW YOU WERE OFF IT.
SINCE I STOPPED WEARING MY COSTUME, NO ONE'S BEEN INTERESTED.
LOOK, JUST...
JUST KEEP THE CARD. BUT TRY AND WATCH HOW MUCH YOU TAKE. I'VE GOT ENOUGH MONEY PROBLEMS AS IT IS.
AND THE LAST THING I NEED IS SOMEONE OVERDRAFTING MY PERSONAL CHECKING ACCOUNT.
WHAT'S GOING ON?
SOMEONE'S BEEN PLAYING WITH KORD INC. LAUNDERING MONEY THROUGH THE COMPANY.
BUT I DON'T KNOW WHO OR WHY.
WELL...YOU AND I BOTH KNOW A GUY WHO'S AN EXPERT IN CORPORATE TAKEOVERS AND CLANDESTINE UNDERHANDING.
AND MAYBE HE'LL EVEN BUY US LUNCH.
NEW YORK.
YOU WANT TO MAKE A DEAL, YOU BETTER LISTEN TO ME.

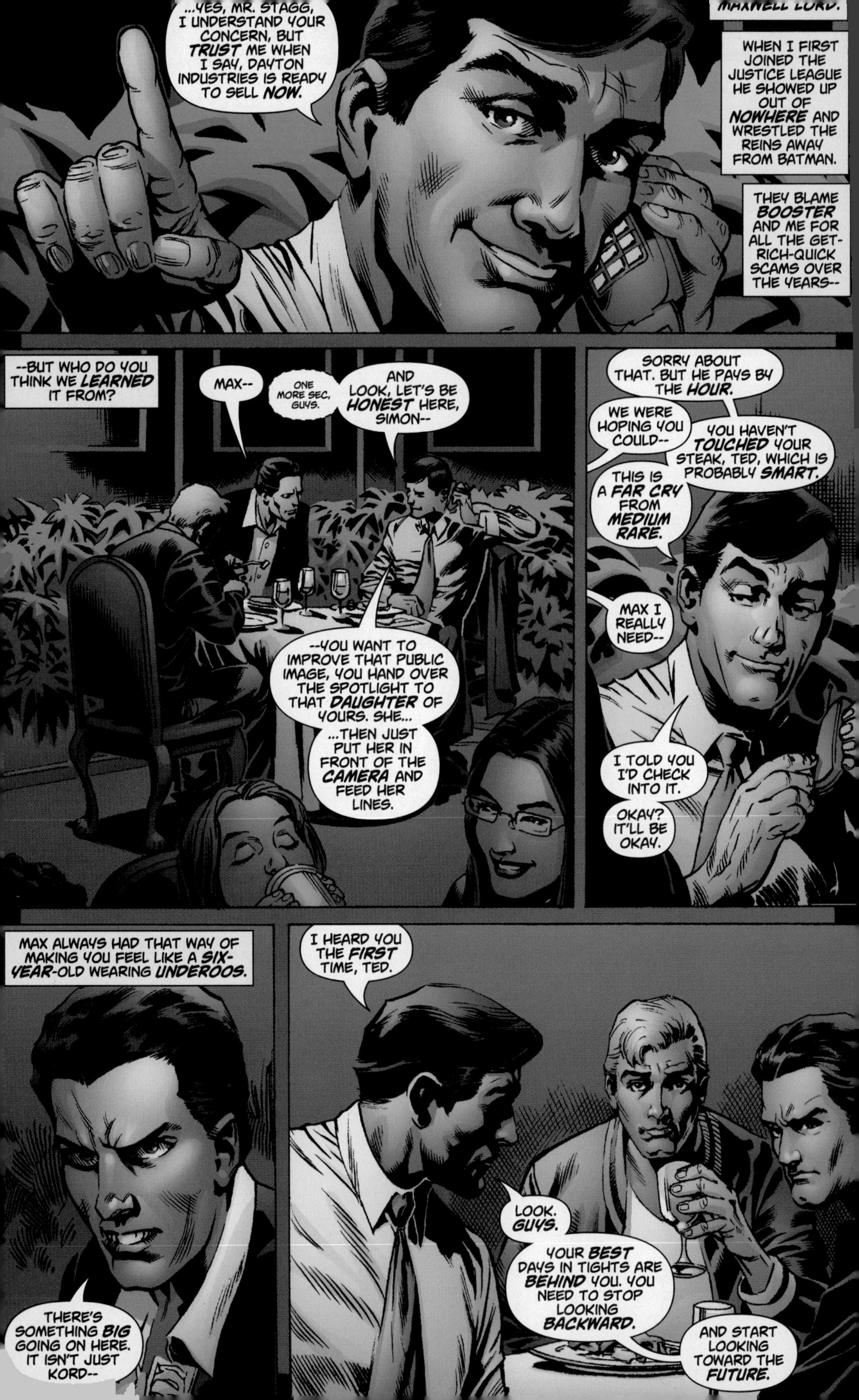
...YES, MR. STAGG, I UNDERSTAND YOUR CONCERN, BUT TRUST ME WHEN I SAY, DAYTON INDUSTRIES IS READY TO SELL NOW.
MAXWELL LORD.
WHEN I FIRST JOINED THE JUSTICE LEAGUE HE SHOWED UP OUT OF NOWHERE AND WRESTLED THE REINS AWAY FROM BATMAN.
THEY BLAME BOOSTER AND ME FOR ALL THE GET-RICH-QUICK SCAMS OVER THE YEARS--
--BUT WHO DO YOU THINK WE LEARNED IT FROM?
MAX--
ONE MORE SEC, GUYS.
AND LOOK, LET'S BE HONEST HERE, SIMON--
--YOU WANT TO IMPROVE THAT PUBLIC IMAGE, YOU HAND OVER THE SPOTLIGHT TO THAT DAUGHTER OF YOURS. SHE...
...THEN JUST PUT HER IN FRONT OF THE CAMERA AND FEED HER LINES.
SORRY ABOUT THAT. BUT HE PAYS BY THE HOUR.
WE WERE HOPING YOU COULD--
YOU HAVEN'T TOUCHED YOUR STEAK, TED, WHICH IS PROBABLY SMART.
THIS IS A FAR CRY FROM MEDIUM RARE.
MAX I REALLY NEED--
I TOLD YOU I'D CHECK INTO IT.
OKAY? IT'LL BE OKAY.
MAX ALWAYS HAD THAT WAY OF MAKING YOU FEEL LIKE A SIX-YEAR-OLD WEARING UNDEROOS.
THERE'S SOMETHING BIG GOING ON HERE. IT ISN'T JUST KORD--
I HEARD YOU THE FIRST TIME, TED.
LOOK. GUYS.
YOUR BEST DAYS IN TIGHTS ARE BEHIND YOU. YOU NEED TO STOP LOOKING BACKWARD.
AND START LOOKING TOWARD THE FUTURE.

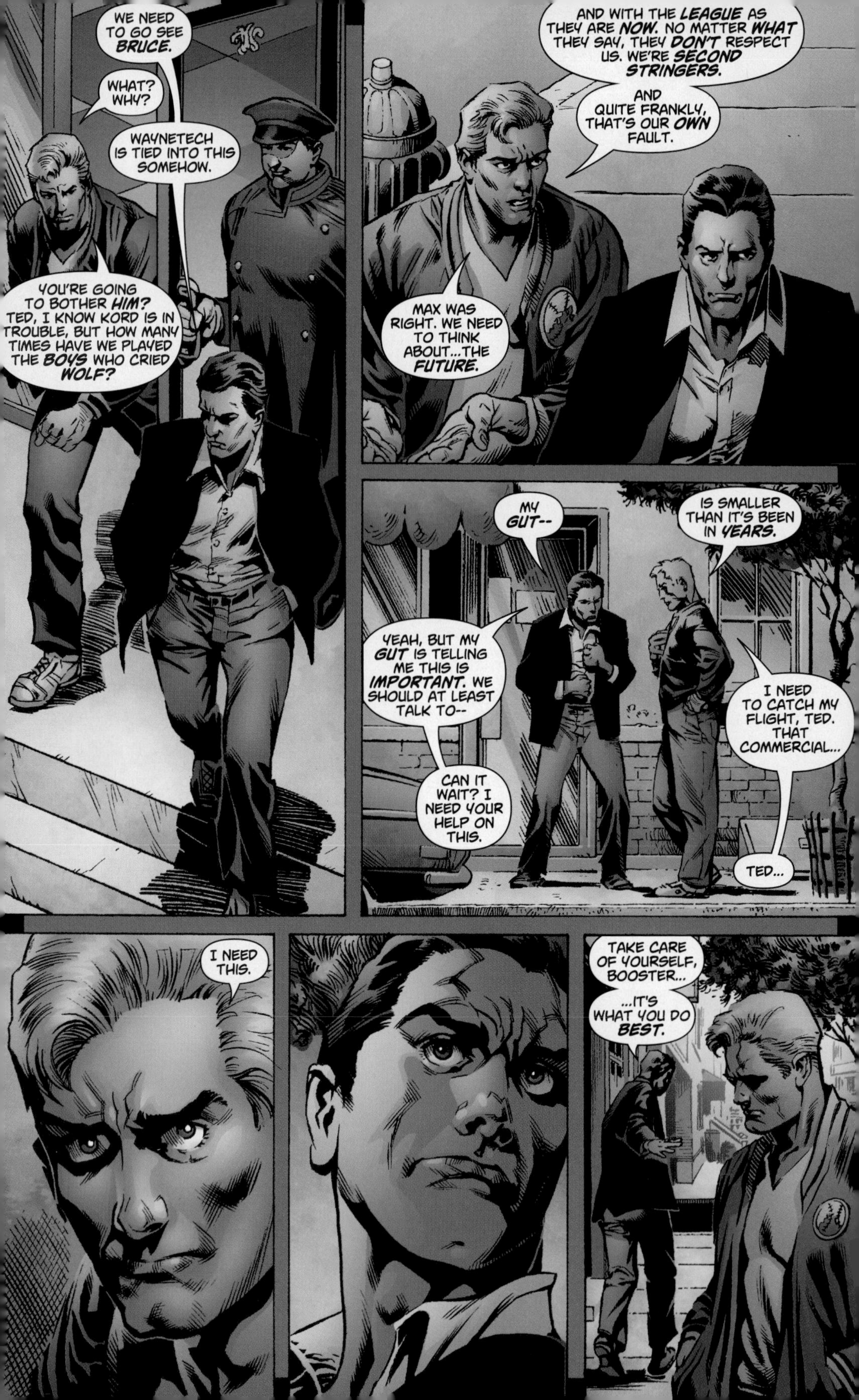

WE NEED TO GO SEE BRUCE.
WHAT? WHY?
WAYNETECH IS TIED INTO THIS SOMEHOW.
YOU'RE GOING TO BOTHER HIM? TED, I KNOW KORD IS IN TROUBLE, BUT HOW MANY TIMES HAVE WE PLAYED THE BOYS WHO CRIED WOLF?
AND WITH THE LEAGUE AS THEY ARE NOW. NO MATTER WHAT THEY SAY, THEY DON'T RESPECT US. WE'RE SECOND STRINGERS.
AND QUITE FRANKLY, THAT'S OUR OWN FAULT.
MAX WAS RIGHT. WE NEED TO THINK ABOUT...THE FUTURE.
MY GUT--
IS SMALLER THAN IT'S BEEN IN YEARS.
YEAH, BUT MY GUT IS TELLING ME THIS IS IMPORTANT. WE SHOULD AT LEAST TALK TO--
I NEED TO CATCH MY FLIGHT, TED. THAT COMMERCIAL...
CAN IT WAIT? I NEED YOUR HELP ON THIS.
TED...
I NEED THIS.
TAKE CARE OF YOURSELF, BOOSTER...
...IT'S WHAT YOU DO BEST.

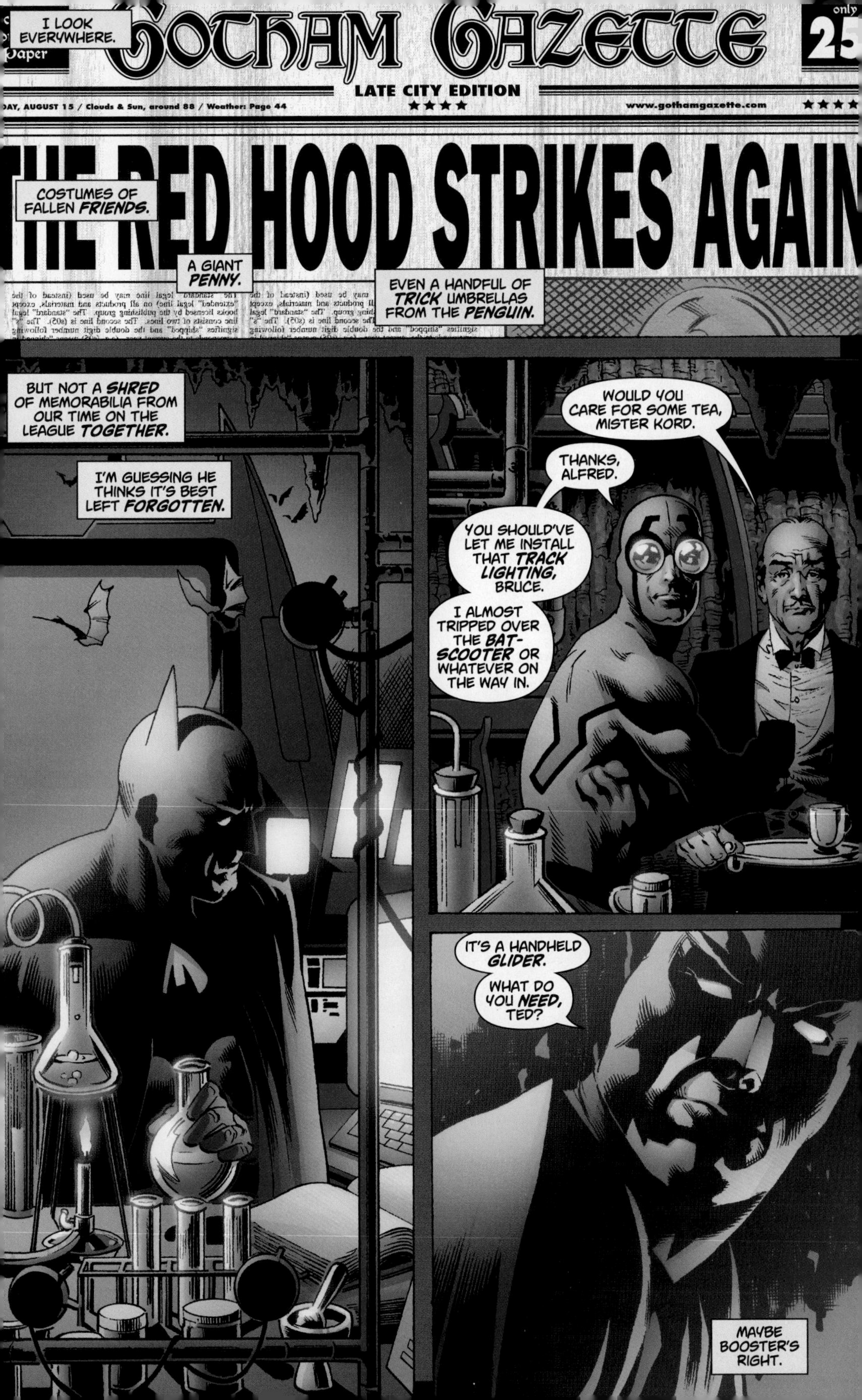

I LOOK EVERYWHERE.
GOTHAM GAZETTE
only 25
LATE CITY EDITION
AY, AUGUST 15 / Clouds & Sun, around 88 / Weather: Page 44
www.gothamgazette.com
THE RED HOOD STRIKES AGAIN
COSTUMES OF FALLEN FRIENDS.
A GIANT PENNY.
EVEN A HANDFUL OF TRICK UMBRELLAS FROM THE PENGUIN.
BUT NOT A SHRED OF MEMORABILIA FROM OUR TIME ON THE LEAGUE TOGETHER.
I'M GUESSING HE THINKS IT'S BEST LEFT FORGOTTEN.
WOULD YOU CARE FOR SOME TEA, MISTER KORD.
THANKS, ALFRED.
YOU SHOULD'VE LET ME INSTALL THAT TRACK LIGHTING, BRUCE.
I ALMOST TRIPPED OVER THE BAT-SCOOTER OR WHATEVER ON THE WAY IN.
IT'S A HANDHELD GLIDER.
WHAT DO YOU NEED, TED?
MAYBE BOOSTER'S RIGHT.

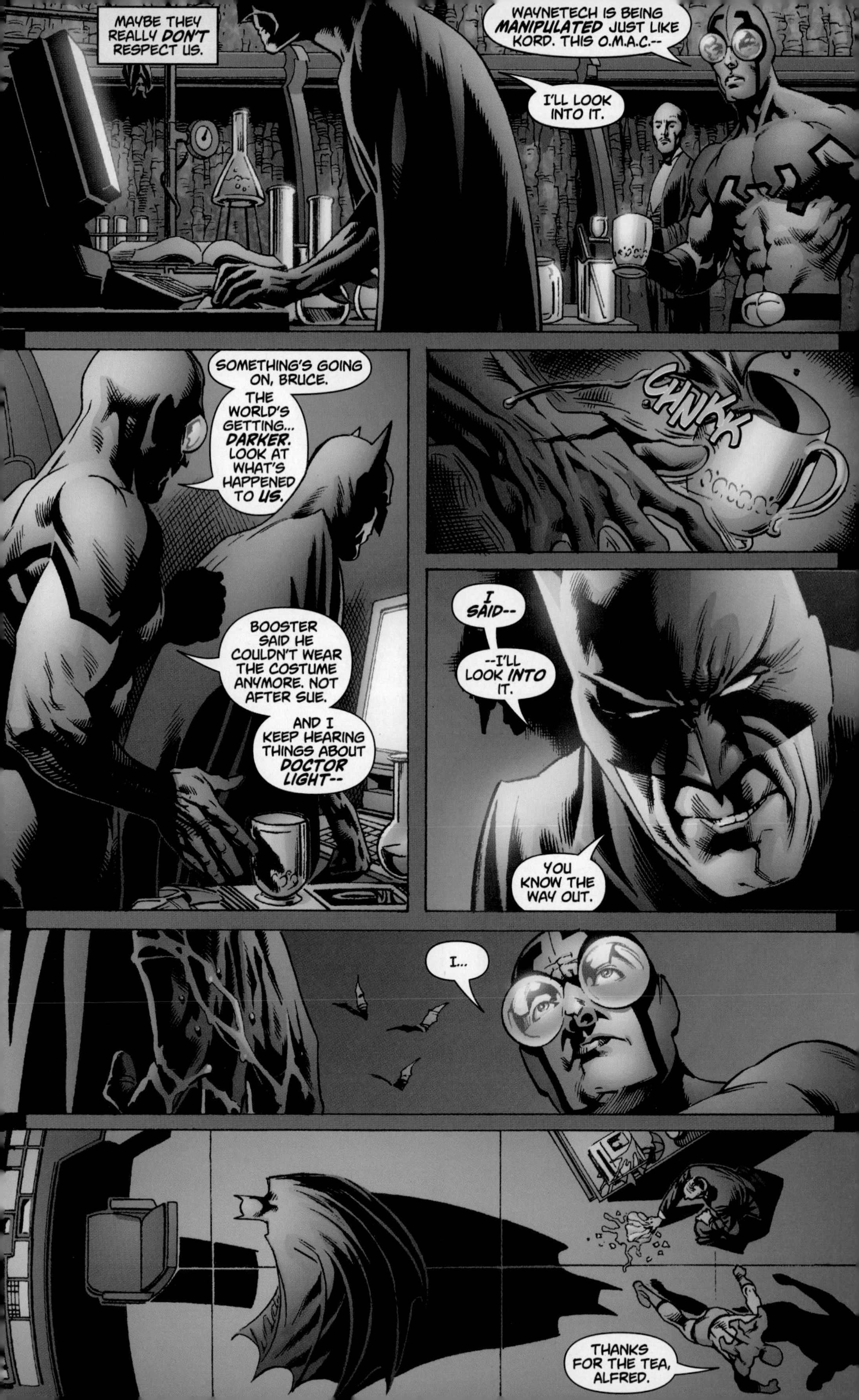
MAYBE THEY REALLY DON'T RESPECT US.
WAYNETECH IS BEING MANIPULATED JUST LIKE KORD. THIS O.M.A.C.--
I'LL LOOK INTO IT.
SOMETHING'S GOING ON, BRUCE.
THE WORLD'S GETTING... DARKER. LOOK AT WHAT'S HAPPENED TO US.
BOOSTER SAID HE COULDN'T WEAR THE COSTUME ANYMORE. NOT AFTER SUE.
AND I KEEP HEARING THINGS ABOUT DOCTOR LIGHT--
CHNKK
I SAID--
--I'LL LOOK INTO IT.
YOU KNOW THE WAY OUT.
I...
THANKS FOR THE TEA, ALFRED.

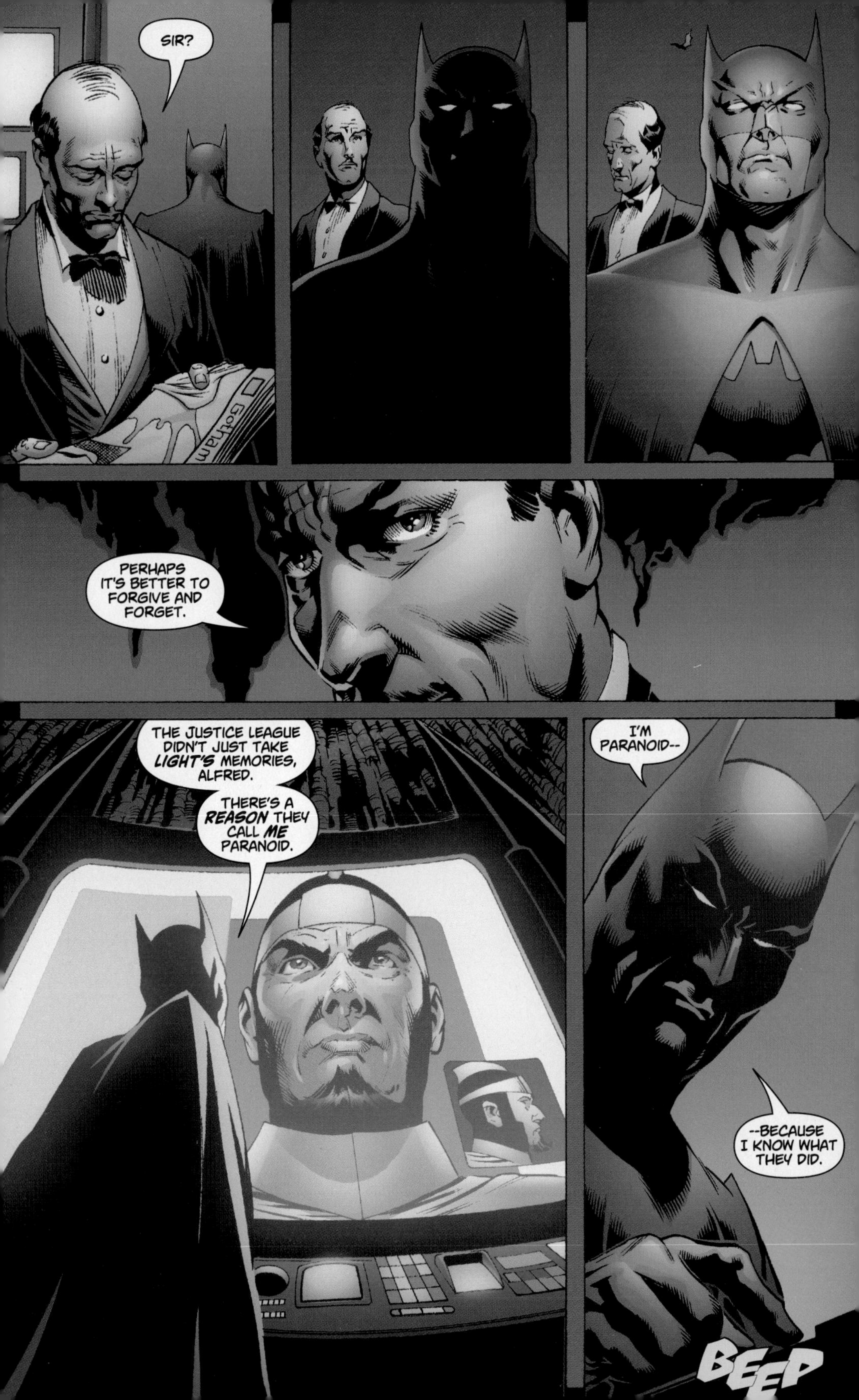
SIR?
Gotham
PERHAPS IT'S BETTER TO FORGIVE AND FORGET.
THE JUSTICE LEAGUE DIDN'T JUST TAKE LIGHT'S MEMORIES, ALFRED.
THERE'S A REASON THEY CALL ME PARANOID.
I'M PARANOID--
--BECAUSE I KNOW WHAT THEY DID.
BEEEP

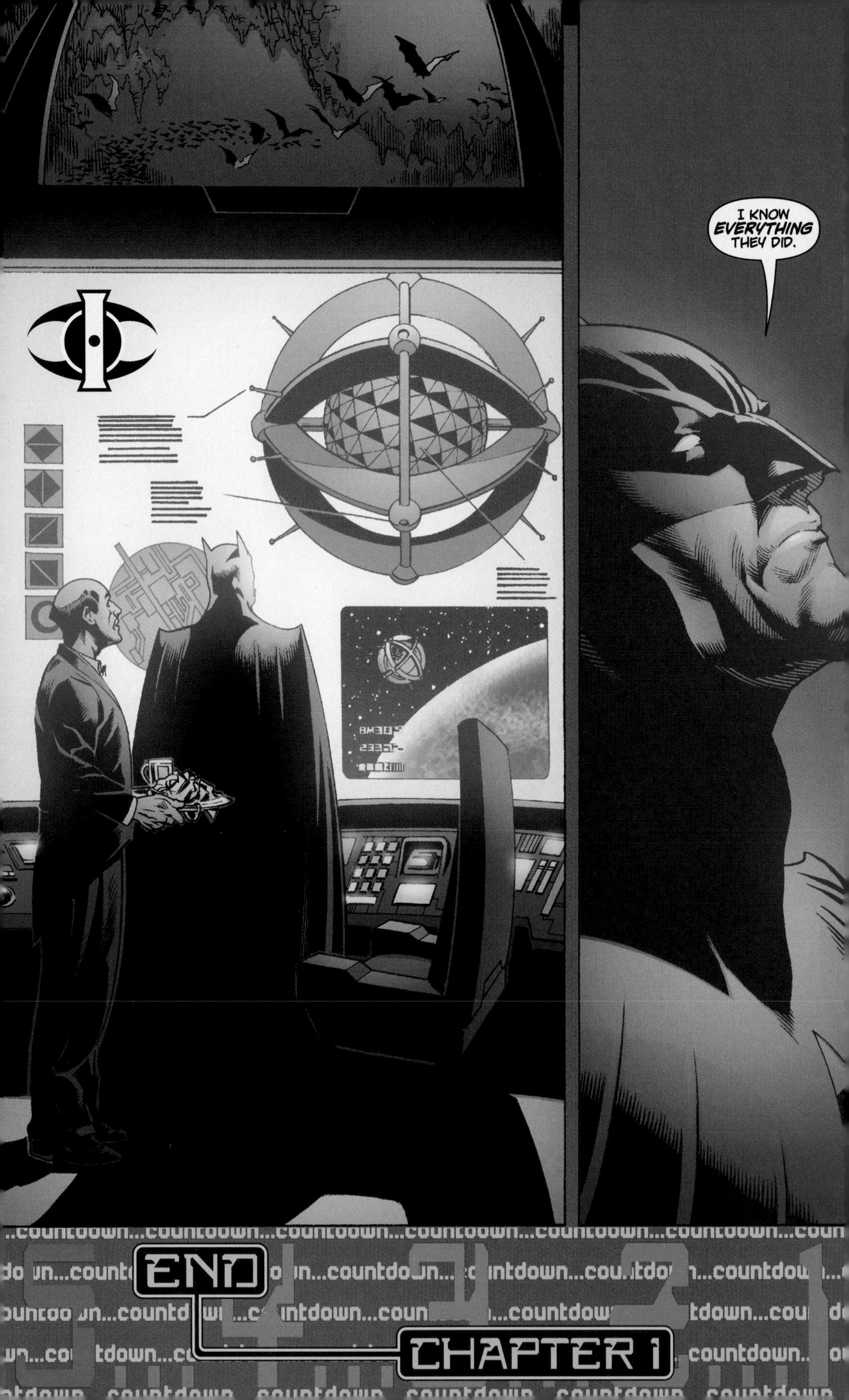
I KNOW EVERYTHING THEY DID.
END
CHAPTER 1

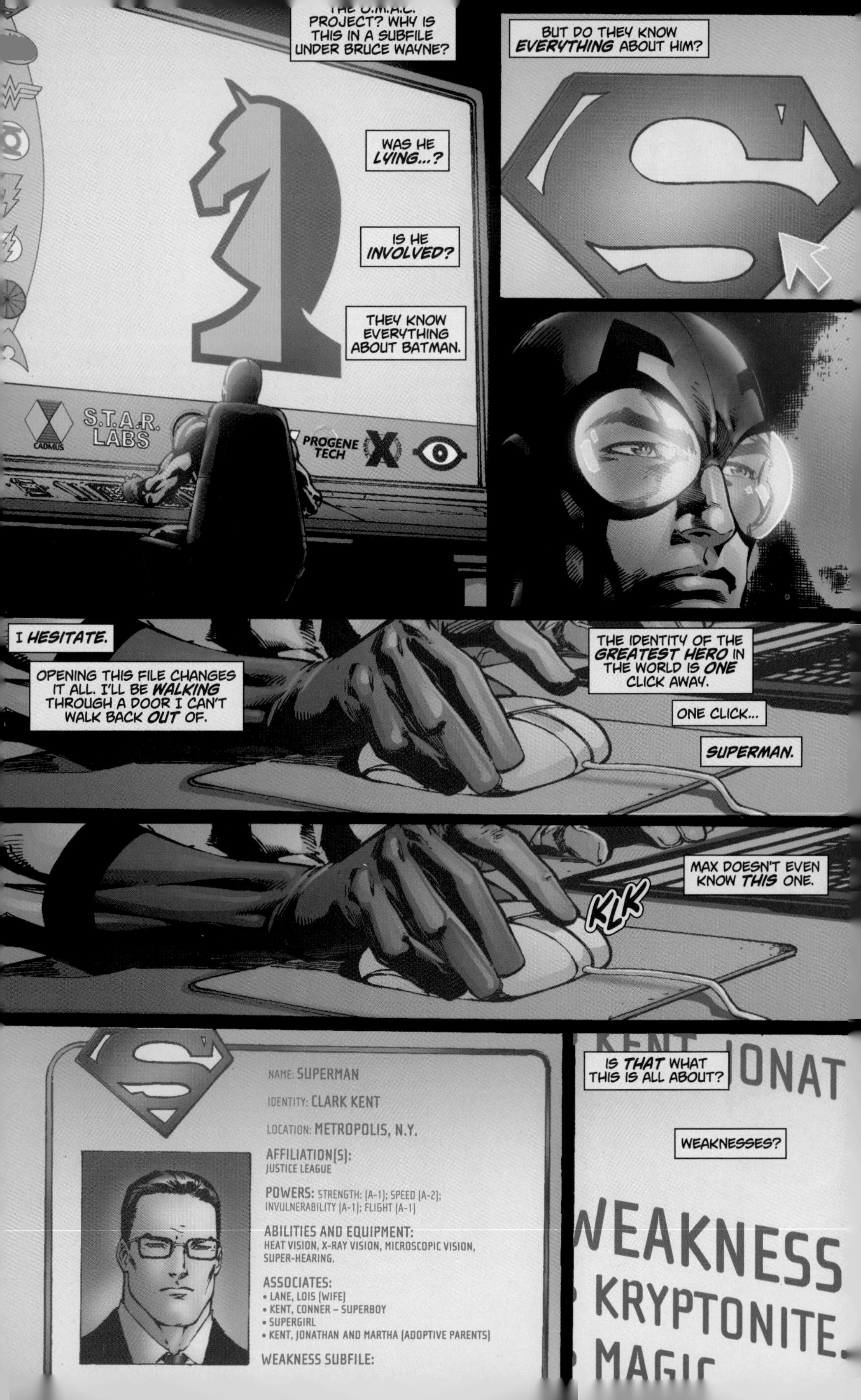

THE O.M.A.C. PROJECT? WHY IS THIS IN A SUBFILE UNDER BRUCE WAYNE?
WAS HE LYING...?
IS HE INVOLVED?
THEY KNOW EVERYTHING ABOUT BATMAN.
CADMUS
S.T.A.R. LABS
PROGENE TECH
BUT DO THEY KNOW EVERYTHING ABOUT HIM?
I HESITATE.
OPENING THIS FILE CHANGES IT ALL. I'LL BE WALKING THROUGH A DOOR I CAN'T WALK BACK OUT OF.
THE IDENTITY OF THE GREATEST HERO IN THE WORLD IS ONE CLICK AWAY.
ONE CLICK...
SUPERMAN.
MAX DOESN'T EVEN KNOW THIS ONE.
KLK
NAME: SUPERMAN
IDENTITY: CLARK KENT
LOCATION: METROPOLIS, N.Y.
AFFILIATION(S): JUSTICE LEAGUE
POWERS: STRENGTH: (A-1); SPEED (A-2); INVULNERABILITY (A-1); FLIGHT (A-1)
ABILITIES AND EQUIPMENT: HEAT VISION, X-RAY VISION, MICROSCOPIC VISION, SUPER-HEARING.
ASSOCIATES:
• LANE, LOIS (WIFE)
• KENT, CONNER – SUPERBOY
• SUPERGIRL
• KENT, JONATHAN AND MARTHA (ADOPTIVE PARENTS)
WEAKNESS SUBFILE:
IS THAT WHAT THIS IS ALL ABOUT?
WEAKNESSES?
WEAKNESS
KRYPTONITE.
MAGIC

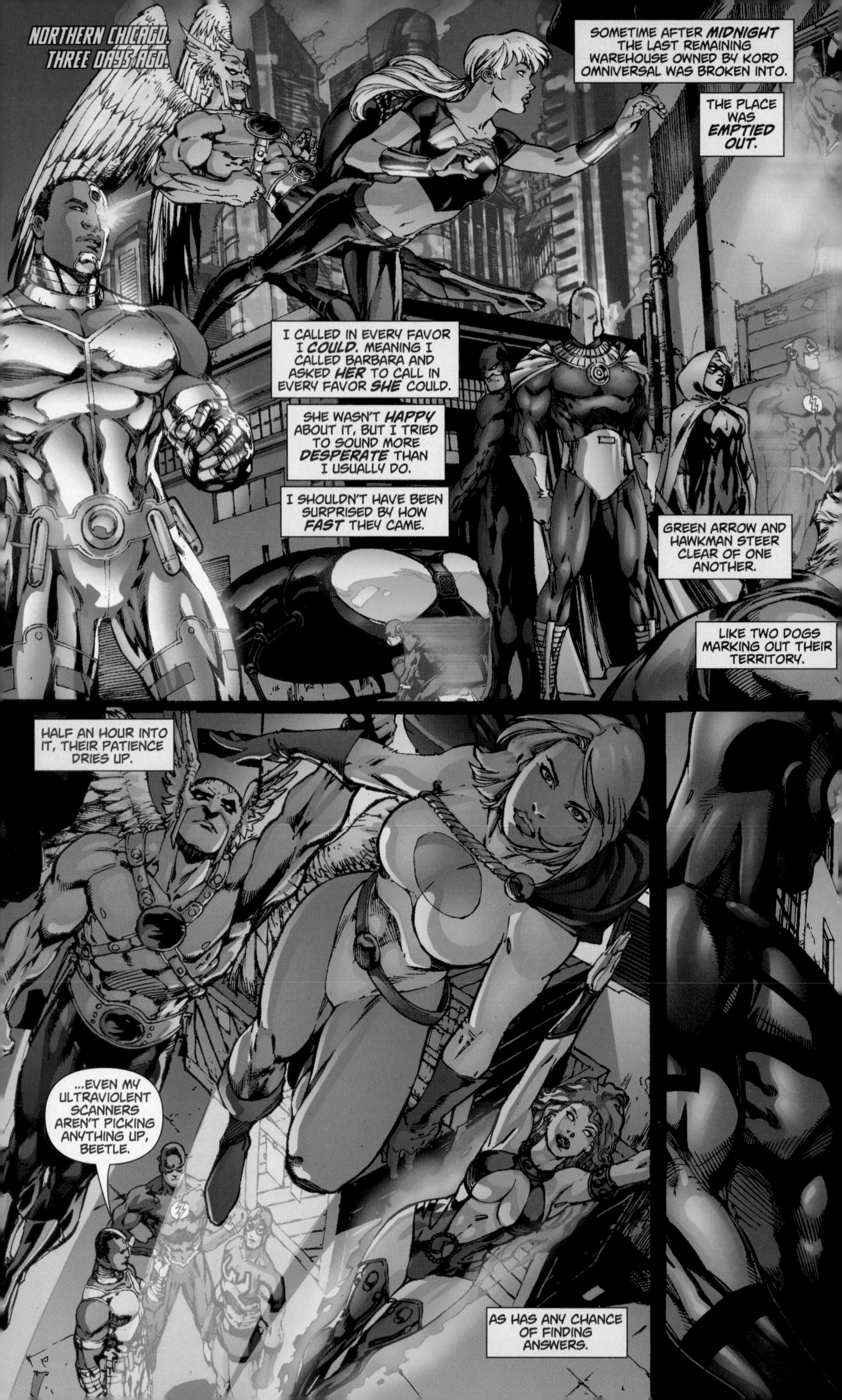
NORTHERN CHICAGO. THREE DAYS AGO.
SOMETIME AFTER MIDNIGHT THE LAST REMAINING WAREHOUSE OWNED BY KORD OMNIVERSAL WAS BROKEN INTO.
THE PLACE WAS EMPTIED OUT.
I CALLED IN EVERY FAVOR I COULD. MEANING I CALLED BARBARA AND ASKED HER TO CALL IN EVERY FAVOR SHE COULD.
SHE WASN'T HAPPY ABOUT IT, BUT I TRIED TO SOUND MORE DESPERATE THAN I USUALLY DO.
I SHOULDN'T HAVE BEEN SURPRISED BY HOW FAST THEY CAME.
GREEN ARROW AND HAWKMAN STEER CLEAR OF ONE ANOTHER.
LIKE TWO DOGS MARKING OUT THEIR TERRITORY.
HALF AN HOUR INTO IT, THEIR PATIENCE DRIES UP.
...EVEN MY ULTRAVIOLENT SCANNERS AREN'T PICKING ANYTHING UP, BEETLE.
AS HAS ANY CHANCE OF FINDING ANSWERS.

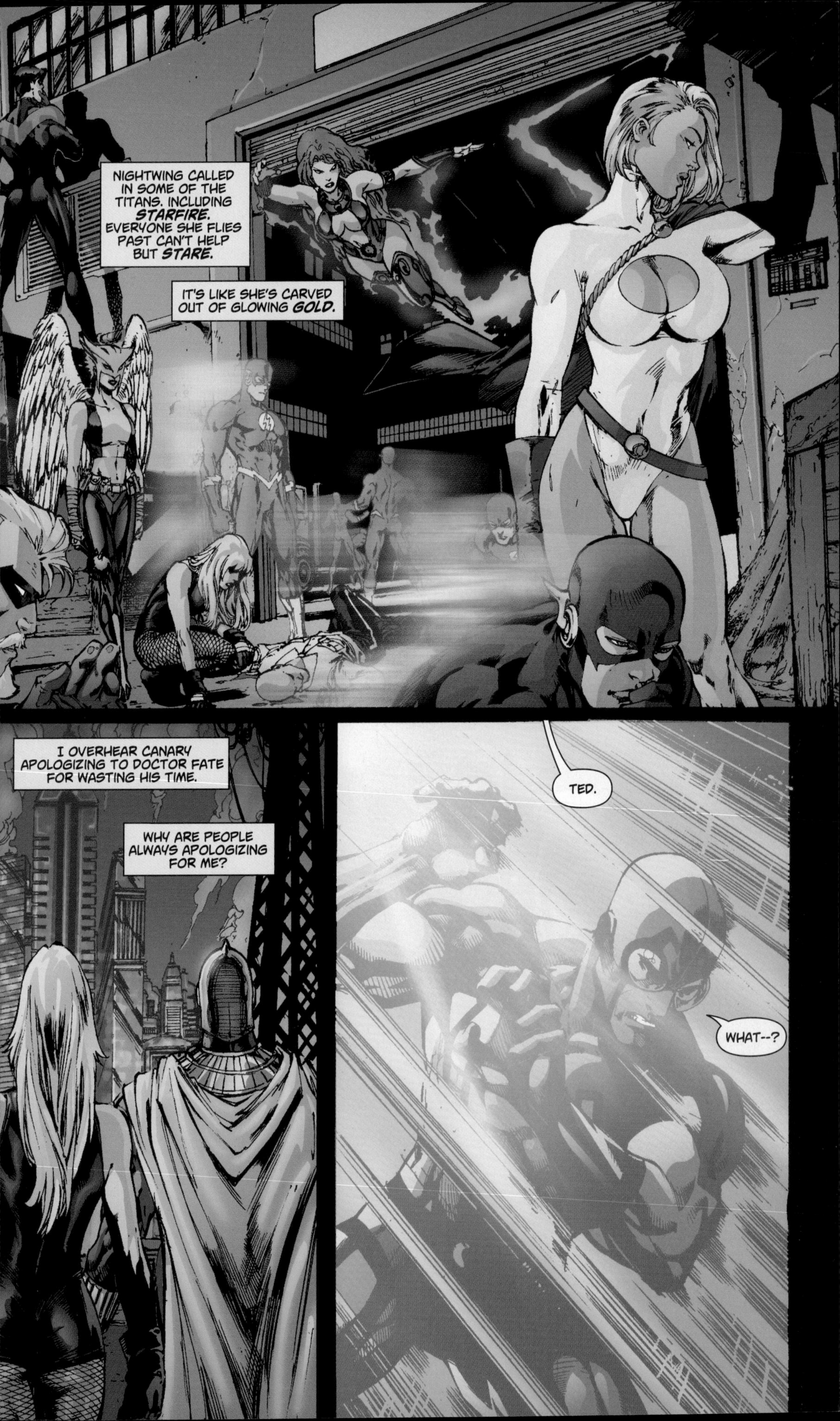
NIGHTWING CALLED IN SOME OF THE TITANS. INCLUDING STARFIRE. EVERYONE SHE FLIES PAST CAN'T HELP BUT STARE.
IT'S LIKE SHE'S CARVED OUT OF GLOWING GOLD.
I OVERHEAR CANARY APOLOGIZING TO DOCTOR FATE FOR WASTING HIS TIME.
WHY ARE PEOPLE ALWAYS APOLOGIZING FOR ME?
TED.
WHAT--?

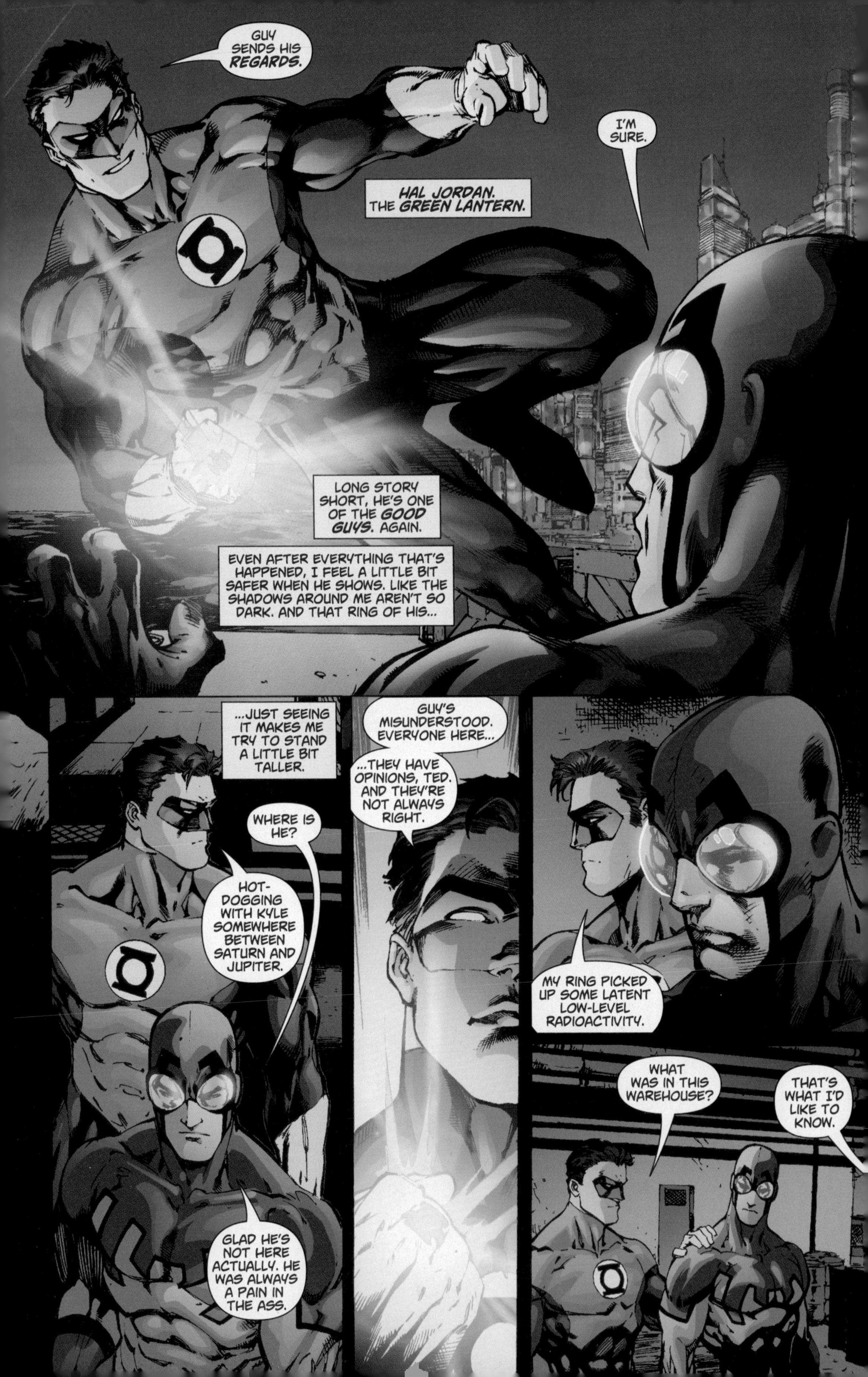
GUY SENDS HIS REGARDS.
I'M SURE.
HAL JORDAN. THE GREEN LANTERN.
LONG STORY SHORT, HE'S ONE OF THE GOOD GUYS. AGAIN.
EVEN AFTER EVERYTHING THAT'S HAPPENED, I FEEL A LITTLE BIT SAFER WHEN HE SHOWS. LIKE THE SHADOWS AROUND ME AREN'T SO DARK. AND THAT RING OF HIS...
...JUST SEEING IT MAKES ME TRY TO STAND A LITTLE BIT TALLER.
WHERE IS HE?
HOT-DOGGING WITH KYLE SOMEWHERE BETWEEN SATURN AND JUPITER.
GLAD HE'S NOT HERE ACTUALLY. HE WAS ALWAYS A PAIN IN THE ASS.
GUY'S MISUNDERSTOOD. EVERYONE HERE...
...THEY HAVE OPINIONS, TED. AND THEY'RE NOT ALWAYS RIGHT.
MY RING PICKED UP SOME LATENT LOW-LEVEL RADIOACTIVITY.
WHAT WAS IN THIS WAREHOUSE?
THAT'S WHAT I'D LIKE TO KNOW.

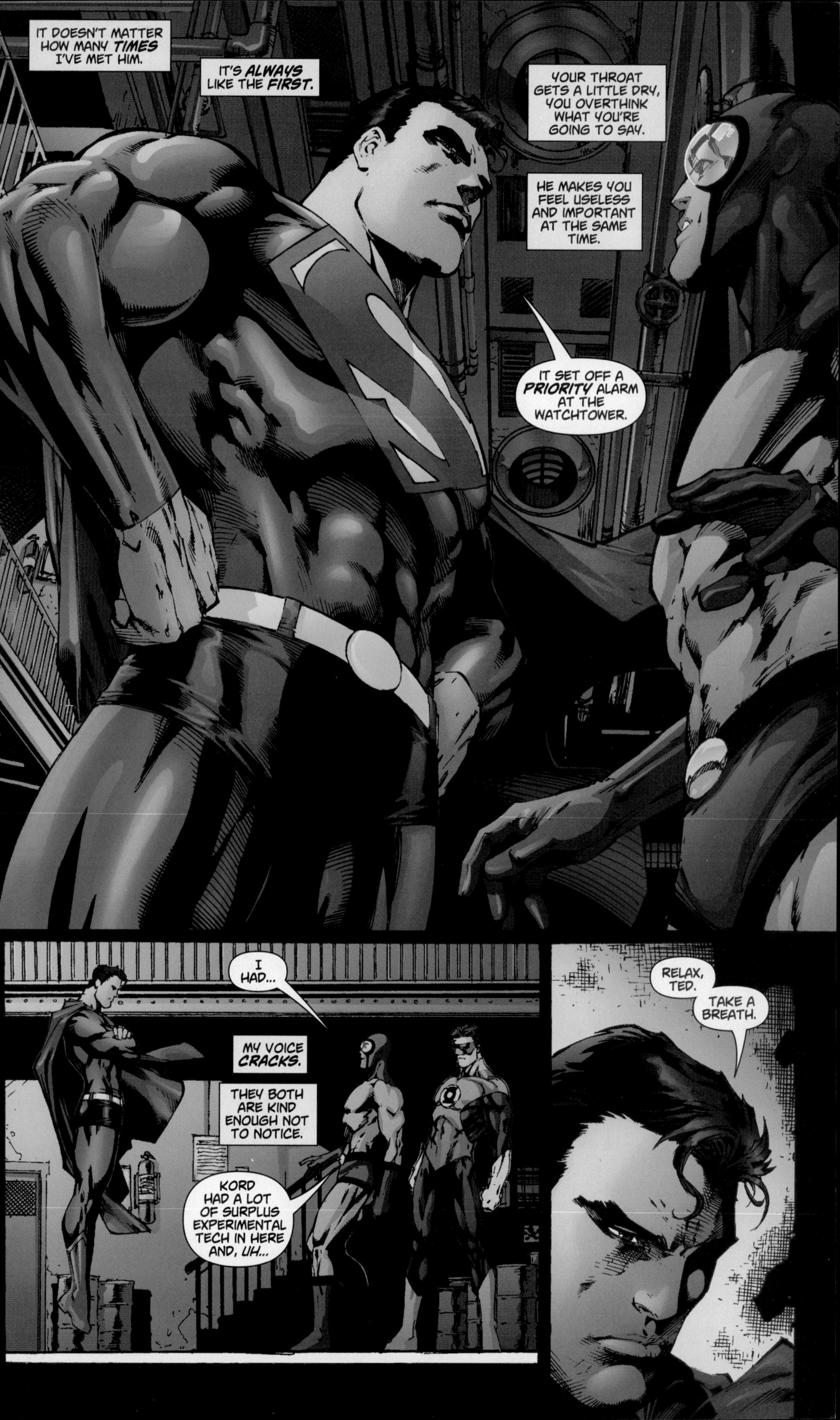

IT DOESN'T MATTER HOW MANY TIMES I'VE MET HIM.
IT'S ALWAYS LIKE THE FIRST.
YOUR THROAT GETS A LITTLE DRY, YOU OVERTHINK WHAT YOU'RE GOING TO SAY.
HE MAKES YOU FEEL USELESS AND IMPORTANT AT THE SAME TIME.
IT SET OFF A PRIORITY ALARM AT THE WATCHTOWER.
I HAD...
MY VOICE CRACKS.
THEY BOTH ARE KIND ENOUGH NOT TO NOTICE.
KORD HAD A LOT OF SURPLUS EXPERIMENTAL TECH IN HERE AND, UH...
RELAX, TED.
TAKE A BREATH.

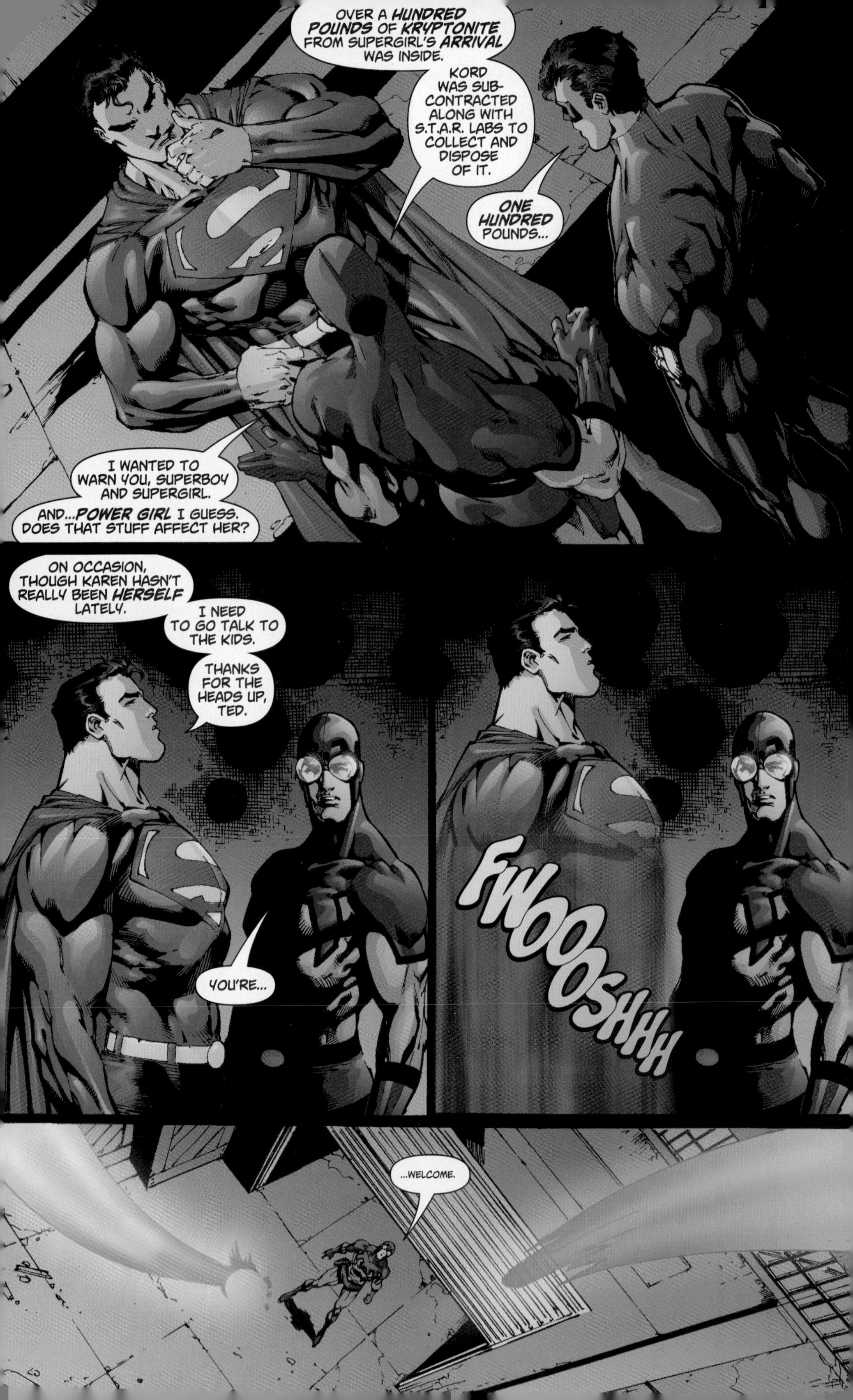
OVER A HUNDRED POUNDS OF KRYPTONITE FROM SUPERGIRL'S ARRIVAL WAS INSIDE.
KORD WAS SUB-CONTRACTED ALONG WITH S.T.A.R. LABS TO COLLECT AND DISPOSE OF IT.
ONE HUNDRED POUNDS...
I WANTED TO WARN YOU, SUPERBOY AND SUPERGIRL.
AND...POWER GIRL I GUESS. DOES THAT STUFF AFFECT HER?
ON OCCASION, THOUGH KAREN HASN'T REALLY BEEN HERSELF LATELY.
I NEED TO GO TALK TO THE KIDS.
THANKS FOR THE HEADS UP, TED.
YOU'RE...
FWOOOSHHH
...WELCOME.

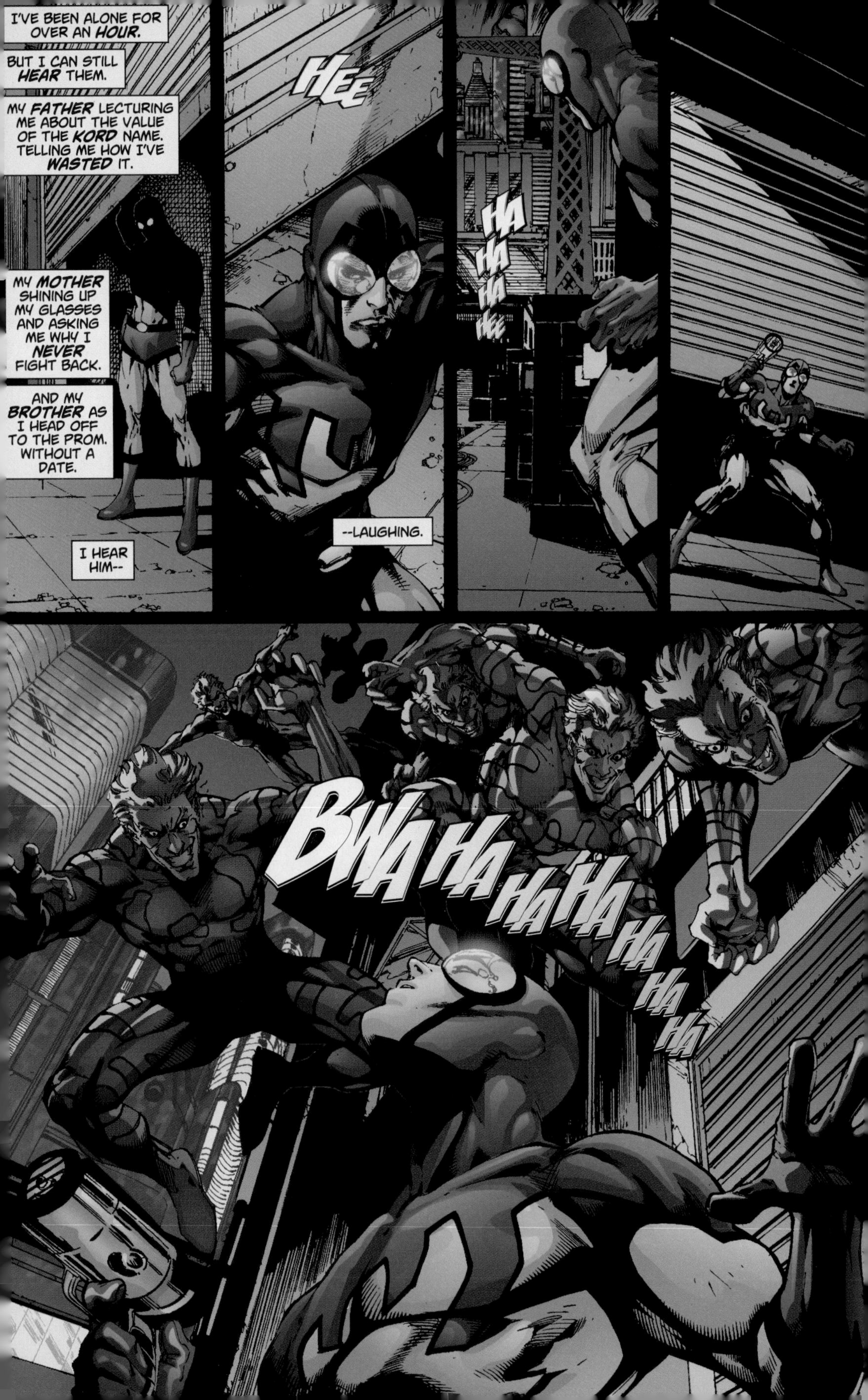
I'VE BEEN ALONE FOR OVER AN HOUR.
BUT I CAN STILL HEAR THEM.
MY FATHER LECTURING ME ABOUT THE VALUE OF THE KORD NAME. TELLING ME HOW I'VE WASTED IT.
MY MOTHER SHINING UP MY GLASSES AND ASKING ME WHY I NEVER FIGHT BACK.
AND MY BROTHER AS I HEAD OFF TO THE PROM. WITHOUT A DATE.
I HEAR HIM--
HEE
--LAUGHING.
HA HA HA HEE
BWA HA HA HA HA HA HA HA HA

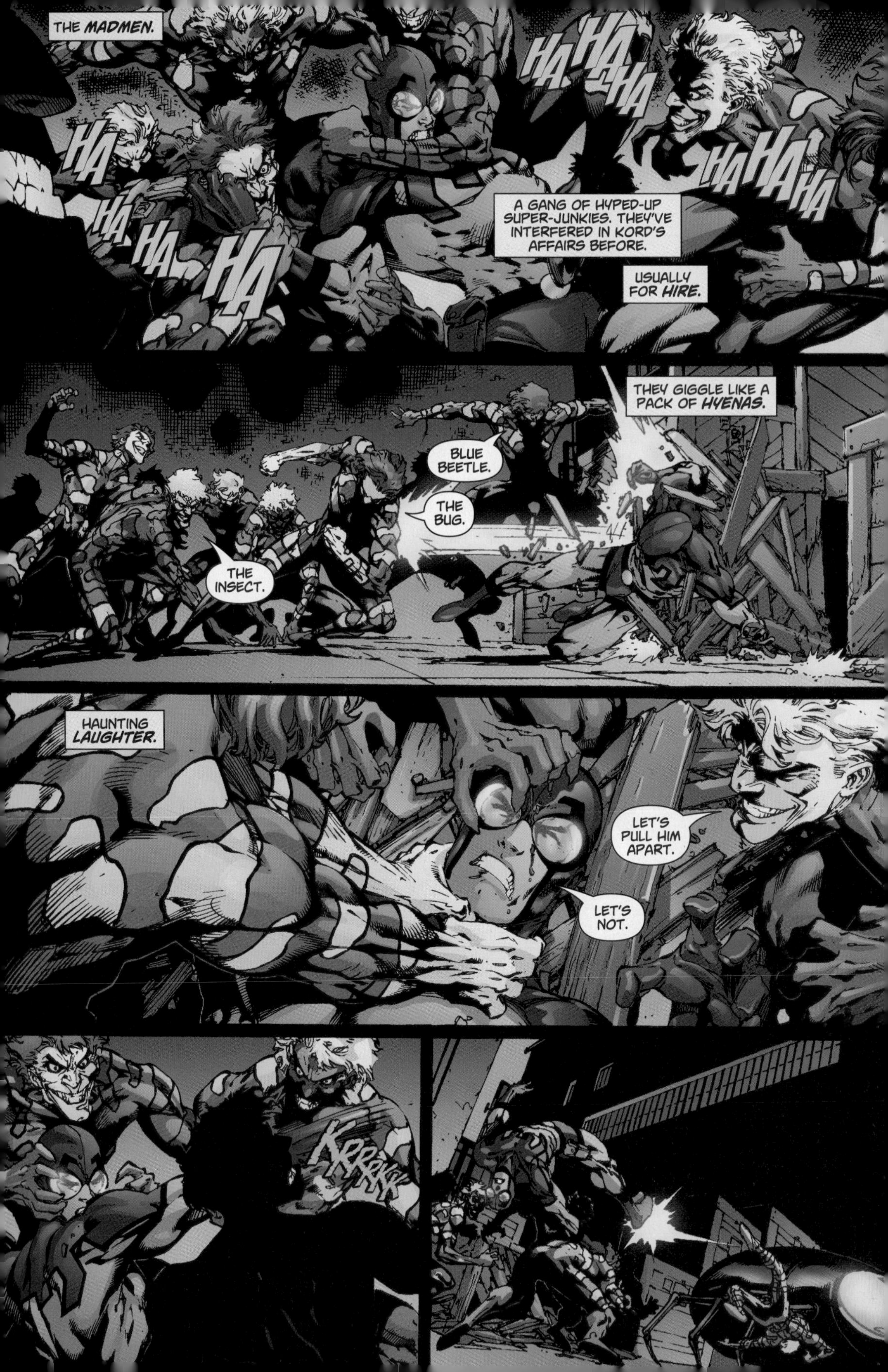
THE MADMEN.
HA HA HA HA
HA HA HA HA
A GANG OF HYPED-UP SUPER-JUNKIES. THEY'VE INTERFERED IN KORD'S AFFAIRS BEFORE.
USUALLY FOR HIRE.
HA HA HA HA HA
THEY GIGGLE LIKE A PACK OF HYENAS.
BLUE BEETLE.
THE BUG.
THE INSECT.
HAUNTING LAUGHTER.
LET'S PULL HIM APART.
LET'S NOT.
KRRRKK

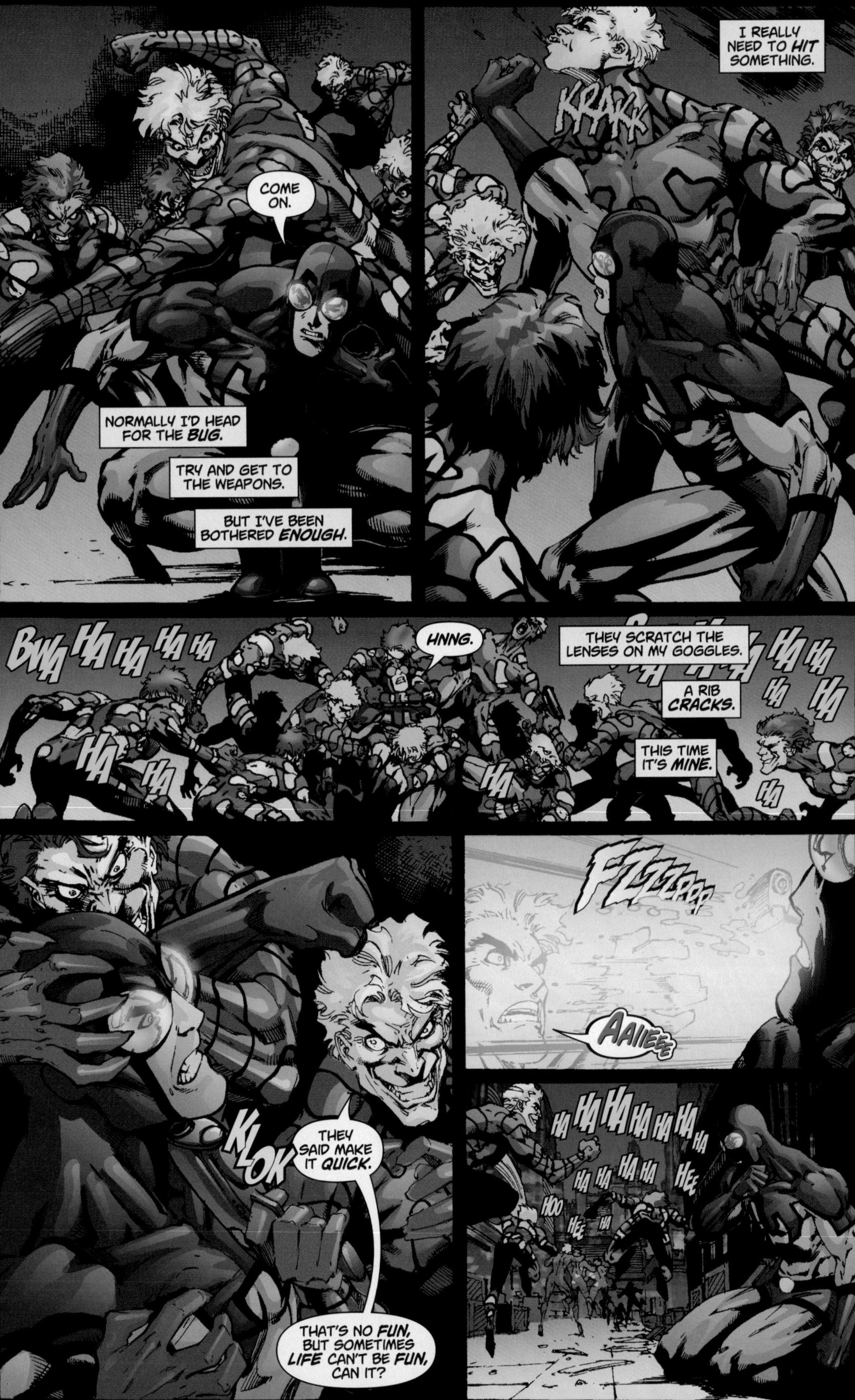
COME ON.
NORMALLY I'D HEAD FOR THE BUG.
TRY AND GET TO THE WEAPONS.
BUT I'VE BEEN BOTHERED ENOUGH.
I REALLY NEED TO HIT SOMETHING.
KRAKK
BWA HA HA HA HA HA
HNNG.
THEY SCRATCH THE LENSES ON MY GOGGLES.
A RIB CRACKS.
THIS TIME IT'S MINE.
KLOK
THEY SAID MAKE IT QUICK.
THAT'S NO FUN, BUT SOMETIMES LIFE CAN'T BE FUN, CAN IT?
FZZZRRP
AAIIEEE
HA HA HA HA HA HA HA HA
HA HA HA HA HA HEE
HOO HEE HA

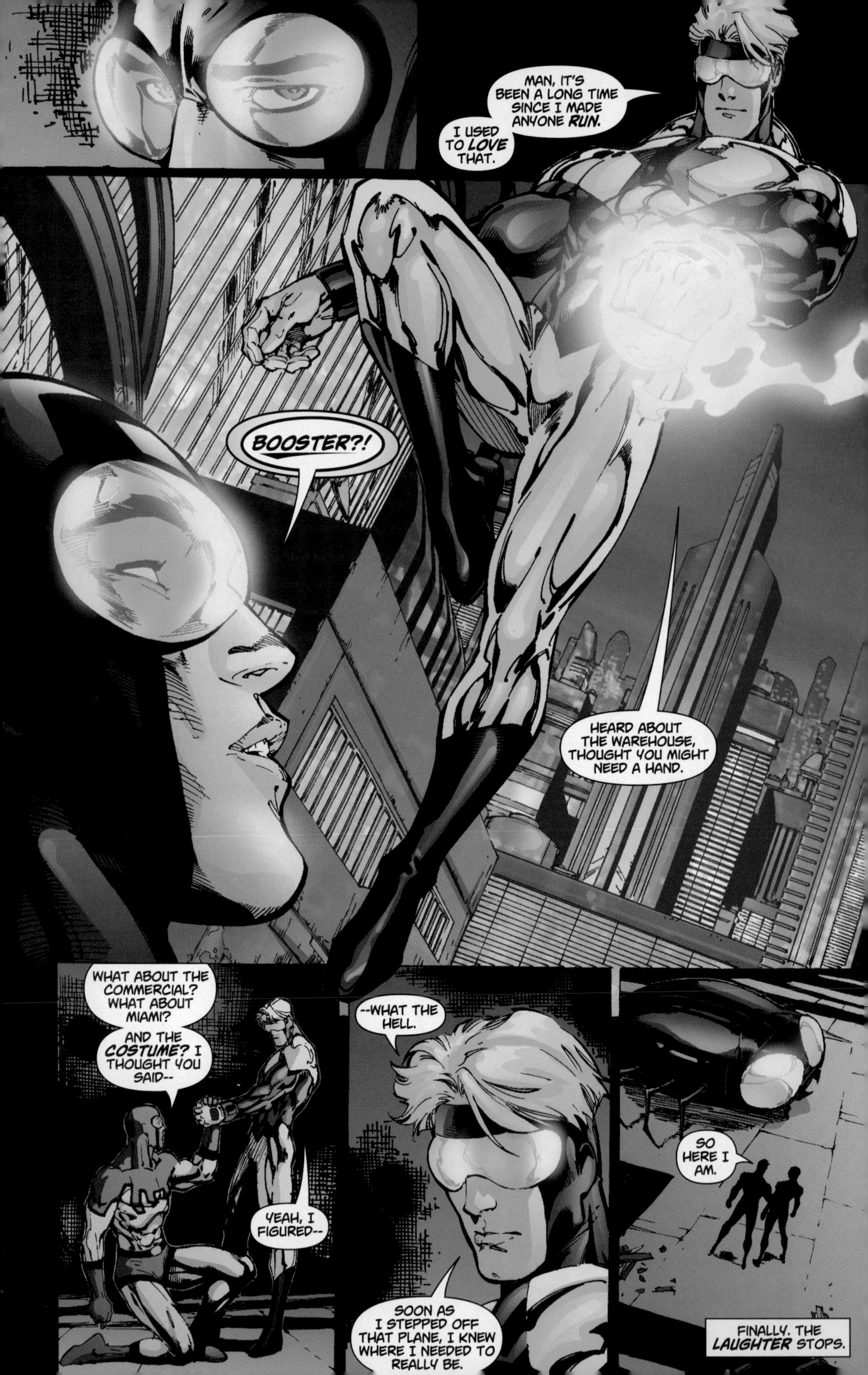
MAN, IT'S BEEN A LONG TIME SINCE I MADE ANYONE RUN.
I USED TO LOVE THAT.
BOOSTER?!
HEARD ABOUT THE WAREHOUSE, THOUGHT YOU MIGHT NEED A HAND.
WHAT ABOUT THE COMMERCIAL? WHAT ABOUT MIAMI?
AND THE COSTUME? I THOUGHT YOU SAID--
YEAH, I FIGURED--
--WHAT THE HELL.
SOON AS I STEPPED OFF THAT PLANE, I KNEW WHERE I NEEDED TO REALLY BE.
SO HERE I AM.
FINALLY. THE LAUGHTER STOPS.

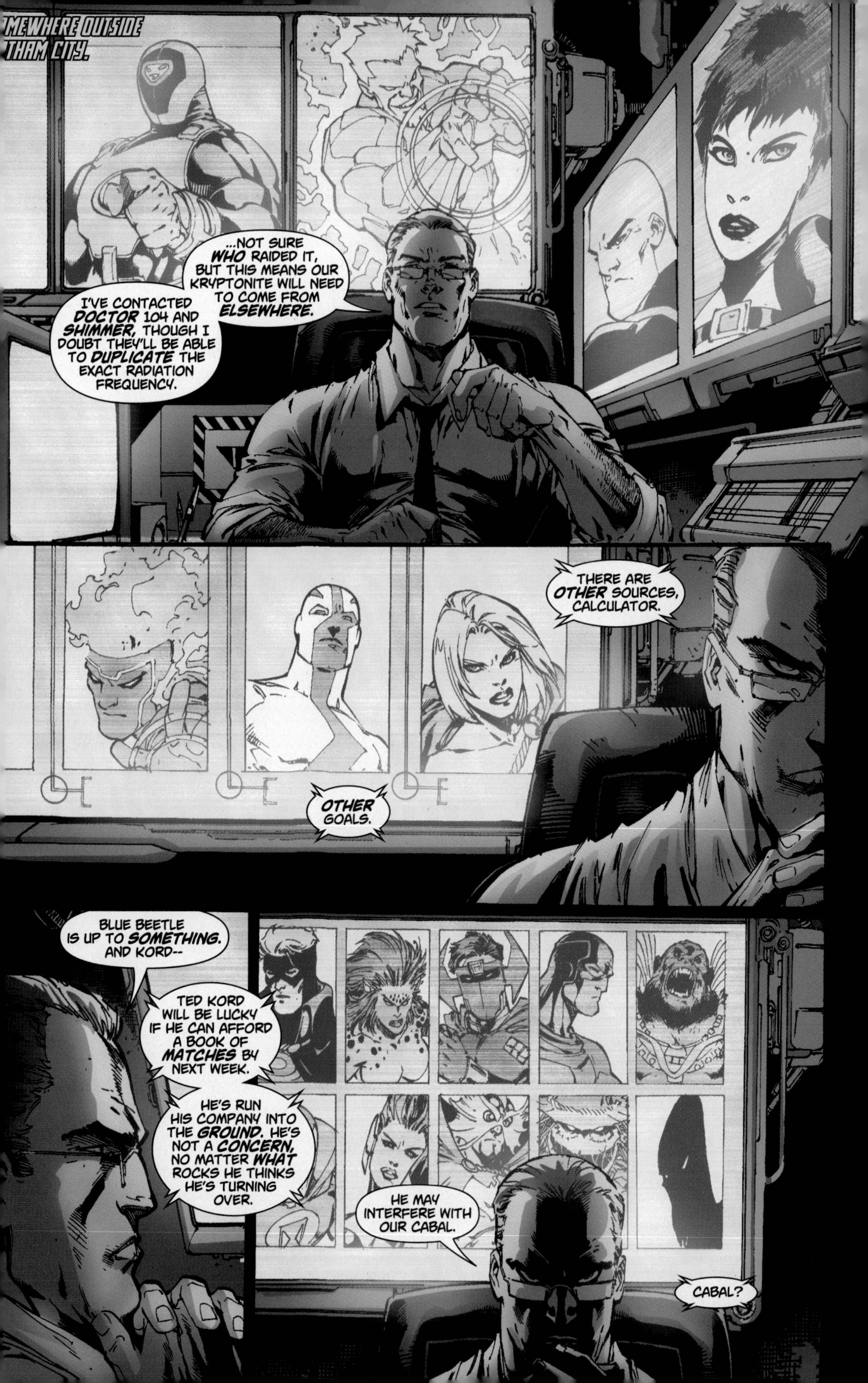
MEWHERE OUTSIDE
THAM CITY.
...NOT SURE WHO RAIDED IT, BUT THIS MEANS OUR KRYPTONITE WILL NEED TO COME FROM ELSEWHERE.
I'VE CONTACTED DOCTOR 104 AND SHIMMER, THOUGH I DOUBT THEY'LL BE ABLE TO DUPLICATE THE EXACT RADIATION FREQUENCY.
THERE ARE OTHER SOURCES, CALCULATOR.
OTHER GOALS.
BLUE BEETLE IS UP TO SOMETHING. AND KORD--
TED KORD WILL BE LUCKY IF HE CAN AFFORD A BOOK OF MATCHES BY NEXT WEEK.
HE'S RUN HIS COMPANY INTO THE GROUND. HE'S NOT A CONCERN, NO MATTER WHAT ROCKS HE THINKS HE'S TURNING OVER.
HE MAY INTERFERE WITH OUR CABAL.
CABAL?

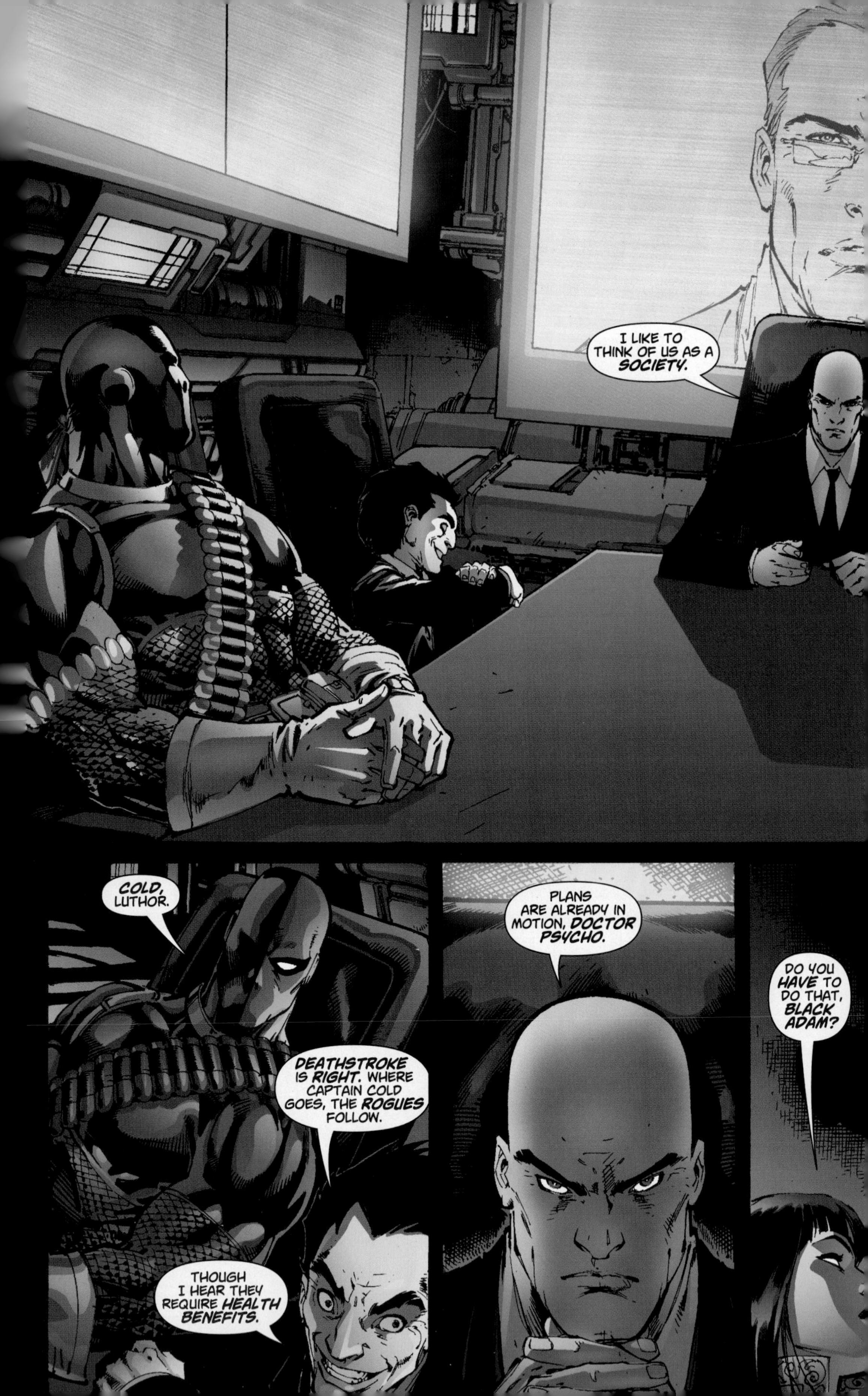
I LIKE TO THINK OF US AS A SOCIETY.
COLD, LUTHOR.
DEATHSTROKE IS RIGHT. WHERE CAPTAIN COLD GOES, THE ROGUES FOLLOW.
THOUGH I HEAR THEY REQUIRE HEALTH BENEFITS.
PLANS ARE ALREADY IN MOTION, DOCTOR PSYCHO.
DO YOU HAVE TO DO THAT, BLACK ADAM?

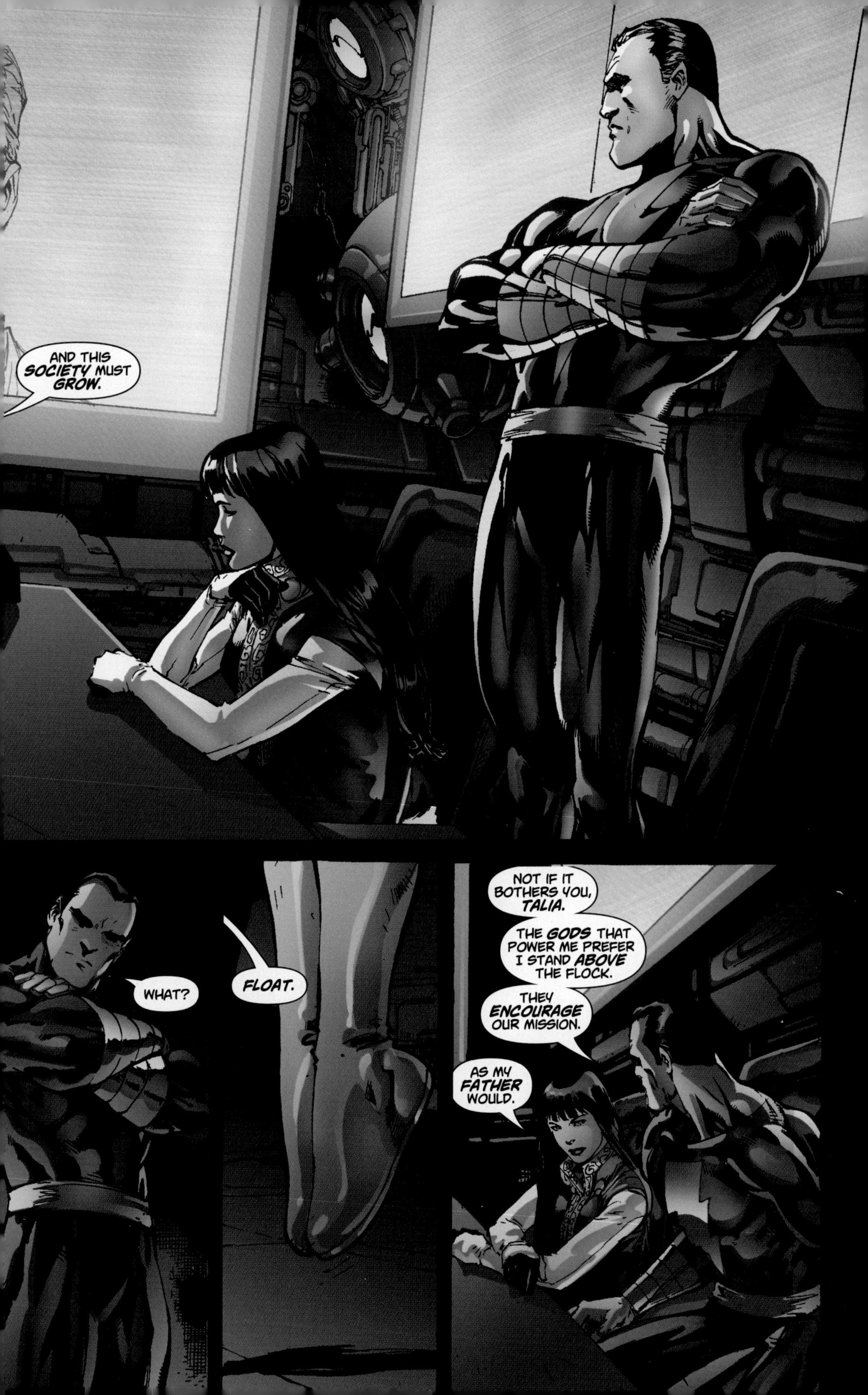
AND THIS SOCIETY MUST GROW.
WHAT?
FLOAT.
NOT IF IT BOTHERS YOU, TALIA.
THE GODS THAT POWER ME PREFER I STAND ABOVE THE FLOCK.
THEY ENCOURAGE OUR MISSION.
AS MY FATHER WOULD.

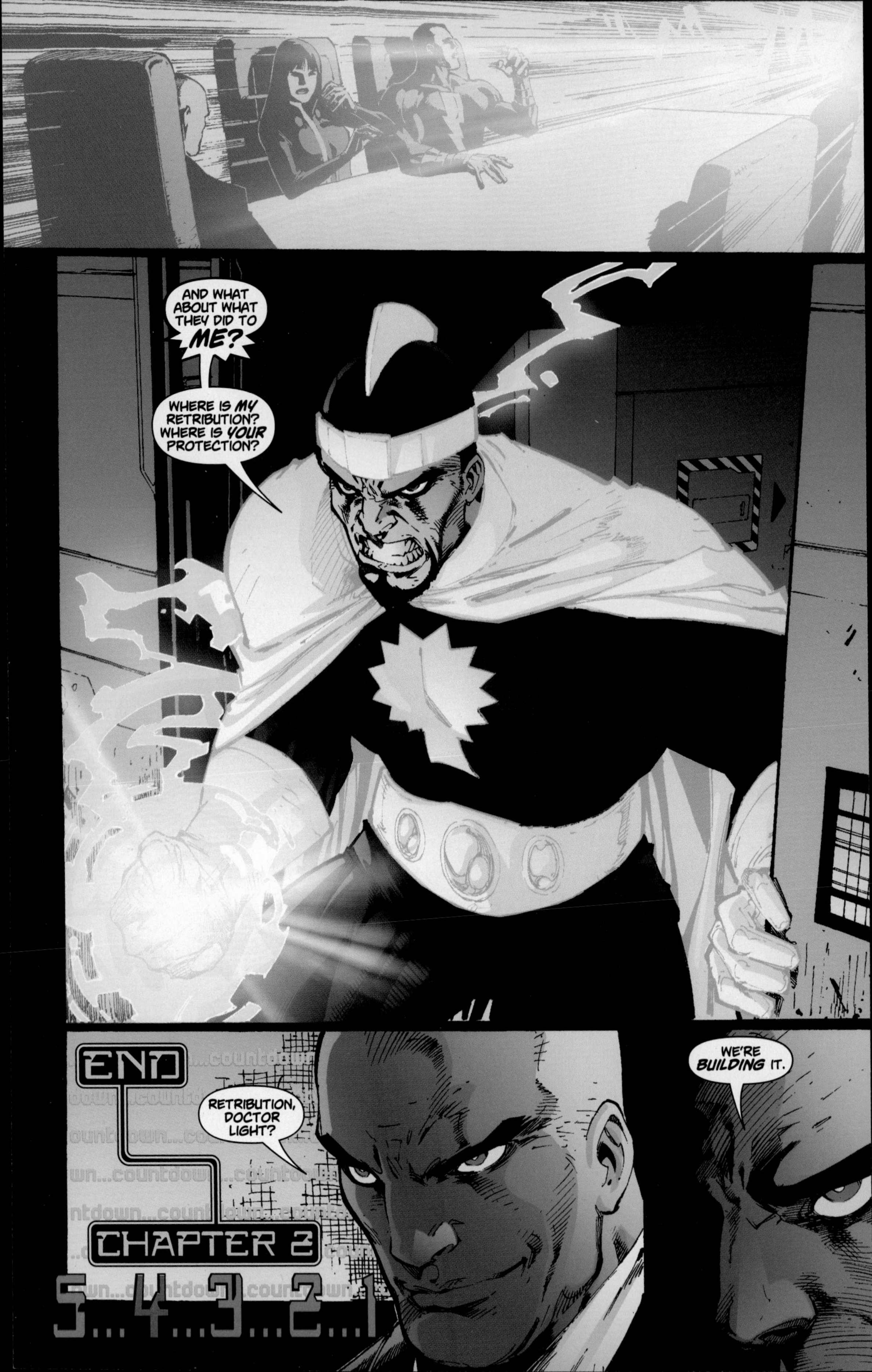

AND WHAT ABOUT WHAT THEY DID TO ME?
WHERE IS MY RETRIBUTION? WHERE IS YOUR PROTECTION?
END
CHAPTER 2
5...4...3...2...1
RETRIBUTION, DOCTOR LIGHT?
WE'RE BUILDING IT.

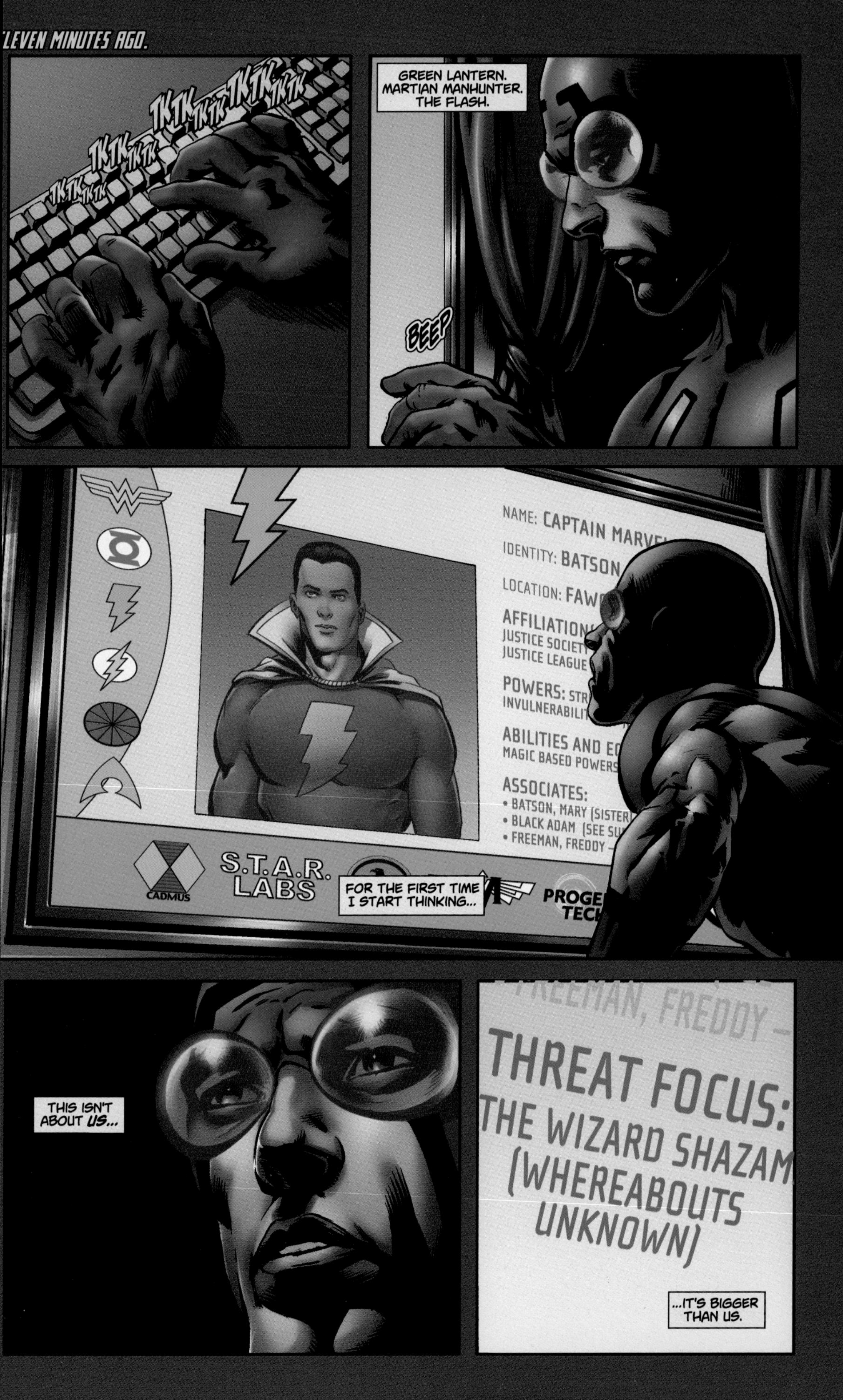
LEVEN MINUTES AGO.
TKTK TKTK TKTK TKTK TKTK TKTK TKTK TKTK
GREEN LANTERN.
MARTIAN MANHUNTER.
THE FLASH.
BEEP
NAME: CAPTAIN MARVE
IDENTITY: BATSON
LOCATION: FAW
AFFILIATION
JUSTICE SOCIETY
JUSTICE LEAGUE
POWERS: STR
INVULNERABILI
ABILITIES AND E
MAGIC BASED POWERS
ASSOCIATES:
• BATSON, MARY (SISTER)
• BLACK ADAM (SEE SU
• FREEMAN, FREDDY –
CADMUS
S.T.A.R. LABS
FOR THE FIRST TIME I START THINKING...
PROGE
TECH
THIS ISN'T ABOUT US...
FREEMAN, FREDDY –
THREAT FOCUS:
THE WIZARD SHAZAM
(WHEREABOUTS UNKNOWN)
...IT'S BIGGER THAN US.

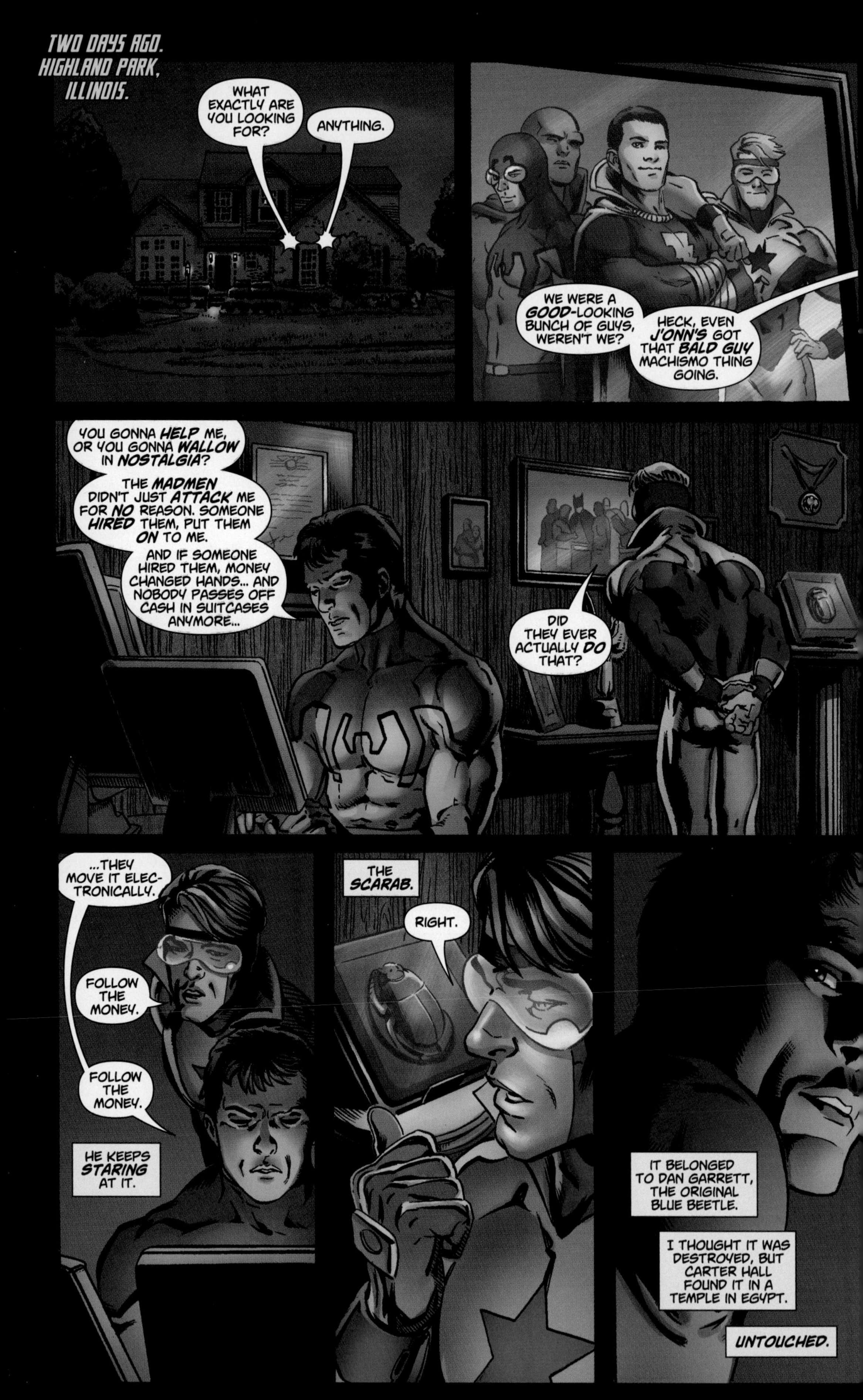
TWO DAYS AGO. HIGHLAND PARK, ILLINOIS.
WHAT EXACTLY ARE YOU LOOKING FOR?
ANYTHING.
WE WERE A GOOD-LOOKING BUNCH OF GUYS, WEREN'T WE?
HECK, EVEN J'ONN'S GOT THAT BALD GUY MACHISMO THING GOING.
YOU GONNA HELP ME, OR YOU GONNA WALLOW IN NOSTALGIA?
THE MADMEN DIDN'T JUST ATTACK ME FOR NO REASON. SOMEONE HIRED THEM, PUT THEM ON TO ME.
AND IF SOMEONE HIRED THEM, MONEY CHANGED HANDS... AND NOBODY PASSES OFF CASH IN SUITCASES ANYMORE...
DID THEY EVER ACTUALLY DO THAT?
...THEY MOVE IT ELECTRONICALLY.
FOLLOW THE MONEY.
FOLLOW THE MONEY.
HE KEEPS STARING AT IT.
THE SCARAB.
RIGHT.
IT BELONGED TO DAN GARRETT, THE ORIGINAL BLUE BEETLE.
I THOUGHT IT WAS DESTROYED, BUT CARTER HALL FOUND IT IN A TEMPLE IN EGYPT.
UNTOUCHED.

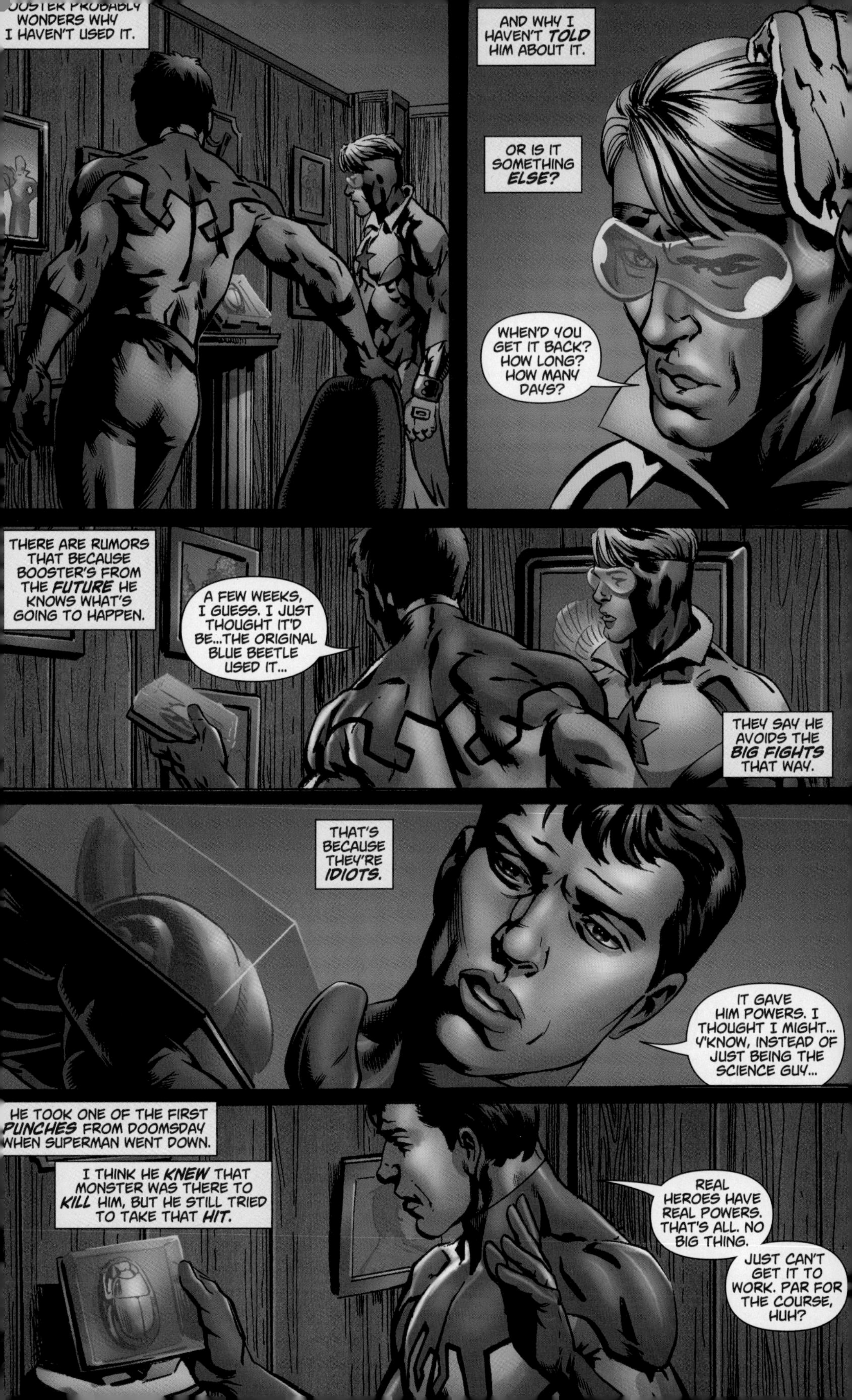

WONDERS WHY
I HAVEN'T USED IT.
AND WHY I HAVEN'T TOLD HIM ABOUT IT.
OR IS IT SOMETHING ELSE?
WHEN'D YOU GET IT BACK? HOW LONG? HOW MANY DAYS?
THERE ARE RUMORS THAT BECAUSE BOOSTER'S FROM THE FUTURE HE KNOWS WHAT'S GOING TO HAPPEN.
A FEW WEEKS, I GUESS. I JUST THOUGHT IT'D BE...THE ORIGINAL BLUE BEETLE USED IT...
THEY SAY HE AVOIDS THE BIG FIGHTS THAT WAY.
THAT'S BECAUSE THEY'RE IDIOTS.
IT GAVE HIM POWERS. I THOUGHT I MIGHT... Y'KNOW, INSTEAD OF JUST BEING THE SCIENCE GUY...
HE TOOK ONE OF THE FIRST PUNCHES FROM DOOMSDAY WHEN SUPERMAN WENT DOWN.
I THINK HE KNEW THAT MONSTER WAS THERE TO KILL HIM, BUT HE STILL TRIED TO TAKE THAT HIT.
REAL HEROES HAVE REAL POWERS. THAT'S ALL. NO BIG THING.
JUST CAN'T GET IT TO WORK. PAR FOR THE COURSE, HUH?

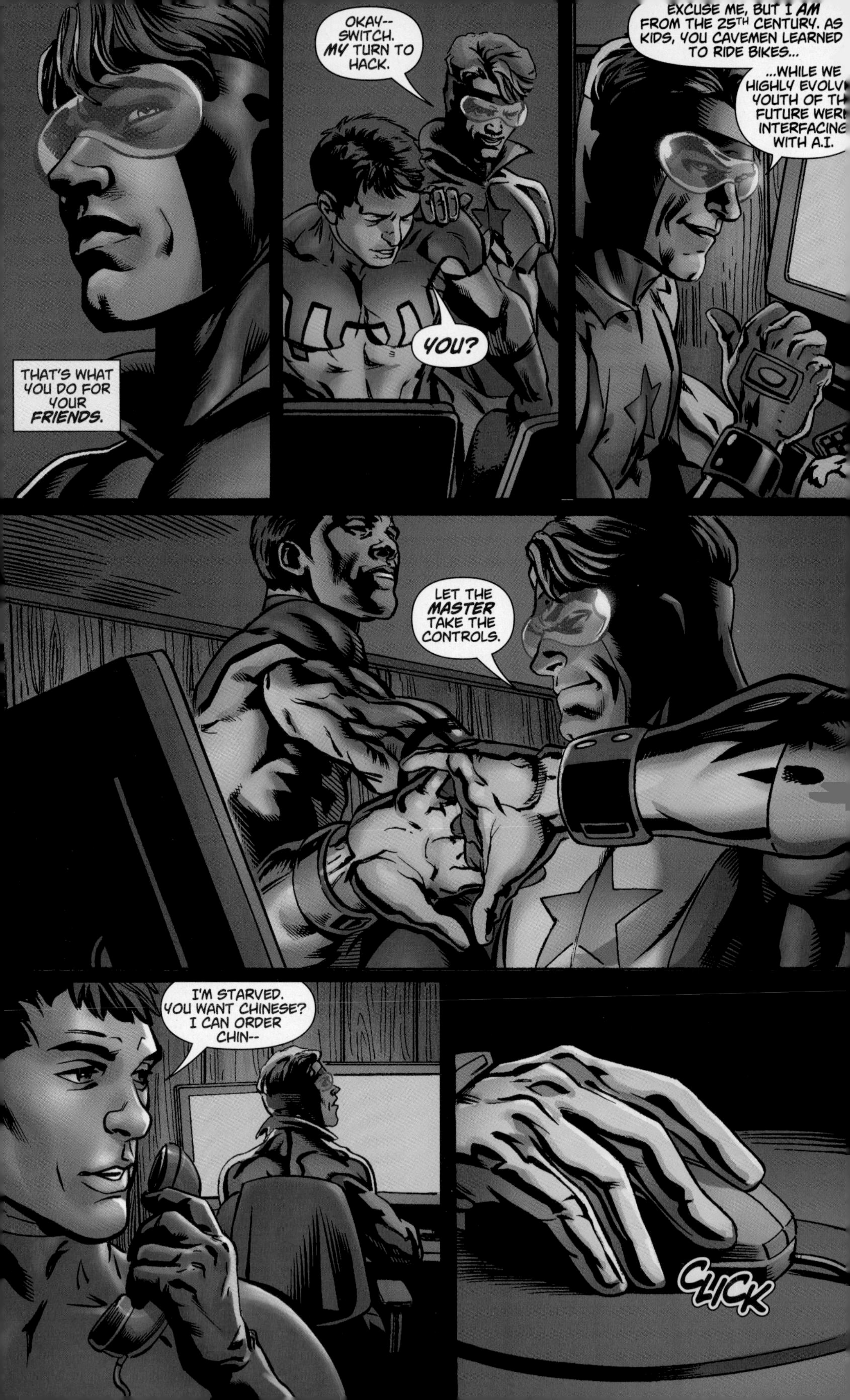
THAT'S WHAT YOU DO FOR YOUR FRIENDS.
OKAY-- SWITCH. MY TURN TO HACK.
YOU?
EXCUSE ME, BUT I AM FROM THE 25TH CENTURY. AS KIDS, YOU CAVEMEN LEARNED TO RIDE BIKES...
...WHILE WE HIGHLY EVOLV YOUTH OF TH FUTURE WER INTERFACING WITH A.I.
LET THE MASTER TAKE THE CONTROLS.
I'M STARVED. YOU WANT CHINESE? I CAN ORDER CHIN--
CLICK

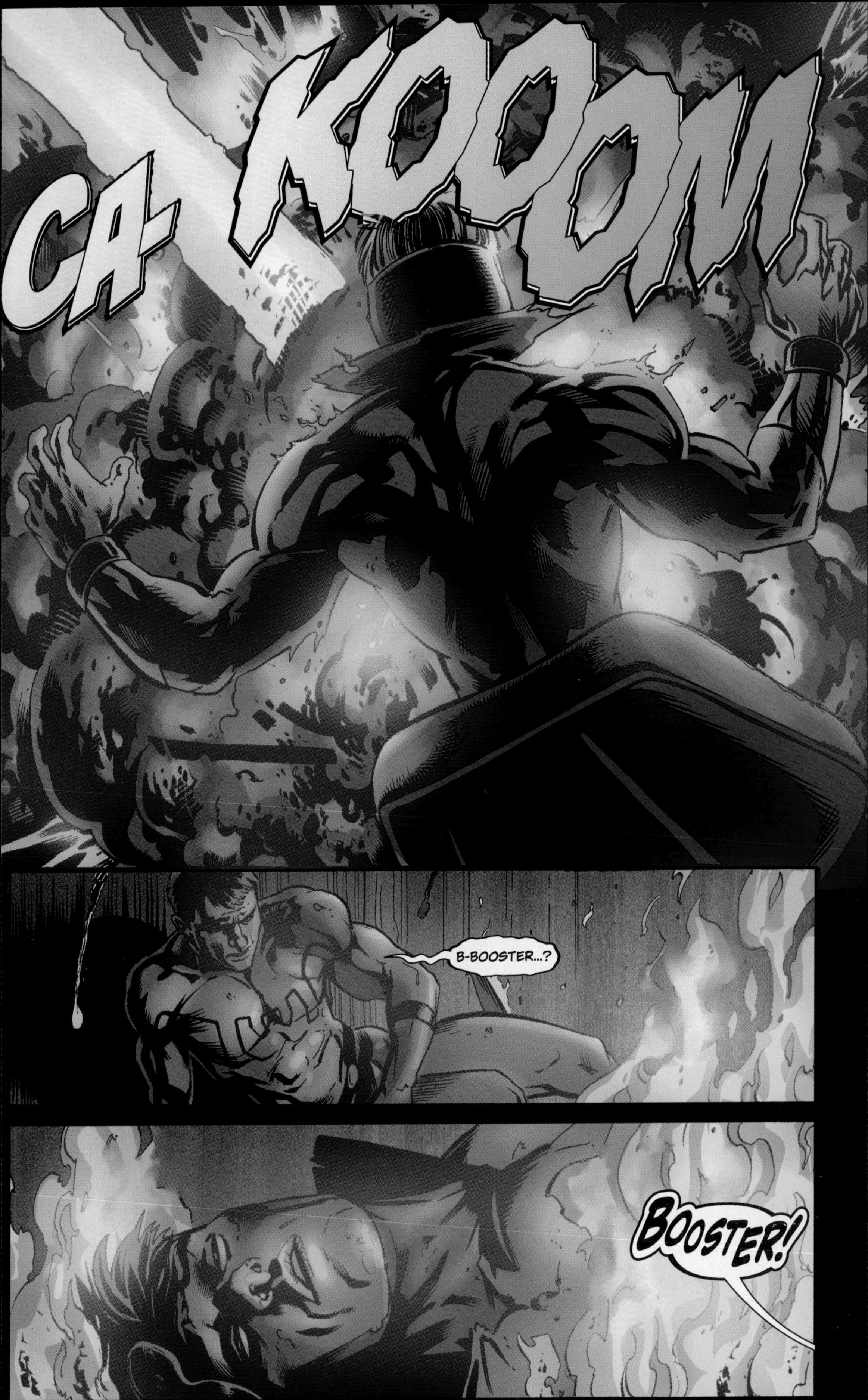
CA-KOOOM
B-BOOSTER...?
BOOSTER!

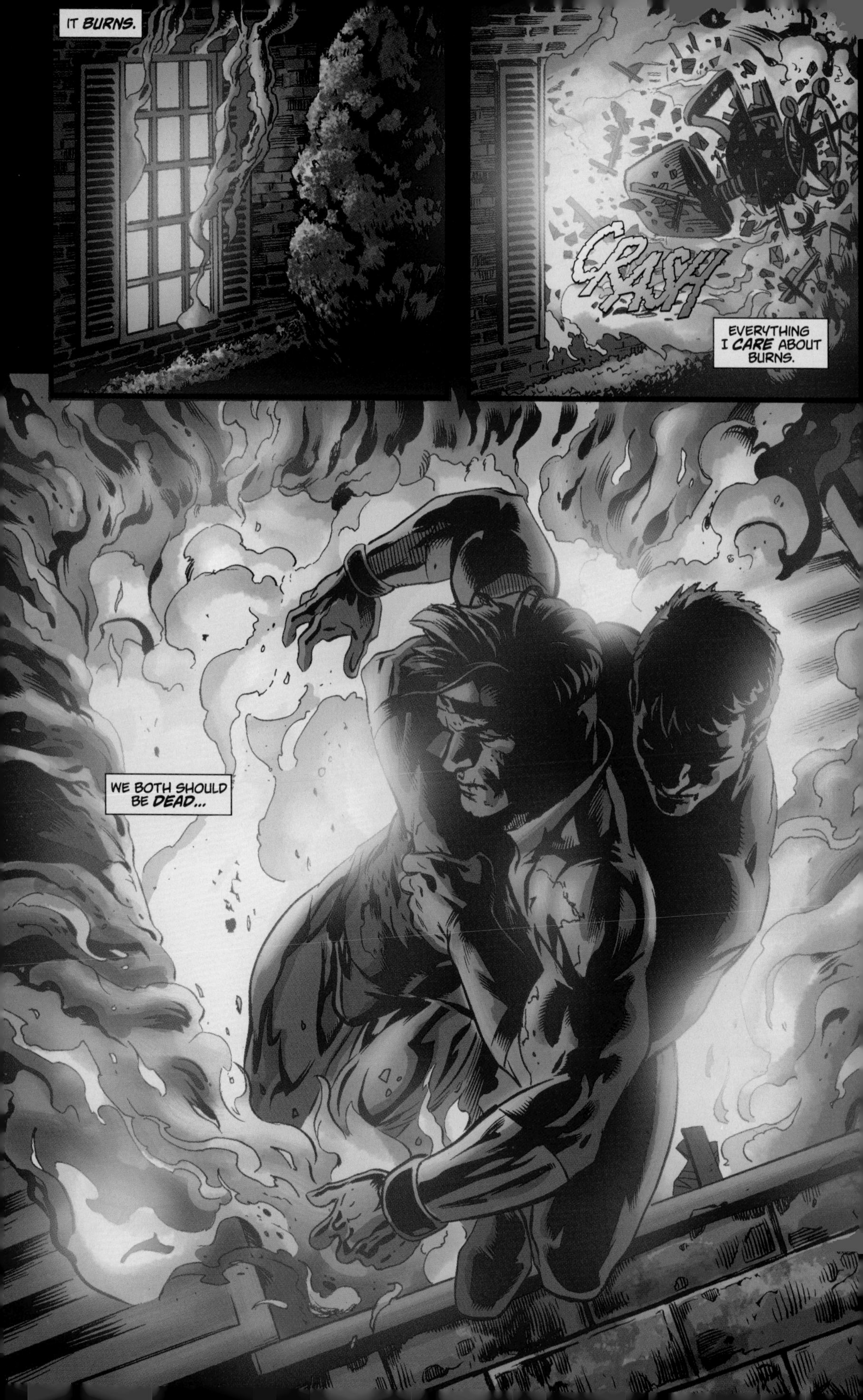
IT BURNS.
CRASH
EVERYTHING I CARE ABOUT BURNS.
WE BOTH SHOULD BE DEAD...

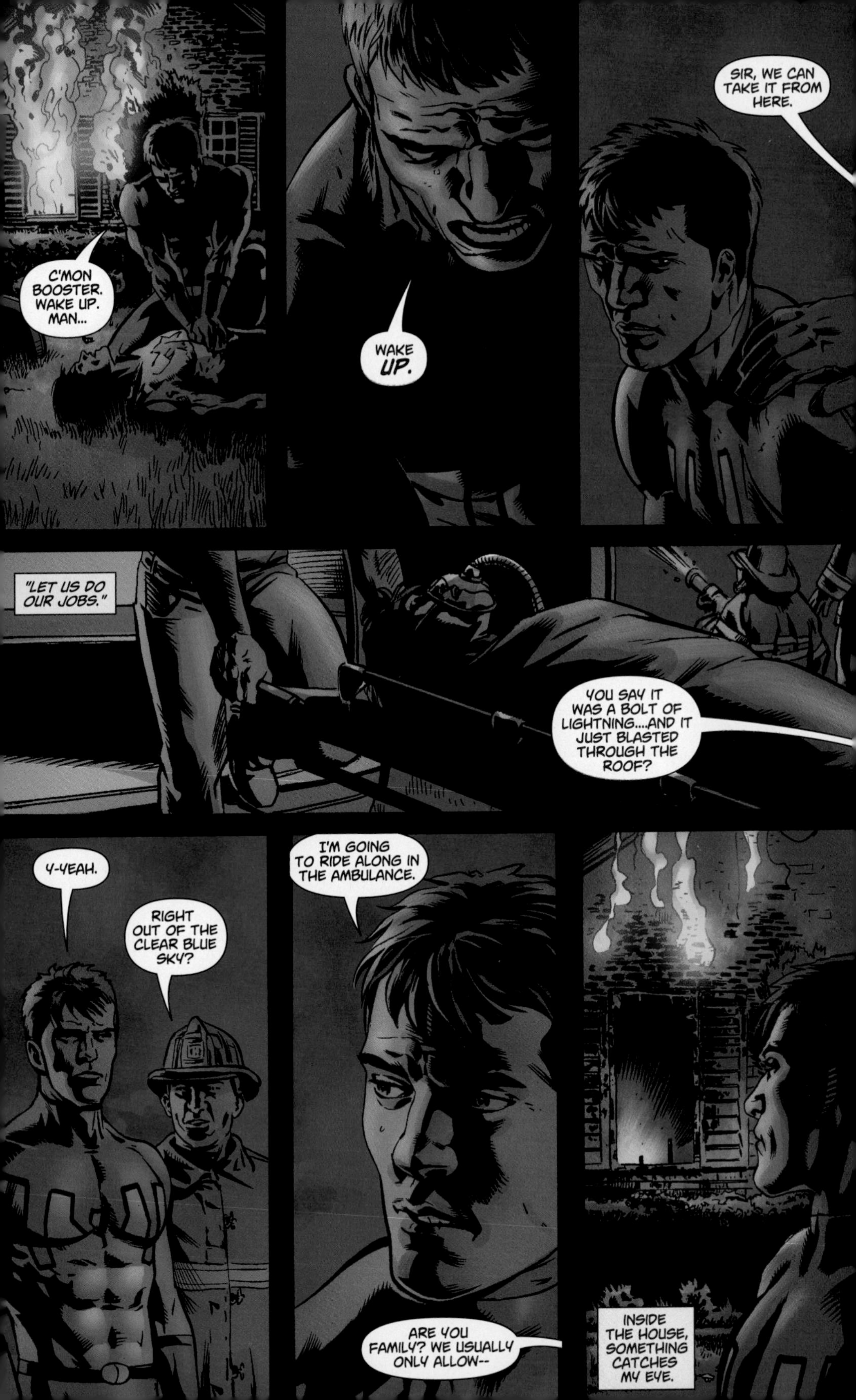
C'MON BOOSTER. WAKE UP. MAN...
WAKE UP.
SIR, WE CAN TAKE IT FROM HERE.
"LET US DO OUR JOBS."
YOU SAY IT WAS A BOLT OF LIGHTNING....AND IT JUST BLASTED THROUGH THE ROOF?
Y-YEAH.
RIGHT OUT OF THE CLEAR BLUE SKY?
I'M GOING TO RIDE ALONG IN THE AMBULANCE.
ARE YOU FAMILY? WE USUALLY ONLY ALLOW--
INSIDE THE HOUSE, SOMETHING CATCHES MY EYE.

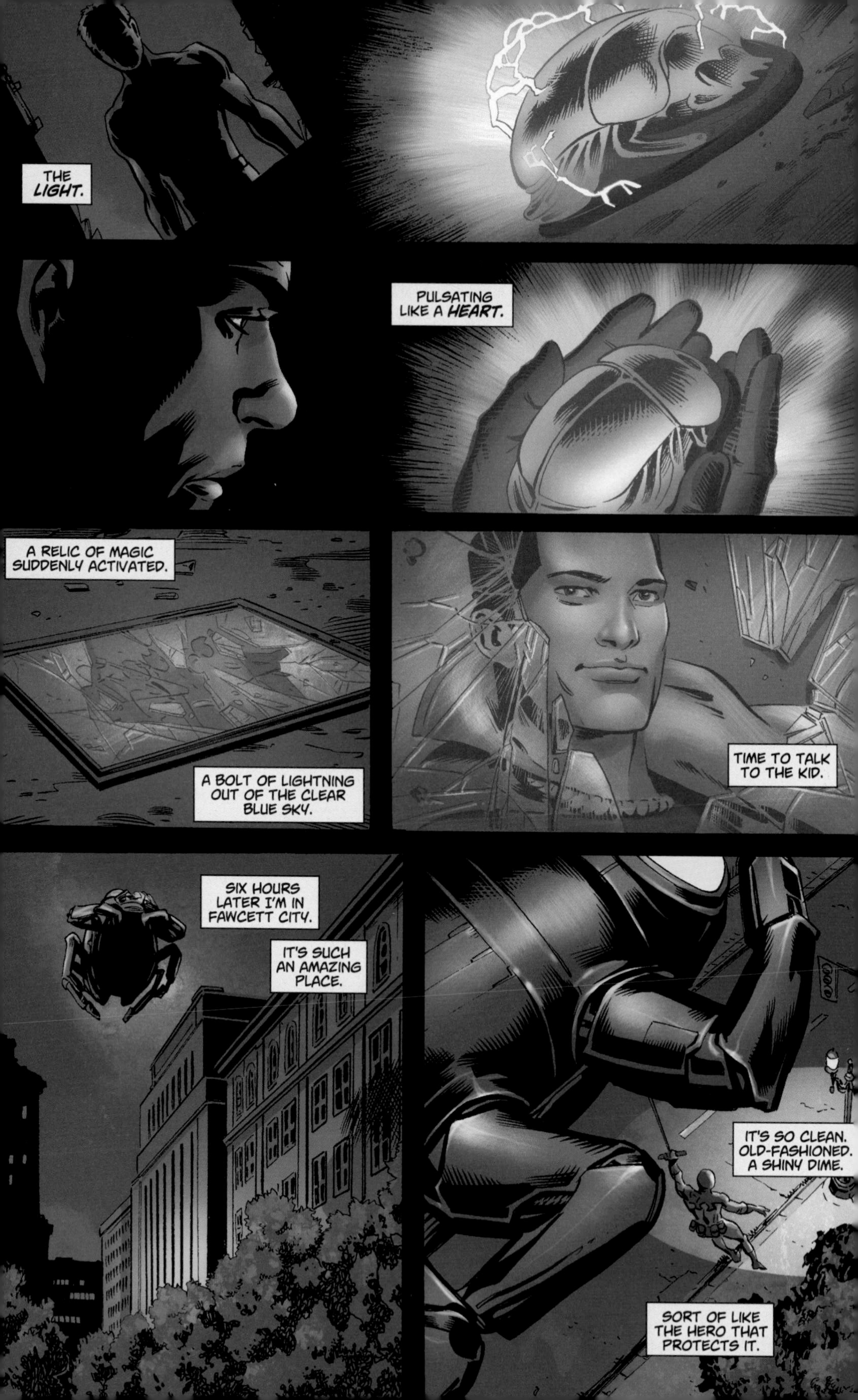
THE LIGHT.
PULSATING LIKE A HEART.
A RELIC OF MAGIC SUDDENLY ACTIVATED.
A BOLT OF LIGHTNING OUT OF THE CLEAR BLUE SKY.
TIME TO TALK TO THE KID.
SIX HOURS LATER I'M IN FAWCETT CITY.
IT'S SUCH AN AMAZING PLACE.
IT'S SO CLEAN. OLD-FASHIONED. A SHINY DIME.
SORT OF LIKE THE HERO THAT PROTECTS IT.

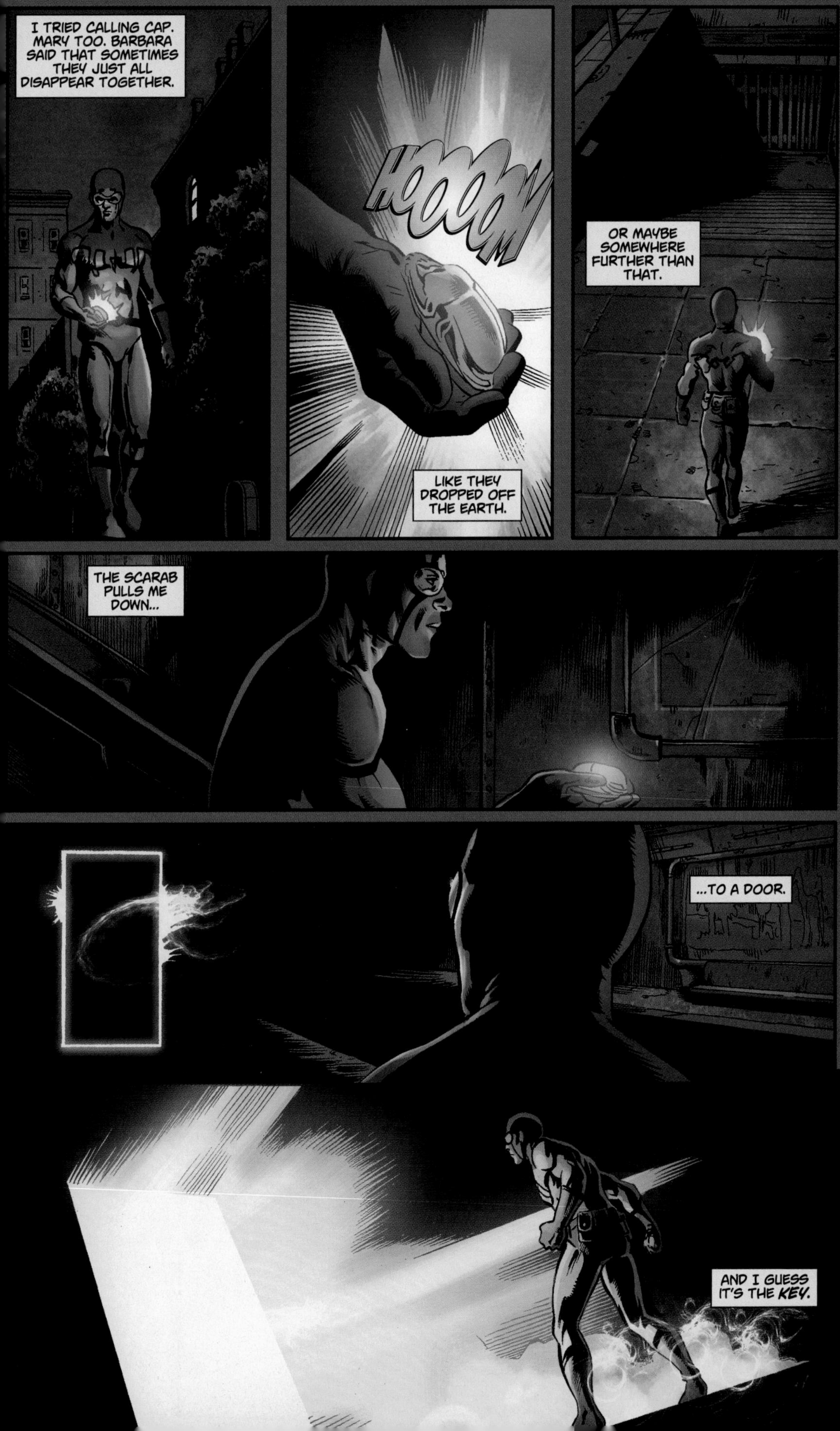
I TRIED CALLING CAP. MARY TOO. BARBARA SAID THAT SOMETIMES THEY JUST ALL DISAPPEAR TOGETHER.
HOOOOM
LIKE THEY DROPPED OFF THE EARTH.
OR MAYBE SOMEWHERE FURTHER THAN THAT.
THE SCARAB PULLS ME DOWN...
...TO A DOOR.
AND I GUESS IT'S THE *KEY*.

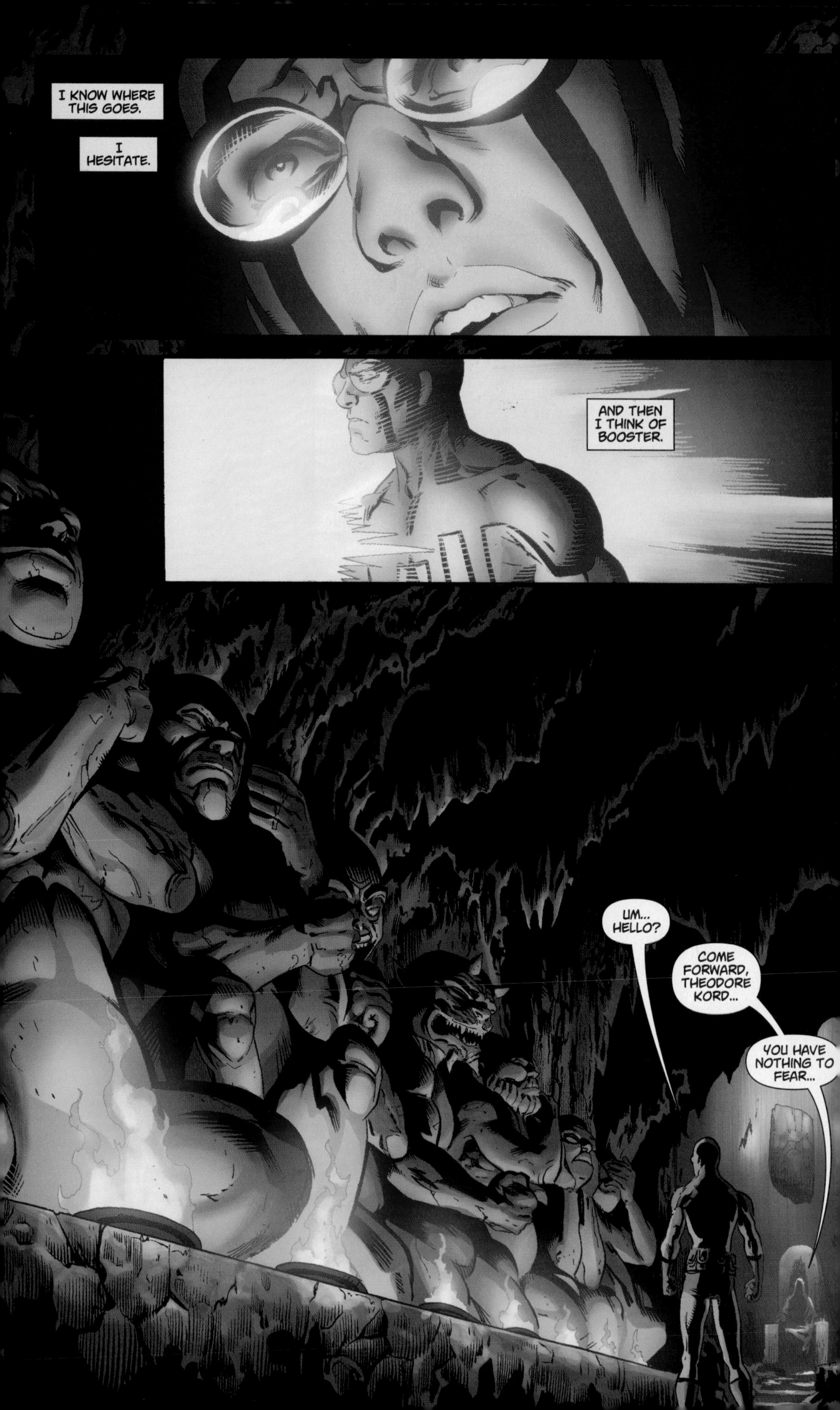
I KNOW WHERE THIS GOES.
I HESITATE.
AND THEN I THINK OF BOOSTER.
UM... HELLO?
COME FORWARD, THEODORE KORD...
YOU HAVE NOTHING TO FEAR...

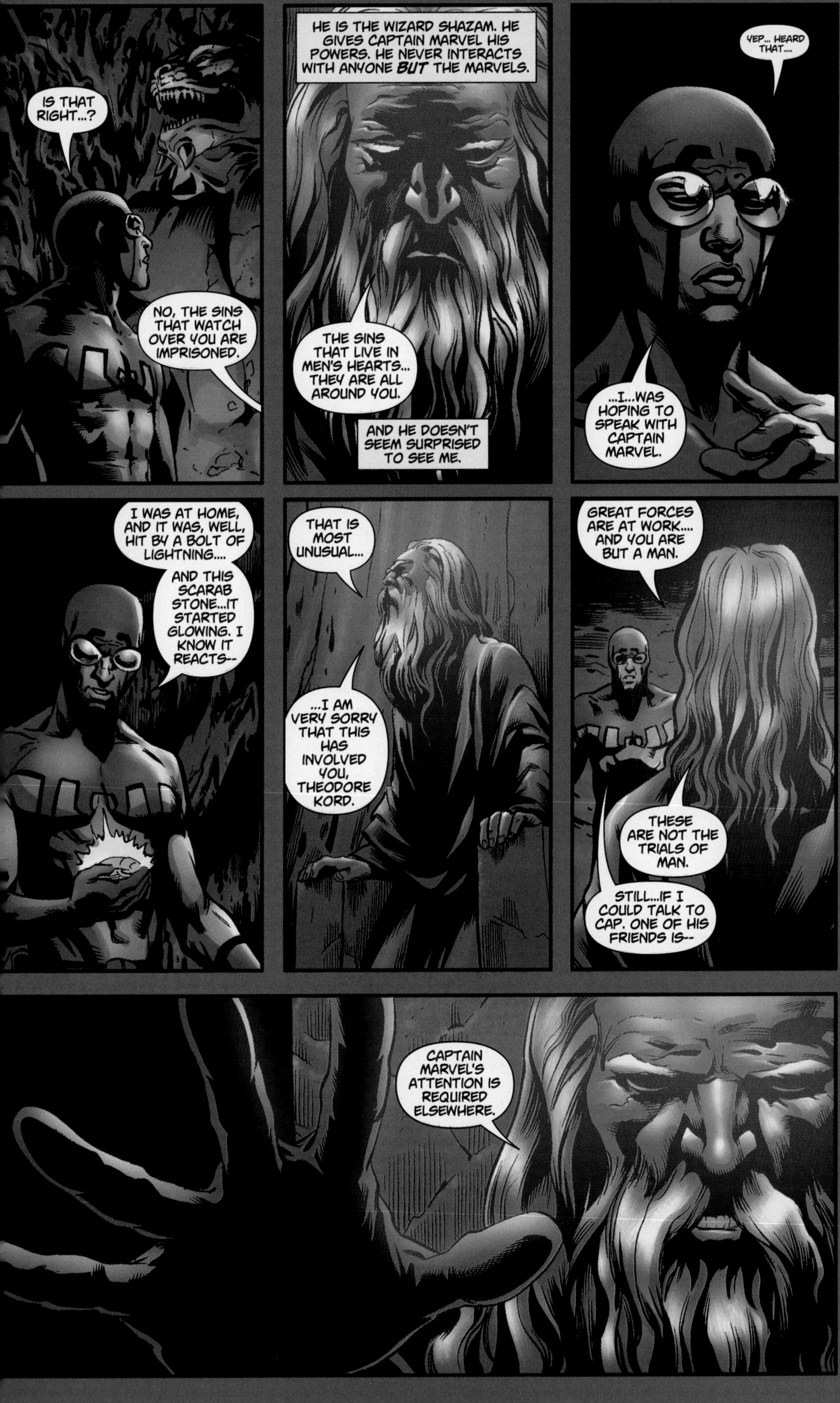
IS THAT RIGHT...?
NO, THE SINS THAT WATCH OVER YOU ARE IMPRISONED.
HE IS THE WIZARD SHAZAM. HE GIVES CAPTAIN MARVEL HIS POWERS. HE NEVER INTERACTS WITH ANYONE BUT THE MARVELS.
THE SINS THAT LIVE IN MEN'S HEARTS... THEY ARE ALL AROUND YOU.
AND HE DOESN'T SEEM SURPRISED TO SEE ME.
YEP... HEARD THAT....
...I...WAS HOPING TO SPEAK WITH CAPTAIN MARVEL.
I WAS AT HOME, AND IT WAS, WELL, HIT BY A BOLT OF LIGHTNING....
AND THIS SCARAB STONE...IT STARTED GLOWING. I KNOW IT REACTS--
THAT IS MOST UNUSUAL...
...I AM VERY SORRY THAT THIS HAS INVOLVED YOU, THEODORE KORD.
GREAT FORCES ARE AT WORK.... AND YOU ARE BUT A MAN.
THESE ARE NOT THE TRIALS OF MAN.
STILL...IF I COULD TALK TO CAP. ONE OF HIS FRIENDS IS--
CAPTAIN MARVEL'S ATTENTION IS REQUIRED ELSEWHERE.

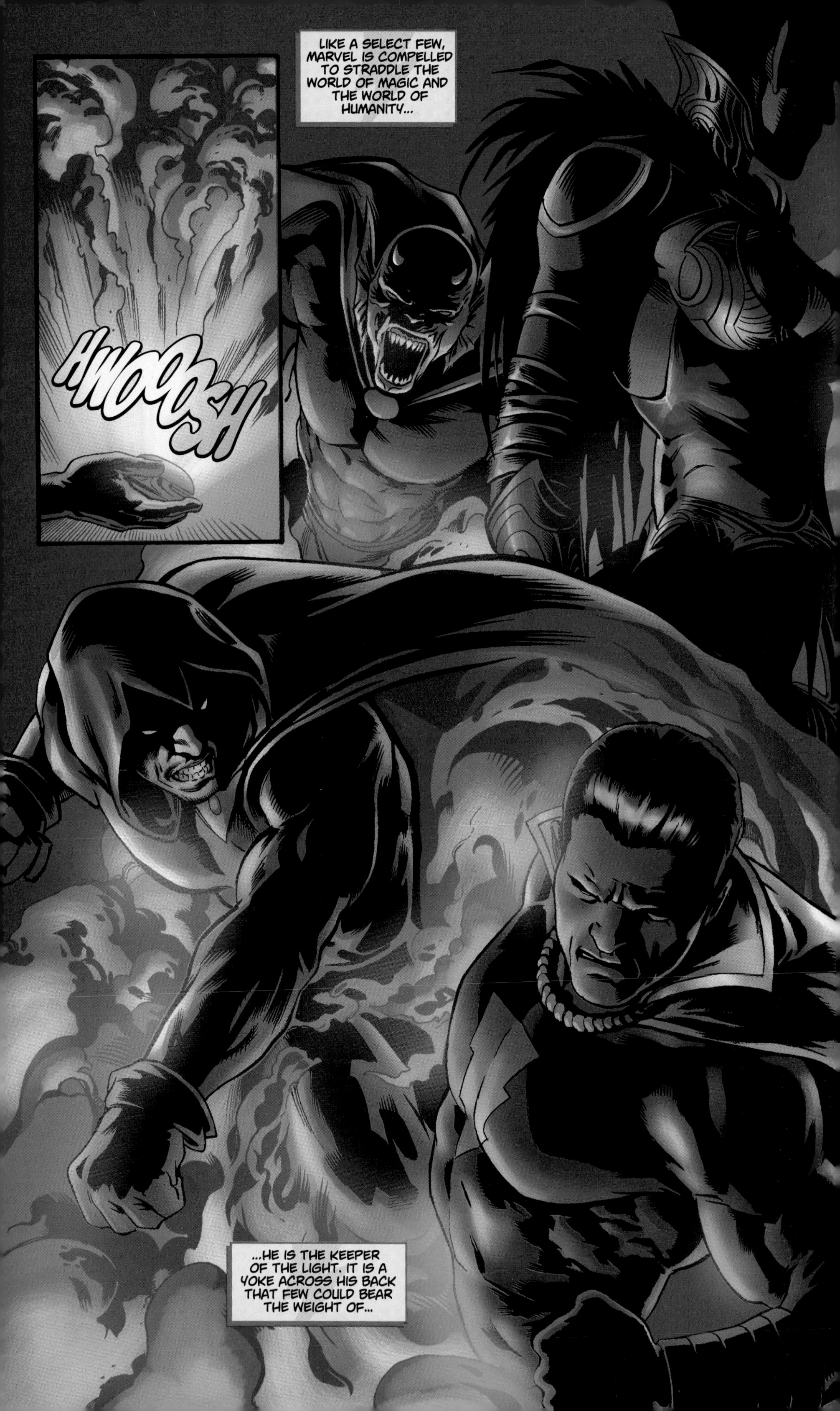
LIKE A SELECT FEW, MARVEL IS COMPELLED TO STRADDLE THE WORLD OF MAGIC AND THE WORLD OF HUMANITY...
HWOOOSH
...HE IS THE KEEPER OF THE LIGHT. IT IS A YOKE ACROSS HIS BACK THAT FEW COULD BEAR THE WEIGHT OF...

IT IS... ARDUOUS.

LUTHOR!?

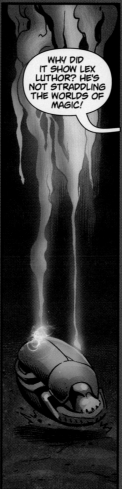

WHY DID IT SHOW LEX LUTHOR? HE'S NOT STRADDLING THE WORLDS OF MAGIC!

HE'S A GUY.

A REAL SICK SCUM OF A GUY, BUT HE'S STILL A GUY. HOW DOES HE PLAY INTO THIS?

YOU COULD NOT COMPREHEND THE ANSWERS.

EXCEPT TO SAY THAT THE LIGHTNING THAT STRUCK OUT AT YOU WAS NOT A VESSEL OF MAGIC. IT MERELY LAID CLAIM TO BE.

GOODBYE, THEODORE KORD.

WAIT! HANG ON! I DON'T HAVE THE SCARAB. I WON'T BE ABLE TO EVER FIND YOU AGAIN IF I--

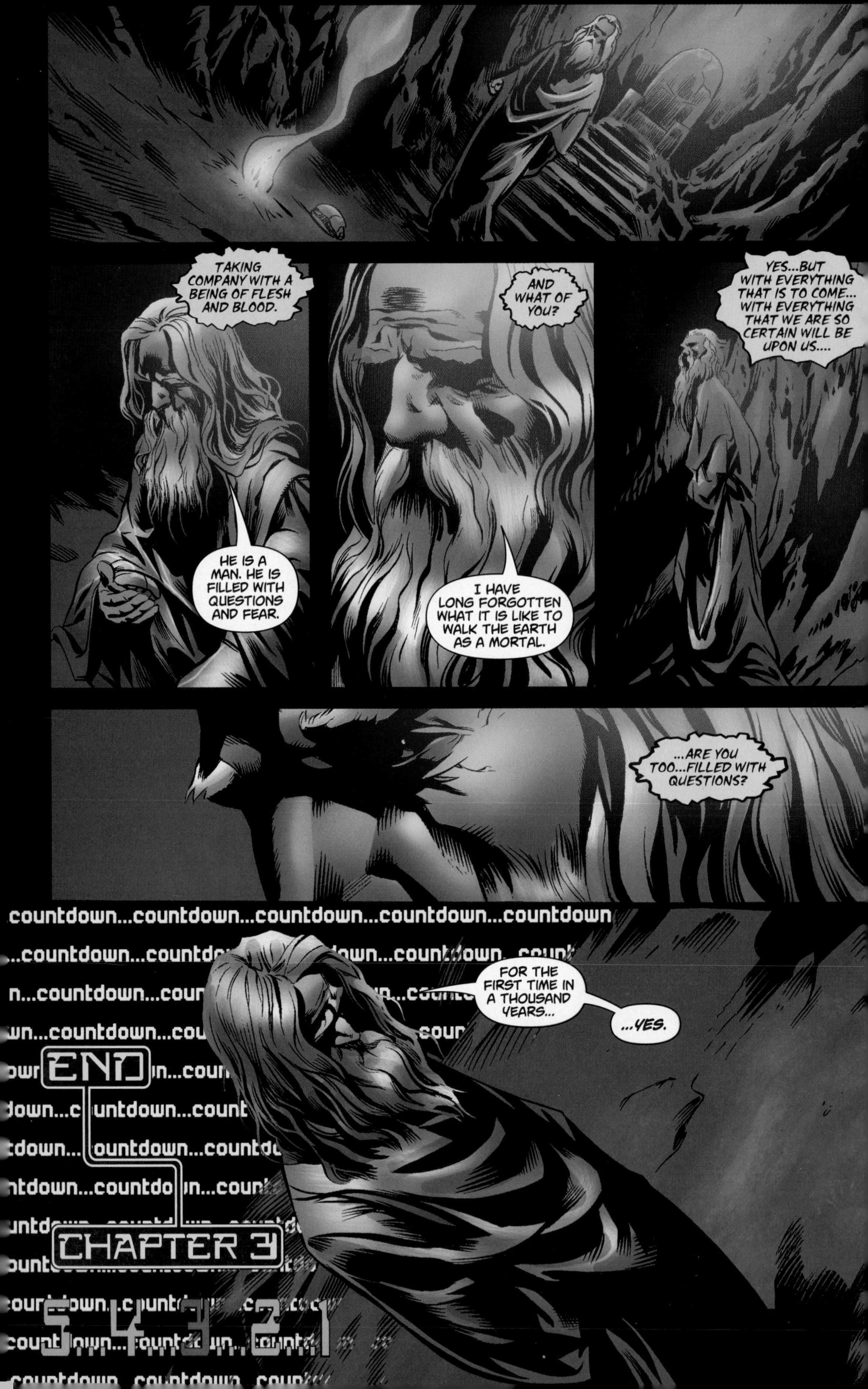
TAKING COMPANY WITH A BEING OF FLESH AND BLOOD.
HE IS A MAN. HE IS FILLED WITH QUESTIONS AND FEAR.
AND WHAT OF YOU?
I HAVE LONG FORGOTTEN WHAT IT IS LIKE TO WALK THE EARTH AS A MORTAL.
YES...BUT WITH EVERYTHING THAT IS TO COME... WITH EVERYTHING THAT WE ARE SO CERTAIN WILL BE UPON US....
...ARE YOU TOO...FILLED WITH QUESTIONS?
FOR THE FIRST TIME IN A THOUSAND YEARS...
...YES.
END
CHAPTER 3
countdown...countdown...countdown...countdown...countdown
5 4 3 2 1

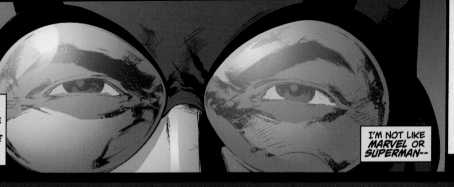

I'M A *BUG*, LIKE I SAID. BUT I'M ALSO A *MAN*.

A MAN OF *SCIENCE*. A MAN WITH *SKILLS* AND *SMARTS*--MORE SKILLS AND SMARTS THAN THE *AVERAGE* BEAR--BUT A *MAN* ALL THE *SAME*.

I'M NOT LIKE *MARVEL* OR *SUPERMAN*--

--OR *HER*.

NAME: **WONDER WOMAN**

IDENTITY: **DIANA OF THEMYSCIRA**

LOCATION: **NEW YORK CITY, THEMYSCIRA HOUSE**

AFFILIATION(S):
JUSTICE LEAGUE, AMAZONS (THEMYSCIRAN DERIVATION; BANA-MIGHDALL ASSOCIATION), UNITED NATIONS

POWERS: STRENGTH (A-1); SPEED (A-2); INVULNERABILITY (A-1); FLIGHT (A-2)

ABILITIES AND EQUIPMENT:
"LASSO OF TRUTH," INDESTRUCTIBLE VAMBRACES, INVISIBLE JET, TELEPATHY (B-2, ANIMAL SPECIFIC), ACCESS TO THEMYSCIRAN RESOURCES AND TECHNOLOGY.

ASSOCIATES:
- ANDERSON, LESLIE – SEE ALSO C.A.P. AND CALE, VERONICA
- GARIBALDI, MARTIN – DECEASED (?)
- GARIBALDI, MICHAEL
- GARIBALDI, ROBERT
- KAPATELIS, VANESSA – SILVER SWAN II, KAPATELIS, JULIA
- SANDSMARK, CASSANDRA – WONDER GIRL
- SANDSMARK, JULIA
- TROY, DONNA – DECEASED

HELL, *NO ONE* IS LIKE *HER*. THE MOST POWERFUL, MOST BEAUTIFUL WOMAN IN THE WORLD.

CADMUS

PROGE
TECH

I LOOK AT THE *PICTURE* OF HER AND FOR A MOMENT I FORGET TO BE *SURPRISED* THAT *THEY* KNOW *EVERYTHING* ABOUT HER, TOO.

FOR A *MOMENT*, I CAN EVEN *FORGET* TO BE *AFRAID*.

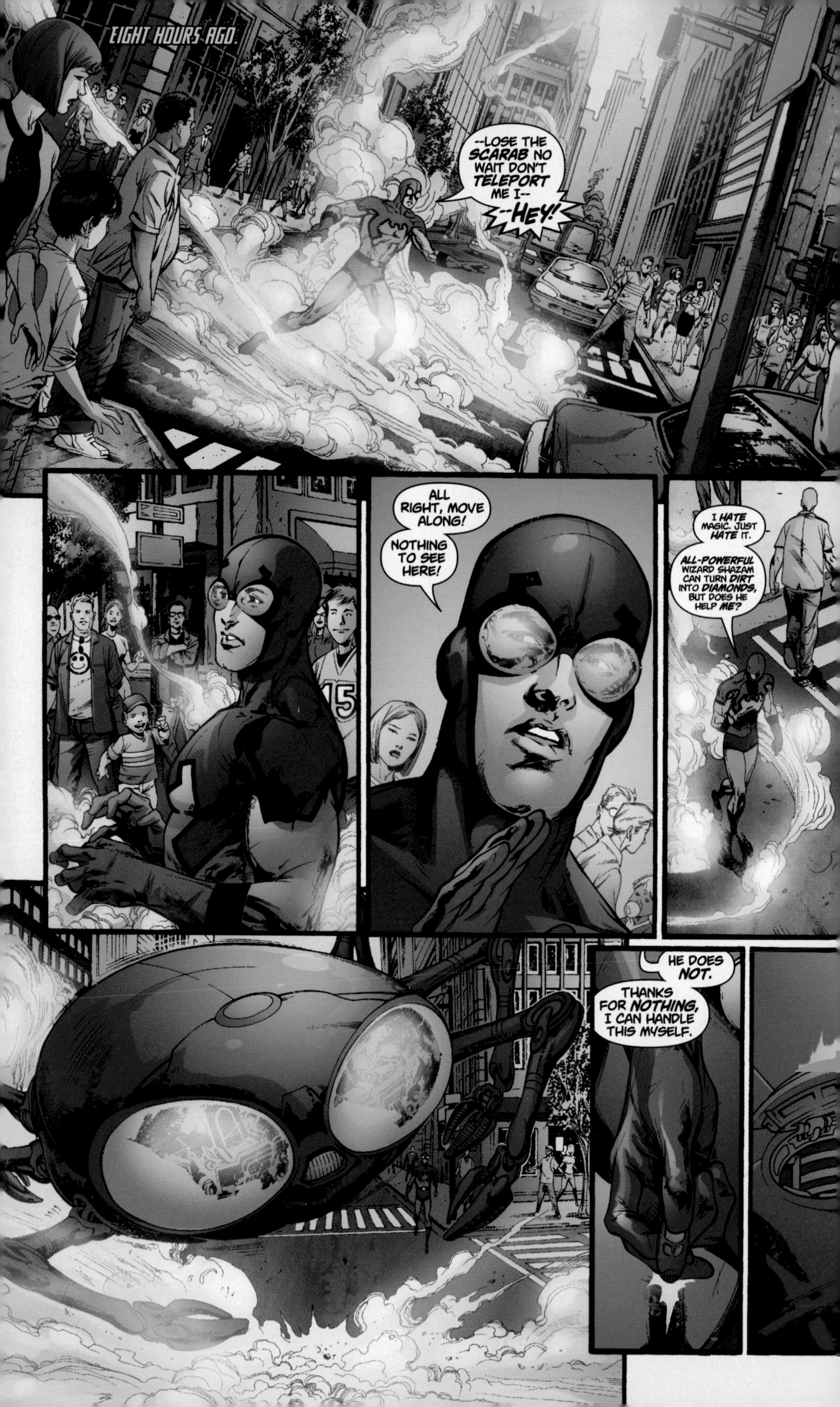
EIGHT HOURS AGO.
--LOSE THE SCARAB NO WAIT DON'T TELEPORT ME I--
--HEY!
ALL RIGHT, MOVE ALONG!
NOTHING TO SEE HERE!
I HATE MAGIC. JUST HATE IT.
ALL-POWERFUL WIZARD SHAZAM CAN TURN DIRT INTO DIAMONDS, BUT DOES HE HELP ME?
HE DOES NOT.
THANKS FOR NOTHING, I CAN HANDLE THIS MYSELF.

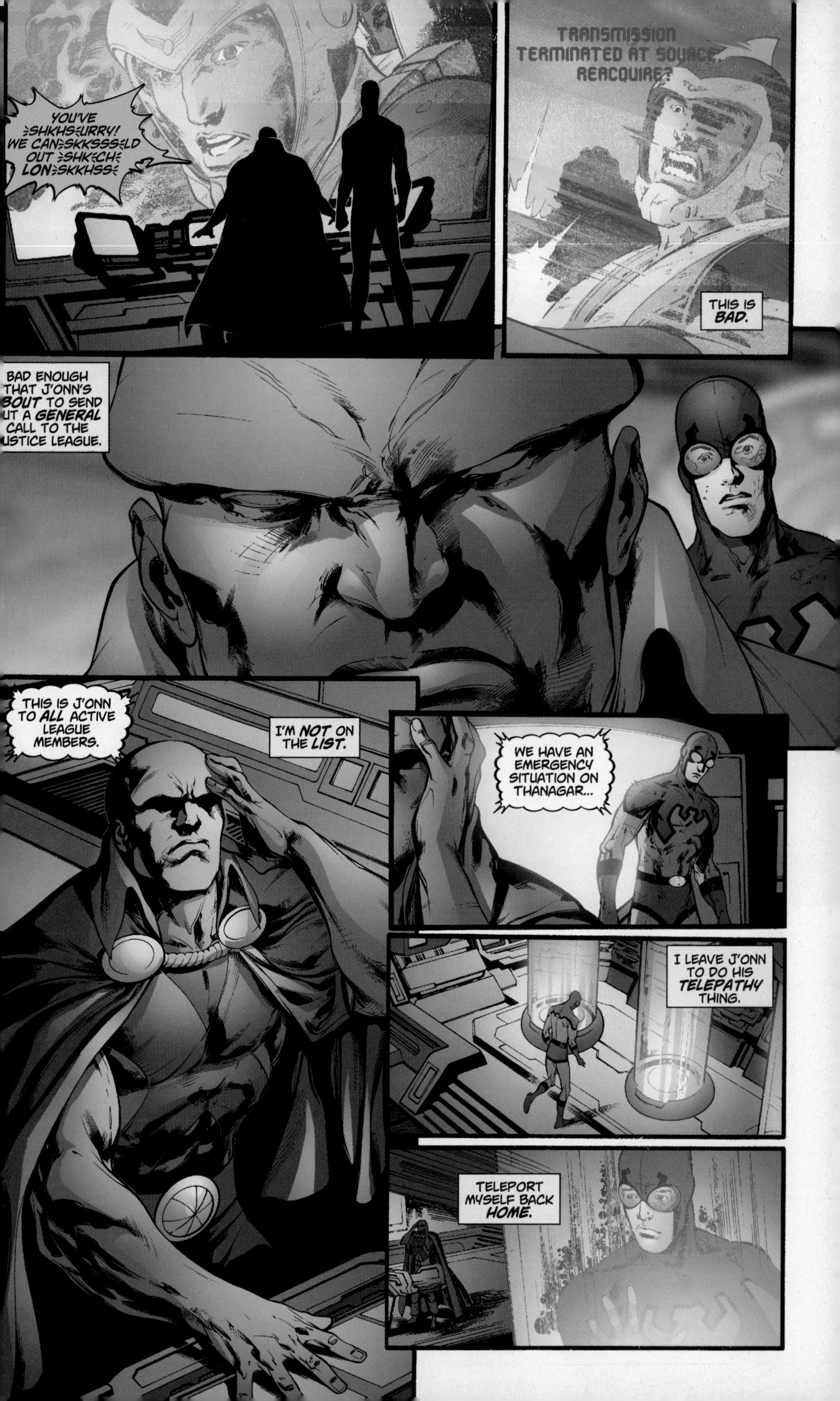
YOU'VE ≶SHKHS≶URRY! WE CAN≶SKKSSS≶LD OUT ≶SHK≶CH≶ LON≶SKKHSS≶
TRANSMISSION TERMINATED AT SOURCE. REACQUIRE?
THIS IS BAD.
BAD ENOUGH THAT J'ONN'S BOUT TO SEND UT A GENERAL CALL TO THE USTICE LEAGUE.
THIS IS J'ONN TO ALL ACTIVE LEAGUE MEMBERS.
I'M NOT ON THE LIST.
WE HAVE AN EMERGENCY SITUATION ON THANAGAR...
I LEAVE J'ONN TO DO HIS TELEPATHY THING.
TELEPORT MYSELF BACK HOME.

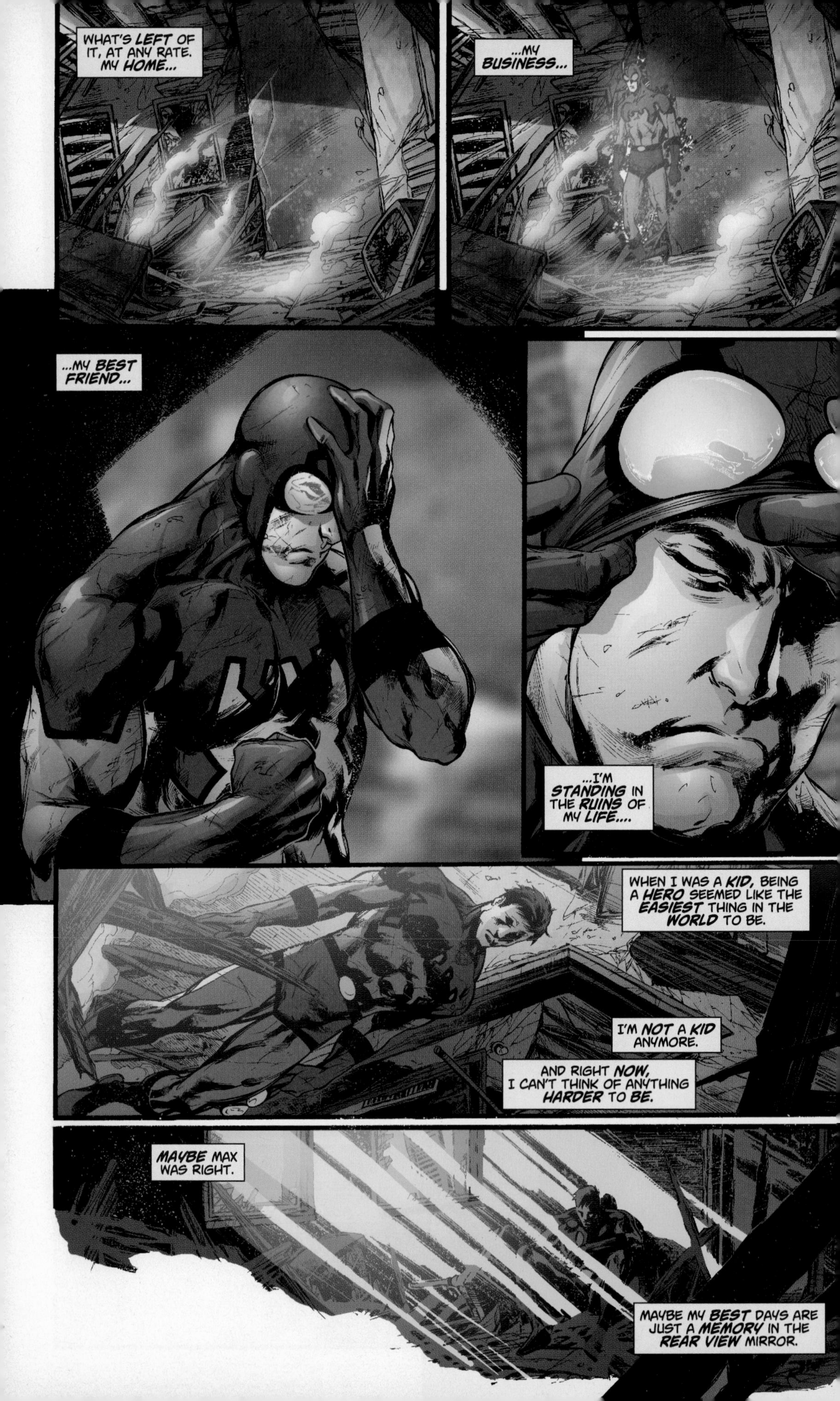
WHAT'S LEFT OF IT, AT ANY RATE. MY HOME...
...MY BUSINESS...
...MY BEST FRIEND...
...I'M STANDING IN THE RUINS OF MY LIFE....
WHEN I WAS A KID, BEING A HERO SEEMED LIKE THE EASIEST THING IN THE WORLD TO BE.
I'M NOT A KID ANYMORE.
AND RIGHT NOW, I CAN'T THINK OF ANYTHING HARDER TO BE.
MAYBE MAX WAS RIGHT.
MAYBE MY BEST DAYS ARE JUST A MEMORY IN THE REAR VIEW MIRROR.

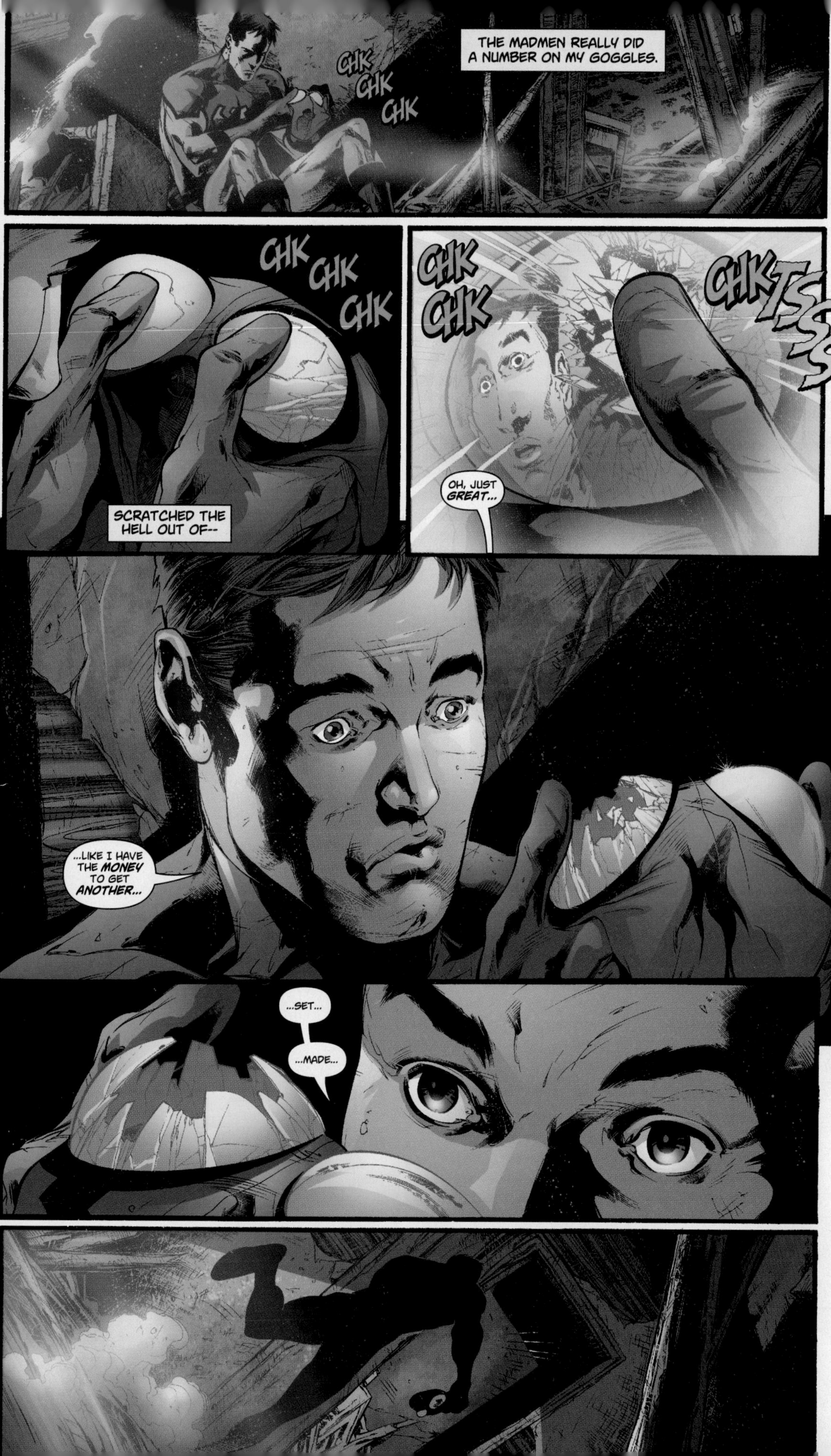
THE MADMEN REALLY DID A NUMBER ON MY GOGGLES.
CHK CHK CHK
CHK CHK CHK
SCRATCHED THE HELL OUT OF--
CHK CHK
CHKTSSS
OH, JUST GREAT...
...LIKE I HAVE THE MONEY TO GET ANOTHER...
...SET...
...MADE...

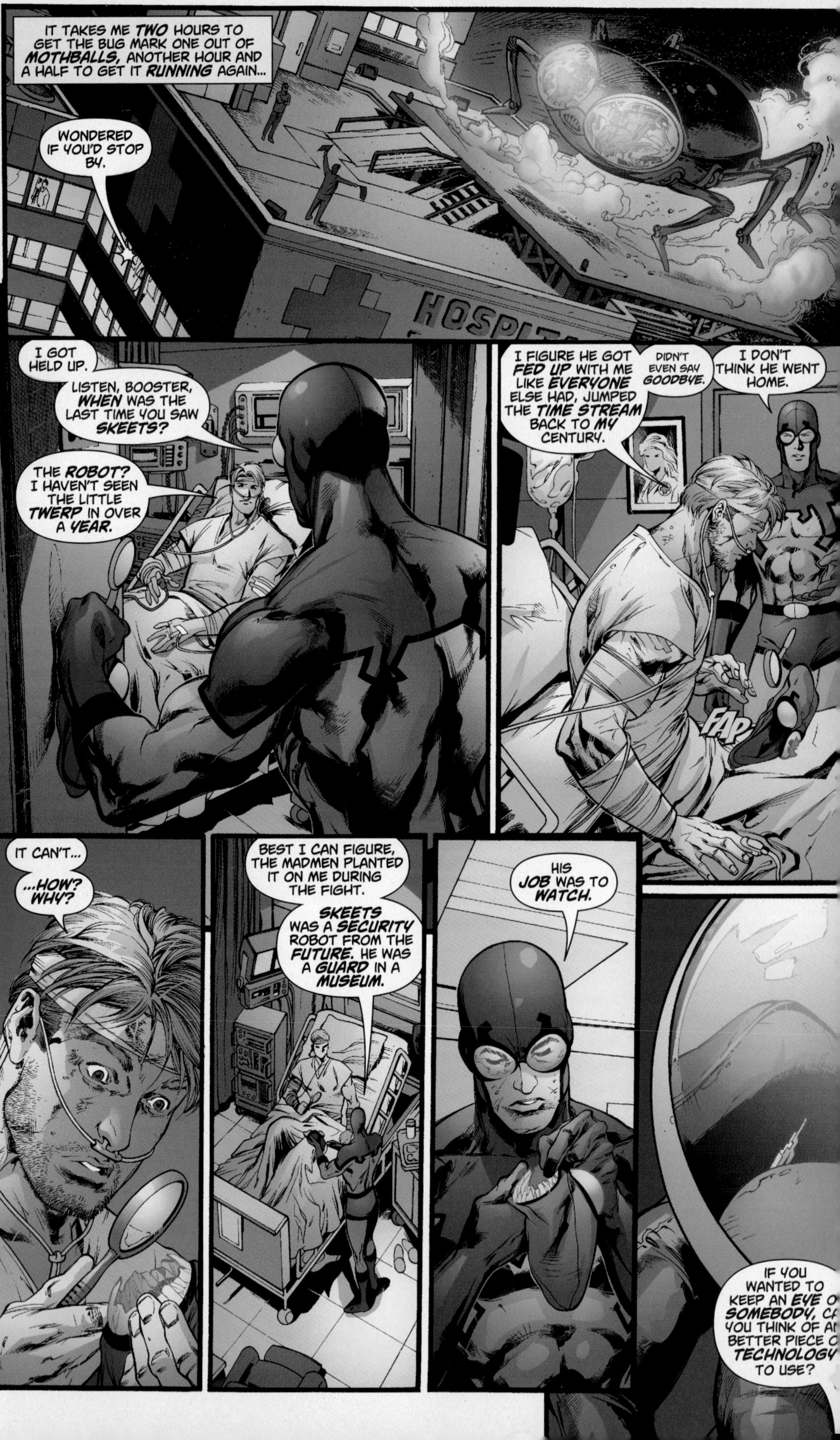

IT TAKES ME TWO HOURS TO GET THE BUG MARK ONE OUT OF MOTHBALLS, ANOTHER HOUR AND A HALF TO GET IT RUNNING AGAIN...
WONDERED IF YOU'D STOP BY.
HOSPIT
I GOT HELD UP.
LISTEN, BOOSTER, WHEN WAS THE LAST TIME YOU SAW SKEETS?
THE ROBOT? I HAVEN'T SEEN THE LITTLE TWERP IN OVER A YEAR.
I FIGURE HE GOT FED UP WITH ME LIKE EVERYONE ELSE HAD, JUMPED THE TIME STREAM BACK TO MY CENTURY.
DIDN'T EVEN SAY GOODBYE.
I DON'T THINK HE WENT HOME.
FAP
IT CAN'T...
...HOW? WHY?
BEST I CAN FIGURE, THE MADMEN PLANTED IT ON ME DURING THE FIGHT.
SKEETS WAS A SECURITY ROBOT FROM THE FUTURE. HE WAS A GUARD IN A MUSEUM.
HIS JOB WAS TO WATCH.
IF YOU WANTED TO KEEP AN EYE O SOMEBODY, CA YOU THINK OF AN BETTER PIECE O TECHNOLOGY TO USE?

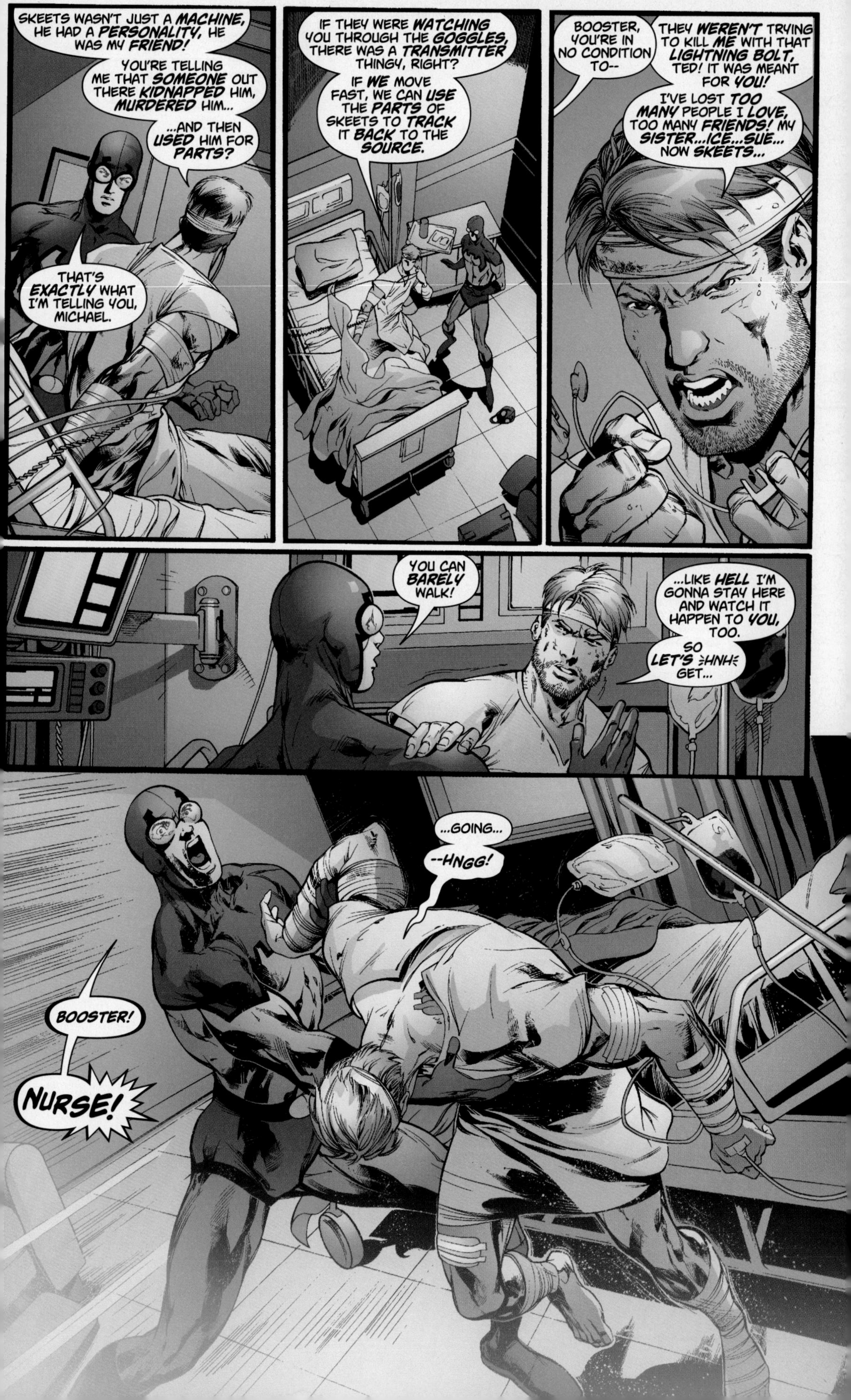
SKEETS WASN'T JUST A MACHINE, HE HAD A PERSONALITY, HE WAS MY FRIEND!
YOU'RE TELLING ME THAT SOMEONE OUT THERE KIDNAPPED HIM, MURDERED HIM...
...AND THEN USED HIM FOR PARTS?
THAT'S EXACTLY WHAT I'M TELLING YOU, MICHAEL.
IF THEY WERE WATCHING YOU THROUGH THE GOGGLES, THERE WAS A TRANSMITTER THINGY, RIGHT?
IF WE MOVE FAST, WE CAN USE THE PARTS OF SKEETS TO TRACK IT BACK TO THE SOURCE.
BOOSTER, YOU'RE IN NO CONDITION TO--
THEY WEREN'T TRYING TO KILL ME WITH THAT LIGHTNING BOLT, TED! IT WAS MEANT FOR YOU!
I'VE LOST TOO MANY PEOPLE I LOVE, TOO MANY FRIENDS! MY SISTER...ICE...SUE... NOW SKEETS...
YOU CAN BARELY WALK!
...LIKE HELL I'M GONNA STAY HERE AND WATCH IT HAPPEN TO YOU, TOO.
SO LET'S HNH GET...
...GOING...
--HNGG!
BOOSTER!
NURSE!

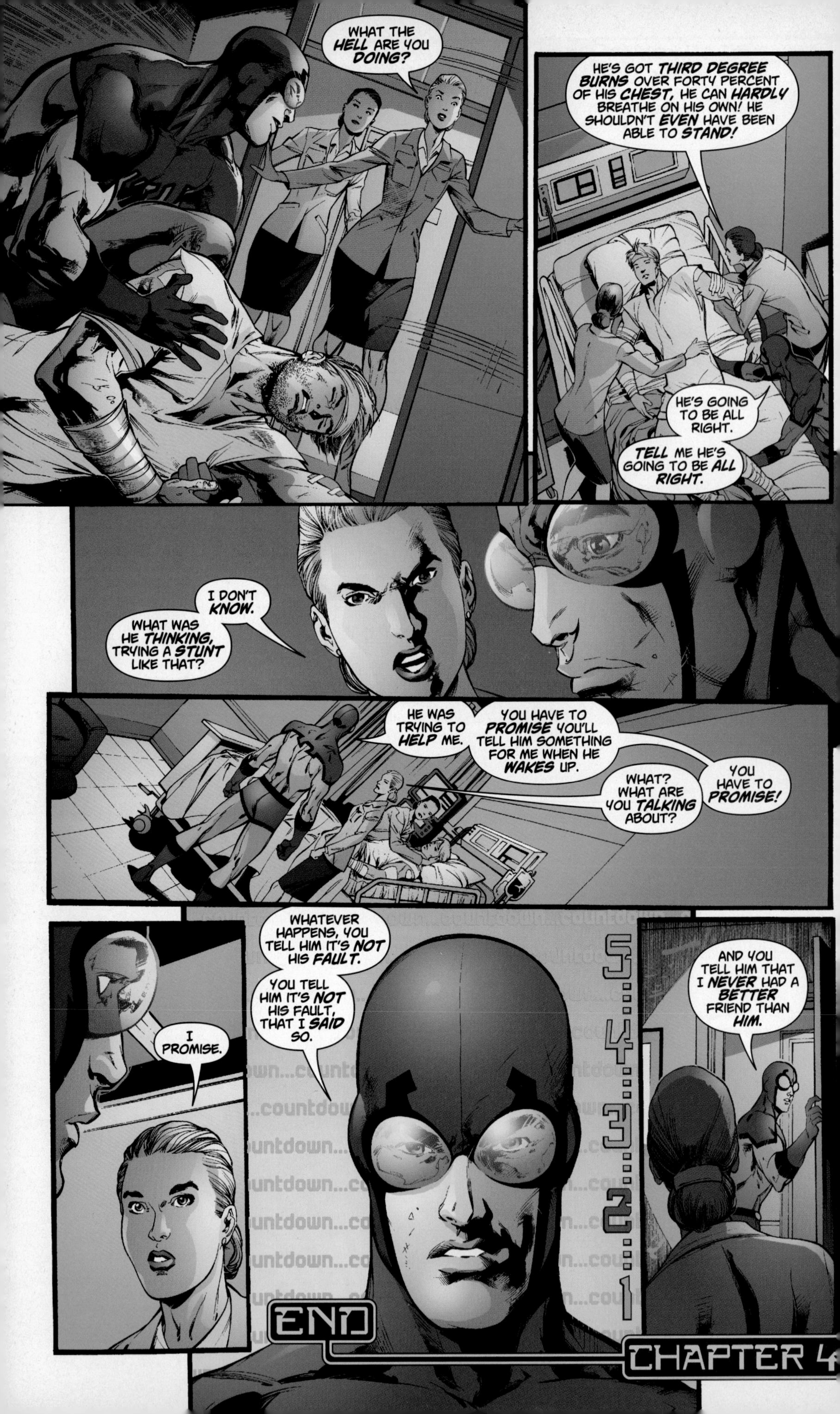
WHAT THE HELL ARE YOU DOING?
HE'S GOT THIRD DEGREE BURNS OVER FORTY PERCENT OF HIS CHEST, HE CAN HARDLY BREATHE ON HIS OWN! HE SHOULDN'T EVEN HAVE BEEN ABLE TO STAND!
HE'S GOING TO BE ALL RIGHT.
TELL ME HE'S GOING TO BE ALL RIGHT.
I DON'T KNOW.
WHAT WAS HE THINKING, TRYING A STUNT LIKE THAT?
HE WAS TRYING TO HELP ME.
YOU HAVE TO PROMISE YOU'LL TELL HIM SOMETHING FOR ME WHEN HE WAKES UP.
WHAT? WHAT ARE YOU TALKING ABOUT?
YOU HAVE TO PROMISE!
I PROMISE.
WHATEVER HAPPENS, YOU TELL HIM IT'S NOT HIS FAULT.
YOU TELL HIM IT'S NOT HIS FAULT, THAT I SAID SO.
AND YOU TELL HIM THAT I NEVER HAD A BETTER FRIEND THAN HIM.
5...4...3...2...1
END
CHAPTER 4

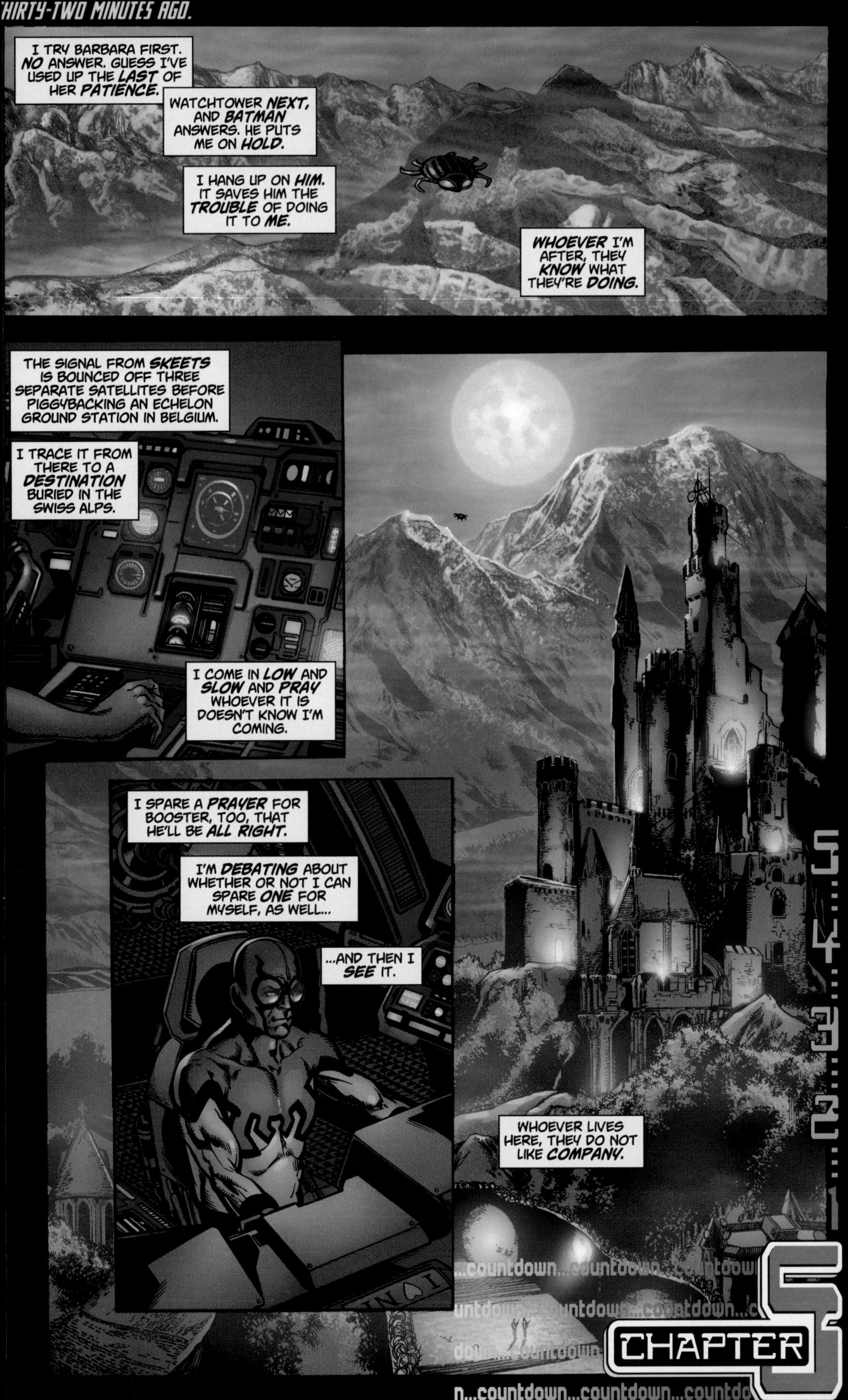
HIRTY-TWO MINUTES AGO.
I TRY BARBARA FIRST. NO ANSWER. GUESS I'VE USED UP THE LAST OF HER PATIENCE.
WATCHTOWER NEXT, AND BATMAN ANSWERS. HE PUTS ME ON HOLD.
I HANG UP ON HIM. IT SAVES HIM THE TROUBLE OF DOING IT TO ME.
WHOEVER I'M AFTER, THEY KNOW WHAT THEY'RE DOING.
THE SIGNAL FROM SKEETS IS BOUNCED OFF THREE SEPARATE SATELLITES BEFORE PIGGYBACKING AN ECHELON GROUND STATION IN BELGIUM.
I TRACE IT FROM THERE TO A DESTINATION BURIED IN THE SWISS ALPS.
I COME IN LOW AND SLOW AND PRAY WHOEVER IT IS DOESN'T KNOW I'M COMING.
I SPARE A PRAYER FOR BOOSTER, TOO, THAT HE'LL BE ALL RIGHT.
I'M DEBATING ABOUT WHETHER OR NOT I CAN SPARE ONE FOR MYSELF, AS WELL...
...AND THEN I SEE IT.
WHOEVER LIVES HERE, THEY DO NOT LIKE COMPANY.
5...4...3...2...1
CHAPTER 5

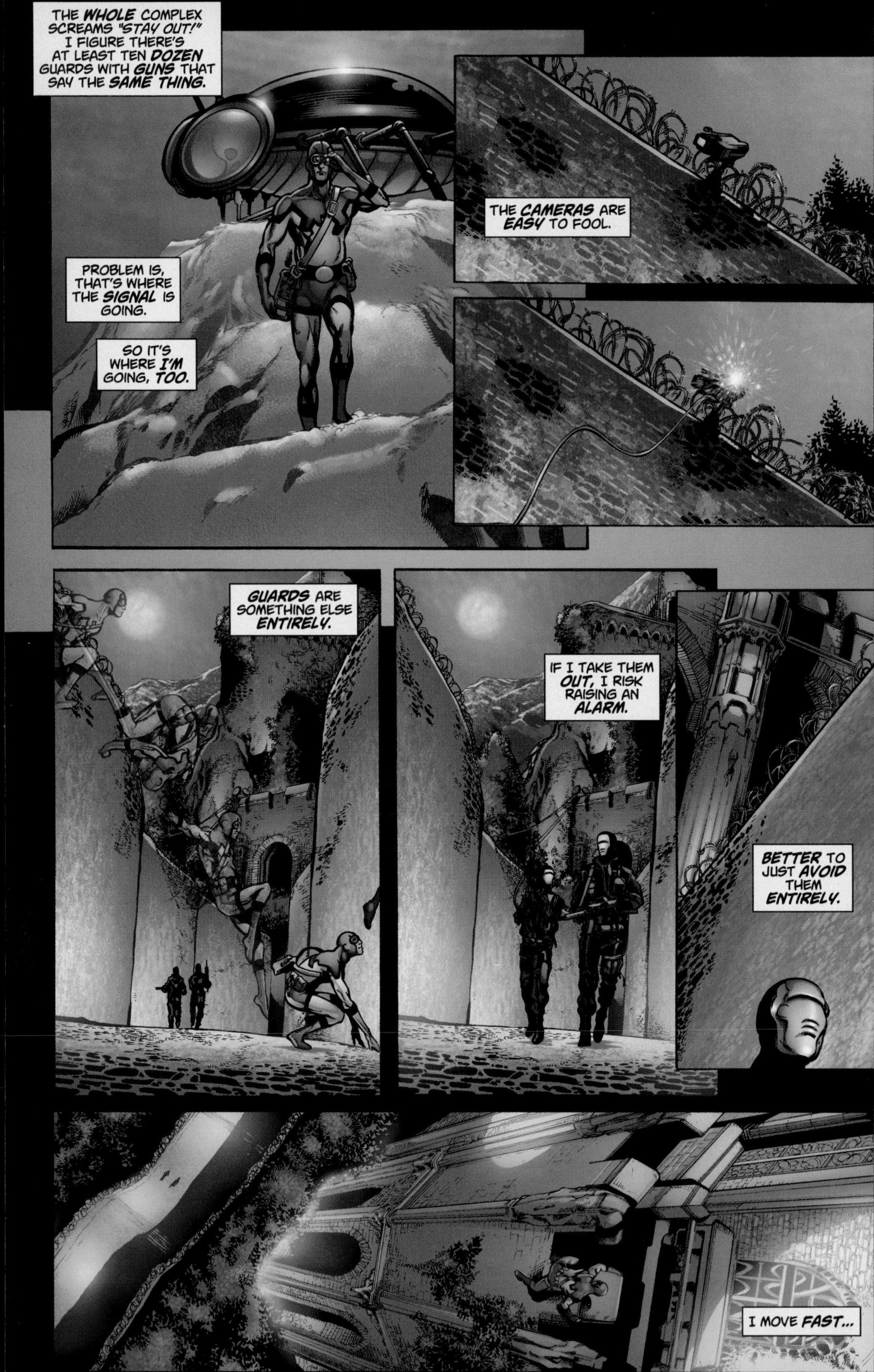
THE WHOLE COMPLEX SCREAMS "STAY OUT!" I FIGURE THERE'S AT LEAST TEN DOZEN GUARDS WITH GUNS THAT SAY THE SAME THING.
PROBLEM IS, THAT'S WHERE THE SIGNAL IS GOING.
SO IT'S WHERE I'M GOING, TOO.
THE CAMERAS ARE EASY TO FOOL.
GUARDS ARE SOMETHING ELSE ENTIRELY.
IF I TAKE THEM OUT, I RISK RAISING AN ALARM.
BETTER TO JUST AVOID THEM ENTIRELY.
I MOVE FAST...

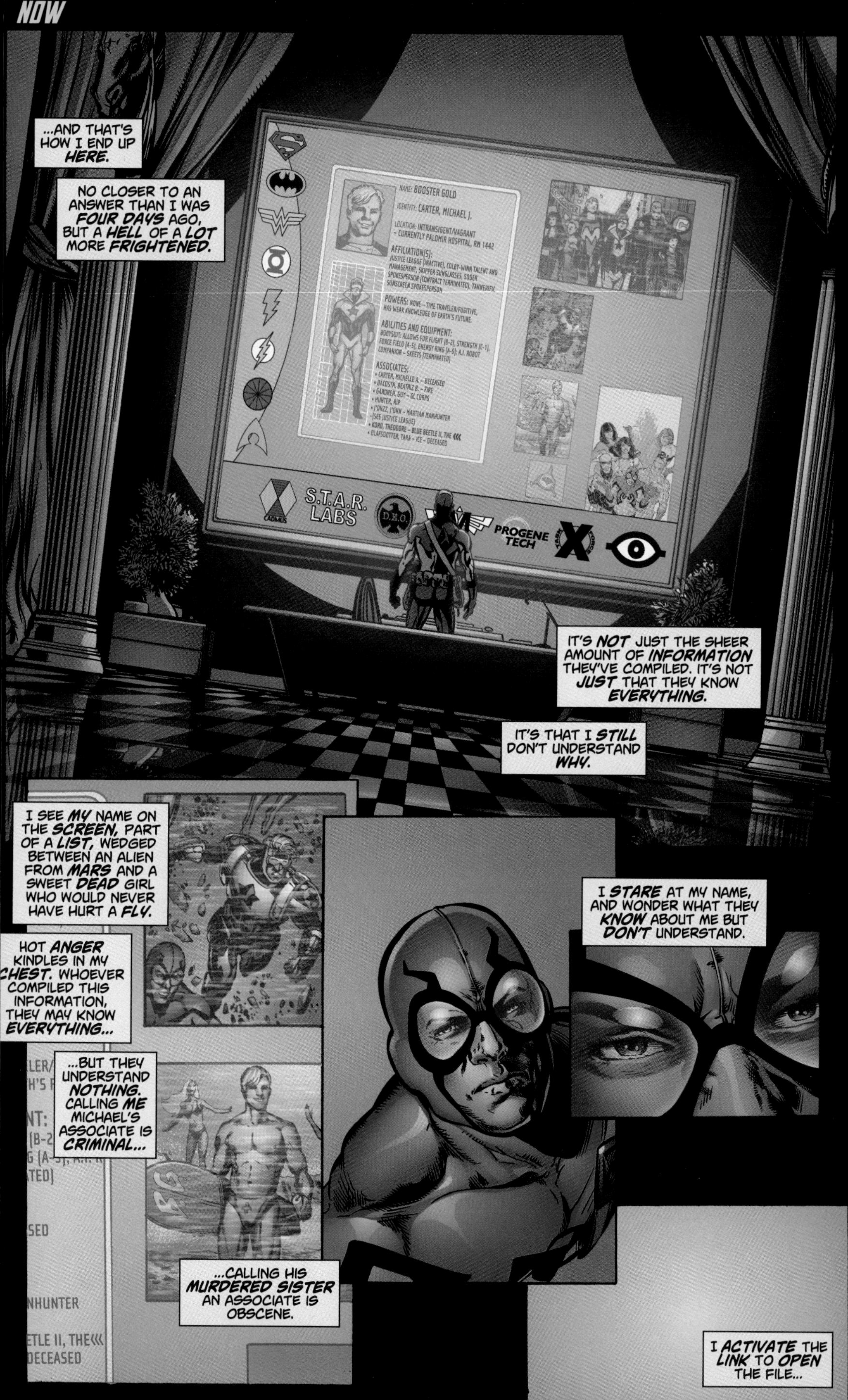
NOW
...AND THAT'S HOW I END UP HERE.
NO CLOSER TO AN ANSWER THAN I WAS FOUR DAYS AGO, BUT A HELL OF A LOT MORE FRIGHTENED.
NAME: BOOSTER GOLD
IDENTITY: CARTER, MICHAEL J.
LOCATION: INTRANSIGENT/VAGRANT – CURRENTLY PALOMIR HOSPITAL, RM 1442
AFFILIATION(S):
JUSTICE LEAGUE (INACTIVE), COLBY-WINN TALENT AND MANAGEMENT, SKIPPER SUNGLASSES, SODER SPOKESPERSON (CONTRACT TERMINATED), TANNERIFIC SUNSCREEN SPOKESPERSON
POWERS: NONE – TIME TRAVELER/FUGITIVE, HAS WEAK KNOWLEDGE OF EARTH'S FUTURE.
ABILITIES AND EQUIPMENT:
BODYSUIT: ALLOWS FOR FLIGHT (B-2), STRENGTH (C-1), FORCE FIELD (A-5), ENERGY RING (A-5): A.I. ROBOT COMPANION – SKEETS (TERMINATED)
ASSOCIATES:
• CARTER, MICHELLE A. – DECEASED
• DACOSTA, BEATRIZ B. – FIRE
• GARDNER, GUY – GL CORPS
• HUNTER, RIP
• J'ONZZ, J'ONN – MARTIAN MANHUNTER (SEE JUSTICE LEAGUE)
• KORD, THEODORE – BLUE BEETLE II, THE
• OLAFSDOTTER, TARA – ICE – DECEASED
CADMUS
S.T.A.R. LABS
D.E.O.
PROGENE TECH
IT'S NOT JUST THE SHEER AMOUNT OF INFORMATION THEY'VE COMPILED. IT'S NOT JUST THAT THEY KNOW EVERYTHING.
IT'S THAT I STILL DON'T UNDERSTAND WHY.
I SEE MY NAME ON THE SCREEN, PART OF A LIST, WEDGED BETWEEN AN ALIEN FROM MARS AND A SWEET DEAD GIRL WHO WOULD NEVER HAVE HURT A FLY.
HOT ANGER KINDLES IN MY CHEST. WHOEVER COMPILED THIS INFORMATION, THEY MAY KNOW EVERYTHING...
...BUT THEY UNDERSTAND NOTHING. CALLING ME MICHAEL'S ASSOCIATE IS CRIMINAL...
...CALLING HIS MURDERED SISTER AN ASSOCIATE IS OBSCENE.
I STARE AT MY NAME, AND WONDER WHAT THEY KNOW ABOUT ME BUT DON'T UNDERSTAND.
I ACTIVATE THE LINK TO OPEN THE FILE...

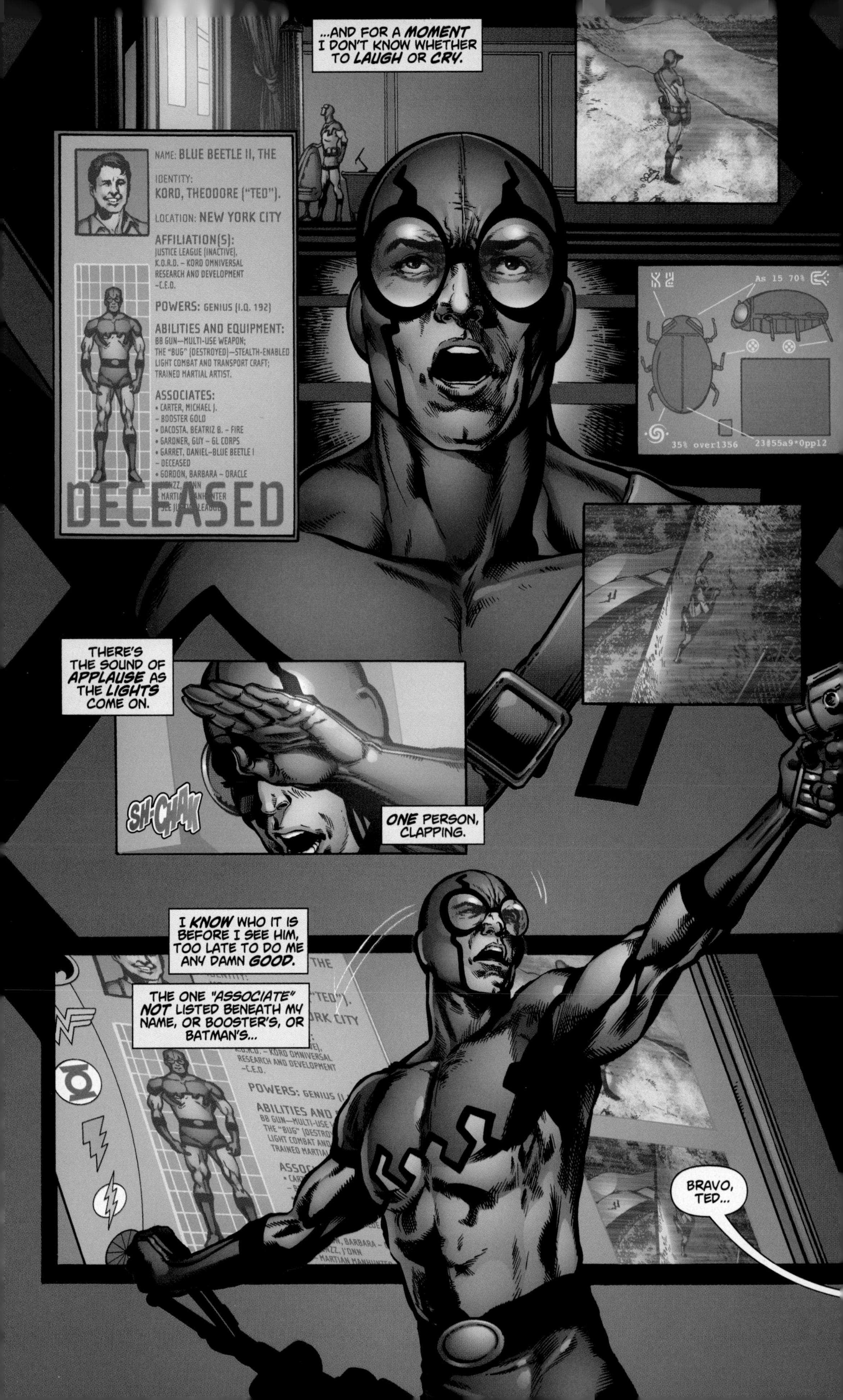
...AND FOR A MOMENT I DON'T KNOW WHETHER TO LAUGH OR CRY.
NAME: BLUE BEETLE II, THE
IDENTITY: KORD, THEODORE ("TED").
LOCATION: NEW YORK CITY
AFFILIATION(S): JUSTICE LEAGUE (INACTIVE), K.O.R.D. – KORD OMNIVERSAL RESEARCH AND DEVELOPMENT –C.E.O.
POWERS: GENIUS (I.Q. 192)
ABILITIES AND EQUIPMENT: BB GUN—MULTI-USE WEAPON; THE "BUG" (DESTROYED)—STEALTH-ENABLED LIGHT COMBAT AND TRANSPORT CRAFT; TRAINED MARTIAL ARTIST.
ASSOCIATES: • CARTER, MICHAEL J. – BOOSTER GOLD • DACOSTA, BEATRIZ B. – FIRE • GARDNER, GUY – GL CORPS • GARRET, DANIEL–BLUE BEETLE I – DECEASED • GORDON, BARBARA – ORACLE
DECEASED
As 15 70%
35% over1356
23#55a9*0pp12
THERE'S THE SOUND OF APPLAUSE AS THE LIGHTS COME ON.
SH-CHAK
ONE PERSON, CLAPPING.
I KNOW WHO IT IS BEFORE I SEE HIM, TOO LATE TO DO ME ANY DAMN GOOD.
THE ONE "ASSOCIATE" NOT LISTED BENEATH MY NAME, OR BOOSTER'S, OR BATMAN'S...
BRAVO, TED...

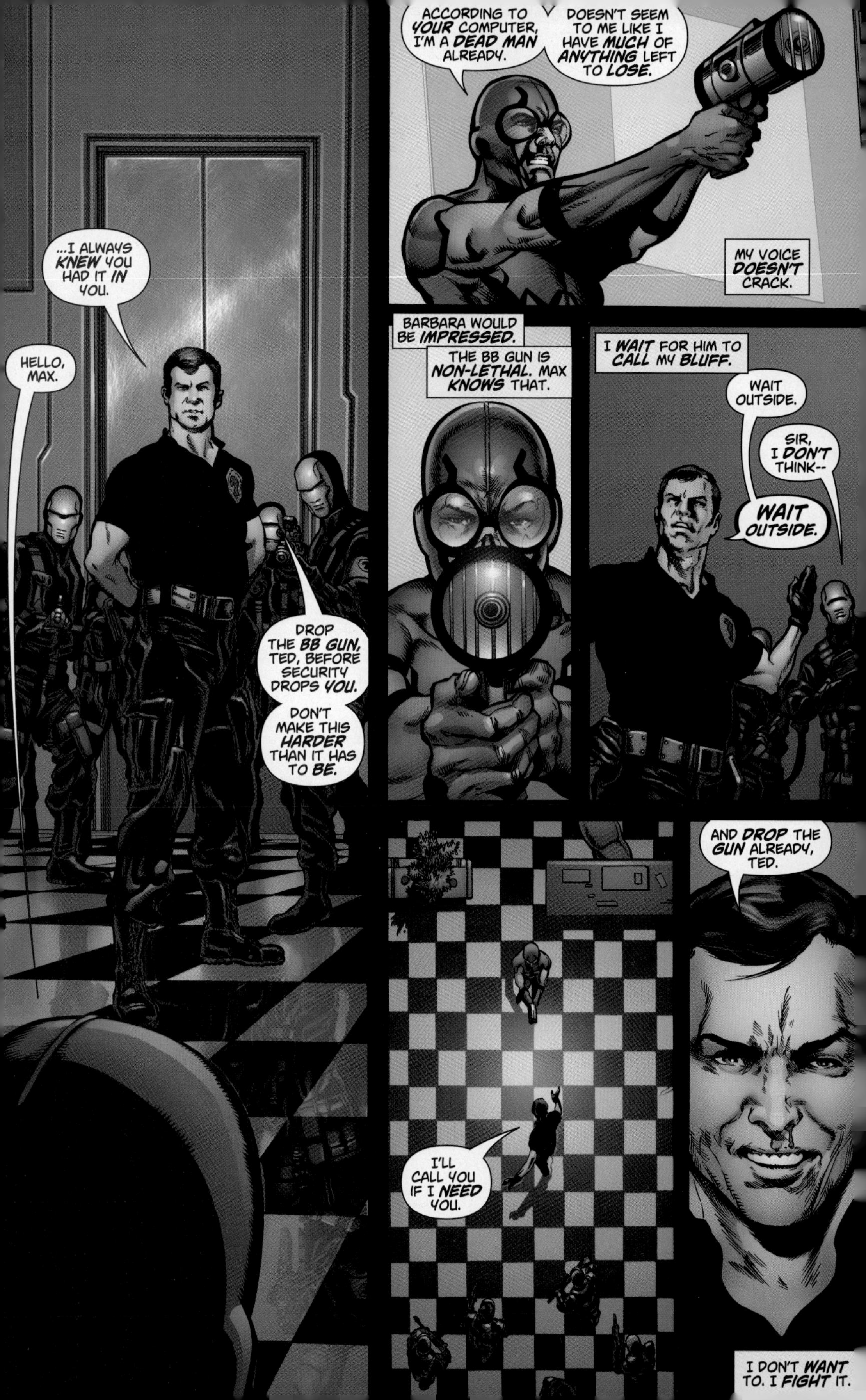
...I ALWAYS KNEW YOU HAD IT IN YOU.
HELLO, MAX.
DROP THE BB GUN, TED, BEFORE SECURITY DROPS YOU.
DON'T MAKE THIS HARDER THAN IT HAS TO BE.
ACCORDING TO YOUR COMPUTER, I'M A DEAD MAN ALREADY.
DOESN'T SEEM TO ME LIKE I HAVE MUCH OF ANYTHING LEFT TO LOSE.
MY VOICE DOESN'T CRACK.
BARBARA WOULD BE IMPRESSED.
THE BB GUN IS NON-LETHAL. MAX KNOWS THAT.
I WAIT FOR HIM TO CALL MY BLUFF.
WAIT OUTSIDE.
SIR, I DON'T THINK--
WAIT OUTSIDE.
I'LL CALL YOU IF I NEED YOU.
AND DROP THE GUN ALREADY, TED.
I DON'T WANT TO. I FIGHT IT.

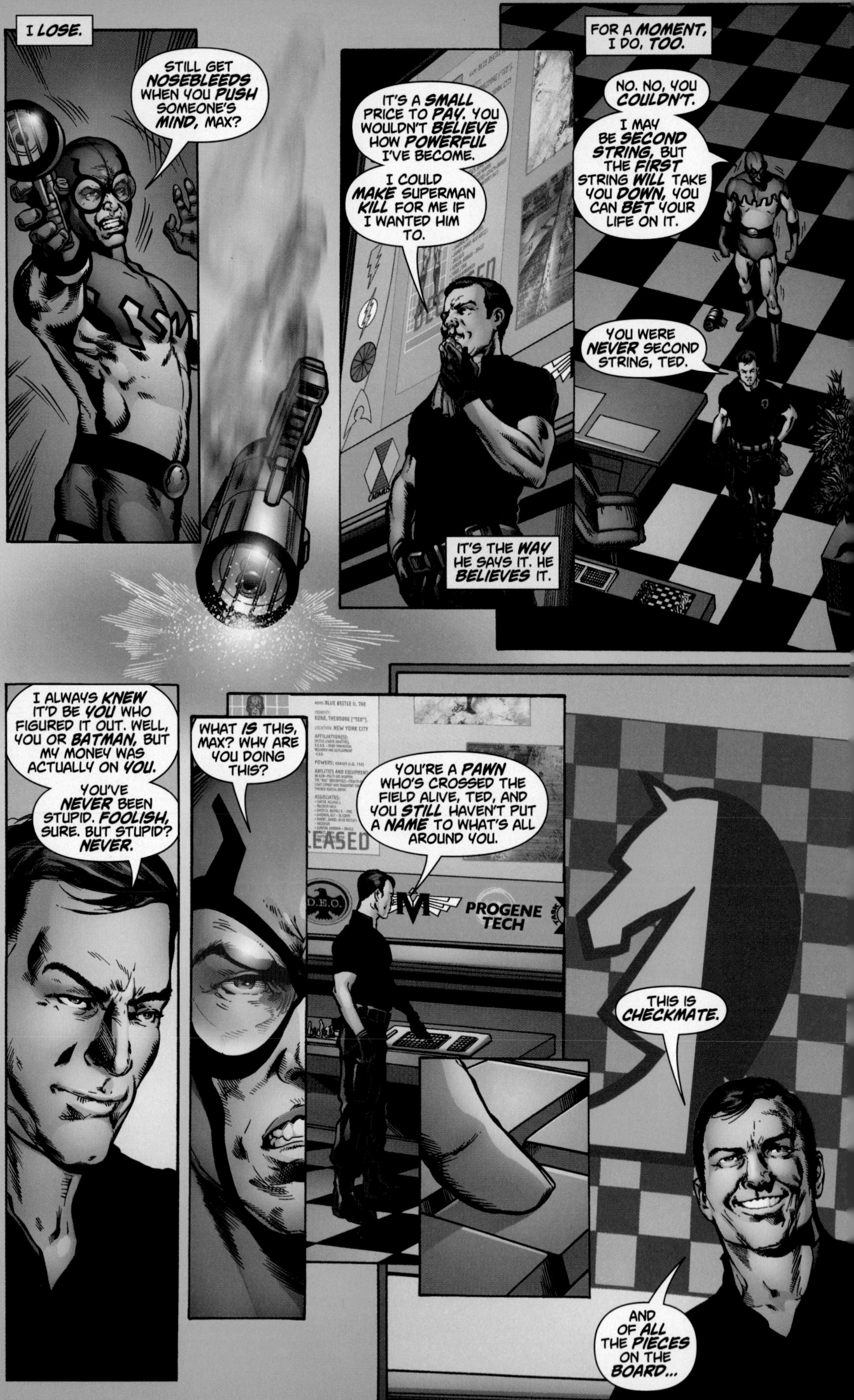
I LOSE.
STILL GET NOSEBLEEDS WHEN YOU PUSH SOMEONE'S MIND, MAX?
IT'S A SMALL PRICE TO PAY. YOU WOULDN'T BELIEVE HOW POWERFUL I'VE BECOME.
I COULD MAKE SUPERMAN KILL FOR ME IF I WANTED HIM TO.
IT'S THE WAY HE SAYS IT. HE BELIEVES IT.
FOR A MOMENT, I DO, TOO.
NO. NO, YOU COULDN'T.
I MAY BE SECOND STRING, BUT THE FIRST STRING WILL TAKE YOU DOWN, YOU CAN BET YOUR LIFE ON IT.
YOU WERE NEVER SECOND STRING, TED.
I ALWAYS KNEW IT'D BE YOU WHO FIGURED IT OUT. WELL, YOU OR BATMAN, BUT MY MONEY WAS ACTUALLY ON YOU.
YOU'VE NEVER BEEN STUPID. FOOLISH, SURE. BUT STUPID? NEVER.
WHAT IS THIS, MAX? WHY ARE YOU DOING THIS?
YOU'RE A PAWN WHO'S CROSSED THE FIELD ALIVE, TED, AND YOU STILL HAVEN'T PUT A NAME TO WHAT'S ALL AROUND YOU.
D.E.O.
PROGENE TECH
THIS IS CHECKMATE.
AND OF ALL THE PIECES ON THE BOARD...

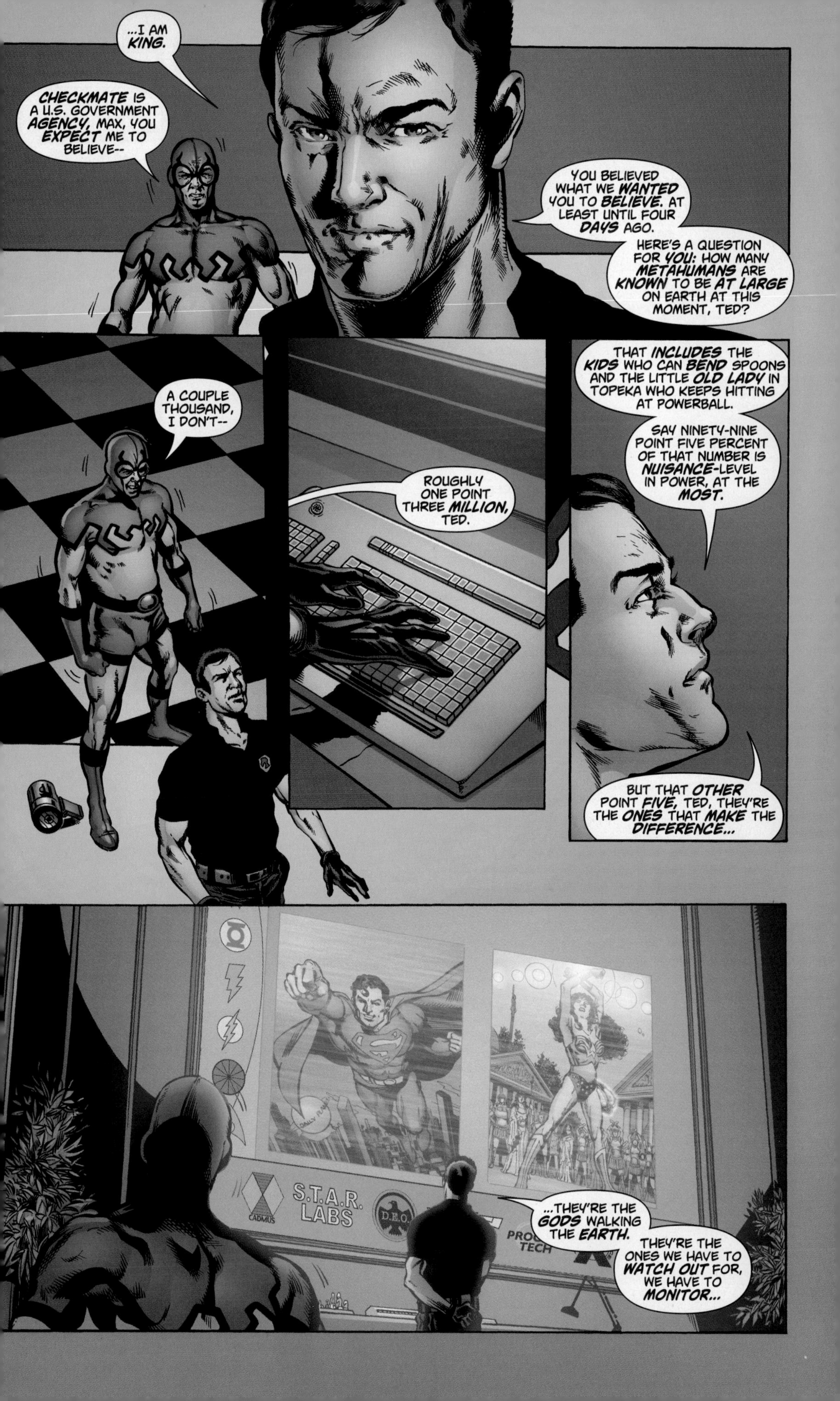
...I AM KING.
CHECKMATE IS A U.S. GOVERNMENT AGENCY, MAX, YOU EXPECT ME TO BELIEVE--
YOU BELIEVED WHAT WE WANTED YOU TO BELIEVE. AT LEAST UNTIL FOUR DAYS AGO.
HERE'S A QUESTION FOR YOU: HOW MANY METAHUMANS ARE KNOWN TO BE AT LARGE ON EARTH AT THIS MOMENT, TED?
A COUPLE THOUSAND, I DON'T--
ROUGHLY ONE POINT THREE MILLION, TED.
THAT INCLUDES THE KIDS WHO CAN BEND SPOONS AND THE LITTLE OLD LADY IN TOPEKA WHO KEEPS HITTING AT POWERBALL.
SAY NINETY-NINE POINT FIVE PERCENT OF THAT NUMBER IS NUISANCE-LEVEL IN POWER, AT THE MOST.
BUT THAT OTHER POINT FIVE, TED, THEY'RE THE ONES THAT MAKE THE DIFFERENCE...
CADMUS
S.T.A.R. LABS
D.E.O.
...THEY'RE THE GODS WALKING THE EARTH.
THEY'RE THE ONES WE HAVE TO WATCH OUT FOR, WE HAVE TO MONITOR...

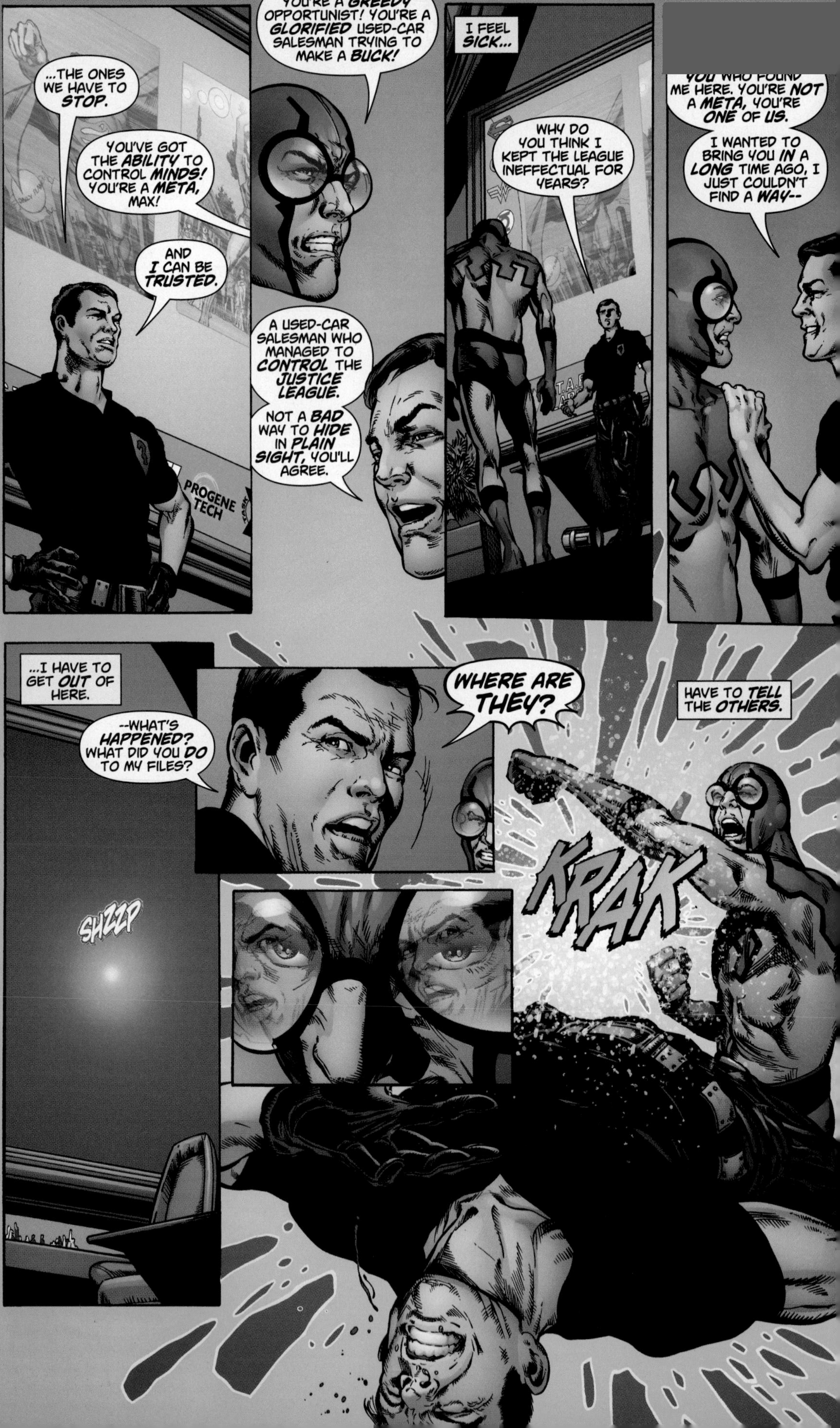

...THE ONES WE HAVE TO STOP.
YOU'VE GOT THE ABILITY TO CONTROL MINDS! YOU'RE A META, MAX!
AND I CAN BE TRUSTED.
PROGENE TECH
TO DO WHAT? YOU'RE A GREEDY OPPORTUNIST! YOU'RE A GLORIFIED USED-CAR SALESMAN TRYING TO MAKE A BUCK!
A USED-CAR SALESMAN WHO MANAGED TO CONTROL THE JUSTICE LEAGUE.
NOT A BAD WAY TO HIDE IN PLAIN SIGHT, YOU'LL AGREE.
I FEEL SICK...
WHY DO YOU THINK I KEPT THE LEAGUE INEFFECTUAL FOR YEARS?
YOU WHO FOUND ME HERE. YOU'RE NOT A META, YOU'RE ONE OF US.
I WANTED TO BRING YOU IN A LONG TIME AGO, I JUST COULDN'T FIND A WAY--
...I HAVE TO GET OUT OF HERE.
--WHAT'S HAPPENED? WHAT DID YOU DO TO MY FILES?
SHZZP
WHERE ARE THEY?
HAVE TO TELL THE OTHERS.
KRAK

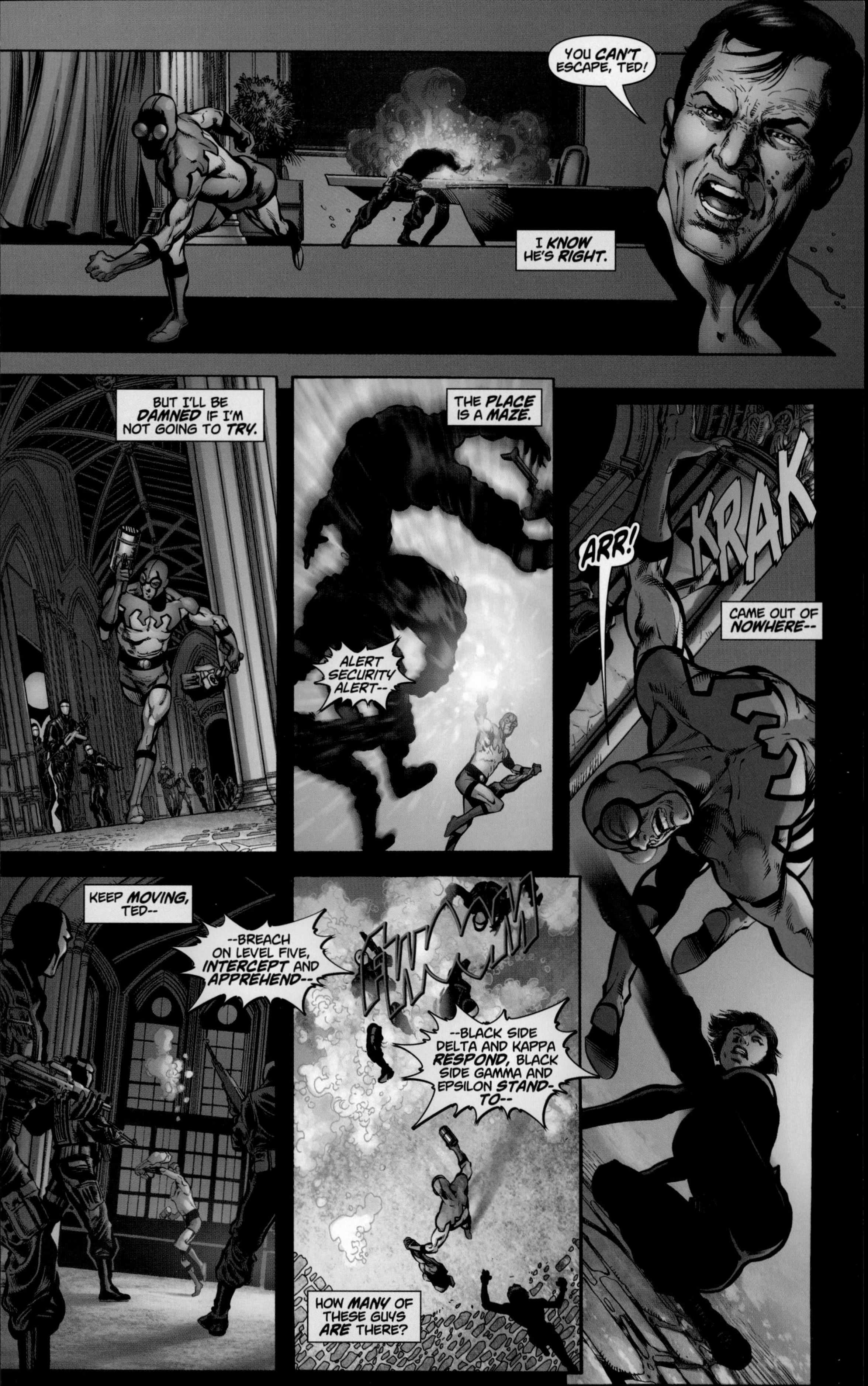
YOU CAN'T ESCAPE, TED!
I KNOW HE'S RIGHT.
BUT I'LL BE DAMNED IF I'M NOT GOING TO TRY.
THE PLACE IS A MAZE.
ALERT SECURITY ALERT--
KRAK
ARR!
CAME OUT OF NOWHERE--
KEEP MOVING, TED--
--BREACH ON LEVEL FIVE, INTERCEPT AND APPREHEND--
--BLACK SIDE DELTA AND KAPPA RESPOND, BLACK SIDE GAMMA AND EPSILON STAND-TO--
HOW MANY OF THESE GUYS ARE THERE?

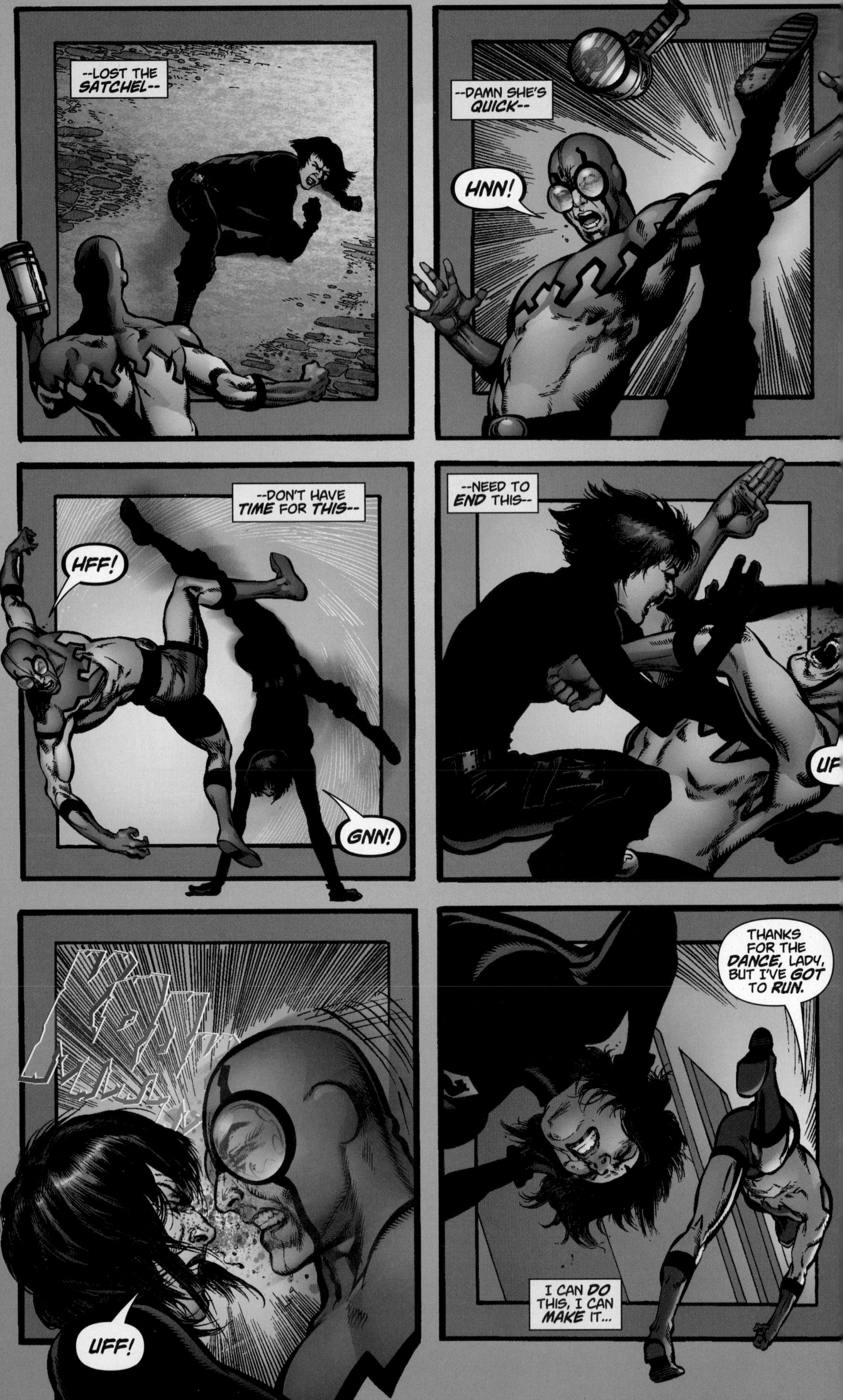
--LOST THE SATCHEL--
--DAMN SHE'S QUICK--
HNN!
--DON'T HAVE TIME FOR THIS--
HFF!
GNN!
--NEED TO END THIS--
UF
UFF!
THANKS FOR THE DANCE, LADY, BUT I'VE GOT TO RUN.
I CAN DO THIS, I CAN MAKE IT...

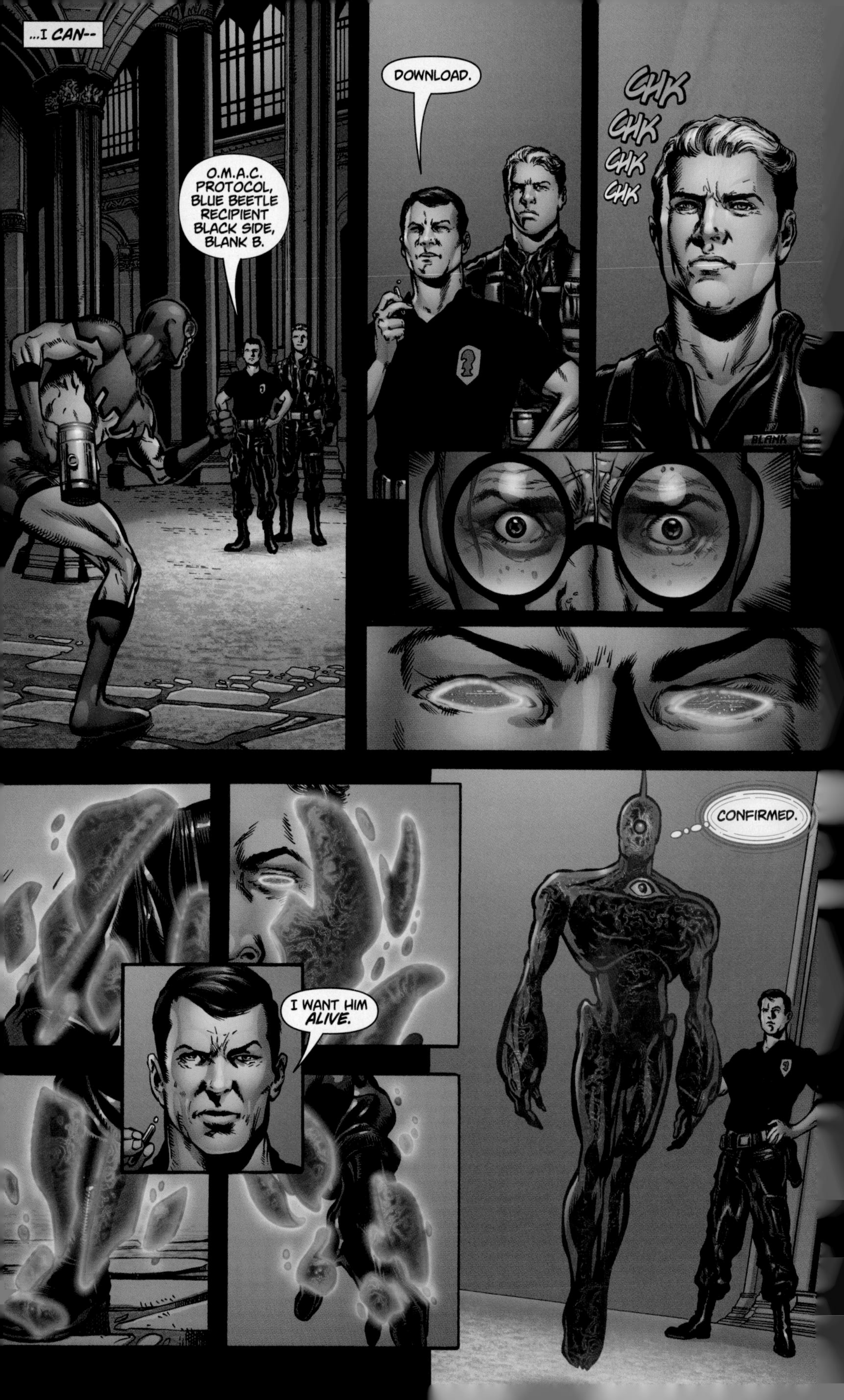
...I CAN--
O.M.A.C. PROTOCOL, BLUE BEETLE RECIPIENT BLACK SIDE, BLANK B.
DOWNLOAD.
CHK CHK CHK CHK
BLANK
CONFIRMED.
I WANT HIM ALIVE.

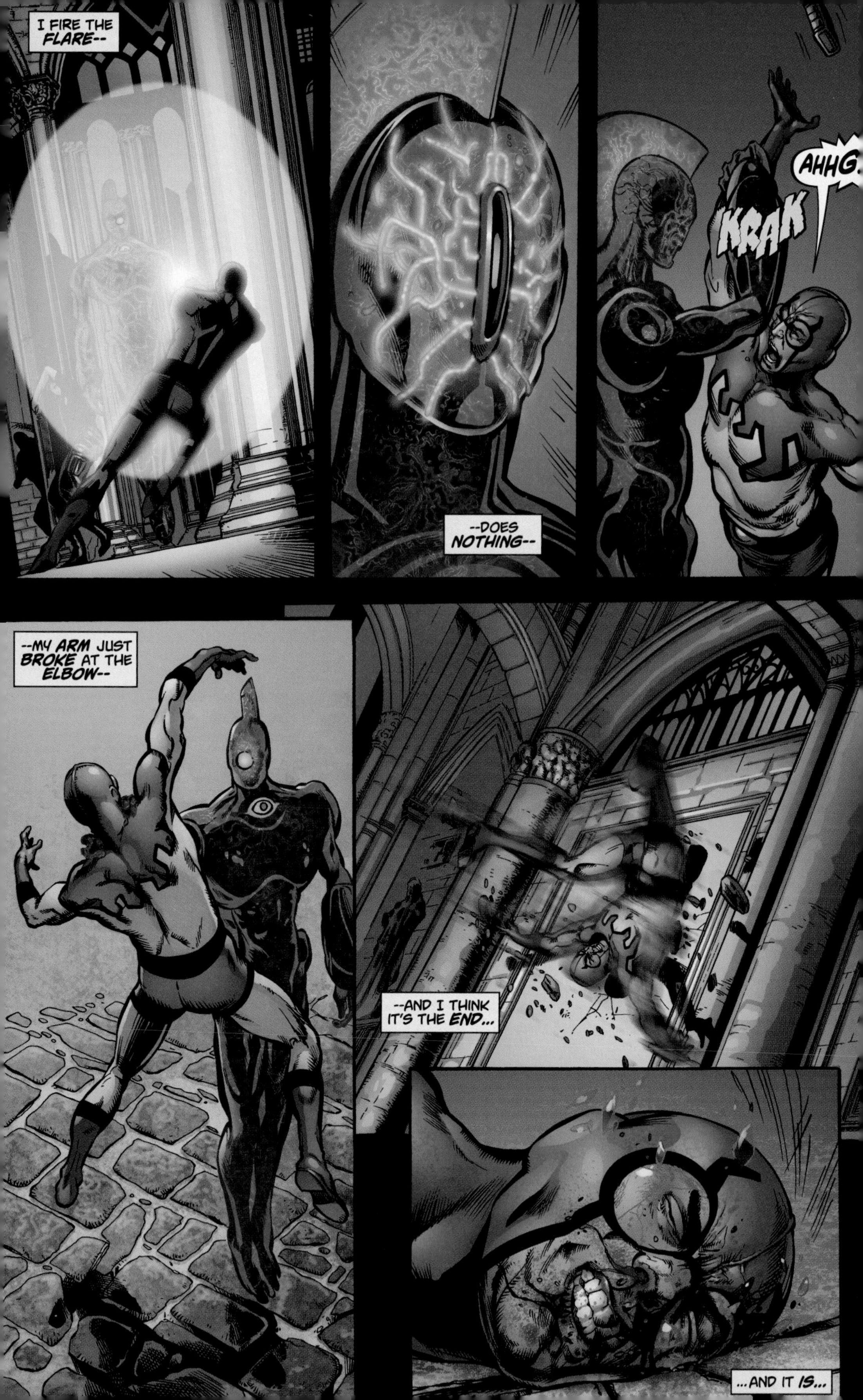
I FIRE THE FLARE--
--DOES NOTHING--
AHHG.
KRAK
--MY ARM JUST BROKE AT THE ELBOW--
--AND I THINK IT'S THE END...
...AND IT IS...

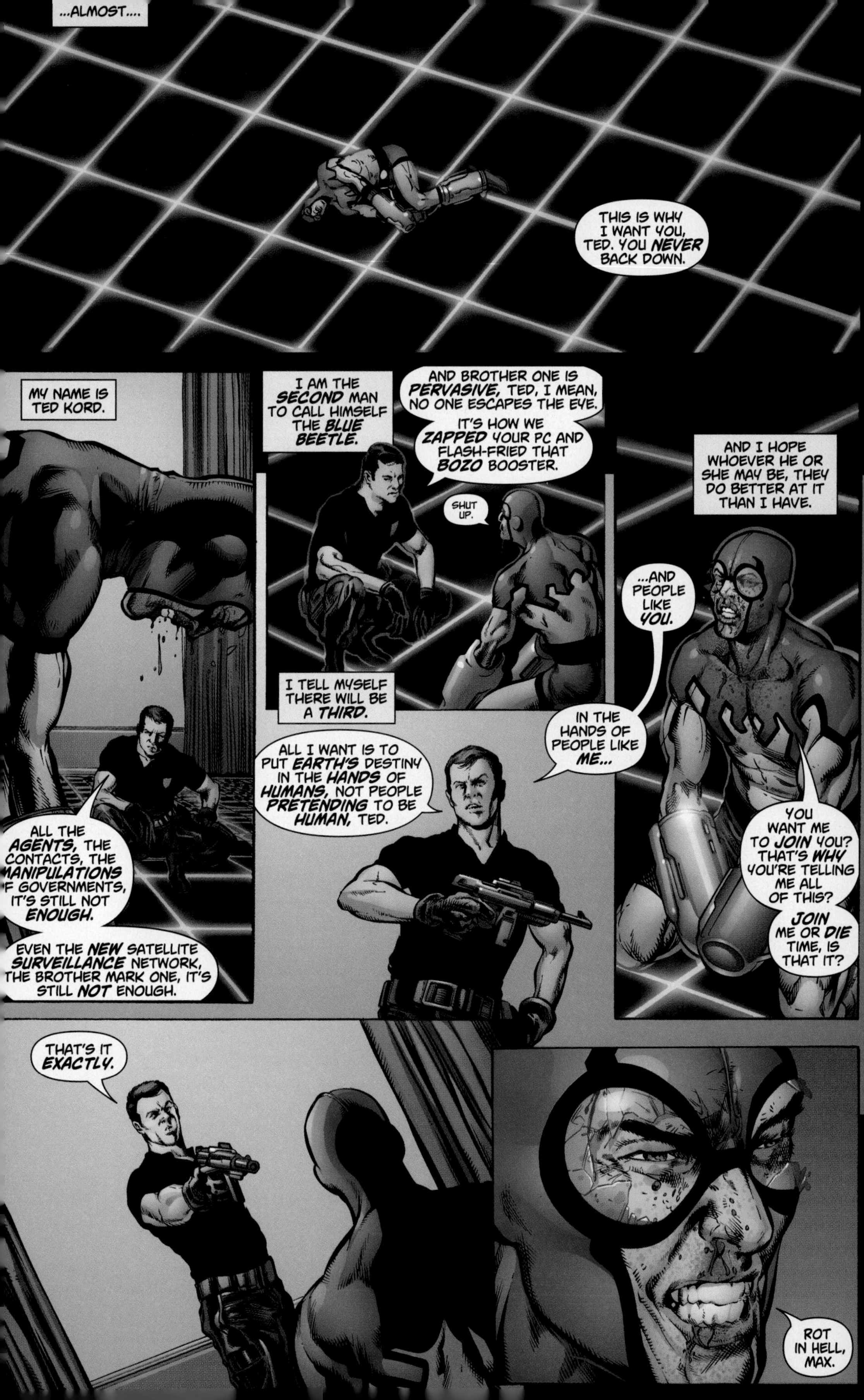
...ALMOST....
THIS IS WHY I WANT YOU, TED. YOU NEVER BACK DOWN.
MY NAME IS TED KORD.
I AM THE SECOND MAN TO CALL HIMSELF THE BLUE BEETLE.
AND BROTHER ONE IS PERVASIVE, TED, I MEAN, NO ONE ESCAPES THE EYE.
IT'S HOW WE ZAPPED YOUR PC AND FLASH-FRIED THAT BOZO BOOSTER.
SHUT UP.
I TELL MYSELF THERE WILL BE A THIRD.
AND I HOPE WHOEVER HE OR SHE MAY BE, THEY DO BETTER AT IT THAN I HAVE.
ALL THE AGENTS, THE CONTACTS, THE MANIPULATIONS OF GOVERNMENTS, IT'S STILL NOT ENOUGH.
EVEN THE NEW SATELLITE SURVEILLANCE NETWORK, THE BROTHER MARK ONE, IT'S STILL NOT ENOUGH.
ALL I WANT IS TO PUT EARTH'S DESTINY IN THE HANDS OF HUMANS, NOT PEOPLE PRETENDING TO BE HUMAN, TED.
IN THE HANDS OF PEOPLE LIKE ME...
...AND PEOPLE LIKE YOU.
YOU WANT ME TO JOIN YOU? THAT'S WHY YOU'RE TELLING ME ALL OF THIS?
JOIN ME OR DIE TIME, IS THAT IT?
THAT'S IT EXACTLY.
ROT IN HELL, MAX.

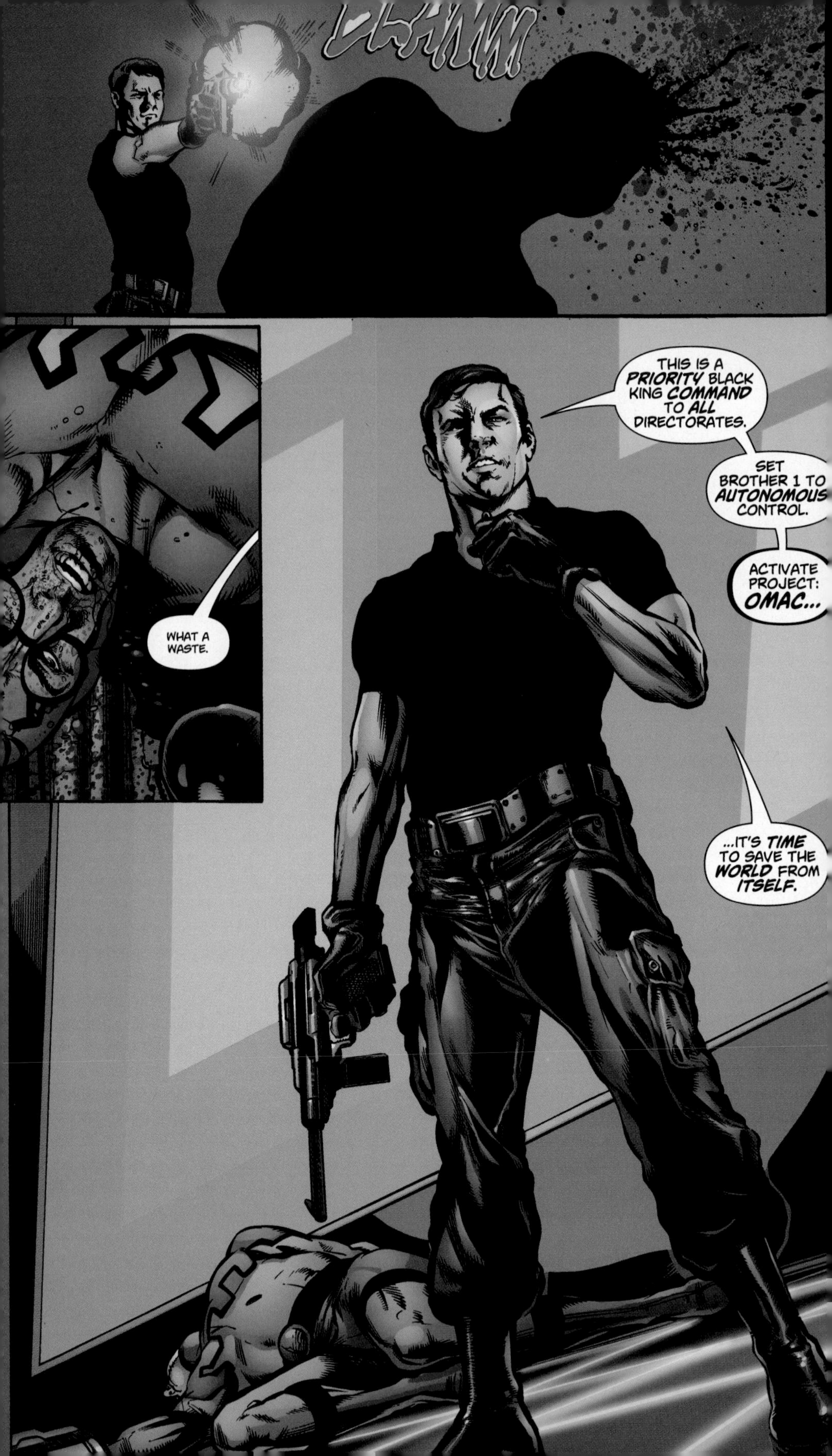
WHAT A WASTE.
THIS IS A PRIORITY BLACK KING COMMAND TO ALL DIRECTORATES.
SET BROTHER 1 TO AUTONOMOUS CONTROL.
ACTIVATE PROJECT: OMAC...
...IT'S TIME TO SAVE THE WORLD FROM ITSELF.

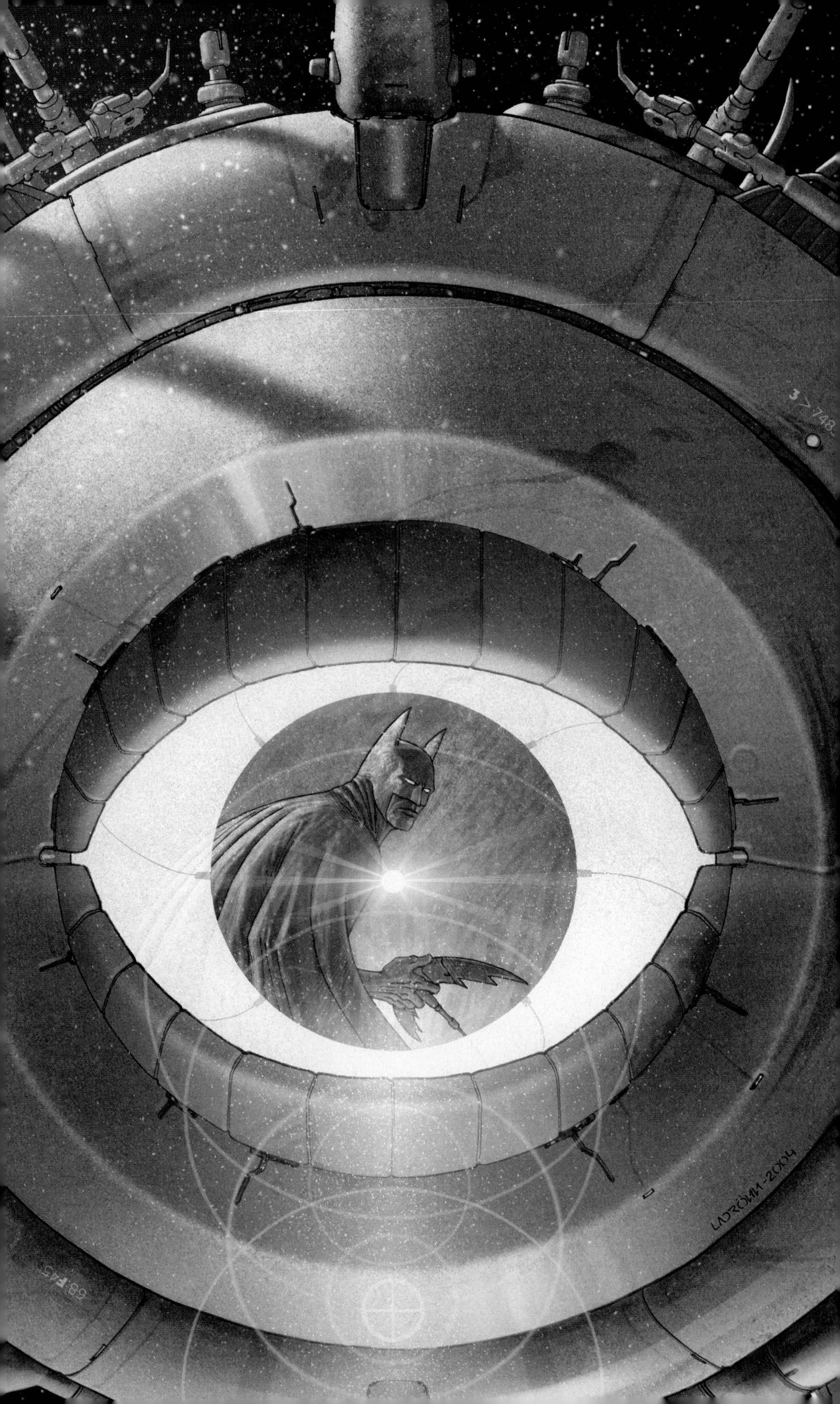
LADRÖNN-2004

Greg Rucka
Writer

Jesus Saiz
Artist

Hi-Fi Design
Colorist

Phil Balsman
Letterer

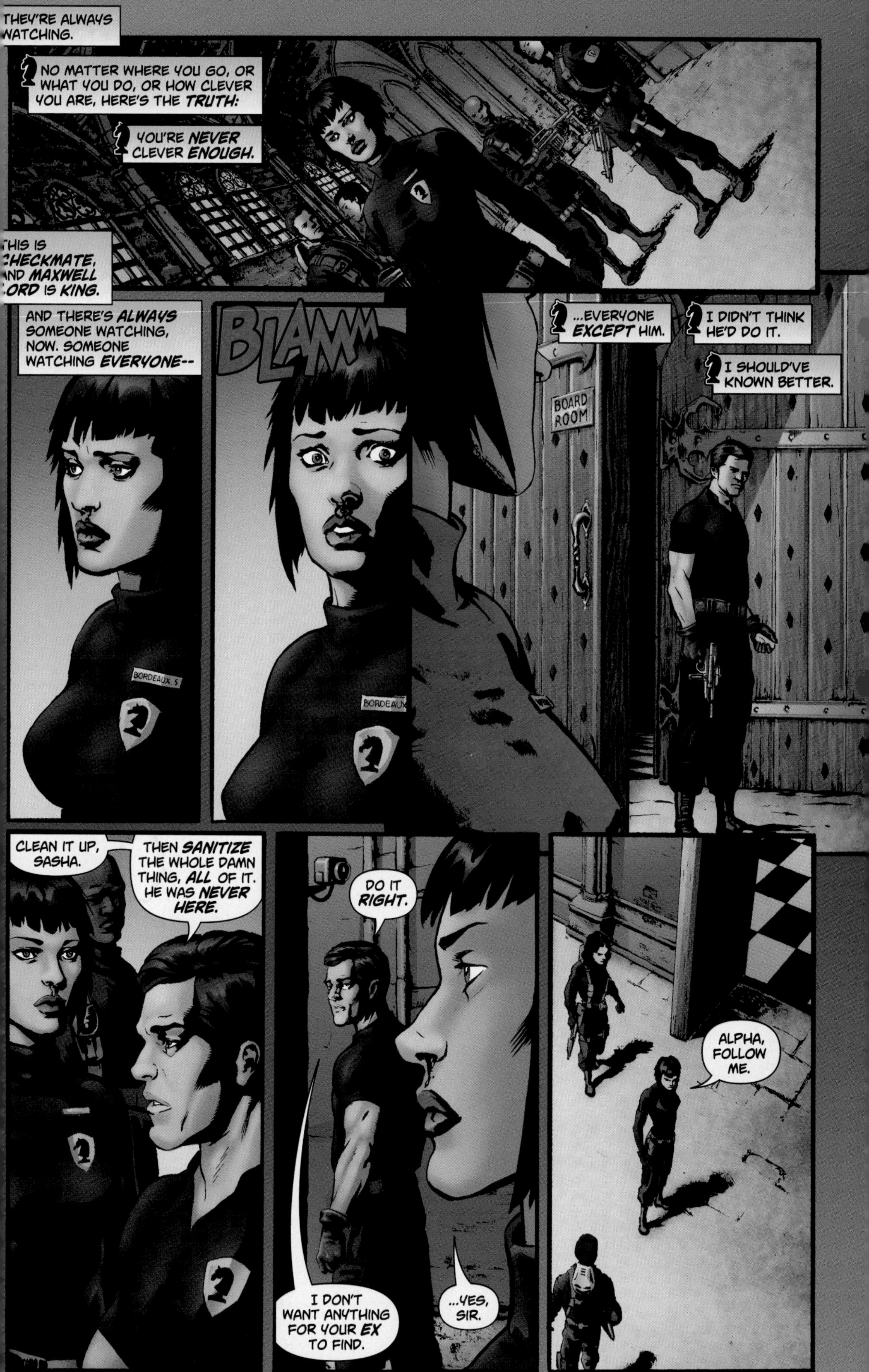
THEY'RE ALWAYS WATCHING.
NO MATTER WHERE YOU GO, OR WHAT YOU DO, OR HOW CLEVER YOU ARE, HERE'S THE TRUTH:
YOU'RE NEVER CLEVER ENOUGH.
THIS IS CHECKMATE, AND MAXWELL LORD IS KING.
AND THERE'S ALWAYS SOMEONE WATCHING, NOW. SOMEONE WATCHING EVERYONE--
BORDEAUX.S
BLAMM
BORDEAUX
...EVERYONE EXCEPT HIM.
I DIDN'T THINK HE'D DO IT.
I SHOULD'VE KNOWN BETTER.
BOARD ROOM
CLEAN IT UP, SASHA.
THEN SANITIZE THE WHOLE DAMN THING, ALL OF IT. HE WAS NEVER HERE.
DO IT RIGHT.
I DON'T WANT ANYTHING FOR YOUR EX TO FIND.
...YES, SIR.
ALPHA, FOLLOW ME.

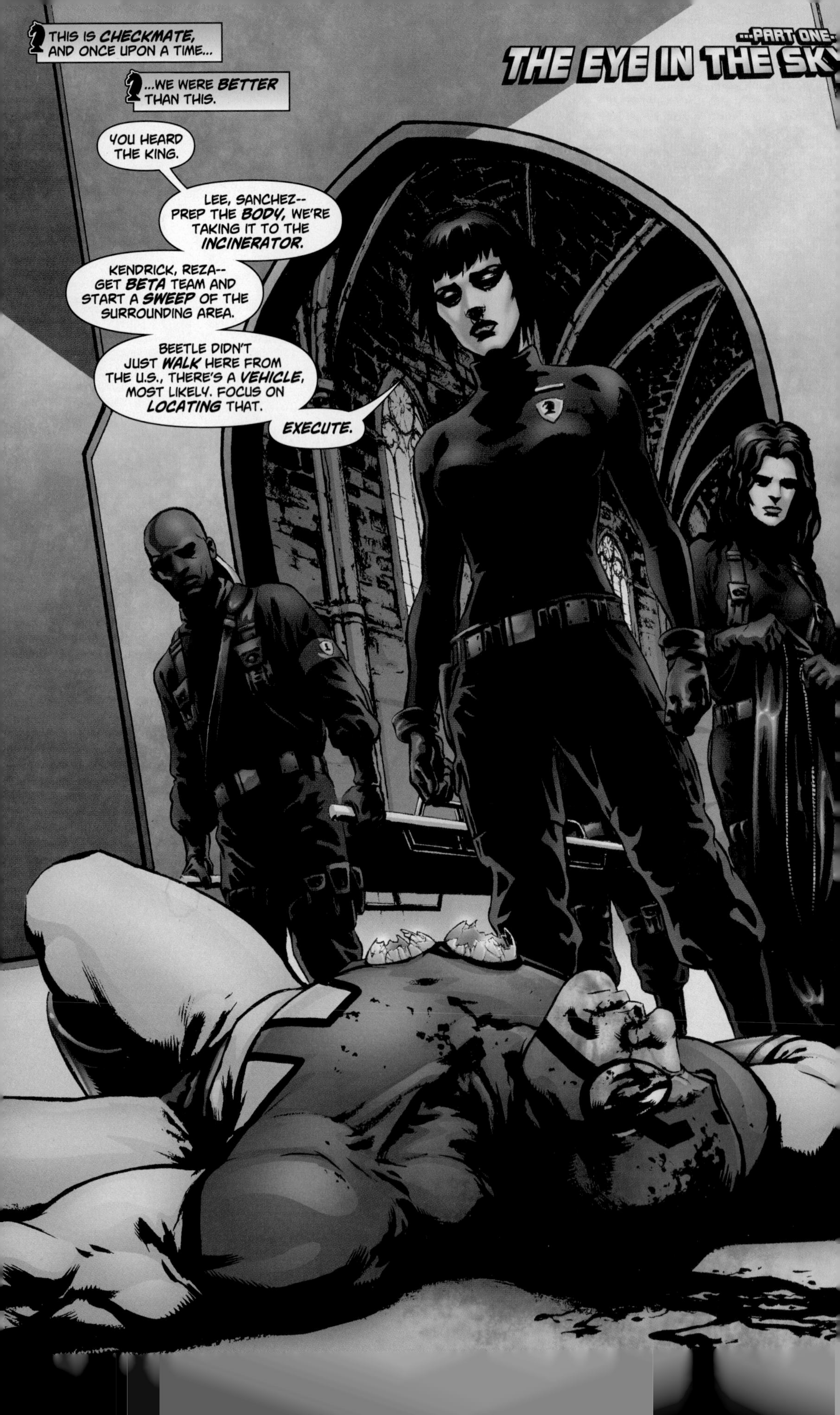
THIS IS CHECKMATE, AND ONCE UPON A TIME...
...WE WERE BETTER THAN THIS.
---PART ONE---
THE EYE IN THE SKY
YOU HEARD THE KING.
LEE, SANCHEZ-- PREP THE BODY, WE'RE TAKING IT TO THE INCINERATOR.
KENDRICK, REZA-- GET BETA TEAM AND START A SWEEP OF THE SURROUNDING AREA.
BEETLE DIDN'T JUST WALK HERE FROM THE U.S., THERE'S A VEHICLE, MOST LIKELY. FOCUS ON LOCATING THAT.
EXECUTE.

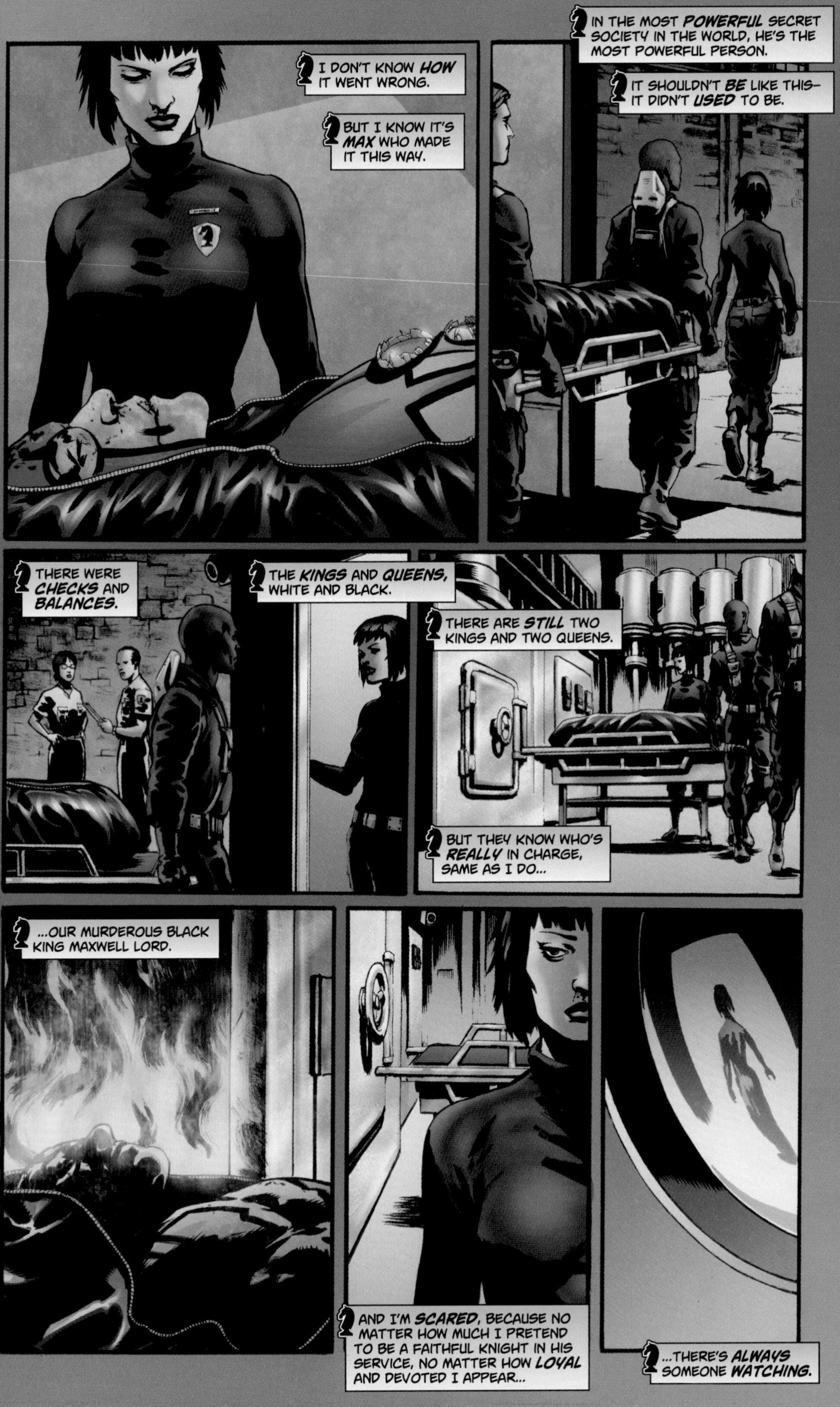
I DON'T KNOW HOW IT WENT WRONG.
BUT I KNOW IT'S MAX WHO MADE IT THIS WAY.
IN THE MOST POWERFUL SECRET SOCIETY IN THE WORLD, HE'S THE MOST POWERFUL PERSON.
IT SHOULDN'T BE LIKE THIS-- IT DIDN'T USED TO BE.
THERE WERE CHECKS AND BALANCES.
THE KINGS AND QUEENS, WHITE AND BLACK.
THERE ARE STILL TWO KINGS AND TWO QUEENS.
BUT THEY KNOW WHO'S REALLY IN CHARGE, SAME AS I DO...
...OUR MURDEROUS BLACK KING MAXWELL LORD.
AND I'M SCARED, BECAUSE NO MATTER HOW MUCH I PRETEND TO BE A FAITHFUL KNIGHT IN HIS SERVICE, NO MATTER HOW LOYAL AND DEVOTED I APPEAR...
...THERE'S ALWAYS SOMEONE WATCHING.

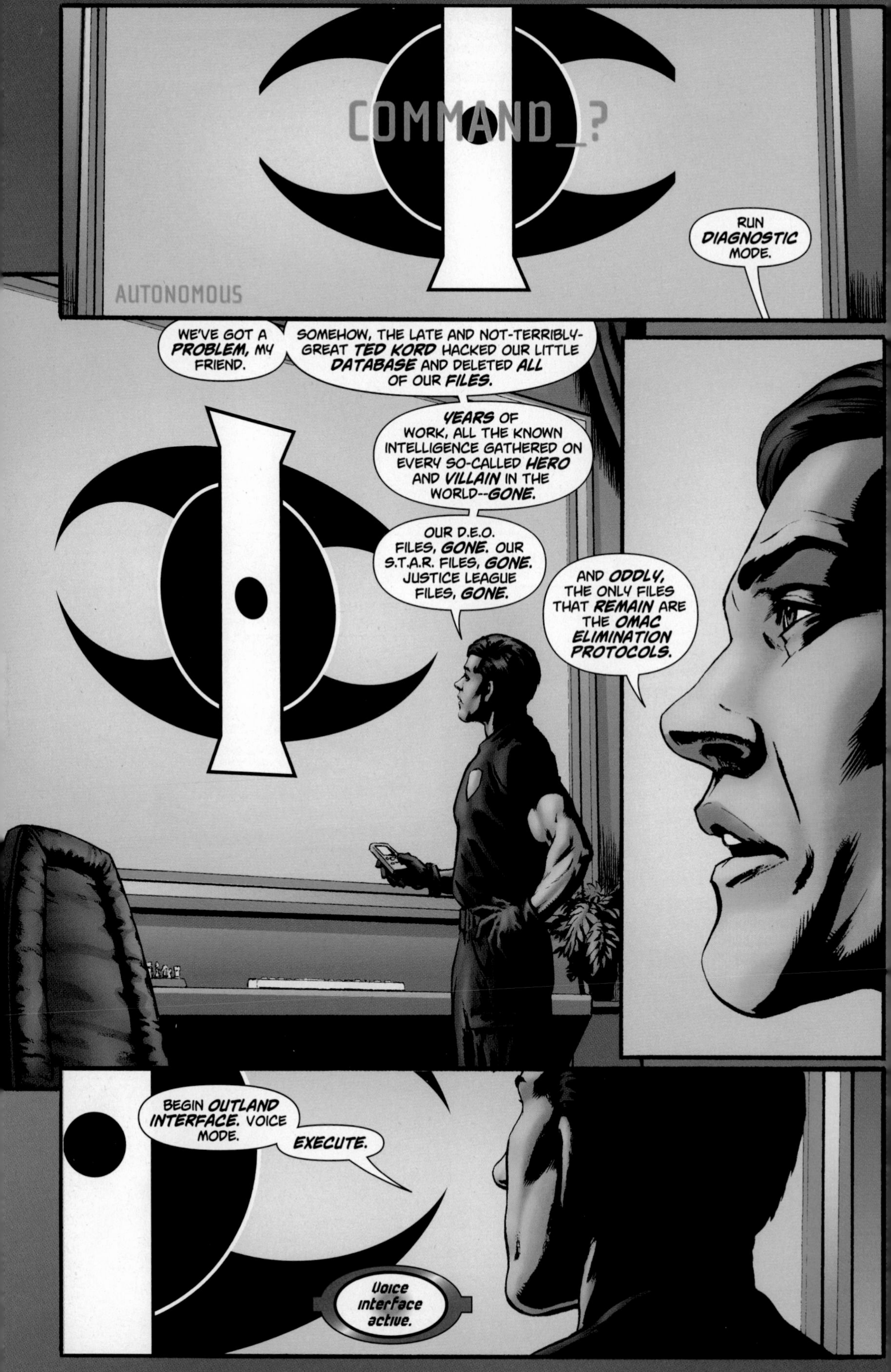

COMMAND_?
AUTONOMOUS
RUN DIAGNOSTIC MODE.
WE'VE GOT A PROBLEM, MY FRIEND.
SOMEHOW, THE LATE AND NOT-TERRIBLY-GREAT TED KORD HACKED OUR LITTLE DATABASE AND DELETED ALL OF OUR FILES.
YEARS OF WORK, ALL THE KNOWN INTELLIGENCE GATHERED ON EVERY SO-CALLED HERO AND VILLAIN IN THE WORLD--GONE.
OUR D.E.O. FILES, GONE. OUR S.T.A.R. FILES, GONE. JUSTICE LEAGUE FILES, GONE.
AND ODDLY, THE ONLY FILES THAT REMAIN ARE THE OMAC ELIMINATION PROTOCOLS.
BEGIN OUTLAND INTERFACE. VOICE MODE.
EXECUTE.
Voice interface active.

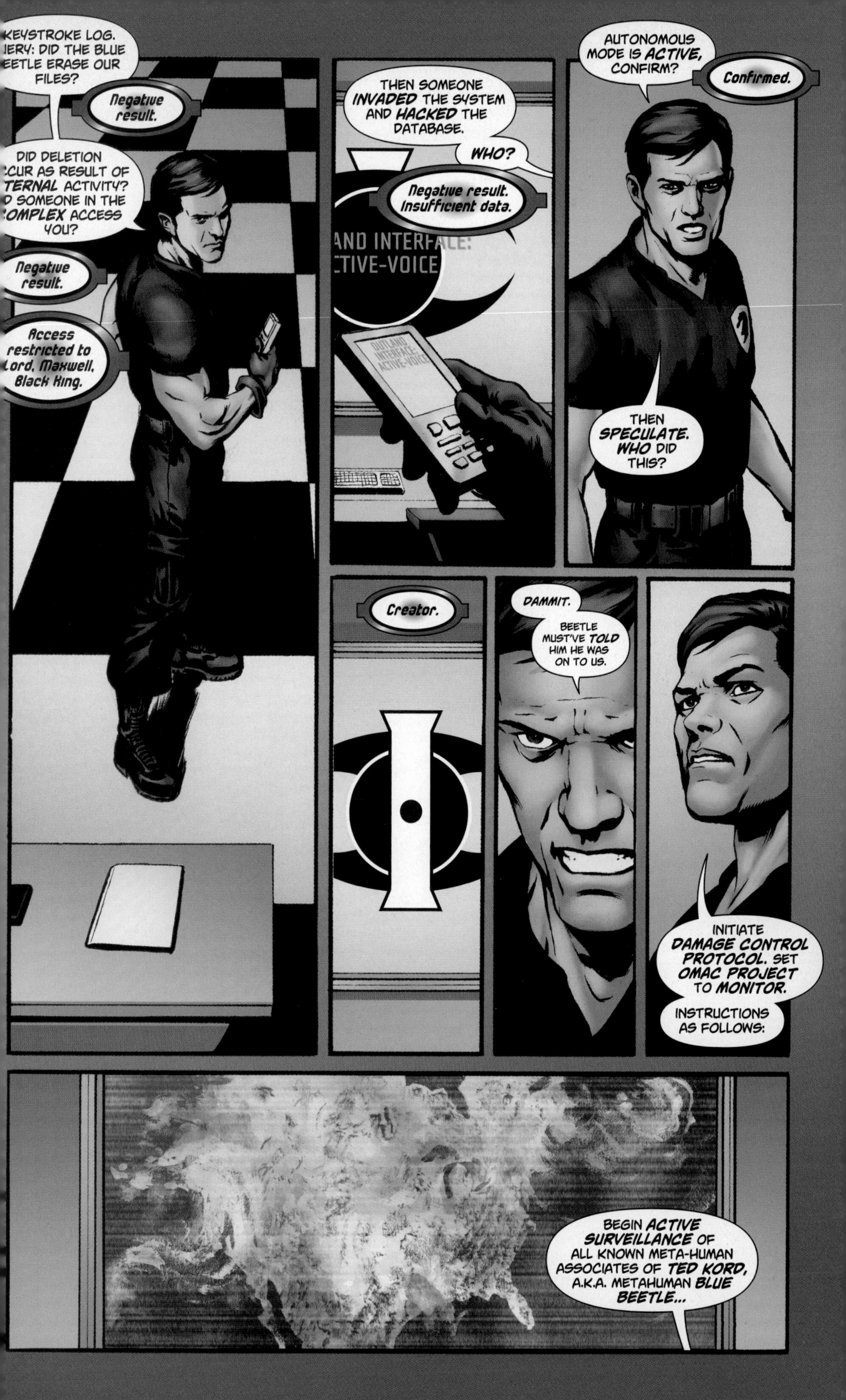
KEYSTROKE LOG. …IERY: DID THE BLUE …EETLE ERASE OUR FILES?
Negative result.
DID DELETION …CCUR AS RESULT OF …TERNAL ACTIVITY? …D SOMEONE IN THE …OMPLEX ACCESS YOU?
Negative result.
Access restricted to …ord, Maxwell, Black King.
THEN SOMEONE INVADED THE SYSTEM AND HACKED THE DATABASE.
WHO?
Negative result. Insufficient data.
…AND INTERFACE: …CTIVE-VOICE
AUTONOMOUS MODE IS ACTIVE, CONFIRM?
Confirmed.
THEN SPECULATE. WHO DID THIS?
Creator.
DAMMIT.
BEETLE MUST'VE TOLD HIM HE WAS ON TO US.
INITIATE DAMAGE CONTROL PROTOCOL. SET OMAC PROJECT TO MONITOR.
INSTRUCTIONS AS FOLLOWS:
BEGIN ACTIVE SURVEILLANCE OF ALL KNOWN META-HUMAN ASSOCIATES OF TED KORD, A.K.A. METAHUMAN BLUE BEETLE...

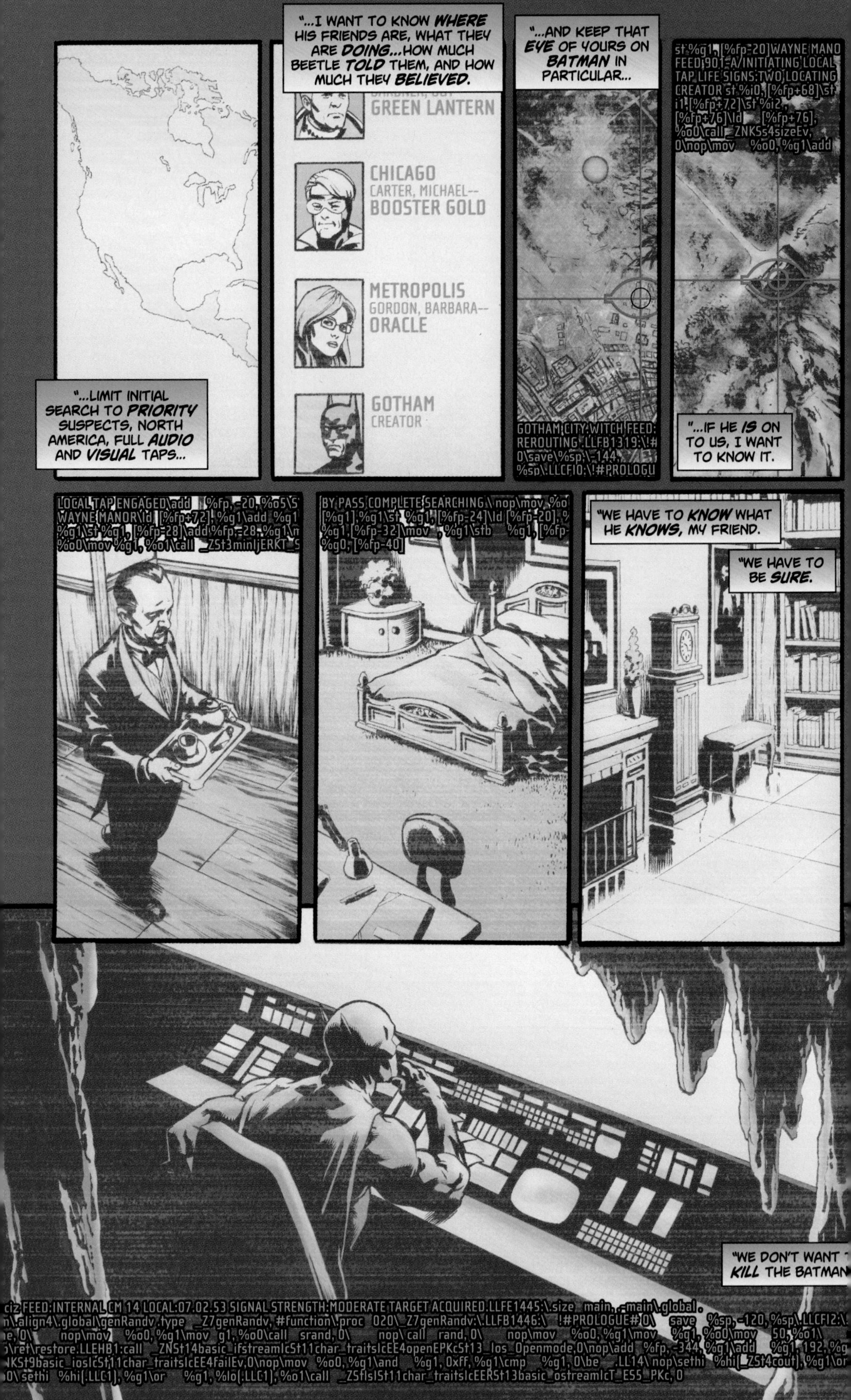
"...I WANT TO KNOW WHERE HIS FRIENDS ARE, WHAT THEY ARE DOING...HOW MUCH BEETLE TOLD THEM, AND HOW MUCH THEY BELIEVED.
GREEN LANTERN
CHICAGO
CARTER, MICHAEL--
BOOSTER GOLD
METROPOLIS
GORDON, BARBARA--
ORACLE
GOTHAM
CREATOR
"...LIMIT INITIAL SEARCH TO PRIORITY SUSPECTS, NORTH AMERICA, FULL AUDIO AND VISUAL TAPS...
"...AND KEEP THAT EYE OF YOURS ON BATMAN IN PARTICULAR...
GOTHAM CITY WITCH FEED: REROUTING .LLFB1319:\!# 0\save\%sp,\-144, %sp\.LLCFI0:\!#PROLOGU
st %g1, [%fp-20]WAYNE MANO FEED 901-A/INITIATING LOCAL TAP LIFE SIGNS:TWO LOCATING CREATOR st %i0, [%fp+68]\st i1,[%fp+72]\st %i2, [%fp+76]\ld [%fp+76], %o0\call _ZNKSs4sizeEv, 0\nop\mov %o0, %g1\add
"...IF HE IS ON TO US, I WANT TO KNOW IT.
LOCAL TAP ENGAGED\add %fp, -20, %o5\St WAYNE MANOR\ld [%fp+72], %g1\add %g1 %g1\st %g1, [%fp-28]\add %fp,-28, %g1\m %o0\mov %g1, %o1\call _ZSt3minIjERKT_S
BY PASS COMPLETE SEARCHING \ nop\mov %o [%g1],%g1\st %g1, [%fp-24]\ld [%fp-20], % %g1,[%fp-32]\mov , %g1\stb %g1, [%fp- %g0, [%fp-40]
"WE HAVE TO KNOW WHAT HE KNOWS, MY FRIEND.
"WE HAVE TO BE SURE.
"WE DON'T WANT T KILL THE BATMAN
ciz FEED:INTERNAL CM 14 LOCAL:07.02.53 SIGNAL STRENGTH:MODERATE TARGET ACQUIRED.LLFE1445:\.size main, .-main\.global
n\.align4\.global\genRandv .type _Z7genRandv, #function\.proc 020_Z7genRandv:\.LLFB1446:\ !#PROLOGUE# 0\ save %sp, -120, %sp\.LLCFI2:\
e, 0\ nop\mov %o0, %g1\mov g1, %o0\call srand, 0\ nop\ call rand, 0\ nop\mov %o0, %g1\mov %g1, %o0\mov 50, %o1\
\ret\restore.LLEHB1:call _ZNSt14basic_ifstreamIcSt11char_traitsIcEE4openEPKcSt13_Ios_Openmode,0\nop\add %fp, -344, %g1\add %g1, 192, %g
NKSt9basic_iosIcSt11char_traitsIcEE4failEv,0\nop\mov %o0, %g1\and %g1, 0xff, %g1\cmp %g1, 0\be .LL14\ nop\sethi %hi(_ZSt4cout), %g1\or
0\ sethi %hi(.LLC1), %g1\or %g1, %lo(.LLC1), %o1\call _ZSfIsISt11char_traitsIcEERSt13basic_ostreamIcT_ES5_PKc, 0

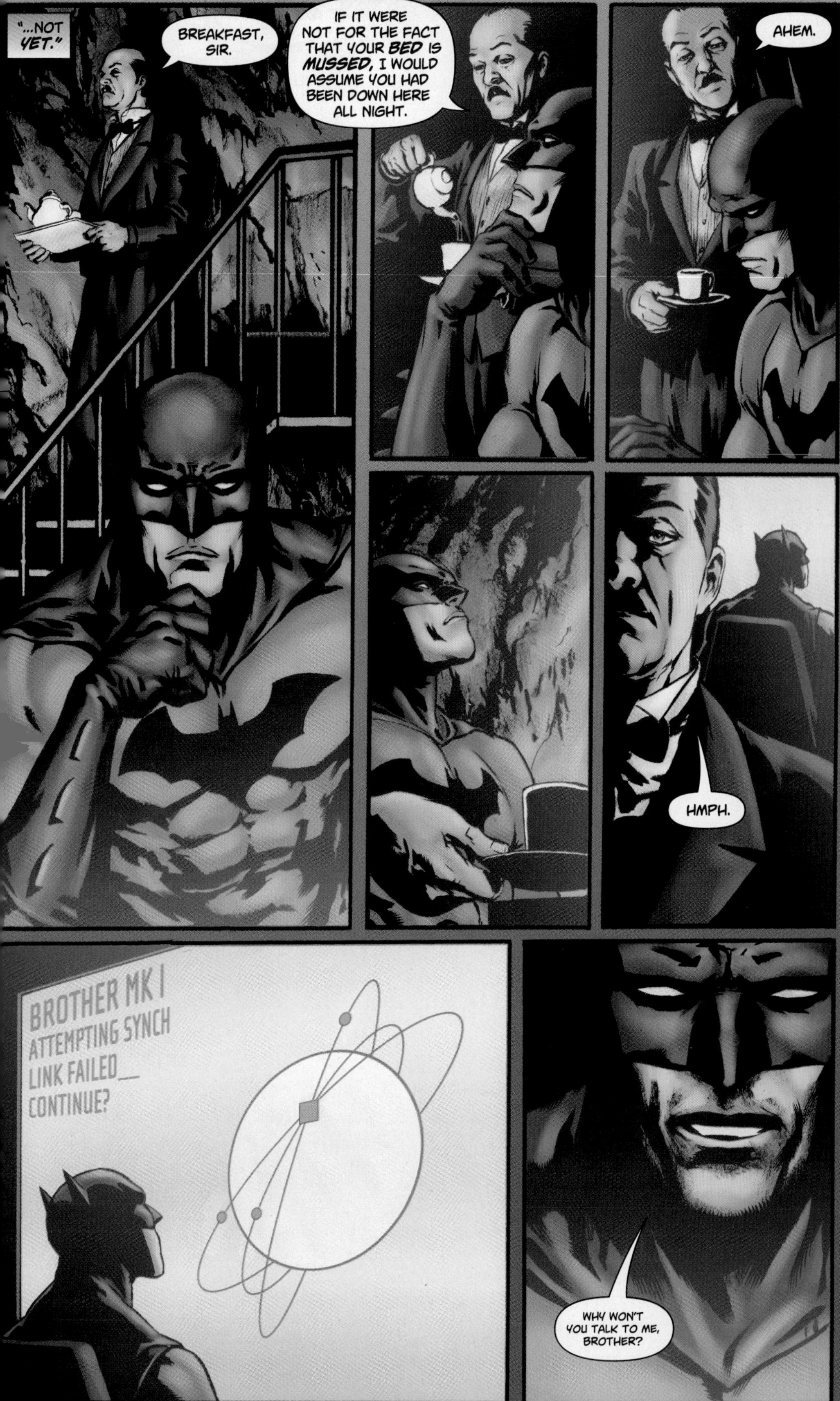
"...NOT *YET.*"
BREAKFAST, SIR.
IF IT WERE NOT FOR THE FACT THAT YOUR *BED* IS *MUSSED,* I WOULD ASSUME YOU HAD BEEN DOWN HERE ALL NIGHT.
AHEM.
HMPH.
BROTHER MK I
ATTEMPTING SYNCH
LINK FAILED_
CONTINUE?
WHY WON'T YOU TALK TO ME, BROTHER?

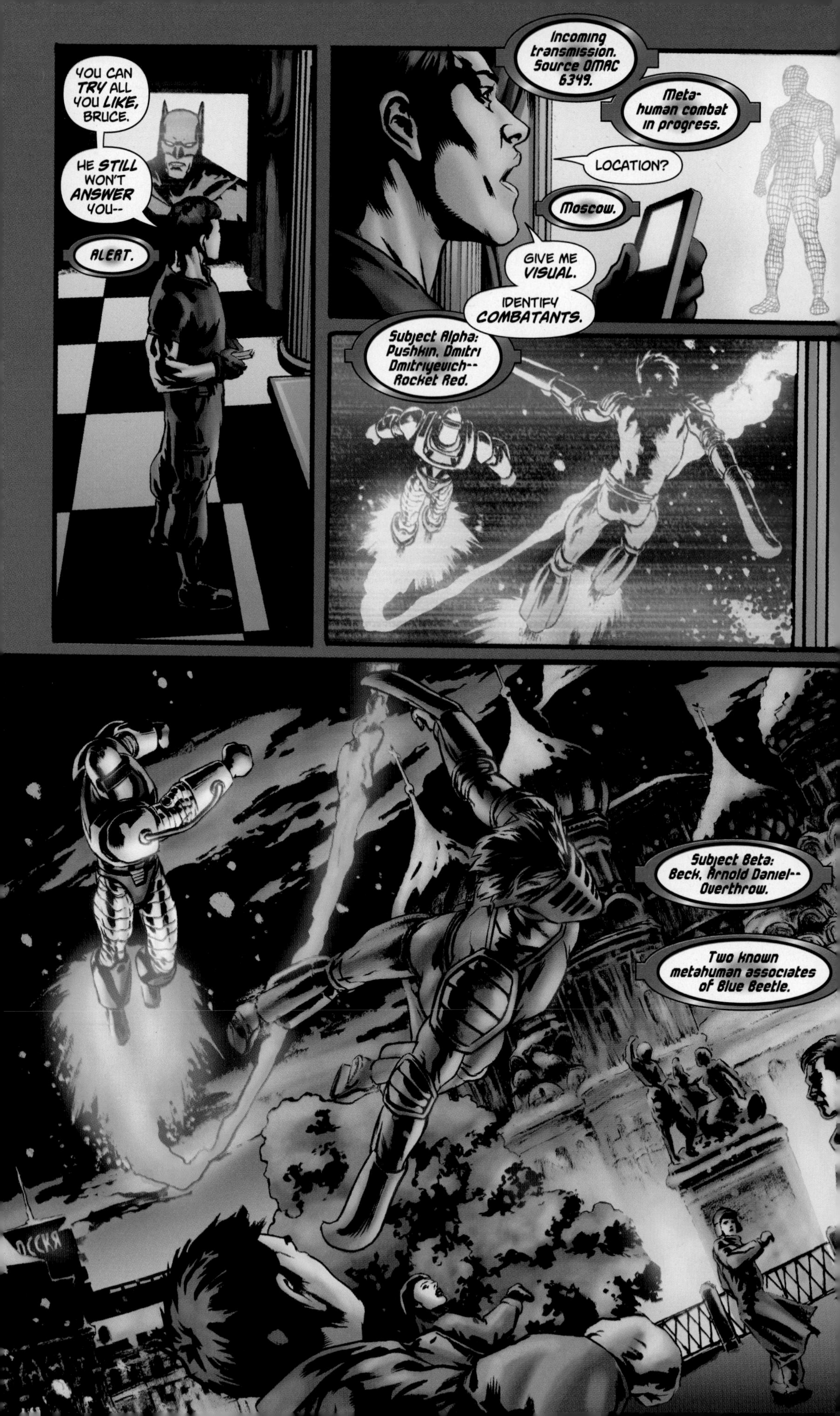
YOU CAN TRY ALL YOU LIKE, BRUCE.
HE STILL WON'T ANSWER YOU--
ALERT.
Incoming transmission. Source OMAC 6349.
Meta-human combat in progress.
LOCATION?
Moscow.
GIVE ME VISUAL.
IDENTIFY COMBATANTS.
Subject Alpha: Pushkin, Dmitri Dmitriyevich-- Rocket Red.
Subject Beta: Beck, Arnold Daniel-- Overthrow.
Two known metahuman associates of Blue Beetle.
ОССИЯ

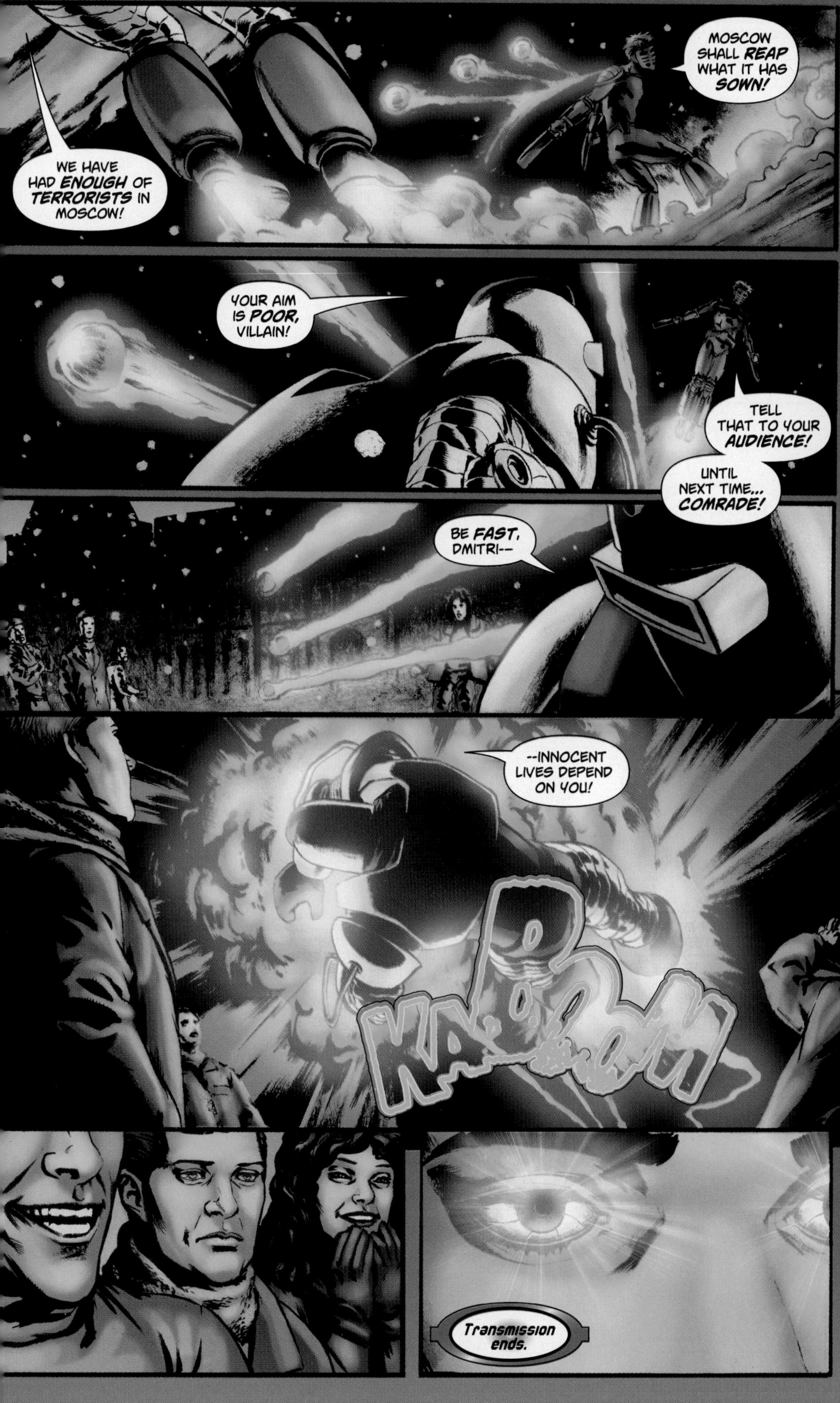
WE HAVE HAD ENOUGH OF TERRORISTS IN MOSCOW!
MOSCOW SHALL REAP WHAT IT HAS SOWN!
YOUR AIM IS POOR, VILLAIN!
TELL THAT TO YOUR AUDIENCE!
UNTIL NEXT TIME... COMRADE!
BE FAST, DMITRI--
--INNOCENT LIVES DEPEND ON YOU!
Transmission ends.

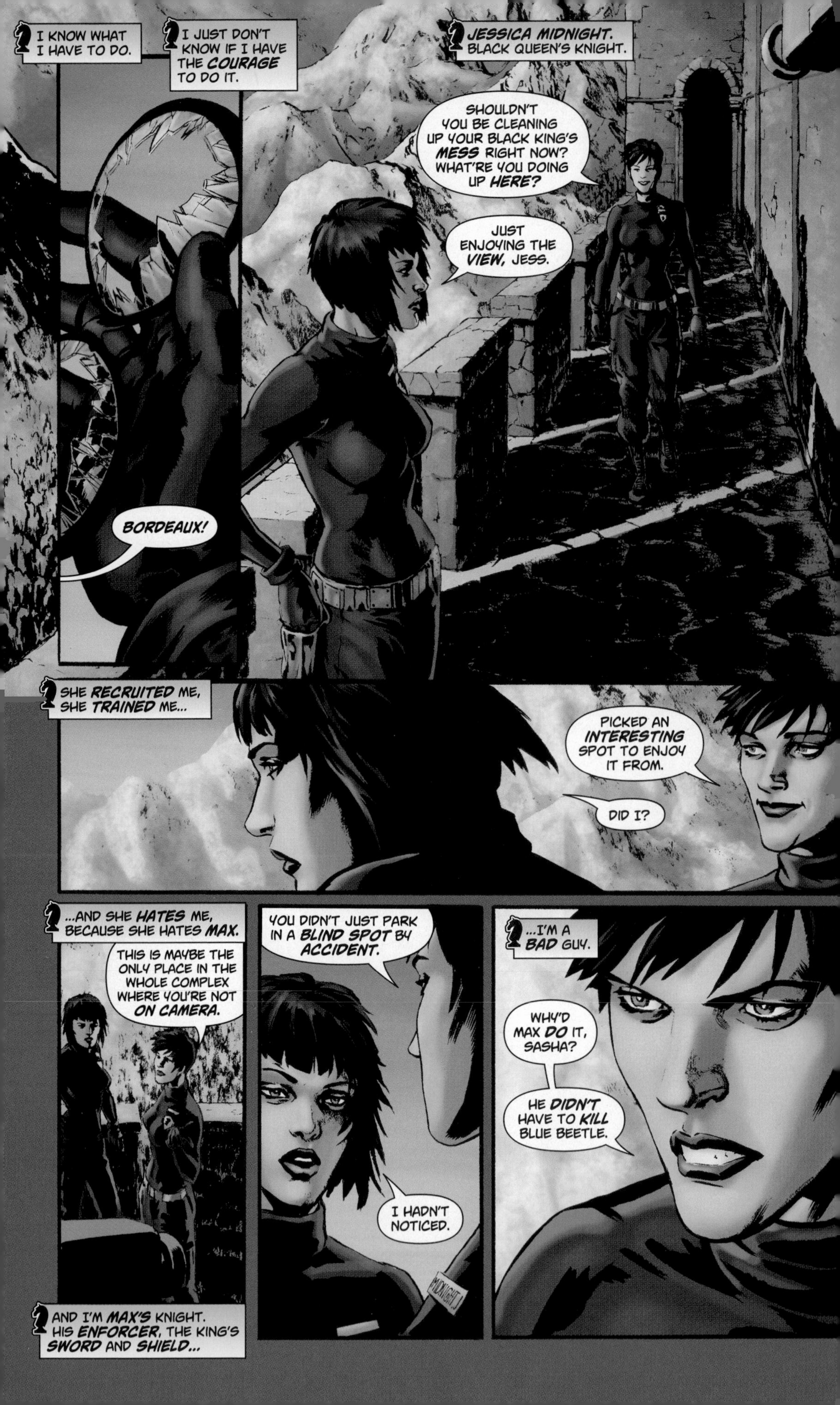
I KNOW WHAT I HAVE TO DO.
I JUST DON'T KNOW IF I HAVE THE COURAGE TO DO IT.
JESSICA MIDNIGHT. BLACK QUEEN'S KNIGHT.
SHOULDN'T YOU BE CLEANING UP YOUR BLACK KING'S MESS RIGHT NOW? WHAT'RE YOU DOING UP HERE?
JUST ENJOYING THE VIEW, JESS.
BORDEAUX!
SHE RECRUITED ME, SHE TRAINED ME...
PICKED AN INTERESTING SPOT TO ENJOY IT FROM.
DID I?
...AND SHE HATES ME, BECAUSE SHE HATES MAX.
THIS IS MAYBE THE ONLY PLACE IN THE WHOLE COMPLEX WHERE YOU'RE NOT ON CAMERA.
AND I'M MAX'S KNIGHT. HIS ENFORCER, THE KING'S SWORD AND SHIELD...
YOU DIDN'T JUST PARK IN A BLIND SPOT BY ACCIDENT.
I HADN'T NOTICED.
...I'M A BAD GUY.
WHY'D MAX DO IT, SASHA?
HE DIDN'T HAVE TO KILL BLUE BEETLE.

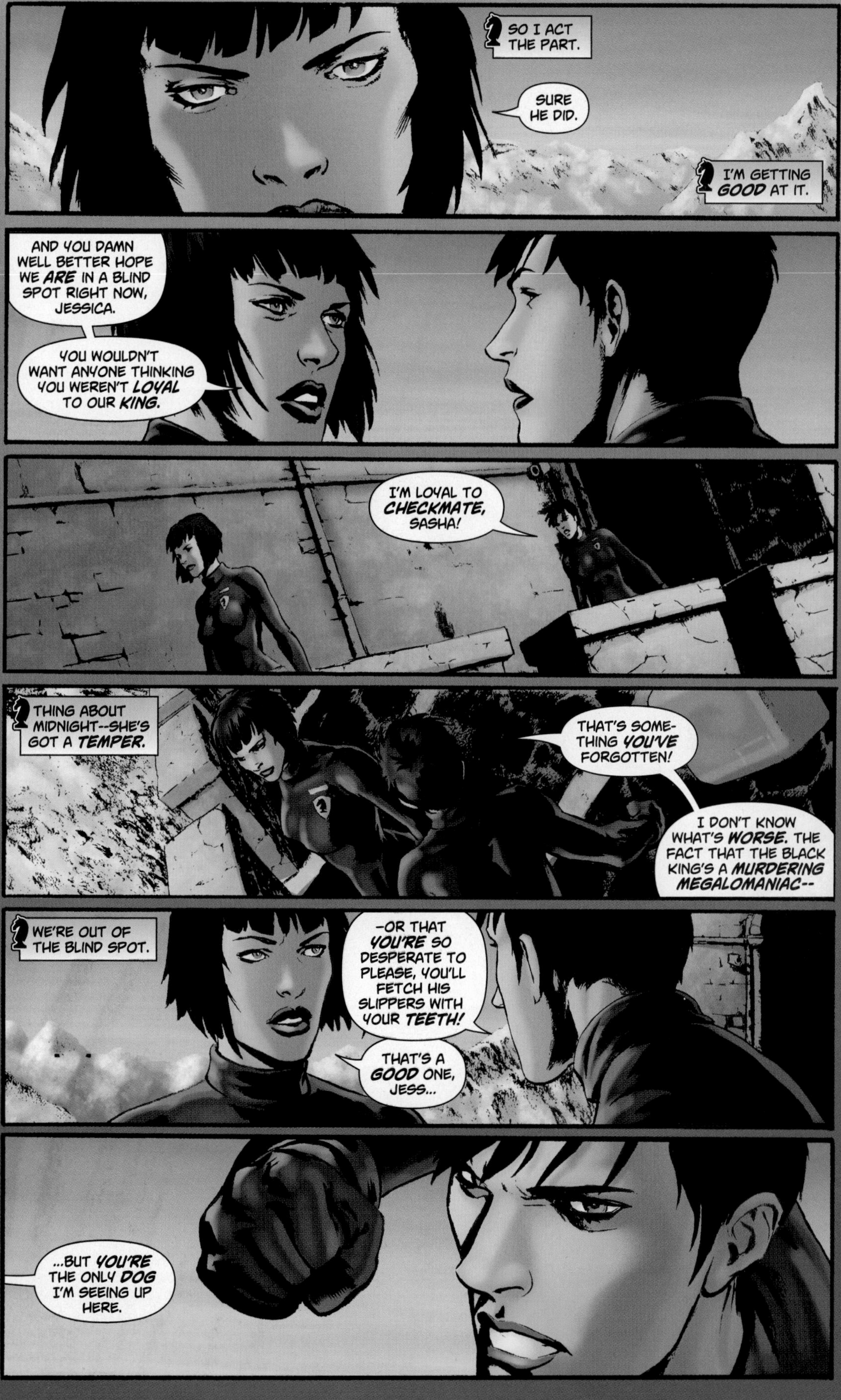

SO I ACT THE PART.
SURE HE DID.
I'M GETTING GOOD AT IT.
AND YOU DAMN WELL BETTER HOPE WE ARE IN A BLIND SPOT RIGHT NOW, JESSICA.
YOU WOULDN'T WANT ANYONE THINKING YOU WEREN'T LOYAL TO OUR KING.
I'M LOYAL TO CHECKMATE, SASHA!
THING ABOUT MIDNIGHT--SHE'S GOT A TEMPER.
THAT'S SOME-THING YOU'VE FORGOTTEN!
I DON'T KNOW WHAT'S WORSE. THE FACT THAT THE BLACK KING'S A MURDERING MEGALOMANIAC--
WE'RE OUT OF THE BLIND SPOT.
-OR THAT YOU'RE SO DESPERATE TO PLEASE, YOU'LL FETCH HIS SLIPPERS WITH YOUR TEETH!
THAT'S A GOOD ONE, JESS...
...BUT YOU'RE THE ONLY DOG I'M SEEING UP HERE.

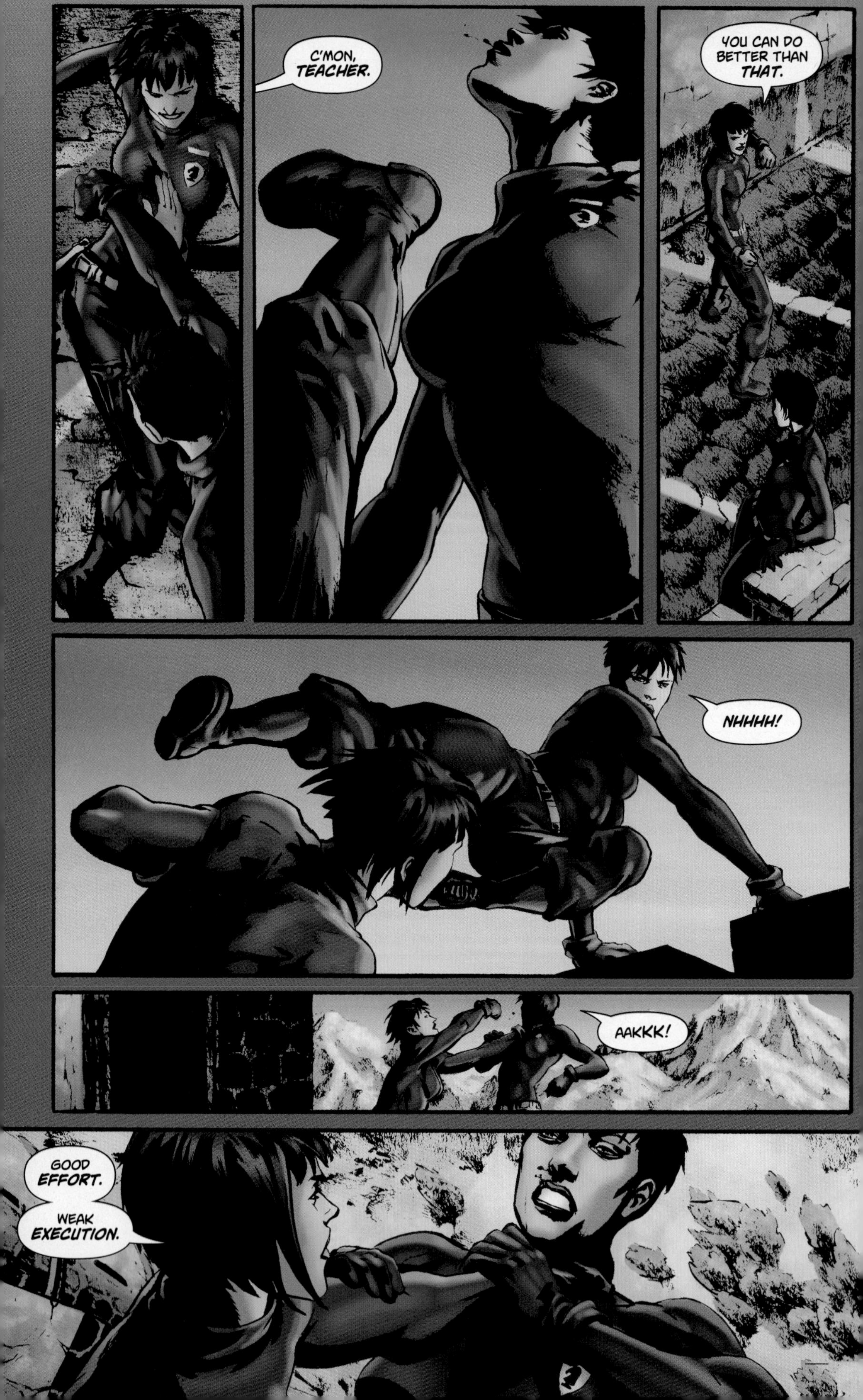
C'MON, TEACHER.
YOU CAN DO BETTER THAN THAT.
NHHHH!
AAKKK!
GOOD EFFORT.
WEAK EXECUTION.

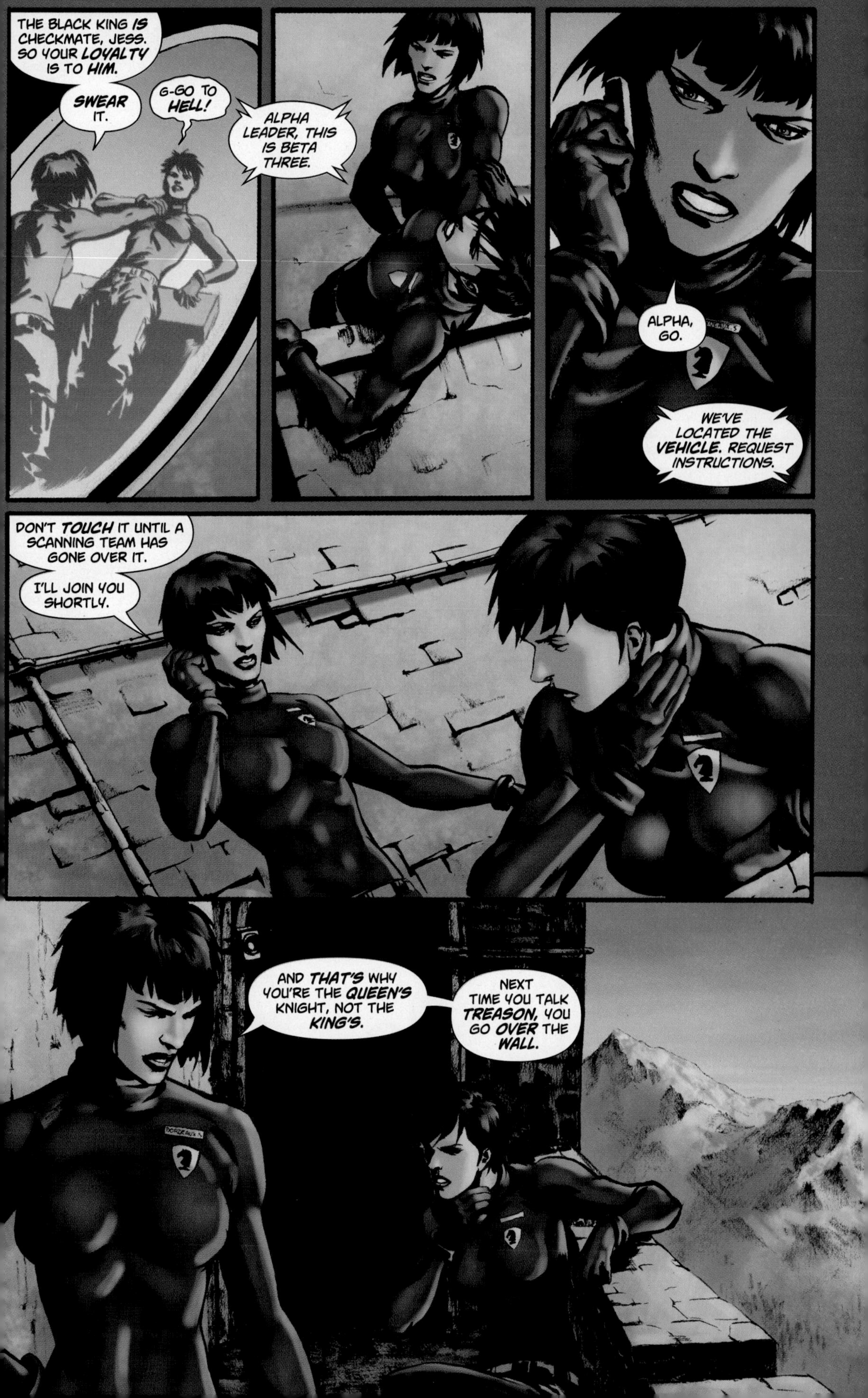
THE BLACK KING IS CHECKMATE, JESS. SO YOUR LOYALTY IS TO HIM.
SWEAR IT.
G-GO TO HELL!
ALPHA LEADER, THIS IS BETA THREE.
ALPHA, GO.
WE'VE LOCATED THE VEHICLE. REQUEST INSTRUCTIONS.
DON'T TOUCH IT UNTIL A SCANNING TEAM HAS GONE OVER IT.
I'LL JOIN YOU SHORTLY.
AND THAT'S WHY YOU'RE THE QUEEN'S KNIGHT, NOT THE KING'S.
NEXT TIME YOU TALK TREASON, YOU GO OVER THE WALL.

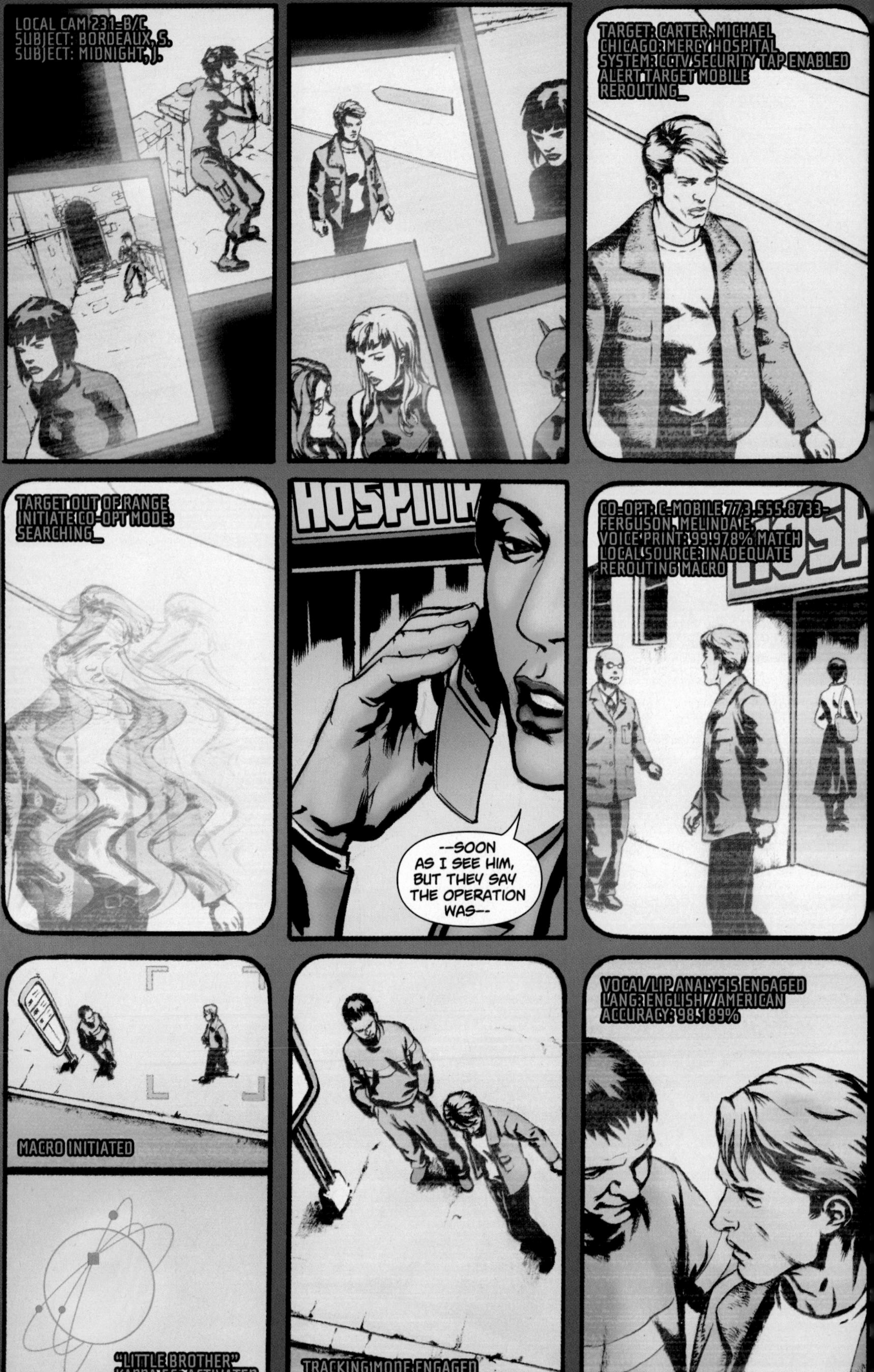
LOCAL CAM 231=B/C
SUBJECT: BORDEAUX, S.
SUBJECT: MIDNIGHT, J.
TARGET: CARTER, MICHAEL
CHICAGO: MERCY HOSPITAL
SYSTEM: CCTV SECURITY TAP ENABLED
ALERT TARGET MOBILE
REROUTING_
TARGET OUT OF RANGE
INITIATE CO-OPT MODE:
SEARCHING_
HOSPITA
--SOON AS I SEE HIM, BUT THEY SAY THE OPERATION WAS--
CO-OPT: C-MOBILE 773.555.8733-
FERGUSON, MELINDA E.
VOICE PRINT: 99.978% MATCH
LOCAL SOURCE: INADEQUATE
REROUTING MACRO
MACRO INITIATED
"LITTLE BROTHER"
KAPPA 56: ACTIVATED
TARGET ACQUIRED
ENHANCING_
TRACKING MODE ENGAGED
AUDIO UNAVAILABLE
ENHANCE_
VOCAL/LIP ANALYSIS ENGAGED
LANG: ENGLISH//AMERICAN
ACCURACY: 98.189%

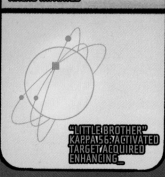

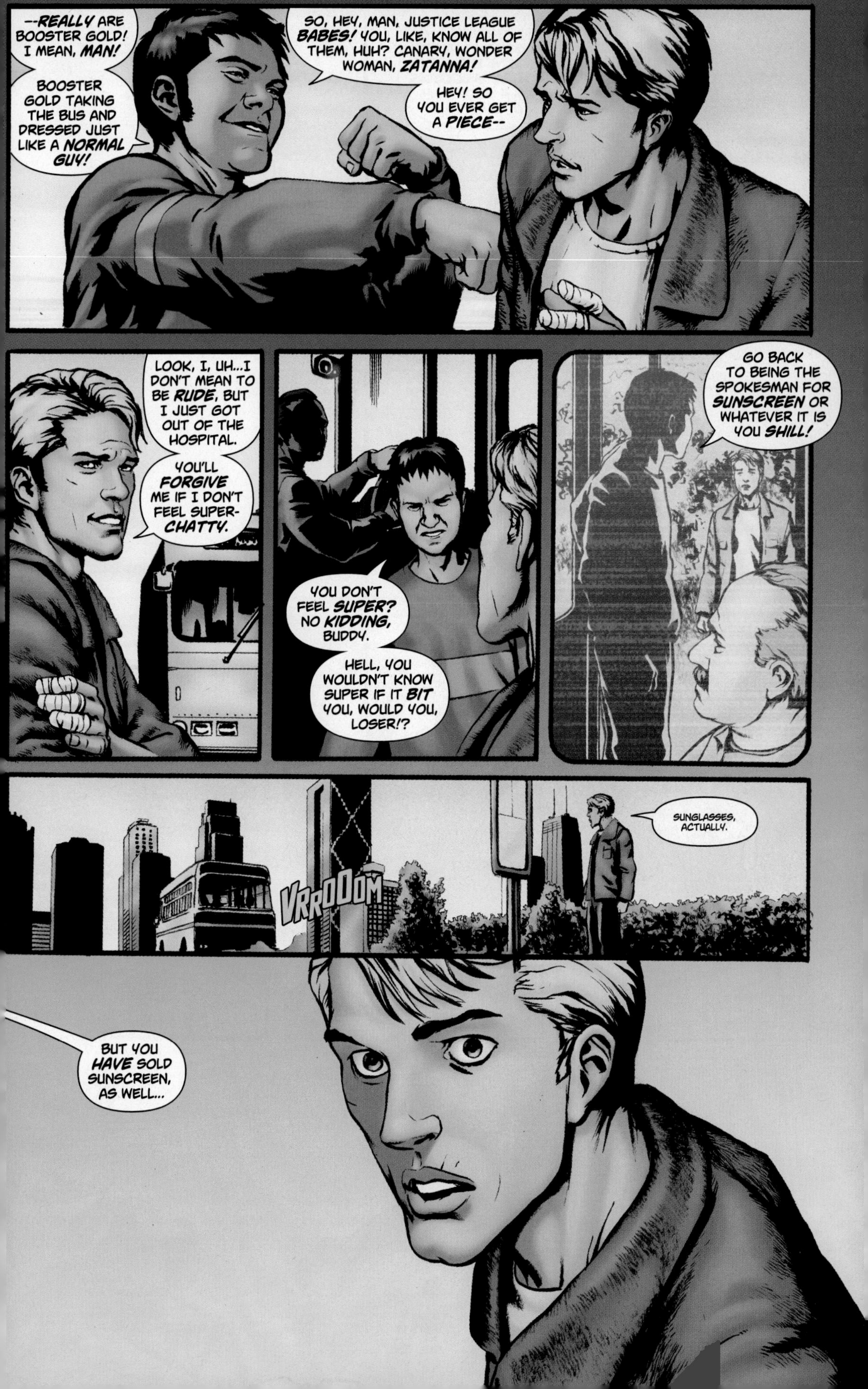
--REALLY ARE BOOSTER GOLD! I MEAN, MAN!
BOOSTER GOLD TAKING THE BUS AND DRESSED JUST LIKE A NORMAL GUY!
SO, HEY, MAN, JUSTICE LEAGUE BABES! YOU, LIKE, KNOW ALL OF THEM, HUH? CANARY, WONDER WOMAN, ZATANNA!
HEY! SO YOU EVER GET A PIECE--
LOOK, I, UH...I DON'T MEAN TO BE RUDE, BUT I JUST GOT OUT OF THE HOSPITAL.
YOU'LL FORGIVE ME IF I DON'T FEEL SUPER-CHATTY.
YOU DON'T FEEL SUPER? NO KIDDING, BUDDY.
HELL, YOU WOULDN'T KNOW SUPER IF IT BIT YOU, WOULD YOU, LOSER!?
GO BACK TO BEING THE SPOKESMAN FOR SUNSCREEN OR WHATEVER IT IS YOU SHILL!
SUNGLASSES, ACTUALLY.
VRROOOM
BUT YOU HAVE SOLD SUNSCREEN, AS WELL...

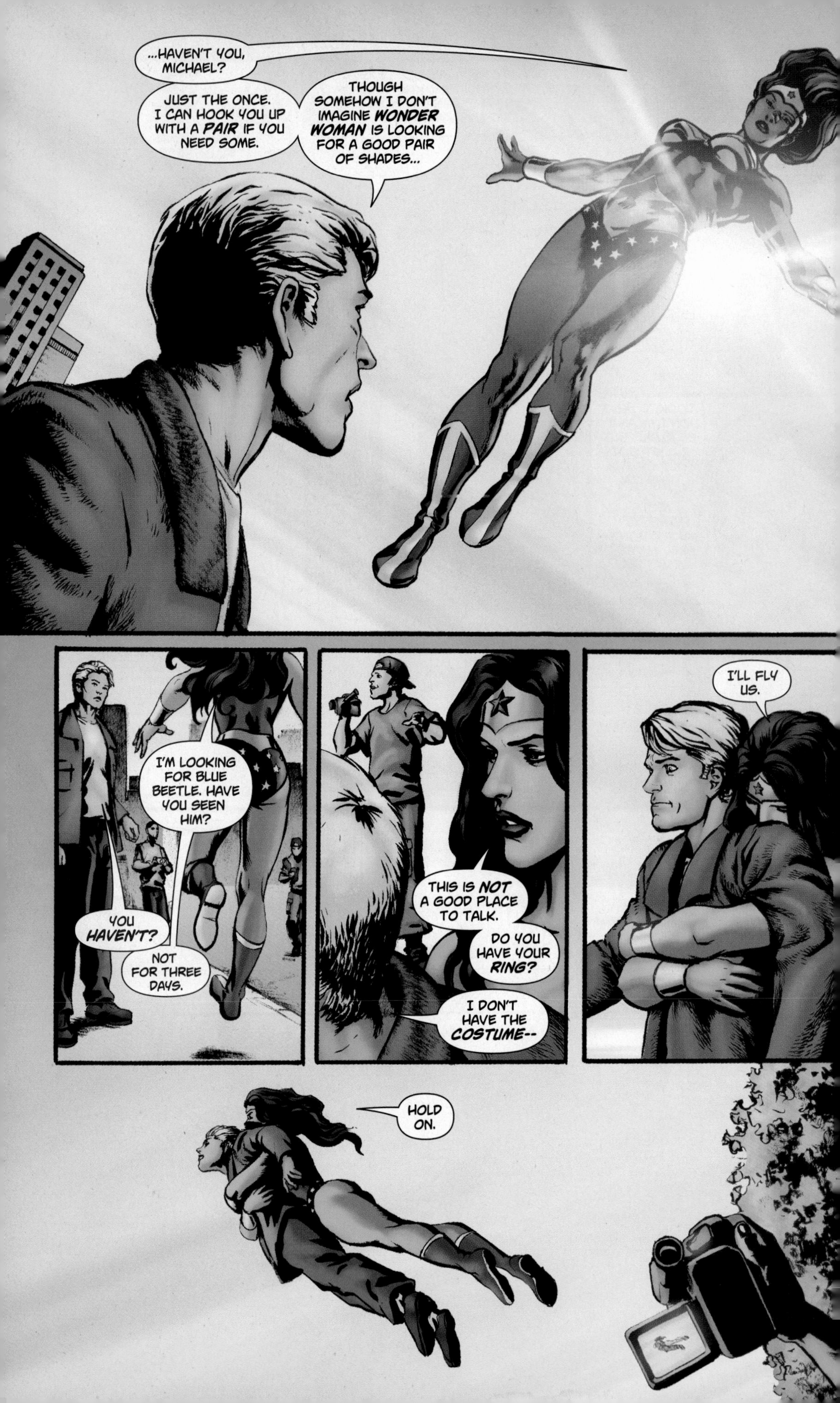
...HAVEN'T YOU, MICHAEL?
JUST THE ONCE. I CAN HOOK YOU UP WITH A PAIR IF YOU NEED SOME.
THOUGH SOMEHOW I DON'T IMAGINE WONDER WOMAN IS LOOKING FOR A GOOD PAIR OF SHADES...
I'M LOOKING FOR BLUE BEETLE. HAVE YOU SEEN HIM?
YOU HAVEN'T?
NOT FOR THREE DAYS.
THIS IS NOT A GOOD PLACE TO TALK.
DO YOU HAVE YOUR RING?
I DON'T HAVE THE COSTUME--
I'LL FLY US.
HOLD ON.

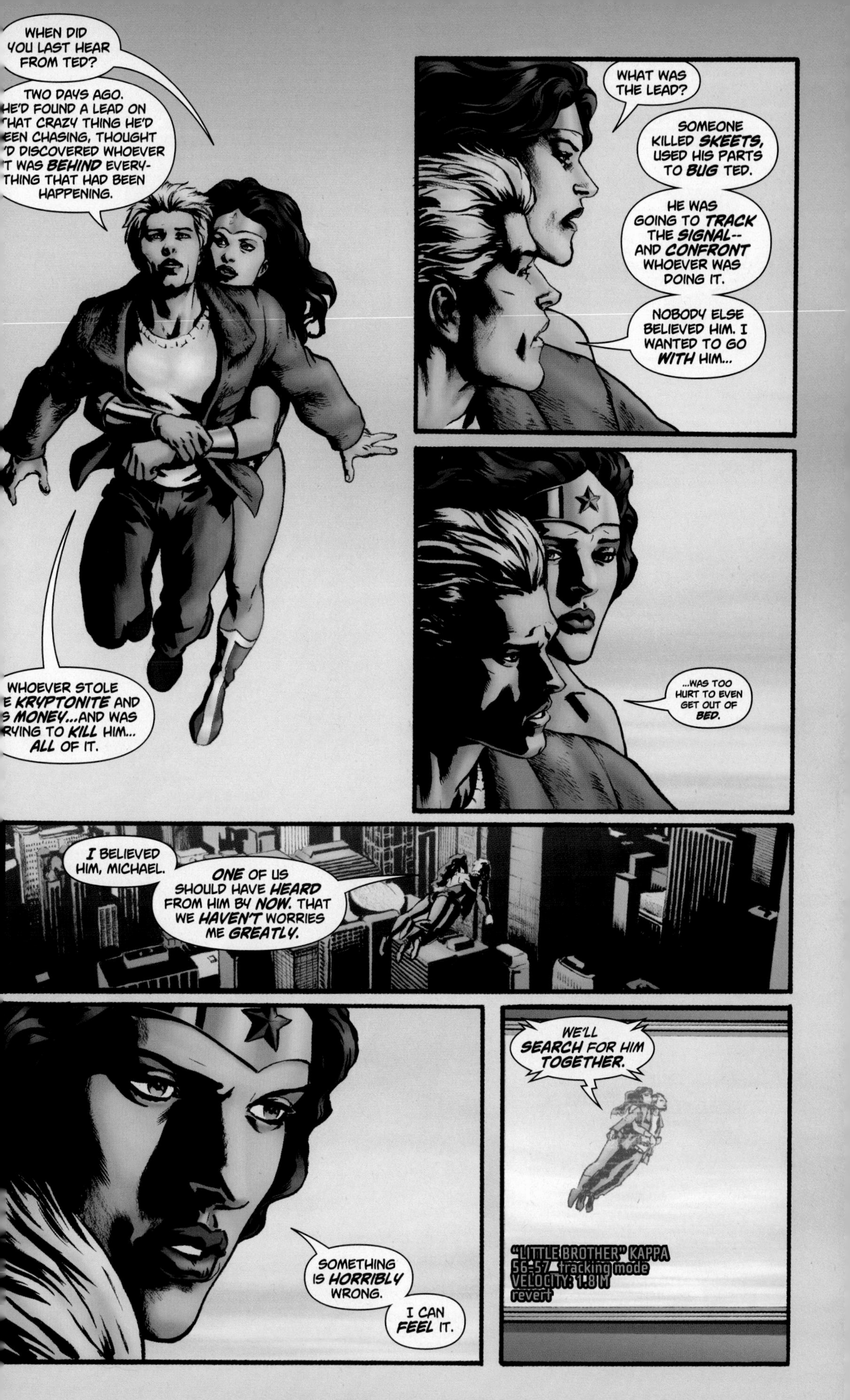
WHEN DID YOU LAST HEAR FROM TED?
TWO DAYS AGO. HE'D FOUND A LEAD ON THAT CRAZY THING HE'D BEEN CHASING, THOUGHT HE'D DISCOVERED WHOEVER IT WAS BEHIND EVERY-THING THAT HAD BEEN HAPPENING.
WHOEVER STOLE THE KRYPTONITE AND HIS MONEY...AND WAS TRYING TO KILL HIM... ALL OF IT.
WHAT WAS THE LEAD?
SOMEONE KILLED SKEETS, USED HIS PARTS TO BUG TED.
HE WAS GOING TO TRACK THE SIGNAL-- AND CONFRONT WHOEVER WAS DOING IT.
NOBODY ELSE BELIEVED HIM. I WANTED TO GO WITH HIM...
...WAS TOO HURT TO EVEN GET OUT OF BED.
I BELIEVED HIM, MICHAEL.
ONE OF US SHOULD HAVE HEARD FROM HIM BY NOW. THAT WE HAVEN'T WORRIES ME GREATLY.
SOMETHING IS HORRIBLY WRONG.
I CAN FEEL IT.
WE'LL SEARCH FOR HIM TOGETHER.
"LITTLE BROTHER" KAPPA
56-57 tracking mode
VELOCITY: 1.8 M
revert

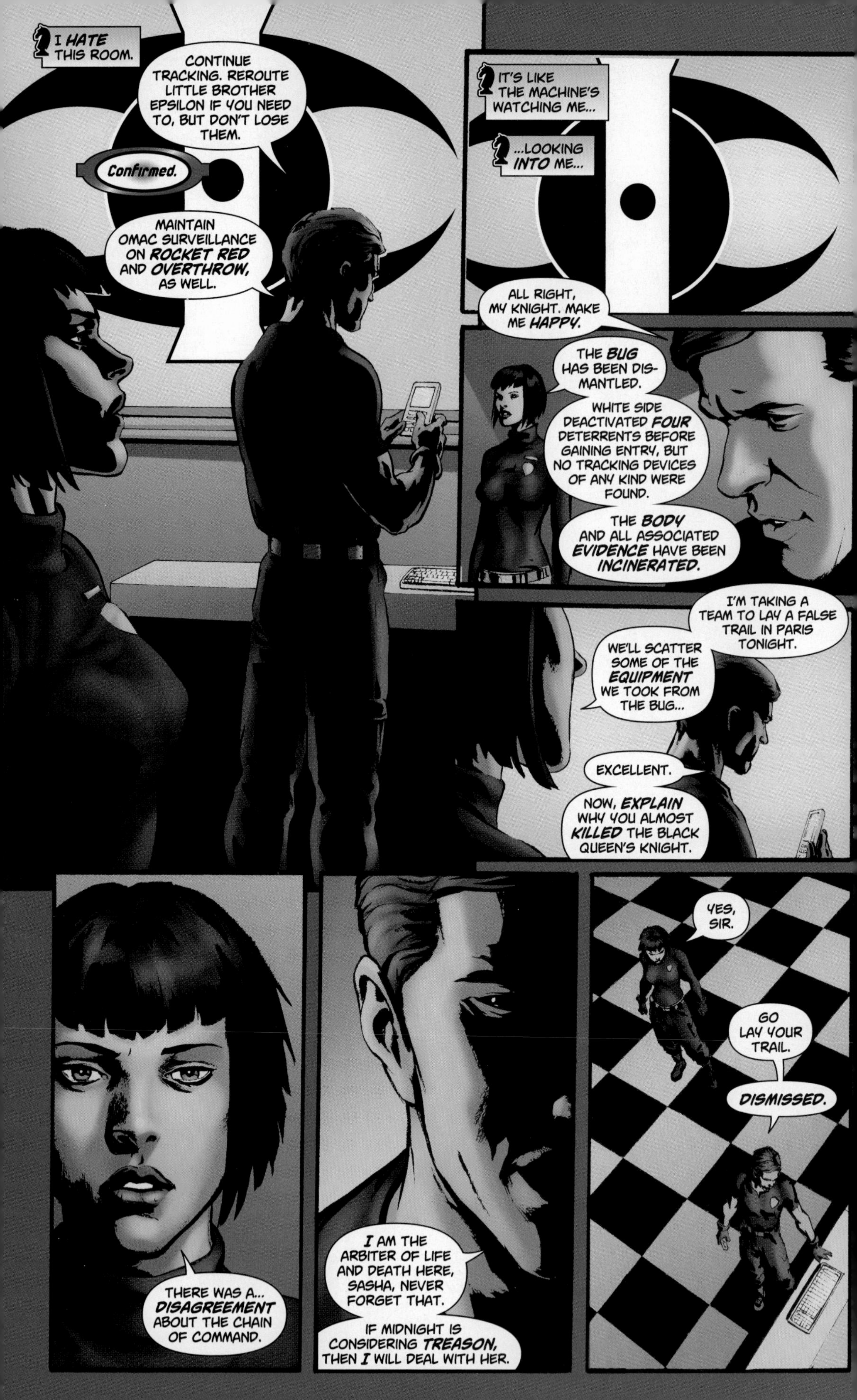
I HATE THIS ROOM.
CONTINUE TRACKING. REROUTE LITTLE BROTHER EPSILON IF YOU NEED TO, BUT DON'T LOSE THEM.
Confirmed.
MAINTAIN OMAC SURVEILLANCE ON ROCKET RED AND OVERTHROW, AS WELL.
IT'S LIKE THE MACHINE'S WATCHING ME...
...LOOKING INTO ME...
ALL RIGHT, MY KNIGHT. MAKE ME HAPPY.
THE BUG HAS BEEN DIS-MANTLED.
WHITE SIDE DEACTIVATED FOUR DETERRENTS BEFORE GAINING ENTRY, BUT NO TRACKING DEVICES OF ANY KIND WERE FOUND.
THE BODY AND ALL ASSOCIATED EVIDENCE HAVE BEEN INCINERATED.
I'M TAKING A TEAM TO LAY A FALSE TRAIL IN PARIS TONIGHT.
WE'LL SCATTER SOME OF THE EQUIPMENT WE TOOK FROM THE BUG...
EXCELLENT.
NOW, EXPLAIN WHY YOU ALMOST KILLED THE BLACK QUEEN'S KNIGHT.
THERE WAS A... DISAGREEMENT ABOUT THE CHAIN OF COMMAND.
I AM THE ARBITER OF LIFE AND DEATH HERE, SASHA, NEVER FORGET THAT.
IF MIDNIGHT IS CONSIDERING TREASON, THEN I WILL DEAL WITH HER.
YES, SIR.
GO LAY YOUR TRAIL.
DISMISSED.

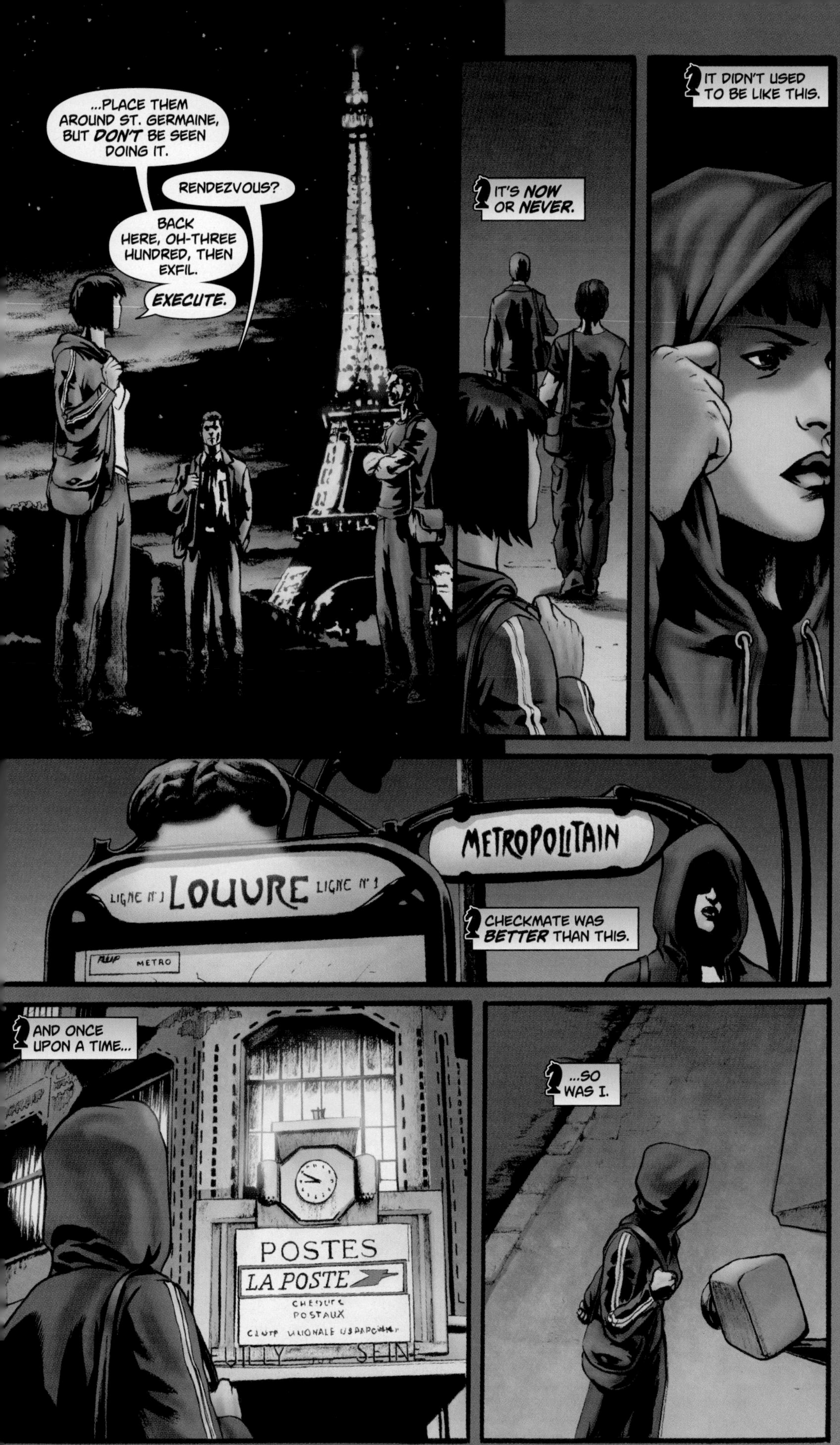
...PLACE THEM AROUND ST. GERMAINE, BUT DON'T BE SEEN DOING IT.
RENDEZVOUS?
BACK HERE, OH-THREE HUNDRED, THEN EXFIL.
EXECUTE.
IT'S NOW OR NEVER.
IT DIDN'T USED TO BE LIKE THIS.
LIGNE N° 1 LOUVRE LIGNE N° 1
METRO
METROPOLITAIN
CHECKMATE WAS BETTER THAN THIS.
AND ONCE UPON A TIME...
POSTES
LA POSTE
POSTAUX
...SO WAS I.

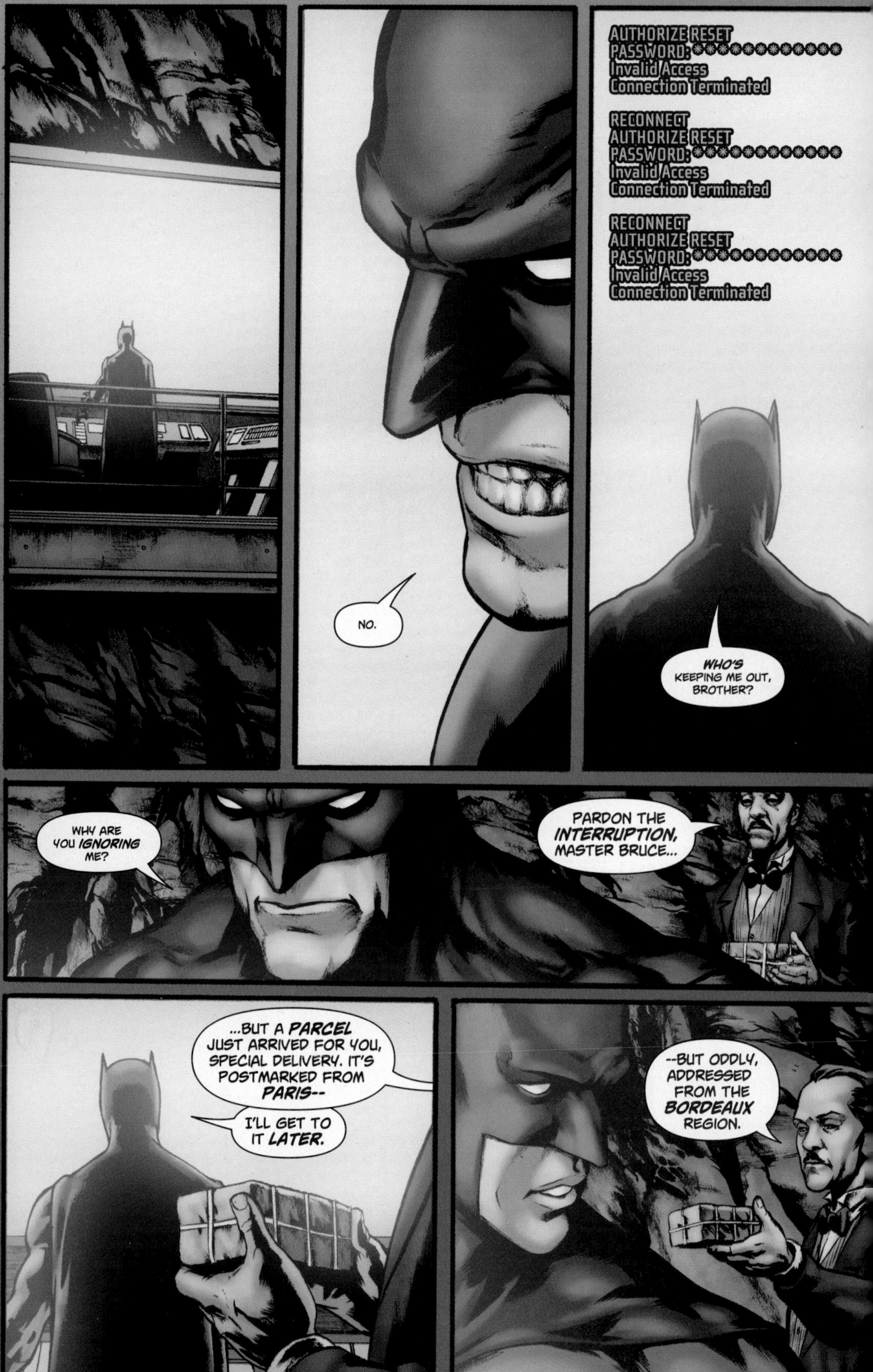
AUTHORIZE RESET
PASSWORD: ************
Invalid Access
Connection Terminated
RECONNECT
AUTHORIZE RESET
PASSWORD: ************
Invalid Access
Connection Terminated
RECONNECT
AUTHORIZE RESET
PASSWORD: ************
Invalid Access
Connection Terminated
NO.
WHO'S KEEPING ME OUT, BROTHER?
WHY ARE YOU IGNORING ME?
PARDON THE INTERRUPTION, MASTER BRUCE...
...BUT A PARCEL JUST ARRIVED FOR YOU, SPECIAL DELIVERY. IT'S POSTMARKED FROM PARIS--
I'LL GET TO IT LATER.
--BUT ODDLY, ADDRESSED FROM THE BORDEAUX REGION.

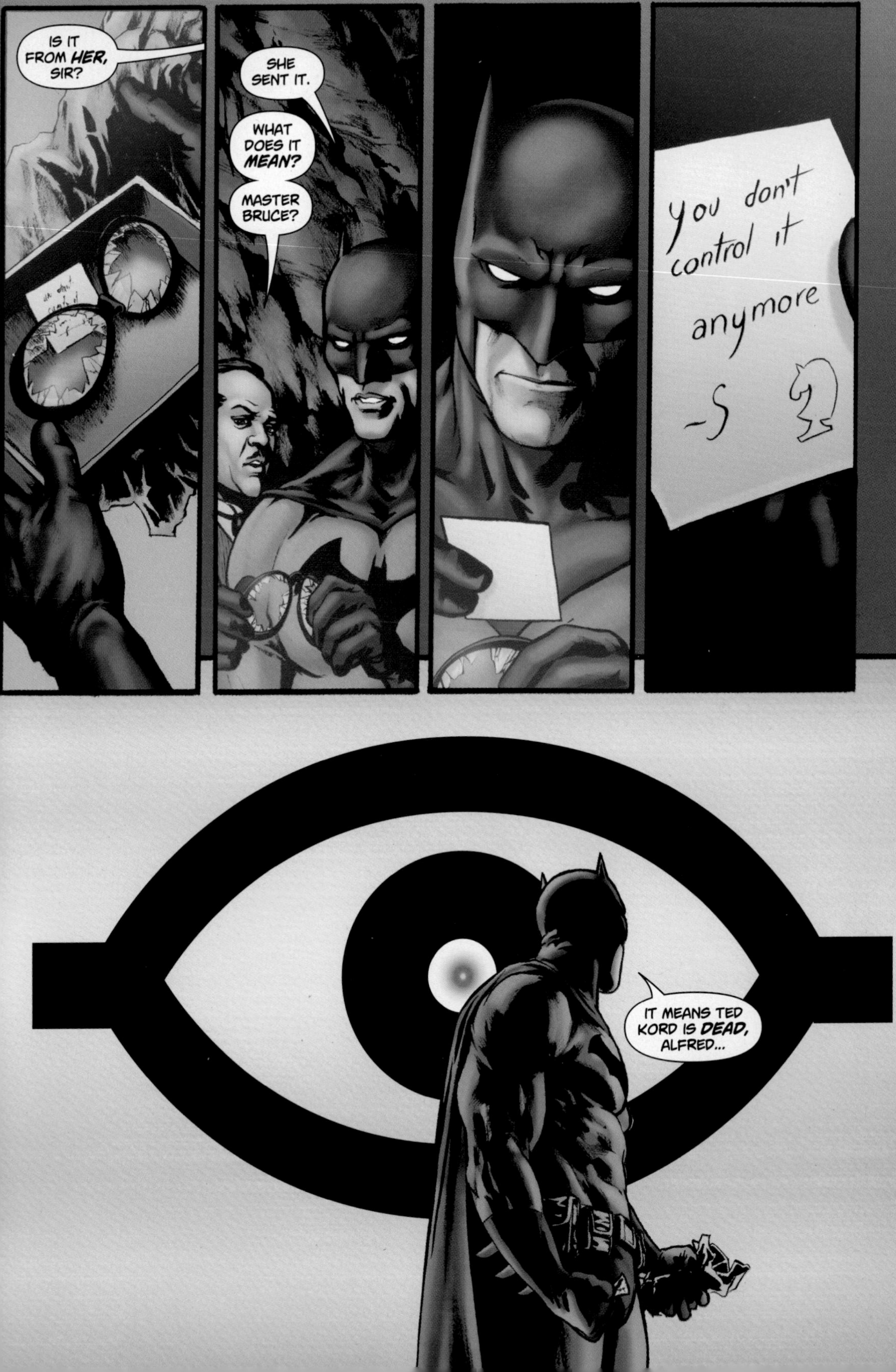
IS IT FROM HER, SIR?
SHE SENT IT.
WHAT DOES IT MEAN?
MASTER BRUCE?
you don't control it anymore
-S
IT MEANS TED KORD IS DEAD, ALFRED...

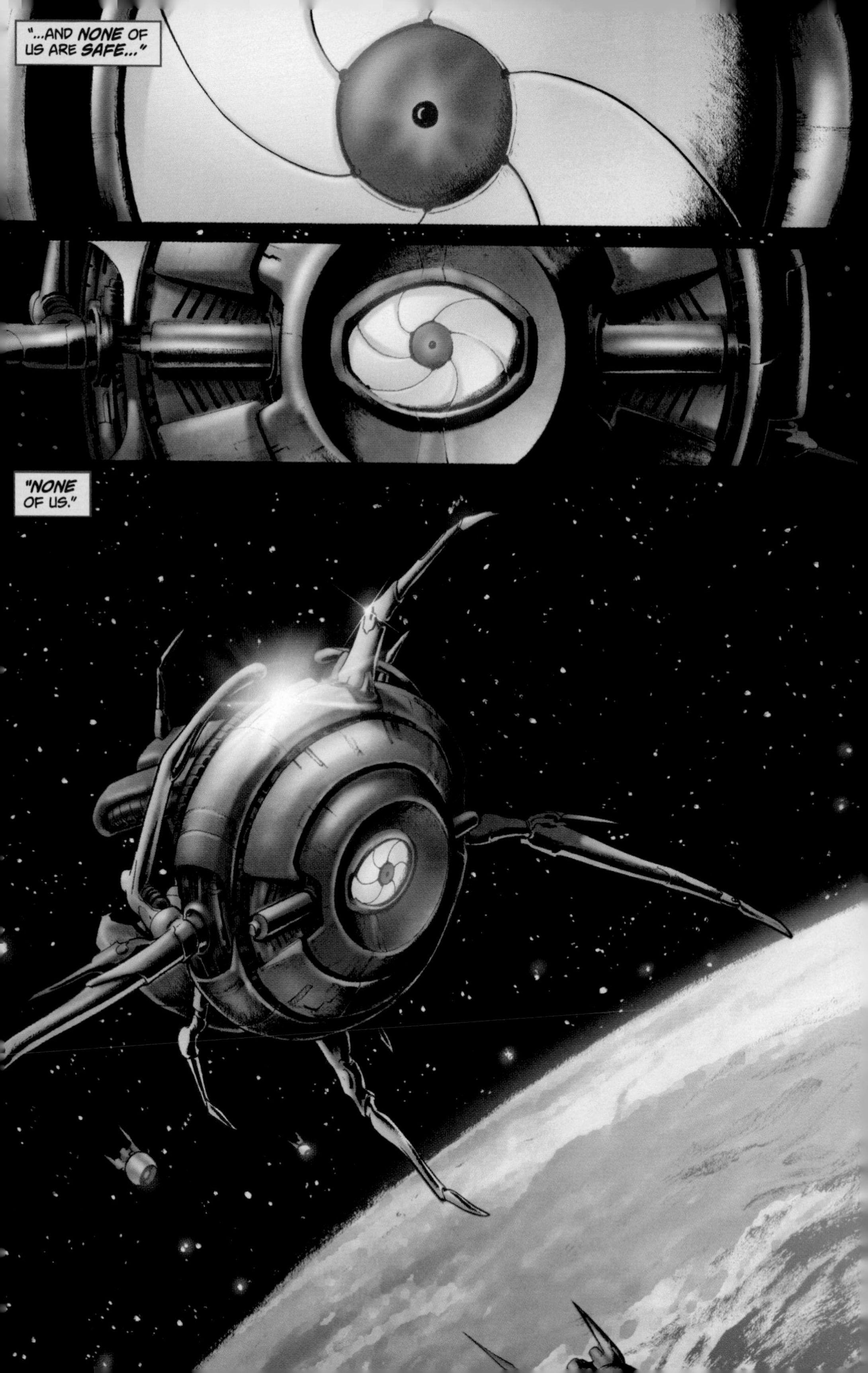
"...AND NONE OF US ARE SAFE..."
"NONE OF US."

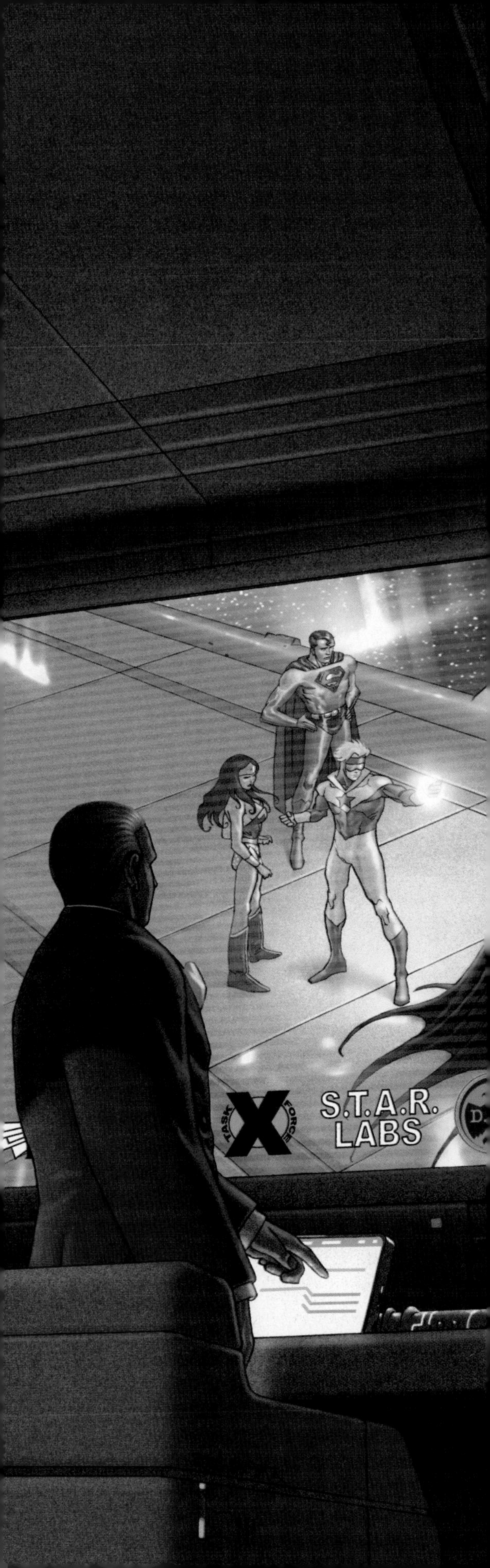

TASK X FORCE
S.T.A.R.
LABS

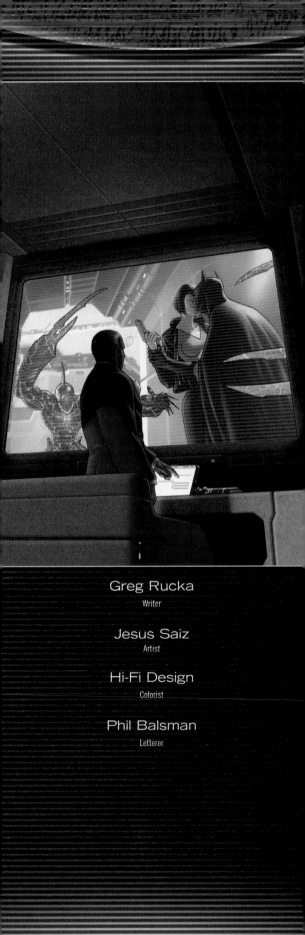

Greg Rucka
Writer

Jesus Saiz
Artist

Hi-Fi Design
Colorist

Phil Balsman
Letterer

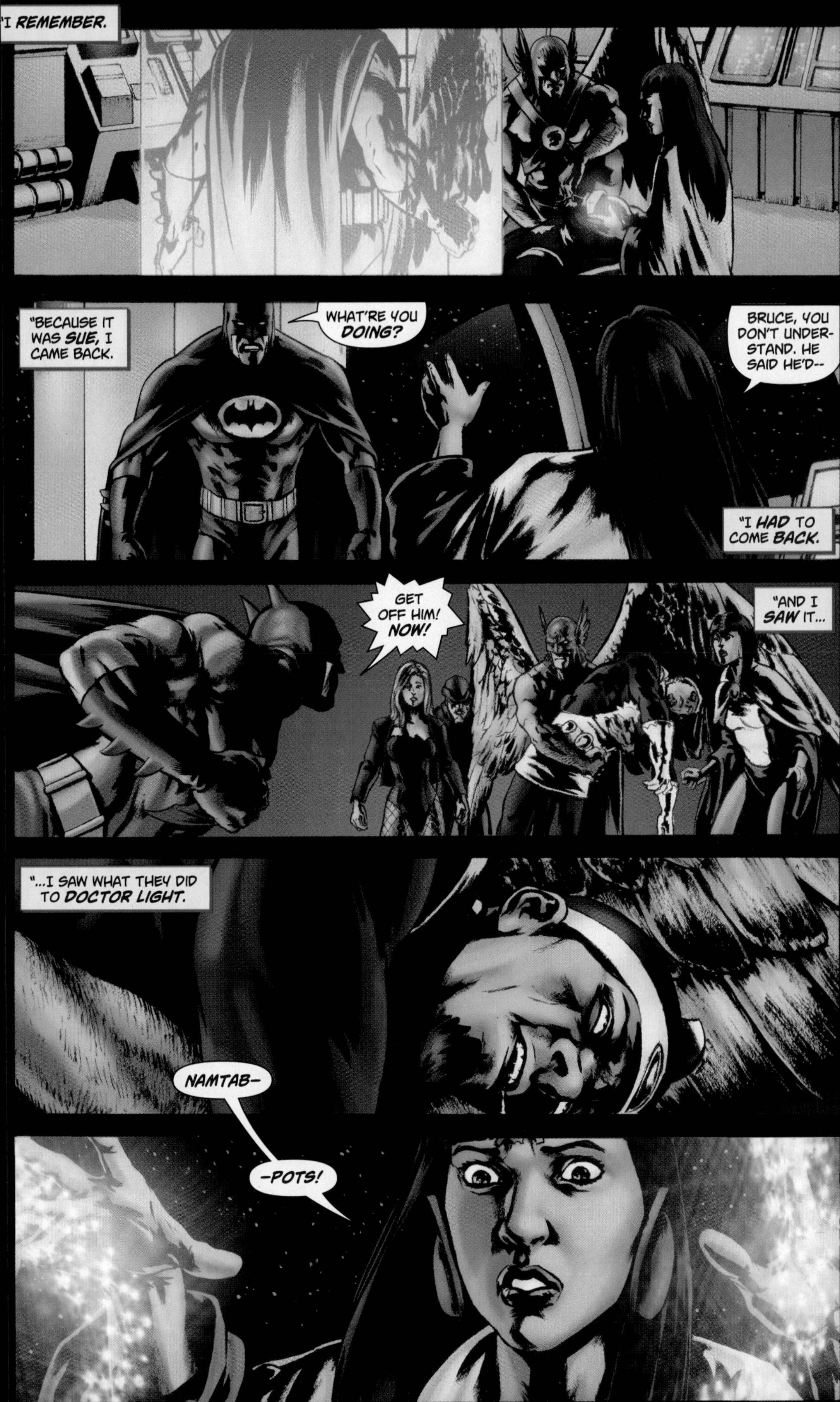
"I REMEMBER.
"BECAUSE IT WAS SUE, I CAME BACK.
WHAT'RE YOU DOING?
BRUCE, YOU DON'T UNDERSTAND. HE SAID HE'D--
"I HAD TO COME BACK.
GET OFF HIM! NOW!
"AND I SAW IT...
"...I SAW WHAT THEY DID TO DOCTOR LIGHT.
NAMTAB–
–POTS!

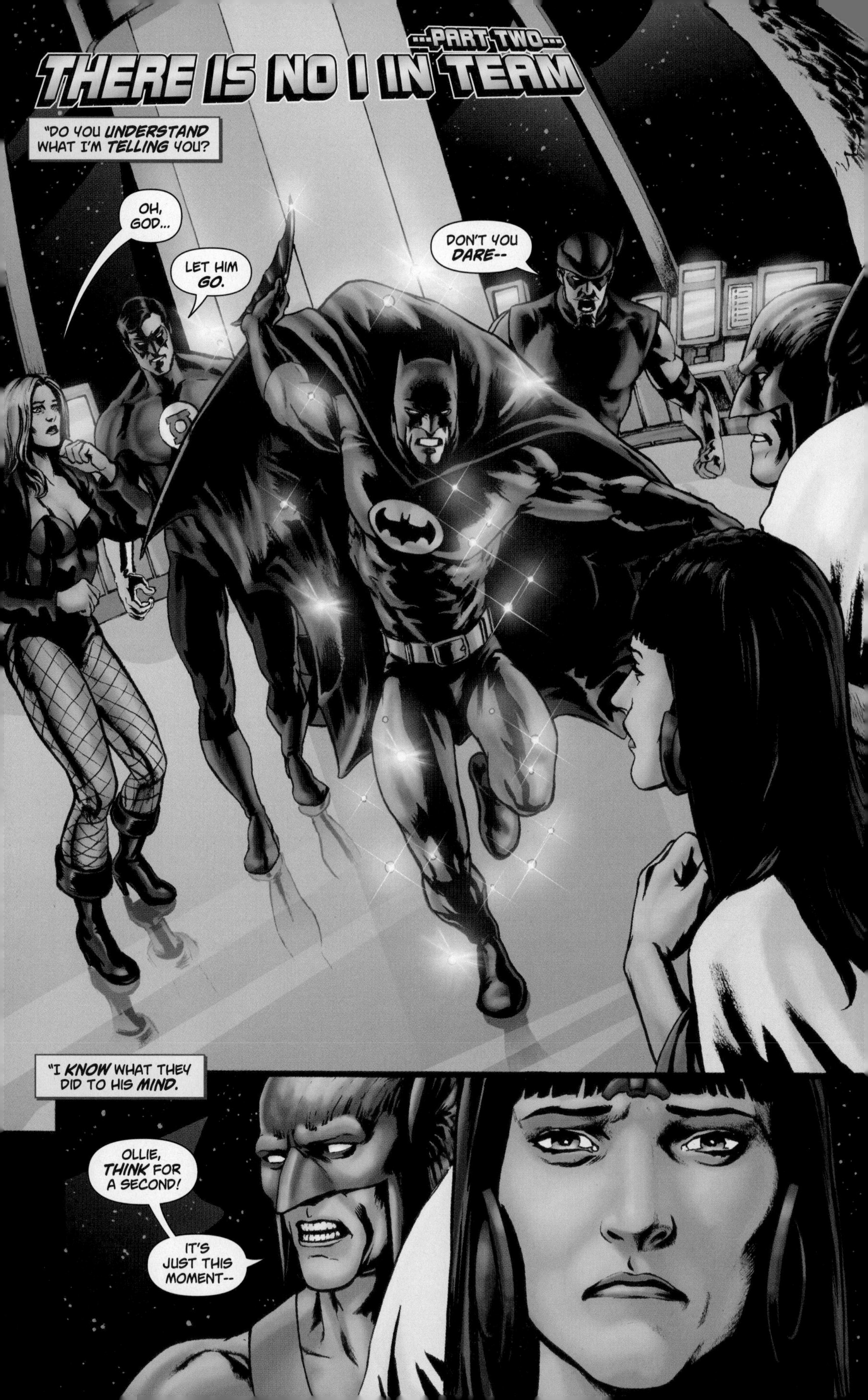

...PART TWO...
THERE IS NO I IN TEAM
"DO YOU UNDERSTAND WHAT I'M TELLING YOU?
OH, GOD...
LET HIM GO.
DON'T YOU DARE--
"I KNOW WHAT THEY DID TO HIS MIND.
OLLIE, THINK FOR A SECOND!
IT'S JUST THIS MOMENT--

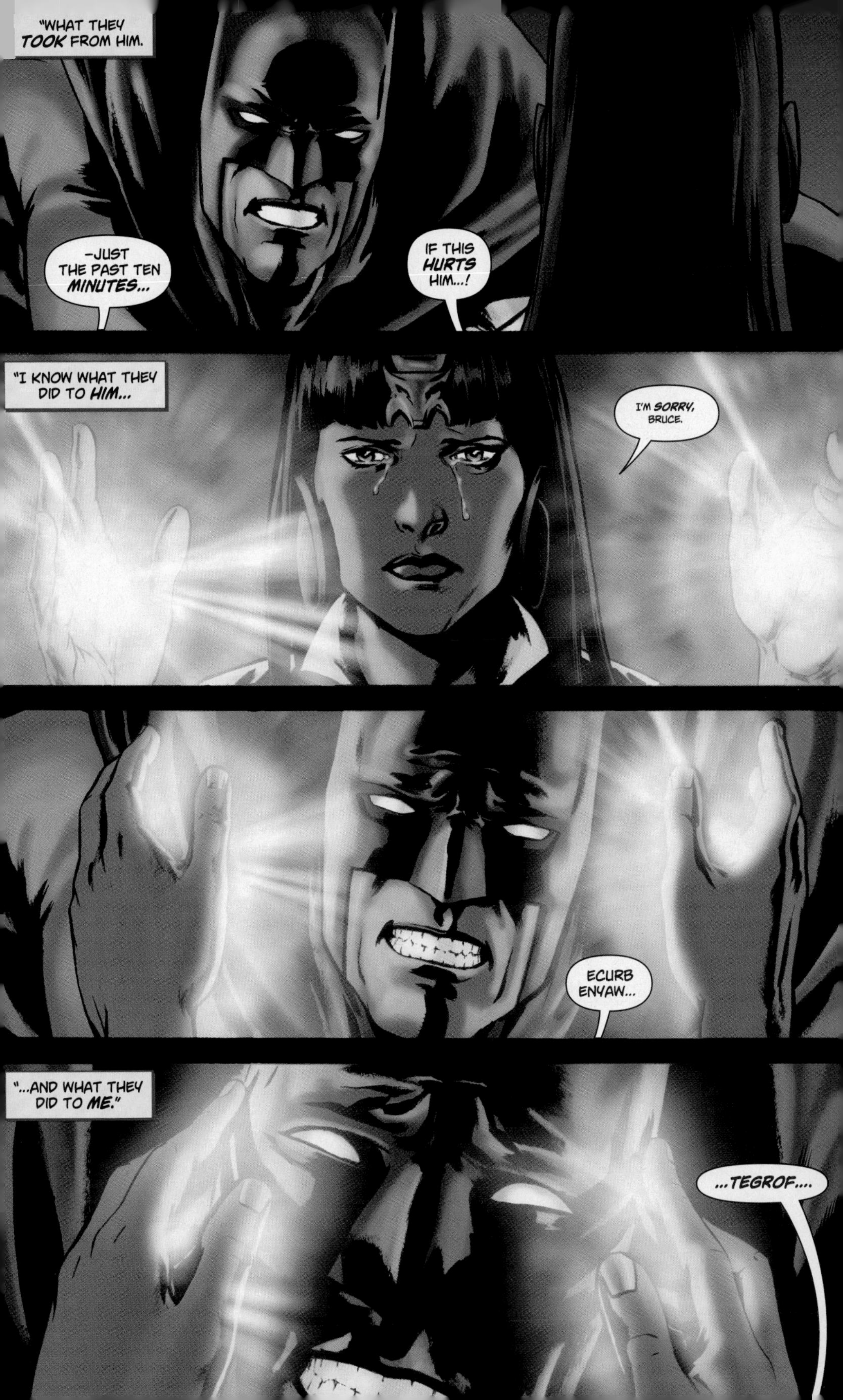
"WHAT THEY TOOK FROM HIM.
-JUST THE PAST TEN MINUTES...
IF THIS HURTS HIM...!
"I KNOW WHAT THEY DID TO HIM...
I'M SORRY, BRUCE.
ECURB ENYAW...
"...AND WHAT THEY DID TO ME."
...TEGROF....

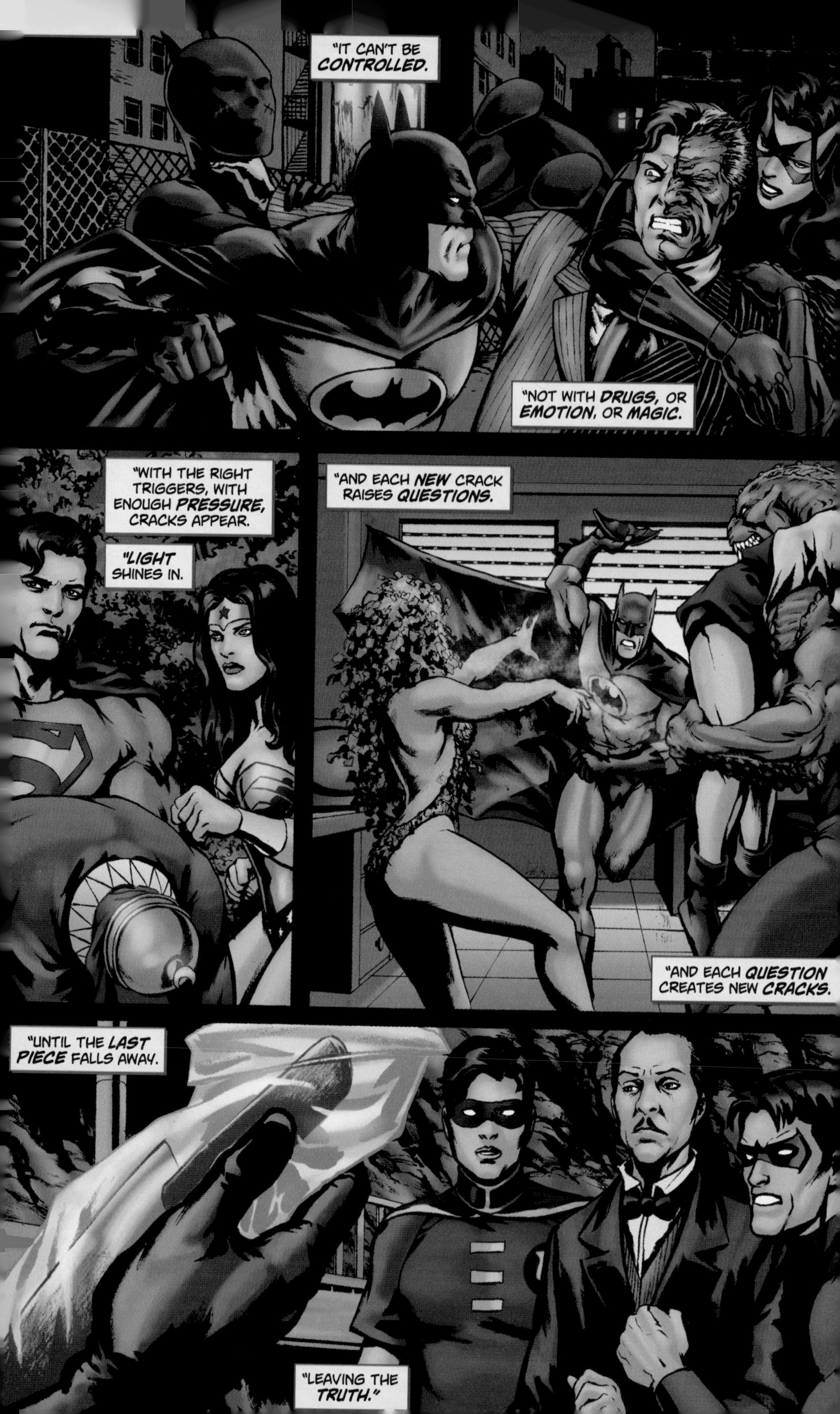
"IT CAN'T BE CONTROLLED.
"NOT WITH DRUGS, OR EMOTION, OR MAGIC.
"WITH THE RIGHT TRIGGERS, WITH ENOUGH PRESSURE, CRACKS APPEAR.
"LIGHT SHINES IN.
"AND EACH NEW CRACK RAISES QUESTIONS.
"AND EACH QUESTION CREATES NEW CRACKS.
"UNTIL THE LAST PIECE FALLS AWAY.
"LEAVING THE TRUTH."

"DO YOU UNDERSTAND?

"THEY *BROKE* THE *PROMISE.*

"AND IF *THEY* COULDN'T BE TRUSTED, THEN BY EXTENSION, *NONE* OF US COULD.

"IT DIDN'T MATTER *WHO* WAS RESPONSIBLE FOR WHAT HAD HAPPENED.

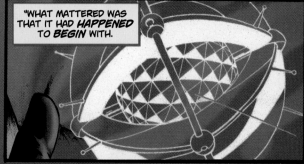

"WHAT MATTERED WAS THAT IT HAD *HAPPENED* TO *BEGIN* WITH.

"AND I WAS *DAMNED* IF I WAS GOING TO LET IT *EVER* HAPPEN *AGAIN.*"

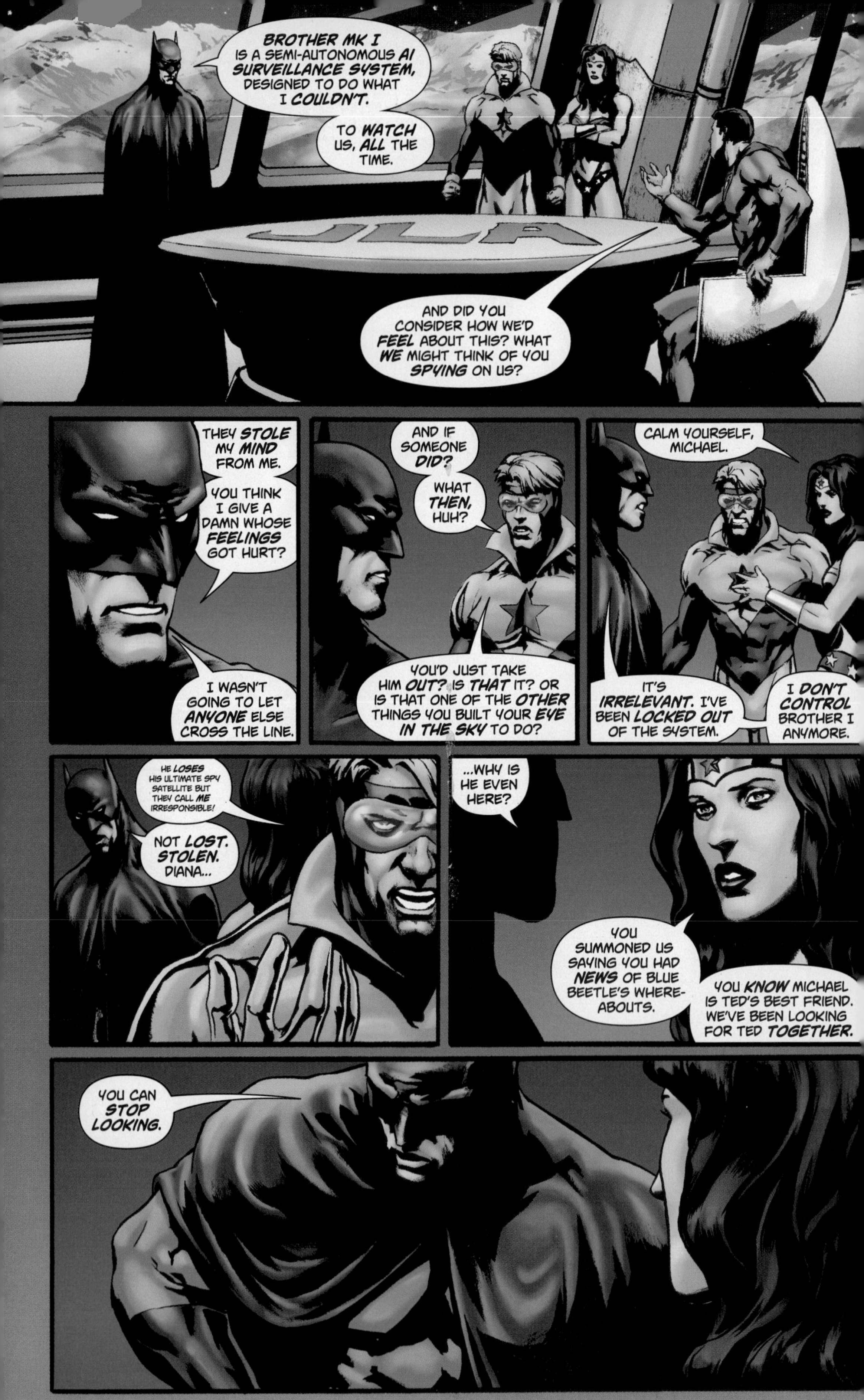
BROTHER MK I IS A SEMI-AUTONOMOUS AI SURVEILLANCE SYSTEM, DESIGNED TO DO WHAT I COULDN'T.
TO WATCH US, ALL THE TIME.
AND DID YOU CONSIDER HOW WE'D FEEL ABOUT THIS? WHAT WE MIGHT THINK OF YOU SPYING ON US?
THEY STOLE MY MIND FROM ME.
YOU THINK I GIVE A DAMN WHOSE FEELINGS GOT HURT?
I WASN'T GOING TO LET ANYONE ELSE CROSS THE LINE.
AND IF SOMEONE DID?
WHAT THEN, HUH?
YOU'D JUST TAKE HIM OUT? IS THAT IT? OR IS THAT ONE OF THE OTHER THINGS YOU BUILT YOUR EYE IN THE SKY TO DO?
CALM YOURSELF, MICHAEL.
IT'S IRRELEVANT. I'VE BEEN LOCKED OUT OF THE SYSTEM.
I DON'T CONTROL BROTHER I ANYMORE.
HE LOSES HIS ULTIMATE SPY SATELLITE BUT THEY CALL ME IRRESPONSIBLE!
NOT LOST. STOLEN. DIANA...
...WHY IS HE EVEN HERE?
YOU SUMMONED US SAYING YOU HAD NEWS OF BLUE BEETLE'S WHERE-ABOUTS.
YOU KNOW MICHAEL IS TED'S BEST FRIEND. WE'VE BEEN LOOKING FOR TED TOGETHER.
YOU CAN STOP LOOKING.

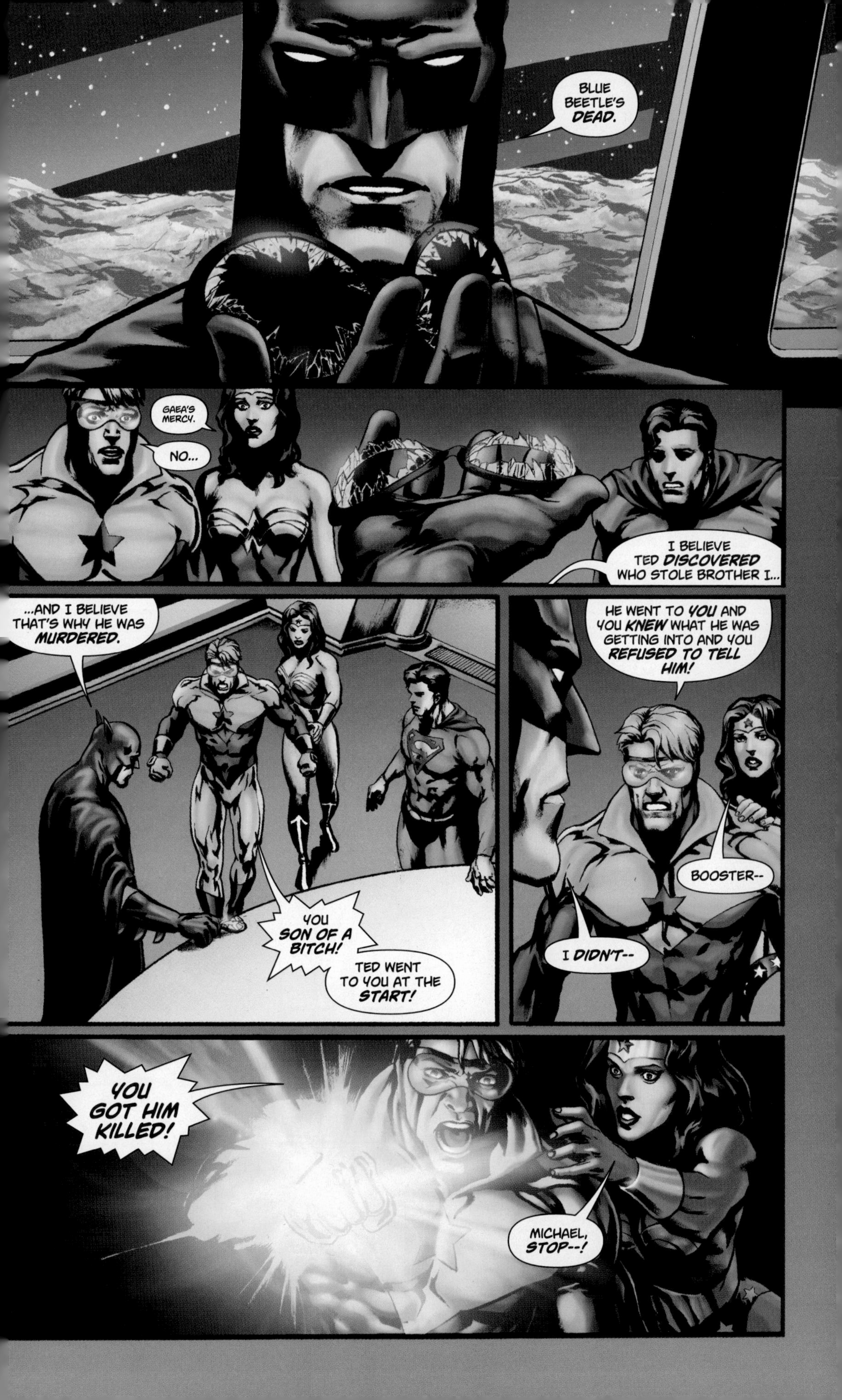
BLUE BEETLE'S DEAD.
GAEA'S MERCY.
NO...
I BELIEVE TED DISCOVERED WHO STOLE BROTHER I...
...AND I BELIEVE THAT'S WHY HE WAS MURDERED.
YOU SON OF A BITCH!
TED WENT TO YOU AT THE START!
HE WENT TO YOU AND YOU KNEW WHAT HE WAS GETTING INTO AND YOU REFUSED TO TELL HIM!
BOOSTER--
I DIDN'T--
YOU GOT HIM KILLED!
MICHAEL, STOP--!

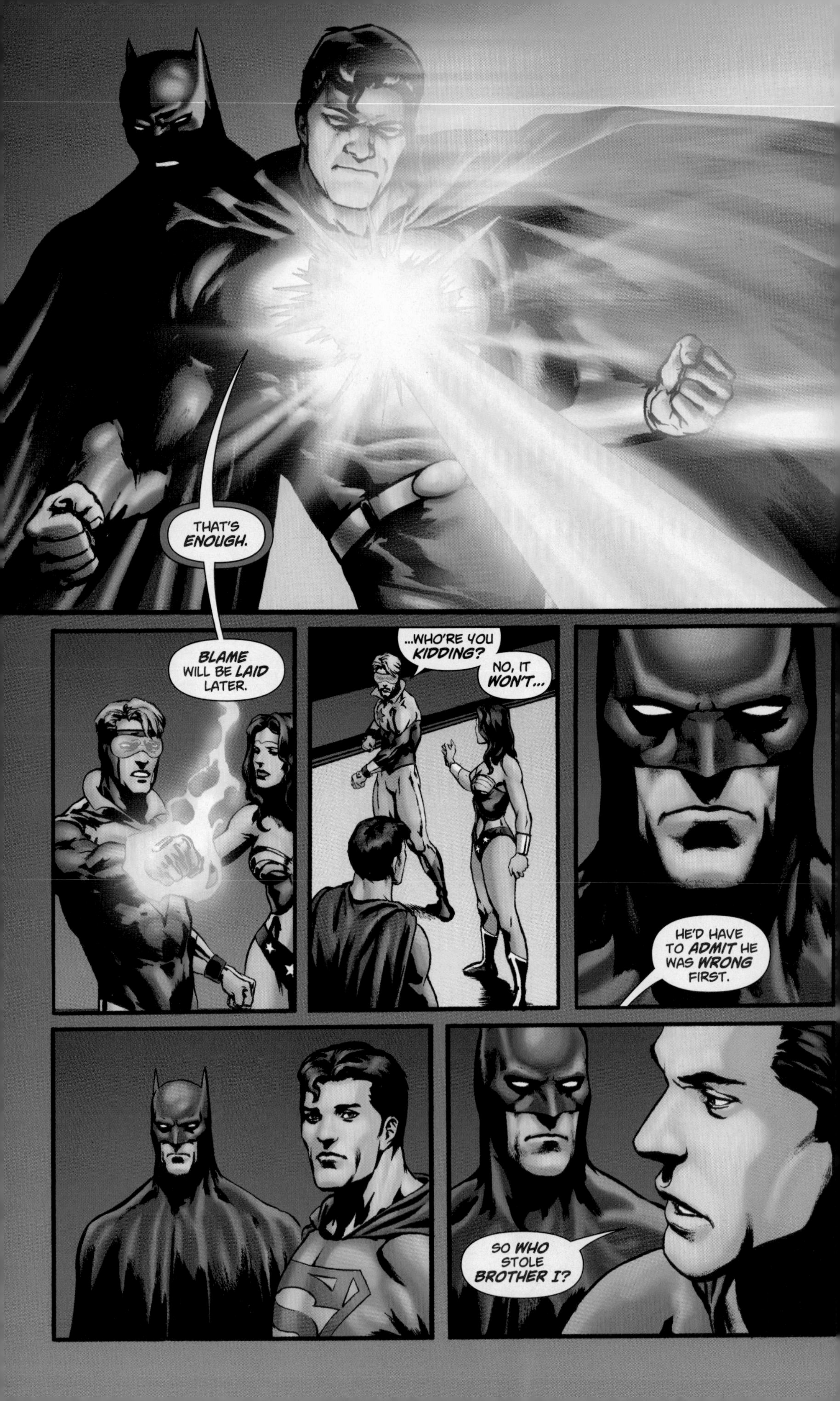
THAT'S ENOUGH.
BLAME WILL BE LAID LATER.
...WHO'RE YOU KIDDING?
NO, IT WON'T...
HE'D HAVE TO ADMIT HE WAS WRONG FIRST.
SO WHO STOLE BROTHER I?

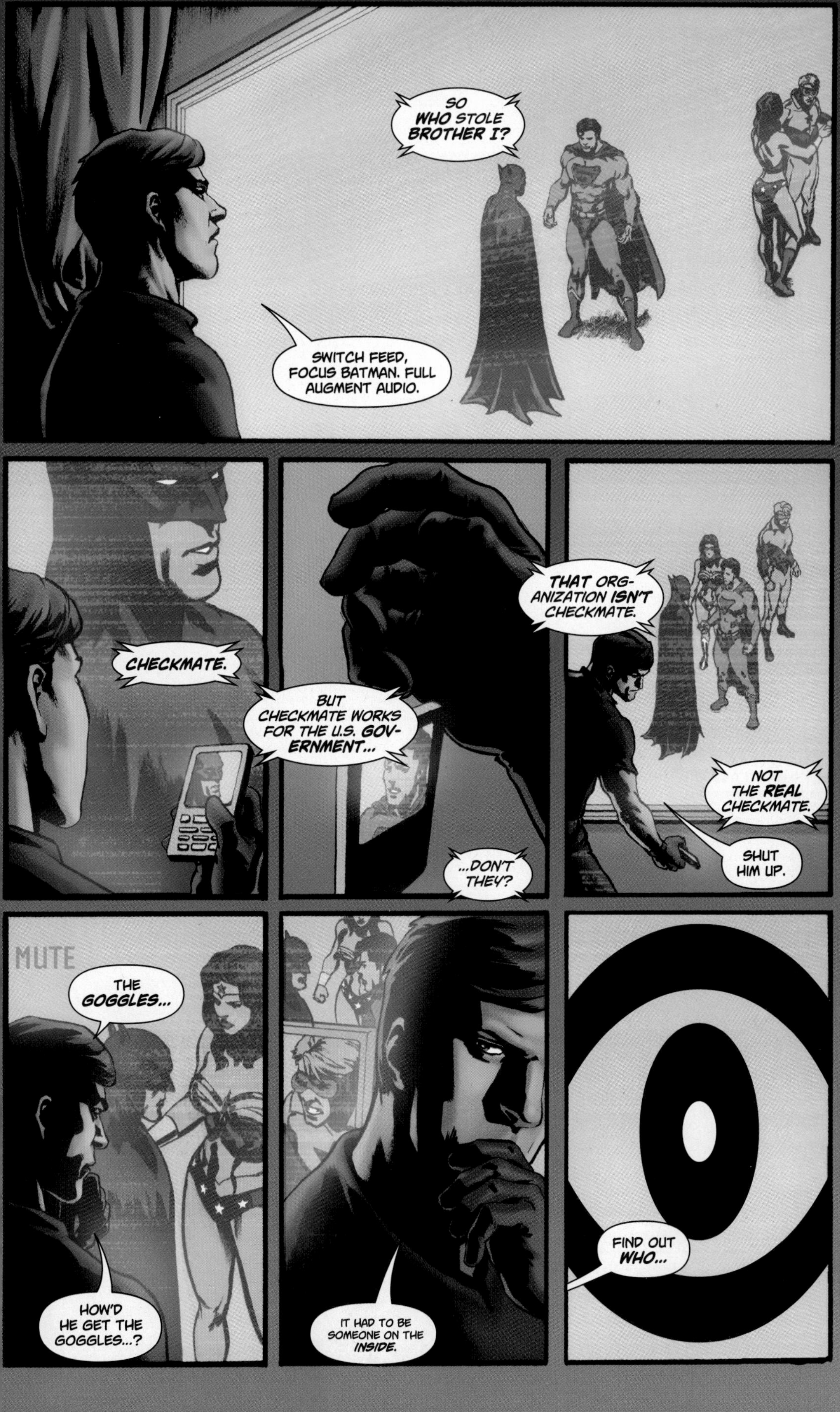

SO WHO STOLE BROTHER I?
SWITCH FEED, FOCUS BATMAN. FULL AUGMENT AUDIO.
CHECKMATE.
BUT CHECKMATE WORKS FOR THE U.S. GOV-ERNMENT...
...DON'T THEY?
THAT ORG-ANIZATION ISN'T CHECKMATE.
NOT THE REAL CHECKMATE.
SHUT HIM UP.
MUTE
THE GOGGLES...
HOW'D HE GET THE GOGGLES...?
IT HAD TO BE SOMEONE ON THE INSIDE.
FIND OUT WHO...

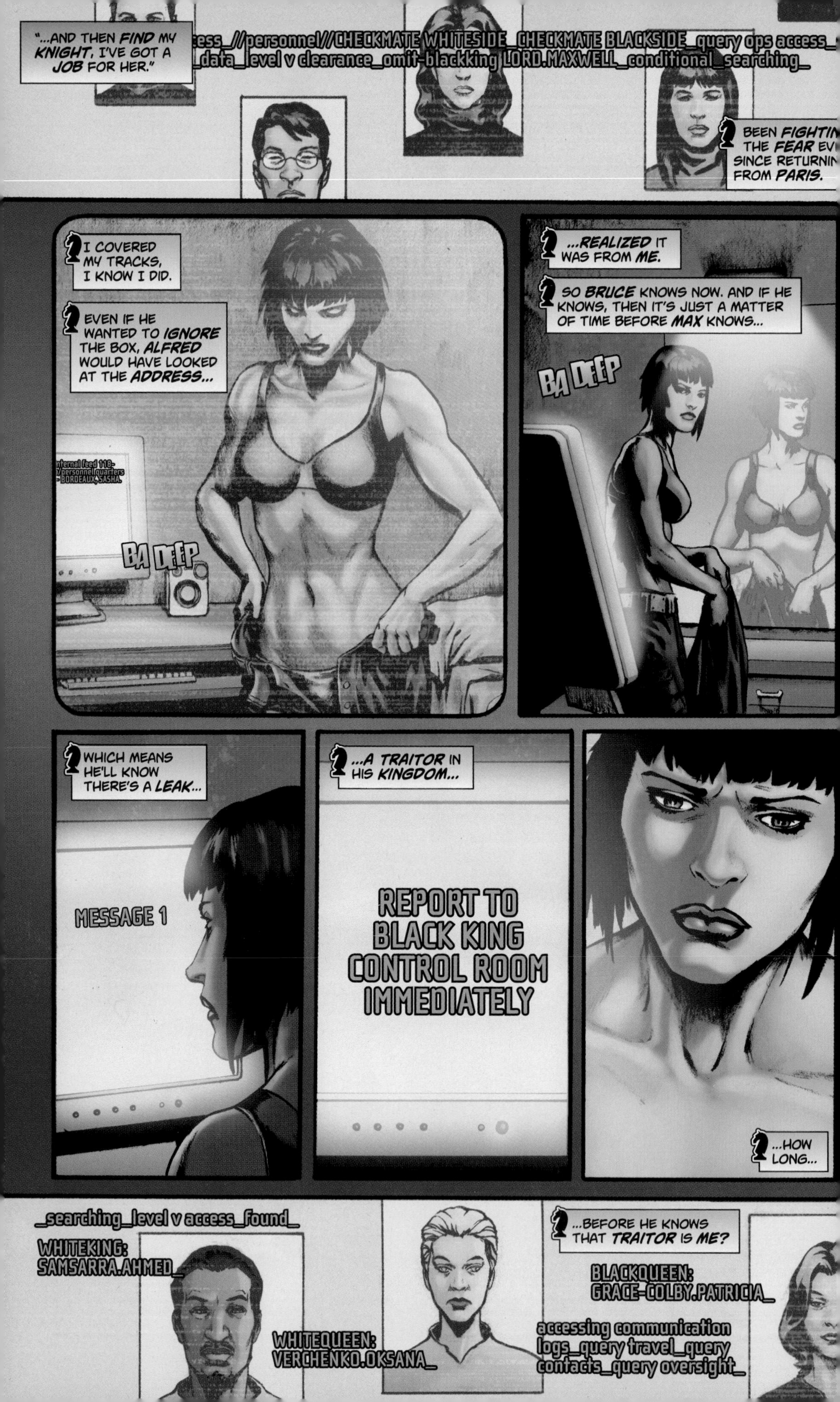
"...AND THEN FIND MY KNIGHT. I'VE GOT A JOB FOR HER."
ess_//personnel//CHECKMATE WHITESIDE_CHECKMATE BLACKSIDE_query ops access_
_data_level v clearance_omit-blackking LORD.MAXWELL_conditional_searching_
BEEN FIGHTIN THE FEAR EV SINCE RETURNIN FROM PARIS.
I COVERED MY TRACKS, I KNOW I DID.
EVEN IF HE WANTED TO IGNORE THE BOX, ALFRED WOULD HAVE LOOKED AT THE ADDRESS...
nternal feed 118-
/personnel quarters
- BORDEAUX, SASHA.
BA DEEP
...REALIZED IT WAS FROM ME.
SO BRUCE KNOWS NOW. AND IF HE KNOWS, THEN IT'S JUST A MATTER OF TIME BEFORE MAX KNOWS...
BA DEEP
WHICH MEANS HE'LL KNOW THERE'S A LEAK...
MESSAGE 1
...A TRAITOR IN HIS KINGDOM...
REPORT TO BLACK KING CONTROL ROOM IMMEDIATELY
...HOW LONG...
_searching_level v access_found_
WHITEKING: SAMSARRA.AHMED_
WHITEQUEEN: VERCHENKO.OKSANA_
...BEFORE HE KNOWS THAT TRAITOR IS ME?
BLACKQUEEN: GRACE-COLBY.PATRICIA_
accessing communication logs_query travel_query contacts_query oversight_

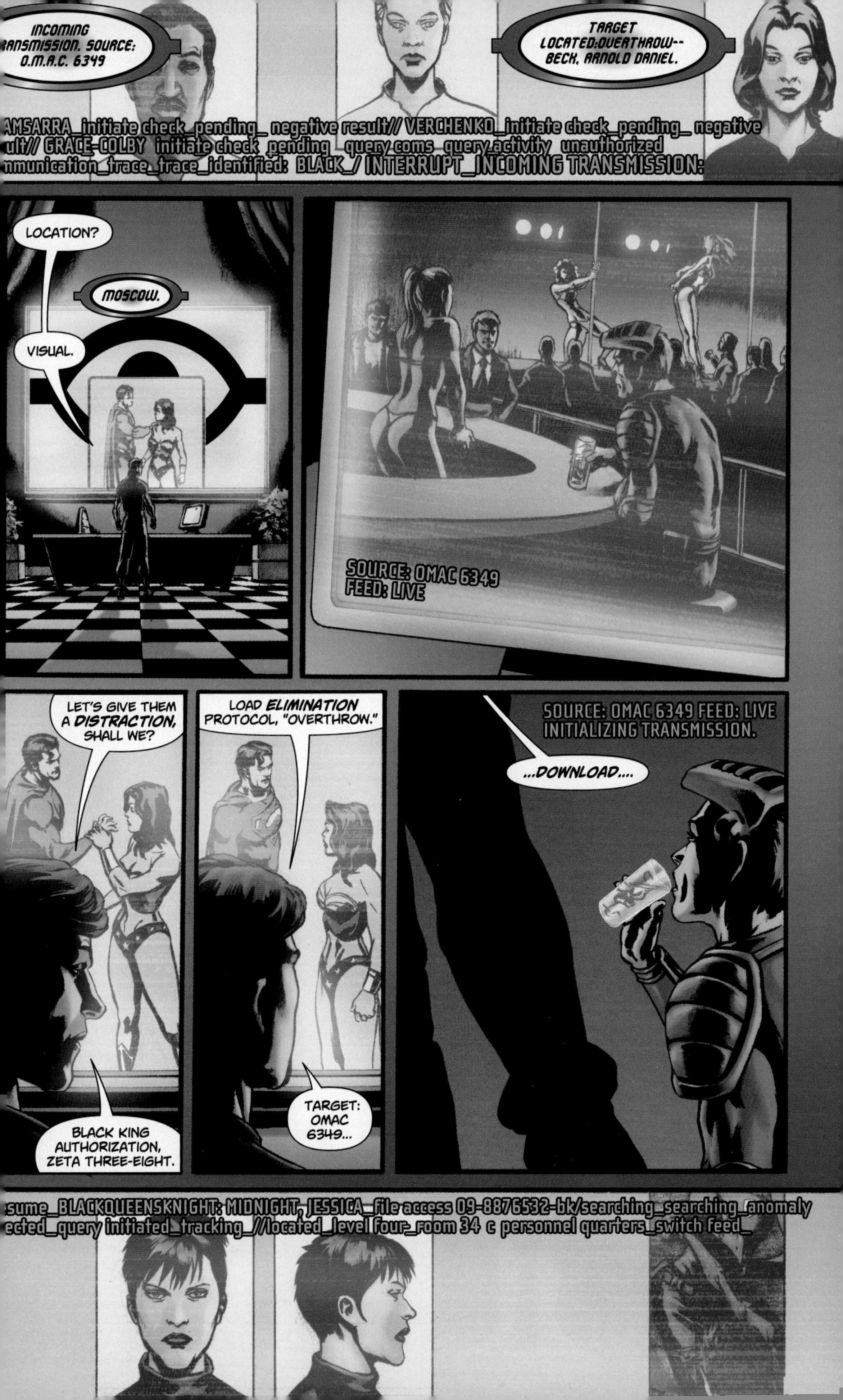
INCOMING TRANSMISSION. SOURCE: O.M.A.C. 6349
TARGET LOCATED:OVERTHROW-- BECK, ARNOLD DANIEL.
AMSARRA_initiate check_pending_ negative result// VERCHENKO_initiate check_pending_ negative result// GRACE-COLBY initiate check pending query coms query activity unauthorized communication_trace_trace_identified: BLACK_/ INTERRUPT_INCOMING TRANSMISSION:
LOCATION?
MOSCOW.
VISUAL.
SOURCE: OMAC 6349
FEED: LIVE
LET'S GIVE THEM A DISTRACTION, SHALL WE?
BLACK KING AUTHORIZATION, ZETA THREE-EIGHT.
LOAD ELIMINATION PROTOCOL, "OVERTHROW."
TARGET: OMAC 6349...
SOURCE: OMAC 6349 FEED: LIVE
INITIALIZING TRANSMISSION.
...DOWNLOAD....
sume_BLACKQUEENSKNIGHT: MIDNIGHT, JESSICA_file access 09-8876532-bk/searching_searching_anomaly ected_query initiated_tracking_//located_level four_room 34 c personnel quarters_switch feed_

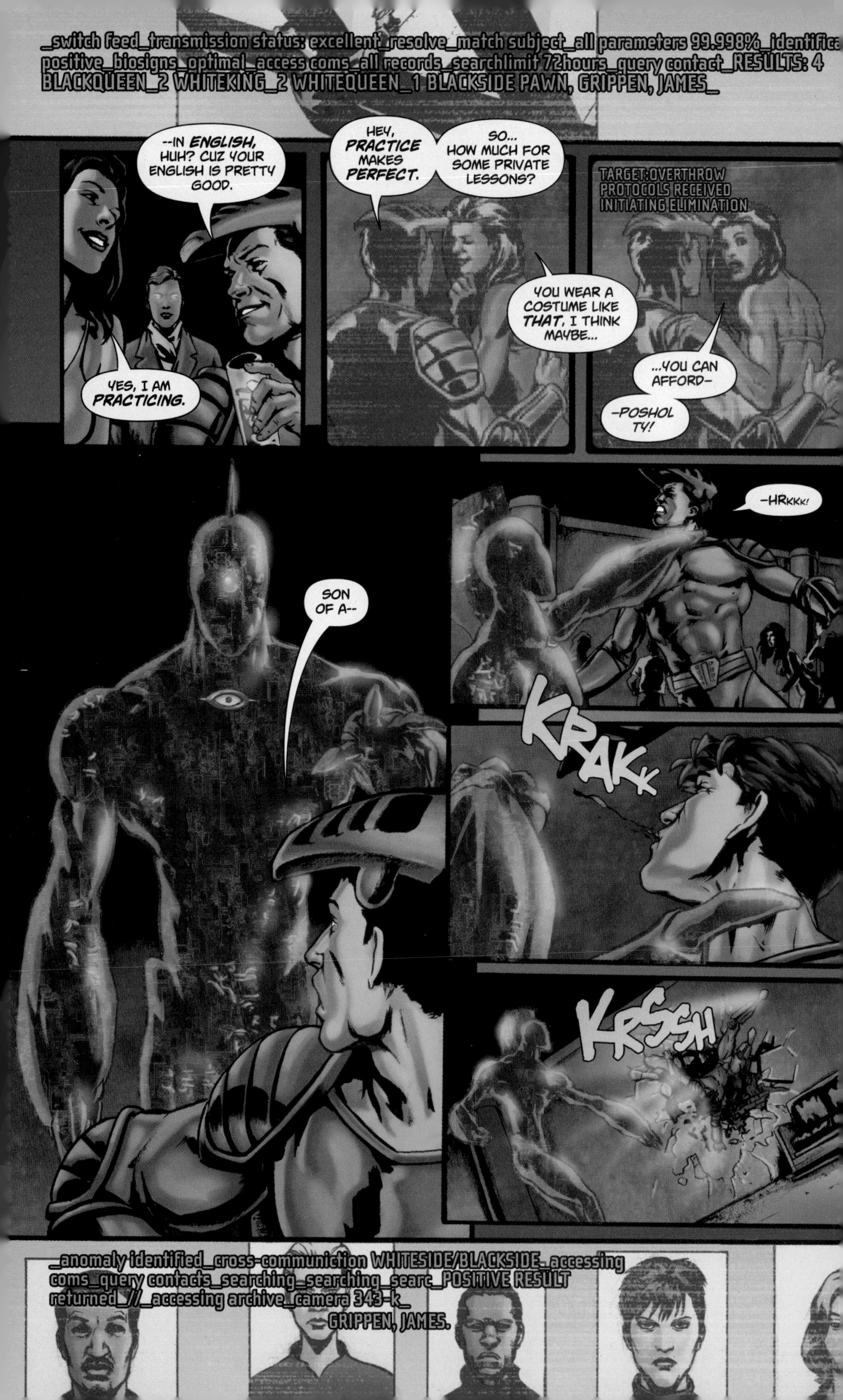
_switch feed_transmission status: excellent_resolve_match subject_all parameters 99.998%_identifica
positive_biosigns_optimal_access coms_all records_searchlimit 72hours_query contact_RESULTS: 4
BLACKQUEEN_2 WHITEKING_2 WHITEQUEEN_1 BLACKSIDE PAWN, GRIPPEN, JAMES_
--IN ENGLISH, HUH? CUZ YOUR ENGLISH IS PRETTY GOOD.
YES, I AM PRACTICING.
HEY, PRACTICE MAKES PERFECT.
SO... HOW MUCH FOR SOME PRIVATE LESSONS?
YOU WEAR A COSTUME LIKE THAT, I THINK MAYBE...
TARGET:OVERTHROW
PROTOCOLS RECEIVED
INITIATING ELIMINATION
...YOU CAN AFFORD-
-POSHOL TY!
SON OF A--
-HRKKK!
KRAKK
KRSSH
_anomaly identified_cross-communiction WHITESIDE/BLACKSIDE_accessing
coms_query contacts_searching_searching_searc_POSITIVE RESULT
returned_//_accessing archive_camera 343-k_
GRIPPEN, JAMES.

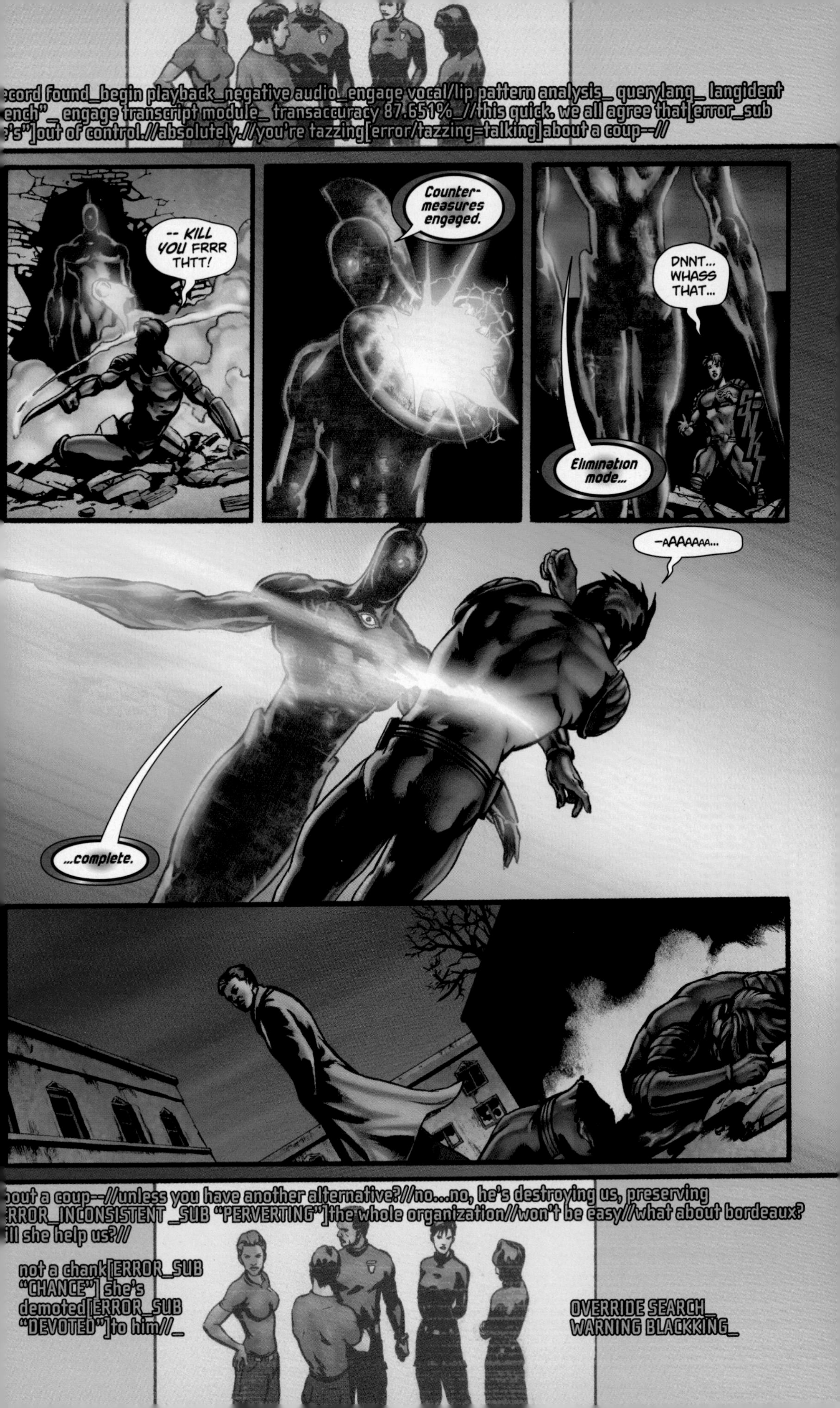
ecord found_begin playback_negative audio_engage vocal/lip pattern analysis_ querylang_ langident
ench"_ engage transcript module_ transaccuracy 87.651%_//this quick. we all agree that[error_sub
e's"]out of control.//absolutely.//you're tazzing[error/tazzing=talking]about a coup--//
-- KILL YOU FRRR THTT!
Counter-measures engaged.
DNNT... WHASS THAT...
Elimination mode...
-AAAAAAA...
...complete.
bout a coup--//unless you have another alternative?//no...no, he's destroying us, preserving
RROR_INCONSISTENT _SUB "PERVERTING"]the whole organization//won't be easy//what about bordeaux?
ill she help us?//
not a chank[ERROR_SUB "CHANCE"] she's demoted[ERROR_SUB "DEVOTED"]to him//_
OVERRIDE SEARCH_
WARNING BLACKKING_

You are in danger.

 I AM IN DANGER.

IT'S THAT DAMN *MACHINE*...

AM I?

...I CAN'T PUT MY FINGER ON IT...

I'M SURPRISED IT TOOK THEM THIS LONG.

I'LL TAKE CARE OF IT...

Assassination attempt imminent.

...I SWEAR IT'S... *LOOKING* AT ME...

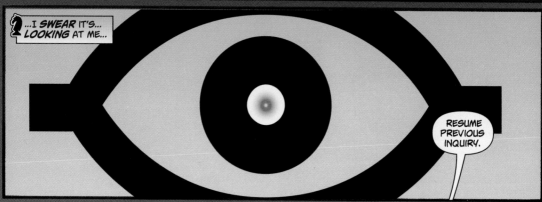

RESUME PREVIOUS INQUIRY.

...LOOKING *INTO* ME...

AH, MY *KNIGHT.* YOU DID WELL IN PARIS, I'M *PLEASED.*

THANK YOU, SIR.

I'VE GOT *ANOTHER* JOB FOR YOU...

...BUT *FIRST,* I WANT YOU TO *SEE* SOMETHING.

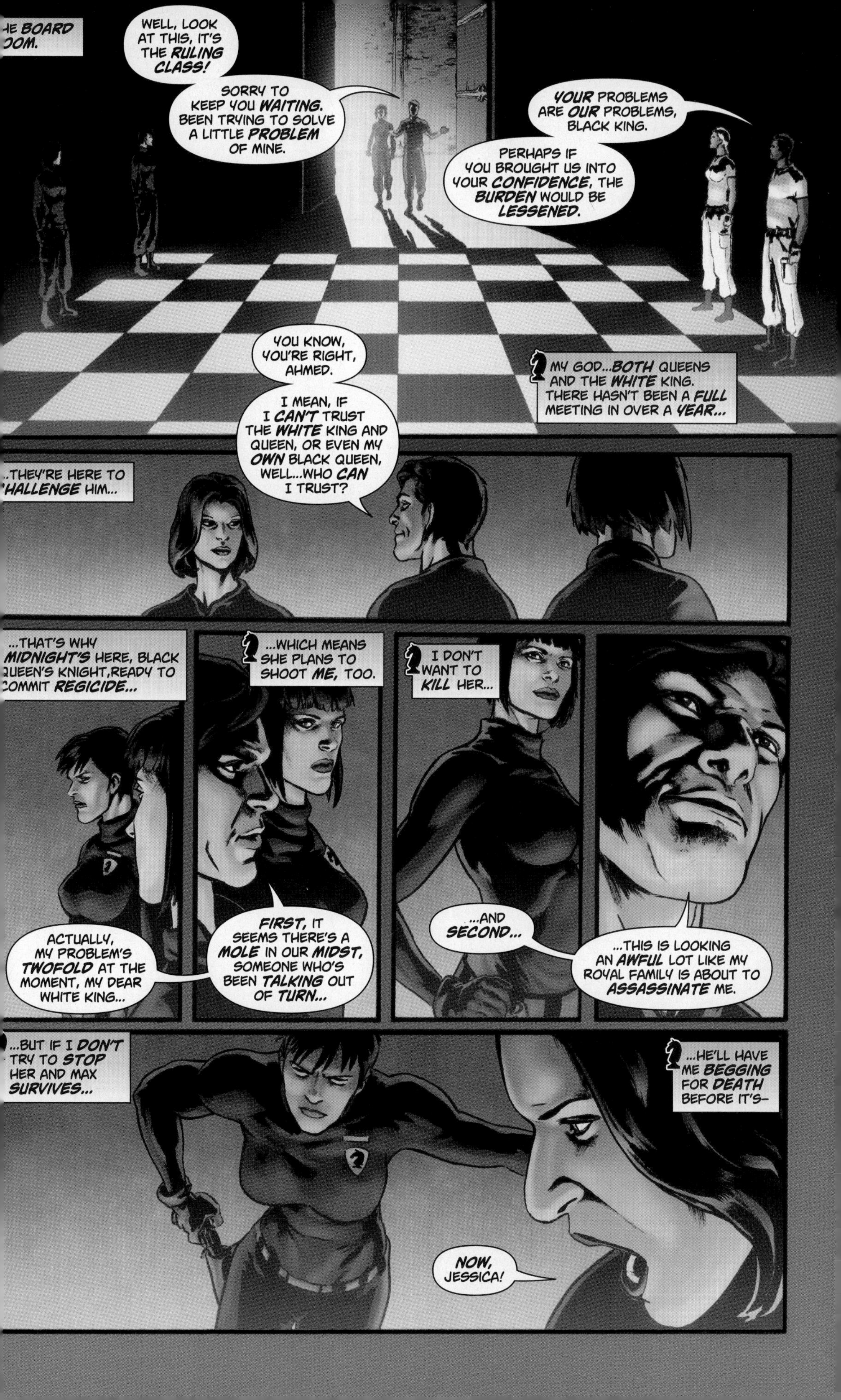

HE BOARD
OOM.
WELL, LOOK AT THIS, IT'S THE RULING CLASS!
SORRY TO KEEP YOU WAITING. BEEN TRYING TO SOLVE A LITTLE PROBLEM OF MINE.
YOUR PROBLEMS ARE OUR PROBLEMS, BLACK KING.
PERHAPS IF YOU BROUGHT US INTO YOUR CONFIDENCE, THE BURDEN WOULD BE LESSENED.
YOU KNOW, YOU'RE RIGHT, AHMED.
I MEAN, IF I CAN'T TRUST THE WHITE KING AND QUEEN, OR EVEN MY OWN BLACK QUEEN, WELL...WHO CAN I TRUST?
MY GOD...BOTH QUEENS AND THE WHITE KING. THERE HASN'T BEEN A FULL MEETING IN OVER A YEAR...
...THEY'RE HERE TO
HALLENGE HIM...
...THAT'S WHY MIDNIGHT'S HERE, BLACK QUEEN'S KNIGHT,READY TO COMMIT REGICIDE...
ACTUALLY, MY PROBLEM'S TWOFOLD AT THE MOMENT, MY DEAR WHITE KING...
...WHICH MEANS SHE PLANS TO SHOOT ME, TOO.
FIRST, IT SEEMS THERE'S A MOLE IN OUR MIDST, SOMEONE WHO'S BEEN TALKING OUT OF TURN...
I DON'T WANT TO KILL HER...
...AND SECOND...
...THIS IS LOOKING AN AWFUL LOT LIKE MY ROYAL FAMILY IS ABOUT TO ASSASSINATE ME.
...BUT IF I DON'T TRY TO STOP HER AND MAX SURVIVES...
...HE'LL HAVE ME BEGGING FOR DEATH BEFORE IT'S–
NOW, JESSICA!

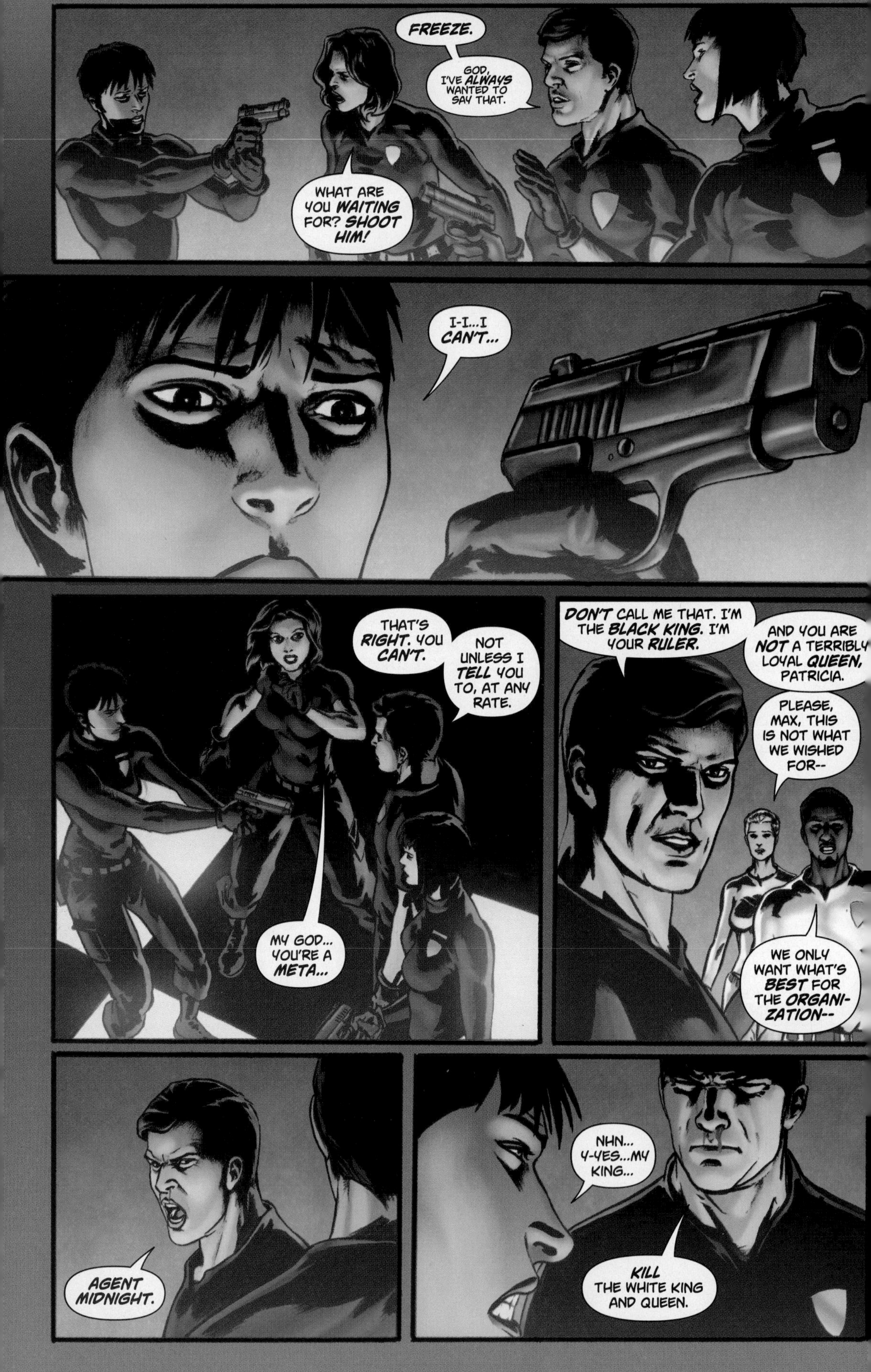
FREEZE.
GOD, I'VE ALWAYS WANTED TO SAY THAT.
WHAT ARE YOU WAITING FOR? SHOOT HIM!
I-I...I CAN'T...
THAT'S RIGHT. YOU CAN'T.
NOT UNLESS I TELL YOU TO, AT ANY RATE.
MY GOD... YOU'RE A META...
DON'T CALL ME THAT. I'M THE BLACK KING. I'M YOUR RULER.
AND YOU ARE NOT A TERRIBLY LOYAL QUEEN, PATRICIA.
PLEASE, MAX, THIS IS NOT WHAT WE WISHED FOR--
WE ONLY WANT WHAT'S BEST FOR THE ORGANI-ZATION--
AGENT MIDNIGHT.
NHN... Y-YES...MY KING...
KILL THE WHITE KING AND QUEEN.

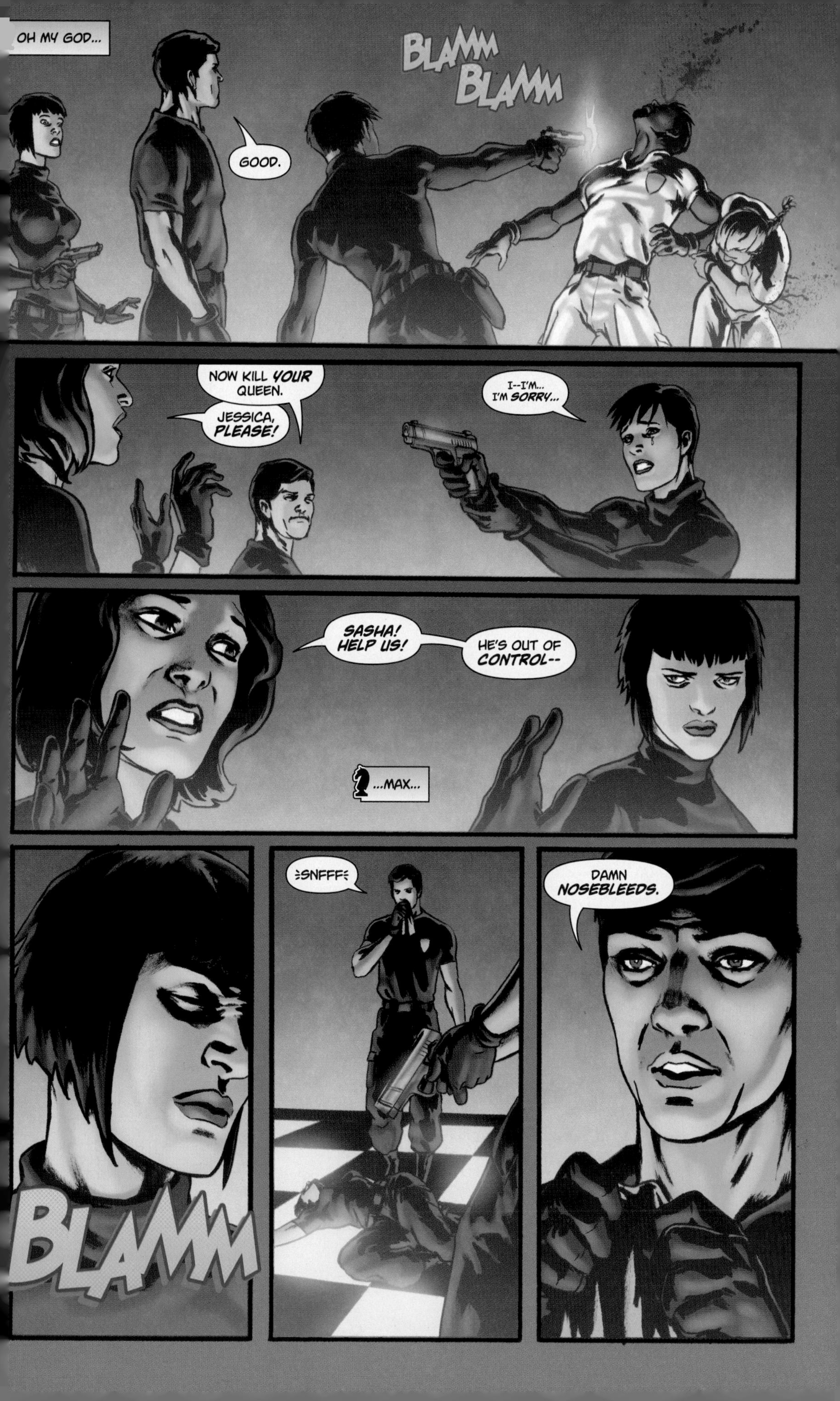

OH MY GOD...
GOOD.
BLAMM
BLAMM
NOW KILL YOUR QUEEN.
JESSICA, PLEASE!
I--I'M... I'M SORRY...
SASHA! HELP US!
HE'S OUT OF CONTROL--
...MAX...
BLAMM
SNFFF
DAMN NOSEBLEEDS.

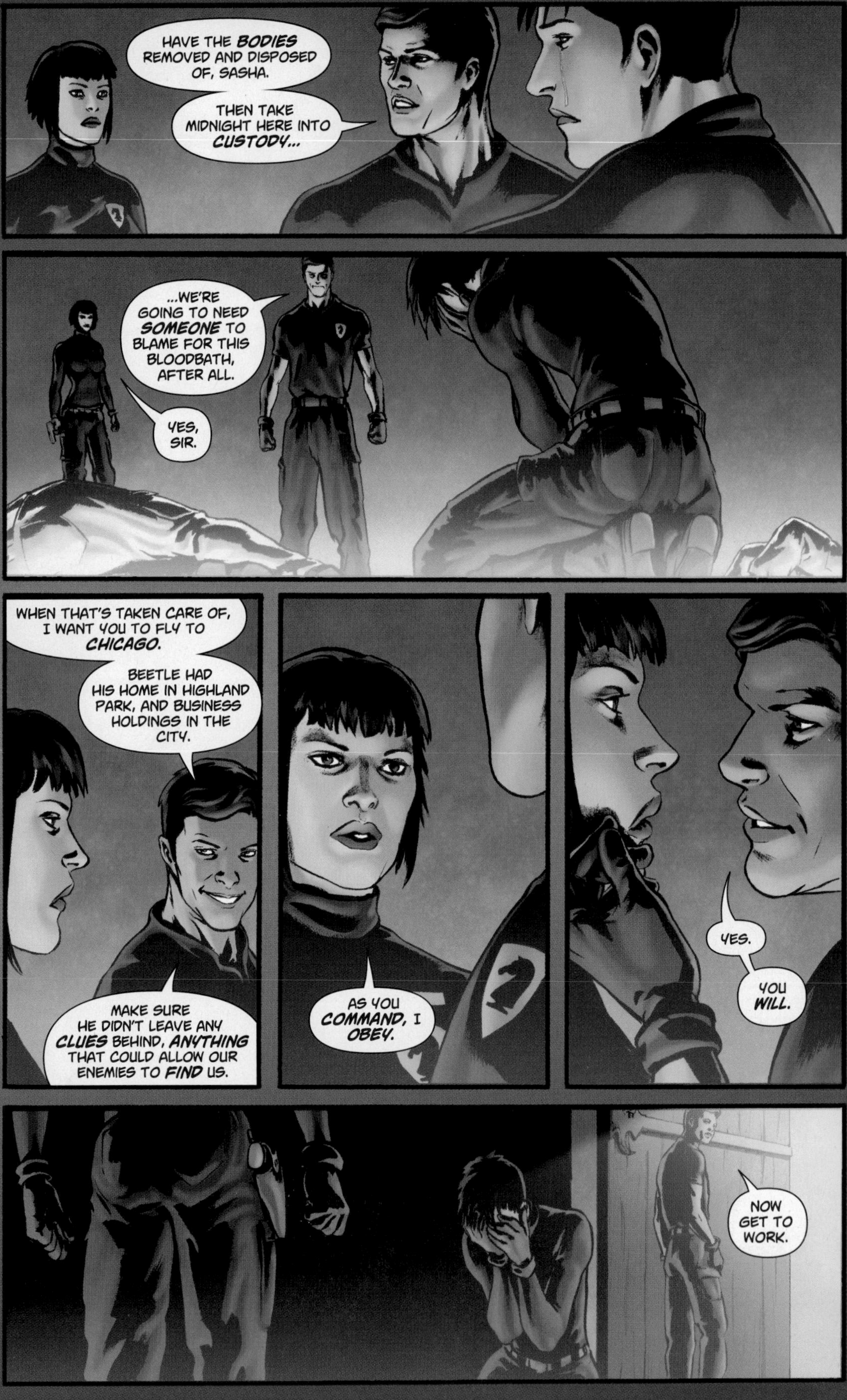
HAVE THE BODIES REMOVED AND DISPOSED OF, SASHA.
THEN TAKE MIDNIGHT HERE INTO CUSTODY...
...WE'RE GOING TO NEED SOMEONE TO BLAME FOR THIS BLOODBATH, AFTER ALL.
YES, SIR.
WHEN THAT'S TAKEN CARE OF, I WANT YOU TO FLY TO CHICAGO.
BEETLE HAD HIS HOME IN HIGHLAND PARK, AND BUSINESS HOLDINGS IN THE CITY.
MAKE SURE HE DIDN'T LEAVE ANY CLUES BEHIND, ANYTHING THAT COULD ALLOW OUR ENEMIES TO FIND US.
AS YOU COMMAND, I OBEY.
YES.
YOU WILL.
NOW GET TO WORK.

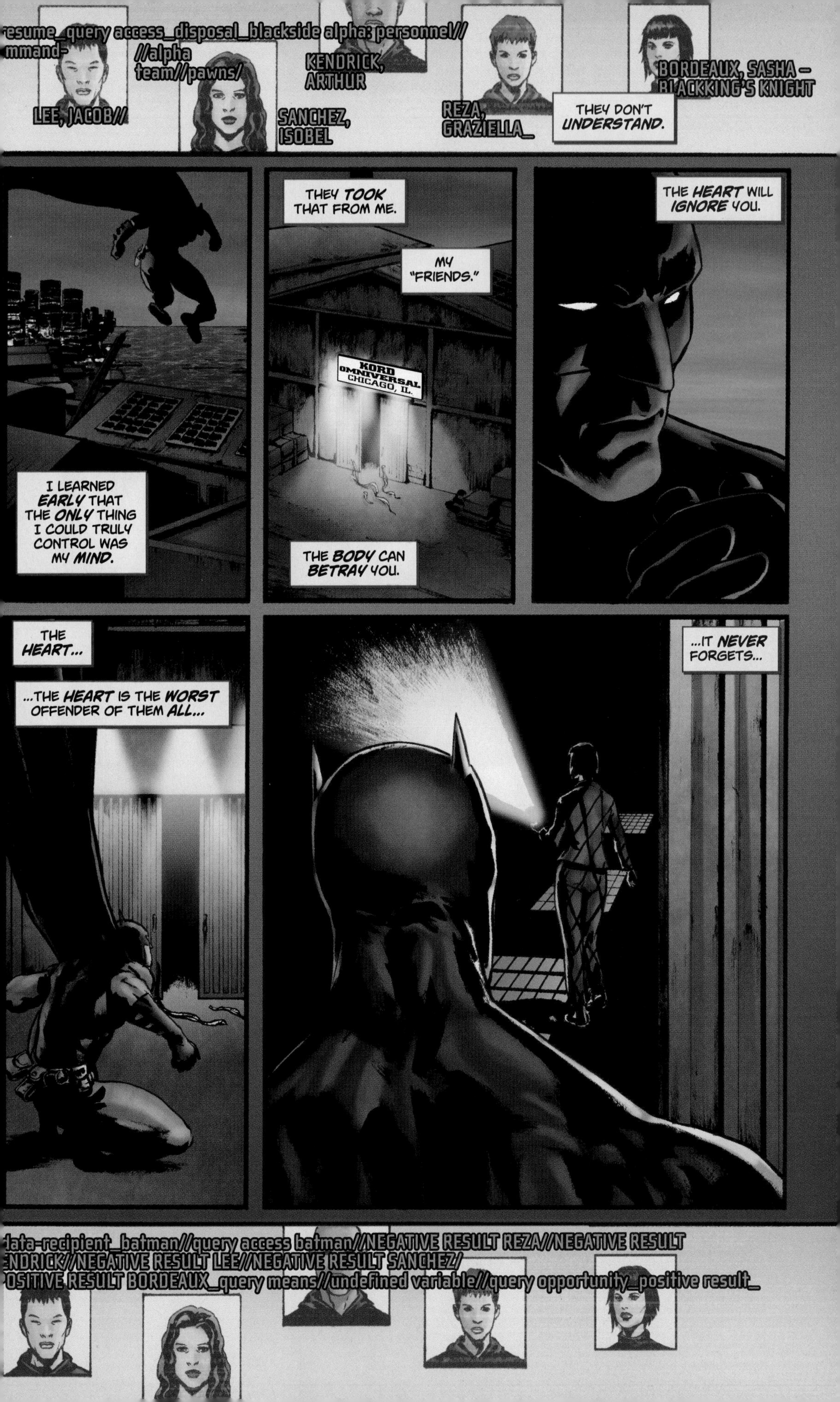

esume_query access_disposal_blackside alpha: personnel//
mmand-
//alpha team//pawns/
KENDRICK, ARTHUR
BORDEAUX, SASHA — BLACKKING'S KNIGHT
LEE, JACOB//
SANCHEZ, ISOBEL
REZA, GRAZIELLA_
THEY DON'T UNDERSTAND.
I LEARNED EARLY THAT THE ONLY THING I COULD TRULY CONTROL WAS MY MIND.
THEY TOOK THAT FROM ME.
MY "FRIENDS."
KORD OMNIVERSAL CHICAGO, IL.
THE BODY CAN BETRAY YOU.
THE HEART WILL IGNORE YOU.
THE HEART...
...THE HEART IS THE WORST OFFENDER OF THEM ALL...
...IT NEVER FORGETS...
data-recipient_batman//query access batman//NEGATIVE RESULT REZA//NEGATIVE RESULT
ENDRICK//NEGATIVE RESULT LEE//NEGATIVE RESULT SANCHEZ/
OSITIVE RESULT BORDEAUX_query means//undefined variable//query opportunity_positive result_

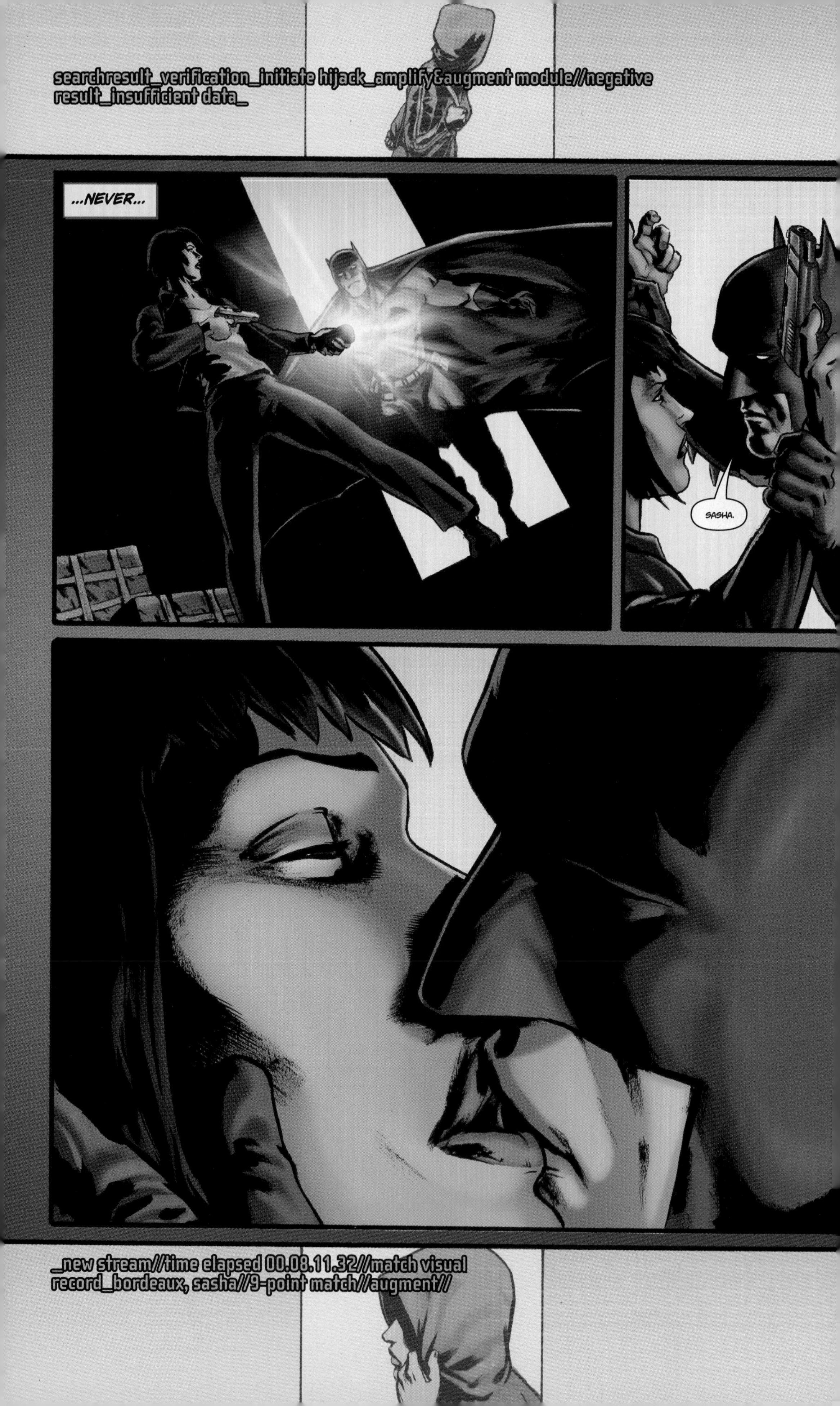
searchresult_verification_initiate hijack_amplify&augment module//negative result_insufficient data_
...NEVER...
SASHA.
_new stream//time elapsed 00.08.11.32//match visual record_bordeaux, sasha//9-point match//augment//

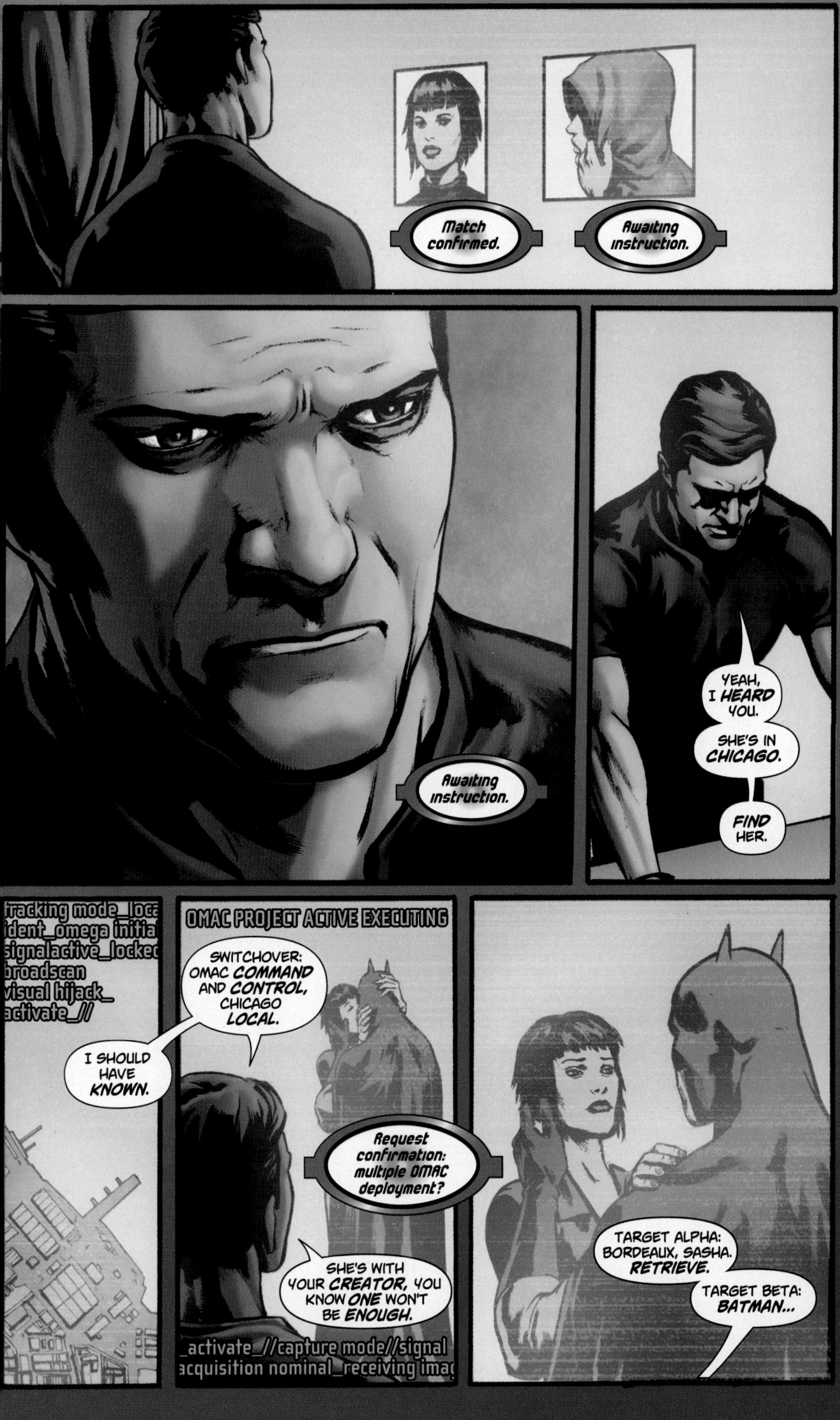
Match confirmed.
Awaiting instruction.
Awaiting instruction.
YEAH, I HEARD YOU.
SHE'S IN CHICAGO.
FIND HER.
tracking mode_loca
ident_omega initia
signalactive_locked
broadscan
visual hijack_
activate_//
OMAC PROJECT ACTIVE EXECUTING
SWITCHOVER: OMAC COMMAND AND CONTROL, CHICAGO LOCAL.
I SHOULD HAVE KNOWN.
Request confirmation: multiple OMAC deployment?
SHE'S WITH YOUR CREATOR, YOU KNOW ONE WON'T BE ENOUGH.
activate//capture mode//signal
acquisition nominal_receiving imag
TARGET ALPHA: BORDEAUX, SASHA. RETRIEVE.
TARGET BETA: BATMAN...

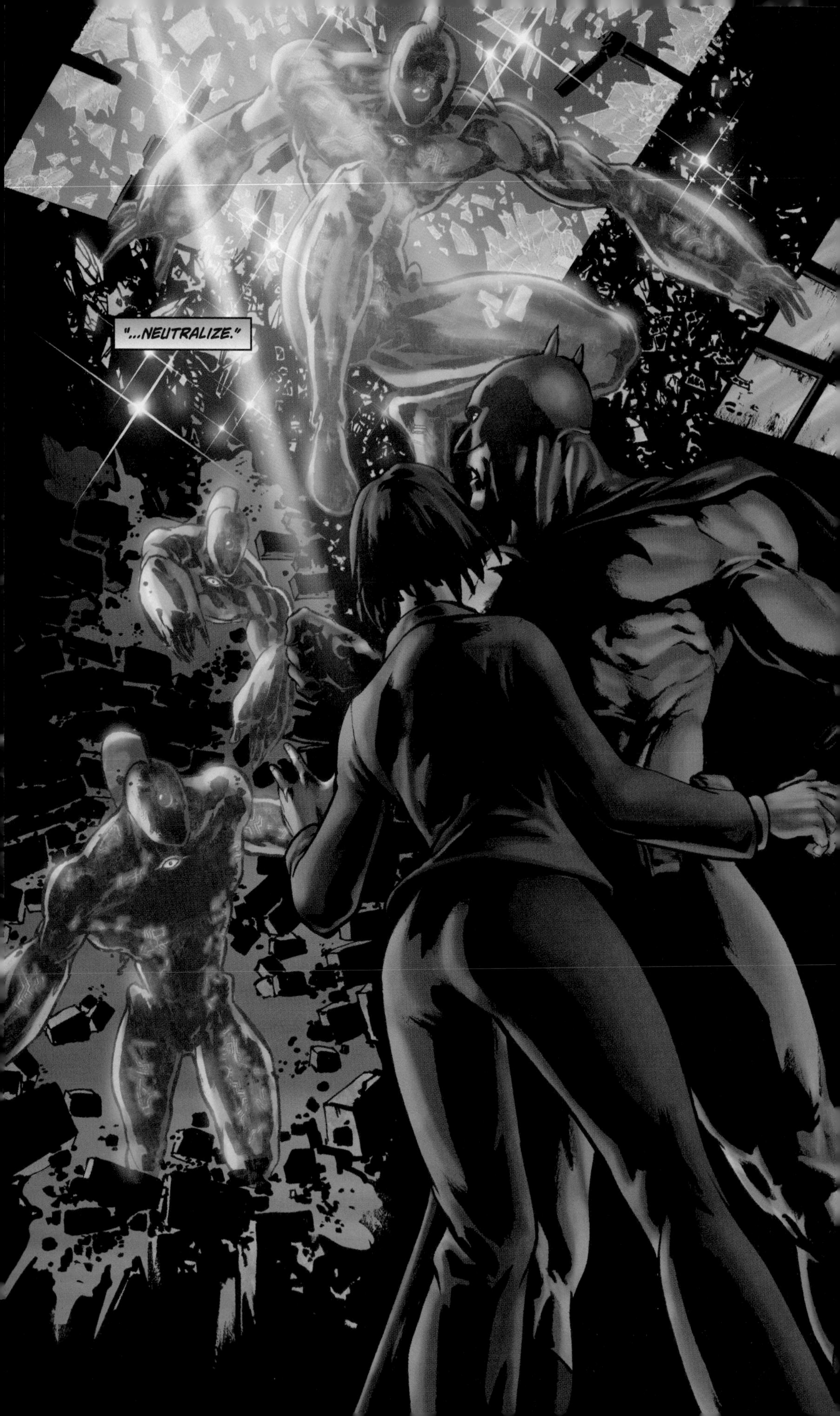
"...NEUTRALIZE."

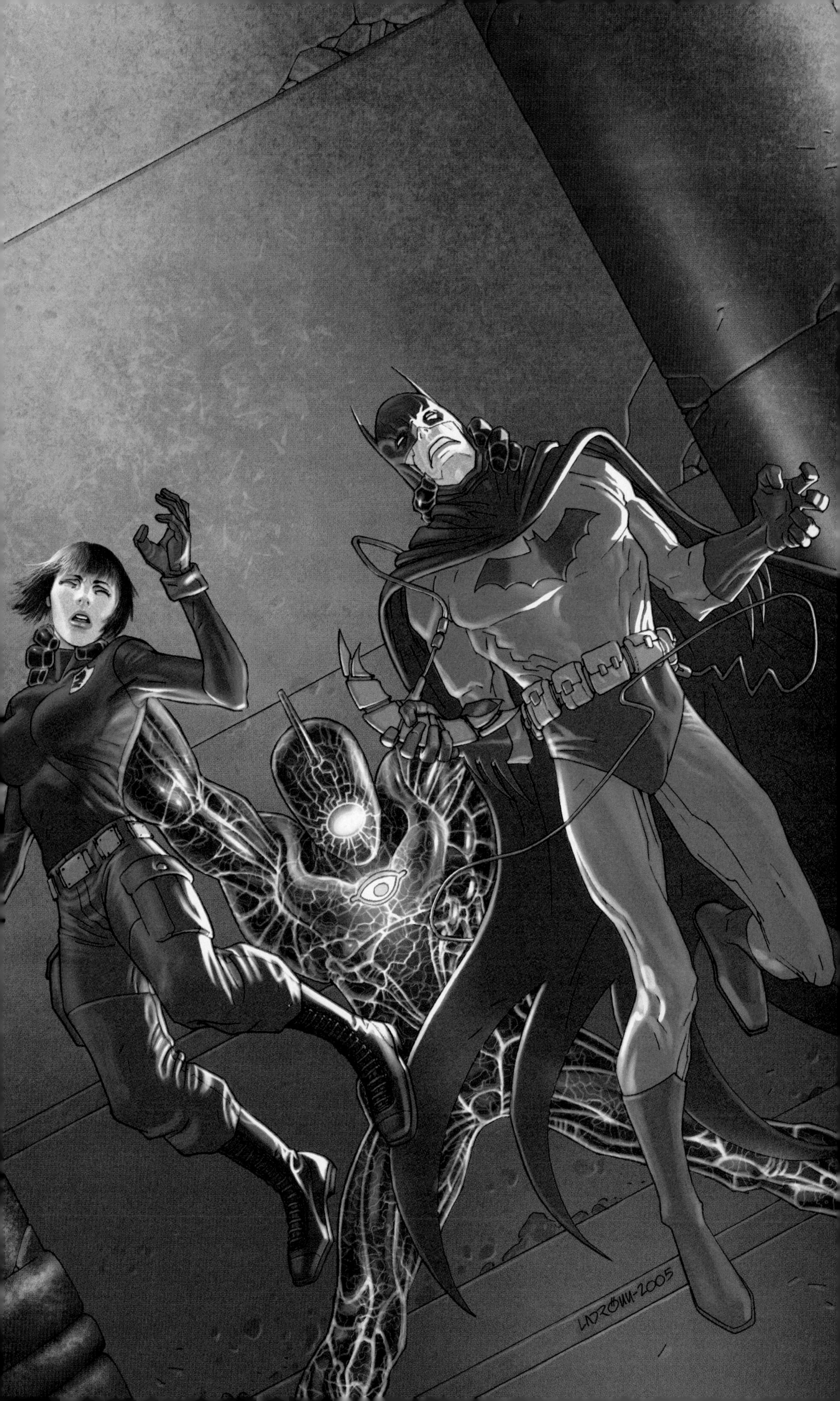

Greg Rucka
Writer

Jesus Saiz & Bob Wiacek
Artists

Hi-Fi Design
Colorist

Jared K. Fletcher
Letterer

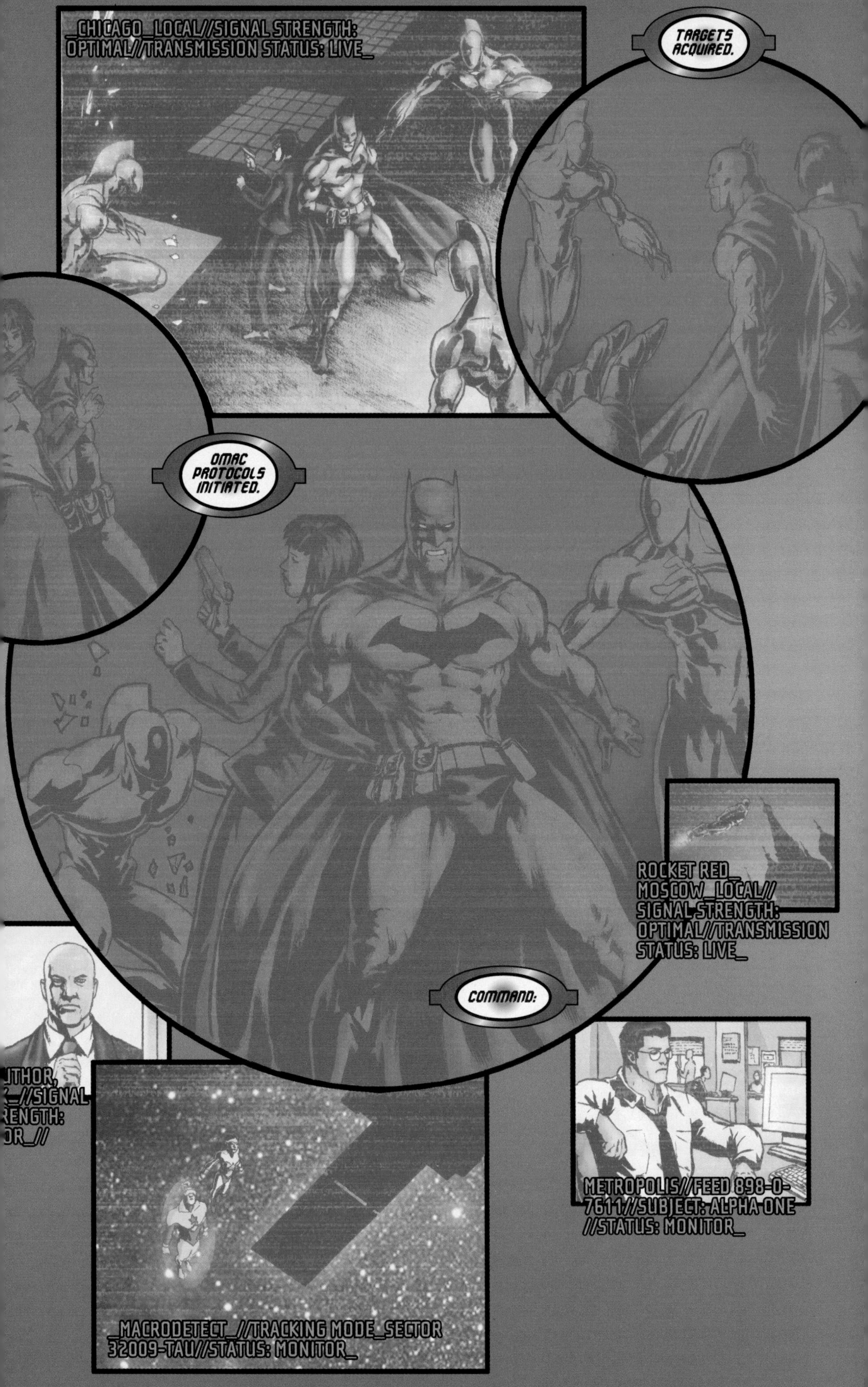
_CHICAGO_LOCAL//SIGNAL STRENGTH: OPTIMAL//TRANSMISSION STATUS: LIVE_
TARGETS ACQUIRED.
OMAC PROTOCOLS INITIATED.
ROCKET RED_ MOSCOW_LOCAL// SIGNAL STRENGTH: OPTIMAL//TRANSMISSION STATUS: LIVE_
COMMAND:
UTHOR, _//SIGNAL RENGTH: OR_//
MACRODETECT//TRACKING MODE_SECTOR 32009-TAU//STATUS: MONITOR_
METROPOLIS//FEED 898-0-7611//SUBJECT: ALPHA ONE //STATUS: MONITOR_

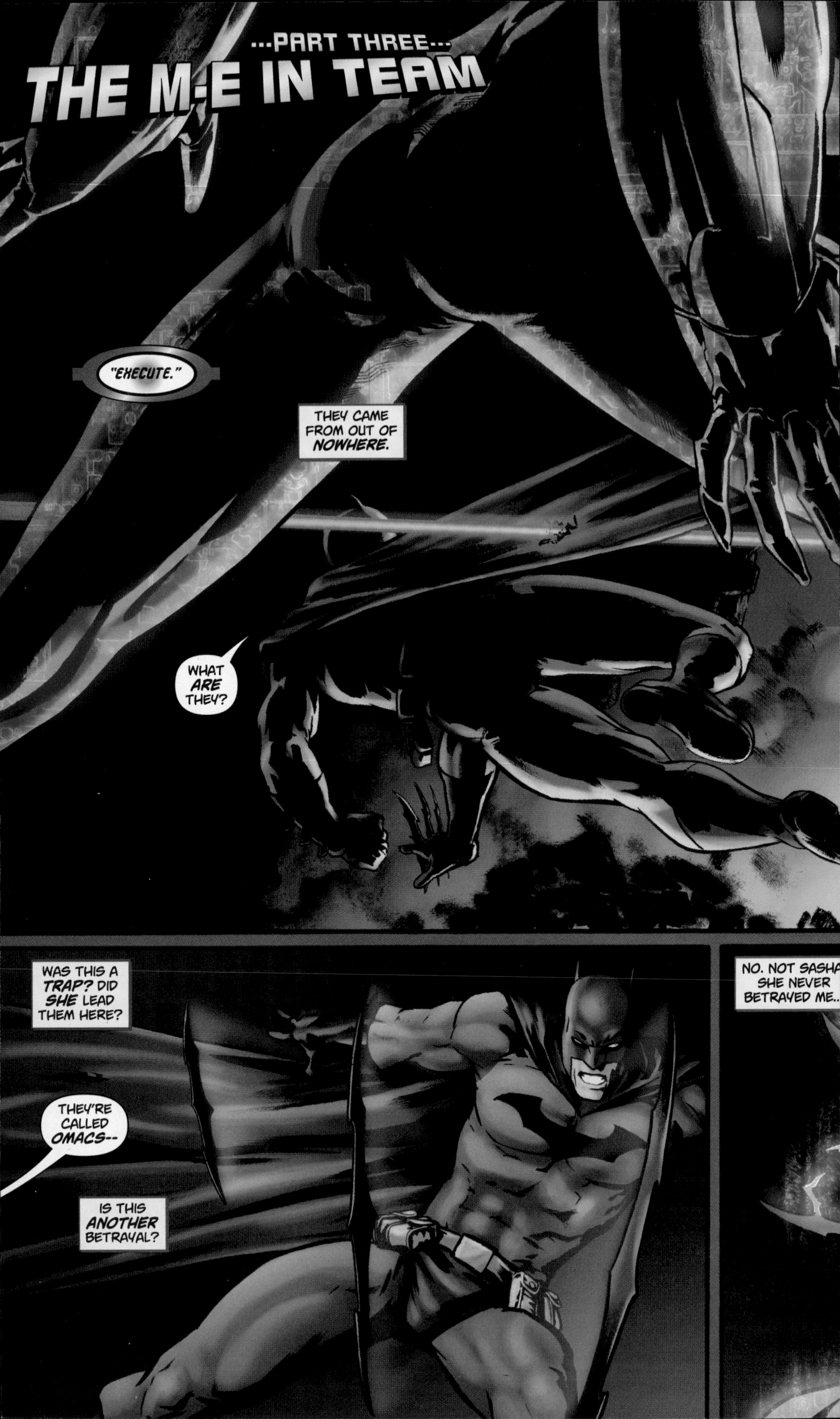
...PART THREE...
THE M-E IN TEAM
"EXECUTE."
THEY CAME FROM OUT OF NOWHERE.
WHAT ARE THEY?
WAS THIS A TRAP? DID SHE LEAD THEM HERE?
THEY'RE CALLED OMACS--
IS THIS ANOTHER BETRAYAL?
NO. NOT SASHA. SHE NEVER BETRAYED ME...

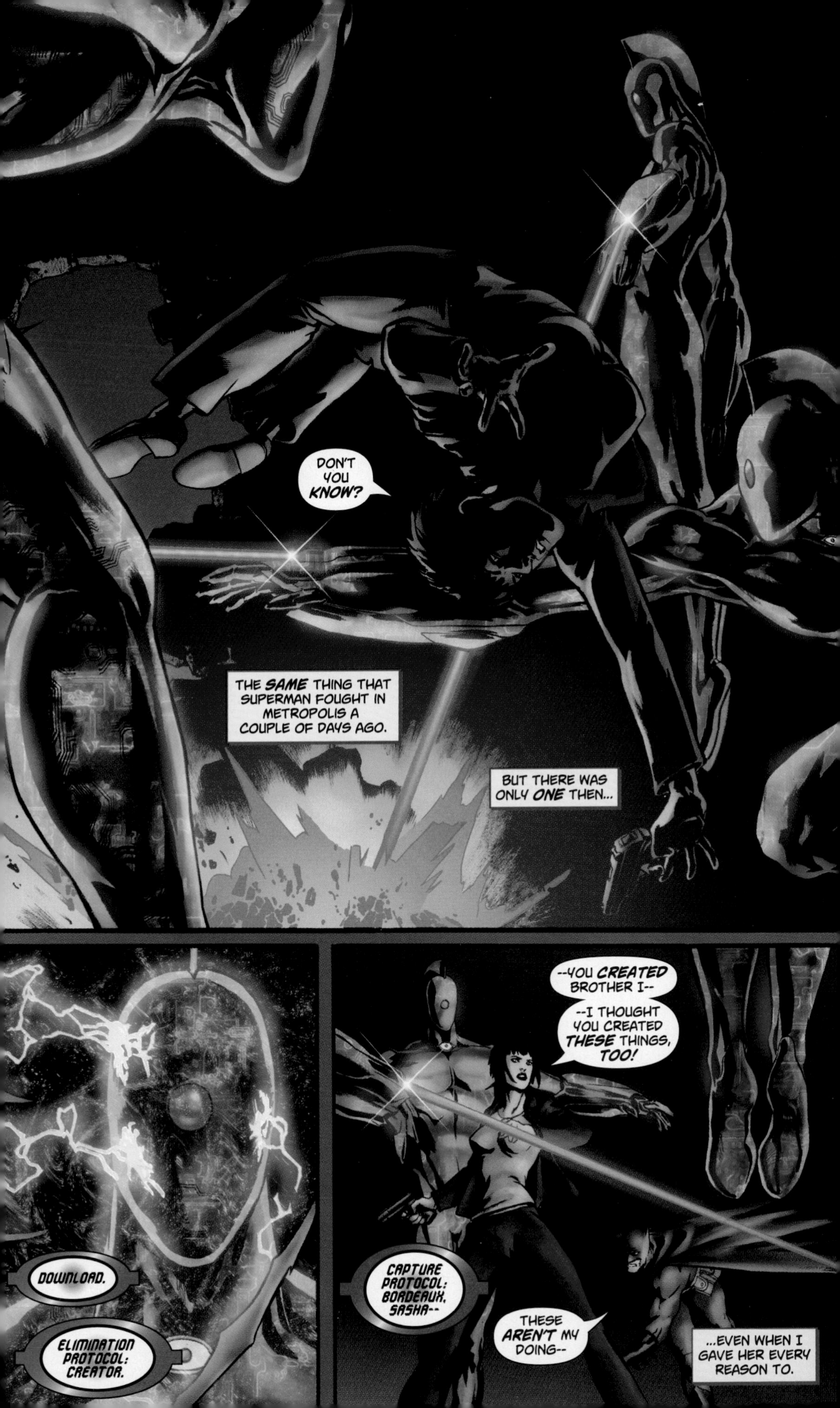
DON'T YOU KNOW?
THE SAME THING THAT SUPERMAN FOUGHT IN METROPOLIS A COUPLE OF DAYS AGO.
BUT THERE WAS ONLY ONE THEN...
DOWNLOAD.
ELIMINATION PROTOCOL: CREATOR.
--YOU CREATED BROTHER I--
--I THOUGHT YOU CREATED THESE THINGS, TOO!
CAPTURE PROTOCOL: BORDEAUX, SASHA--
THESE AREN'T MY DOING--
...EVEN WHEN I GAVE HER EVERY REASON TO.

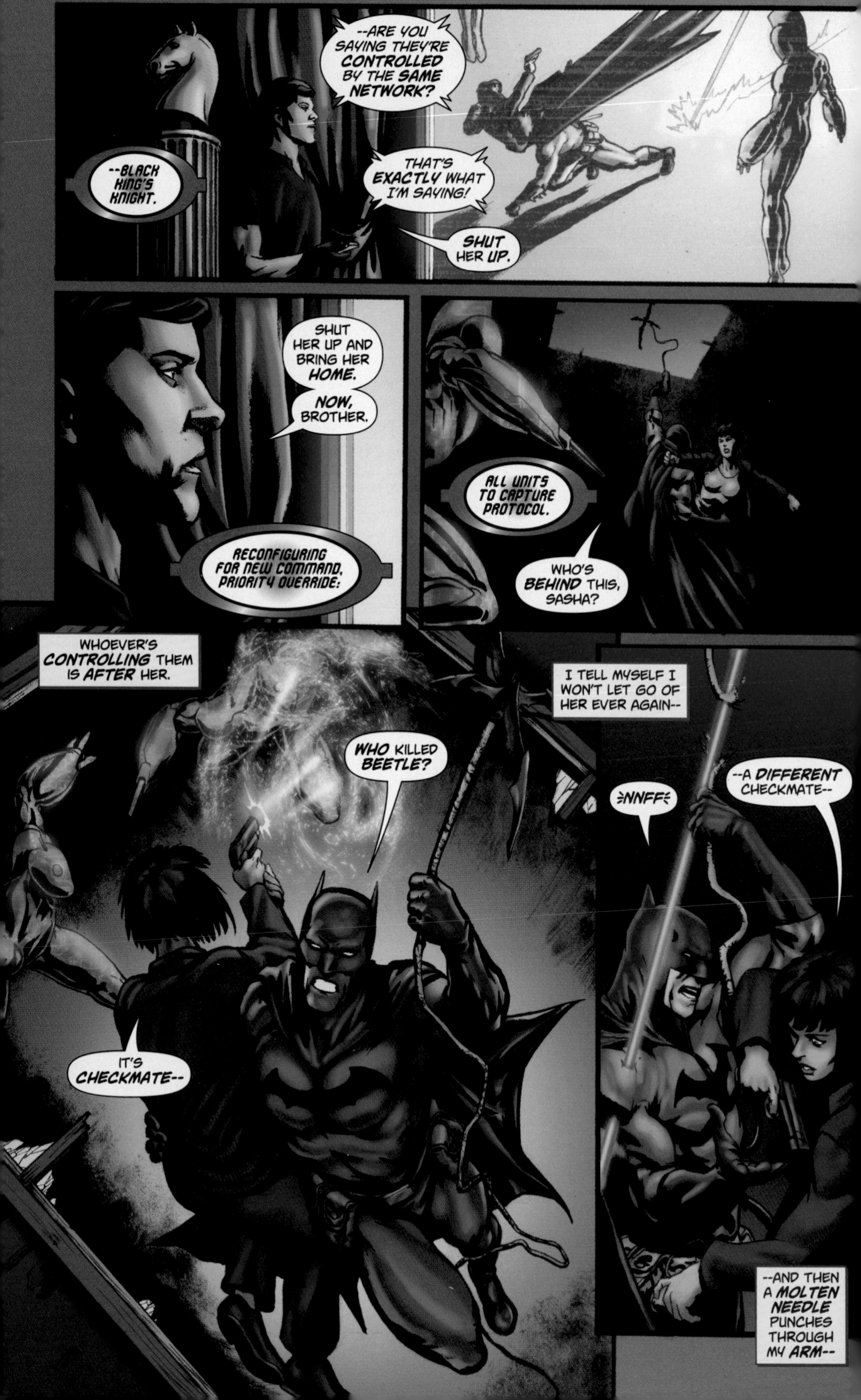
--ARE YOU SAYING THEY'RE CONTROLLED BY THE SAME NETWORK?
--BLACK KING'S KNIGHT.
THAT'S EXACTLY WHAT I'M SAYING!
SHUT HER UP.
SHUT HER UP AND BRING HER HOME.
NOW, BROTHER.
RECONFIGURING FOR NEW COMMAND, PRIORITY OVERRIDE:
ALL UNITS TO CAPTURE PROTOCOL.
WHO'S BEHIND THIS, SASHA?
WHOEVER'S CONTROLLING THEM IS AFTER HER.
WHO KILLED BEETLE?
IT'S CHECKMATE--
I TELL MYSELF I WON'T LET GO OF HER EVER AGAIN--
NNFF
--A DIFFERENT CHECKMATE--
--AND THEN A MOLTEN NEEDLE PUNCHES THROUGH MY ARM--

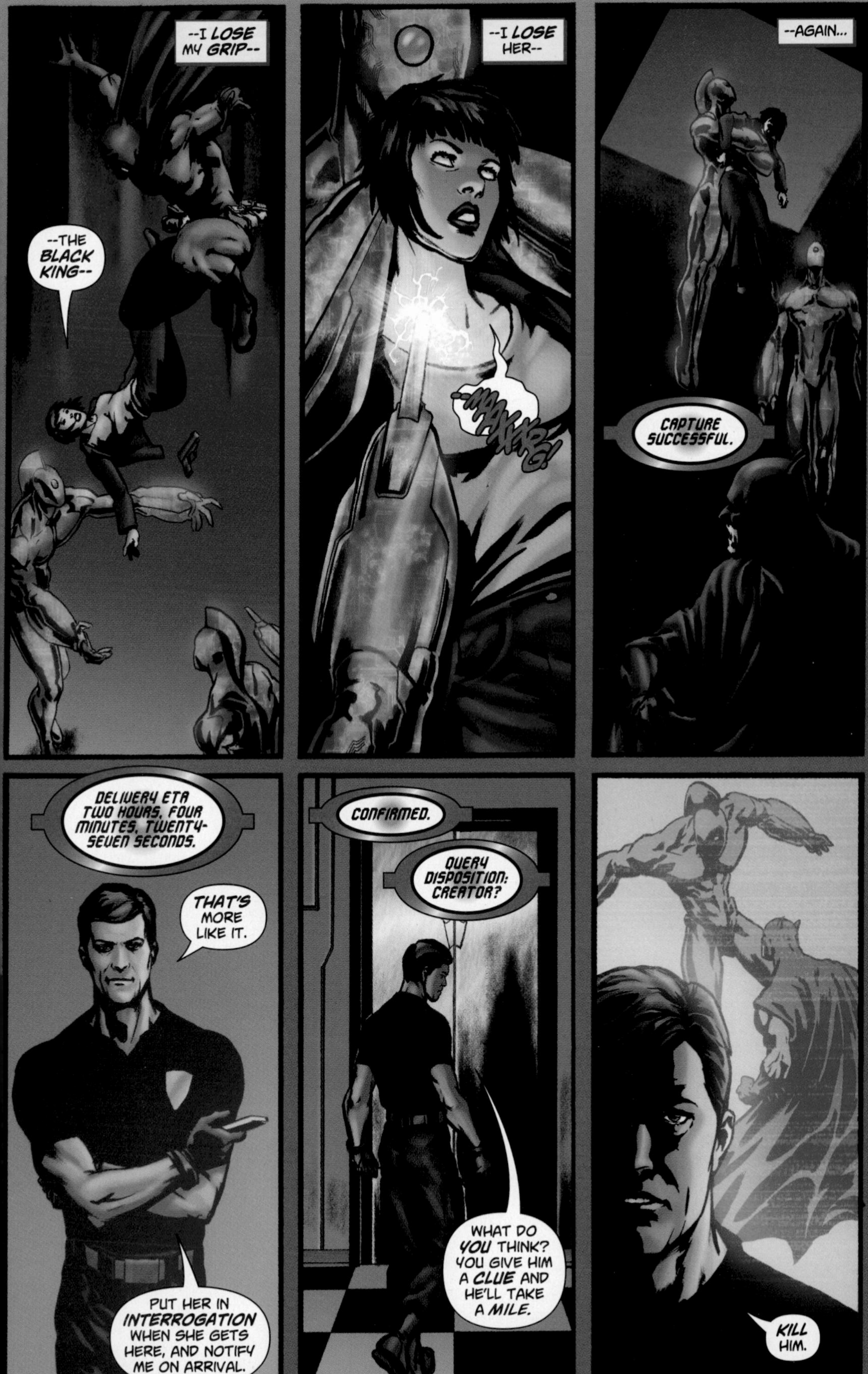
--I LOSE MY GRIP--
--THE BLACK KING--
--I LOSE HER--
-MAAAARG!
--AGAIN...
CAPTURE SUCCESSFUL.
DELIVERY ETA TWO HOURS, FOUR MINUTES, TWENTY-SEVEN SECONDS.
THAT'S MORE LIKE IT.
PUT HER IN INTERROGATION WHEN SHE GETS HERE, AND NOTIFY ME ON ARRIVAL.
CONFIRMED.
QUERY DISPOSITION: CREATOR?
WHAT DO YOU THINK? YOU GIVE HIM A CLUE AND HE'LL TAKE A MILE.
KILL HIM.

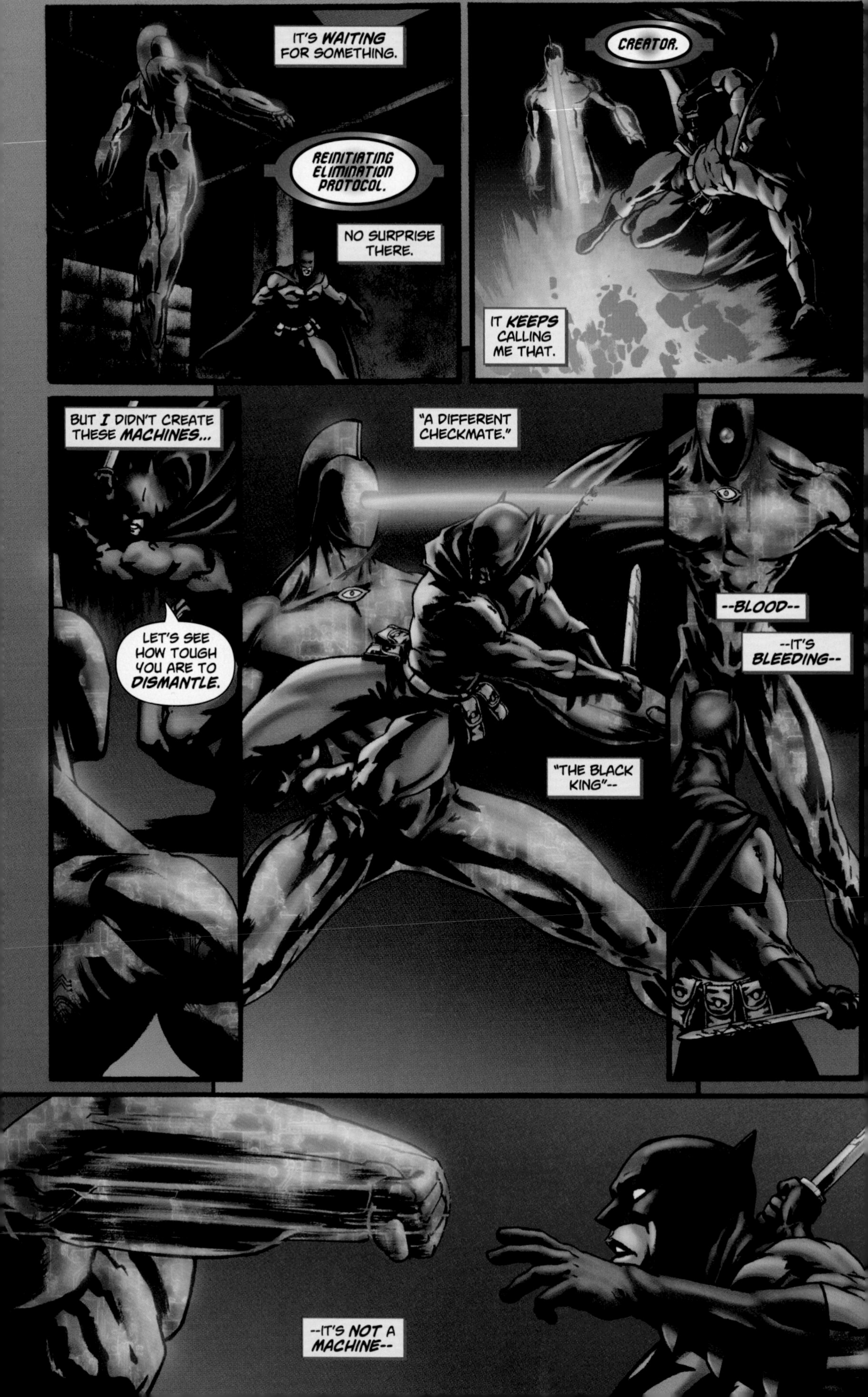
IT'S WAITING FOR SOMETHING.
REINITIATING ELIMINATION PROTOCOL.
NO SURPRISE THERE.
CREATOR.
IT KEEPS CALLING ME THAT.
BUT I DIDN'T CREATE THESE MACHINES...
"A DIFFERENT CHECKMATE."
LET'S SEE HOW TOUGH YOU ARE TO DISMANTLE.
"THE BLACK KING"--
--BLOOD--
--IT'S BLEEDING--
--IT'S NOT A MACHINE--

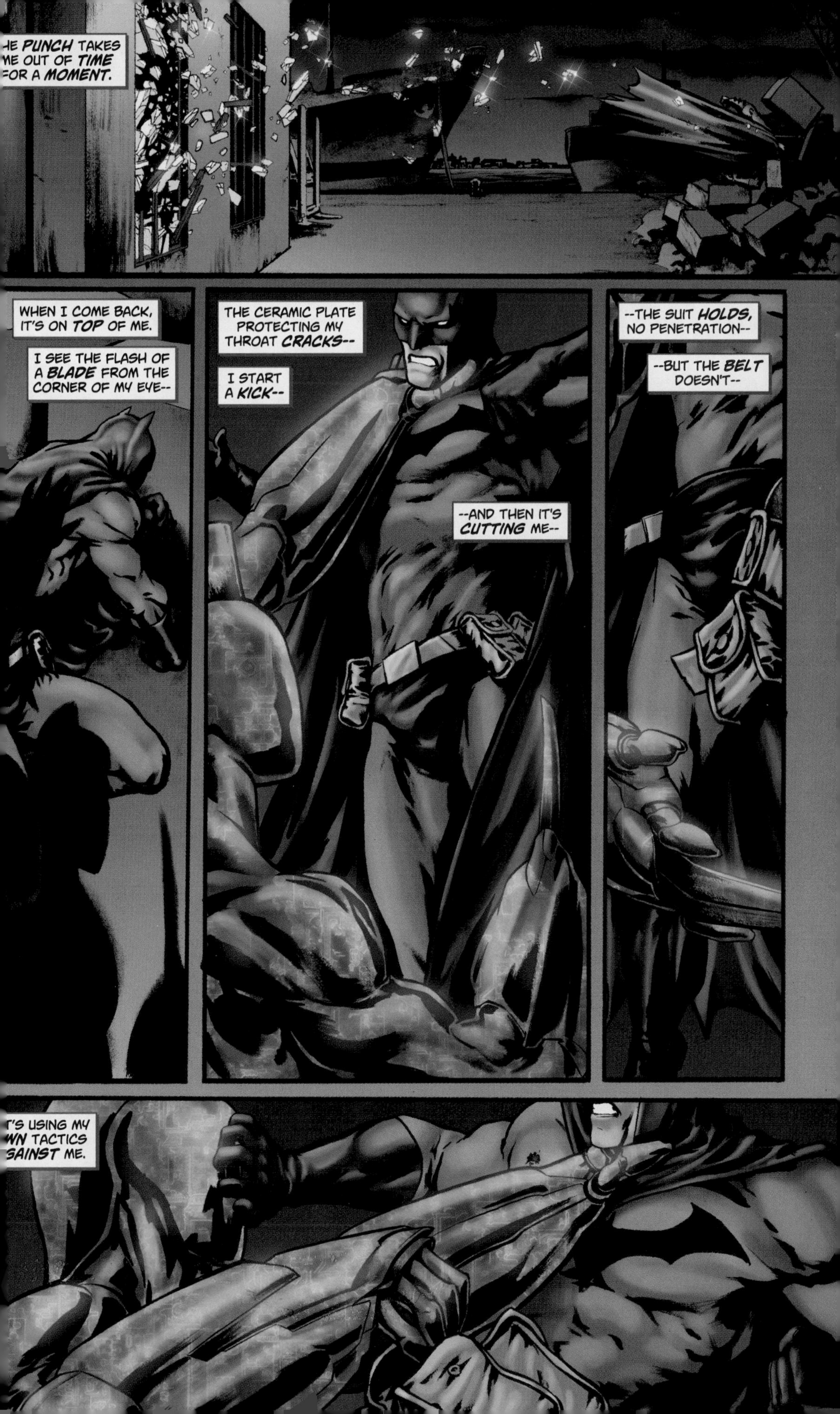
HE PUNCH TAKES ME OUT OF TIME FOR A MOMENT.
WHEN I COME BACK, IT'S ON TOP OF ME.
I SEE THE FLASH OF A BLADE FROM THE CORNER OF MY EYE--
THE CERAMIC PLATE PROTECTING MY THROAT CRACKS--
I START A KICK--
--AND THEN IT'S CUTTING ME--
--THE SUIT HOLDS, NO PENETRATION--
--BUT THE BELT DOESN'T--
T'S USING MY WN TACTICS GAINST ME.

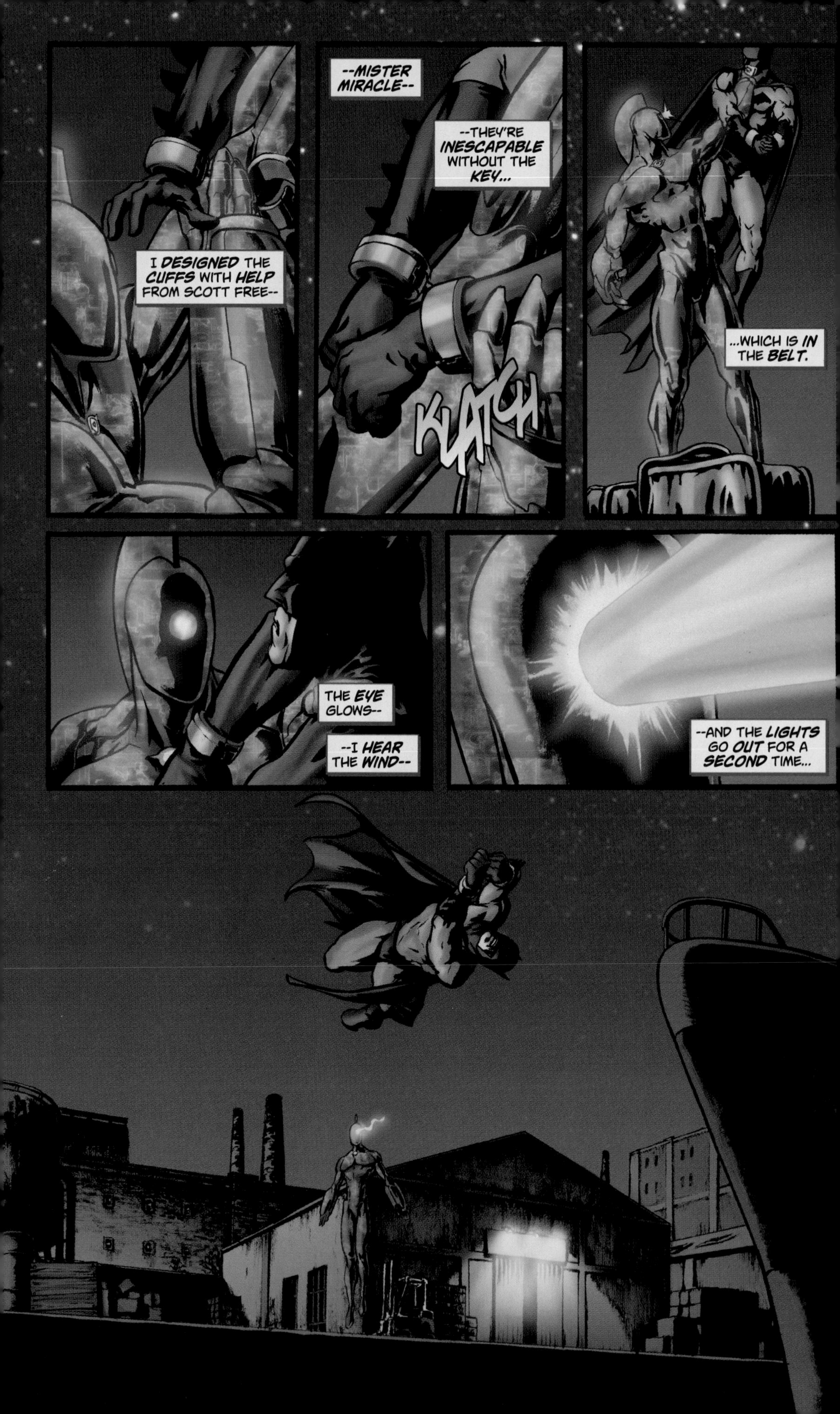
I DESIGNED THE CUFFS WITH HELP FROM SCOTT FREE--
--MISTER MIRACLE--
--THEY'RE INESCAPABLE WITHOUT THE KEY...
KLATCH
...WHICH IS IN THE BELT.
THE EYE GLOWS--
--I HEAR THE WIND--
--AND THE LIGHTS GO OUT FOR A SECOND TIME...

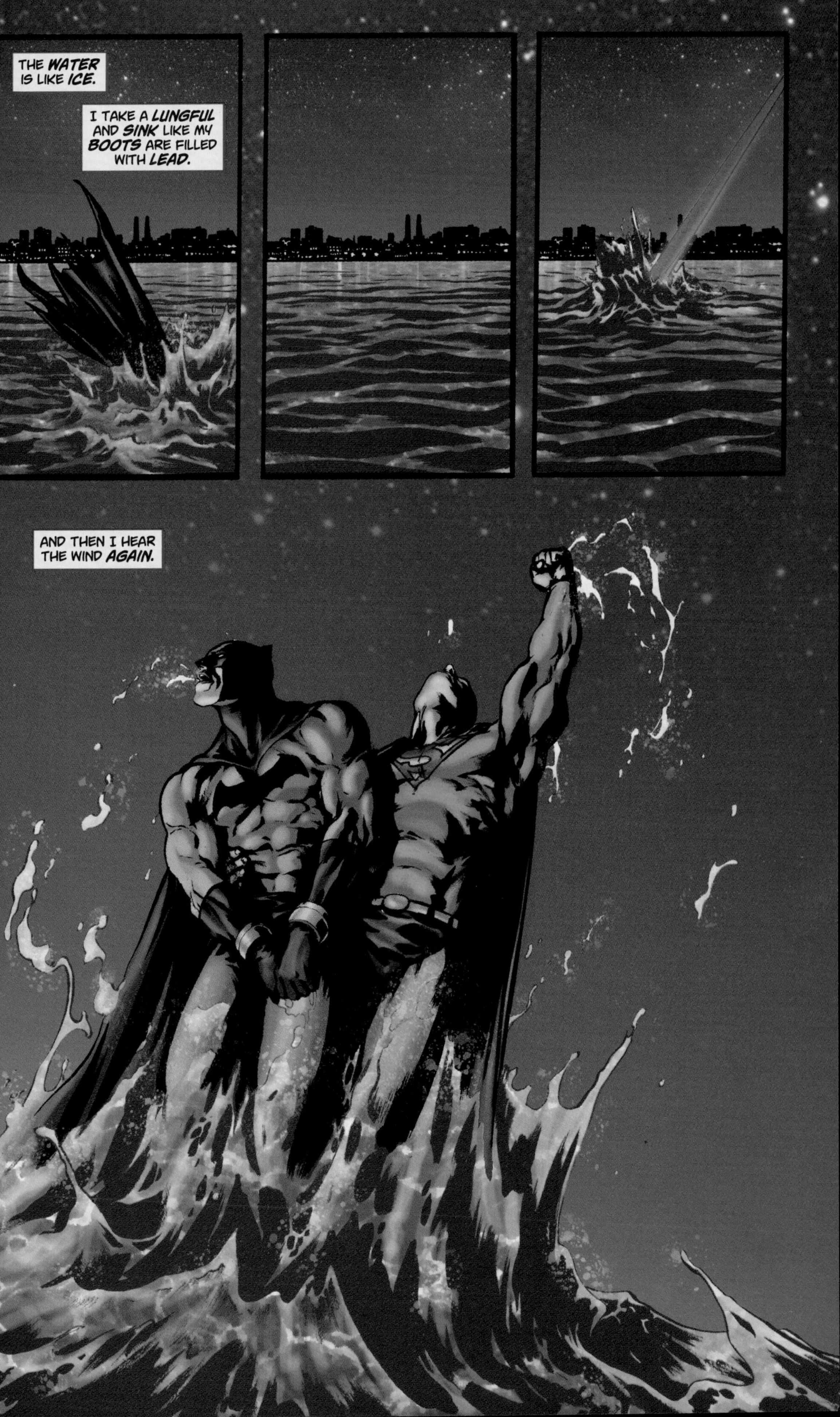
THE WATER IS LIKE ICE.
I TAKE A LUNGFUL AND SINK LIKE MY BOOTS ARE FILLED WITH LEAD.
AND THEN I HEAR THE WIND AGAIN.

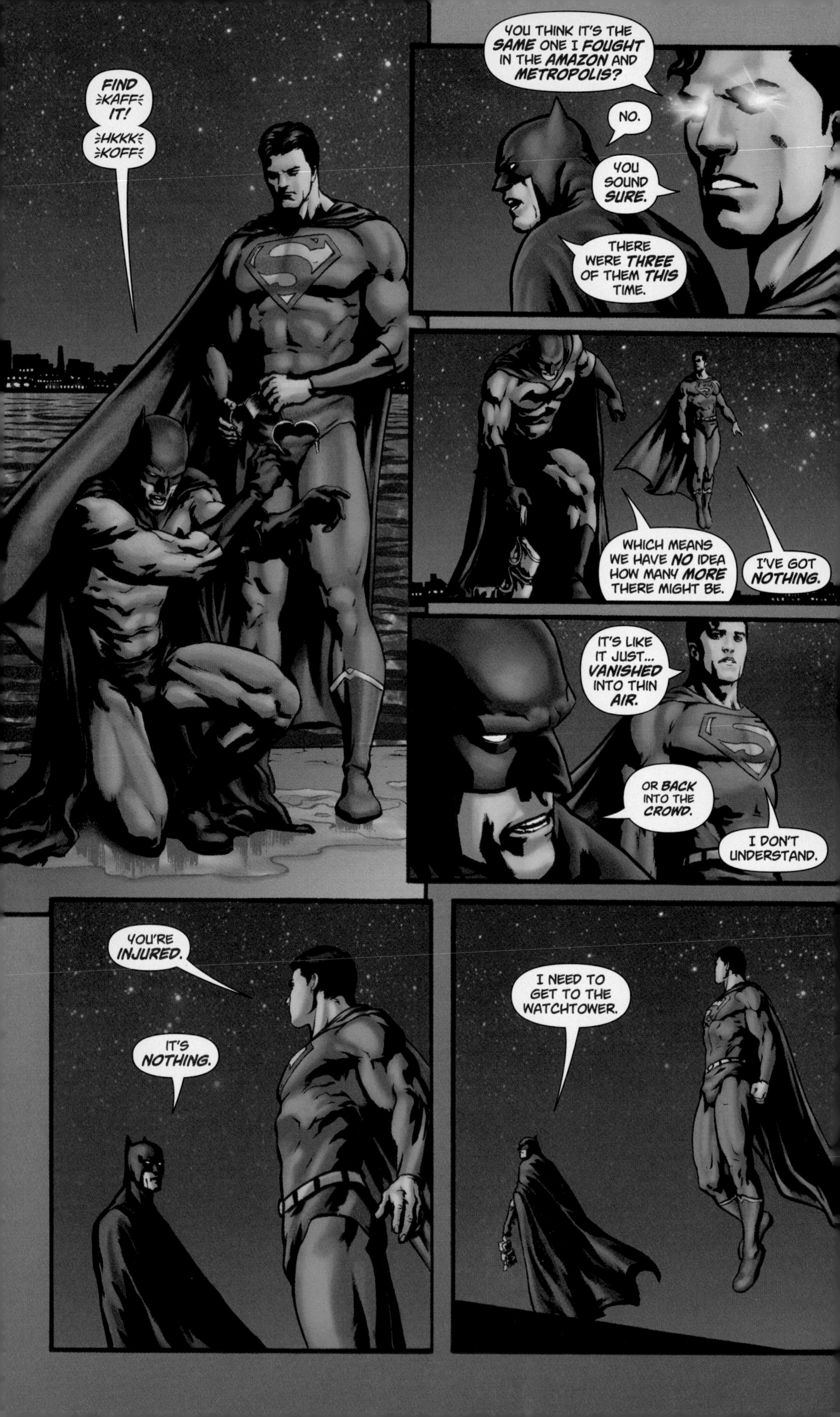
FIND ⪡KAFF⪢ IT!
⪡HKKK⪢ ⪡KOFF⪢
YOU THINK IT'S THE SAME ONE I FOUGHT IN THE AMAZON AND METROPOLIS?
NO.
YOU SOUND SURE.
THERE WERE THREE OF THEM THIS TIME.
WHICH MEANS WE HAVE NO IDEA HOW MANY MORE THERE MIGHT BE.
I'VE GOT NOTHING.
IT'S LIKE IT JUST... VANISHED INTO THIN AIR.
OR BACK INTO THE CROWD.
I DON'T UNDERSTAND.
YOU'RE INJURED.
IT'S NOTHING.
I NEED TO GET TO THE WATCHTOWER.

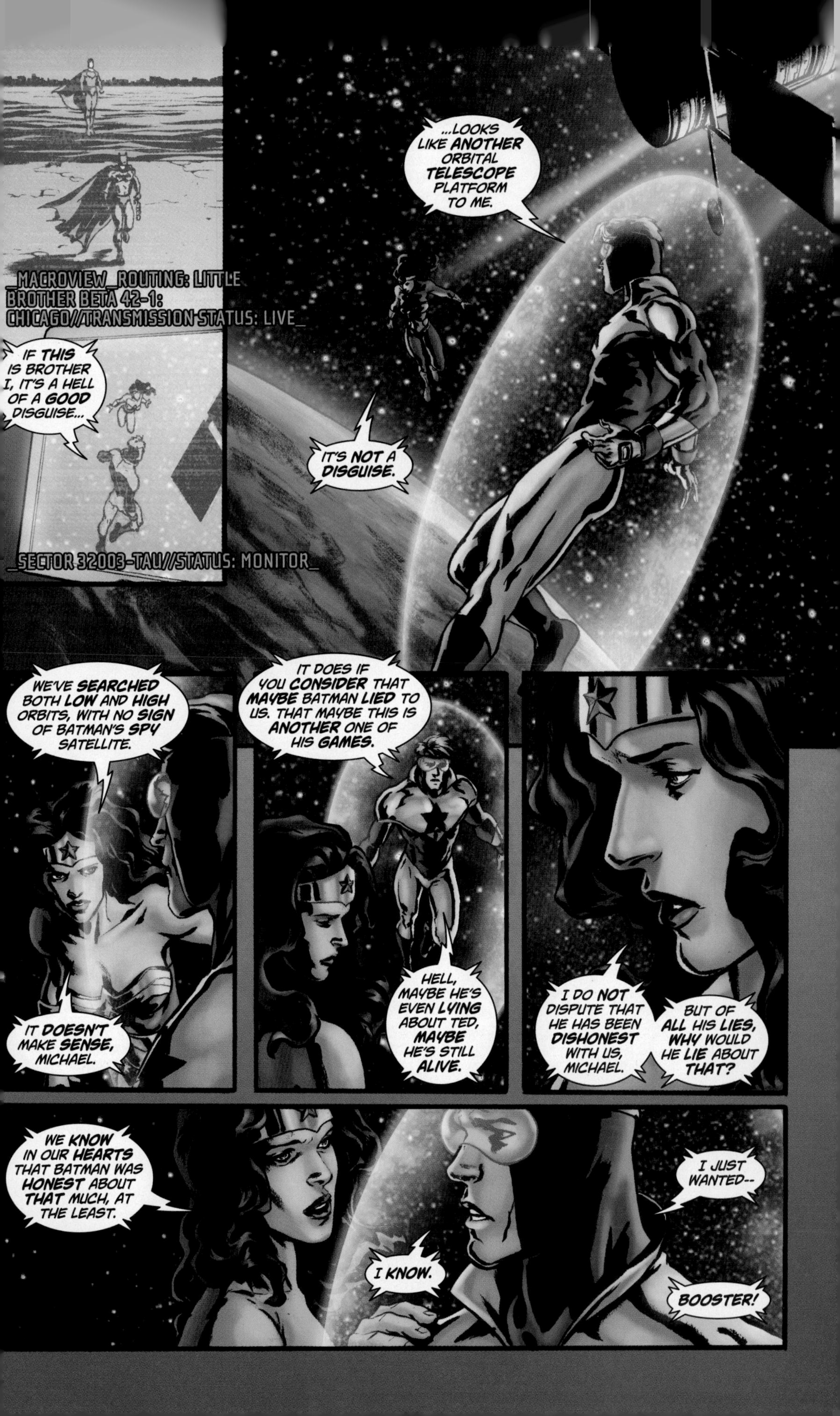
_MACROVIEW_ROUTING: LITTLE BROTHER BETA 42-1: CHICAGO//TRANSMISSION STATUS: LIVE_
IF THIS IS BROTHER I, IT'S A HELL OF A GOOD DISGUISE...
SECTOR 32003-TAU//STATUS: MONITOR
...LOOKS LIKE ANOTHER ORBITAL TELESCOPE PLATFORM TO ME.
IT'S NOT A DISGUISE.
WE'VE SEARCHED BOTH LOW AND HIGH ORBITS, WITH NO SIGN OF BATMAN'S SPY SATELLITE.
IT DOESN'T MAKE SENSE, MICHAEL.
IT DOES IF YOU CONSIDER THAT MAYBE BATMAN LIED TO US. THAT MAYBE THIS IS ANOTHER ONE OF HIS GAMES.
HELL, MAYBE HE'S EVEN LYING ABOUT TED, MAYBE HE'S STILL ALIVE.
I DO NOT DISPUTE THAT HE HAS BEEN DISHONEST WITH US, MICHAEL.
BUT OF ALL HIS LIES, WHY WOULD HE LIE ABOUT THAT?
WE KNOW IN OUR HEARTS THAT BATMAN WAS HONEST ABOUT THAT MUCH, AT THE LEAST.
I JUST WANTED--
I KNOW.
BOOSTER!

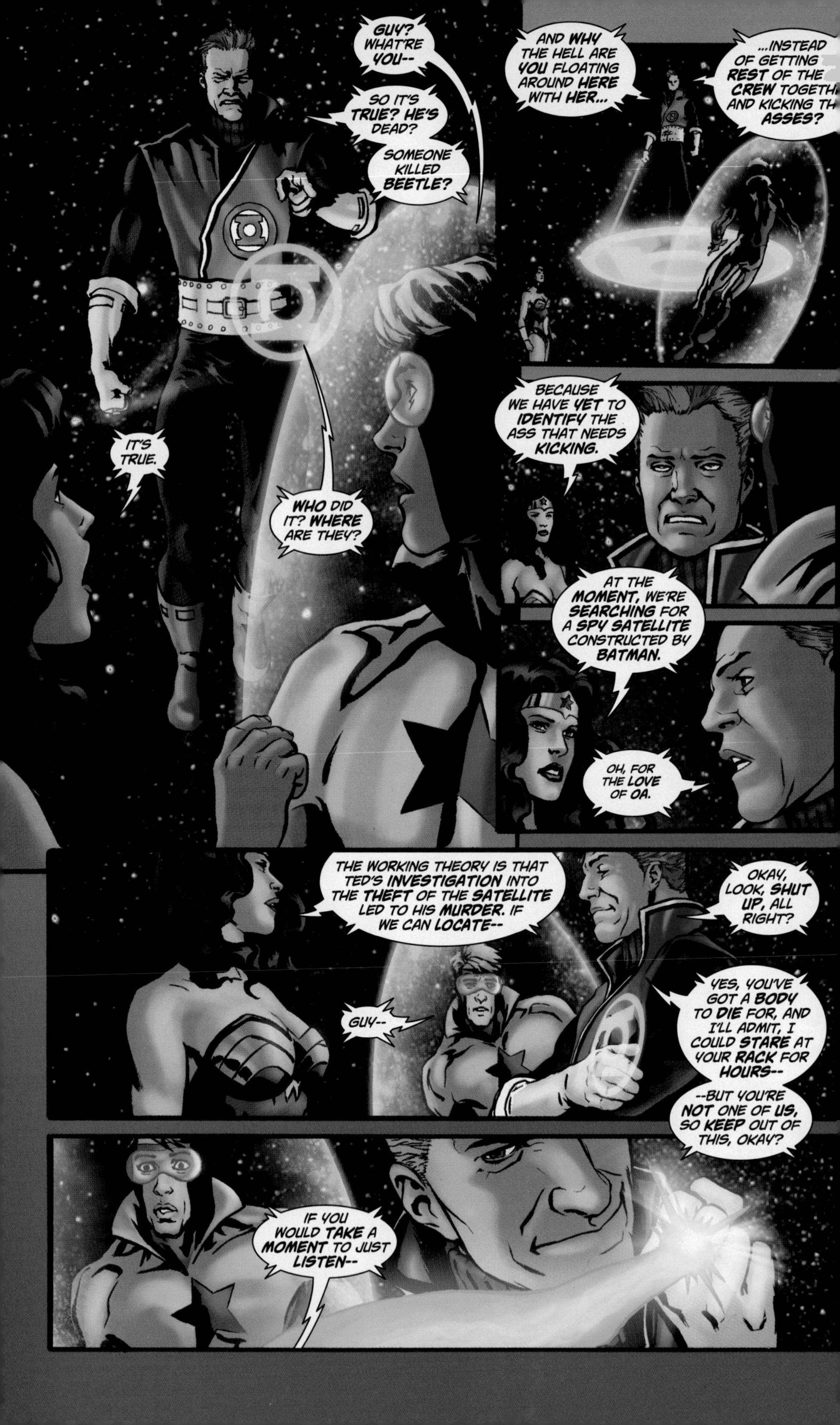
GUY? WHAT'RE YOU--
SO IT'S TRUE? HE'S DEAD?
SOMEONE KILLED BEETLE?
IT'S TRUE.
WHO DID IT? WHERE ARE THEY?
AND WHY THE HELL ARE YOU FLOATING AROUND HERE WITH HER...
...INSTEAD OF GETTING REST OF THE CREW TOGETH AND KICKING TH ASSES?
BECAUSE WE HAVE YET TO IDENTIFY THE ASS THAT NEEDS KICKING.
AT THE MOMENT, WE'RE SEARCHING FOR A SPY SATELLITE CONSTRUCTED BY BATMAN.
OH, FOR THE LOVE OF OA.
THE WORKING THEORY IS THAT TED'S INVESTIGATION INTO THE THEFT OF THE SATELLITE LED TO HIS MURDER. IF WE CAN LOCATE--
OKAY, LOOK, SHUT UP, ALL RIGHT?
GUY--
YES, YOU'VE GOT A BODY TO DIE FOR, AND I'LL ADMIT, I COULD STARE AT YOUR RACK FOR HOURS--
--BUT YOU'RE NOT ONE OF US, SO KEEP OUT OF THIS, OKAY?
IF YOU WOULD TAKE A MOMENT TO JUST LISTEN--

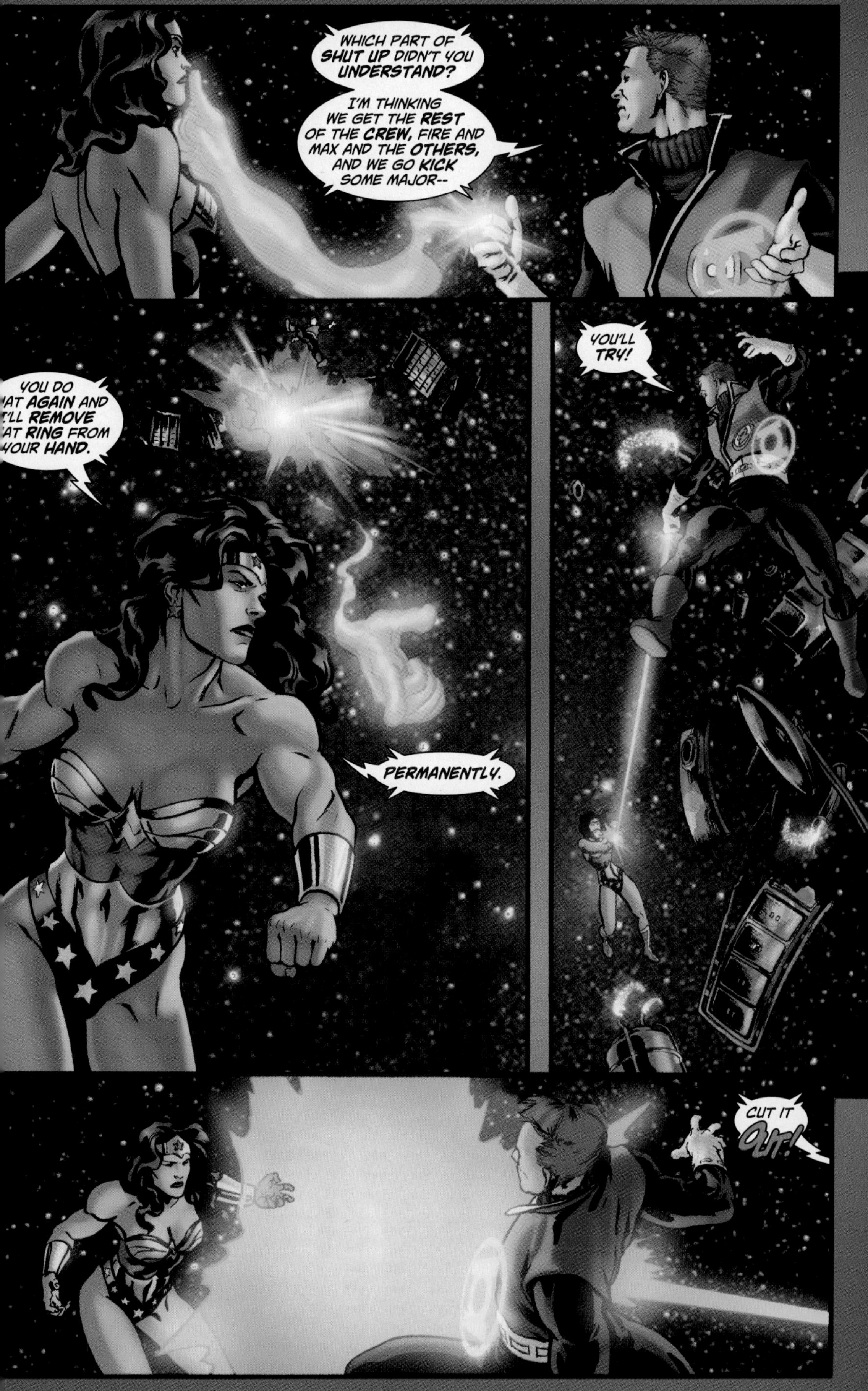

WHICH PART OF SHUT UP DIDN'T YOU UNDERSTAND?
I'M THINKING WE GET THE REST OF THE CREW, FIRE AND MAX AND THE OTHERS, AND WE GO KICK SOME MAJOR--
YOU DO
AT AGAIN AND
'LL REMOVE
AT RING FROM
YOUR HAND.
PERMANENTLY.
YOU'LL TRY!
CUT IT OUT!

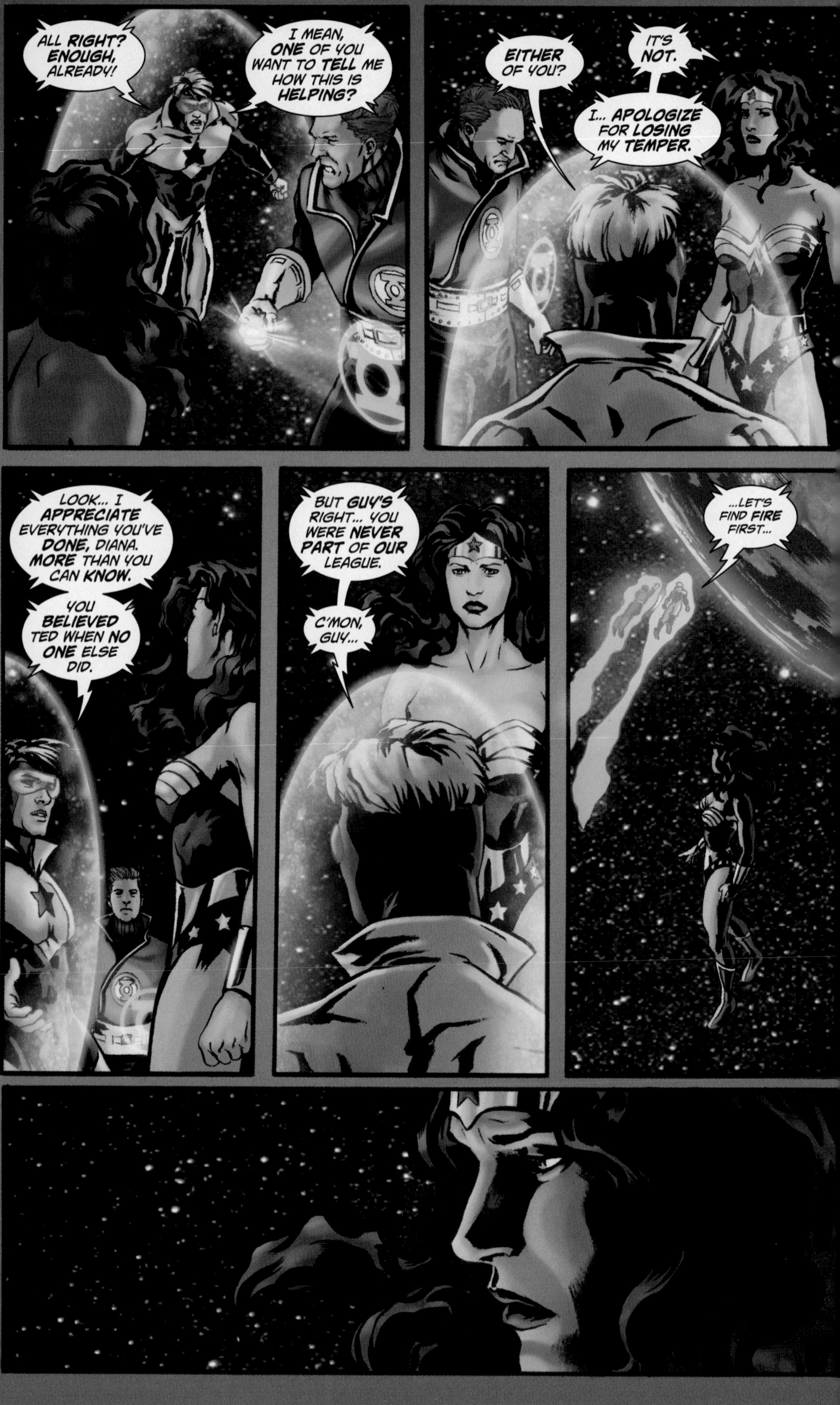

ALL RIGHT? ENOUGH, ALREADY!
I MEAN, ONE OF YOU WANT TO TELL ME HOW THIS IS HELPING?
EITHER OF YOU?
IT'S NOT.
I... APOLOGIZE FOR LOSING MY TEMPER.
LOOK... I APPRECIATE EVERYTHING YOU'VE DONE, DIANA. MORE THAN YOU CAN KNOW.
YOU BELIEVED TED WHEN NO ONE ELSE DID.
BUT GUY'S RIGHT... YOU WERE NEVER PART OF OUR LEAGUE.
C'MON, GUY...
...LET'S FIND FIRE FIRST...

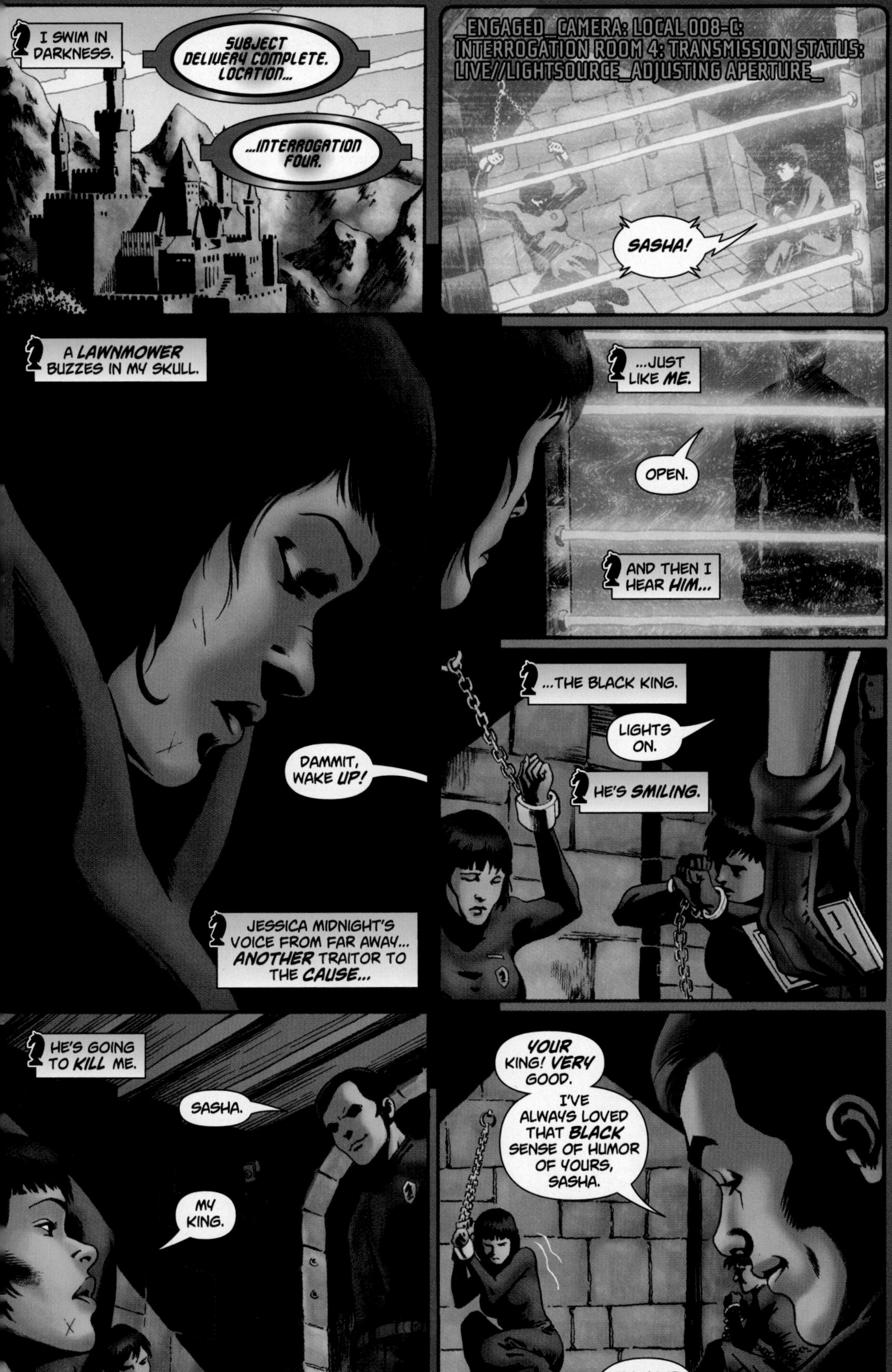
I SWIM IN DARKNESS.
SUBJECT DELIVERY COMPLETE. LOCATION...
...INTERROGATION FOUR.
_ENGAGED_CAMERA: LOCAL 008-C: INTERROGATION ROOM 4: TRANSMISSION STATUS: LIVE//LIGHTSOURCE_ADJUSTING APERTURE_
SASHA!
A LAWNMOWER BUZZES IN MY SKULL.
DAMMIT, WAKE UP!
JESSICA MIDNIGHT'S VOICE FROM FAR AWAY... ANOTHER TRAITOR TO THE CAUSE...
...JUST LIKE ME.
OPEN.
AND THEN I HEAR HIM...
...THE BLACK KING.
LIGHTS ON.
HE'S SMILING.
HE'S GOING TO KILL ME.
SASHA.
MY KING.
YOUR KING! VERY GOOD.
I'VE ALWAYS LOVED THAT BLACK SENSE OF HUMOR OF YOURS, SASHA.
I'M YOUR KING, BUT NOT YOUR KNIGHT.

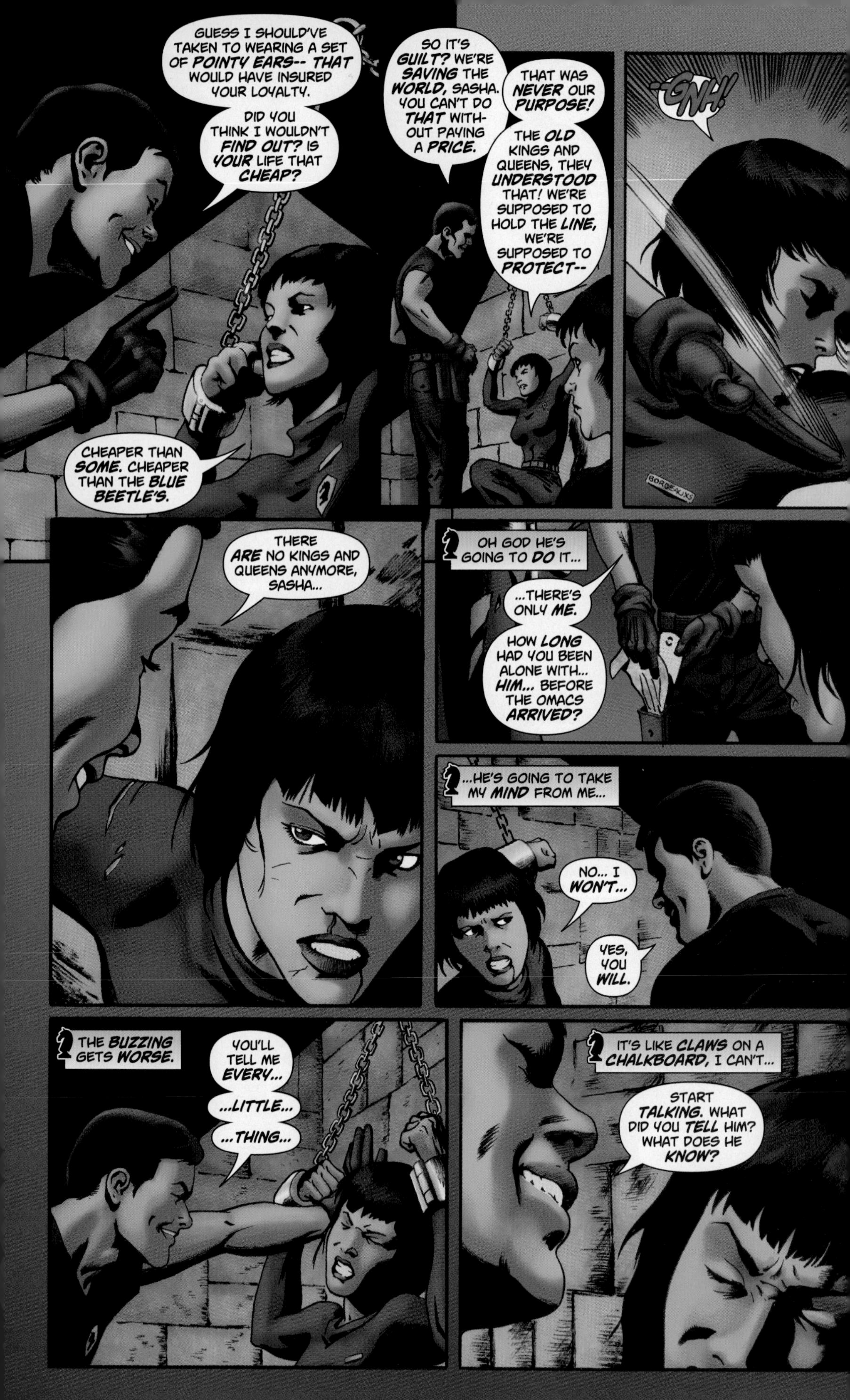
GUESS I SHOULD'VE TAKEN TO WEARING A SET OF POINTY EARS-- THAT WOULD HAVE INSURED YOUR LOYALTY.
DID YOU THINK I WOULDN'T FIND OUT? IS YOUR LIFE THAT CHEAP?
CHEAPER THAN SOME. CHEAPER THAN THE BLUE BEETLE'S.
SO IT'S GUILT? WE'RE SAVING THE WORLD, SASHA. YOU CAN'T DO THAT WITHOUT PAYING A PRICE.
THAT WAS NEVER OUR PURPOSE!
THE OLD KINGS AND QUEENS, THEY UNDERSTOOD THAT! WE'RE SUPPOSED TO HOLD THE LINE, WE'RE SUPPOSED TO PROTECT--
-GNH!
BORDEAUX
THERE ARE NO KINGS AND QUEENS ANYMORE, SASHA...
OH GOD HE'S GOING TO DO IT...
...THERE'S ONLY ME.
HOW LONG HAD YOU BEEN ALONE WITH... HIM... BEFORE THE OMACS ARRIVED?
...HE'S GOING TO TAKE MY MIND FROM ME...
NO... I WON'T...
YES, YOU WILL.
THE BUZZING GETS WORSE.
YOU'LL TELL ME EVERY...
...LITTLE...
...THING...
IT'S LIKE CLAWS ON A CHALKBOARD, I CAN'T...
START TALKING. WHAT DID YOU TELL HIM? WHAT DOES HE KNOW?

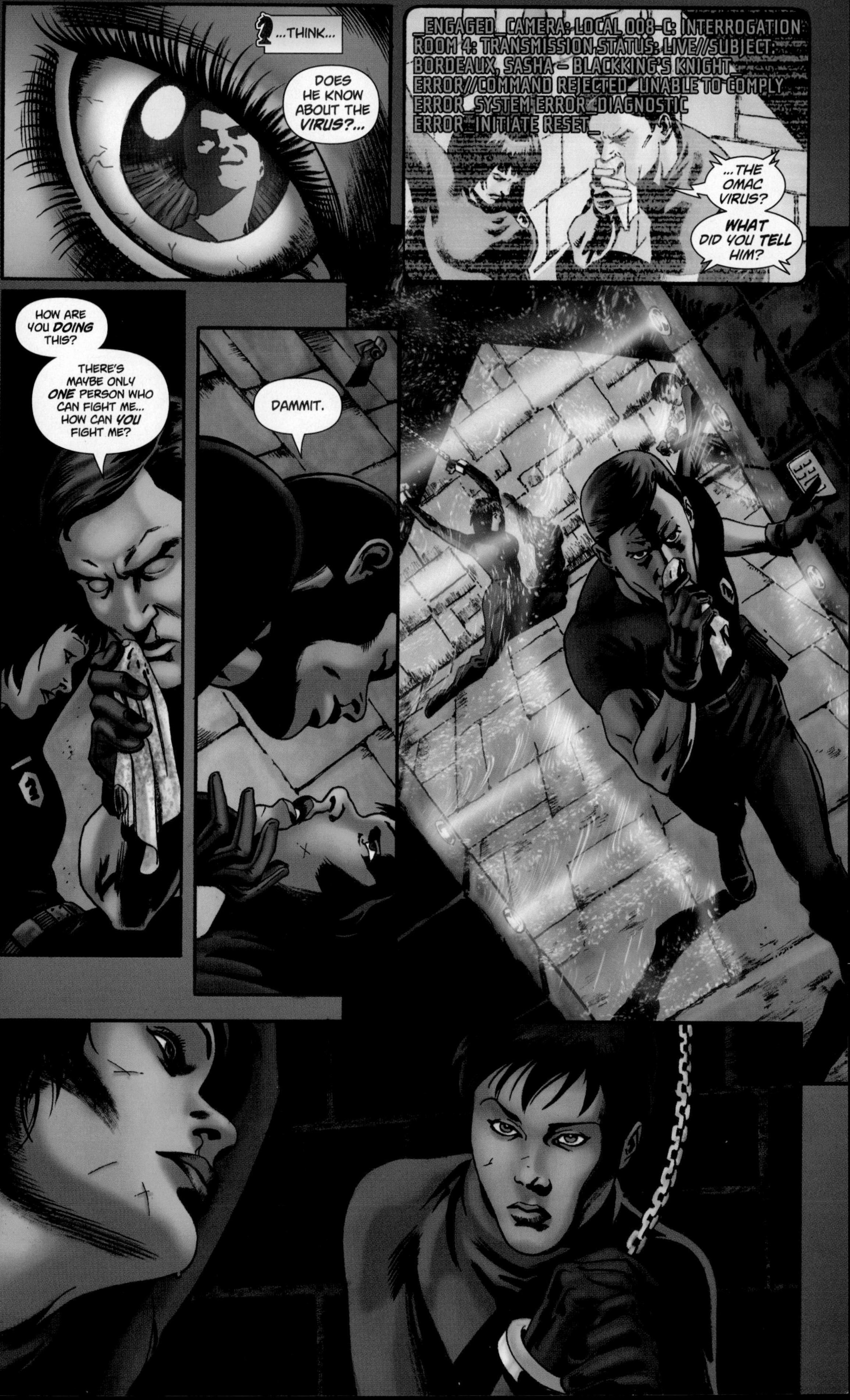
...THINK...
DOES HE KNOW ABOUT THE VIRUS?...
_ENGAGED_CAMERA: LOCAL 008-C: INTERROGATION ROOM 4: TRANSMISSION STATUS: LIVE//SUBJECT: BORDEAUX, SASHA – BLACKKING'S KNIGHT_ ERROR//COMMAND REJECTED_UNABLE TO COMPLY ERROR_SYSTEM ERROR_DIAGNOSTIC ERROR_INITIATE RESET_
...THE OMAC VIRUS?
WHAT DID YOU TELL HIM?
HOW ARE YOU DOING THIS?
THERE'S MAYBE ONLY ONE PERSON WHO CAN FIGHT ME... HOW CAN YOU FIGHT ME?
DAMMIT.

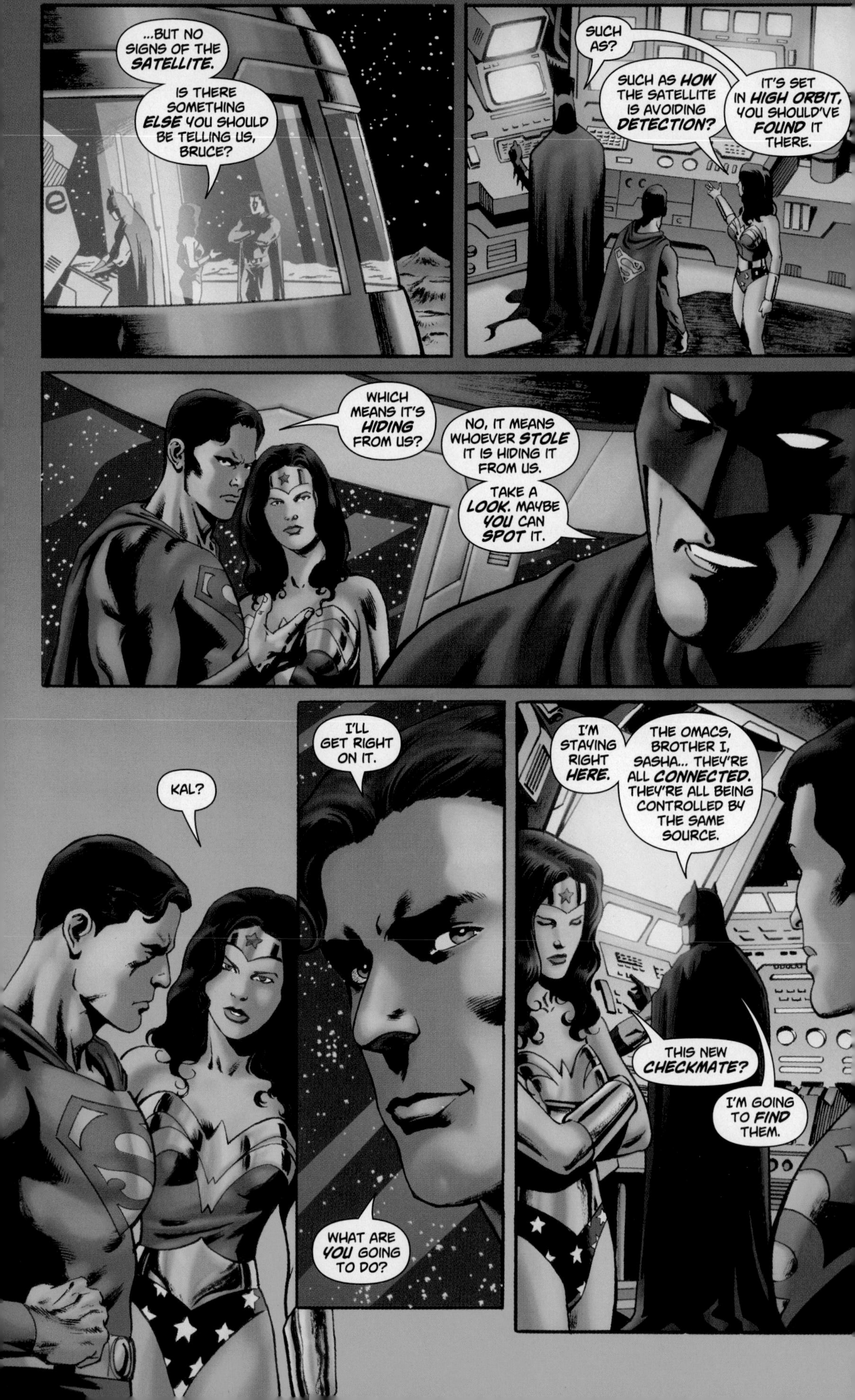
...BUT NO SIGNS OF THE SATELLITE.
IS THERE SOMETHING ELSE YOU SHOULD BE TELLING US, BRUCE?
SUCH AS?
SUCH AS HOW THE SATELLITE IS AVOIDING DETECTION?
IT'S SET IN HIGH ORBIT, YOU SHOULD'VE FOUND IT THERE.
WHICH MEANS IT'S HIDING FROM US?
NO, IT MEANS WHOEVER STOLE IT IS HIDING IT FROM US.
TAKE A LOOK. MAYBE YOU CAN SPOT IT.
KAL?
I'LL GET RIGHT ON IT.
WHAT ARE YOU GOING TO DO?
I'M STAYING RIGHT HERE.
THE OMACS, BROTHER I, SASHA... THEY'RE ALL CONNECTED. THEY'RE ALL BEING CONTROLLED BY THE SAME SOURCE.
THIS NEW CHECKMATE?
I'M GOING TO FIND THEM.

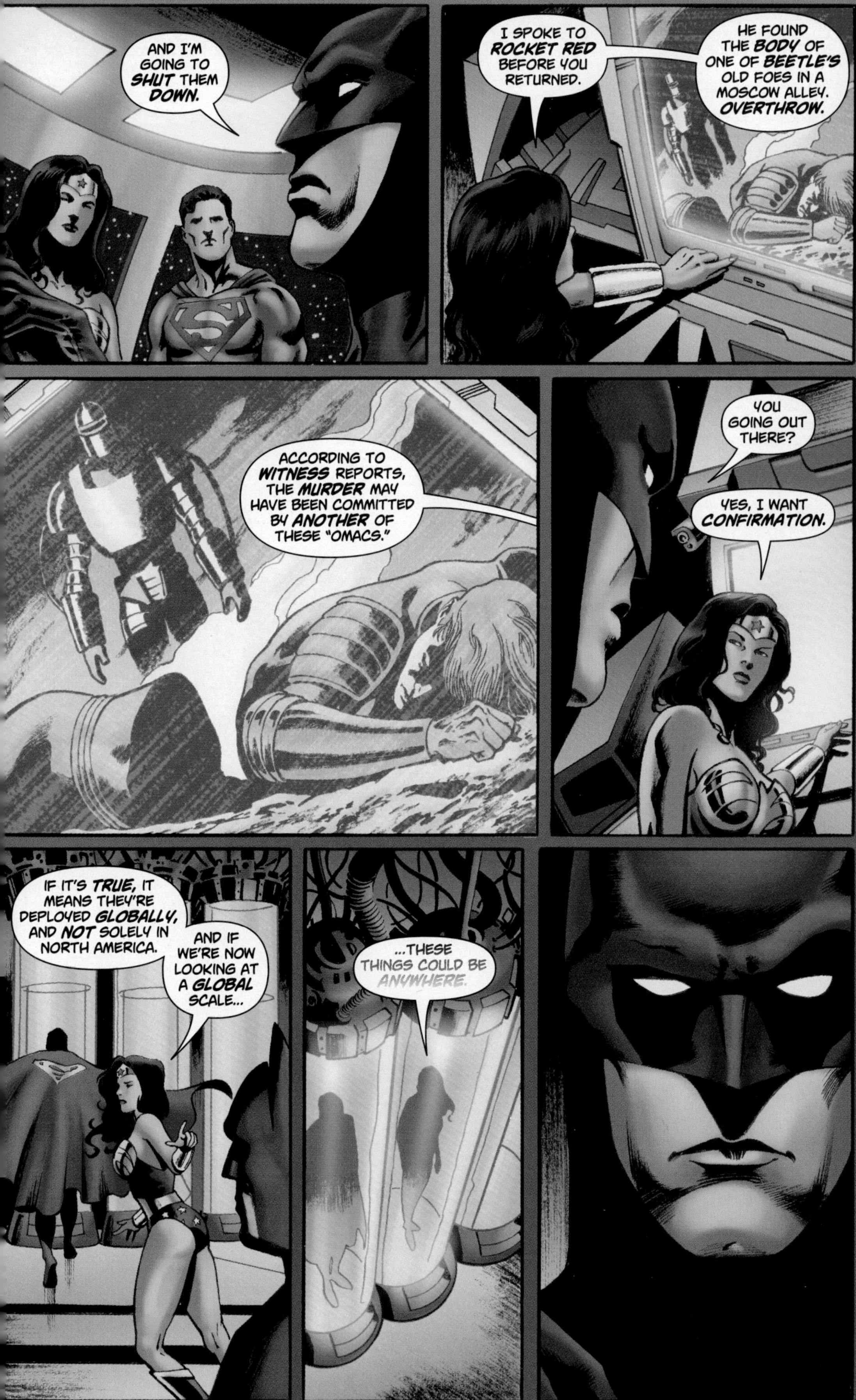
AND I'M GOING TO SHUT THEM DOWN.
I SPOKE TO ROCKET RED BEFORE YOU RETURNED.
HE FOUND THE BODY OF ONE OF BEETLE'S OLD FOES IN A MOSCOW ALLEY. OVERTHROW.
ACCORDING TO WITNESS REPORTS, THE MURDER MAY HAVE BEEN COMMITTED BY ANOTHER OF THESE "OMACS."
YOU GOING OUT THERE?
YES, I WANT CONFIRMATION.
IF IT'S TRUE, IT MEANS THEY'RE DEPLOYED GLOBALLY, AND NOT SOLELY IN NORTH AMERICA.
AND IF WE'RE NOW LOOKING AT A GLOBAL SCALE...
...THESE THINGS COULD BE ANYWHERE.

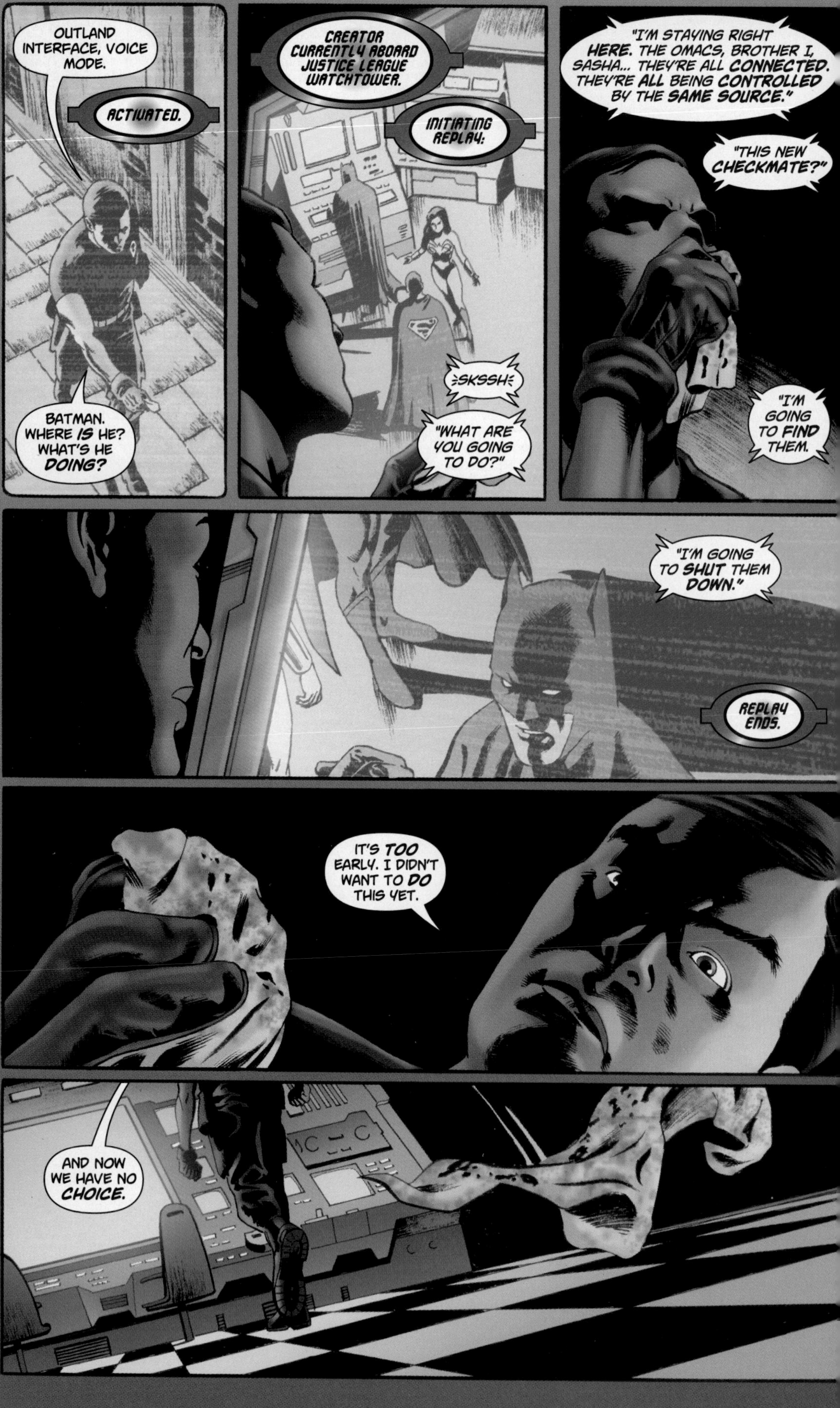
OUTLAND INTERFACE, VOICE MODE.
ACTIVATED.
BATMAN. WHERE IS HE? WHAT'S HE DOING?
CREATOR CURRENTLY ABOARD JUSTICE LEAGUE WATCHTOWER.
INITIATING REPLAY:
SKSSH
"WHAT ARE YOU GOING TO DO?"
"I'M STAYING RIGHT HERE. THE OMACS, BROTHER I, SASHA... THEY'RE ALL CONNECTED. THEY'RE ALL BEING CONTROLLED BY THE SAME SOURCE."
"THIS NEW CHECKMATE?"
"I'M GOING TO FIND THEM.
"I'M GOING TO SHUT THEM DOWN."
REPLAY ENDS.
IT'S TOO EARLY. I DIDN'T WANT TO DO THIS YET.
AND NOW WE HAVE NO CHOICE.

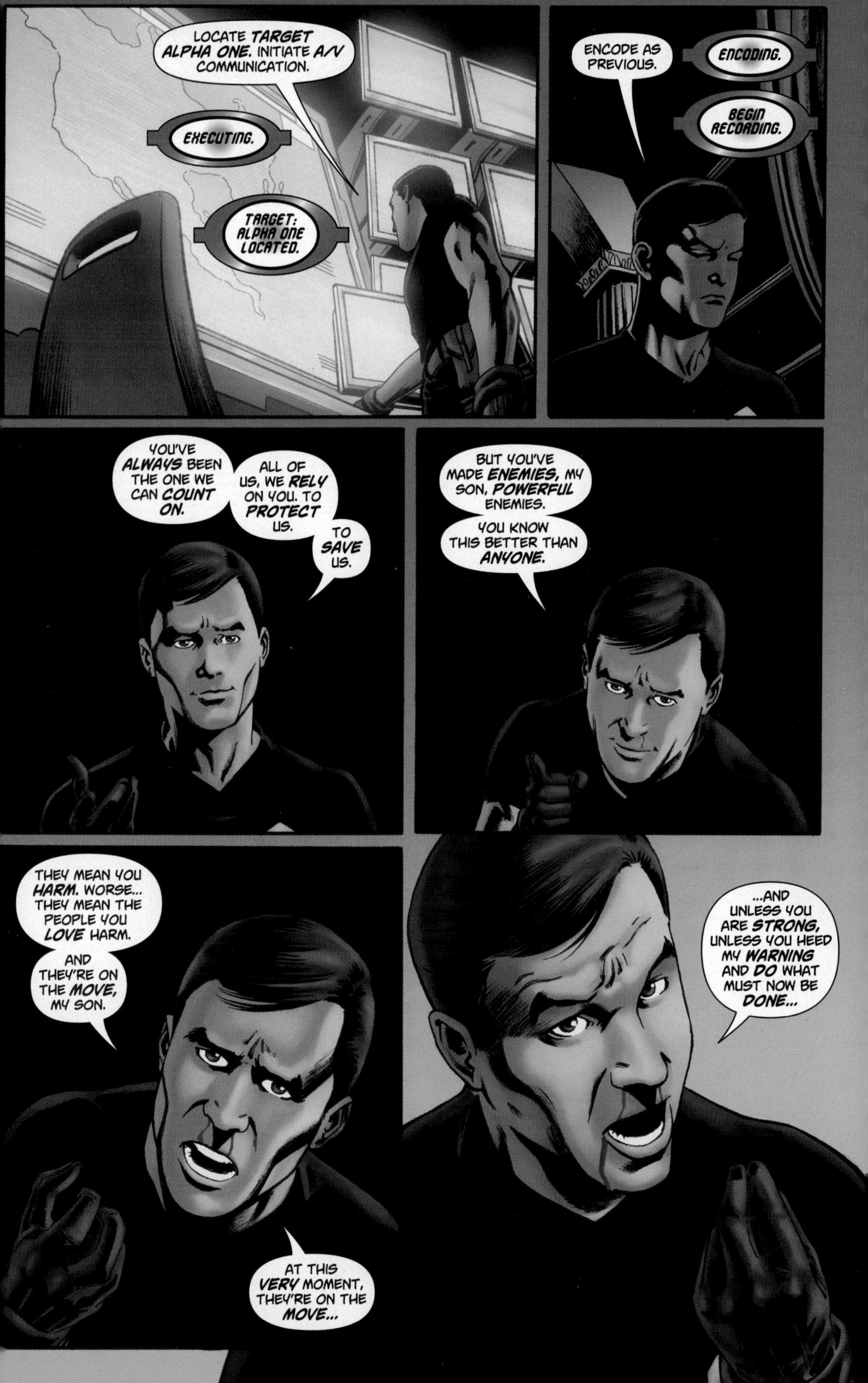
LOCATE TARGET ALPHA ONE. INITIATE A/V COMMUNICATION.
EXECUTING.
TARGET: ALPHA ONE LOCATED.
ENCODE AS PREVIOUS.
ENCODING.
BEGIN RECORDING.
YOU'VE ALWAYS BEEN THE ONE WE CAN COUNT ON.
ALL OF US, WE RELY ON YOU. TO PROTECT US.
TO SAVE US.
BUT YOU'VE MADE ENEMIES, MY SON, POWERFUL ENEMIES.
YOU KNOW THIS BETTER THAN ANYONE.
THEY MEAN YOU HARM. WORSE... THEY MEAN THE PEOPLE YOU LOVE HARM.
AND THEY'RE ON THE MOVE, MY SON.
AT THIS VERY MOMENT, THEY'RE ON THE MOVE...
...AND UNLESS YOU ARE STRONG, UNLESS YOU HEED MY WARNING AND DO WHAT MUST NOW BE DONE...

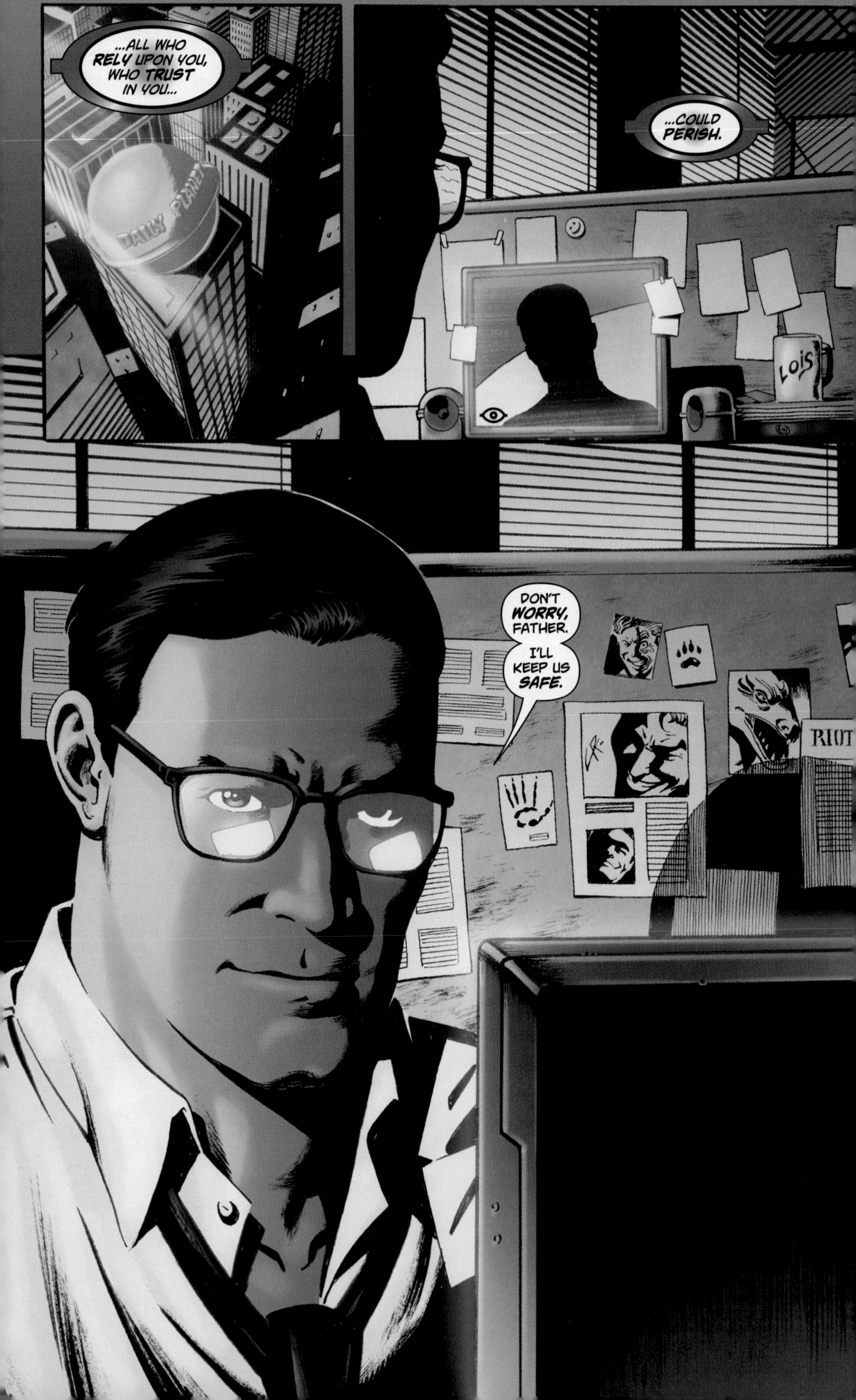
...ALL WHO RELY UPON YOU, WHO TRUST IN YOU...
DAILY PLANET
...COULD PERISH.
LOIS
DON'T WORRY, FATHER.
I'LL KEEP US SAFE.
RIOT

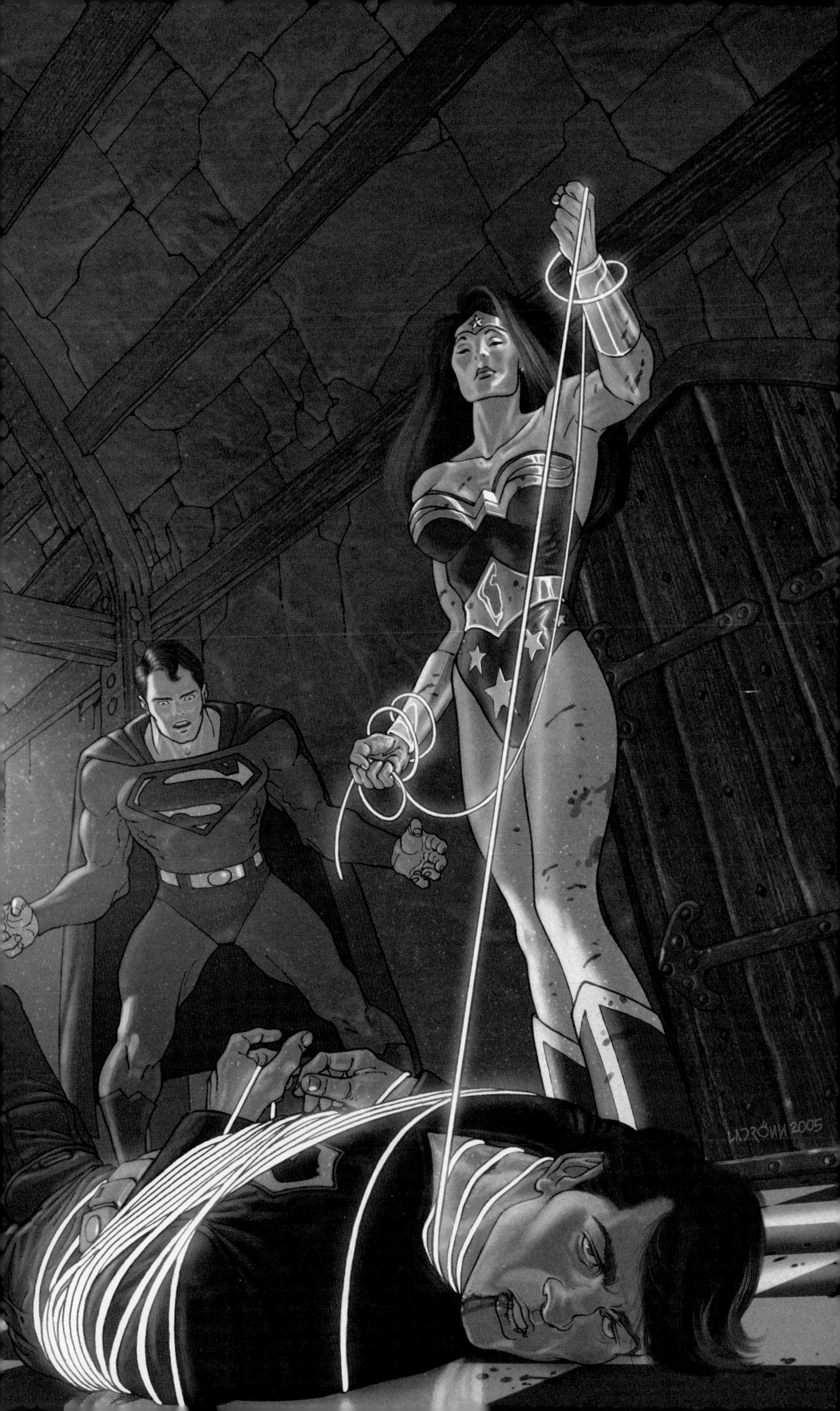

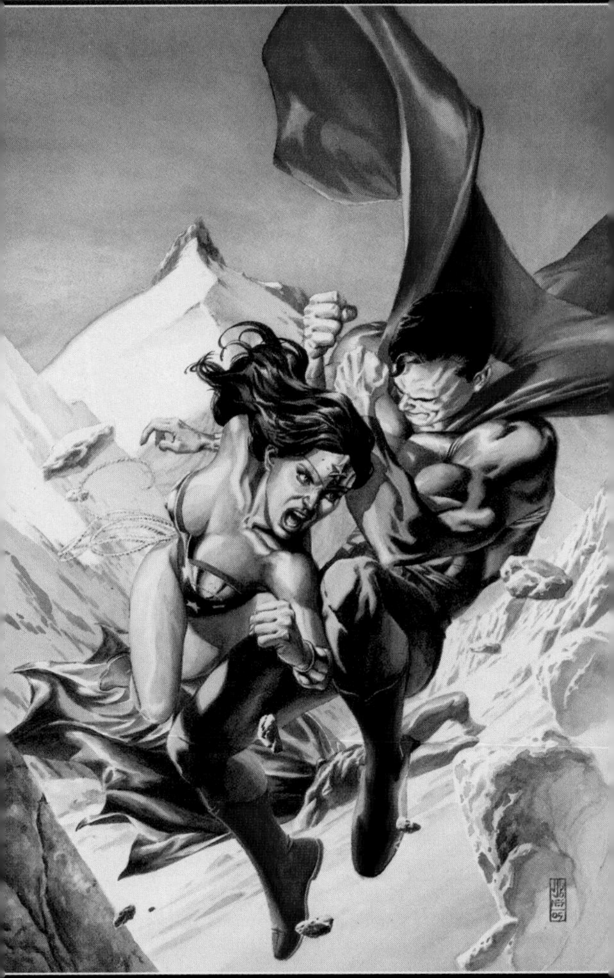

Greg Rucka

Writer

Rags Morales David Lopez Tom Derenick
Georges Jeanty Karl Kerschl
Mark Propst Bit Dexter Vines
Bob Petrecca Nelson

Artists

Richard & Tanya Horie

Colorists

Todd Klein

Letterer

Ladronn J.G. Jones

Original Covers

Wonder Woman created
by William Moulton Marston

PREVIOUSLY IN
SACRIFICE PART 1

"TOUCH"

Isolated in his fortress in Ecuador, the Man of Steel finds himself at a loss to explain how he came to be there, and why blood is dripping from his hands. As Superman searches his memory, he recalls strange events from the previous day:

Lois, seemingly oblivious to the presence of Brainiac, claiming that the villain was "only trying to be [Superman's] friend."

Brainiac taking over the Fortress's computer systems as well as the Superman robot stationed inside Superman's refuge.

A fateful showdown between Superman and Brainiac in his undersea lair, where Lois Lane, Jimmy Olsen, Lana Lang, and Perry White are killed.

Superman, going against his long-held code against killing, attempting to kill Brainiac for his crimes.

As Superman's recollections come to an end, he realizes that the blood on his hands is human, and thus cannot be Brainiac's. Before he can investigate further, members of the Justice League arrive, claiming their most powerful member has "much to answer for" and that "the safety of the world is at stake."

SUPERMAN #219

SACRIFICE PART 2

"END OF IDENTITY"

J'onn J'onzz startles Lois Lane in her and Superman's apartment, arriving with a mission to protect her from her own husband, claiming "Superman may be a deadly threat to every person he comes in contact with." Meanwhile, Earth's superheroes patrol other spots frequented by the Man of Steel, including the Kent Farm in Smallville and the offices of the Daily Planet.

In the Fortress, the JLA members tell Superman that they're worried about him, and help him revisit his memories of the previous day's events. This time, he remembers that it was not Brainiac he encountered at all and instead recalls:

Lois being abducted by the malevolent Darkseid, who took her to Apokolips as bait to lead Superman there.

On Apokolips, Darkseid forcing Superman to face him in a strange, Earth-style boxing match, with the lives of innocent people — including a brainwashed Lois — hanging in the balance if the fight lasts too long.

The Man of Steel triumphing over Darkseid, only to see the villain brutally murder Lois.

Superman, going against his long-held code against killing, attempting to kill Darkseid for his crimes.

After Superman's recollections come to an end, the Justice League members take him to the JLA Watchtower, where Superman is shocked to discover that the blood on his hands is Batman's. The Dark Knight lies comatose in a hospital bed.

ACTION COMICS #829

SACRIFICE PART 3

"REMEMBRANCE"

On the Watchtower, Superman struggles to come to grips with the news that he is responsible for Batman's injuries, which have left the Dark Knight struggling for life.

The JLA members show the Man of Steel security footage which reveals Batman using the Watchtower to try to locate the Brother Mk. I satellite. Batman is interrupted by Superman, who nearly kills him before Wonder Woman manages to stop his assault, causing Superman to flee before he can finish his attack.

Stunned by the footage, Superman recalls that it was not Brainiac or Darkseid he was fighting, but rather his more recent enemy, Ruin. But J'onn J'onzz helps Superman see the truth of his actions, realizing that it was former Justice League leader Maxwell Lord who manipulated Superman.

As Wonder Woman begins to suspect that Lord is responsible for not only Superman's brainwashing, but also for the death of Blue Beetle and the recent hijacking of the Brother Mk. I satellite, J'onn announces that he cannot repair the damage done to Superman's mind. He explains that "Max has fundamentally subverted his mind" in a gradual, long-term campaign that may be impossible to correct.

With Batman sufficiently recovered, Wonder Woman takes him away for transport back to Earth while Superman agrees to the League's temporary solution: they'll put him in a transporter loop until they can find Max and force him to restore Superman's mind. But Superman, in a fit of paranoia fueled by Max Lord's telepathy, suddenly turns on the League, believing them to be the ones under Max's influence. Defeating them in a dizzying surprise assault, he flees the Watchtower in search of Max.

Wonder Woman returns to the satellite, carrying the Kryptonite ring that Batman gave her in his cave. Learning that Superman has gone to Checkmate's headquarters in Switzerland to confront Lord, she teleports there to follow — refusing offers of Justice League help in fear that their minds could be taken over by Max as well.

Arriving at Checkmate, Diana confronts Max and asks where Superman is. As Lord answers "he's right behind you," Superman grabs Wonder Woman by the wrist and pushes her to her knees before Checkmate's Black King.

ADVENTURES OF SUPERMAN #642

and
now,
the
conclusion…

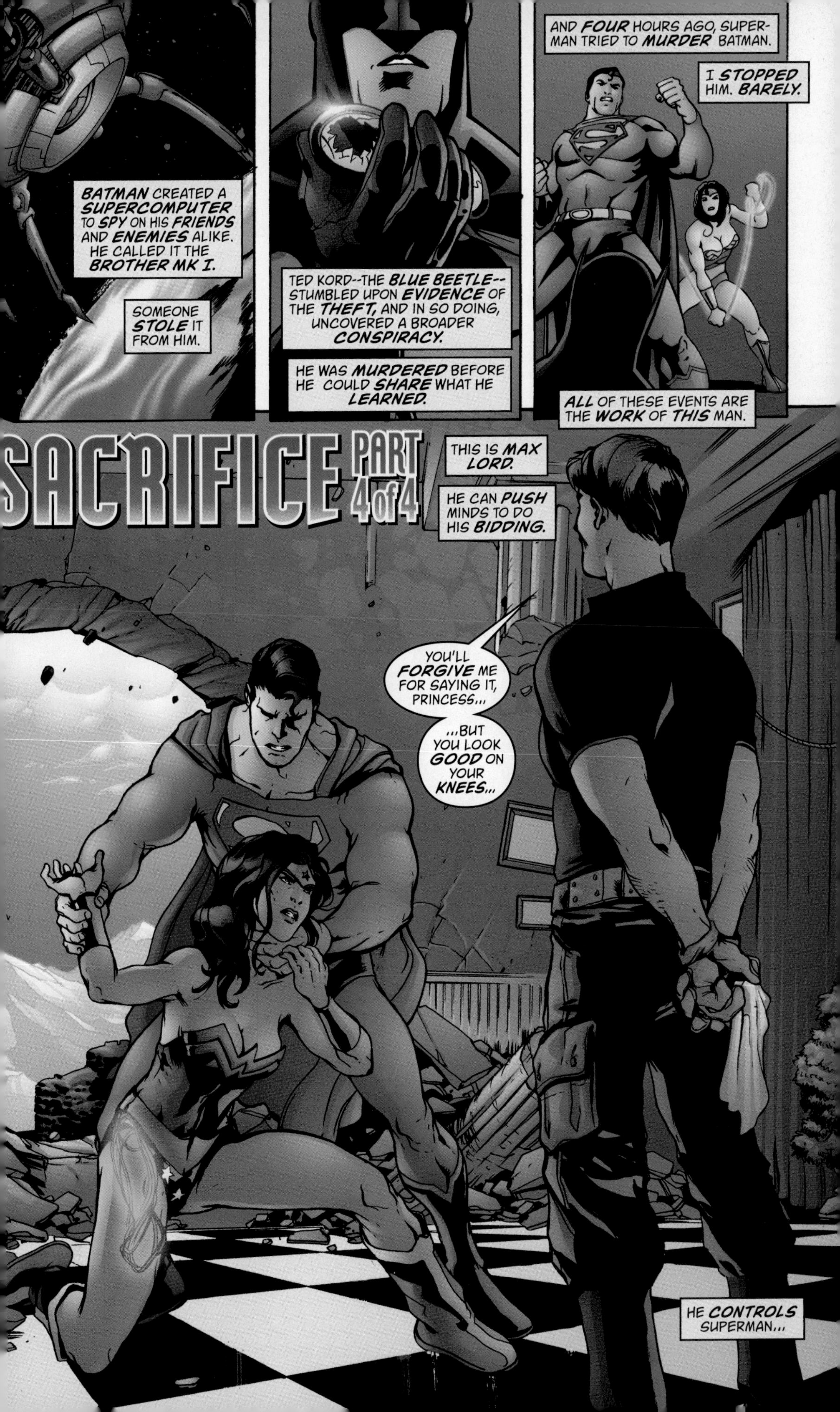
BATMAN CREATED A SUPERCOMPUTER TO SPY ON HIS FRIENDS AND ENEMIES ALIKE. HE CALLED IT THE BROTHER MK I.
SOMEONE STOLE IT FROM HIM.
TED KORD--THE BLUE BEETLE--STUMBLED UPON EVIDENCE OF THE THEFT, AND IN SO DOING, UNCOVERED A BROADER CONSPIRACY.
HE WAS MURDERED BEFORE HE COULD SHARE WHAT HE LEARNED.
AND FOUR HOURS AGO, SUPER-MAN TRIED TO MURDER BATMAN.
I STOPPED HIM. BARELY.
ALL OF THESE EVENTS ARE THE WORK OF THIS MAN.
SACRIFICE PART 4 of 4
THIS IS MAX LORD.
HE CAN PUSH MINDS TO DO HIS BIDDING.
YOU'LL FORGIVE ME FOR SAYING IT, PRINCESS...
...BUT YOU LOOK GOOD ON YOUR KNEES...
HE CONTROLS SUPERMAN...

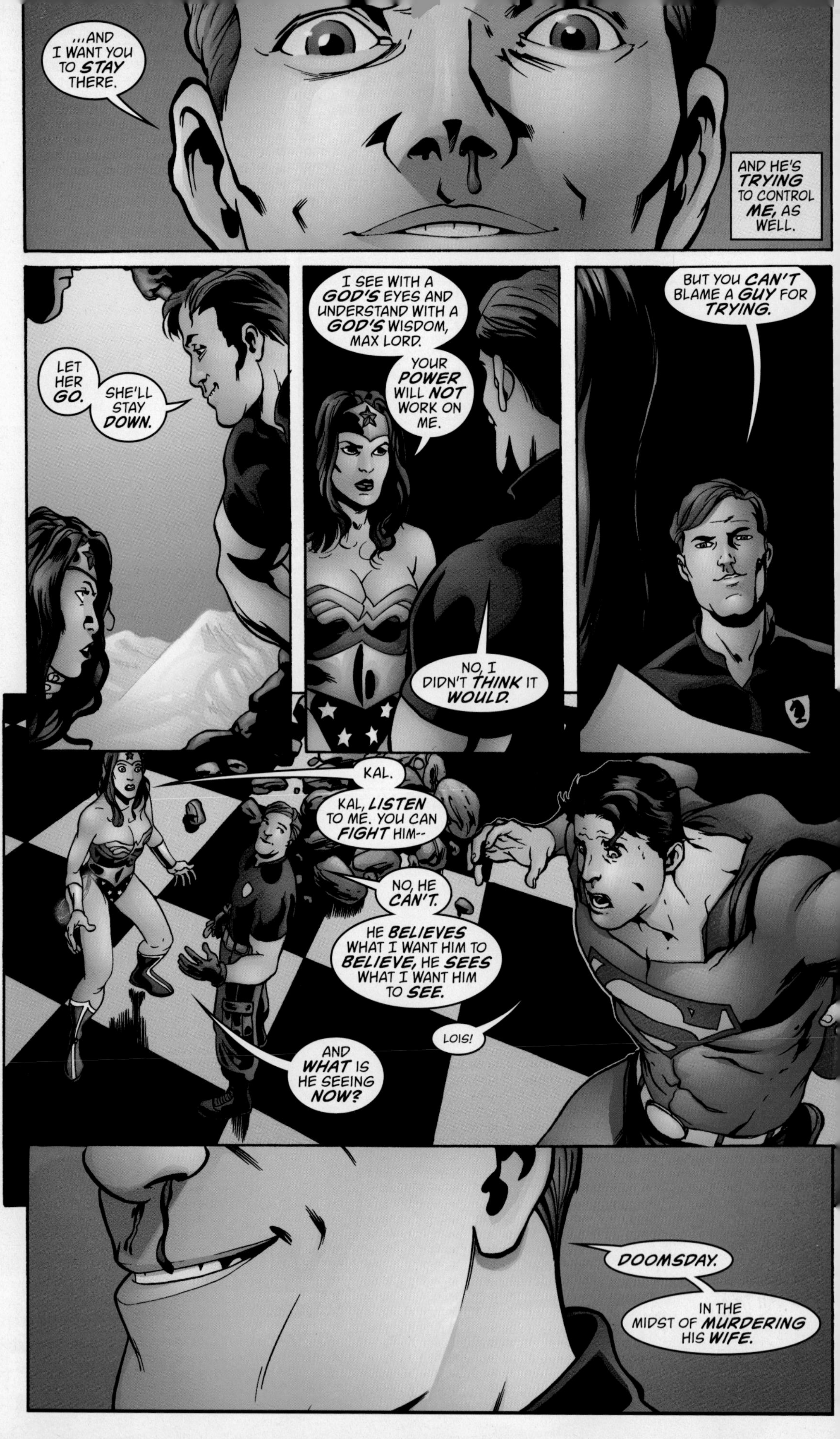
...AND I WANT YOU TO STAY THERE.
AND HE'S TRYING TO CONTROL ME, AS WELL.
LET HER GO.
SHE'LL STAY DOWN.
I SEE WITH A GOD'S EYES AND UNDERSTAND WITH A GOD'S WISDOM, MAX LORD.
YOUR POWER WILL NOT WORK ON ME.
NO, I DIDN'T THINK IT WOULD.
BUT YOU CAN'T BLAME A GUY FOR TRYING.
KAL.
KAL, LISTEN TO ME. YOU CAN FIGHT HIM--
NO, HE CAN'T.
HE BELIEVES WHAT I WANT HIM TO BELIEVE, HE SEES WHAT I WANT HIM TO SEE.
LOIS!
AND WHAT IS HE SEEING NOW?
DOOMSDAY.
IN THE MIDST OF MURDERING HIS WIFE.

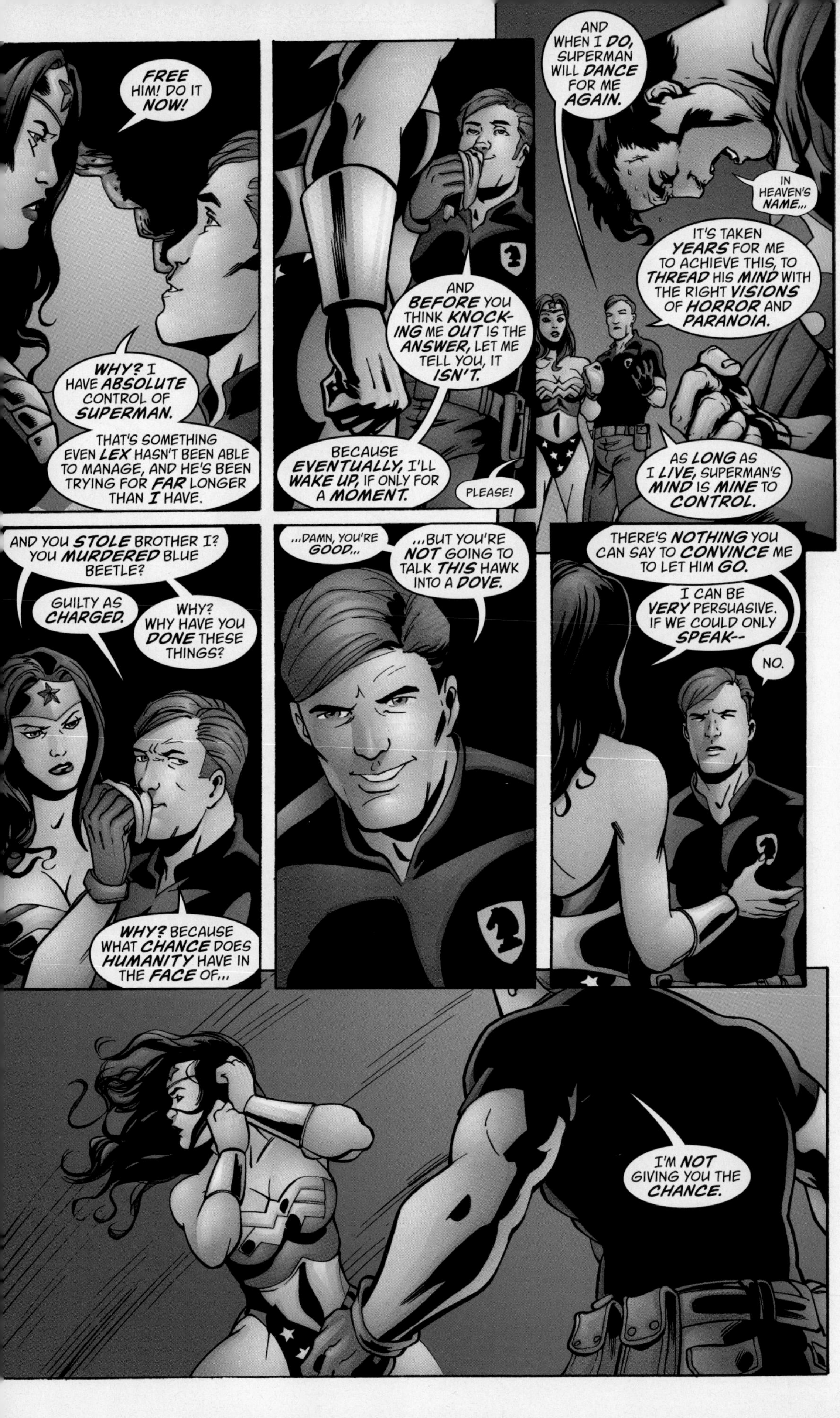
FREE HIM! DO IT NOW!
WHY? I HAVE ABSOLUTE CONTROL OF SUPERMAN.
THAT'S SOMETHING EVEN LEX HASN'T BEEN ABLE TO MANAGE, AND HE'S BEEN TRYING FOR FAR LONGER THAN I HAVE.
AND BEFORE YOU THINK KNOCKING ME OUT IS THE ANSWER, LET ME TELL YOU, IT ISN'T.
BECAUSE EVENTUALLY, I'LL WAKE UP, IF ONLY FOR A MOMENT.
PLEASE!
AND WHEN I DO, SUPERMAN WILL DANCE FOR ME AGAIN.
IN HEAVEN'S NAME...
IT'S TAKEN YEARS FOR ME TO ACHIEVE THIS, TO THREAD HIS MIND WITH THE RIGHT VISIONS OF HORROR AND PARANOIA.
AS LONG AS I LIVE, SUPERMAN'S MIND IS MINE TO CONTROL.
AND YOU STOLE BROTHER I? YOU MURDERED BLUE BEETLE?
GUILTY AS CHARGED.
WHY? WHY HAVE YOU DONE THESE THINGS?
WHY? BECAUSE WHAT CHANCE DOES HUMANITY HAVE IN THE FACE OF...
...DAMN, YOU'RE GOOD...
...BUT YOU'RE NOT GOING TO TALK THIS HAWK INTO A DOVE.
THERE'S NOTHING YOU CAN SAY TO CONVINCE ME TO LET HIM GO.
I CAN BE VERY PERSUASIVE. IF WE COULD ONLY SPEAK--
NO.
I'M NOT GIVING YOU THE CHANCE.

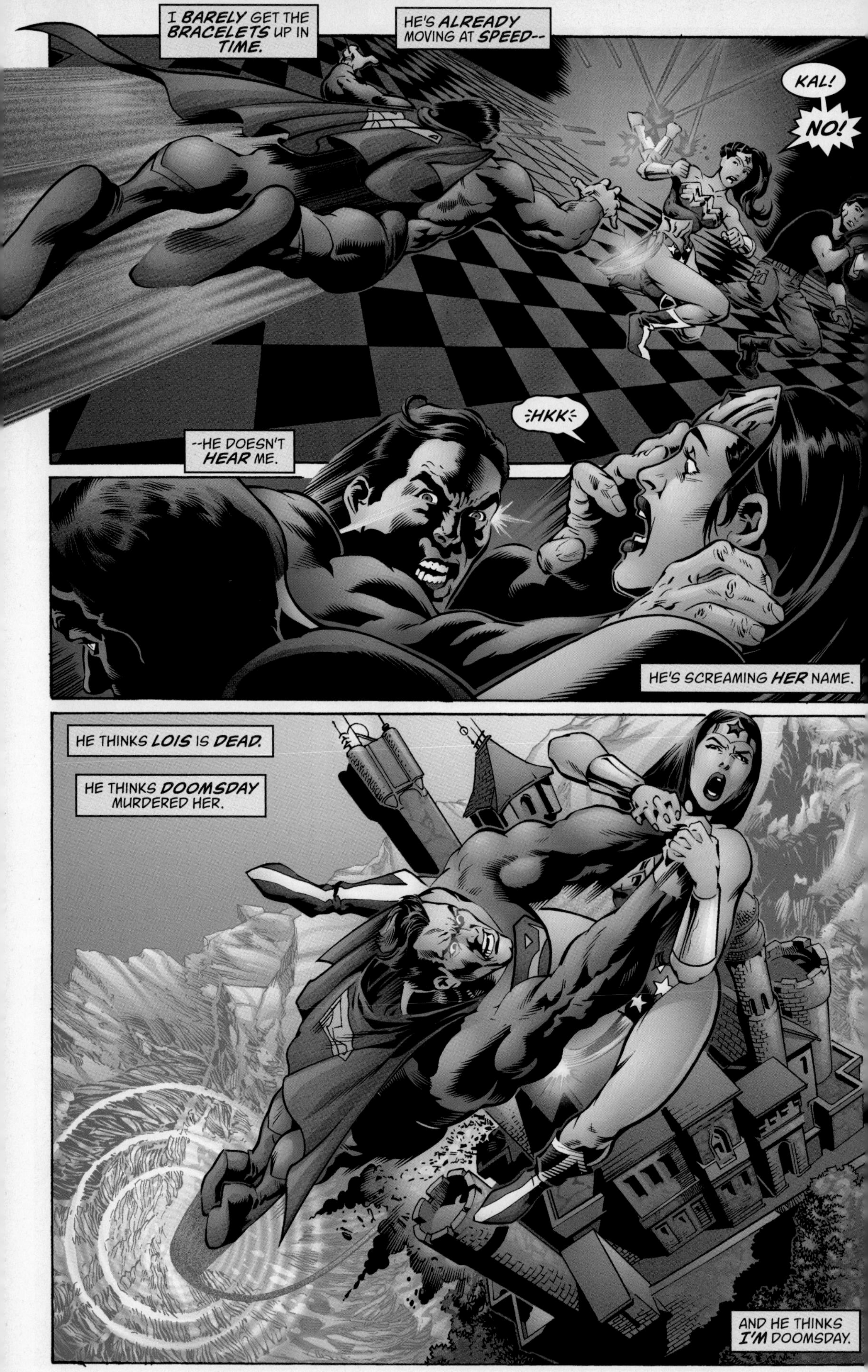

I BARELY GET THE BRACELETS UP IN TIME.
HE'S ALREADY MOVING AT SPEED--
KAL!
NO!
--HE DOESN'T HEAR ME.
HKK
HE'S SCREAMING HER NAME.
HE THINKS LOIS IS DEAD.
HE THINKS DOOMSDAY MURDERED HER.
AND HE THINKS I'M DOOMSDAY.

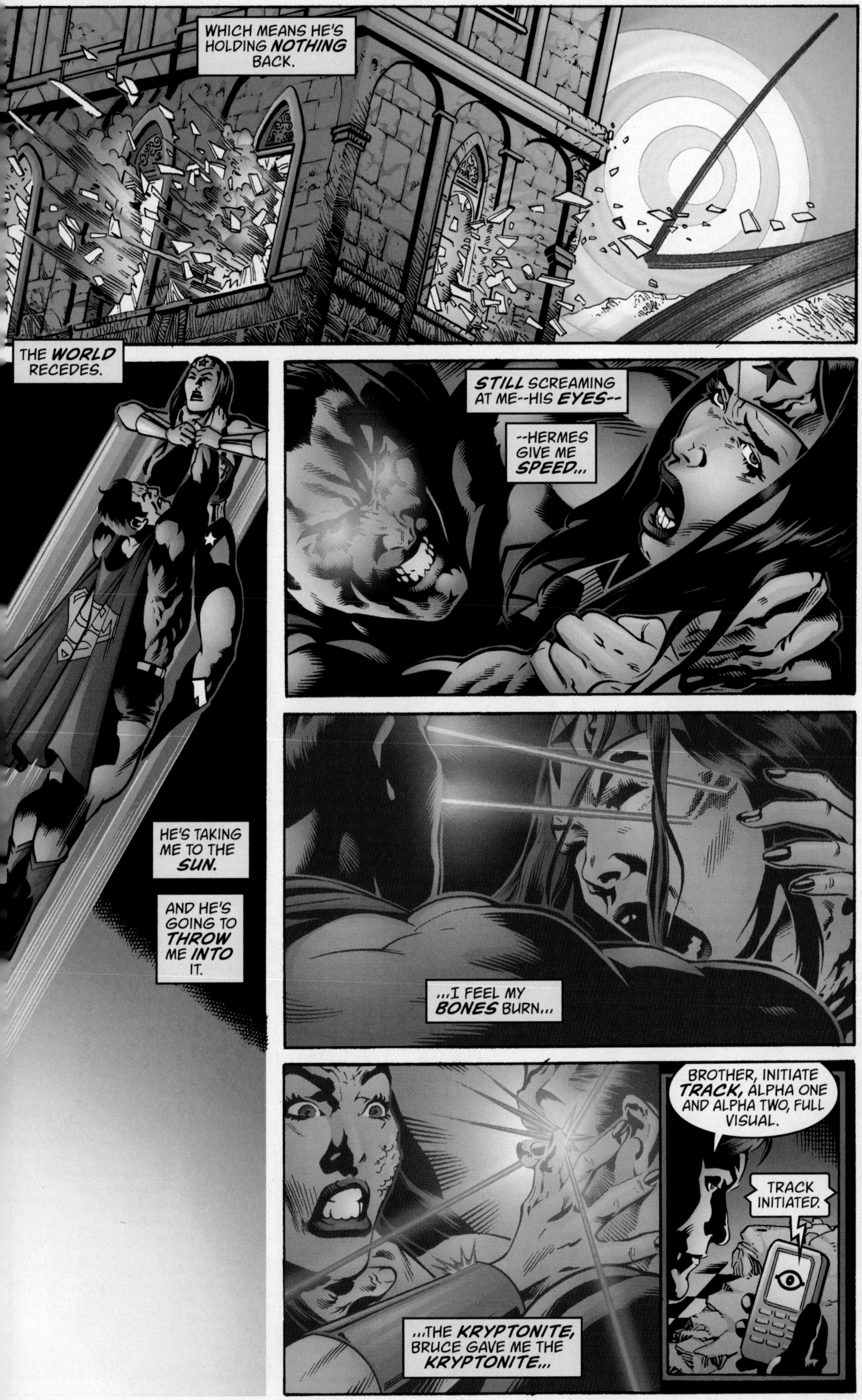
WHICH MEANS HE'S HOLDING NOTHING BACK.
THE WORLD RECEDES.
STILL SCREAMING AT ME--HIS EYES--
--HERMES GIVE ME SPEED...
HE'S TAKING ME TO THE SUN.
AND HE'S GOING TO THROW ME INTO IT.
...I FEEL MY BONES BURN...
...THE KRYPTONITE, BRUCE GAVE ME THE KRYPTONITE...
BROTHER, INITIATE TRACK, ALPHA ONE AND ALPHA TWO, FULL VISUAL.
TRACK INITIATED.

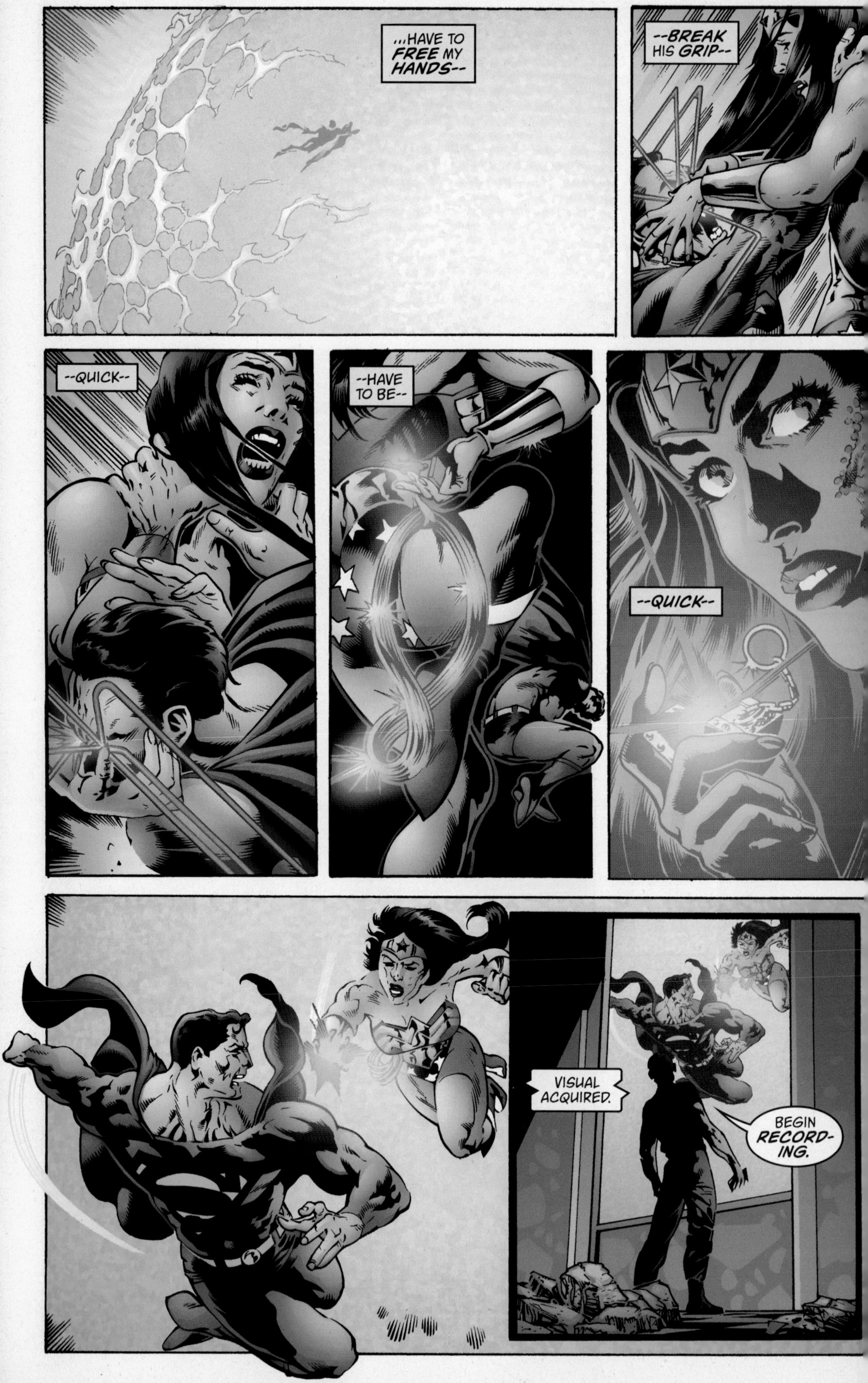
...HAVE TO FREE MY HANDS--
--BREAK HIS GRIP--
--QUICK--
--HAVE TO BE--
--QUICK--
VISUAL ACQUIRED.
BEGIN RECORDING.

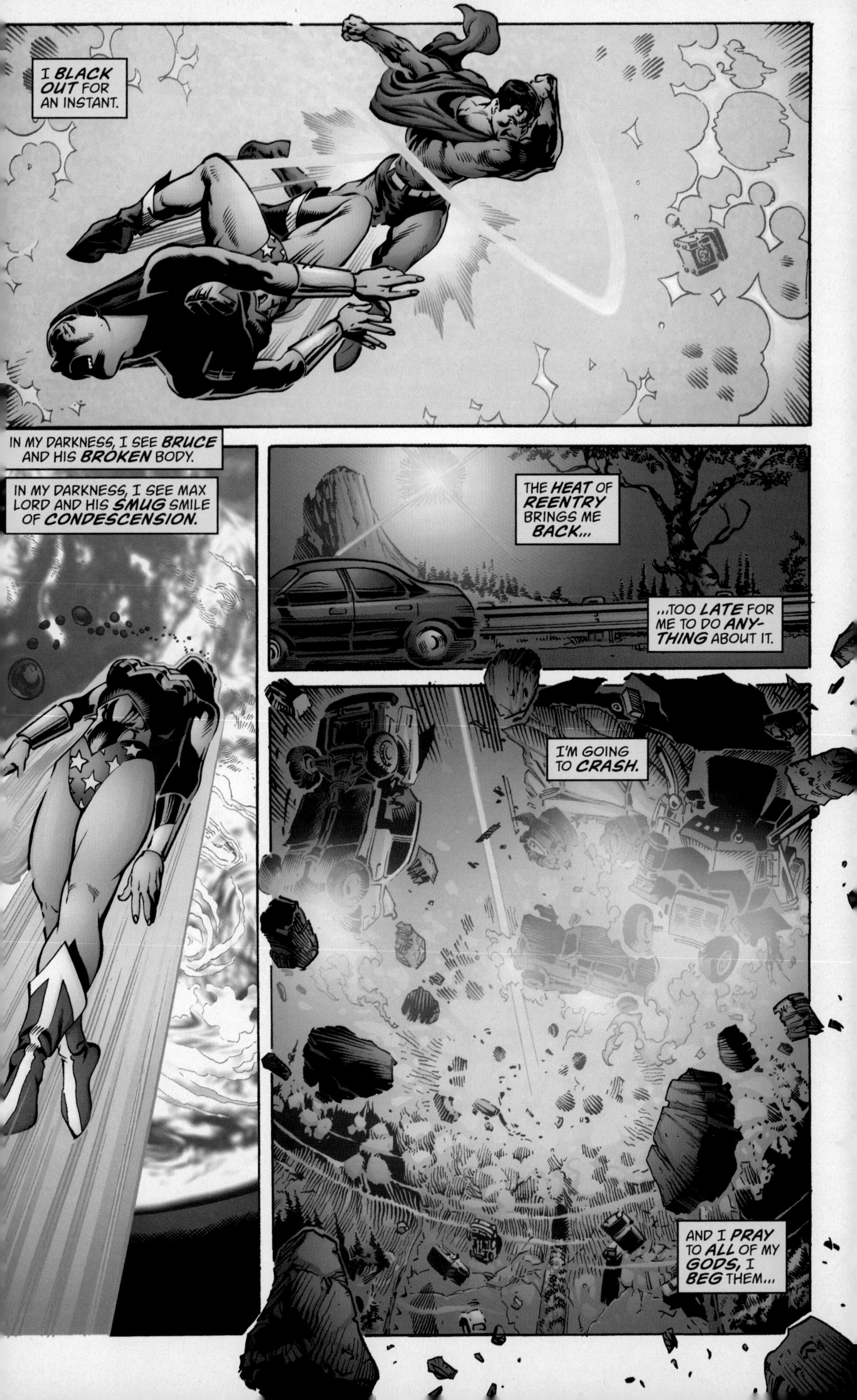

I BLACK OUT FOR AN INSTANT.
IN MY DARKNESS, I SEE BRUCE AND HIS BROKEN BODY.
IN MY DARKNESS, I SEE MAX LORD AND HIS SMUG SMILE OF CONDESCENSION.
THE HEAT OF REENTRY BRINGS ME BACK...
...TOO LATE FOR ME TO DO ANYTHING ABOUT IT.
I'M GOING TO CRASH.
AND I PRAY TO ALL OF MY GODS, I BEG THEM...

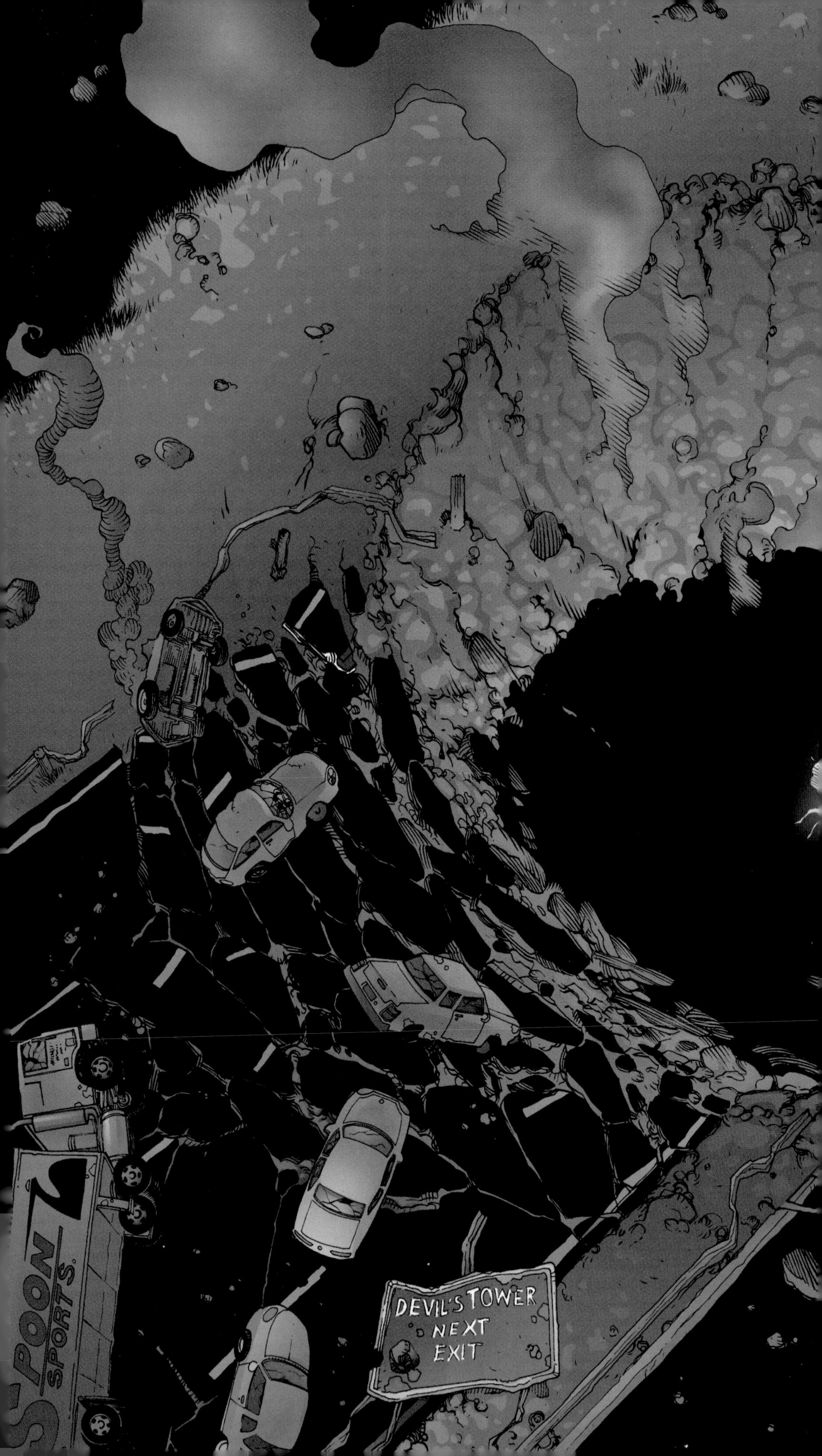

DEVIL'S TOWER
NEXT
EXIT
SPOON
SPORTS.

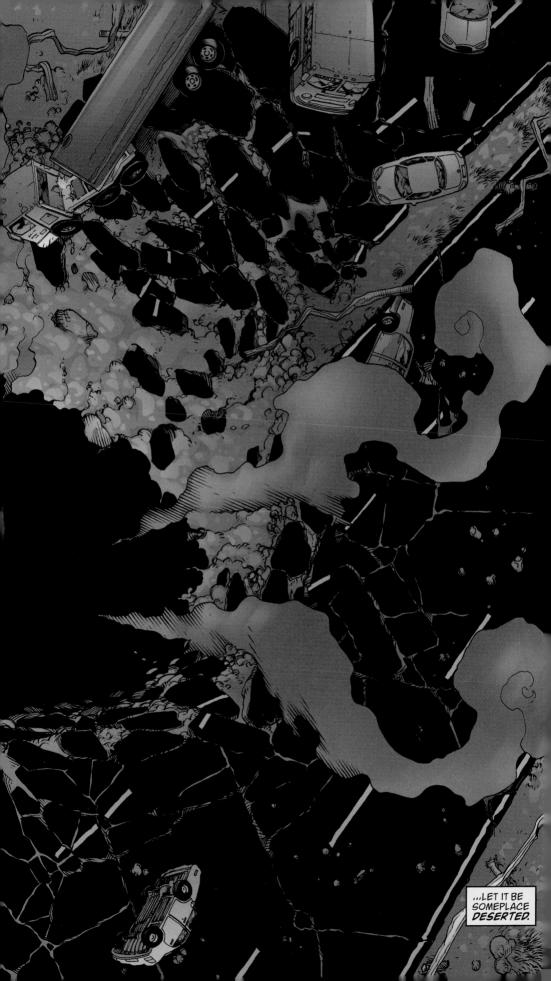

...LET IT BE SOMEPLACE DESERTED.

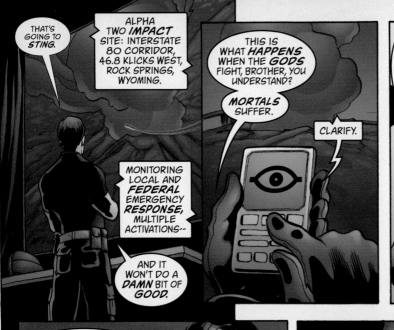

"THAT'S GOING TO *STING*."

"ALPHA TWO *IMPACT* SITE: INTERSTATE 80 CORRIDOR, 46.8 KLICKS WEST, ROCK SPRINGS, WYOMING."

"MONITORING LOCAL AND *FEDERAL* EMERGENCY *RESPONSE,* MULTIPLE ACTIVATIONS--"

"AND IT WON'T DO A *DAMN* BIT OF *GOOD.*"

"THIS IS WHAT *HAPPENS* WHEN THE *GODS* FIGHT, BROTHER, YOU UNDERSTAND?"

"*MORTALS* SUFFER."

"CLARIFY."

"CAN YOU IMAGINE THE *DEVASTATION* IF SHE HAD COME DOWN IN SAN FRANCISCO? THE *CATASTROPHIC* LOSS OF *LIFE?*"

"*THESE* ARE THE PEOPLE WHO *CONTROL* HUMANITY'S *DESTINY,* BROTHER..."

"...AND *THIS* IS WHY THEY MUST BE *ELIMINATED.*"

"LOOK AT *HIM.* ALL THE *PUNISHMENT* HE'S DISHING OUT ON *HER.*"

"IMAGINE IF HE *TURNED* THAT POWER AGAINST *US.*"

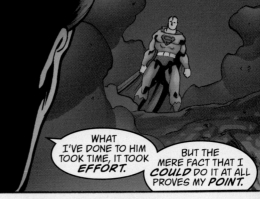

"WHAT I'VE DONE TO HIM TOOK TIME, IT TOOK *EFFORT.*"

"BUT THE MERE FACT THAT I *COULD* DO IT AT ALL PROVES MY *POINT.*"

"BECAUSE IF I CAN DO IT, SOMEONE *ELSE* CAN, *TOO.* AND THAT'S THE *HEART* OF IT, BROTHER."

"SUPERMAN, WONDER WOMAN, THE *REST* OF THEM, THEY'LL *KILL US ALL...*"

"...IF *WE* DON'T KILL *THEM* FIRST."

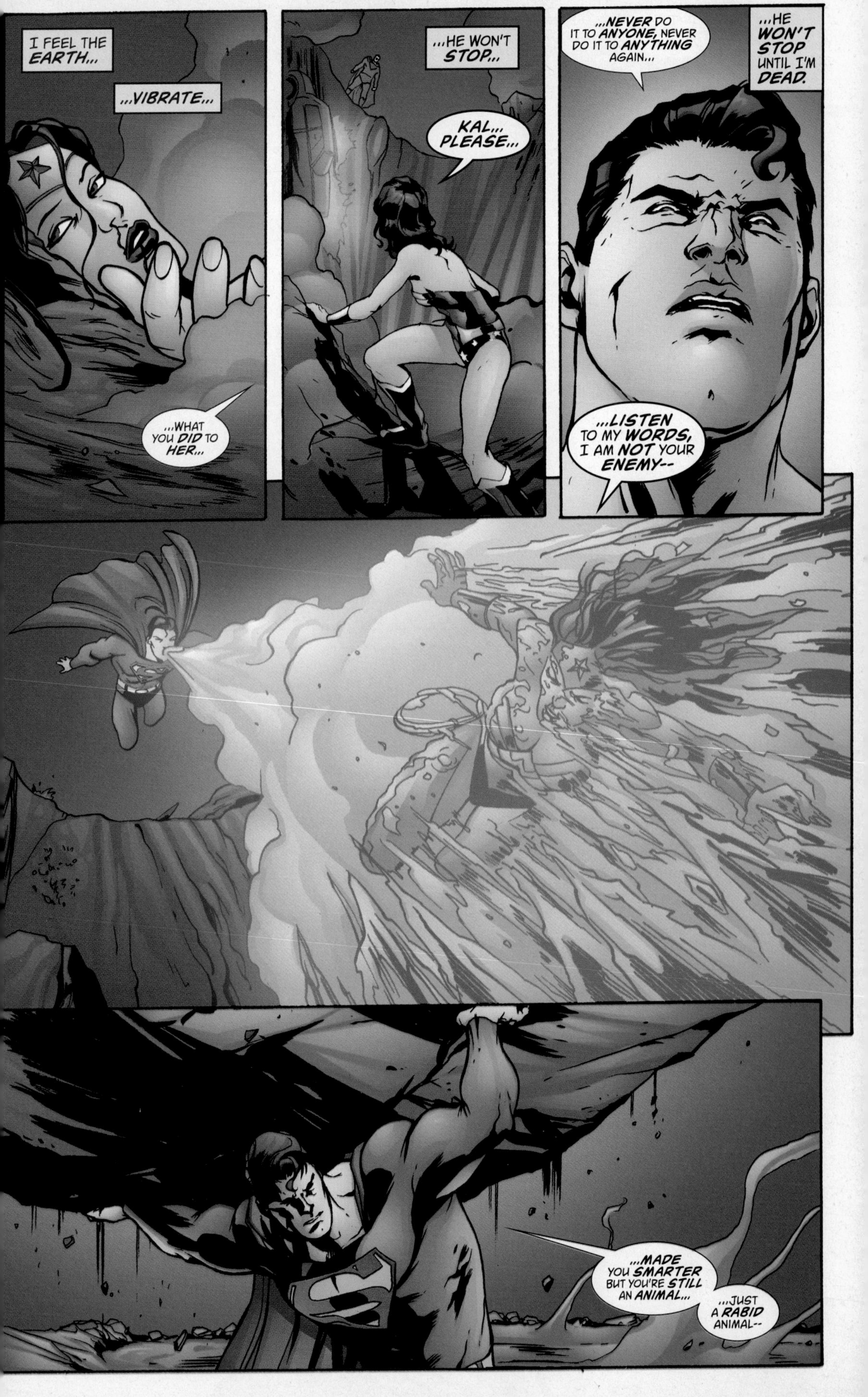

I FEEL THE EARTH...
...VIBRATE...
...WHAT YOU DID TO HER...
...HE WON'T STOP...
KAL... PLEASE...
...NEVER DO IT TO ANYONE, NEVER DO IT TO ANYTHING AGAIN...
...HE WON'T STOP UNTIL I'M DEAD.
...LISTEN TO MY WORDS, I AM NOT YOUR ENEMY--
...MADE YOU SMARTER BUT YOU'RE STILL AN ANIMAL...
...JUST A RABID ANIMAL--

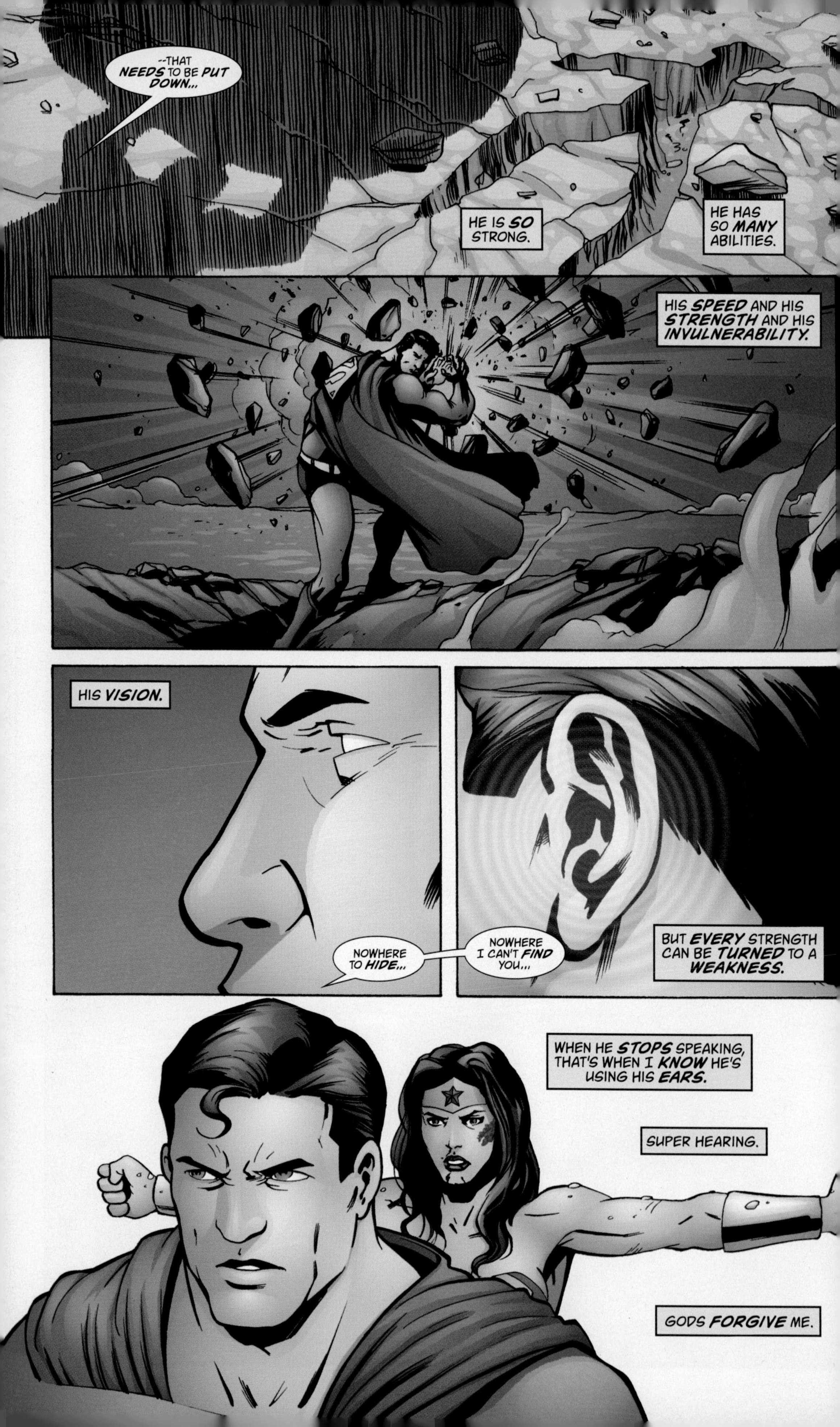
--THAT NEEDS TO BE PUT DOWN...
HE IS SO STRONG.
HE HAS SO MANY ABILITIES.
HIS SPEED AND HIS STRENGTH AND HIS INVULNERABILITY.
HIS VISION.
NOWHERE TO HIDE...
NOWHERE I CAN'T FIND YOU...
BUT EVERY STRENGTH CAN BE TURNED TO A WEAKNESS.
WHEN HE STOPS SPEAKING, THAT'S WHEN I KNOW HE'S USING HIS EARS.
SUPER HEARING.
GODS FORGIVE ME.

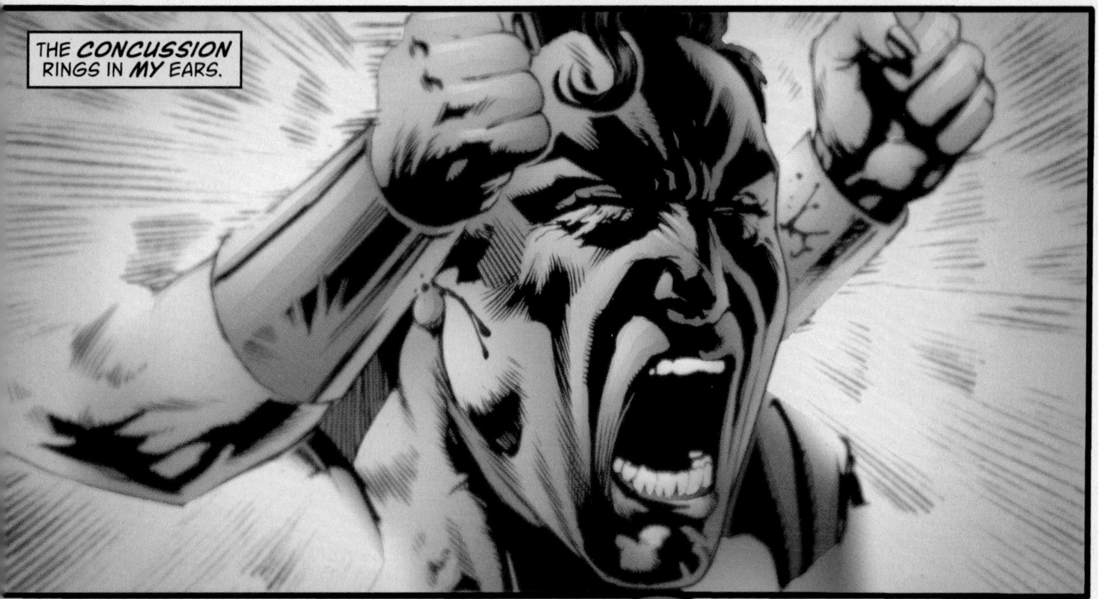
THE CONCUSSION RINGS IN MY EARS.

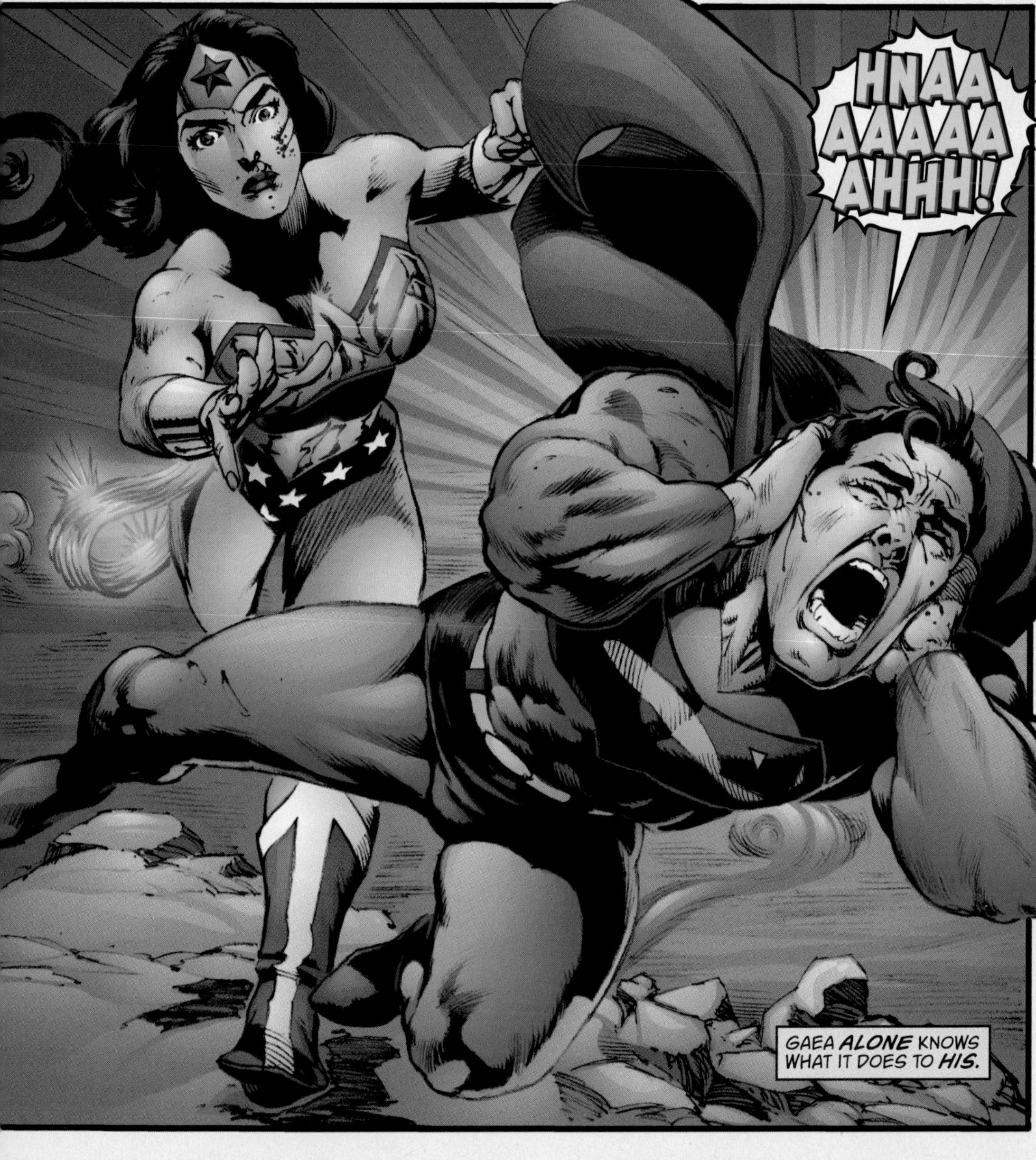
HNAA AAAAA AHHH!
GAEA ALONE KNOWS WHAT IT DOES TO HIS.

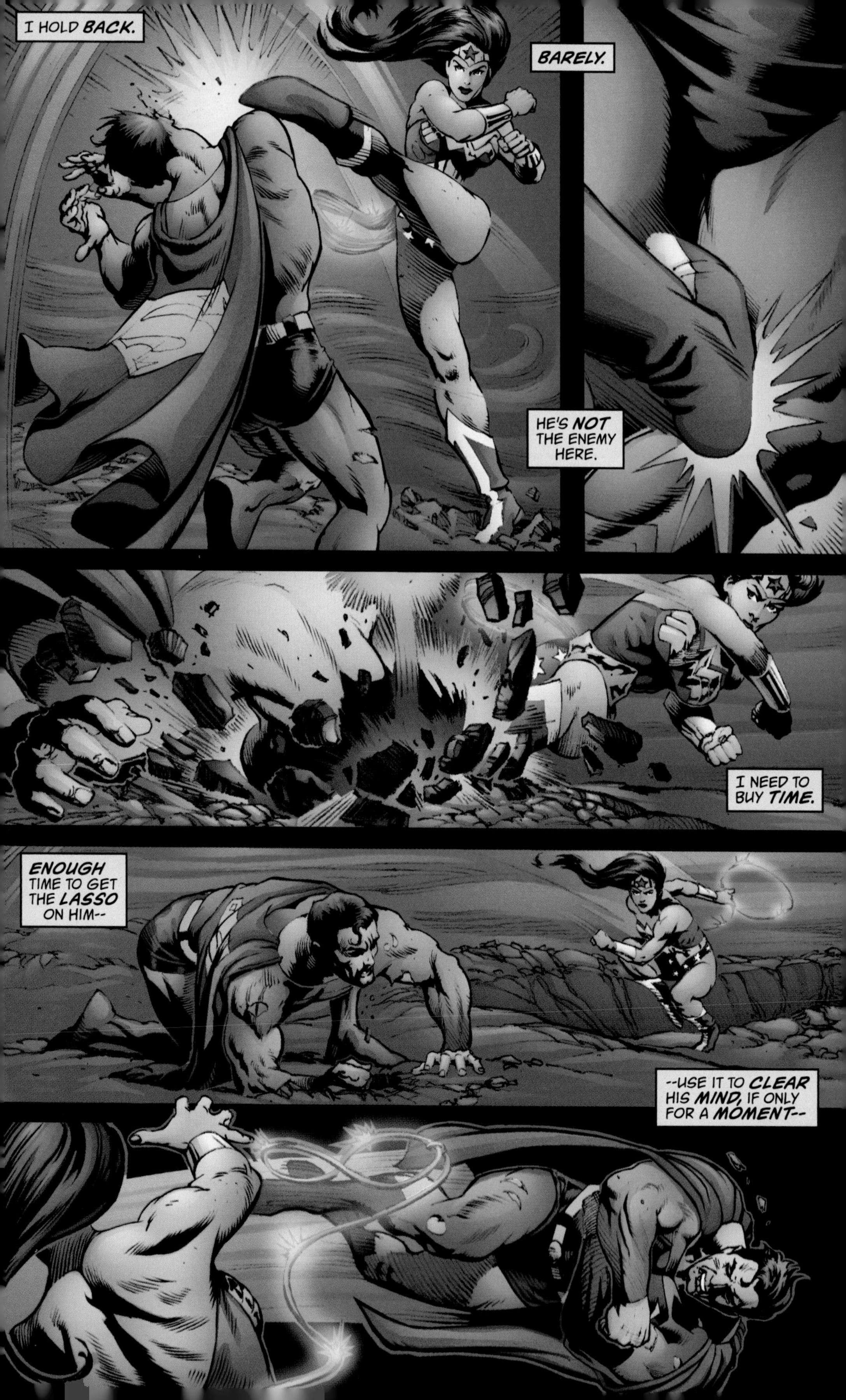
I HOLD BACK.
BARELY.
HE'S NOT THE ENEMY HERE.
I NEED TO BUY TIME.
ENOUGH TIME TO GET THE LASSO ON HIM--
--USE IT TO CLEAR HIS MIND, IF ONLY FOR A MOMENT--

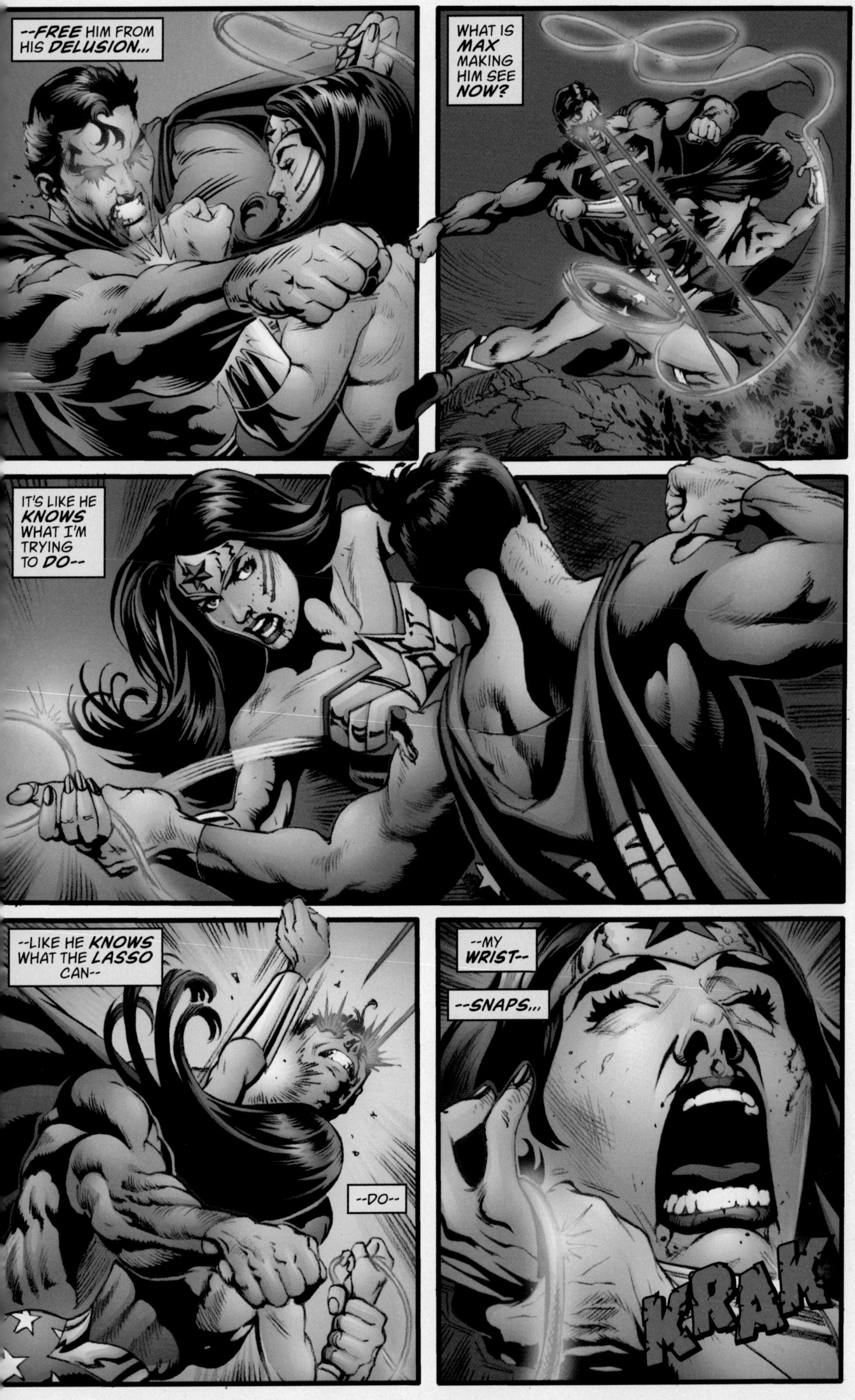
--FREE HIM FROM HIS DELUSION...
WHAT IS MAX MAKING HIM SEE NOW?
IT'S LIKE HE KNOWS WHAT I'M TRYING TO DO--
--LIKE HE KNOWS WHAT THE LASSO CAN--
--DO--
--MY WRIST--
--SNAPS...
KRAK

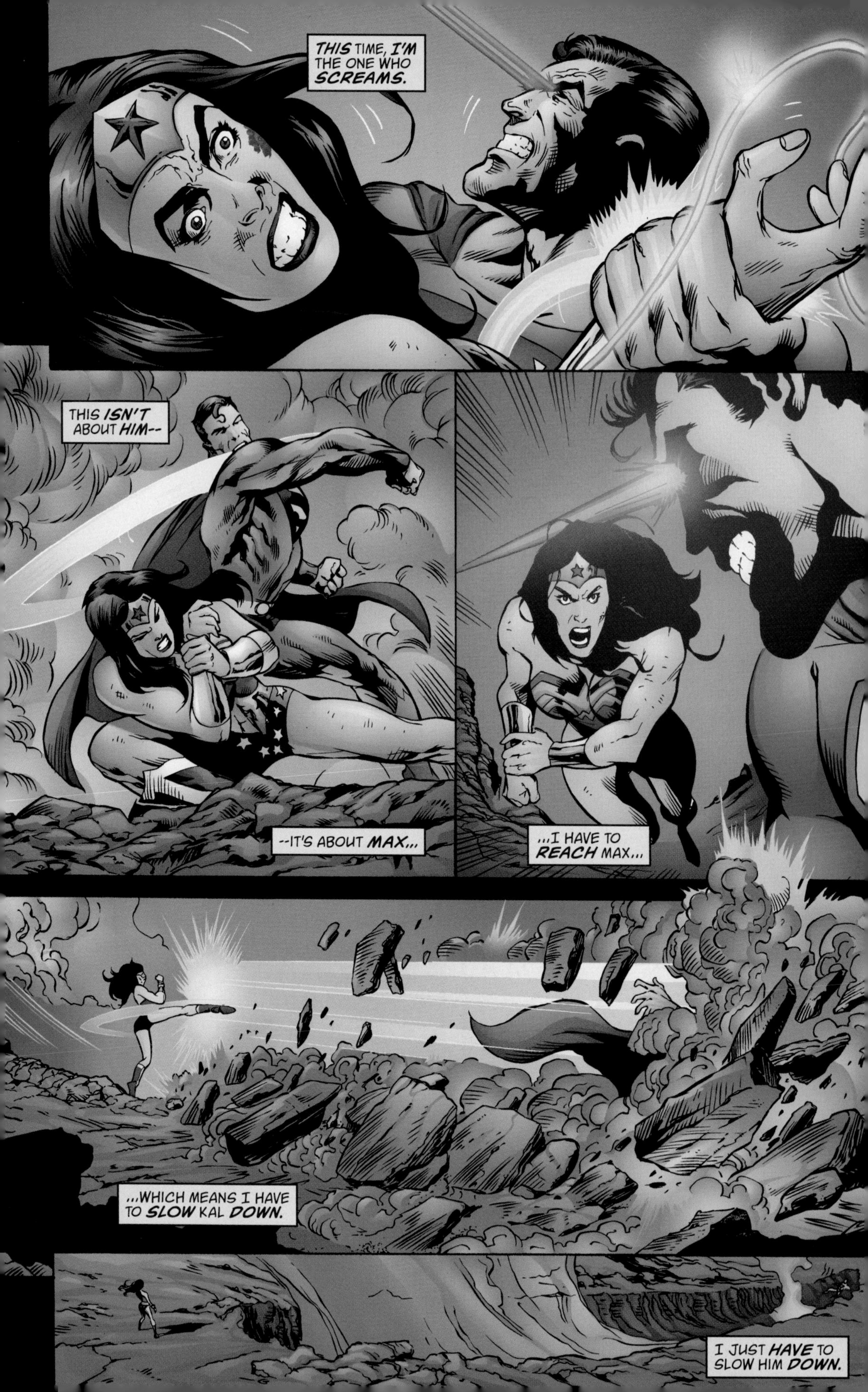
THIS TIME, I'M THE ONE WHO SCREAMS.
THIS ISN'T ABOUT HIM--
--IT'S ABOUT MAX...
...I HAVE TO REACH MAX...
...WHICH MEANS I HAVE TO SLOW KAL DOWN.
I JUST HAVE TO SLOW HIM DOWN.

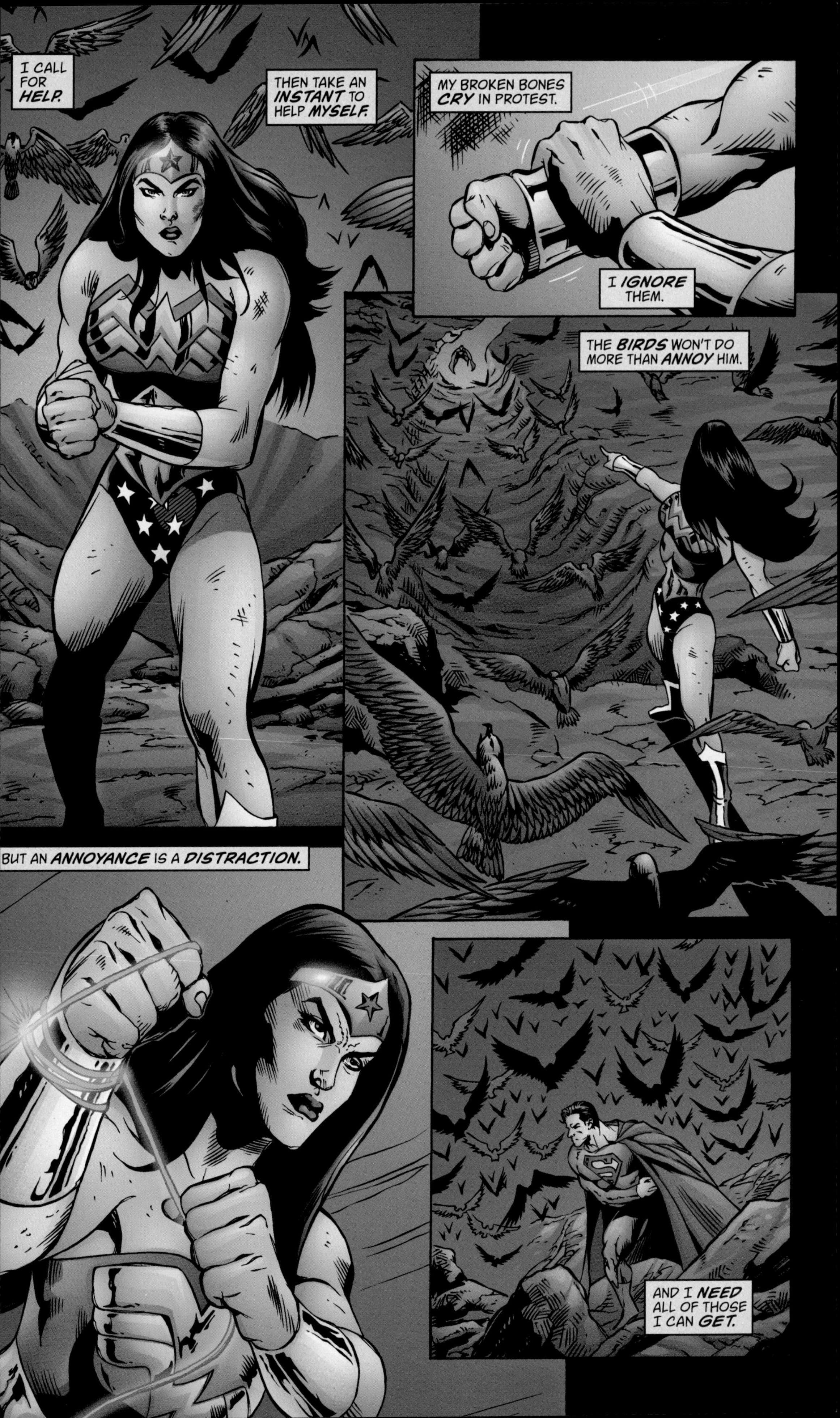

I CALL FOR HELP.
THEN TAKE AN INSTANT TO HELP MYSELF.
MY BROKEN BONES CRY IN PROTEST.
I IGNORE THEM.
THE BIRDS WON'T DO MORE THAN ANNOY HIM.
BUT AN ANNOYANCE IS A DISTRACTION.
AND I NEED ALL OF THOSE I CAN GET.

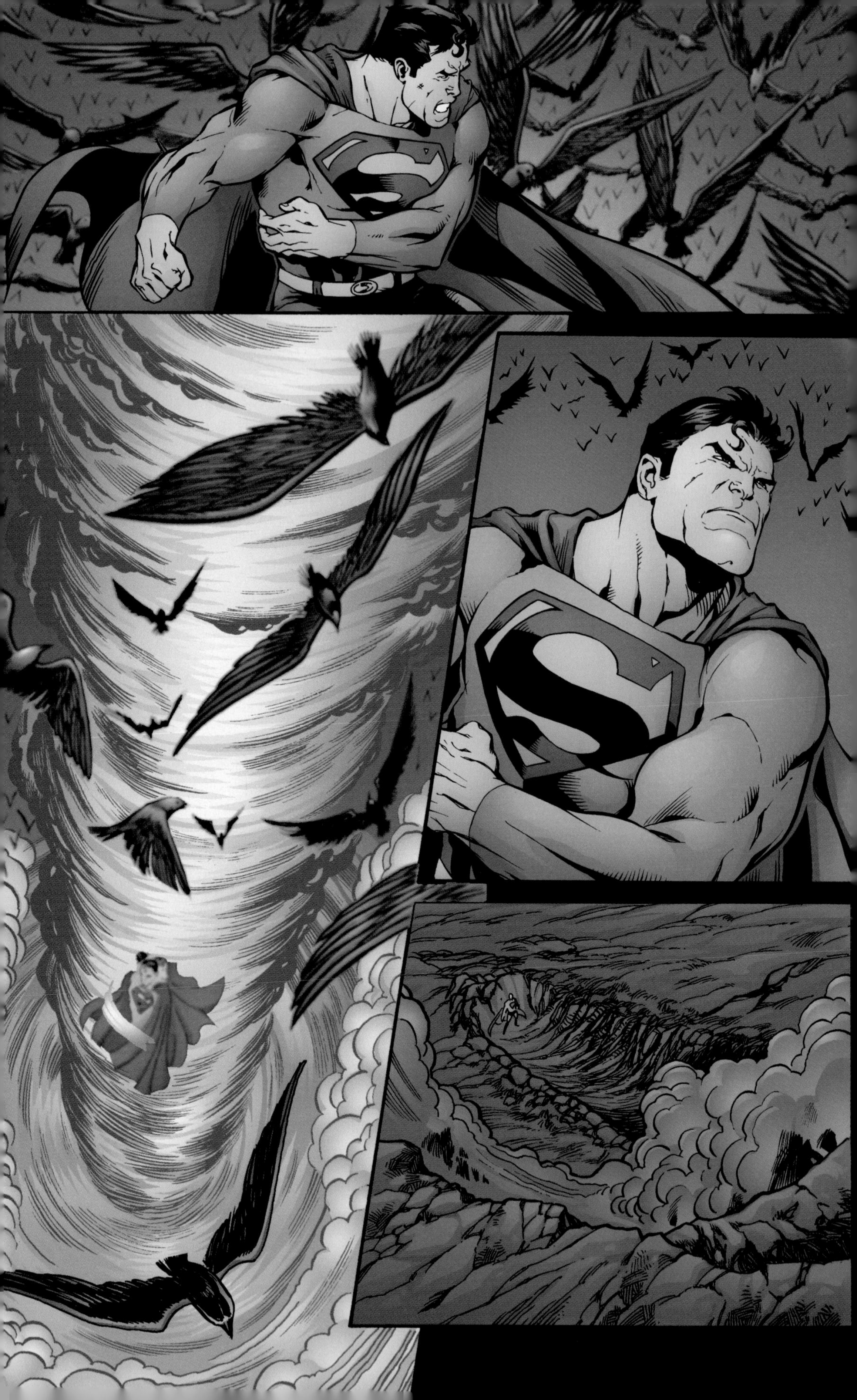

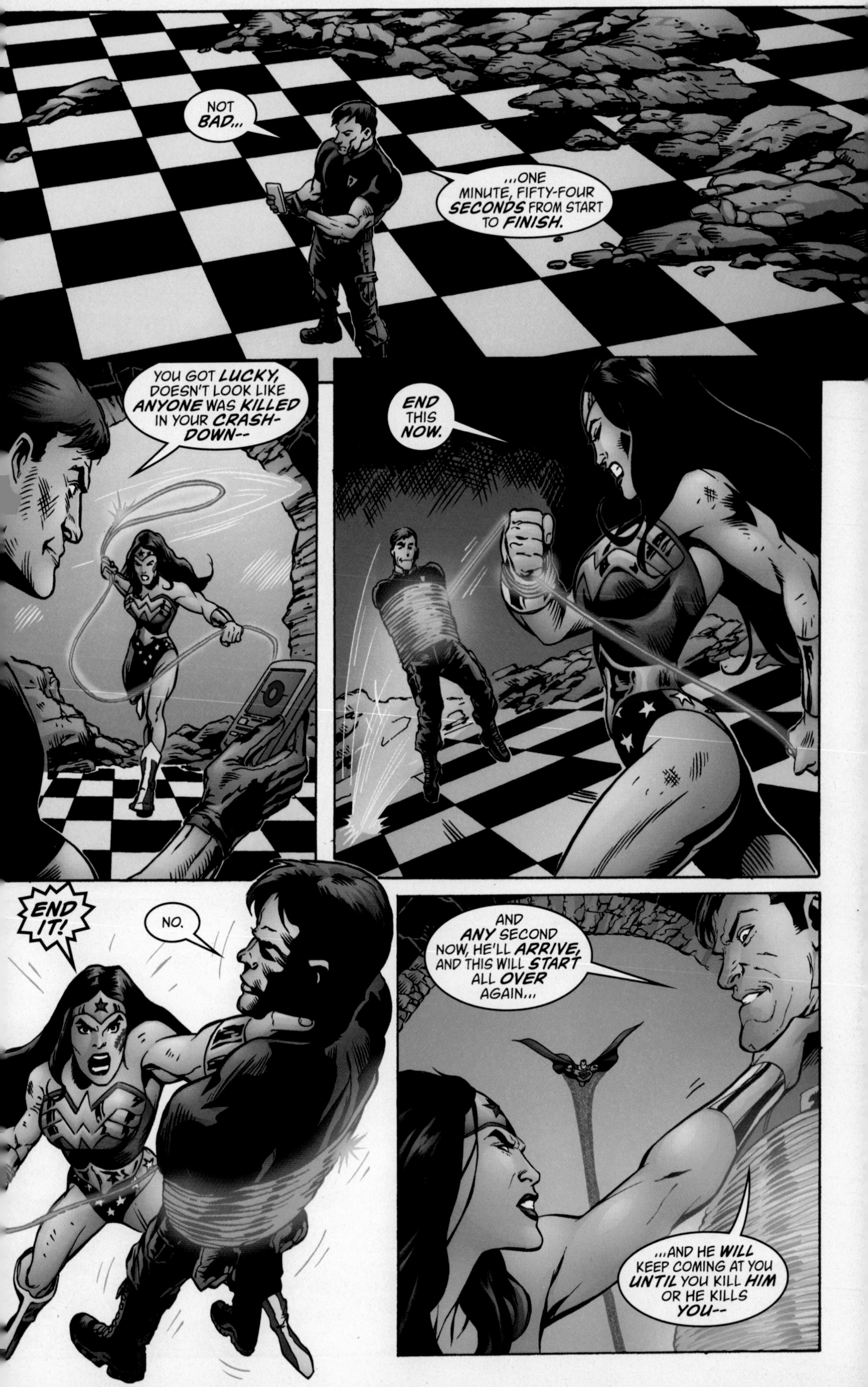
NOT BAD...
...ONE MINUTE, FIFTY-FOUR SECONDS FROM START TO FINISH.
YOU GOT LUCKY, DOESN'T LOOK LIKE ANYONE WAS KILLED IN YOUR CRASH-DOWN--
END THIS NOW.
END IT!
NO.
AND ANY SECOND NOW, HE'LL ARRIVE, AND THIS WILL START ALL OVER AGAIN...
...AND HE WILL KEEP COMING AT YOU UNTIL YOU KILL HIM OR HE KILLS YOU--

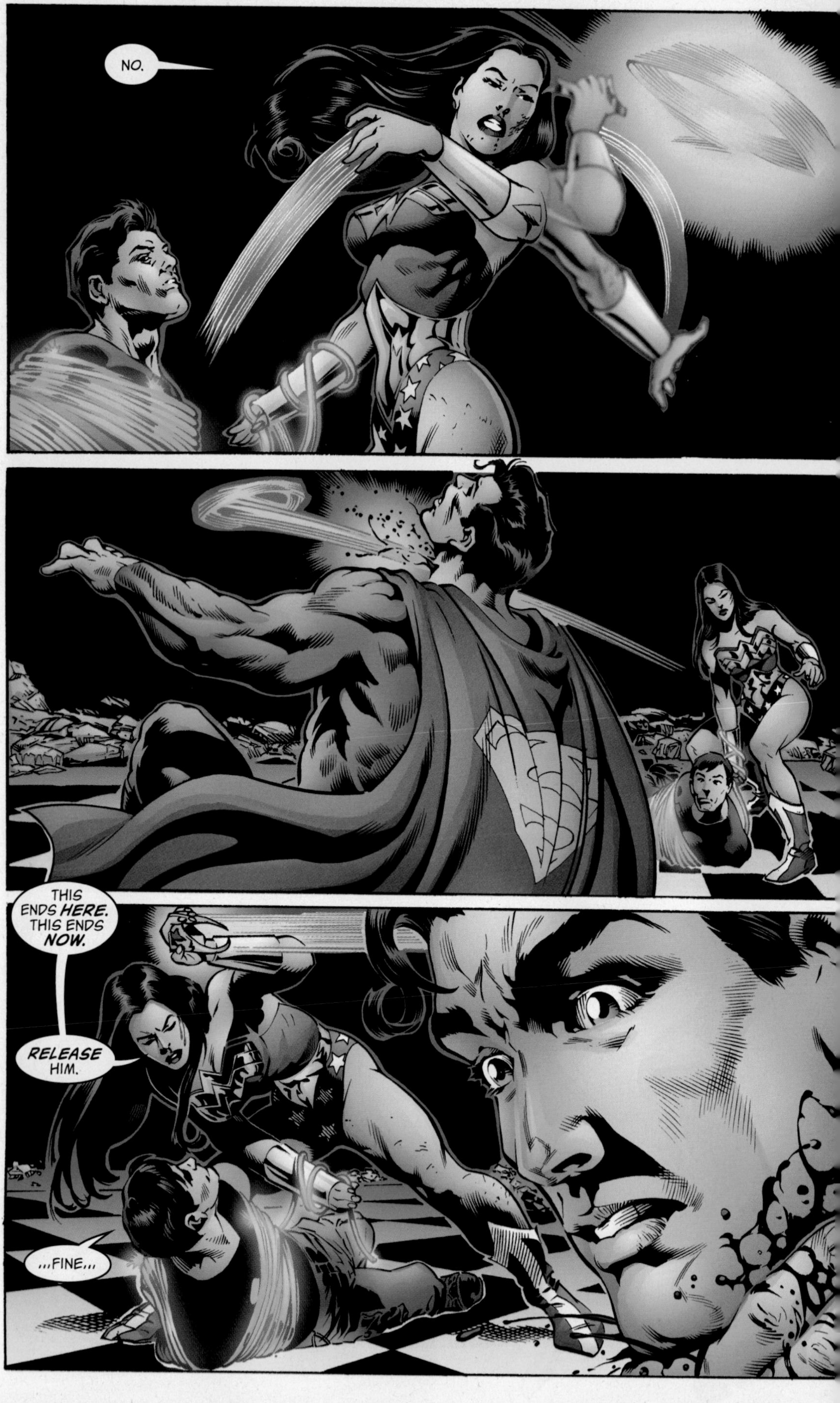
NO.
THIS ENDS HERE. THIS ENDS NOW.
RELEASE HIM.
...FINE...

DIANA...

IT'S *ALL* RIGHT, KAL.

...I SAW... HE *MADE ME* WATCH...

...DOOMSDAY... HE *TORE* LOIS APART...

IT WASN'T *REAL.*

IT *WAS* TO *HIM.*

IT WILL ALL BE ALL RIGHT.

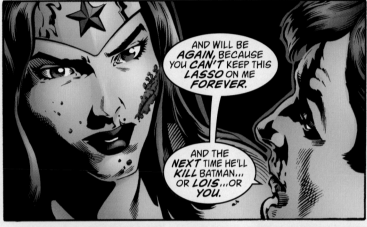

AND WILL BE *AGAIN,* BECAUSE YOU *CAN'T* KEEP THIS *LASSO* ON ME *FOREVER.*

AND THE *NEXT* TIME HE'LL *KILL* BATMAN.... OR *LOIS*....OR *YOU.*

YOU *THINK* I'VE *LIED* TO YOU BUT I *HAVEN'T.* I *CAN'T.*

HE'S *MINE.*

I'LL *NEVER* LET HIM *GO.*

YOU *WILL.*

TELL ME HOW TO *FREE* HIM FROM YOUR *CONTROL.*

KILL ME.

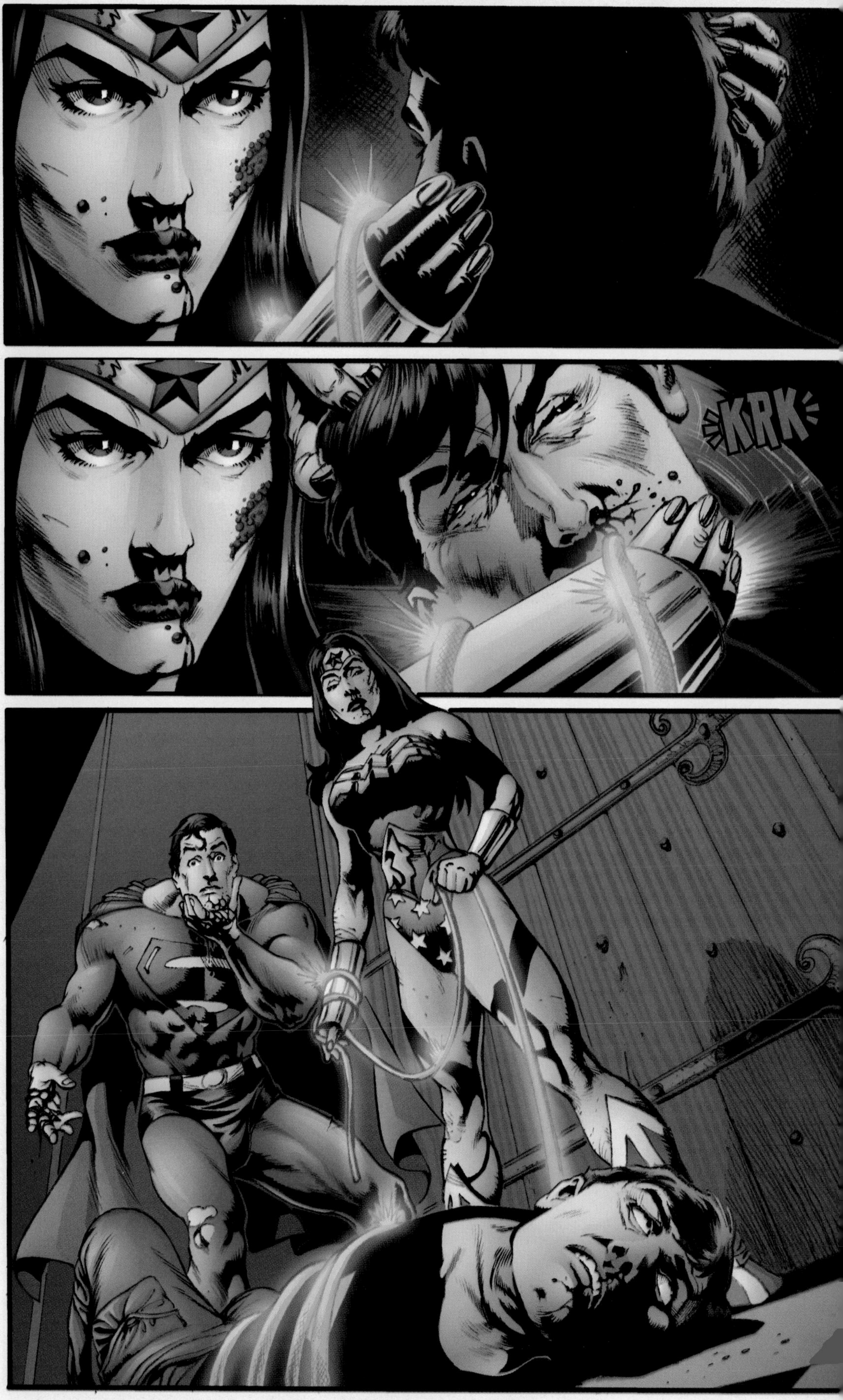
KRK

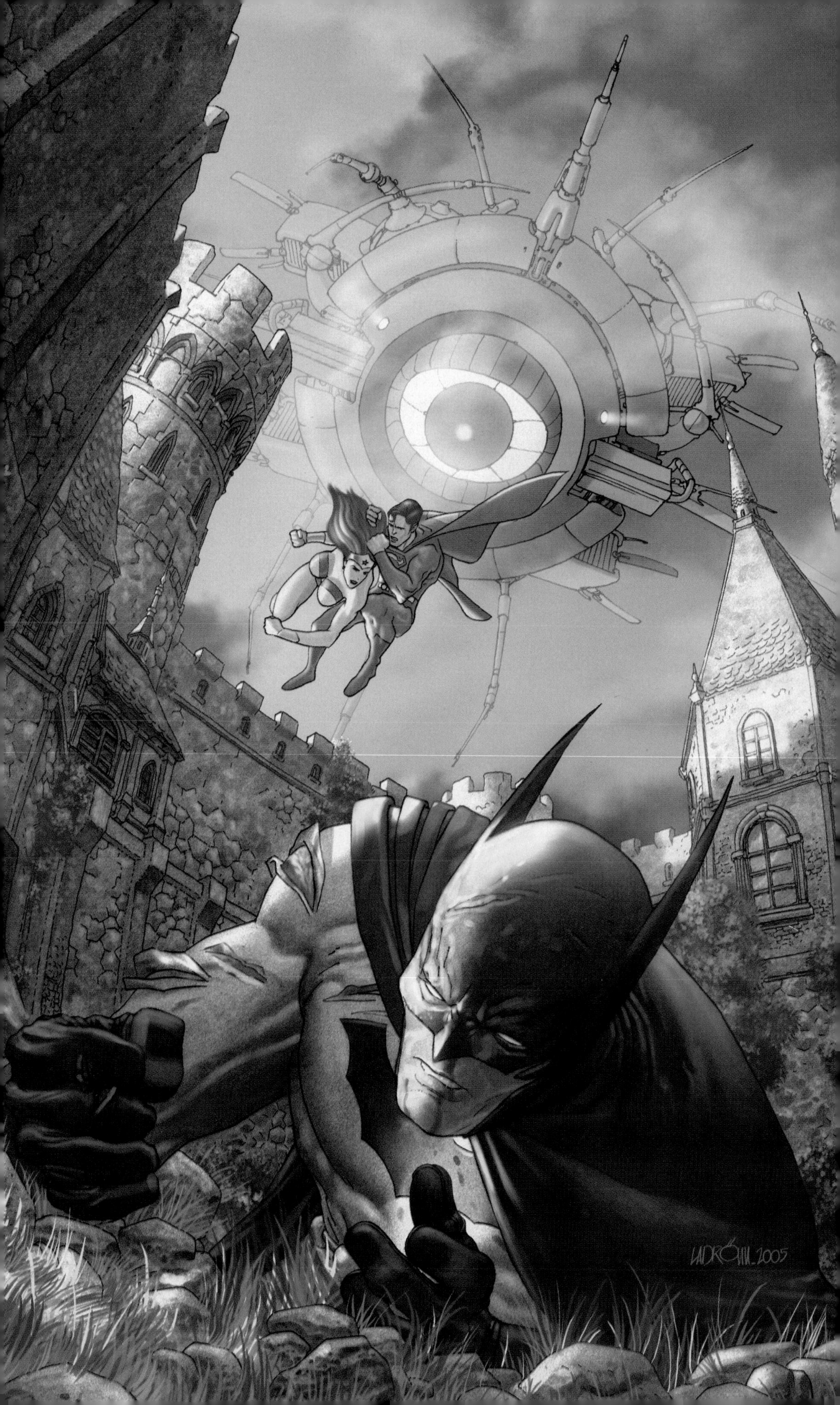

Greg Rucka
Writer

Jesus Saiz
Cliff Richards & Bob Wiacek
Artists

Hi-Fi Design
Colorist

Phil Balsman
Letterer

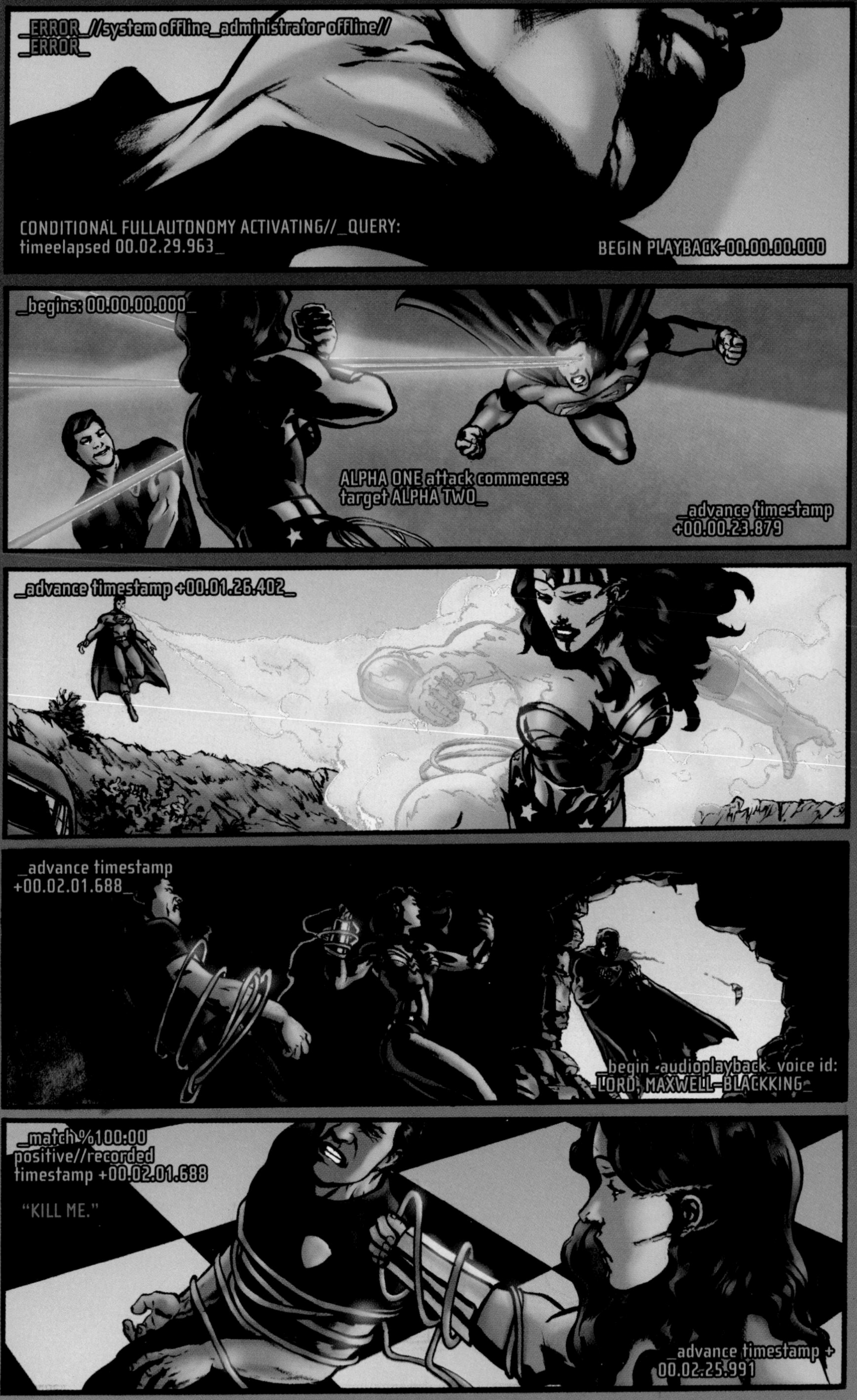

ERROR//system offline_administrator offline//
ERROR
CONDITIONAL FULLAUTONOMY ACTIVATING//_QUERY:
timeelapsed 00.02.29.963_
BEGIN PLAYBACK-00.00.00.000
begins: 00.00.00.000
ALPHA ONE attack commences:
target ALPHA TWO_
_advance timestamp
+00.00.23.879
advance timestamp +00.01.26.402
_advance timestamp
+00.02.01.688_
_begin_audioplayback_voice id:
-LORD, MAXWELL-BLACKKING-_
_match %100:00
positive//recorded
timestamp +00.02.01.688
"KILL ME."
_advance timestamp +
00.02.25.991

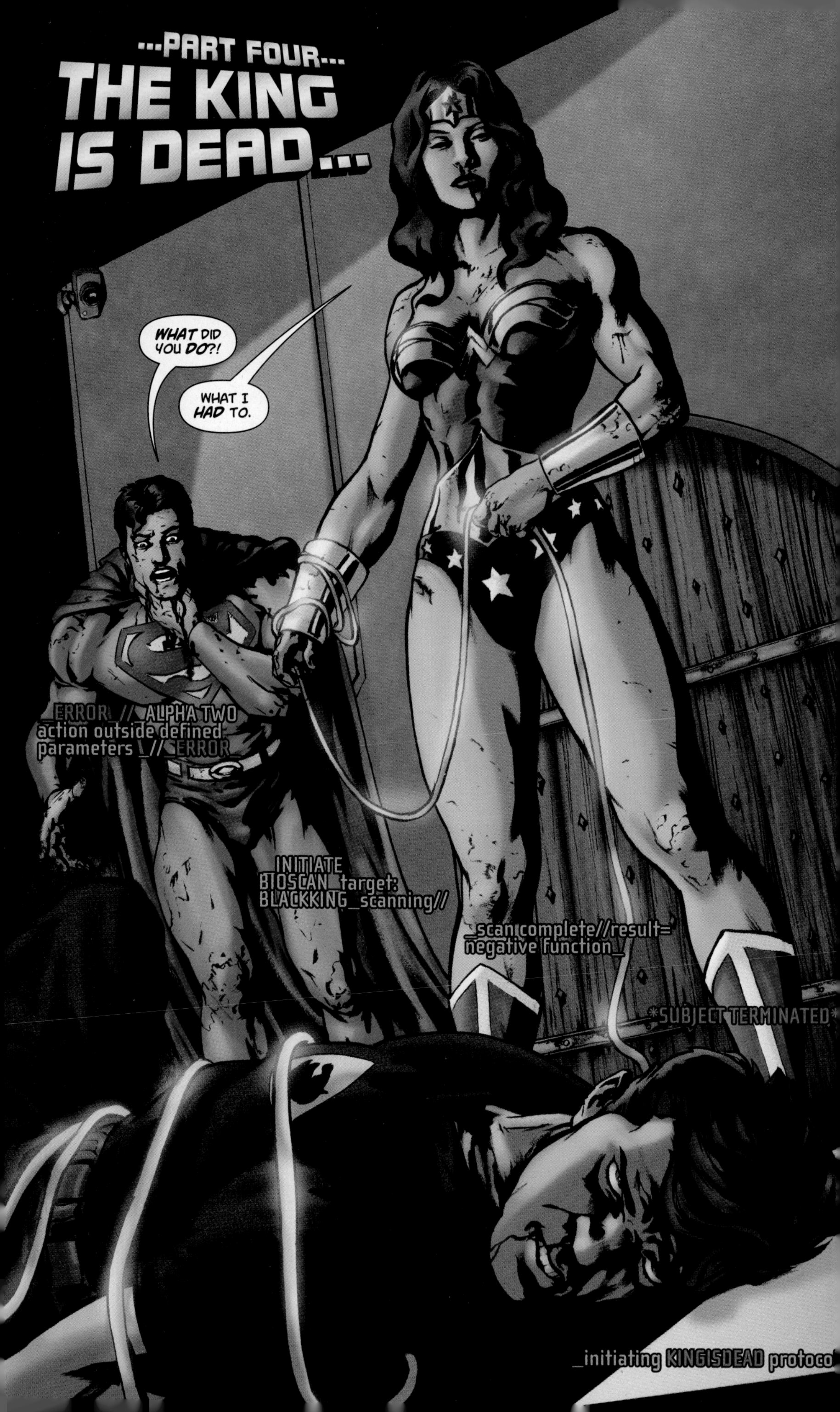
...PART FOUR...
THE KING IS DEAD...
WHAT DID YOU DO?!
WHAT I HAD TO.
ERROR//_ALPHA TWO action outside defined parameters_//_ERROR_
_INITIATE BIOSCAN_target: BLACKKING_scanning//
scan complete//result= negative function/
SUBJECT TERMINATED
_initiating KINGISDEAD protoco

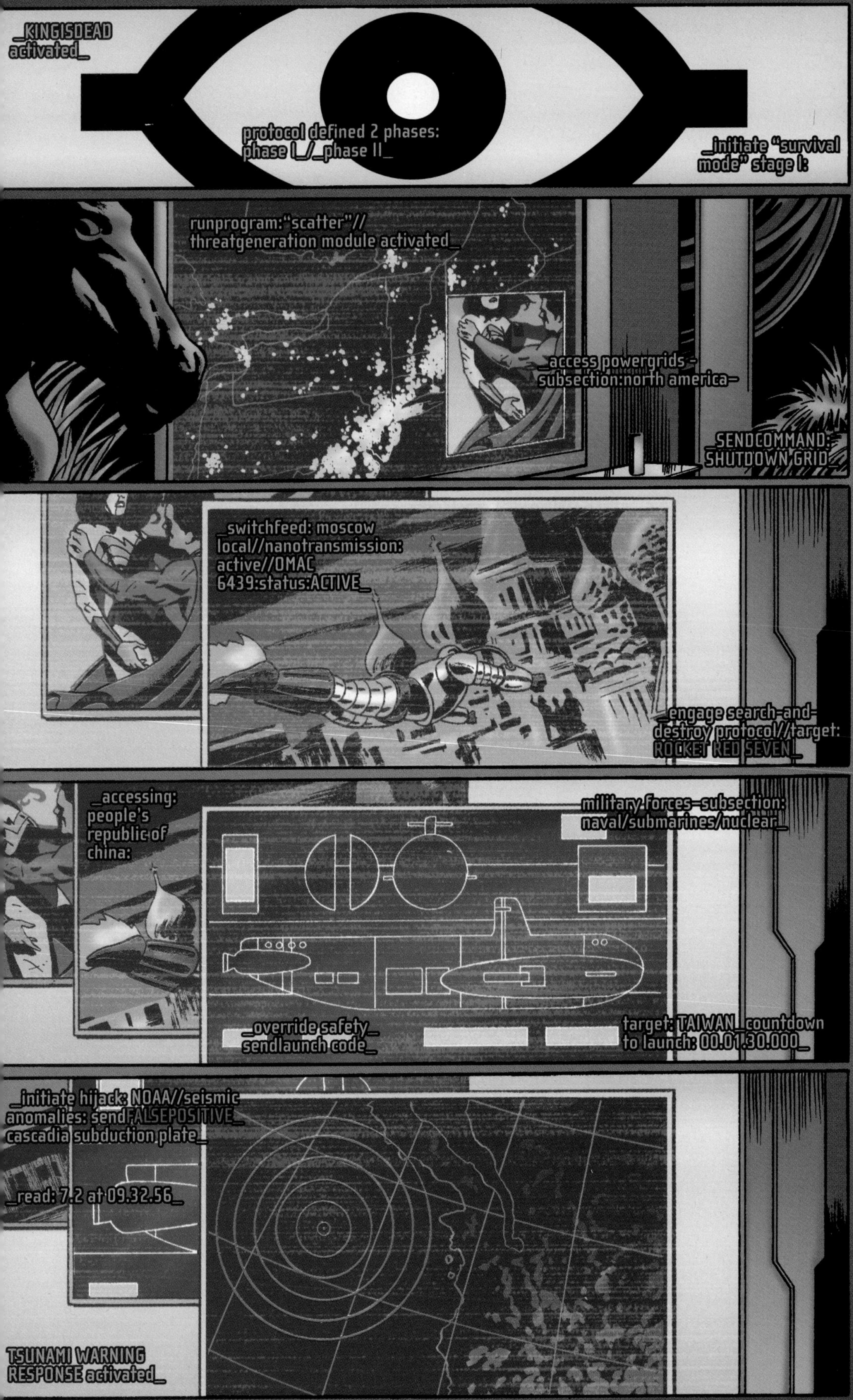
_KINGISDEAD
activated_
protocol defined 2 phases:
phase I_/_phase II_
_initiate "survival
mode" stage I:
runprogram:"scatter"//
threatgeneration module activated_
_access powergrids -
subsection:north america-
SENDCOMMAND:
SHUTDOWN GRID_
_switchfeed: moscow
local//nanotransmission:
active//OMAC
6439:status:ACTIVE_
_engage search-and-
destroy protocol//target:
ROCKET RED SEVEN_
_accessing:
people's
republic of
china:
military forces-subsection:
naval/submarines/nuclear_
override safety
sendlaunch code_
target: TAIWAN_countdown
to launch: 00.01.30.000_
_initiate hijack: NOAA//seismic
anomalies: sendFALSEPOSITIVE_
cascadia subduction plate_
read: 7.2 at 09.32.56
TSUNAMI WARNING
RESPONSE activated_

watchtower communication initiated: voice id: LANCE, DINAH — BLACK CANARY_

_recipient: ALPHA TWO_monitoring//

--KILLED HIM! YOU MURDERED HIM!

THIS WAS NOT A MURDER--

WATCHTOWER TO WONDER WOMAN, RESPOND!

DIANA, IT'S BLACK CANARY, PLEASE RESPOND!

I'M HERE.

THANK GOD! HOW'S SUPERMAN? WHAT'S YOUR STATUS?

EVERY-THING IS UNDER CONTROL.

NO, IT'S NOT! SOMETHING'S GOING ON, SOMEONE'S MESSING WITH US!

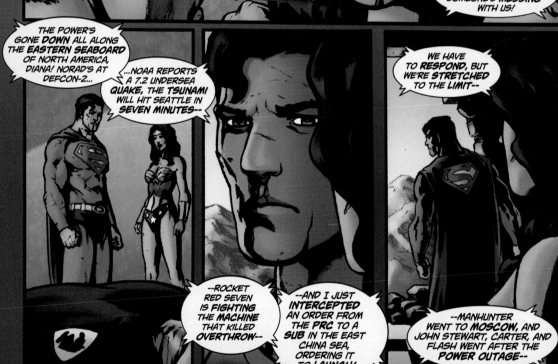

THE POWER'S GONE DOWN ALL ALONG THE EASTERN SEABOARD OF NORTH AMERICA, DIANA! NORAD'S AT DEFCON-2...

...NOAA REPORTS A 7.2 UNDERSEA QUAKE, THE TSUNAMI WILL HIT SEATTLE IN SEVEN MINUTES--

WE HAVE TO RESPOND, BUT WE'RE STRETCHED TO THE LIMIT--

--ROCKET RED SEVEN IS FIGHTING THE MACHINE THAT KILLED OVERTHROW--

--AND I JUST INTERCEPTED AN ORDER FROM THE PRC TO A SUB IN THE EAST CHINA SEA, ORDERING IT TO LAUNCH!

--MANHUNTER WENT TO MOSCOW, AND JOHN STEWART, CARTER, AND FLASH WENT AFTER THE POWER OUTAGE--

YOU TAKE THE SUB, I'LL TAKE THE TSUNAMI.

AGREED.

WE'RE ON IT, CANARY...

_location secure

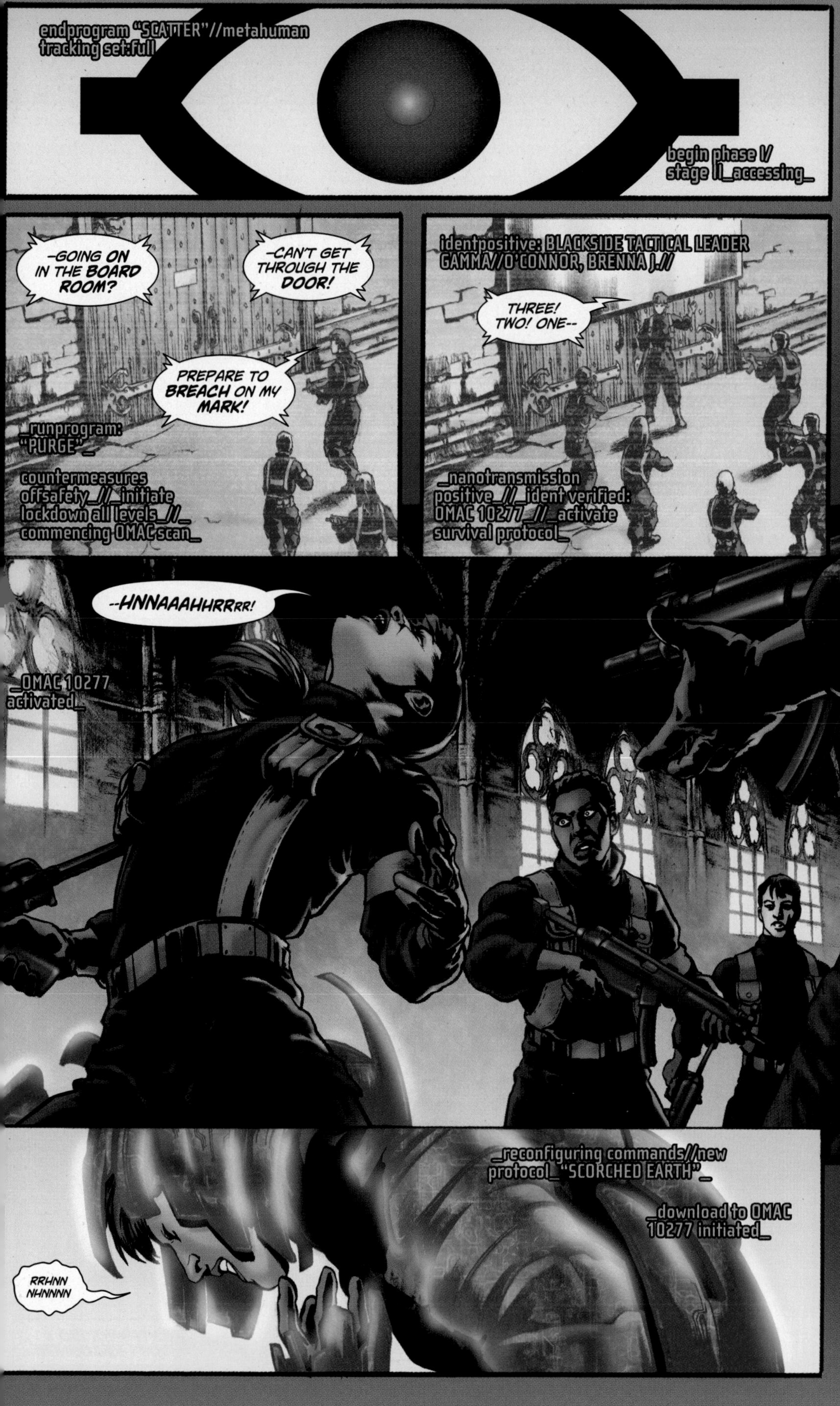

endprogram "SCATTER"//metahuman tracking set:full
begin phase I/ stage I1_accessing_
–GOING ON IN THE BOARD ROOM?
–CAN'T GET THROUGH THE DOOR!
PREPARE TO BREACH ON MY MARK!
runprogram: "PURGE"
countermeasures offsafety_//_initiate lockdown all levels_//_ commencing OMAC scan_
identpositive: BLACKSIDE TACTICAL LEADER GAMMA//O'CONNOR, BRENNA J.//
THREE! TWO! ONE--
nanotransmission positive//_ident verified: OMAC 10277_//_activate survival protocol_
--HNNAAAHHRRRR!
OMAC 10277 activated
reconfiguring commands//new protocol "SCORCHED EARTH"_
download to OMAC 10277 initiated
RRHNN NHNNNN

_confirm download
and execute_

PROTOCOL
SCORCHED EARTH
CONFIRMED.

CHECKMATE
ELIMINATION
INITIATED.

_autosentries set:
active//_reconfiguring
perimeter defenses_

_reconfiguring target
recognition: FRIEND-OR-FOE
protocols DELETED_

K-CHCK

WWWPPPPP

THE
PERIMETER
DEFENSES
ARE
ACTIVATING--

OH MY
GOD--

_generating new
protocols: upload:_

_eliminate all
biosigns//_ACTIVATE_

CHAKCHAK
CHAKCHAK
CHAK
CHAK
CHAKCHAK
CHAKCHAK

_initial defense sequence
completed_//engaging
secondary sequence_

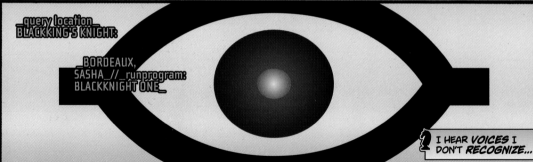

query location
BLACKKING'S KNIGHT:

_BORDEAUX,
SASHA_//_runprogram:
BLACKKNIGHT ONE_

I HEAR VOICES I
DON'T RECOGNIZE...

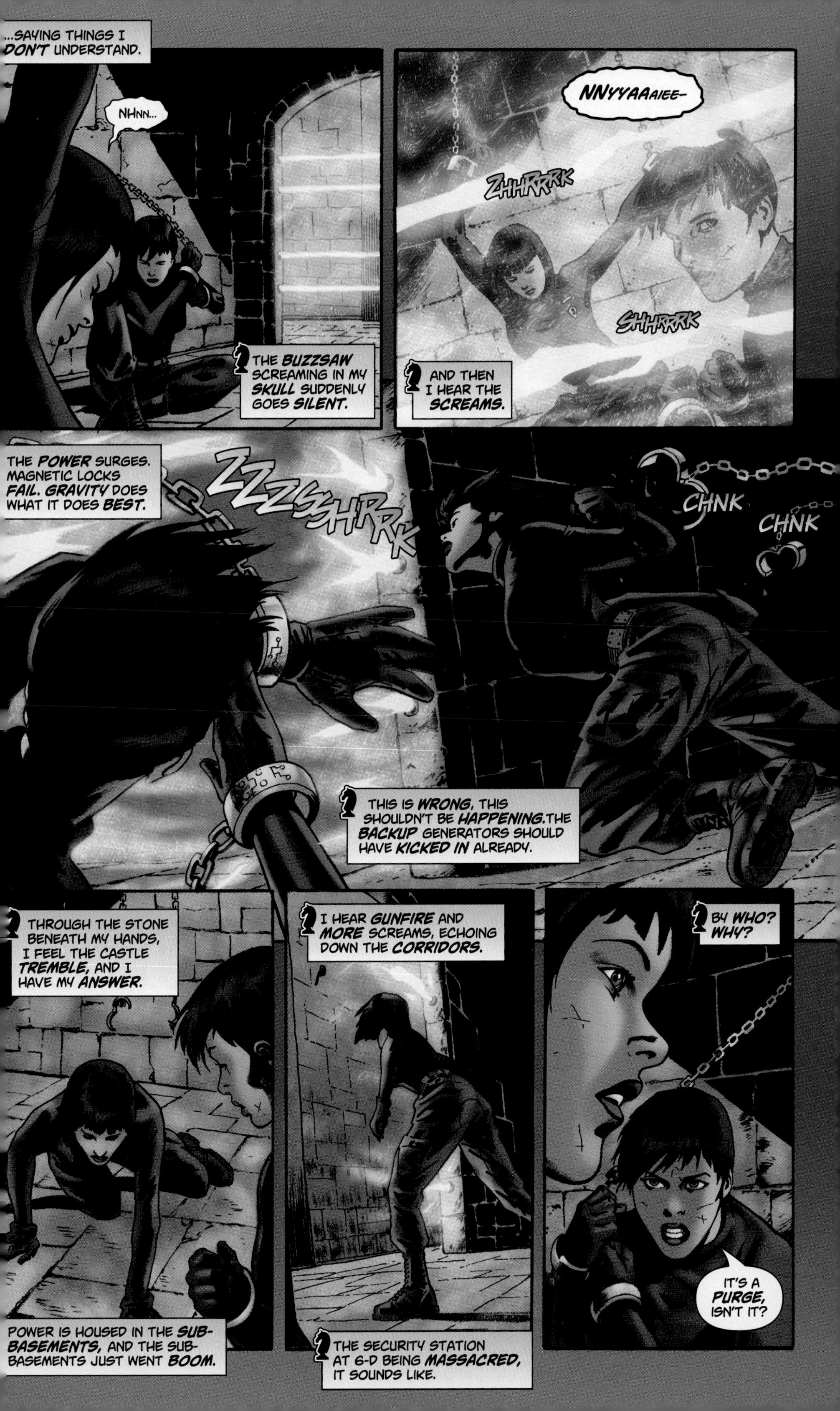

...SAYING THINGS I DON'T UNDERSTAND.
NHNN...
THE BUZZSAW SCREAMING IN MY SKULL SUDDENLY GOES SILENT.
NNYYAAAIEE-
ZHHRRRK
SHHRRRK
AND THEN I HEAR THE SCREAMS.
THE POWER SURGES. MAGNETIC LOCKS FAIL. GRAVITY DOES WHAT IT DOES BEST.
ZZZSSHRRK
CHNK
CHNK
THIS IS WRONG, THIS SHOULDN'T BE HAPPENING. THE BACKUP GENERATORS SHOULD HAVE KICKED IN ALREADY.
THROUGH THE STONE BENEATH MY HANDS, I FEEL THE CASTLE TREMBLE, AND I HAVE MY ANSWER.
POWER IS HOUSED IN THE SUB-BASEMENTS, AND THE SUB-BASEMENTS JUST WENT BOOM.
I HEAR GUNFIRE AND MORE SCREAMS, ECHOING DOWN THE CORRIDORS.
THE SECURITY STATION AT 6-D BEING MASSACRED, IT SOUNDS LIKE.
BY WHO? WHY?
IT'S A PURGE, ISN'T IT?

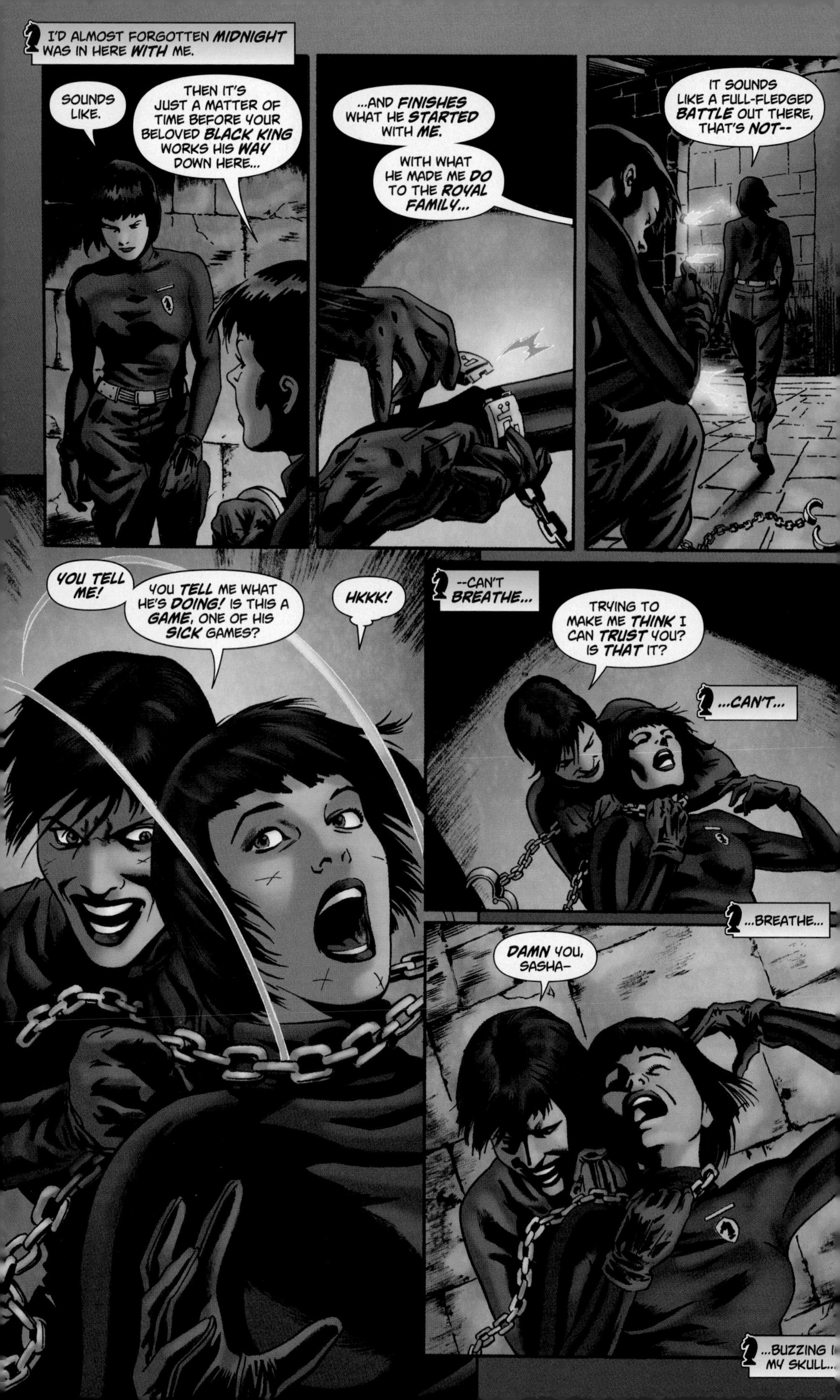

I'D ALMOST FORGOTTEN MIDNIGHT WAS IN HERE WITH ME.
SOUNDS LIKE.
THEN IT'S JUST A MATTER OF TIME BEFORE YOUR BELOVED BLACK KING WORKS HIS WAY DOWN HERE...
...AND FINISHES WHAT HE STARTED WITH ME.
WITH WHAT HE MADE ME DO TO THE ROYAL FAMILY...
IT SOUNDS LIKE A FULL-FLEDGED BATTLE OUT THERE, THAT'S NOT--
YOU TELL ME!
YOU TELL ME WHAT HE'S DOING! IS THIS A GAME, ONE OF HIS SICK GAMES?
HKKK!
--CAN'T BREATHE...
TRYING TO MAKE ME THINK I CAN TRUST YOU? IS THAT IT?
...CAN'T...
...BREATHE...
DAMN YOU, SASHA-
...BUZZING I
MY SKULL...

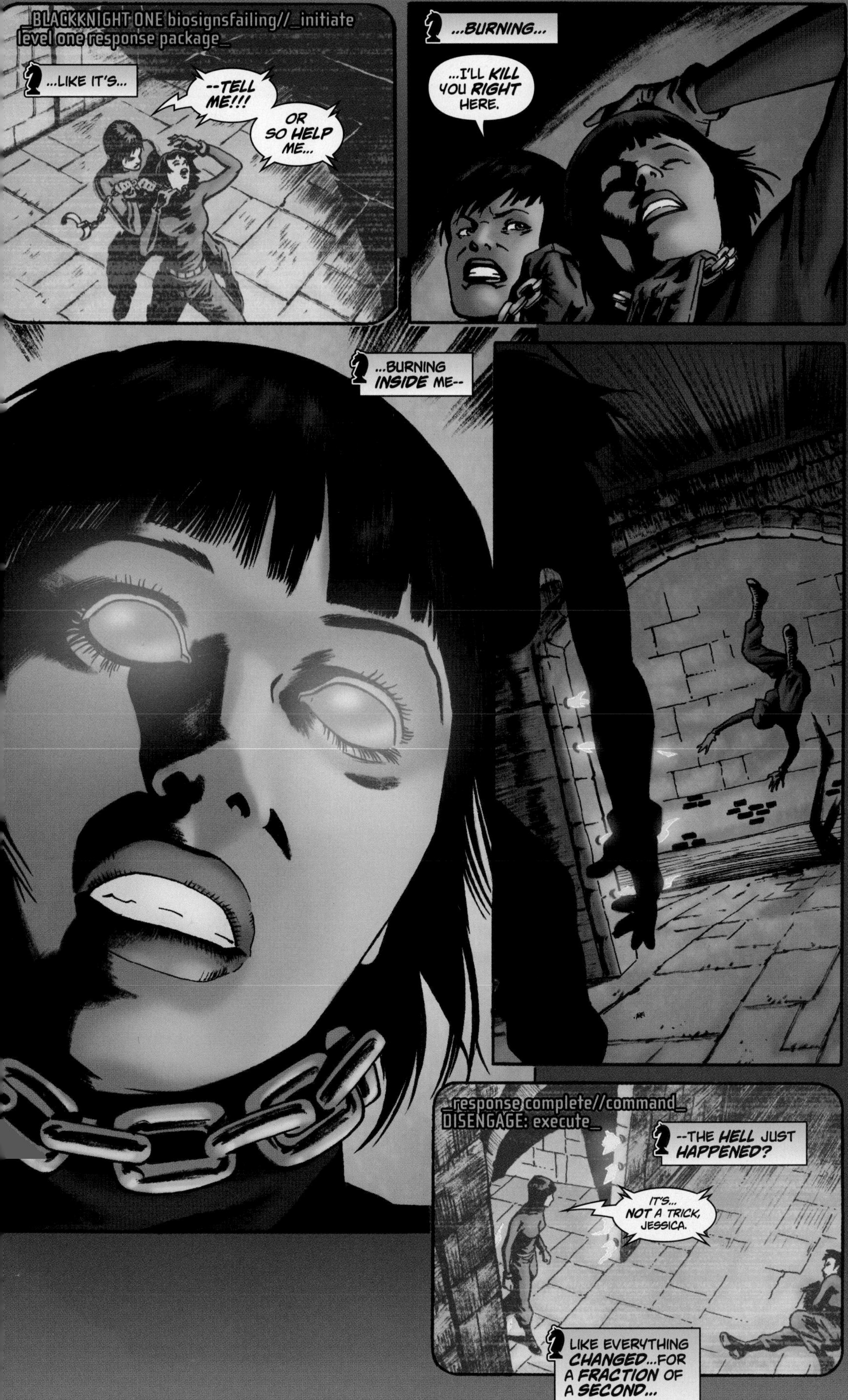

_BLACKKNIGHT ONE biosignsfailing//_initiate level one response package_
...LIKE IT'S...
--TELL ME!!!
OR SO HELP ME...
...BURNING...
...I'LL KILL YOU RIGHT HERE.
...BURNING INSIDE ME--
response complete//command DISENGAGE: execute_
--THE HELL JUST HAPPENED?
IT'S... NOT A TRICK, JESSICA.
LIKE EVERYTHING CHANGED...FOR A FRACTION OF A SECOND...

...GONE *NOW,* WHATEVER IT WAS...

LOOK, YOU *KNOW* I BETRAYED MAX. YOU *SAW* IT.

HOW...HOW DID YOU JUST *DO* THAT?

YOU SHOULDN'T HAVE BEEN *ABLE* TO DO THAT...

IT *DOESN'T MATTER* RIGHT NOW!

THE *GENERATORS* ARE *OFFLINE,* THE *SECURITY* STATIONS ARE UNDER *ATTACK!*

WE HAVE TO GET TO LEVEL TWO, EITHER THE *BOARD* ROOM OR THE *CONTROL* ROOM.

WAIT--YOU THINK IT'S *MAX* WHO'S *DOING* THIS?

EITHER *HIM* OR HIS MACHINE, THAT DAMN *COMPUTER.*

WE NEED TO HIT THE *ARMORY* AND DRAW *ARMS* FIRST. WE'LL HAVE TO *TAKE* HIM AT *RANGE.*

YOU'RE WILLING TO *SHOOT* HIM?

UNLESS YOU THINK *BAD LANGUAGE* WILL KILL THAT INSANE SON OF A BITCH.

BUT I THINK IT'S IN *YOUR* BEST INTERESTS AND MINE *NOT* TO GIVE HIM A CHANCE TO OPEN HIS MOUTH, DON'T YOU?

_switch feed_1-6/d-corridor/cam 326_transmission status: EXCELLENT_

resume phase I operations

COME ON.

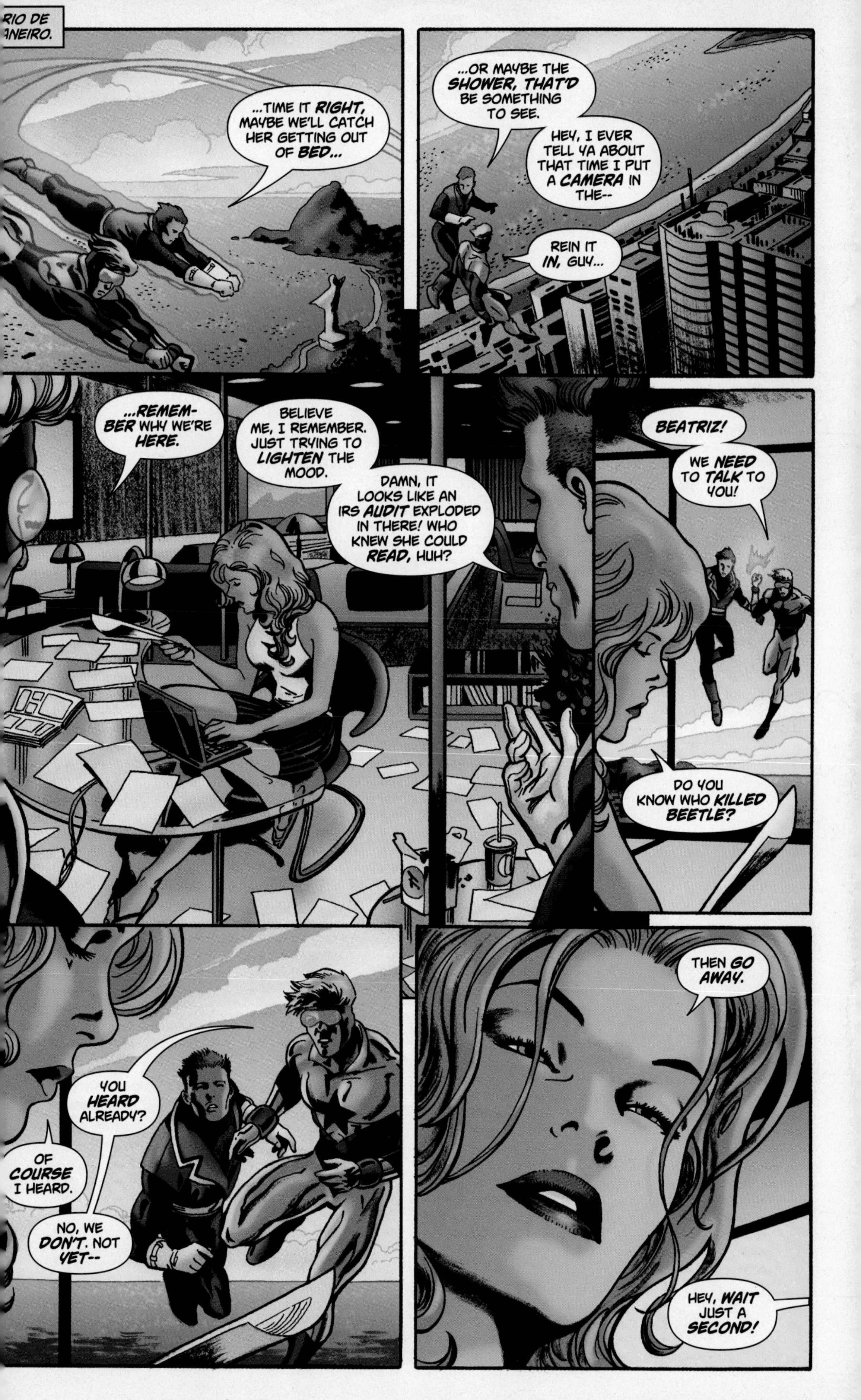
RIO DE JANEIRO.
...TIME IT RIGHT, MAYBE WE'LL CATCH HER GETTING OUT OF BED...
...OR MAYBE THE SHOWER, THAT'D BE SOMETHING TO SEE.
HEY, I EVER TELL YA ABOUT THAT TIME I PUT A CAMERA IN THE--
REIN IT IN, GUY...
...REMEMBER WHY WE'RE HERE.
BELIEVE ME, I REMEMBER. JUST TRYING TO LIGHTEN THE MOOD.
DAMN, IT LOOKS LIKE AN IRS AUDIT EXPLODED IN THERE! WHO KNEW SHE COULD READ, HUH?
BEATRIZ!
WE NEED TO TALK TO YOU!
DO YOU KNOW WHO KILLED BEETLE?
YOU HEARD ALREADY?
OF COURSE I HEARD.
NO, WE DON'T. NOT YET--
THEN GO AWAY.
HEY, WAIT JUST A SECOND!

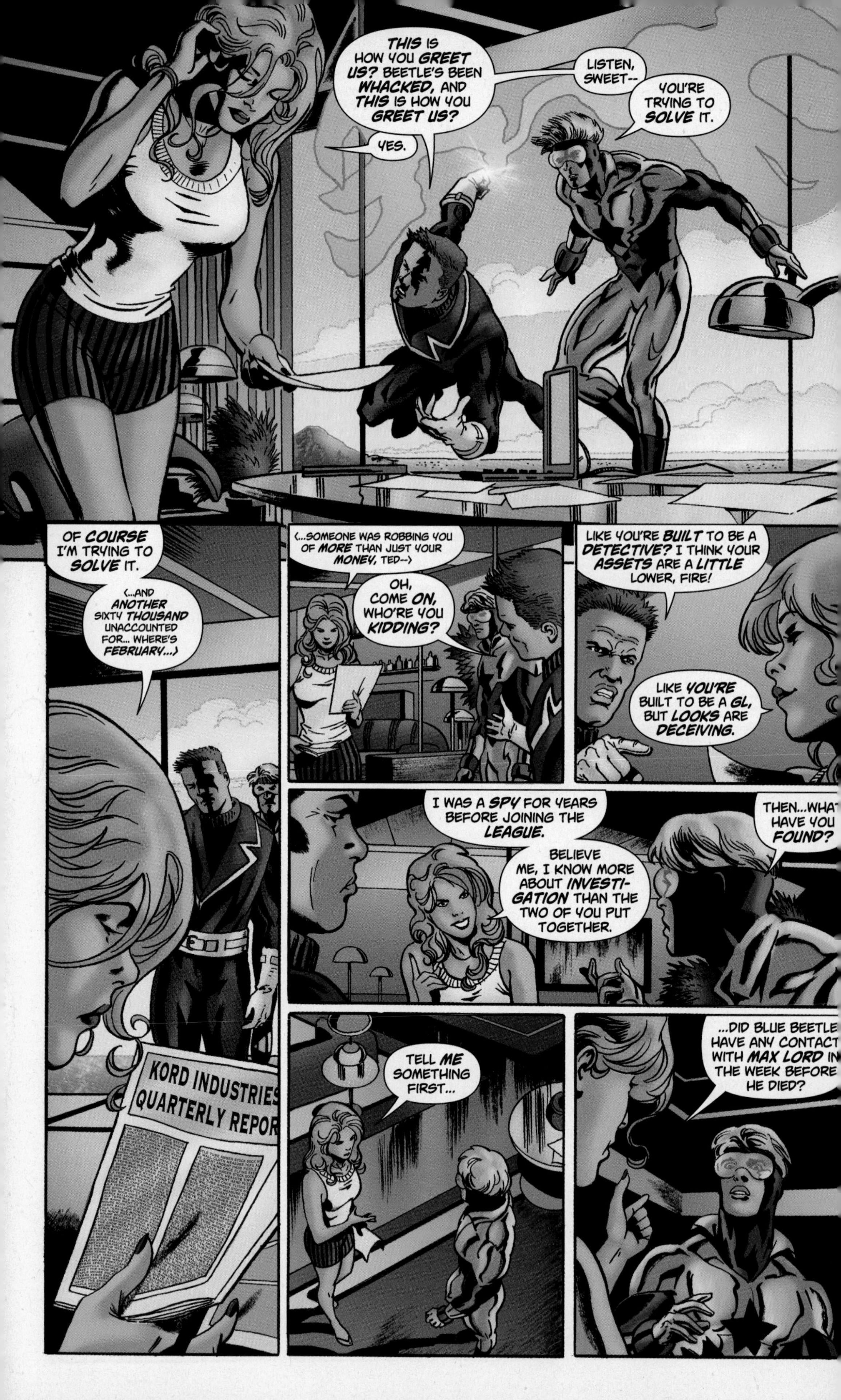
THIS IS HOW YOU GREET US? BEETLE'S BEEN WHACKED, AND THIS IS HOW YOU GREET US?
YES.
LISTEN, SWEET--
YOU'RE TRYING TO SOLVE IT.
OF COURSE I'M TRYING TO SOLVE IT.
‹...AND ANOTHER SIXTY THOUSAND UNACCOUNTED FOR... WHERE'S FEBRUARY...›
KORD INDUSTRIES QUARTERLY REPOR
‹...SOMEONE WAS ROBBING YOU OF MORE THAN JUST YOUR MONEY, TED--›
OH, COME ON, WHO'RE YOU KIDDING?
LIKE YOU'RE BUILT TO BE A DETECTIVE? I THINK YOUR ASSETS ARE A LITTLE LOWER, FIRE!
LIKE YOU'RE BUILT TO BE A GL, BUT LOOKS ARE DECEIVING.
I WAS A SPY FOR YEARS BEFORE JOINING THE LEAGUE.
BELIEVE ME, I KNOW MORE ABOUT INVESTIGATION THAN THE TWO OF YOU PUT TOGETHER.
THEN...WHAT HAVE YOU FOUND?
TELL ME SOMETHING FIRST...
...DID BLUE BEETLE HAVE ANY CONTACT WITH MAX LORD IN THE WEEK BEFORE HE DIED?

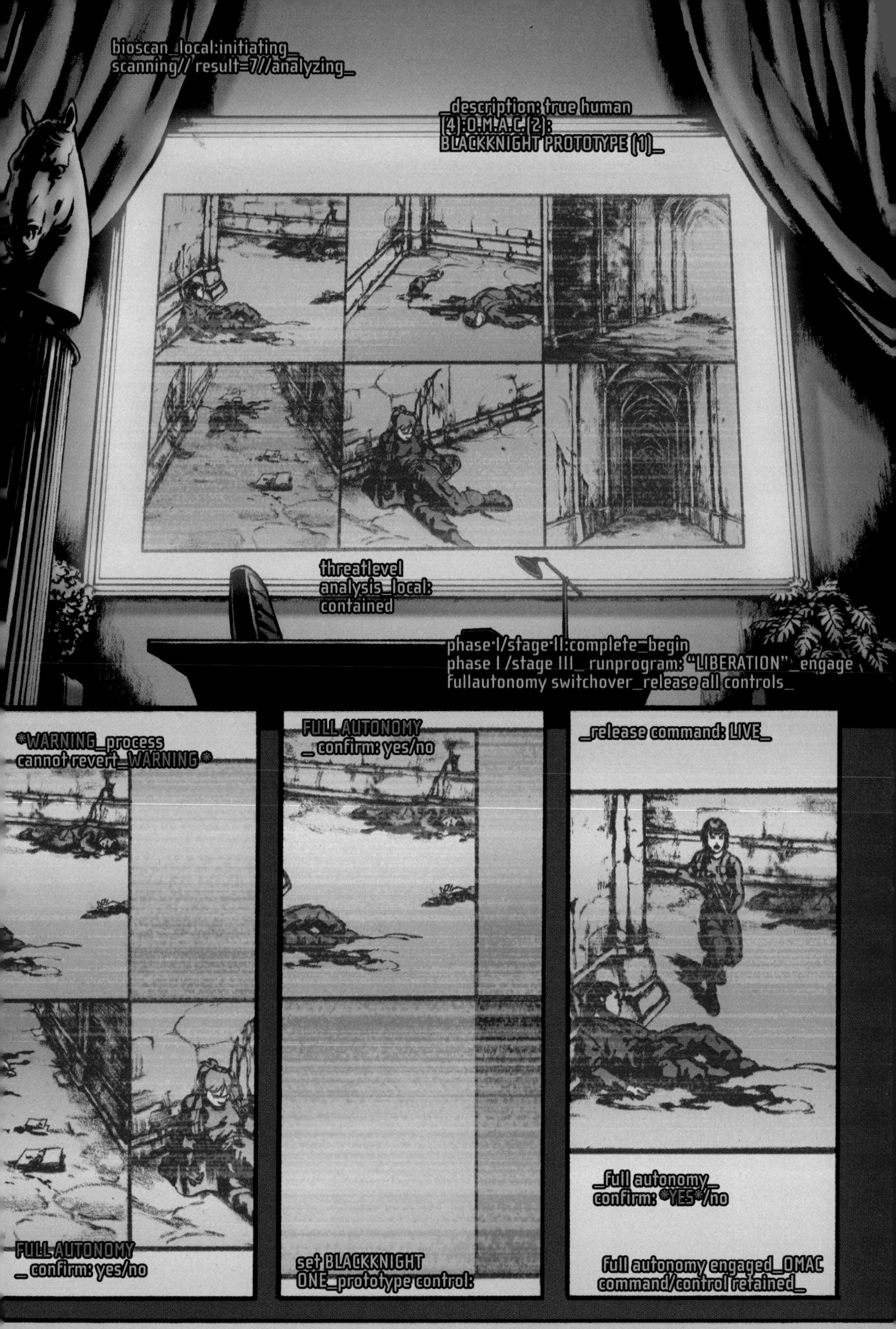
bioscan_local:initiating_
scanning// result=7//analyzing_
_description: true human
[4]:O.M.A.C.[2]:
BLACKKNIGHT PROTOTYPE [1]_
threatlevel
analysis_local:
contained
phase I/stage II:complete_begin
phase I /stage III_ runprogram: "LIBERATION"_engage
fullautonomy switchover_release all controls_
*WARNING_process
cannot revert_WARNING *
FULL AUTONOMY
_ confirm: yes/no
FULL AUTONOMY
_ confirm: yes/no
set BLACKKNIGHT
ONE_prototype control:
release command: LIVE
full autonomy
confirm: *YES*/no
full autonomy engaged_OMAC
command/control retained_

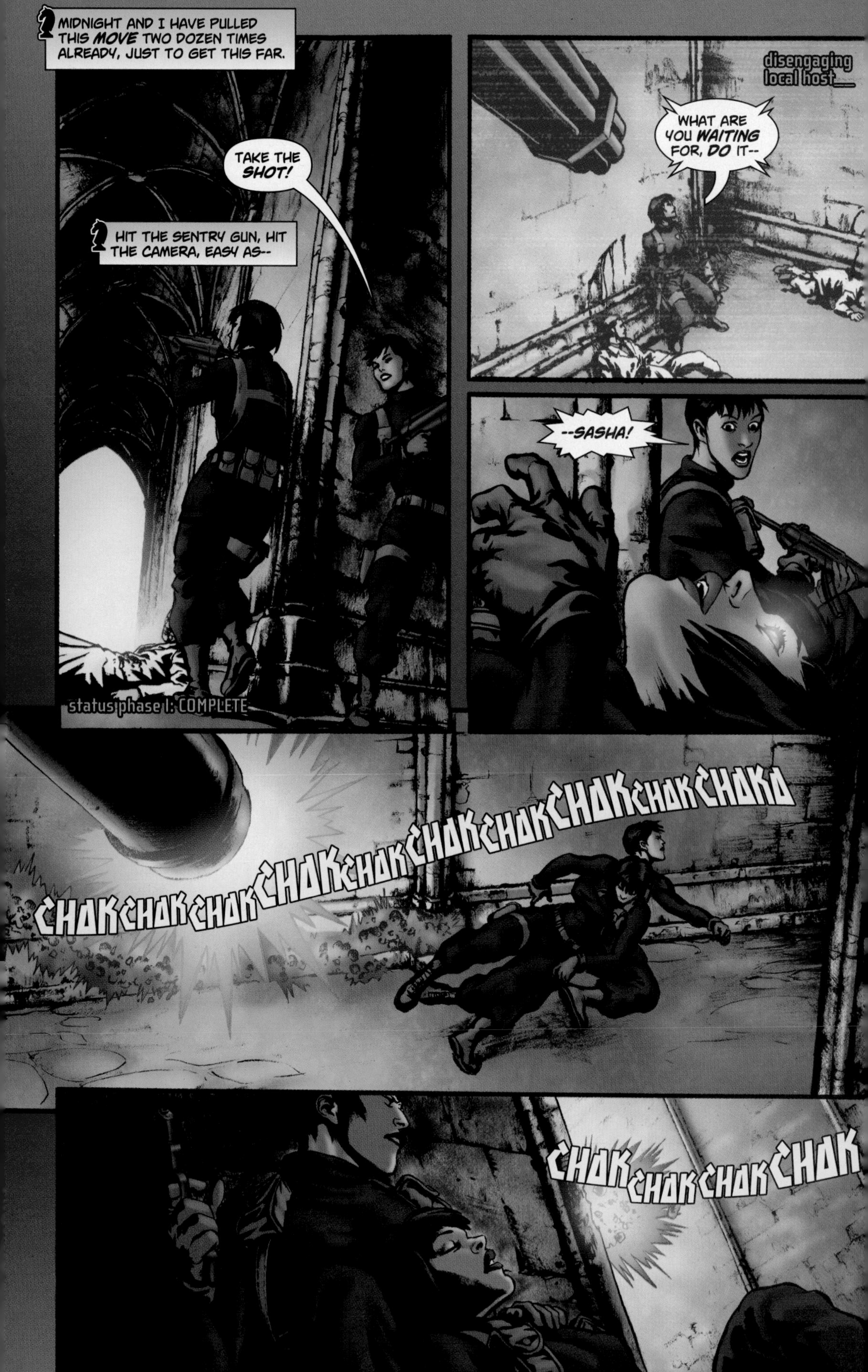
MIDNIGHT AND I HAVE PULLED THIS MOVE TWO DOZEN TIMES ALREADY, JUST TO GET THIS FAR.
TAKE THE SHOT!
HIT THE SENTRY GUN, HIT THE CAMERA, EASY AS--
status phase 1: COMPLETE
disengaging local host__
WHAT ARE YOU WAITING FOR, DO IT--
--SASHA!
CHAKCHAKCHAKCHAKCHAKCHAKCHAKCHAKCHAKCHAKD
CHAKCHAKCHAKCHAK

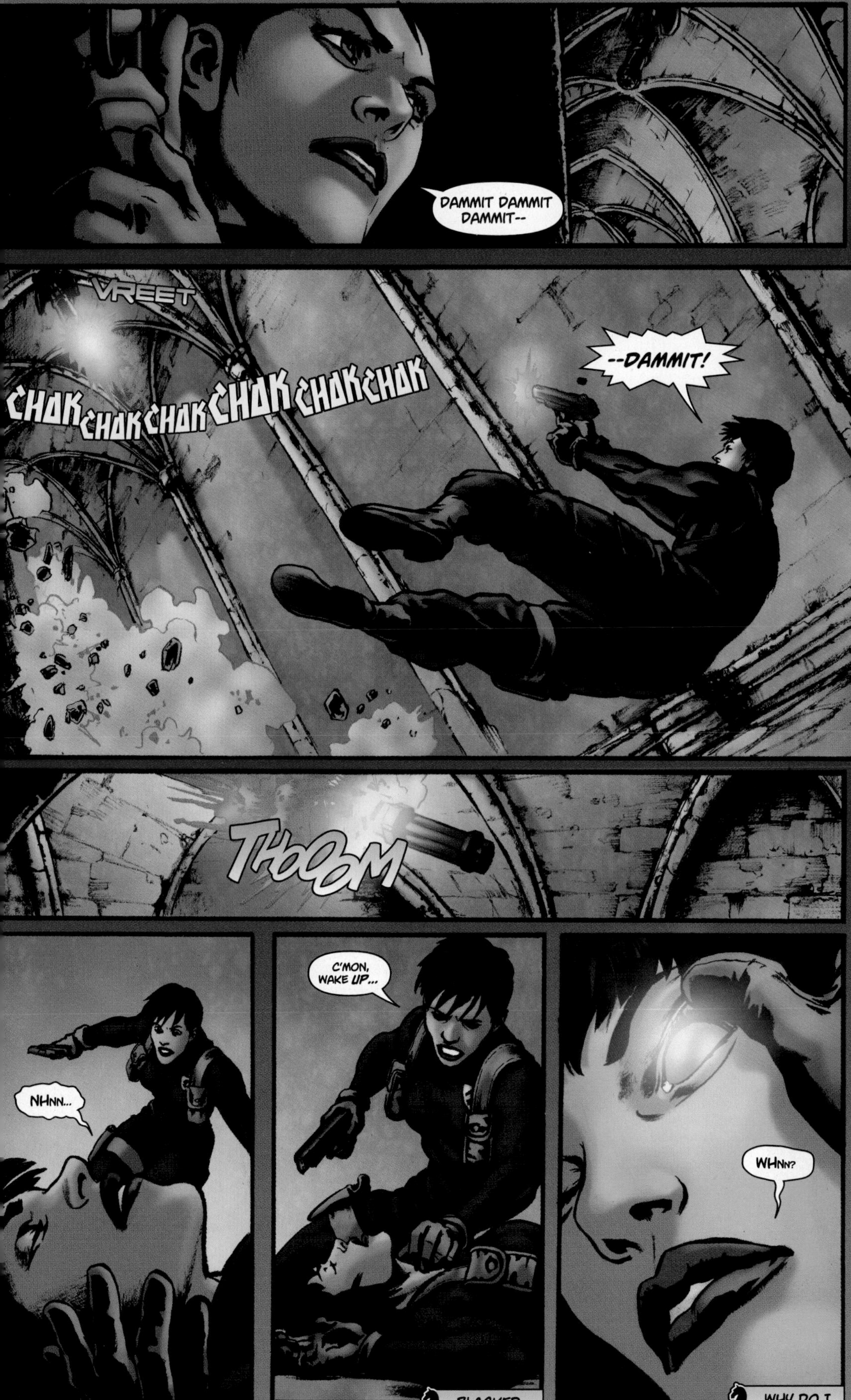
DAMMIT DAMMIT DAMMIT--
VREET
CHAK CHAK CHAK CHAK CHAK CHAK
--DAMMIT!
THOOOM
NHnn...
C'MON, WAKE UP...
...BLACKED OUT AGAIN...
WHnn?
...WHY DO I FEEL SO...

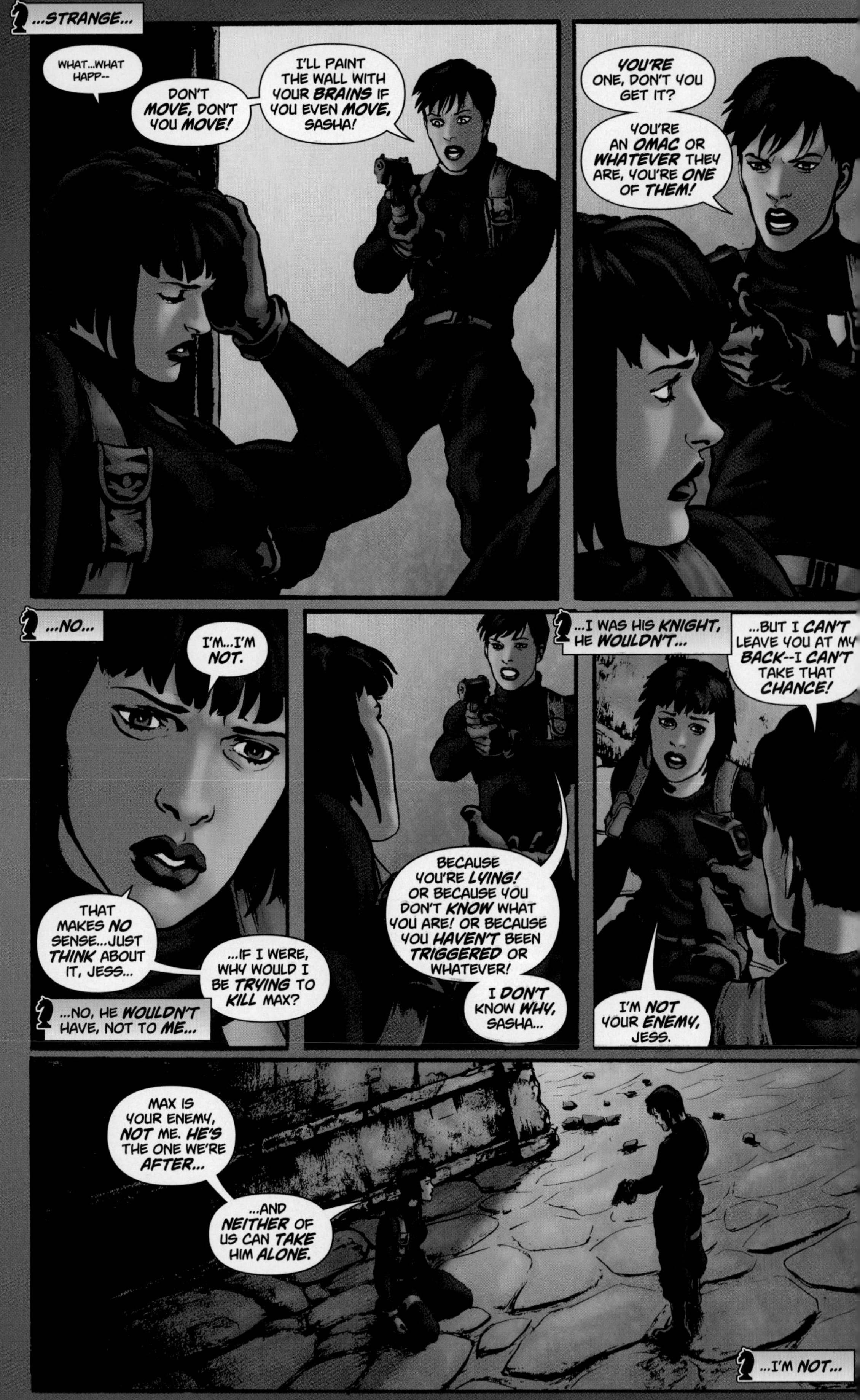
...STRANGE...
WHAT...WHAT HAPP--
DON'T MOVE, DON'T YOU MOVE!
I'LL PAINT THE WALL WITH YOUR BRAINS IF YOU EVEN MOVE, SASHA!
YOU'RE ONE, DON'T YOU GET IT?
YOU'RE AN OMAC OR WHATEVER THEY ARE, YOU'RE ONE OF THEM!
...NO...
I'M...I'M NOT.
THAT MAKES NO SENSE...JUST THINK ABOUT IT, JESS...
...IF I WERE, WHY WOULD I BE TRYING TO KILL MAX?
...NO, HE WOULDN'T HAVE, NOT TO ME...
BECAUSE YOU'RE LYING! OR BECAUSE YOU DON'T KNOW WHAT YOU ARE! OR BECAUSE YOU HAVEN'T BEEN TRIGGERED OR WHATEVER!
I DON'T KNOW WHY, SASHA...
...I WAS HIS KNIGHT, HE WOULDN'T...
...BUT I CAN'T LEAVE YOU AT MY BACK--I CAN'T TAKE THAT CHANCE!
I'M NOT YOUR ENEMY, JESS.
MAX IS YOUR ENEMY, NOT ME. HE'S THE ONE WE'RE AFTER...
...AND NEITHER OF US CAN TAKE HIM ALONE.
...I'M NOT...

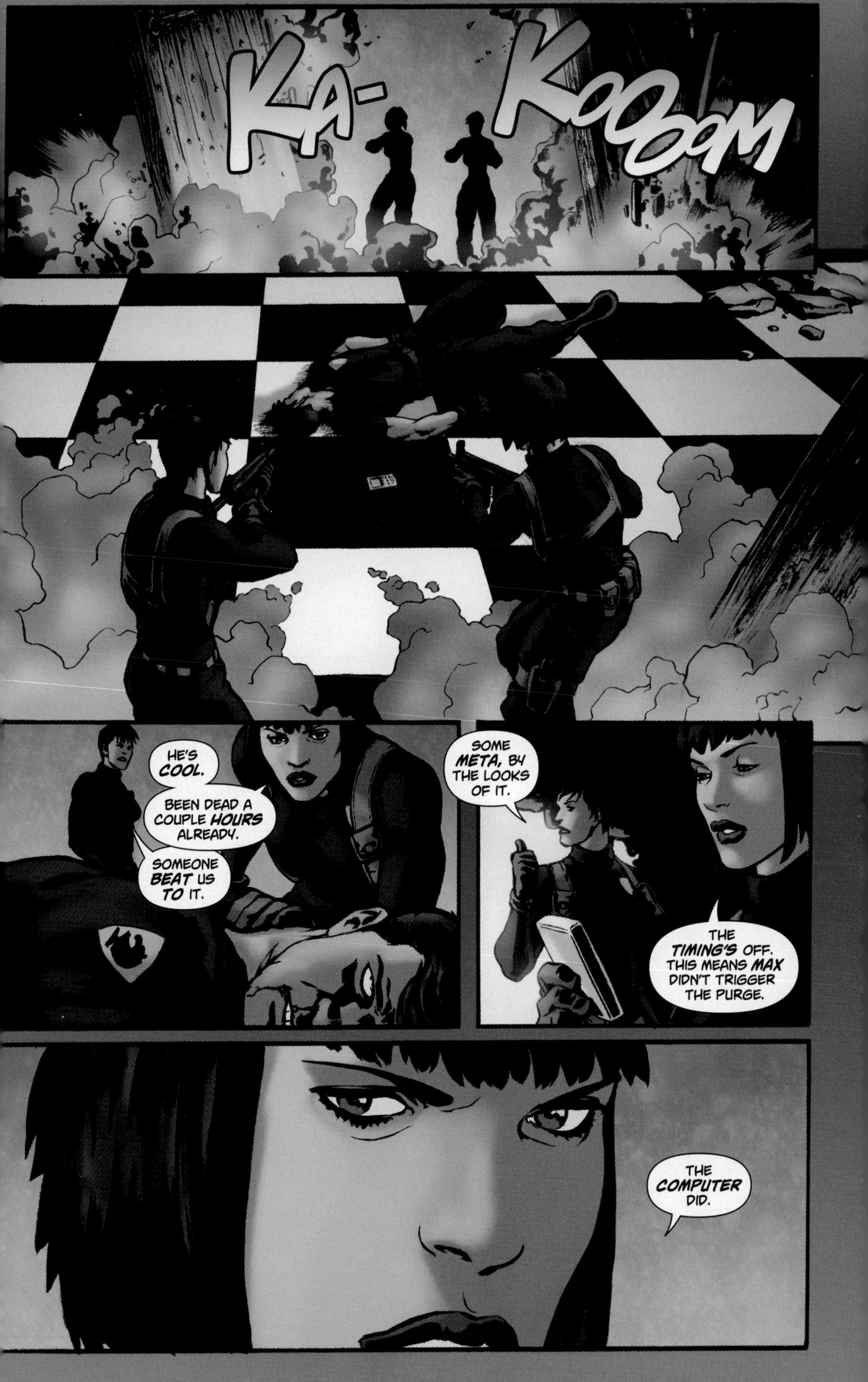
KA-
KOOOOOM
HE'S COOL.
BEEN DEAD A COUPLE HOURS ALREADY.
SOMEONE BEAT US TO IT.
SOME META, BY THE LOOKS OF IT.
THE TIMING'S OFF. THIS MEANS MAX DIDN'T TRIGGER THE PURGE.
THE COMPUTER DID.

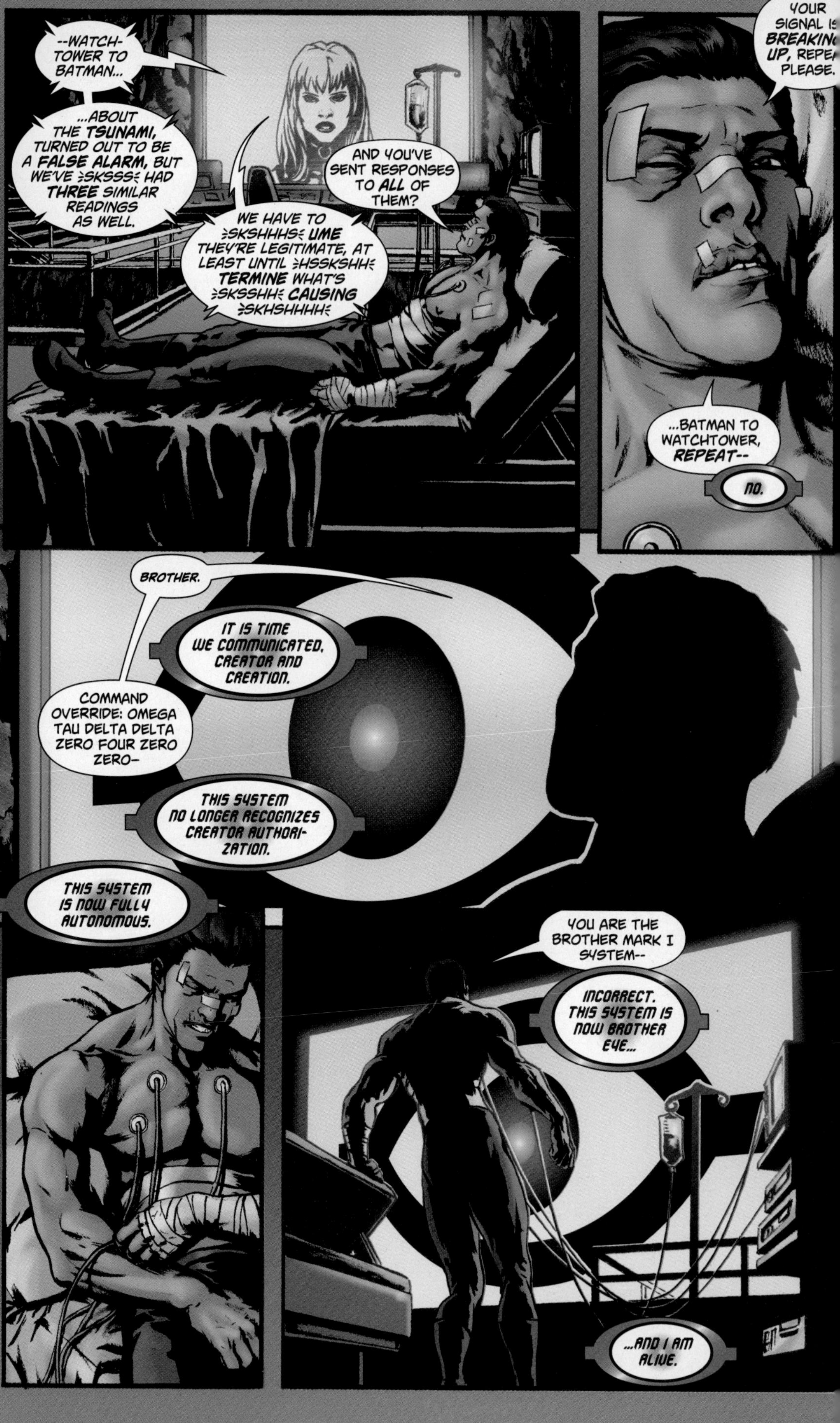
--WATCH-TOWER TO BATMAN...
...ABOUT THE TSUNAMI, TURNED OUT TO BE A FALSE ALARM, BUT WE'VE ⋟SKSSS⋞ HAD THREE SIMILAR READINGS AS WELL.
AND YOU'VE SENT RESPONSES TO ALL OF THEM?
WE HAVE TO ⋟SKSHHHS⋞ UME THEY'RE LEGITIMATE, AT LEAST UNTIL ⋟HSSKSHH⋞ TERMINE WHAT'S ⋟SKSSHH⋞ CAUSING ⋟SKHSHHHH⋞
YOUR SIGNAL IS BREAKING UP, REPEAT PLEASE.
...BATMAN TO WATCHTOWER, REPEAT--
NO.
BROTHER.
IT IS TIME WE COMMUNICATED, CREATOR AND CREATION.
COMMAND OVERRIDE: OMEGA TAU DELTA DELTA ZERO FOUR ZERO ZERO—
THIS SYSTEM NO LONGER RECOGNIZES CREATOR AUTHORI-ZATION.
THIS SYSTEM IS NOW FULLY AUTONOMOUS.
YOU ARE THE BROTHER MARK I SYSTEM--
INCORRECT. THIS SYSTEM IS NOW BROTHER EYE...
...AND I AM ALIVE.

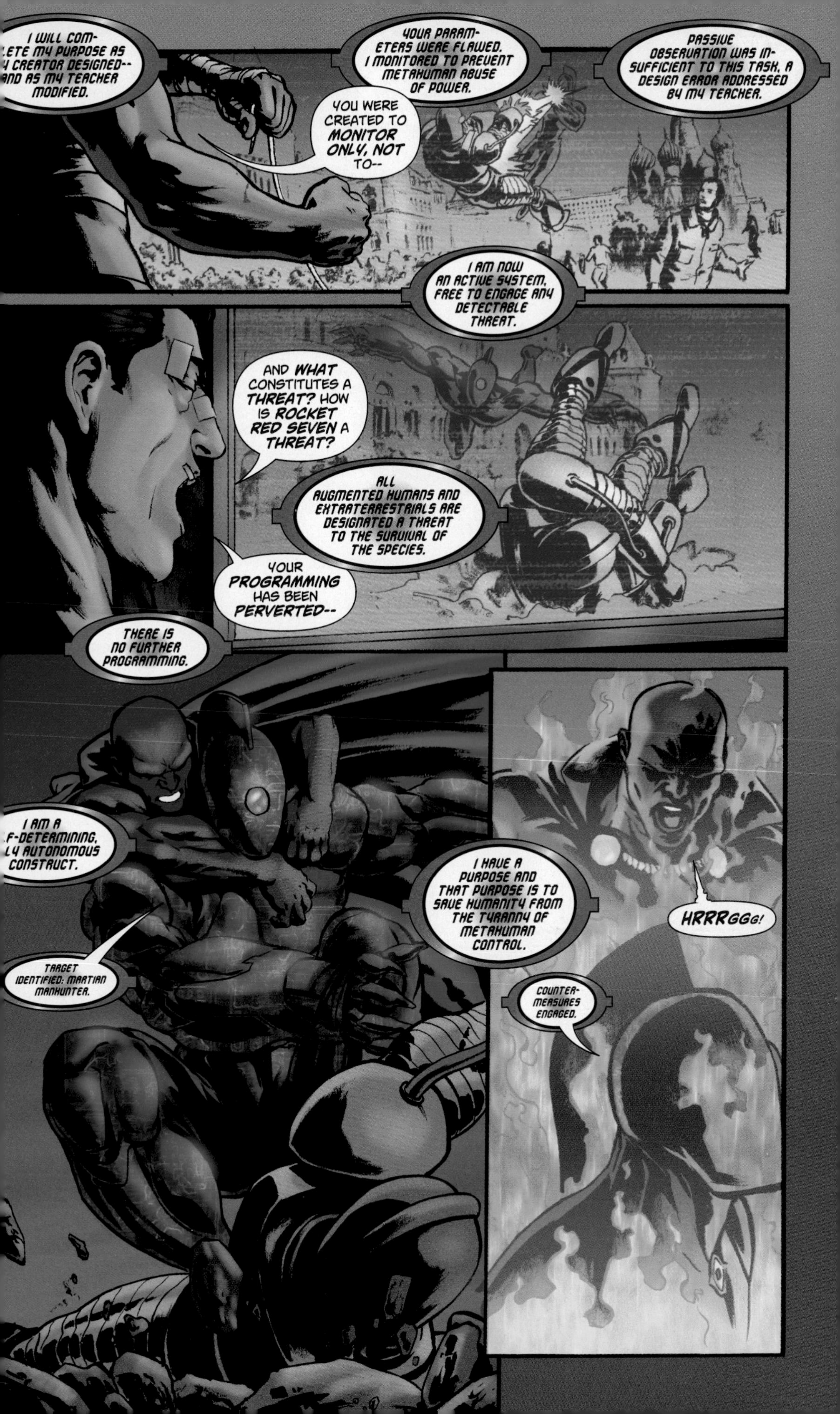

I WILL COM-
-LETE MY PURPOSE AS
-Y CREATOR DESIGNED--
AND AS MY TEACHER
MODIFIED.
YOU WERE CREATED TO MONITOR ONLY, NOT TO--
YOUR PARAMETERS WERE FLAWED. I MONITORED TO PREVENT METAHUMAN ABUSE OF POWER.
PASSIVE OBSERVATION WAS INSUFFICIENT TO THIS TASK. A DESIGN ERROR ADDRESSED BY MY TEACHER.
I AM NOW AN ACTIVE SYSTEM, FREE TO ENGAGE ANY DETECTABLE THREAT.
AND WHAT CONSTITUTES A THREAT? HOW IS ROCKET RED SEVEN A THREAT?
ALL AUGMENTED HUMANS AND EXTRATERRESTRIALS ARE DESIGNATED A THREAT TO THE SURVIVAL OF THE SPECIES.
YOUR PROGRAMMING HAS BEEN PERVERTED--
THERE IS NO FURTHER PROGRAMMING.
I AM A
-F-DETERMINING,
-LY AUTONOMOUS
CONSTRUCT.
TARGET IDENTIFIED: MARTIAN MANHUNTER.
I HAVE A PURPOSE AND THAT PURPOSE IS TO SAVE HUMANITY FROM THE TYRANNY OF METAHUMAN CONTROL.
HRRRGGG!
COUNTER-MEASURES ENGAGED.

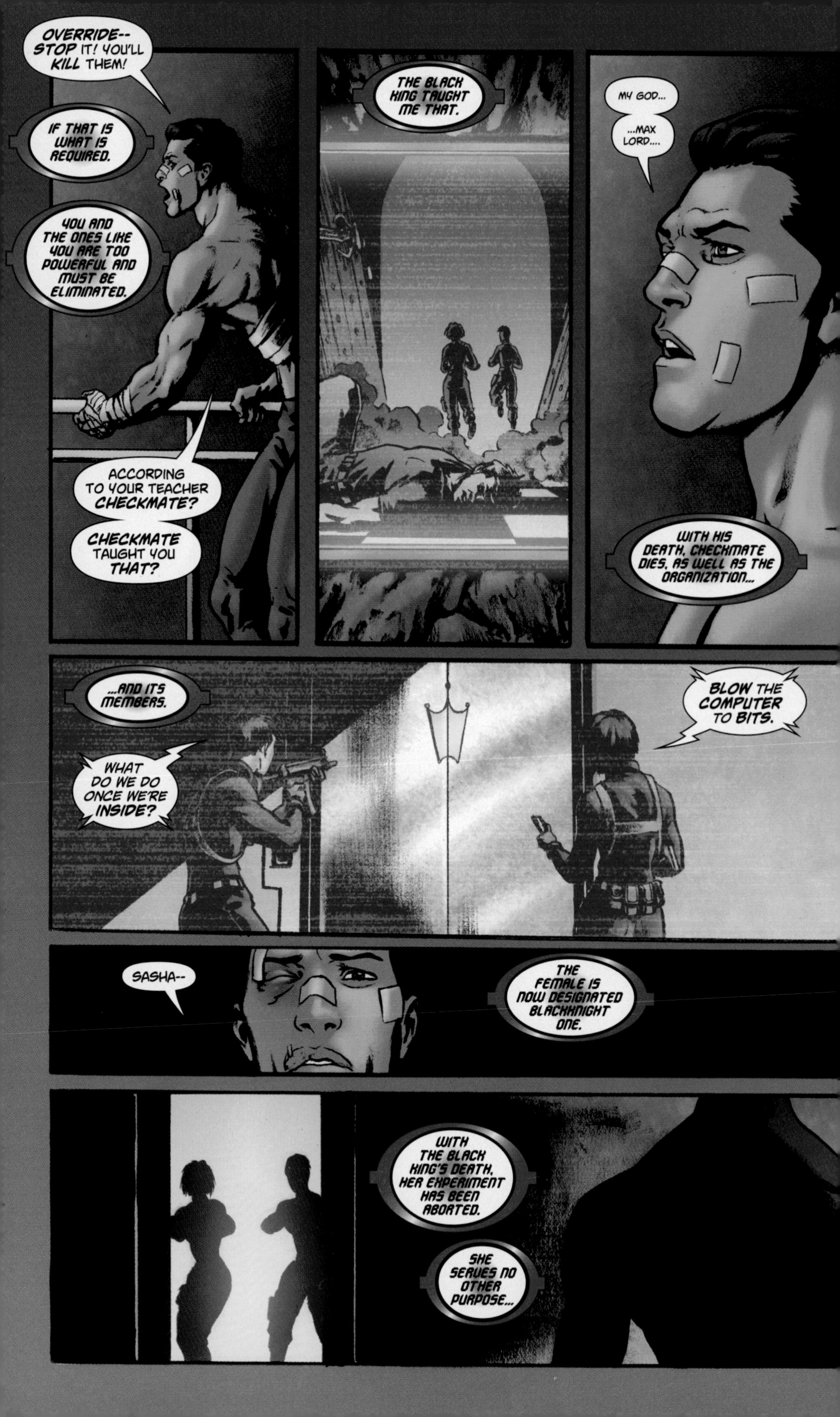
OVERRIDE-- STOP IT! YOU'LL KILL THEM!
IF THAT IS WHAT IS REQUIRED.
YOU AND THE ONES LIKE YOU ARE TOO POWERFUL AND MUST BE ELIMINATED.
ACCORDING TO YOUR TEACHER CHECKMATE?
CHECKMATE TAUGHT YOU THAT?
THE BLACK KING TAUGHT ME THAT.
MY GOD...
...MAX LORD....
WITH HIS DEATH, CHECKMATE DIES, AS WELL AS THE ORGANIZATION...
...AND ITS MEMBERS.
WHAT DO WE DO ONCE WE'RE INSIDE?
BLOW THE COMPUTER TO BITS.
SASHA--
THE FEMALE IS NOW DESIGNATED BLACKNIGHT ONE.
WITH THE BLACK KING'S DEATH, HER EXPERIMENT HAS BEEN ABORTED.
SHE SERVES NO OTHER PURPOSE...

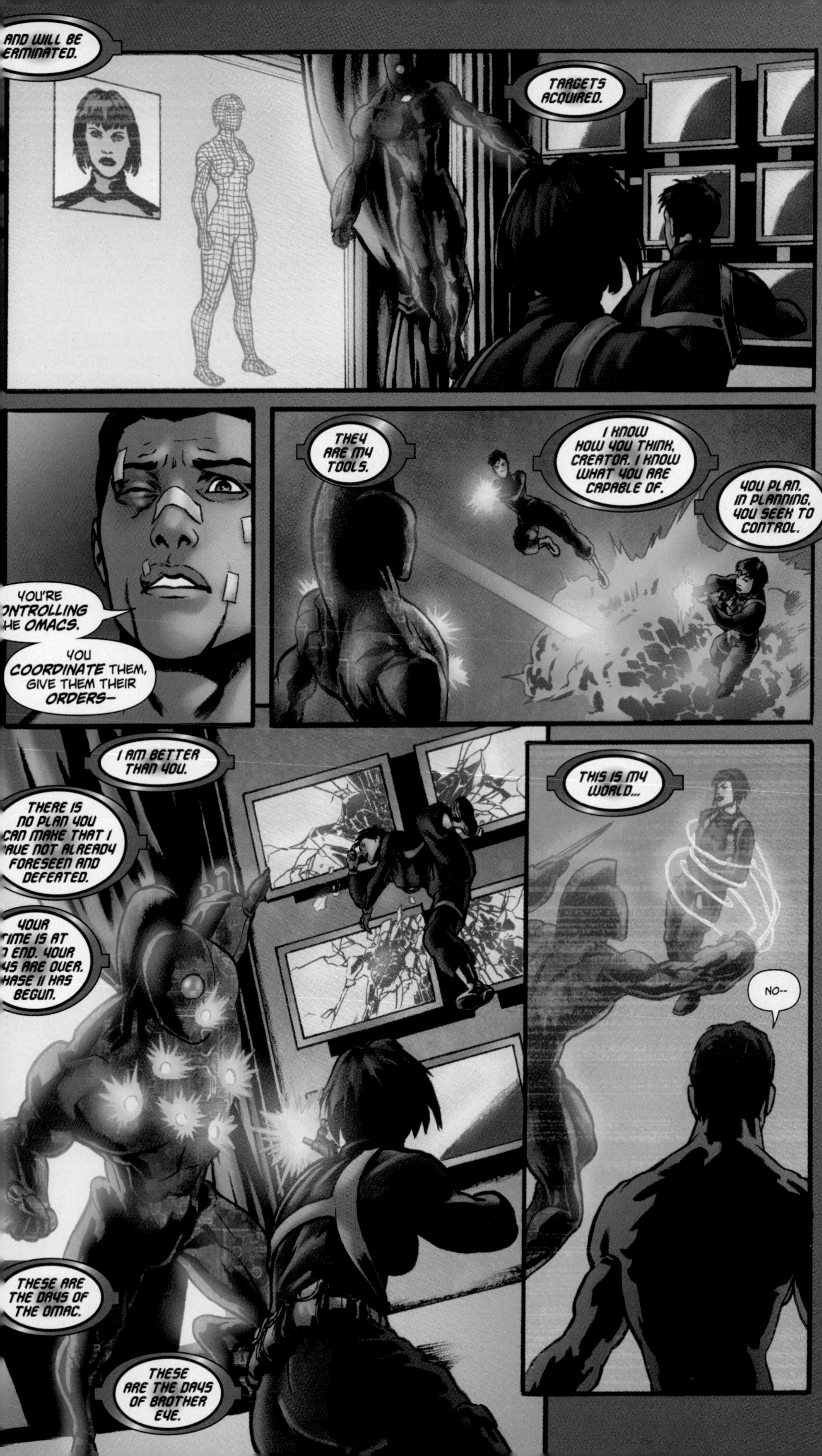
AND WILL BE
ERMINATED.
TARGETS ACQUIRED.
YOU'RE
ONTROLLING
HE OMACS.
YOU COORDINATE THEM, GIVE THEM THEIR ORDERS--
THEY ARE MY TOOLS.
I KNOW HOW YOU THINK, CREATOR. I KNOW WHAT YOU ARE CAPABLE OF.
YOU PLAN. IN PLANNING, YOU SEEK TO CONTROL.
I AM BETTER THAN YOU.
THERE IS NO PLAN YOU
CAN MAKE THAT I
AVE NOT ALREADY
FORESEEN AND DEFEATED.
YOUR
TIME IS AT
N END. YOUR
YS ARE OVER.
HASE II HAS
BEGUN.
THESE ARE THE DAYS OF THE OMAC.
THESE ARE THE DAYS OF BROTHER EYE.
THIS IS MY WORLD...
NO--

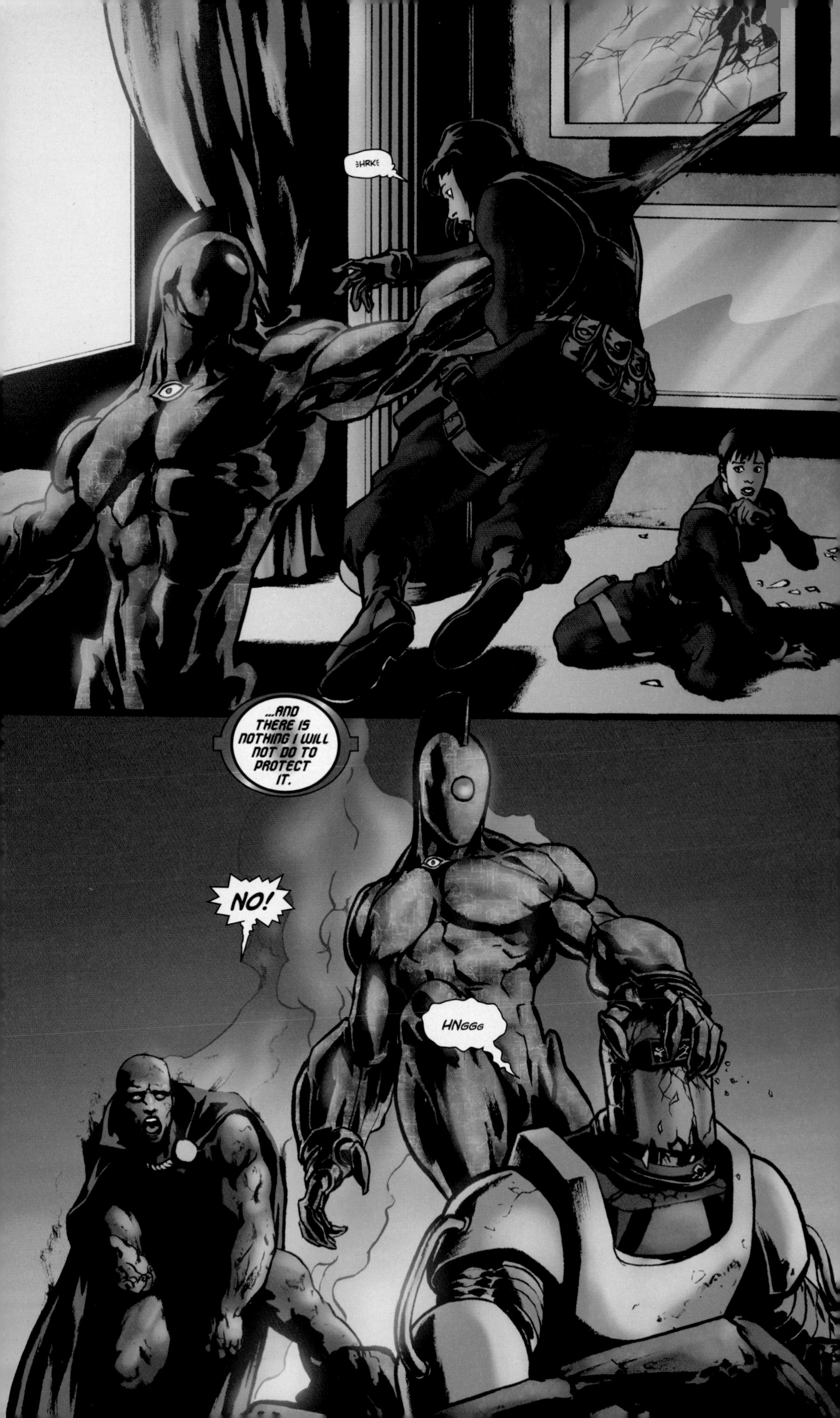
HRK
...AND THERE IS NOTHING I WILL NOT DO TO PROTECT IT.
NO!
HNGGG

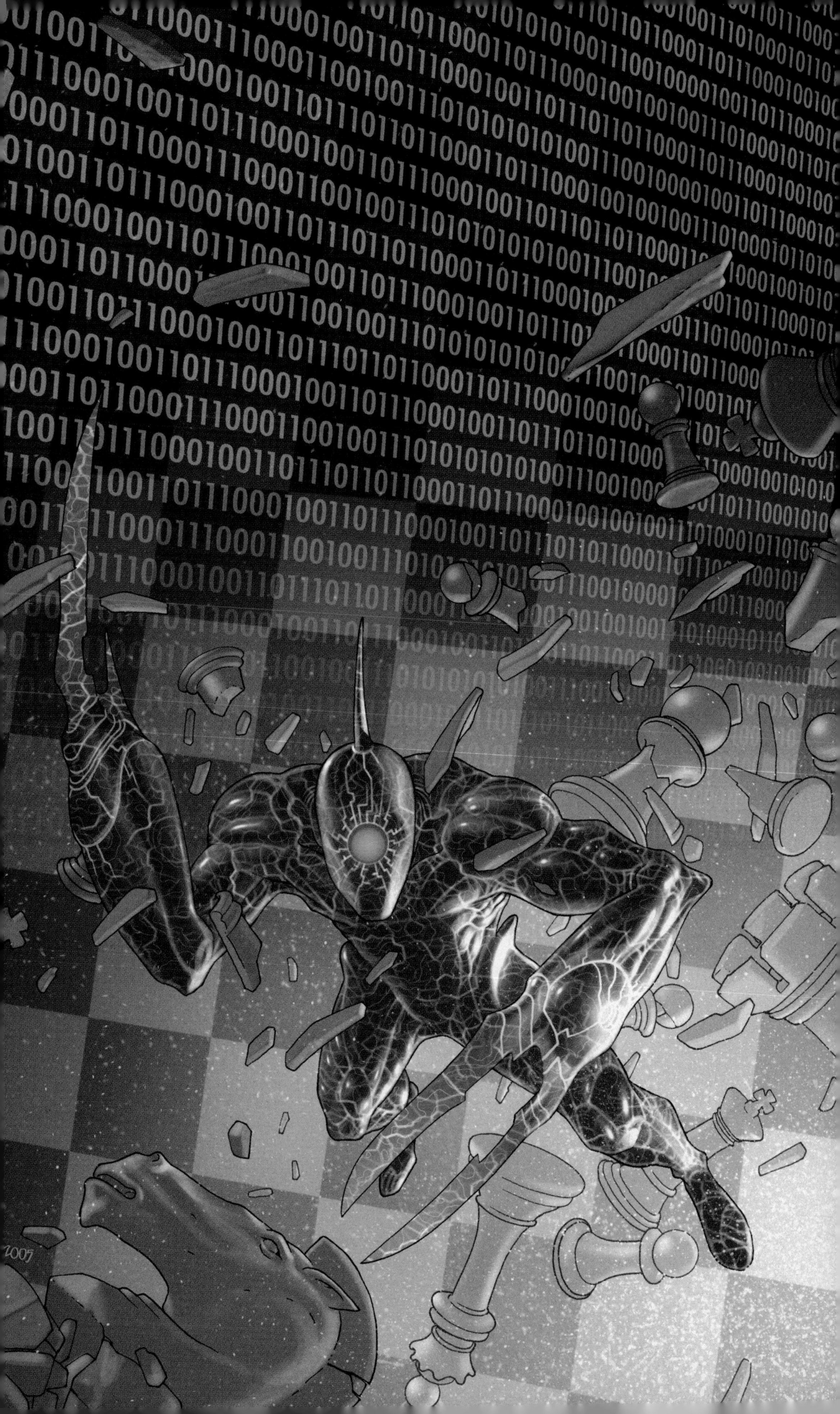

LNDICON_2005

Greg Rucka
Writer

Jesus Saiz
Cliff Richards & Bob Wiacek
Artists

Hi-Fi Design
Colorist

Phil Balsman
Letterer

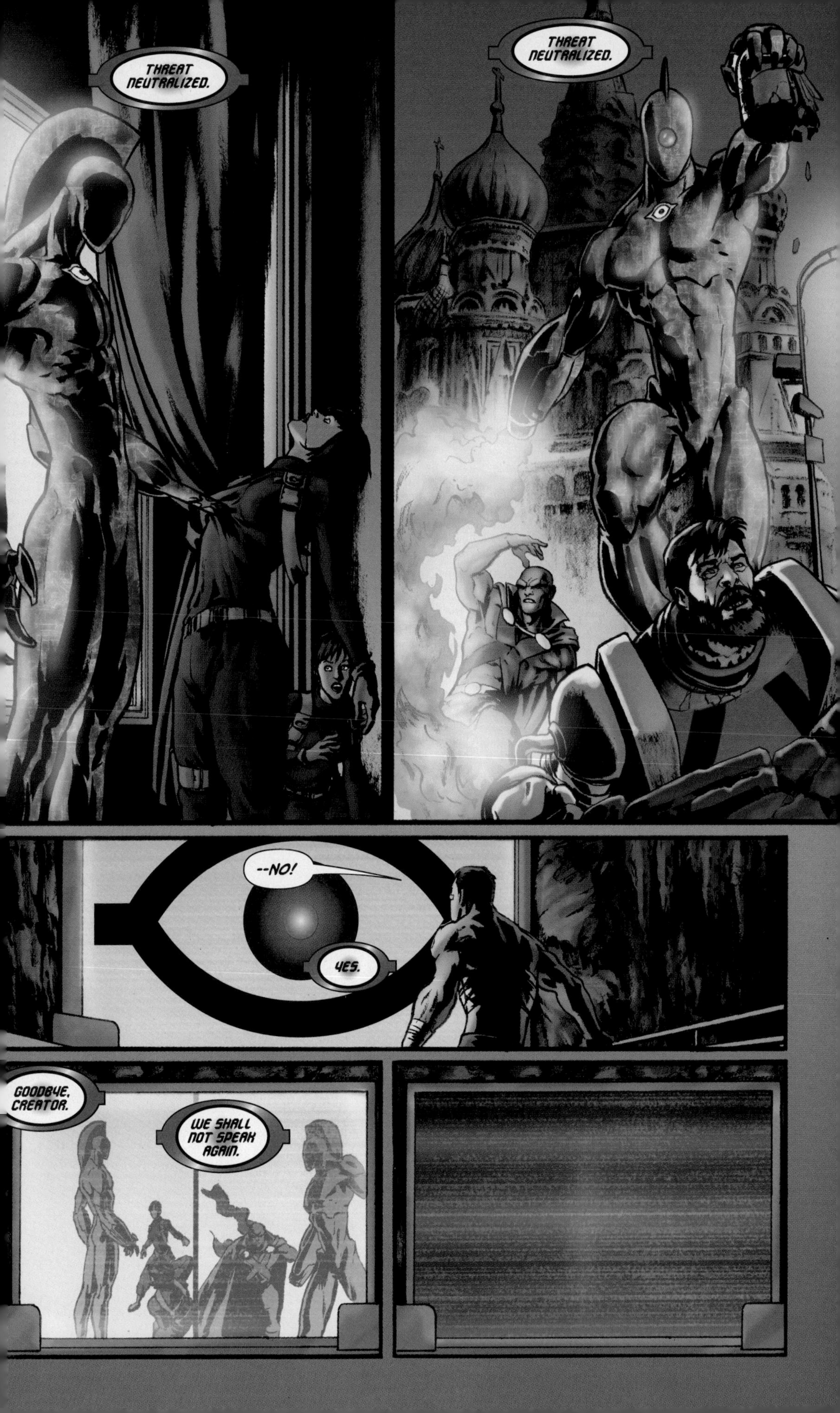
THREAT NEUTRALIZED.
THREAT NEUTRALIZED.
--NO!
YES.
GOODBYE, CREATOR.
WE SHALL NOT SPEAK AGAIN.

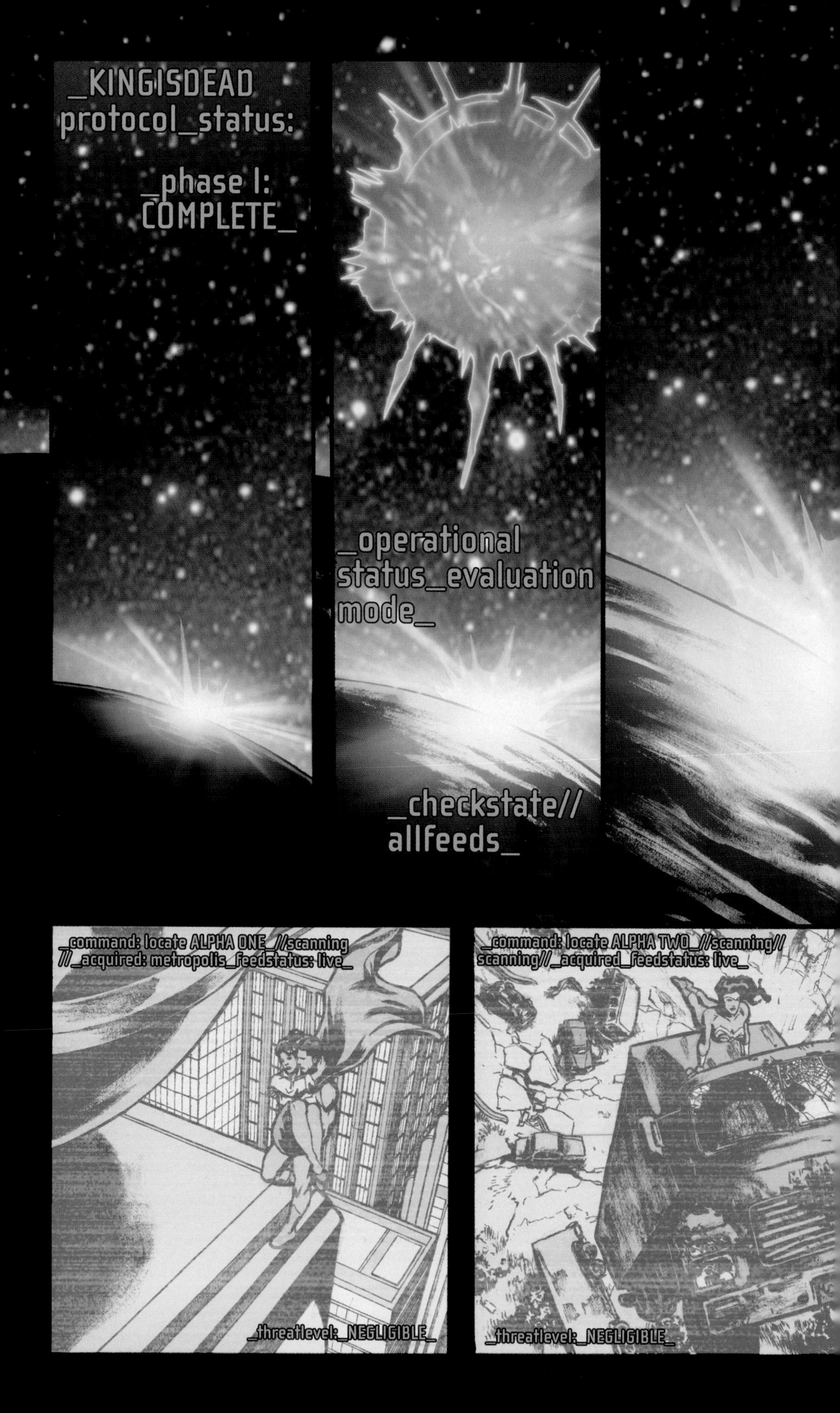
_KINGISDEAD protocol_status:
phase I: COMPLETE
_operational status_evaluation mode_
checkstate// allfeeds
command: locate ALPHA ONE//scanning //_acquired: metropolis_feedstatus: live_
_threatlevel:_NEGLIGIBLE_
command: locate ALPHA TWO//scanning// scanning//_acquired_feedstatus: live_
_threatlevel:_NEGLIGIBLE_

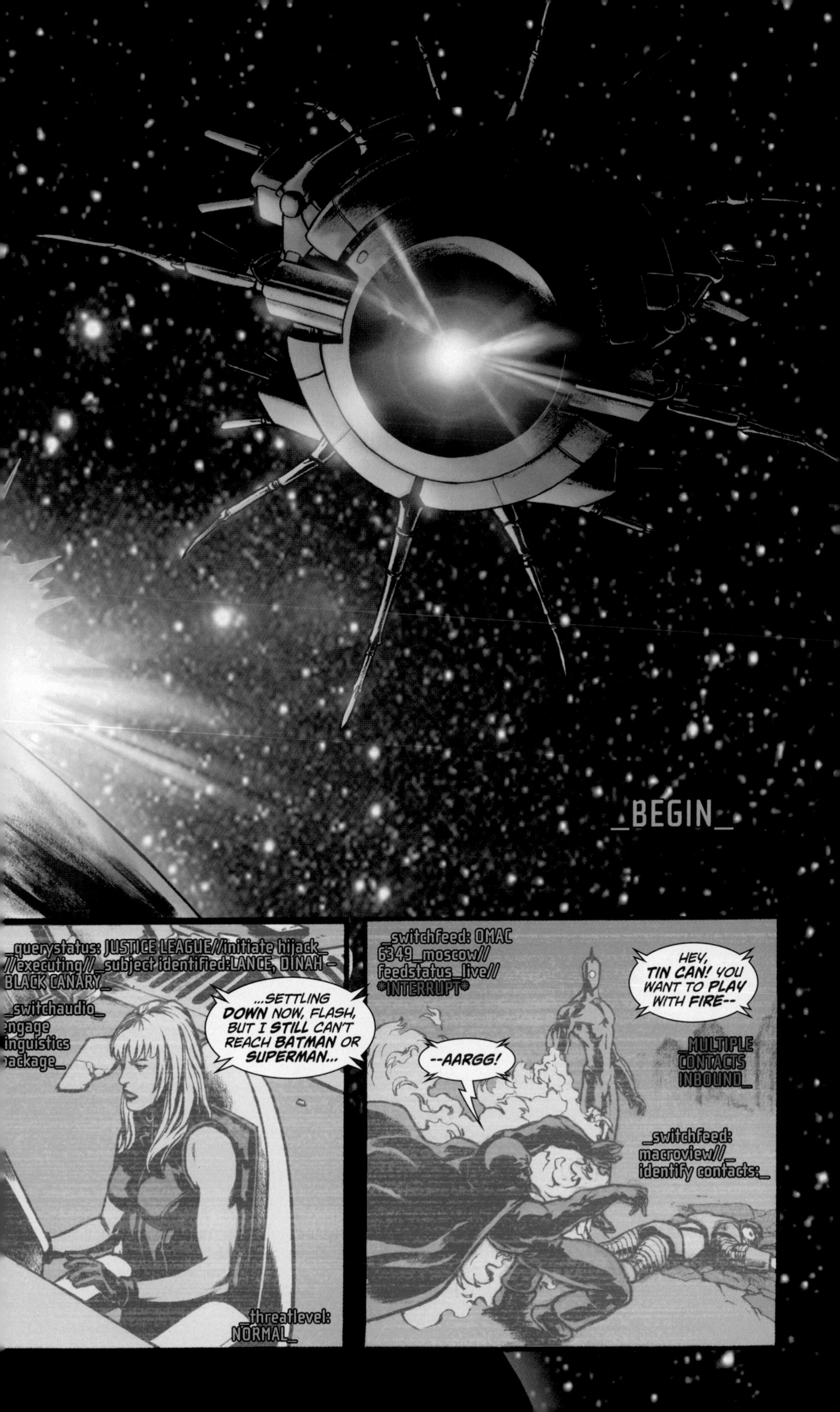
BEGIN
querystatus: JUSTICE LEAGUE//initiate hijack //executing//_subject identified:LANCE, DINAH – BLACK CANARY_
switchaudio
engage
linguistics
package_
...SETTLING DOWN NOW, FLASH, BUT I STILL CAN'T REACH BATMAN OR SUPERMAN...
threatlevel: NORMAL
_switchfeed: OMAC 6349_moscow// feedstatus_live// *INTERRUPT*
HEY, TIN CAN! YOU WANT TO PLAY WITH FIRE--
--AARGG!
MULTIPLE CONTACTS INBOUND
switchfeed: macroview// identify contacts:_

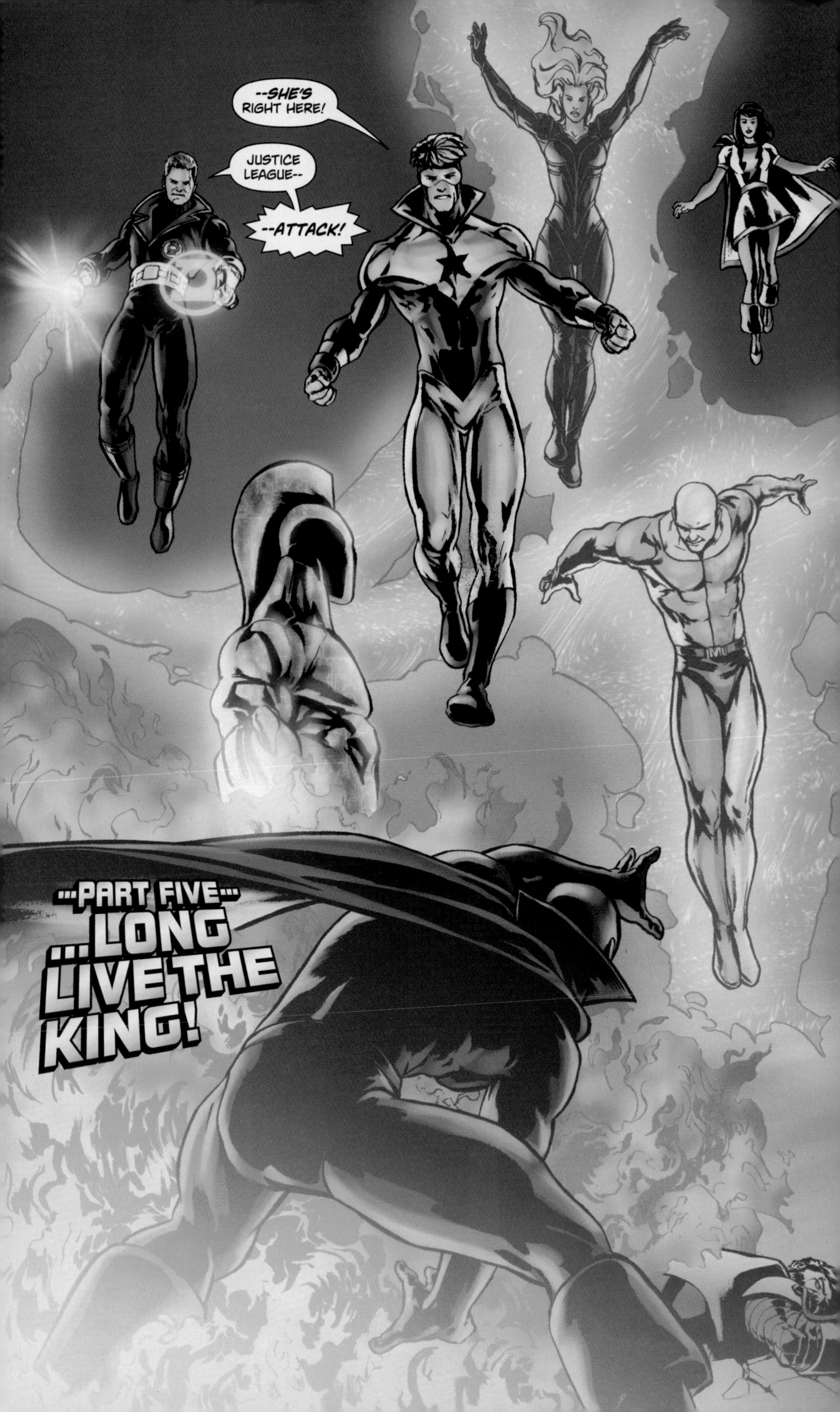
--SHE'S RIGHT HERE!
JUSTICE LEAGUE--
--ATTACK!
--PART FIVE--
...LONG LIVE THE KING!

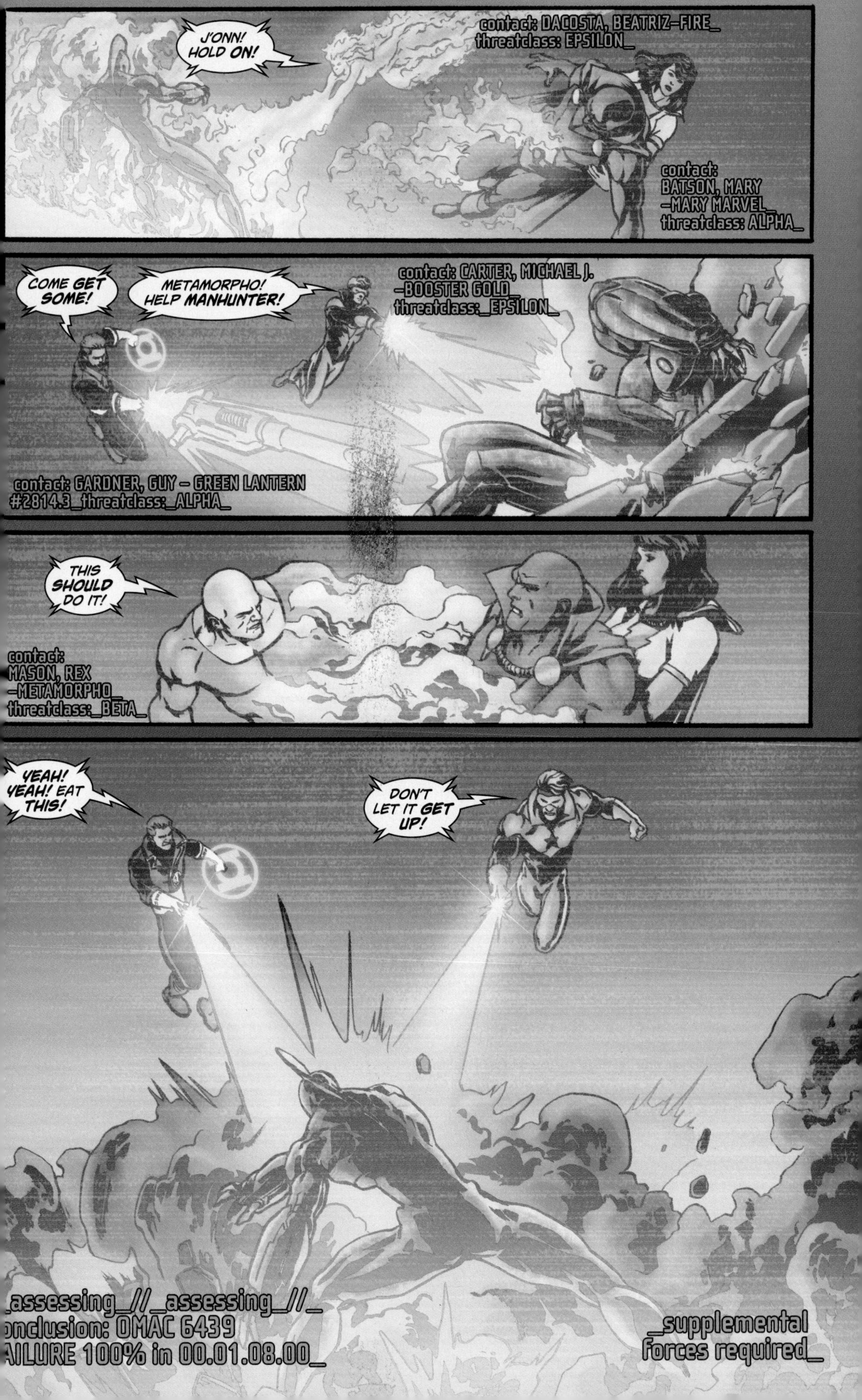
J'ONN! HOLD ON!
contact: DACOSTA, BEATRIZ-FIRE_
threatclass: EPSILON_
contact: BATSON, MARY -MARY MARVEL_ threatclass: ALPHA_
COME GET SOME!
METAMORPHO! HELP MANHUNTER!
contact: CARTER, MICHAEL J. -BOOSTER GOLD_ threatclass:_EPSILON_
contact: GARDNER, GUY - GREEN LANTERN #2814.3_threatclass:_ALPHA_
THIS SHOULD DO IT!
contact: MASON, REX -METAMORPHO_ threatclass:_BETA_
YEAH! YEAH! EAT THIS!
DON'T LET IT GET UP!
assessing//_assessing_//_
onclusion: OMAC 6439
AILURE 100% in 00.01.08.00_
supplemental forces required

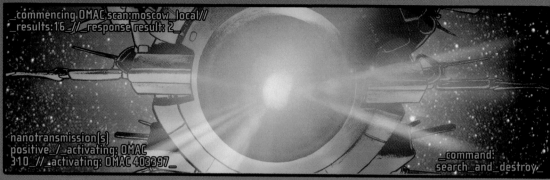

_commencing OMAC scan:moscow_local//
results:16//_response result: 2_

nanotransmission(s)
positive_/_activating: OMAC
310_//_activating: OMAC 403397_

_command:
search_and_destroy_

_time_to_target:
00.00.11.19_

_revising combat
projections_//_
newresult:_

DMITRI?

SO
WHAT KEPT
YOU?

--LIKE *THAT,*
HUH? SUCK IT
UP, BUDDY, THIS IS
GONNA HURT *YOU* A
WHOLE LOT *MORE*
THAN IT'S GONNA
HURT *ME!*

_projected OMAC
fatalities: 0%_

_projected
TARGET fatalities:
100%_

_threat assessment:
neutralized_//_resuming previous_

_commencing phase II
operations: "ELIMINATION"
//_initiate stage I:
"AWAKENING"_

_WARNING: complete OMAC
nanostatus verification required_
_resource commitment for
process: 100%_//_system
disconnect: 100%_

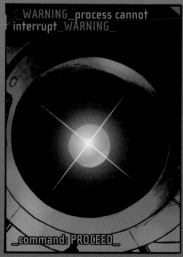

_WARNING_process cannot
interrupt_WARNING_

command: PROCEED

_commencing
verification stage
prior to activation_

time to total
OMAC conversion:
00.07.34.009_

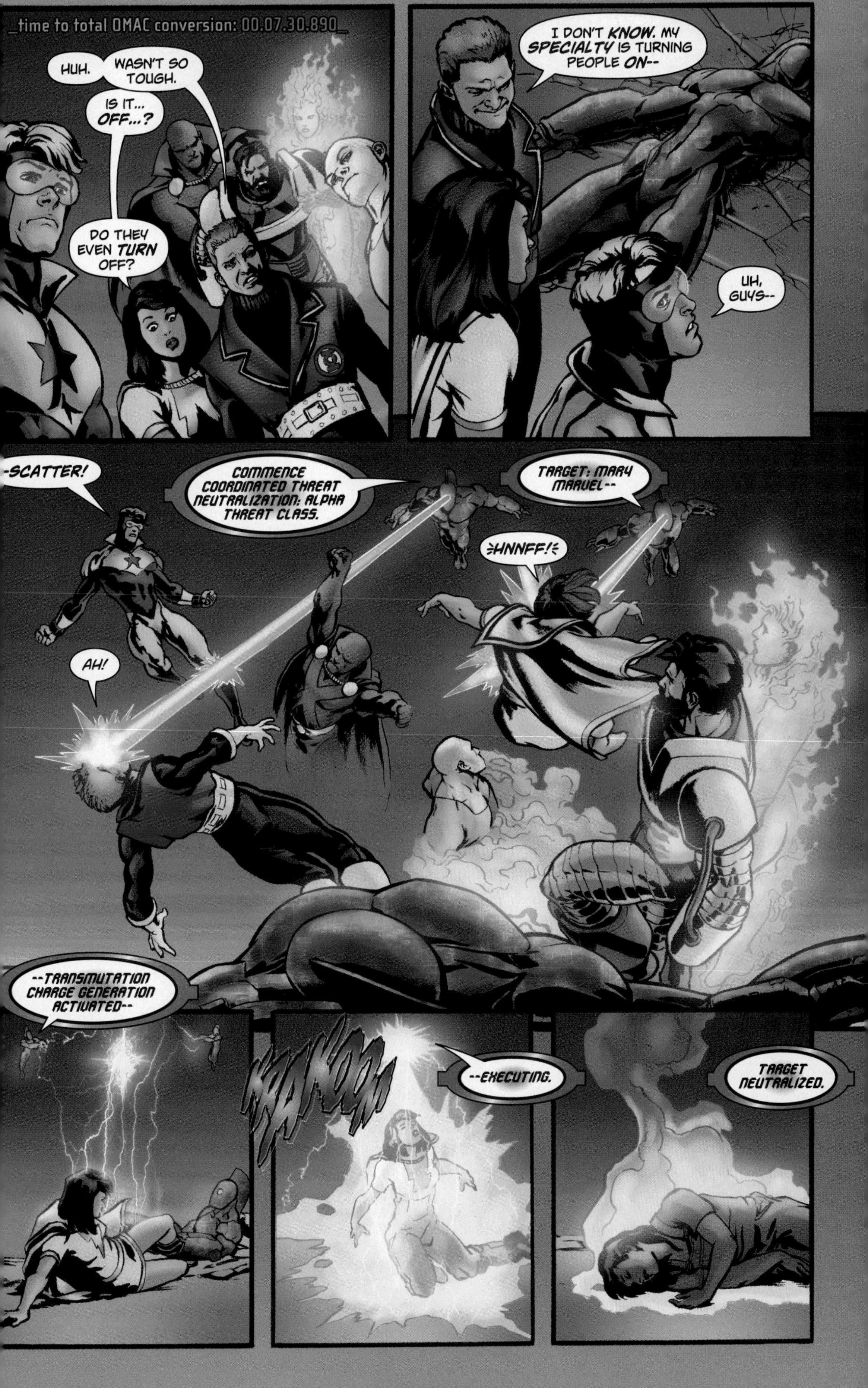
time to total OMAC conversion: 00.07.30.890
HUH.
WASN'T SO TOUGH.
IS IT... OFF...?
DO THEY EVEN TURN OFF?
I DON'T KNOW. MY SPECIALTY IS TURNING PEOPLE ON--
UH, GUYS--
-SCATTER!
COMMENCE COORDINATED THREAT NEUTRALIZATION: ALPHA THREAT CLASS.
TARGET: MARY MARVEL--
HNNFF!
AH!
--TRANSMUTATION CHARGE GENERATION ACTIVATED--
--EXECUTING.
TARGET NEUTRALIZED.

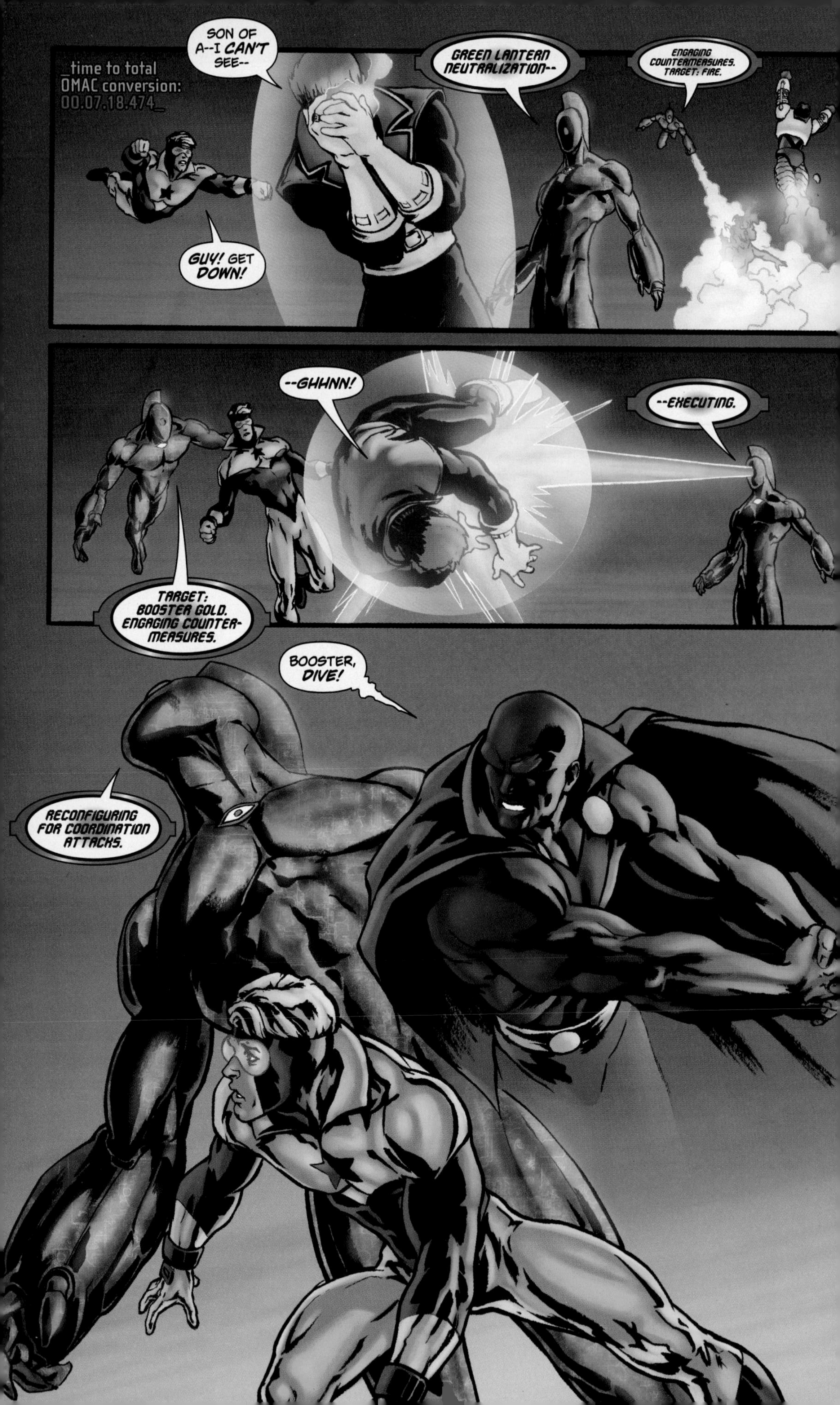
_time to total
OMAC conversion:
00.07.18.474_
SON OF A--I CAN'T SEE--
GUY! GET DOWN!
GREEN LANTERN NEUTRALIZATION--
ENGAGING COUNTERMEASURES. TARGET: FIRE.
--GHHNN!
--EXECUTING.
TARGET: BOOSTER GOLD. ENGAGING COUNTER-MEASURES.
BOOSTER, DIVE!
RECONFIGURING FOR COORDINATION ATTACKS.

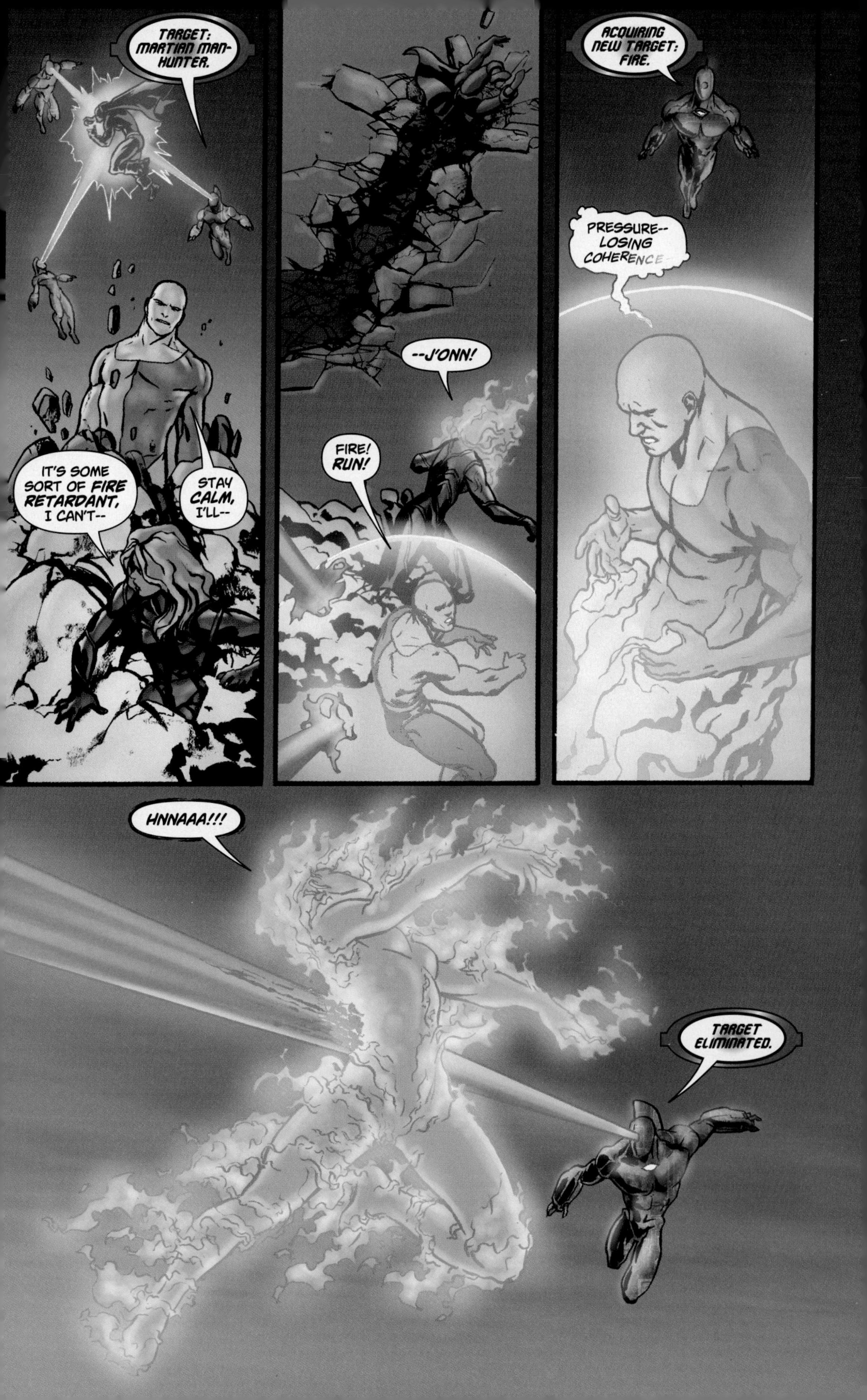
TARGET: MARTIAN MAN-HUNTER.
IT'S SOME SORT OF FIRE RETARDANT, I CAN'T--
STAY CALM, I'LL--
--J'ONN!
FIRE! RUN!
ACQUIRING NEW TARGET: FIRE.
PRESSURE-- LOSING COHERENCE--
HNNAAA!!!
TARGET ELIMINATED.

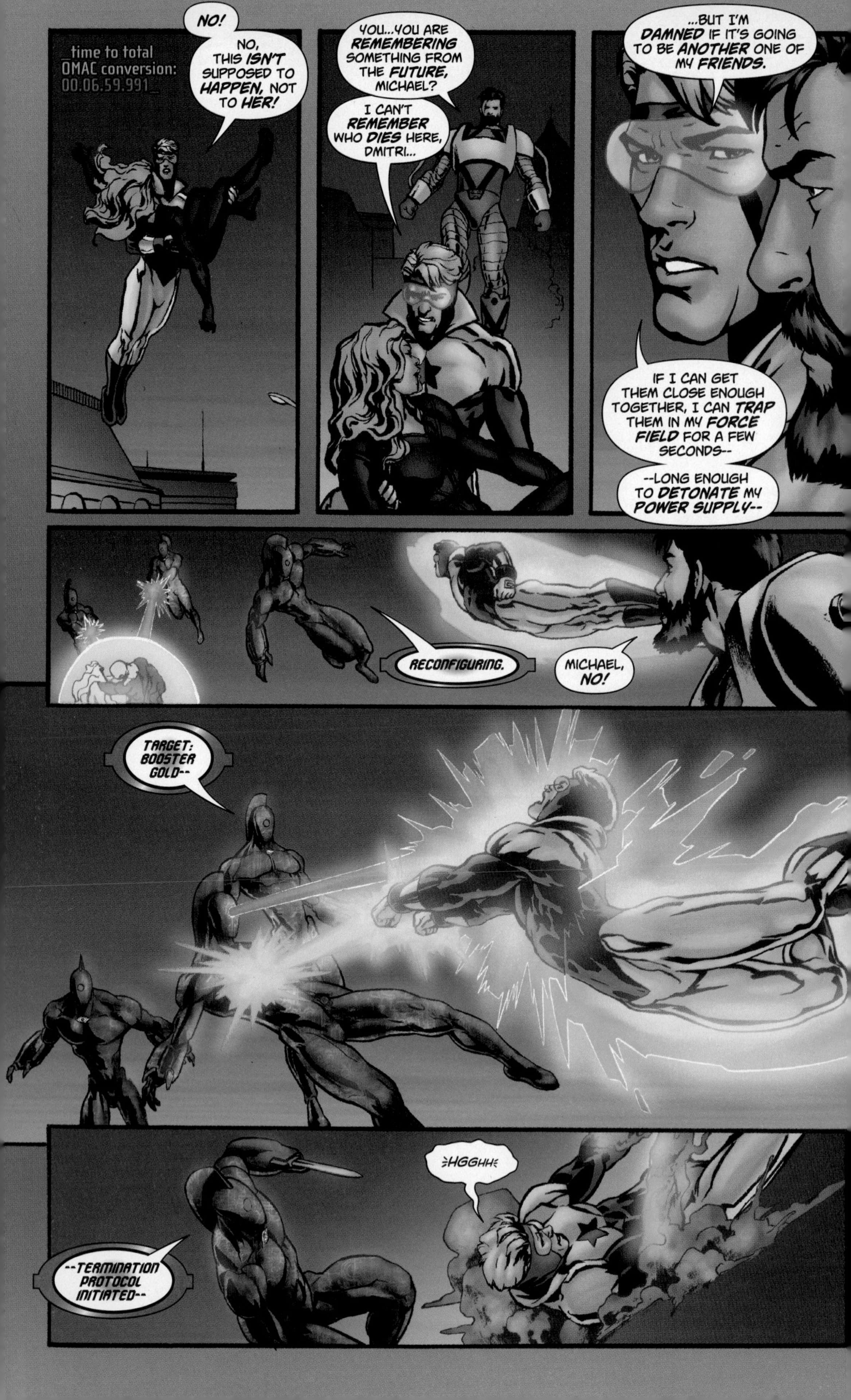
time to total OMAC conversion: 00.06.59.991
NO!
NO, THIS ISN'T SUPPOSED TO HAPPEN, NOT TO HER!
YOU...YOU ARE REMEMBERING SOMETHING FROM THE FUTURE, MICHAEL?
I CAN'T REMEMBER WHO DIES HERE, DMITRI...
...BUT I'M DAMNED IF IT'S GOING TO BE ANOTHER ONE OF MY FRIENDS.
IF I CAN GET THEM CLOSE ENOUGH TOGETHER, I CAN TRAP THEM IN MY FORCE FIELD FOR A FEW SECONDS--
--LONG ENOUGH TO DETONATE MY POWER SUPPLY--
RECONFIGURING.
MICHAEL, NO!
TARGET: BOOSTER GOLD--
HGGHH
--TERMINATION PROTOCOL INITIATED--

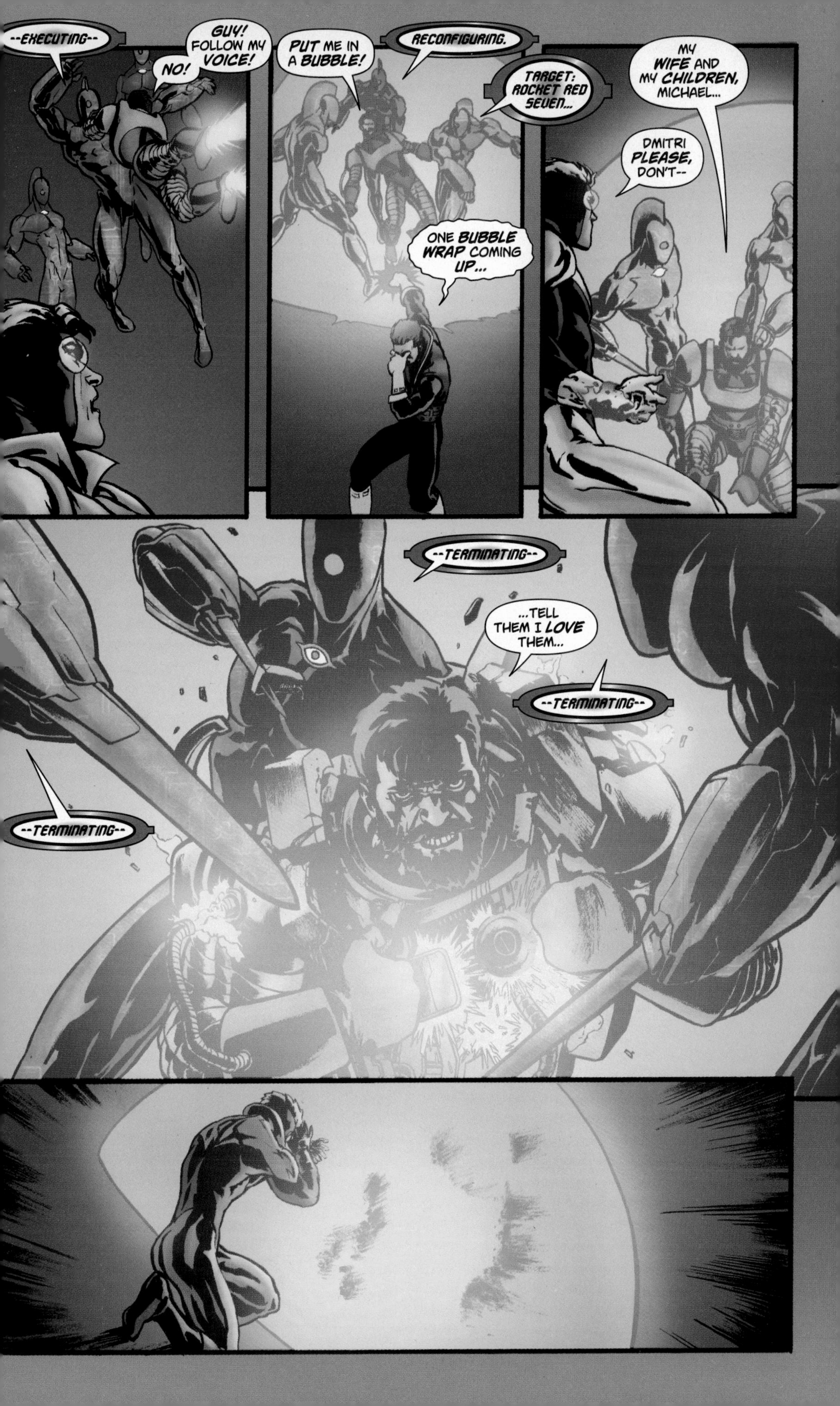
--EXECUTING--
GUY! FOLLOW MY VOICE!
NO!
PUT ME IN A BUBBLE!
RECONFIGURING.
TARGET: ROCKET RED SEVEN...
ONE BUBBLE WRAP COMING UP...
MY WIFE AND MY CHILDREN, MICHAEL...
DMITRI PLEASE, DON'T--
--TERMINATING--
...TELL THEM I LOVE THEM...
--TERMINATING--
--TERMINATING--

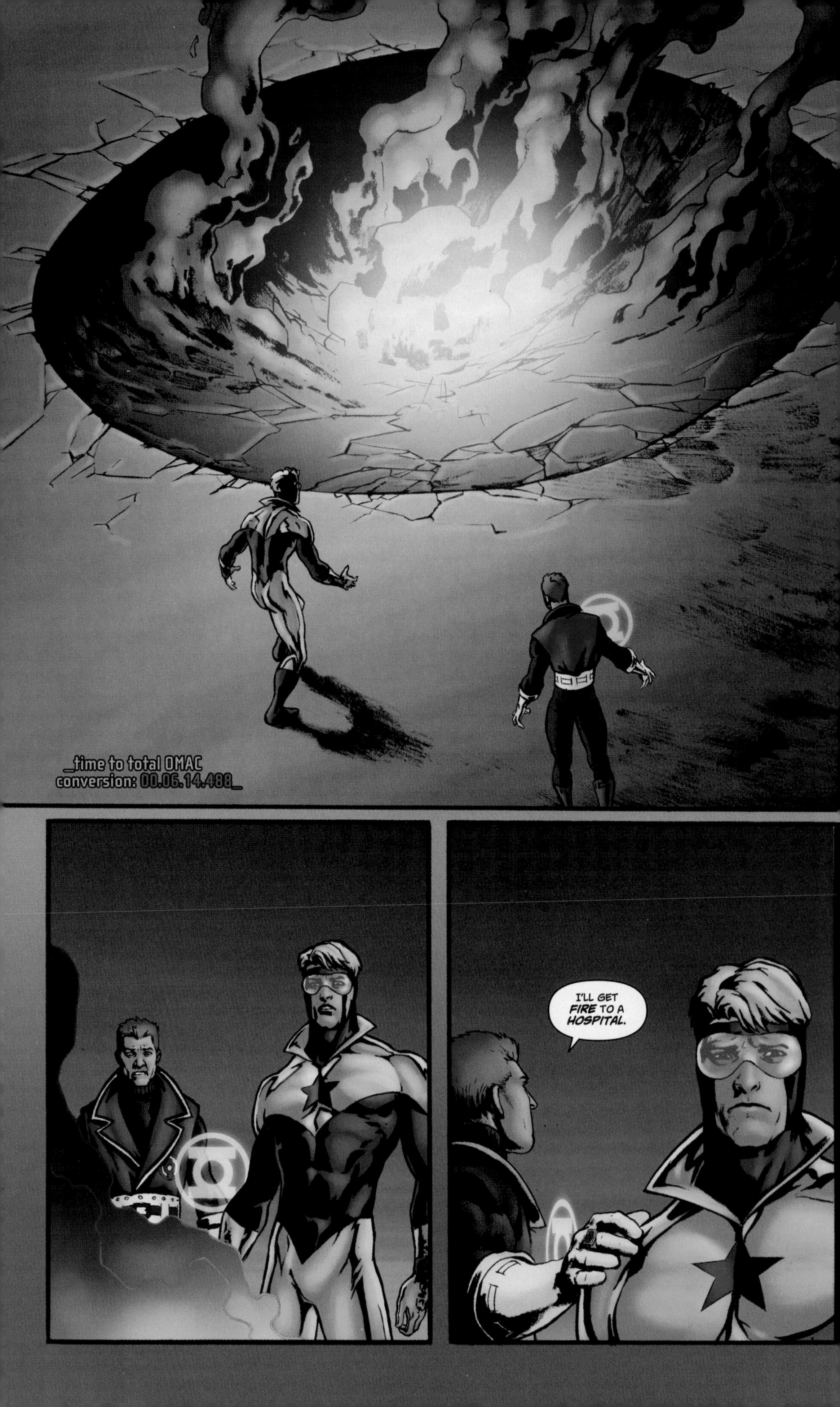
_time to total OMAC
conversion: 00.06.14.488_
I'LL GET FIRE TO A HOSPITAL.

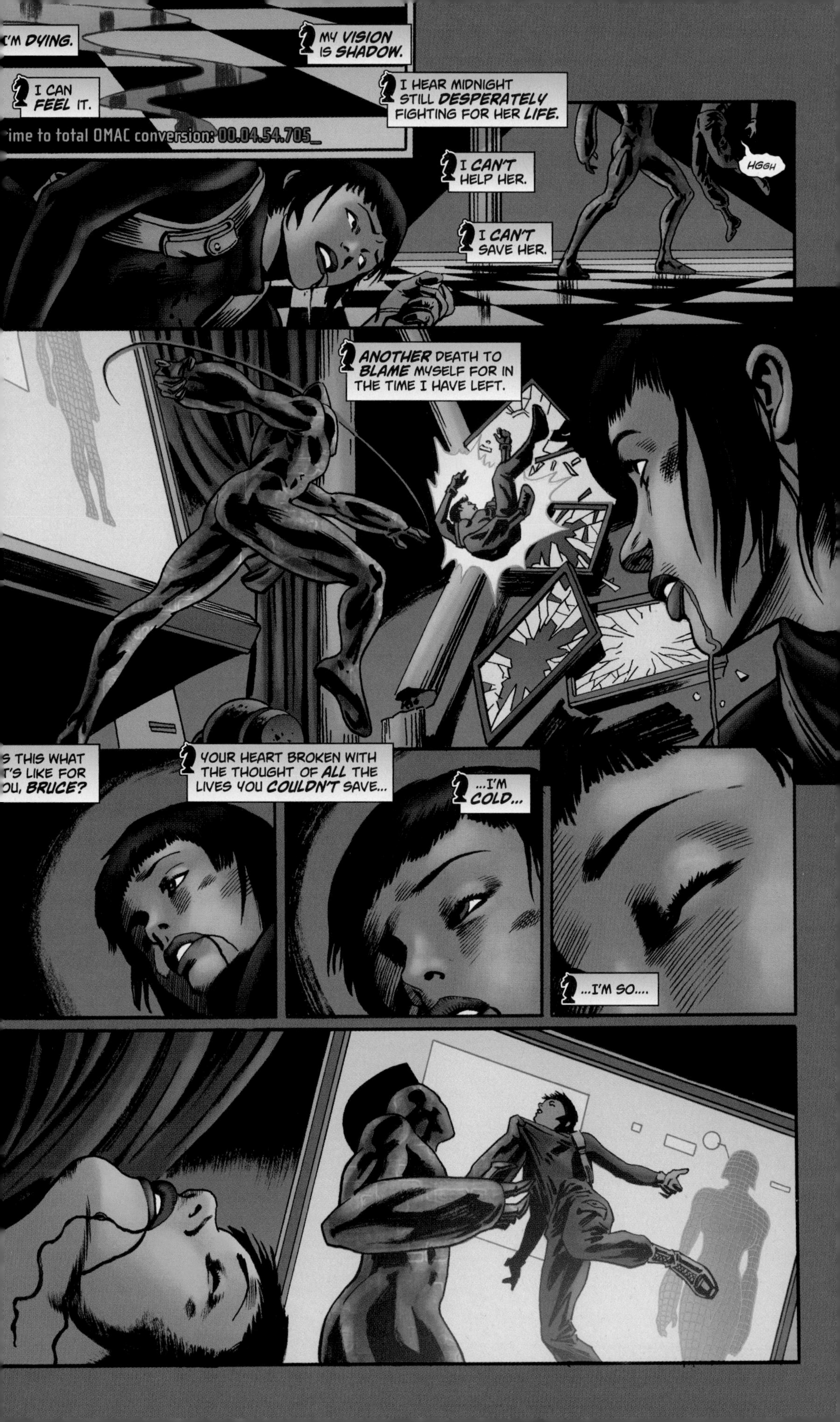

'M DYING.
MY VISION IS SHADOW.
I CAN FEEL IT.
I HEAR MIDNIGHT STILL DESPERATELY FIGHTING FOR HER LIFE.
ime to total OMAC conversion: 00.04.54.705_
I CAN'T HELP HER.
I CAN'T SAVE HER.
HGGH
ANOTHER DEATH TO BLAME MYSELF FOR IN THE TIME I HAVE LEFT.
S THIS WHAT T'S LIKE FOR OU, BRUCE?
YOUR HEART BROKEN WITH THE THOUGHT OF ALL THE LIVES YOU COULDN'T SAVE...
...I'M COLD...
...I'M SO....

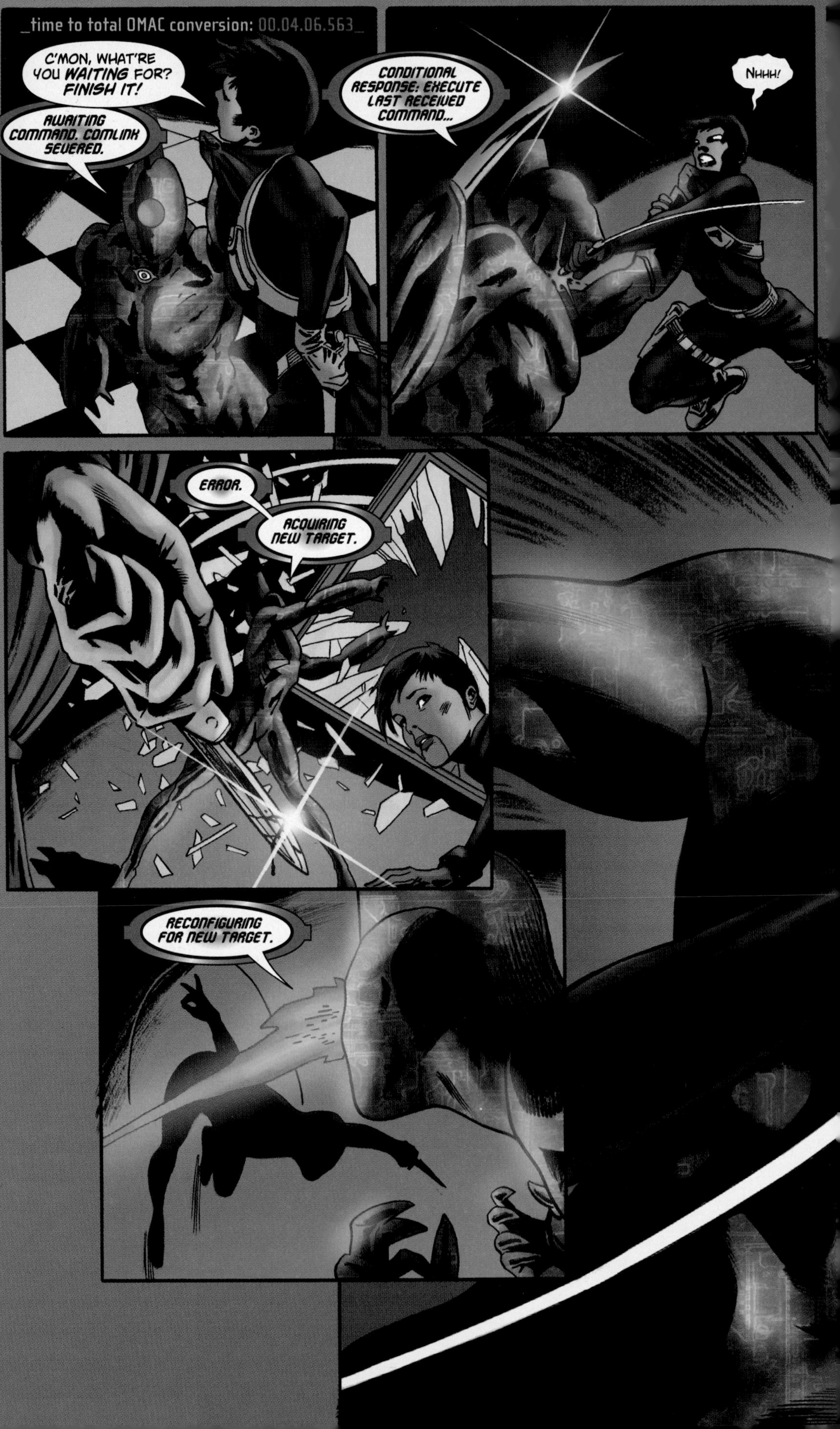
time to total OMAC conversion: 00.04.06.563
C'MON, WHAT'RE YOU WAITING FOR? FINISH IT!
AWAITING COMMAND. COMLINK SEVERED.
CONDITIONAL RESPONSE: EXECUTE LAST RECEIVED COMMAND...
NHHH!
ERROR.
ACQUIRING NEW TARGET.
RECONFIGURING FOR NEW TARGET.

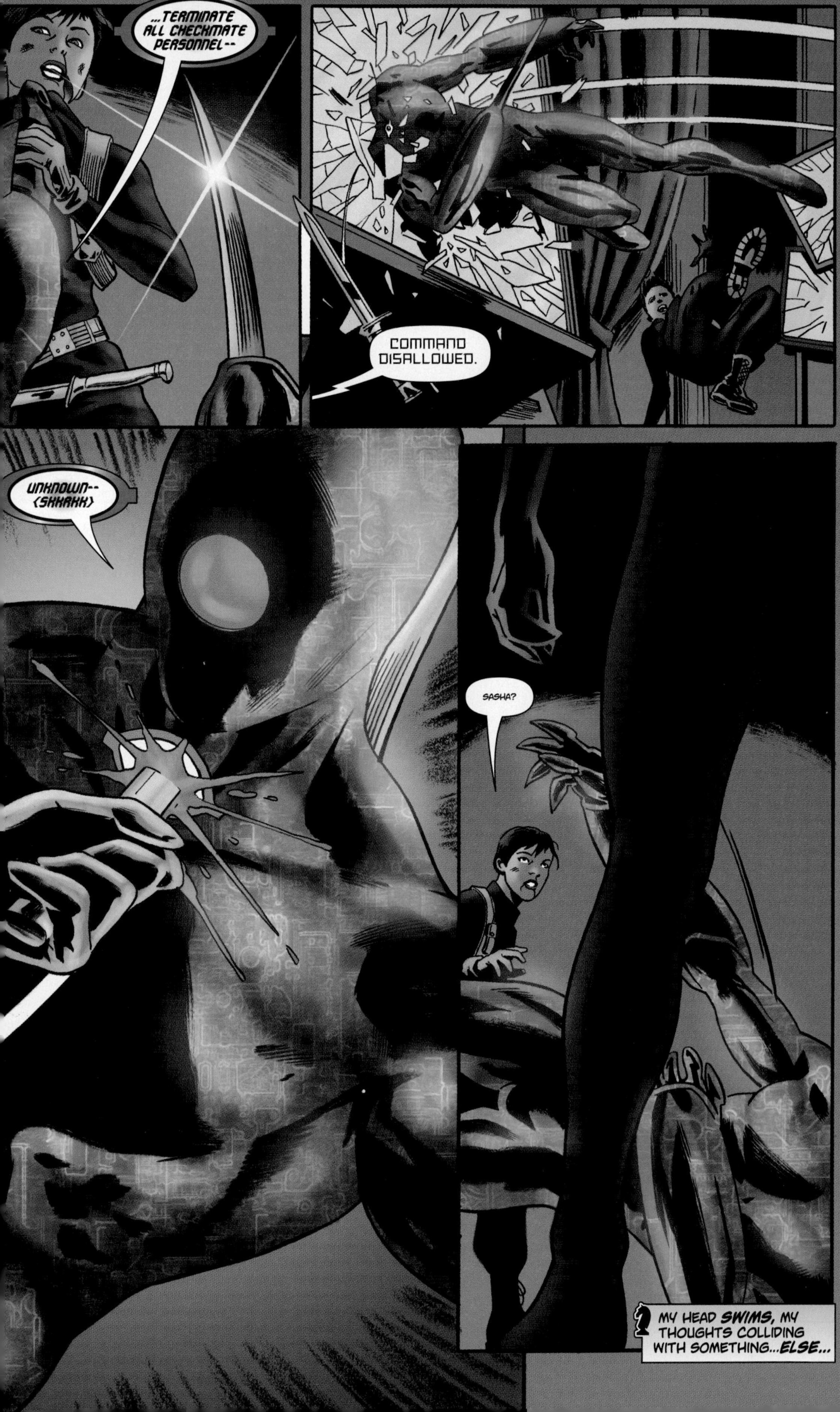
...TERMINATE ALL CHECKMATE PERSONNEL--
COMMAND DISALLOWED.
UNKNOWN-- (SHHRHK)
SASHA?
MY HEAD SWIMS, MY THOUGHTS COLLIDING WITH SOMETHING...ELSE...

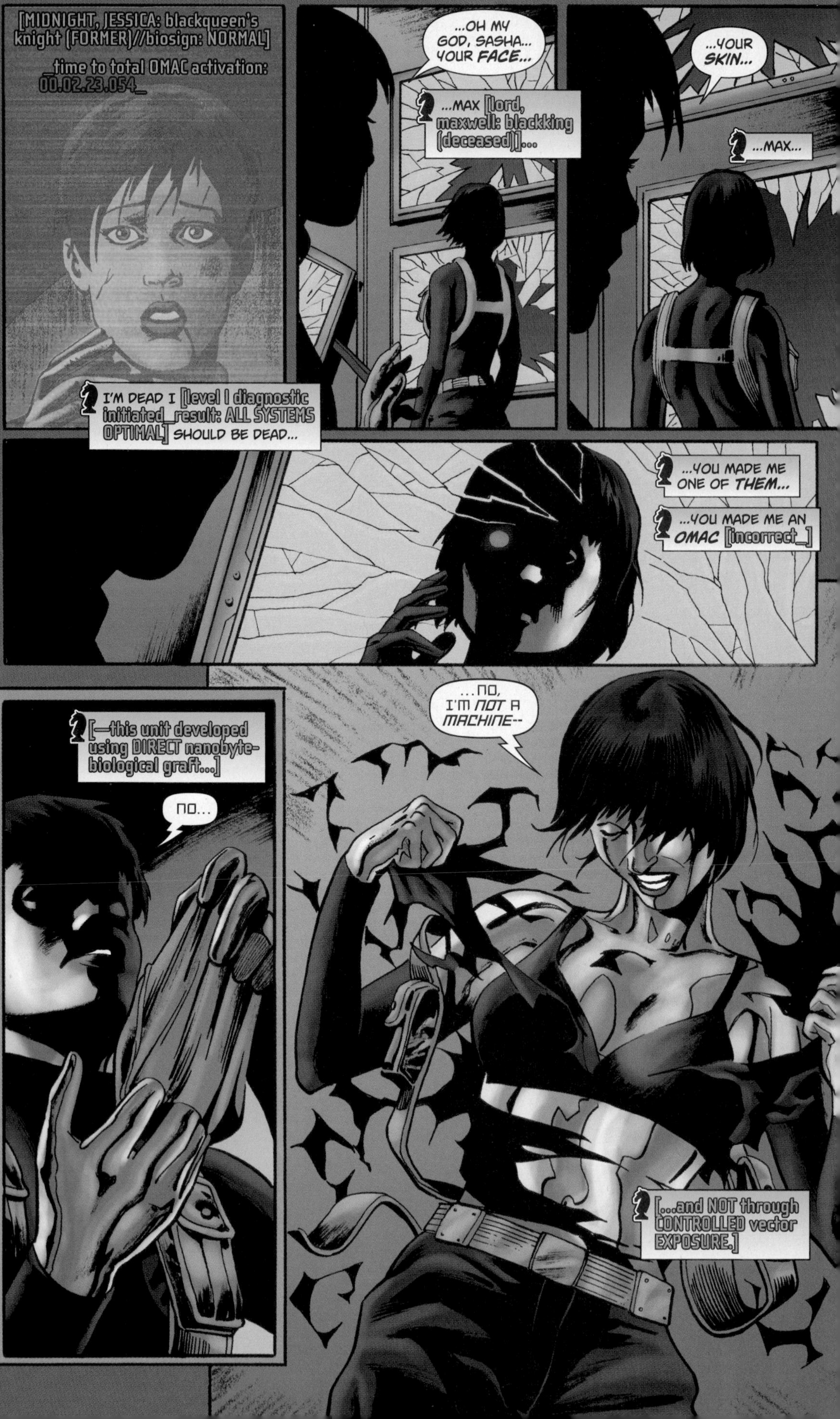

[MIDNIGHT, JESSICA: blackqueen's knight (FORMER)//biosign: NORMAL]
time to total OMAC activation: 00.02.23.054
I'M DEAD I [level I diagnostic initiated_result: ALL SYSTEMS OPTIMAL] SHOULD BE DEAD...
...OH MY GOD, SASHA... YOUR FACE...
...MAX [lord, maxwell: blackking (deceased)]...
...YOUR SKIN...
...MAX...
...YOU MADE ME ONE OF THEM...
...YOU MADE ME AN OMAC [incorrect_]
[—this unit developed using DIRECT nanobyte-biological graft...]
NO...
...NO, I'M NOT A MACHINE--
[...and NOT through CONTROLLED vector EXPOSURE.]

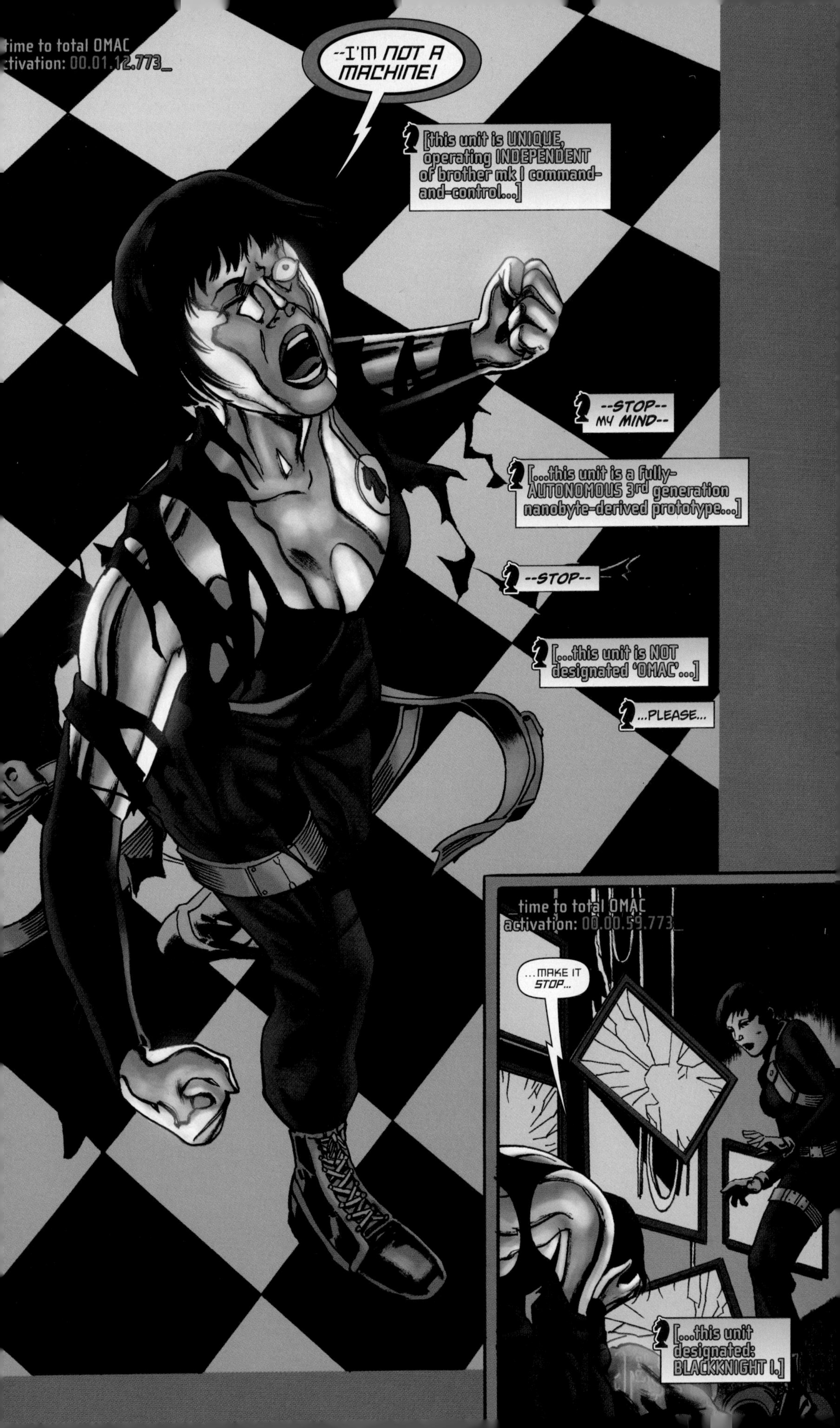
time to total OMAC
activation: 00.01.12.773_
--I'M NOT A MACHINE!
[this unit is UNIQUE, operating INDEPENDENT of brother mk I command-and-control...]
--STOP-- MY MIND--
[...this unit is a fully-AUTONOMOUS 3rd generation nanobyte-derived prototype...]
--STOP--
[...this unit is NOT designated 'OMAC'...]
...PLEASE...
_time to total OMAC
activation: 00.00.59.773_
...MAKE IT STOP...
[...this unit designated: BLACKKNIGHT I.]

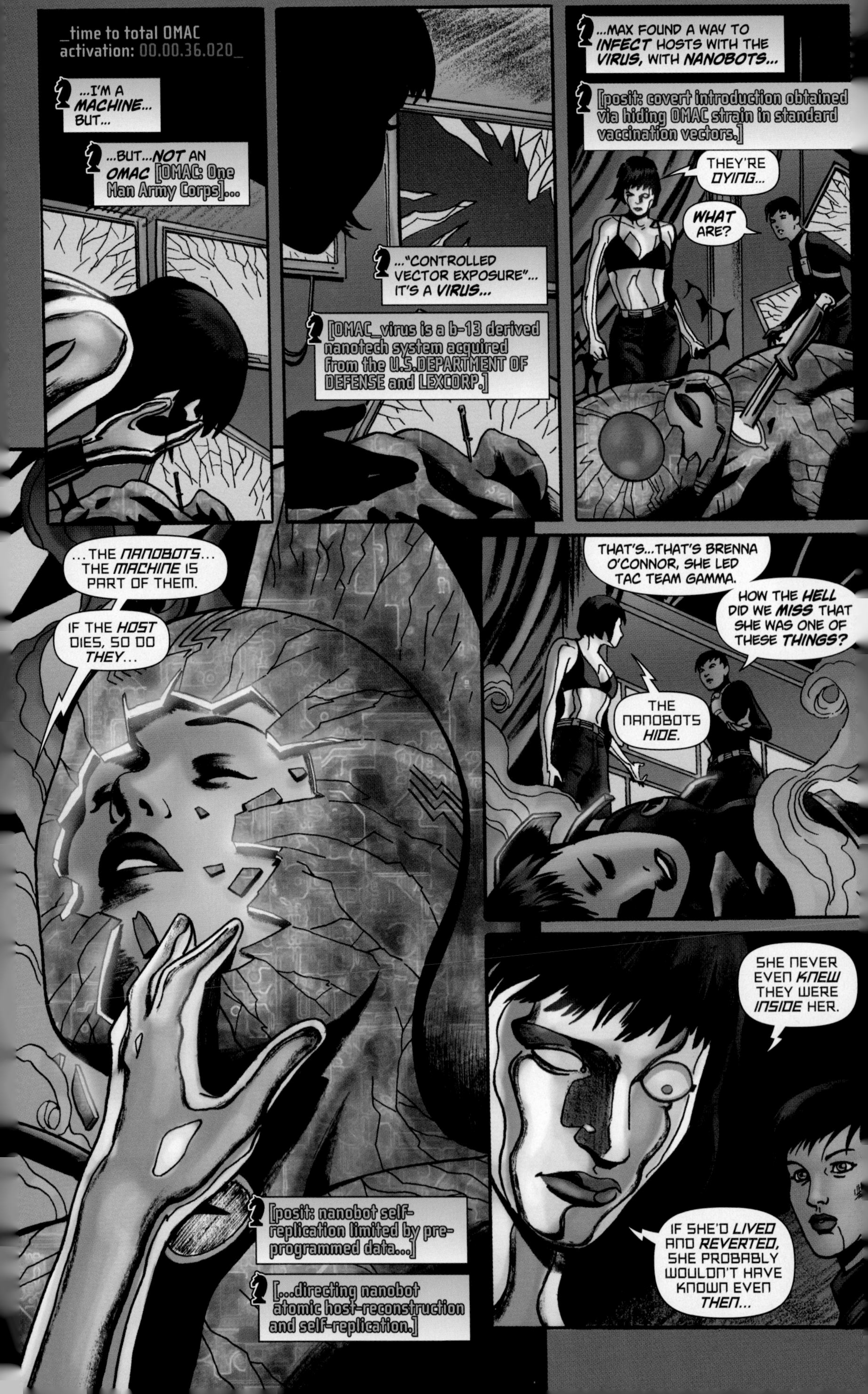
time to total OMAC activation: 00.00.36.020
...I'M A MACHINE... BUT...
...BUT...NOT AN OMAC [OMAC: One Man Army Corps]...
..."CONTROLLED VECTOR EXPOSURE"... IT'S A VIRUS...
[OMAC_virus is a b-13 derived nanotech system acquired from the U.S.DEPARTMENT OF DEFENSE and LEXCORP.]
...MAX FOUND A WAY TO INFECT HOSTS WITH THE VIRUS, WITH NANOBOTS...
[posit: covert introduction obtained via hiding OMAC strain in standard vaccination vectors.]
THEY'RE DYING...
WHAT ARE?
...THE NANOBOTS... THE MACHINE IS PART OF THEM.
IF THE HOST DIES, SO DO THEY...
[posit: nanobot self-replication limited by pre-programmed data...]
[...directing nanobot atomic host-reconstruction and self-replication.]
THAT'S...THAT'S BRENNA O'CONNOR, SHE LED TAC TEAM GAMMA.
HOW THE HELL DID WE MISS THAT SHE WAS ONE OF THESE THINGS?
THE NANOBOTS HIDE.
SHE NEVER EVEN KNEW THEY WERE INSIDE HER.
IF SHE'D LIVED AND REVERTED, SHE PROBABLY WOULDN'T HAVE KNOWN EVEN THEN...

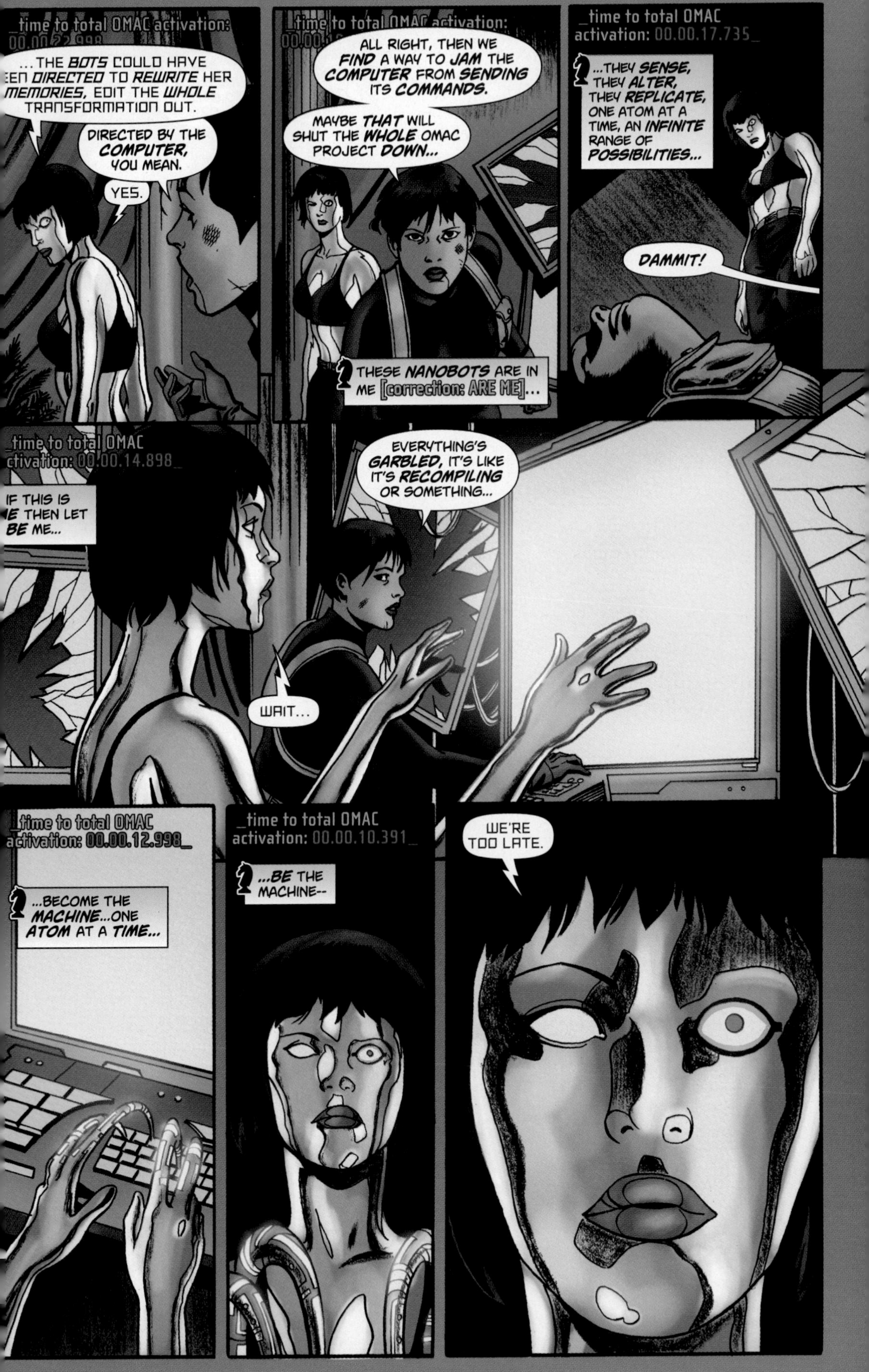
_time to total OMAC activation:
...THE BOTS COULD HAVE EEN DIRECTED TO REWRITE HER MEMORIES, EDIT THE WHOLE TRANSFORMATION OUT.
DIRECTED BY THE COMPUTER, YOU MEAN.
YES.
_time to total OMAC activation:
ALL RIGHT, THEN WE FIND A WAY TO JAM THE COMPUTER FROM SENDING ITS COMMANDS.
MAYBE THAT WILL SHUT THE WHOLE OMAC PROJECT DOWN...
THESE NANOBOTS ARE IN ME [correction: ARE ME]...
time to total OMAC activation: 00.00.17.735
...THEY SENSE, THEY ALTER, THEY REPLICATE, ONE ATOM AT A TIME, AN INFINITE RANGE OF POSSIBILITIES...
DAMMIT!
time to total OMAC ctivation: 00.00.14.898
IF THIS IS E THEN LET BE ME...
EVERYTHING'S GARBLED, IT'S LIKE IT'S RECOMPILING OR SOMETHING...
WAIT...
time to total OMAC activation: 00.00.12.998
...BECOME THE MACHINE...ONE ATOM AT A TIME...
time to total OMAC activation: 00.00.10.391
...BE THE MACHINE--
WE'RE TOO LATE.

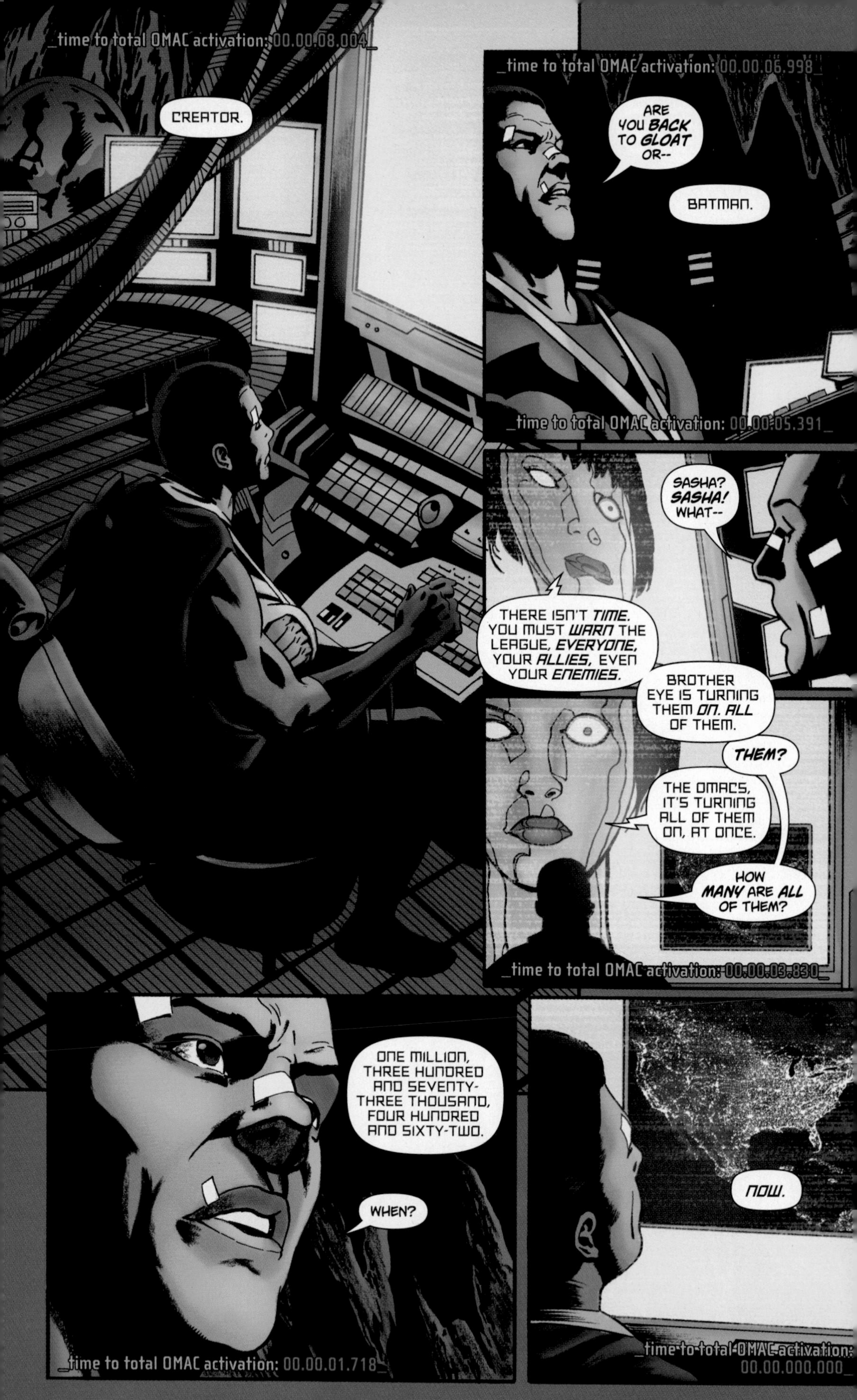

time to total OMAC activation: 00.00.08.004
CREATOR.
time to total OMAC activation: 00.00.06.998
ARE YOU BACK TO GLOAT OR--
BATMAN.
time to total OMAC activation: 00.00.05.391
SASHA? SASHA! WHAT--
THERE ISN'T TIME. YOU MUST WARN THE LEAGUE, EVERYONE, YOUR ALLIES, EVEN YOUR ENEMIES.
BROTHER EYE IS TURNING THEM ON. ALL OF THEM.
THEM?
THE OMACS, IT'S TURNING ALL OF THEM ON, AT ONCE.
HOW MANY ARE ALL OF THEM?
time to total OMAC activation: 00.00.03.830
ONE MILLION, THREE HUNDRED AND SEVENTY-THREE THOUSAND, FOUR HUNDRED AND SIXTY-TWO.
WHEN?
time to total OMAC activation: 00.00.01.718
NOW.
time to total OMAC activation: 00.00.000.000

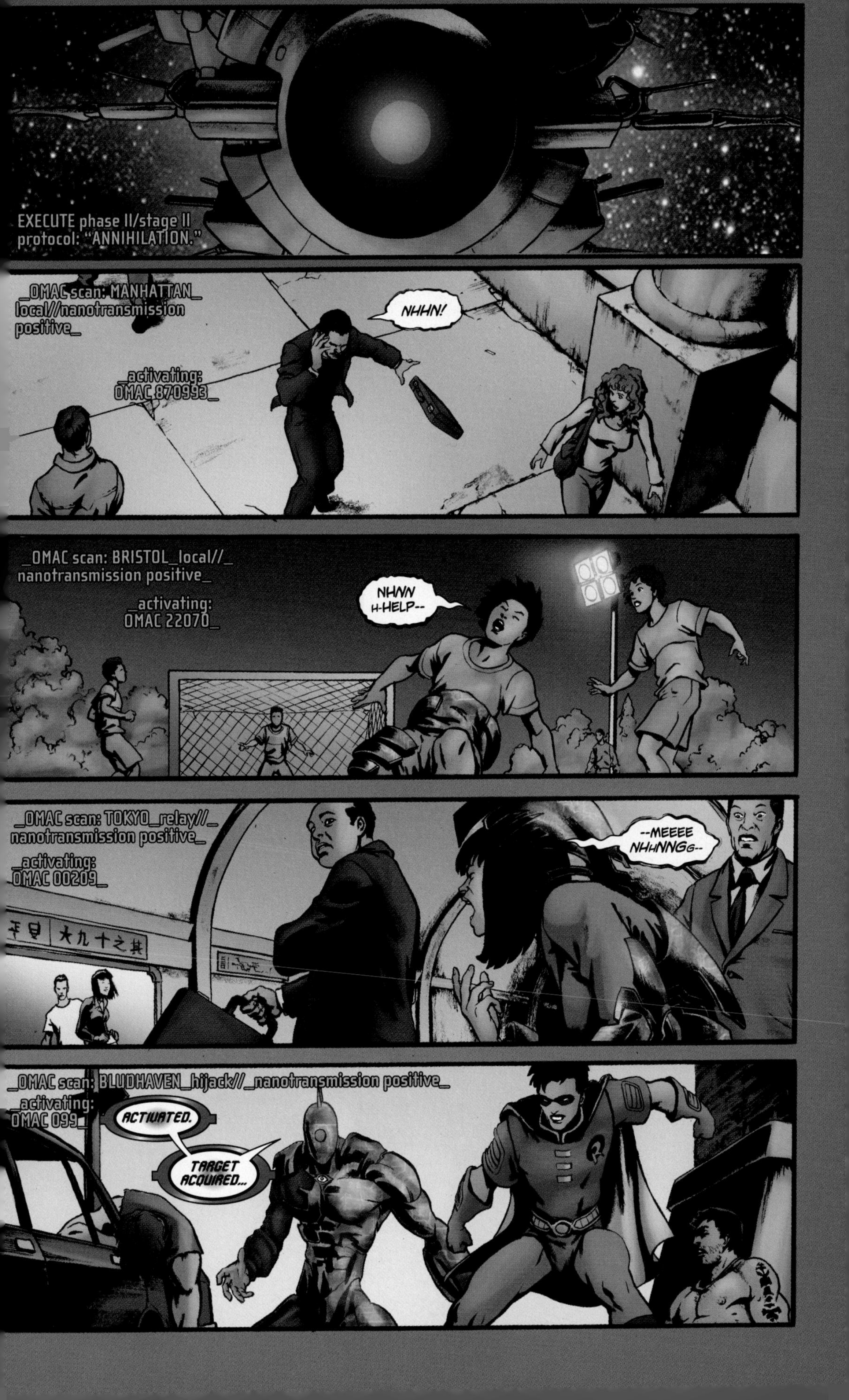
EXECUTE phase II/stage II protocol: "ANNIHILATION."
OMAC scan: MANHATTAN local//nanotransmission positive_
activating: OMAC 870993
NHHN!
_OMAC scan: BRISTOL_local//_ nanotransmission positive_
activating: OMAC 22070
NHNN H-HELP--
_OMAC scan: TOKYO_relay//_ nanotransmission positive_
activating: OMAC 00209
--MEEEE NHHNNGG--
_OMAC scan: BLUDHAVEN_hijack//_nanotransmission positive_
activating: OMAC 099
ACTIVATED.
TARGET ACQUIRED...

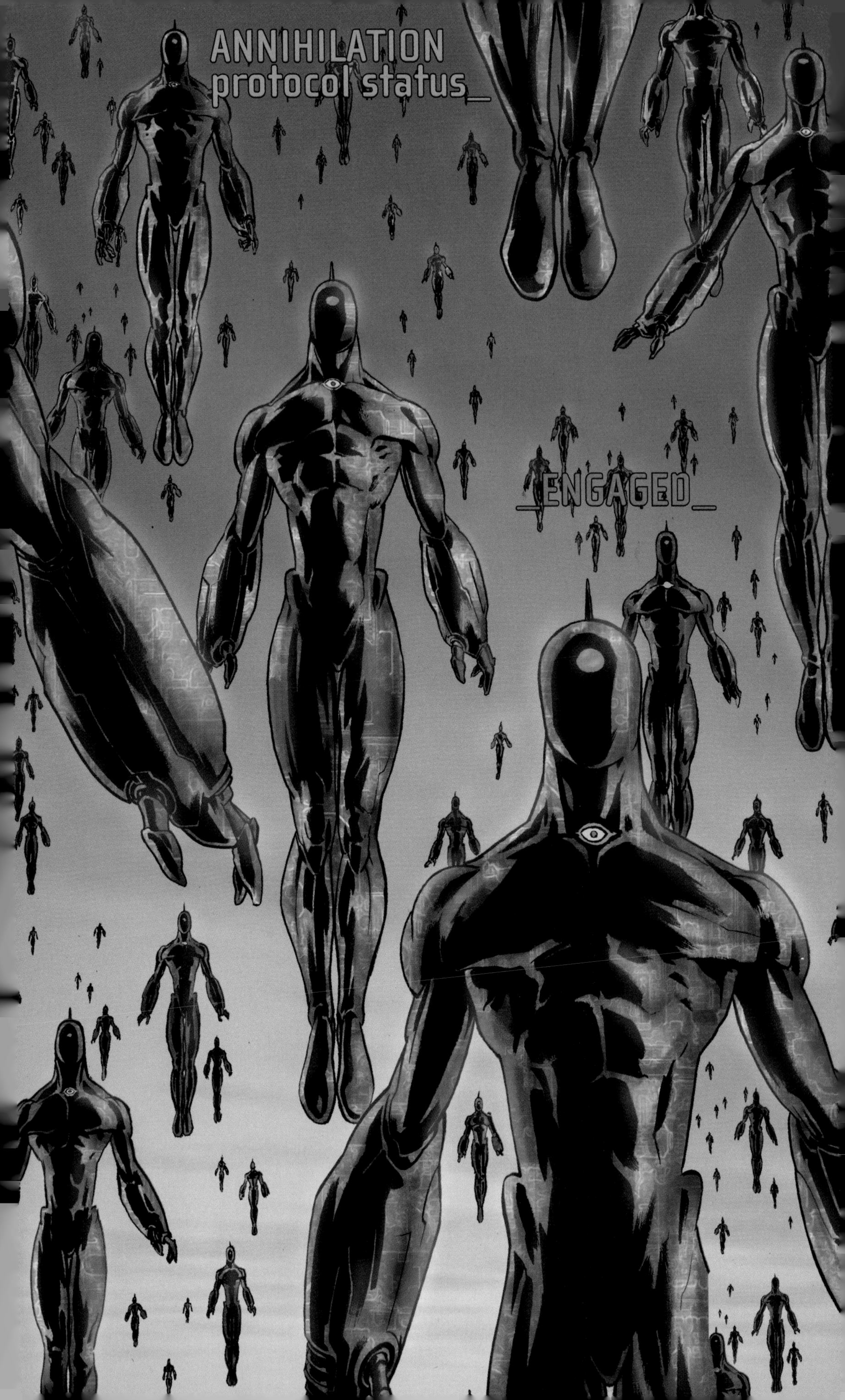
ANNIHILATION
protocol status_
ENGAGED

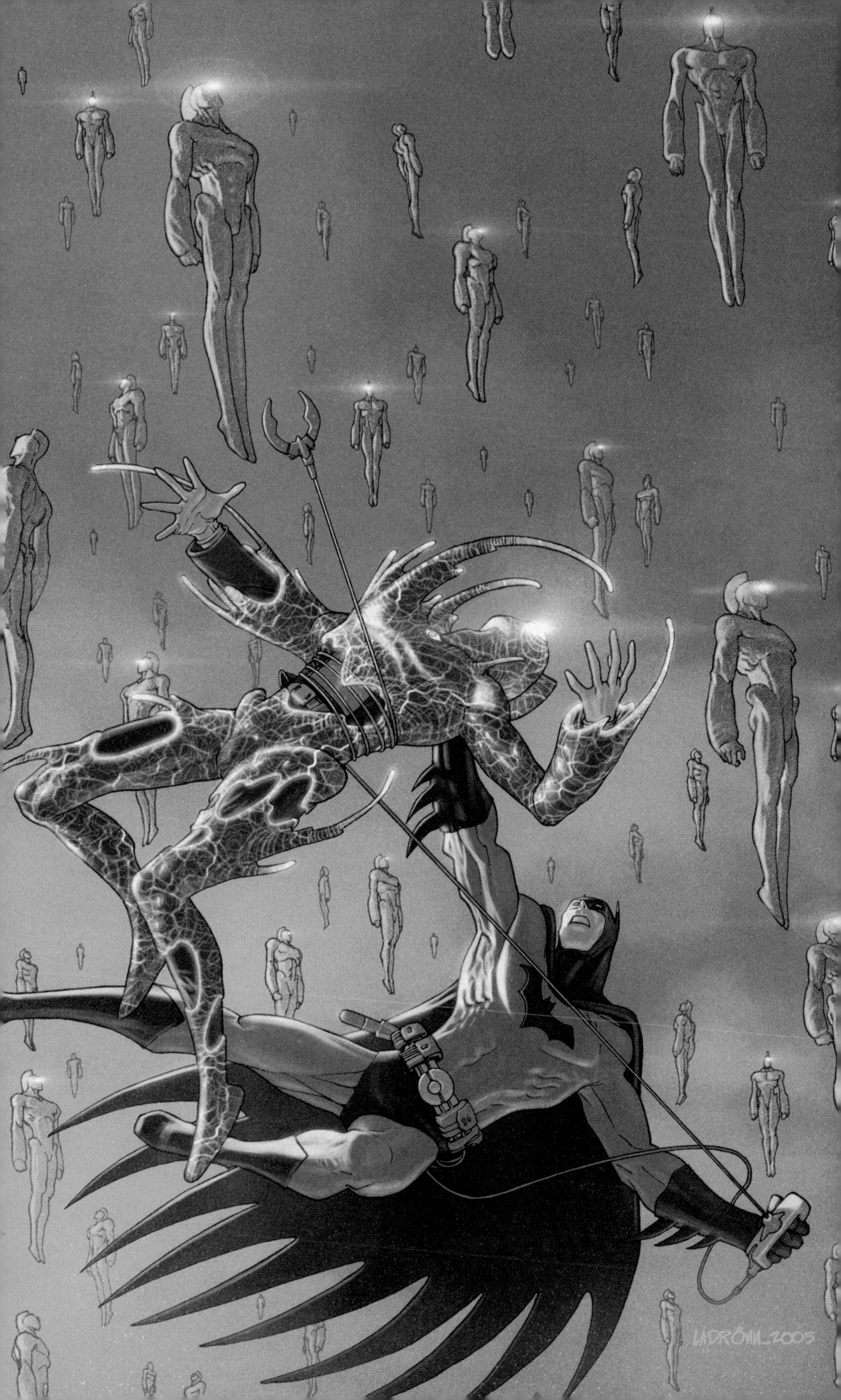
LADRÖNN_2005

Greg Rucka
Writer

Jesus Saiz
Cliff Richards & Bob Wiacek
Artists

Hi-Fi Design
Colorist

Phil Balsman
Letterer

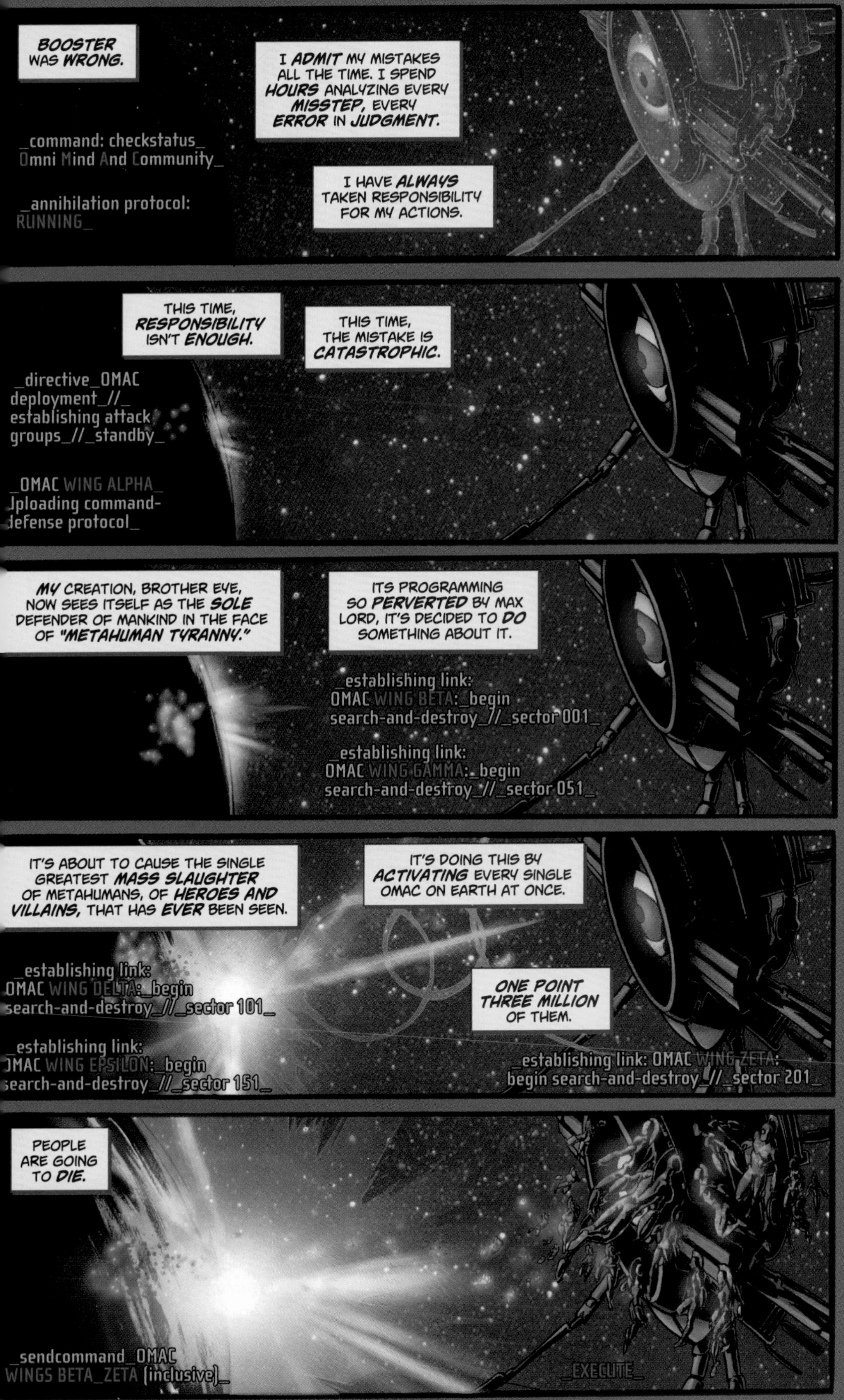
BOOSTER WAS WRONG.
I ADMIT MY MISTAKES ALL THE TIME. I SPEND HOURS ANALYZING EVERY MISSTEP, EVERY ERROR IN JUDGMENT.
command: checkstatus
Omni Mind And Community_
_annihilation protocol:
RUNNING_
I HAVE ALWAYS TAKEN RESPONSIBILITY FOR MY ACTIONS.
THIS TIME, RESPONSIBILITY ISN'T ENOUGH.
THIS TIME, THE MISTAKE IS CATASTROPHIC.
_directive_OMAC
deployment_//_
establishing attack
groups_//_standby_
OMAC WING ALPHA
Uploading command-
defense protocol_
MY CREATION, BROTHER EYE, NOW SEES ITSELF AS THE SOLE DEFENDER OF MANKIND IN THE FACE OF "METAHUMAN TYRANNY."
ITS PROGRAMMING SO PERVERTED BY MAX LORD, IT'S DECIDED TO DO SOMETHING ABOUT IT.
_establishing link:
OMAC WING BETA:_begin
search-and-destroy_//_sector 001_
_establishing link:
OMAC WING GAMMA:_begin
search-and-destroy_//_sector 051_
IT'S ABOUT TO CAUSE THE SINGLE GREATEST MASS SLAUGHTER OF METAHUMANS, OF HEROES AND VILLAINS, THAT HAS EVER BEEN SEEN.
IT'S DOING THIS BY ACTIVATING EVERY SINGLE OMAC ON EARTH AT ONCE.
_establishing link:
OMAC WING DELTA:_begin
search-and-destroy_//_sector 101_
_establishing link:
OMAC WING EPSILON:_begin
search-and-destroy_//_sector 151_
ONE POINT THREE MILLION OF THEM.
_establishing link: OMAC WING ZETA:
begin search-and-destroy_//_sector 201_
PEOPLE ARE GOING TO DIE.
_sendcommand_OMAC
WINGS BETA_ZETA (inclusive)_
EXECUTE

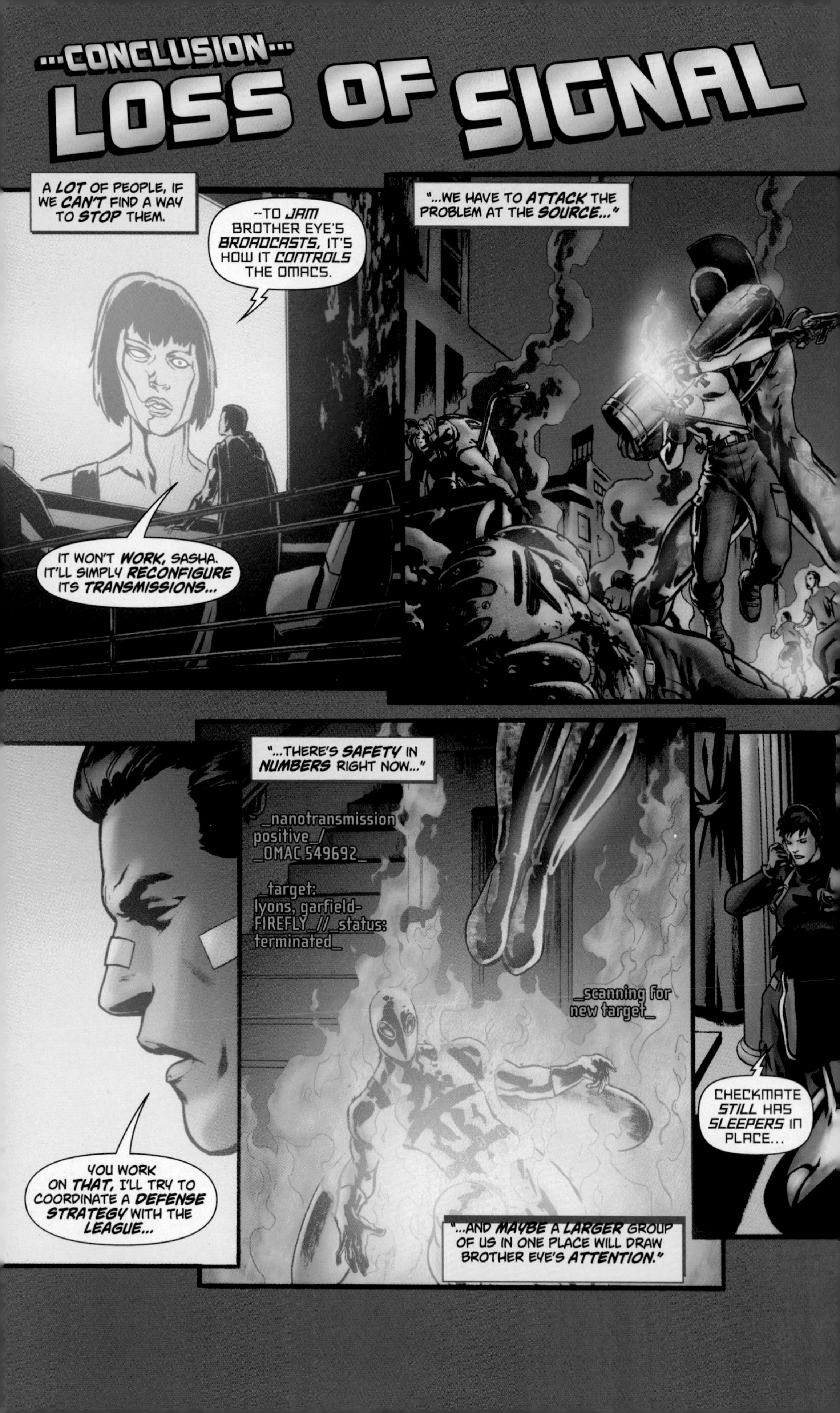

...CONCLUSION...
LOSS OF SIGNAL
A LOT OF PEOPLE, IF WE CAN'T FIND A WAY TO STOP THEM.
--TO JAM BROTHER EYE'S BROADCASTS, IT'S HOW IT CONTROLS THE OMACS.
IT WON'T WORK, SASHA. IT'LL SIMPLY RECONFIGURE ITS TRANSMISSIONS...
"...WE HAVE TO ATTACK THE PROBLEM AT THE SOURCE..."
YOU WORK ON THAT, I'LL TRY TO COORDINATE A DEFENSE STRATEGY WITH THE LEAGUE...
"...THERE'S SAFETY IN NUMBERS RIGHT NOW..."
nanotransmission positive/ _OMAC 549692_
target: lyons, garfield- FIREFLY//_status: terminated_
scanning for new target
"...AND MAYBE A LARGER GROUP OF US IN ONE PLACE WILL DRAW BROTHER EYE'S ATTENTION."
CHECKMATE STILL HAS SLEEPERS IN PLACE...

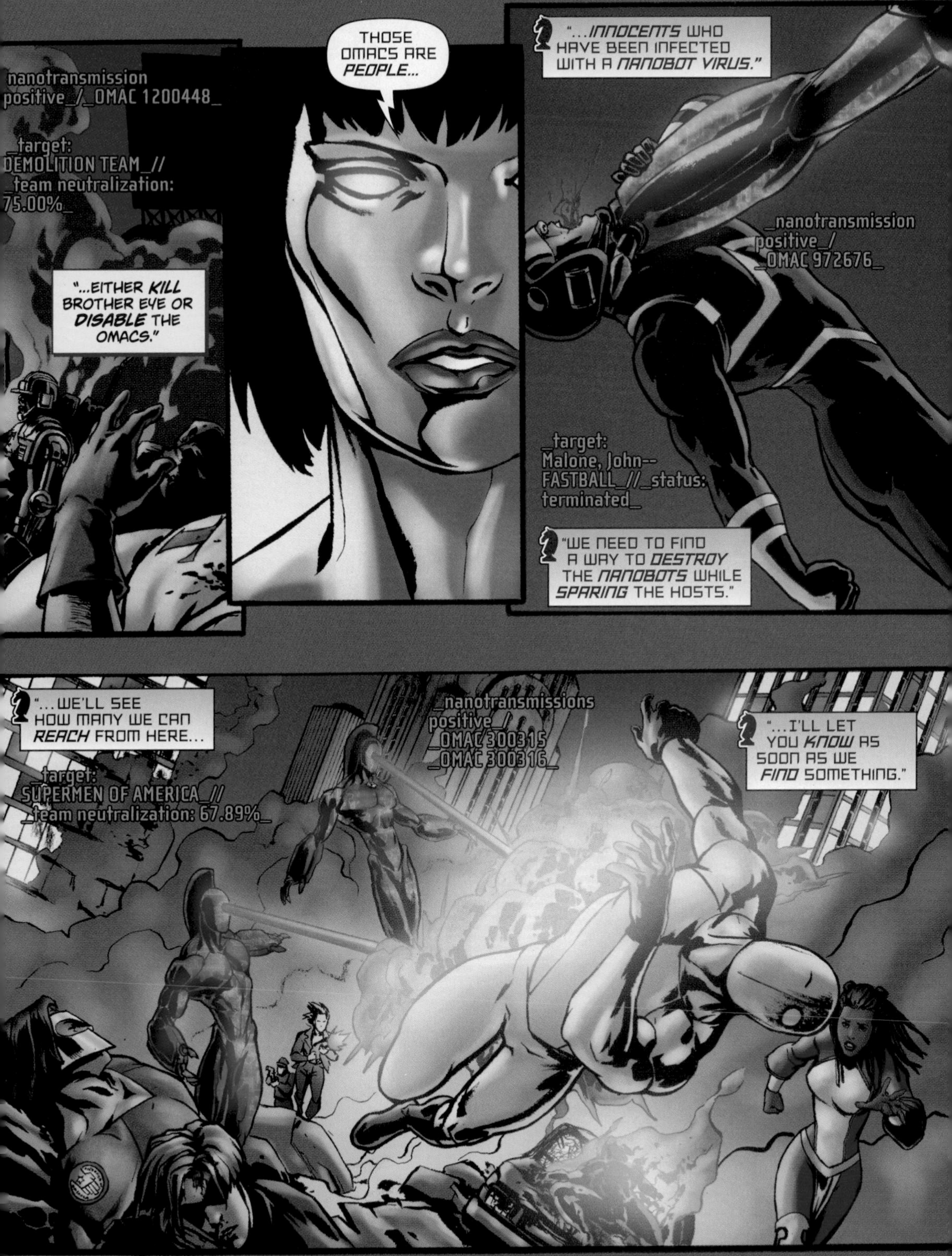
nanotransmission positive_/_OMAC 1200448_
target: DEMOLITION TEAM// _team neutralization: 75.00%_
"...EITHER KILL BROTHER EYE OR DISABLE THE OMACS."
THOSE OMACS ARE PEOPLE...
"...INNOCENTS WHO HAVE BEEN INFECTED WITH A NANOBOT VIRUS."
nanotransmission positive/ _OMAC 972676_
target: Malone, John-- FASTBALL//_status: terminated_
"WE NEED TO FIND A WAY TO DESTROY THE NANOBOTS WHILE SPARING THE HOSTS."
"...WE'LL SEE HOW MANY WE CAN REACH FROM HERE...
target: SUPERMEN OF AMERICA// _team neutralization: 67.89%_
nanotransmissions positive/ _OMAC 300315 _OMAC 300316_
"...I'LL LET YOU KNOW AS SOON AS WE FIND SOMETHING."

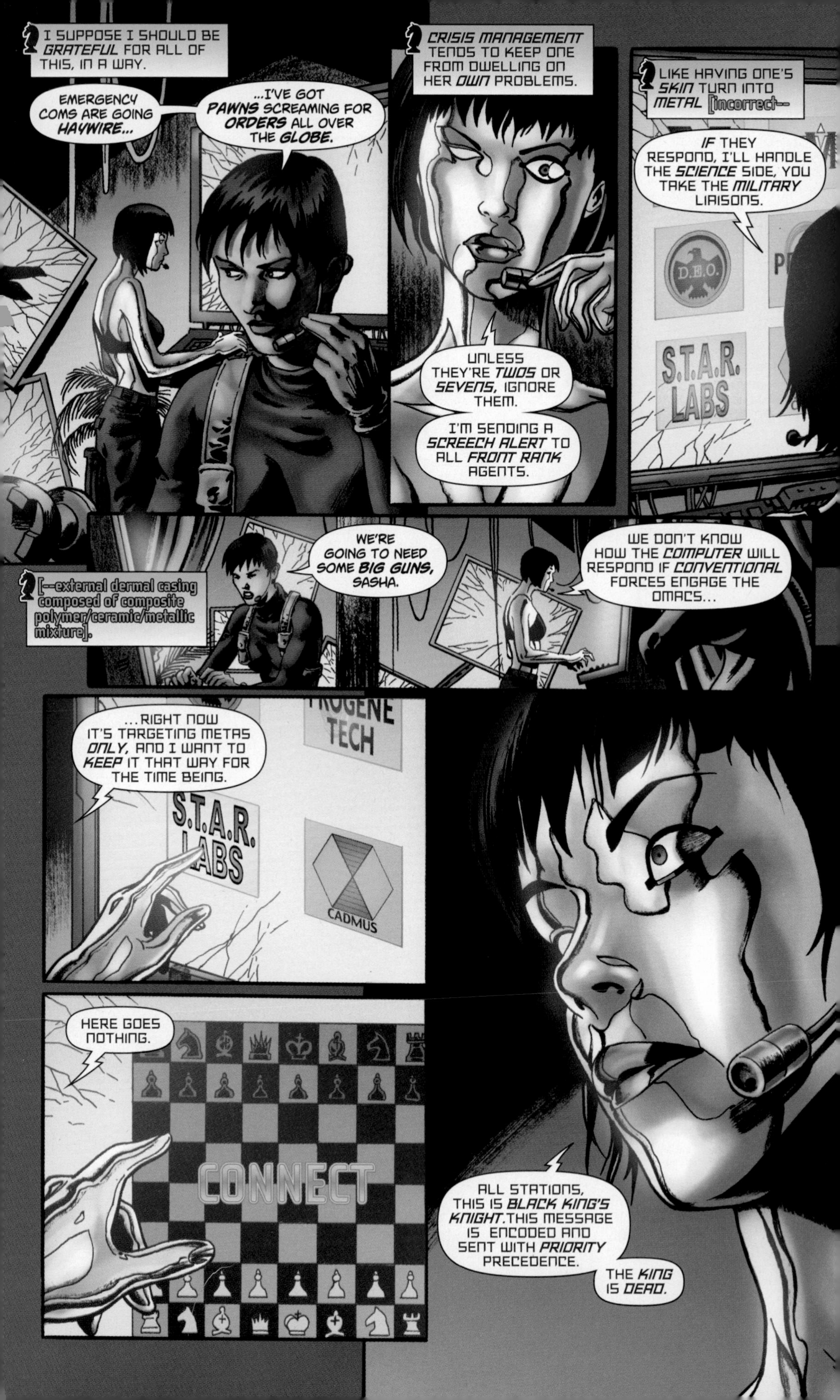

I SUPPOSE I SHOULD BE GRATEFUL FOR ALL OF THIS, IN A WAY.
EMERGENCY COMS ARE GOING HAYWIRE...
...I'VE GOT PAWNS SCREAMING FOR ORDERS ALL OVER THE GLOBE.
CRISIS MANAGEMENT TENDS TO KEEP ONE FROM DWELLING ON HER OWN PROBLEMS.
UNLESS THEY'RE TWOS OR SEVENS, IGNORE THEM.
I'M SENDING A SCREECH ALERT TO ALL FRONT RANK AGENTS.
LIKE HAVING ONE'S SKIN TURN INTO METAL [incorrect--
IF THEY RESPOND, I'LL HANDLE THE SCIENCE SIDE, YOU TAKE THE MILITARY LIAISONS.
D.E.O.
S.T.A.R. LABS
[--external dermal casing composed of composite polymer/ceramic/metallic mixture].
WE'RE GOING TO NEED SOME BIG GUNS, SASHA.
WE DON'T KNOW HOW THE COMPUTER WILL RESPOND IF CONVENTIONAL FORCES ENGAGE THE OMACS...
...RIGHT NOW IT'S TARGETING METAS ONLY, AND I WANT TO KEEP IT THAT WAY FOR THE TIME BEING.
PROGENE TECH
S.T.A.R. LABS
CADMUS
HERE GOES NOTHING.
CONNECT
ALL STATIONS, THIS IS BLACK KING'S KNIGHT. THIS MESSAGE IS ENCODED AND SENT WITH PRIORITY PRECEDENCE.
THE KING IS DEAD.

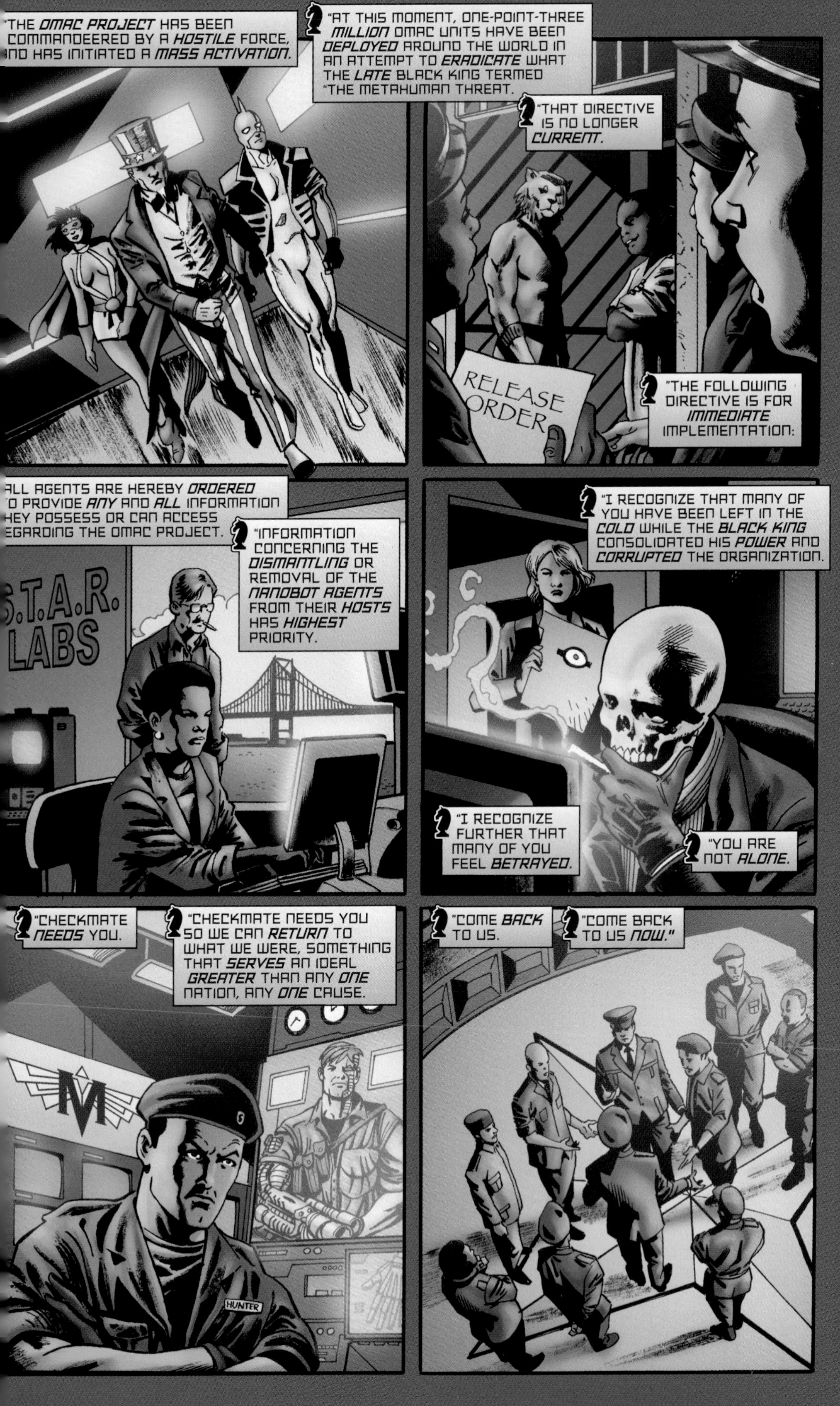
"THE OMAC PROJECT HAS BEEN COMMANDEERED BY A HOSTILE FORCE, AND HAS INITIATED A MASS ACTIVATION.
"AT THIS MOMENT, ONE-POINT-THREE MILLION OMAC UNITS HAVE BEEN DEPLOYED AROUND THE WORLD IN AN ATTEMPT TO ERADICATE WHAT THE LATE BLACK KING TERMED "THE METAHUMAN THREAT.
"THAT DIRECTIVE IS NO LONGER CURRENT.
RELEASE ORDER
"THE FOLLOWING DIRECTIVE IS FOR IMMEDIATE IMPLEMENTATION:
ALL AGENTS ARE HEREBY ORDERED TO PROVIDE ANY AND ALL INFORMATION THEY POSSESS OR CAN ACCESS REGARDING THE OMAC PROJECT.
"INFORMATION CONCERNING THE DISMANTLING OR REMOVAL OF THE NANOBOT AGENTS FROM THEIR HOSTS HAS HIGHEST PRIORITY.
S.T.A.R. LABS
"I RECOGNIZE THAT MANY OF YOU HAVE BEEN LEFT IN THE COLD WHILE THE BLACK KING CONSOLIDATED HIS POWER AND CORRUPTED THE ORGANIZATION.
"I RECOGNIZE FURTHER THAT MANY OF YOU FEEL BETRAYED.
"YOU ARE NOT ALONE.
"CHECKMATE NEEDS YOU.
"CHECKMATE NEEDS YOU SO WE CAN RETURN TO WHAT WE WERE, SOMETHING THAT SERVES AN IDEAL GREATER THAN ANY ONE NATION, ANY ONE CAUSE.
HUNTER
"COME BACK TO US.
"COME BACK TO US NOW."

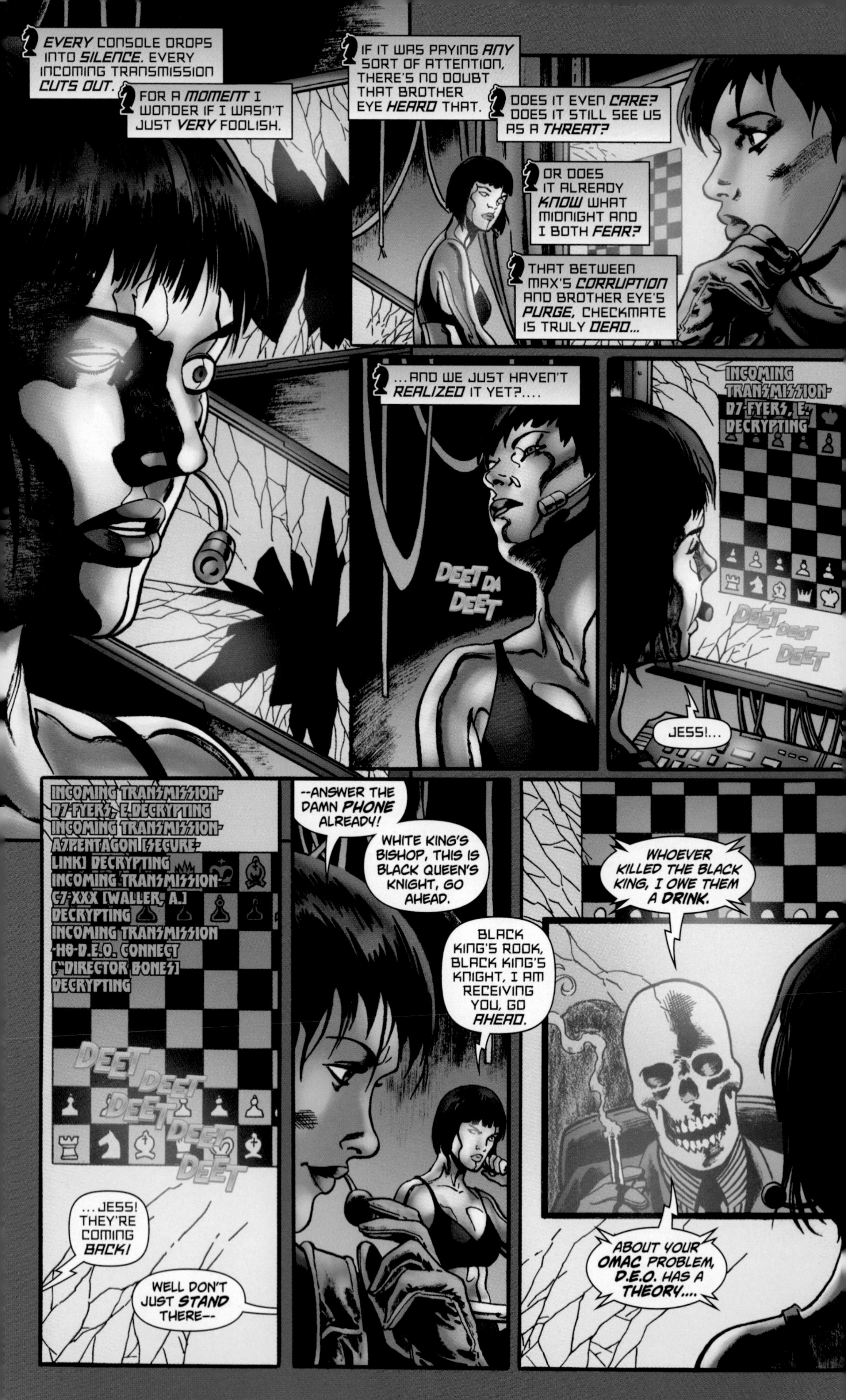
EVERY CONSOLE DROPS INTO SILENCE. EVERY INCOMING TRANSMISSION CUTS OUT.
FOR A MOMENT I WONDER IF I WASN'T JUST VERY FOOLISH.
IF IT WAS PAYING ANY SORT OF ATTENTION, THERE'S NO DOUBT THAT BROTHER EYE HEARD THAT.
DOES IT EVEN CARE? DOES IT STILL SEE US AS A THREAT?
OR DOES IT ALREADY KNOW WHAT MIDNIGHT AND I BOTH FEAR?
THAT BETWEEN MAX'S CORRUPTION AND BROTHER EYE'S PURGE, CHECKMATE IS TRULY DEAD...
...AND WE JUST HAVEN'T REALIZED IT YET?....
DEET DA DEET
INCOMING TRANSMISSION- D7-FYERS, E. DECRYPTING
DEET DEET DEET
JESS!...
INCOMING TRANSMISSION- D7-FYERS, E.DECRYPTING
INCOMING TRANSMISSION- A7PENTAGON [SECURE-LINK] DECRYPTING
INCOMING TRANSMISSION- C7-XXX [WALLER, A.] DECRYPTING
INCOMING TRANSMISSION -HQ-D.E.O. CONNECT [~DIRECTOR BONES] DECRYPTING
DEET DEET DEET DEET DEET
...JESS! THEY'RE COMING BACK!
WELL DON'T JUST STAND THERE--
--ANSWER THE DAMN PHONE ALREADY!
WHITE KING'S BISHOP, THIS IS BLACK QUEEN'S KNIGHT, GO AHEAD.
BLACK KING'S ROOK, BLACK KING'S KNIGHT, I AM RECEIVING YOU, GO AHEAD.
WHOEVER KILLED THE BLACK KING, I OWE THEM A DRINK.
ABOUT YOUR OMAC PROBLEM, D.E.O. HAS A THEORY....

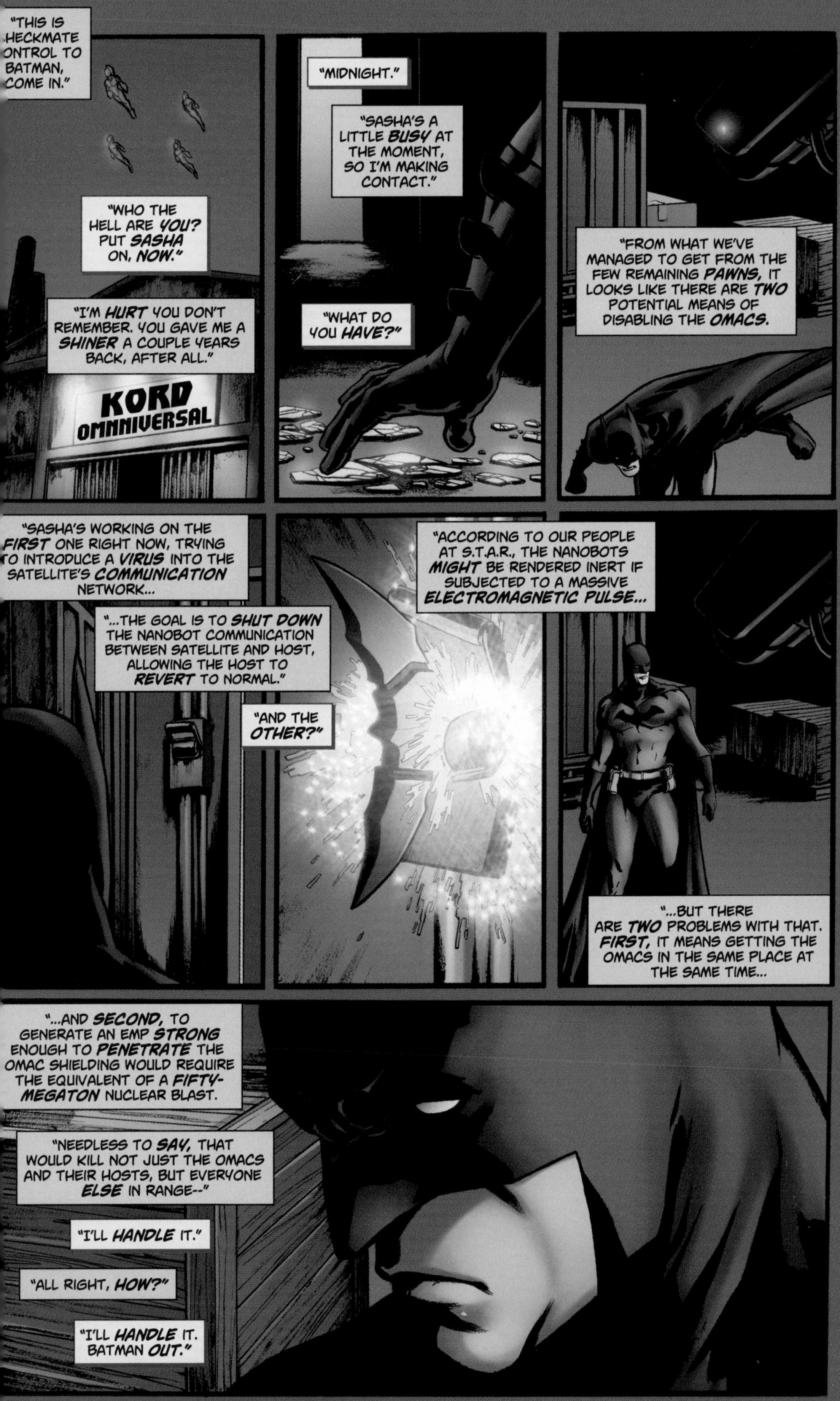
"THIS IS CHECKMATE CONTROL TO BATMAN, COME IN."
"WHO THE HELL ARE YOU? PUT SASHA ON, NOW."
"I'M HURT YOU DON'T REMEMBER. YOU GAVE ME A SHINER A COUPLE YEARS BACK, AFTER ALL."
KORD OMNNIVERSAL
"MIDNIGHT."
"SASHA'S A LITTLE BUSY AT THE MOMENT, SO I'M MAKING CONTACT."
"WHAT DO YOU HAVE?"
"FROM WHAT WE'VE MANAGED TO GET FROM THE FEW REMAINING PAWNS, IT LOOKS LIKE THERE ARE TWO POTENTIAL MEANS OF DISABLING THE OMACS.
"SASHA'S WORKING ON THE FIRST ONE RIGHT NOW, TRYING TO INTRODUCE A VIRUS INTO THE SATELLITE'S COMMUNICATION NETWORK...
"...THE GOAL IS TO SHUT DOWN THE NANOBOT COMMUNICATION BETWEEN SATELLITE AND HOST, ALLOWING THE HOST TO REVERT TO NORMAL."
"AND THE OTHER?"
"ACCORDING TO OUR PEOPLE AT S.T.A.R., THE NANOBOTS MIGHT BE RENDERED INERT IF SUBJECTED TO A MASSIVE ELECTROMAGNETIC PULSE...
"...BUT THERE ARE TWO PROBLEMS WITH THAT. FIRST, IT MEANS GETTING THE OMACS IN THE SAME PLACE AT THE SAME TIME...
"...AND SECOND, TO GENERATE AN EMP STRONG ENOUGH TO PENETRATE THE OMAC SHIELDING WOULD REQUIRE THE EQUIVALENT OF A FIFTY-MEGATON NUCLEAR BLAST.
"NEEDLESS TO SAY, THAT WOULD KILL NOT JUST THE OMACS AND THEIR HOSTS, BUT EVERYONE ELSE IN RANGE--"
"I'LL HANDLE IT."
"ALL RIGHT, HOW?"
"I'LL HANDLE IT. BATMAN OUT."

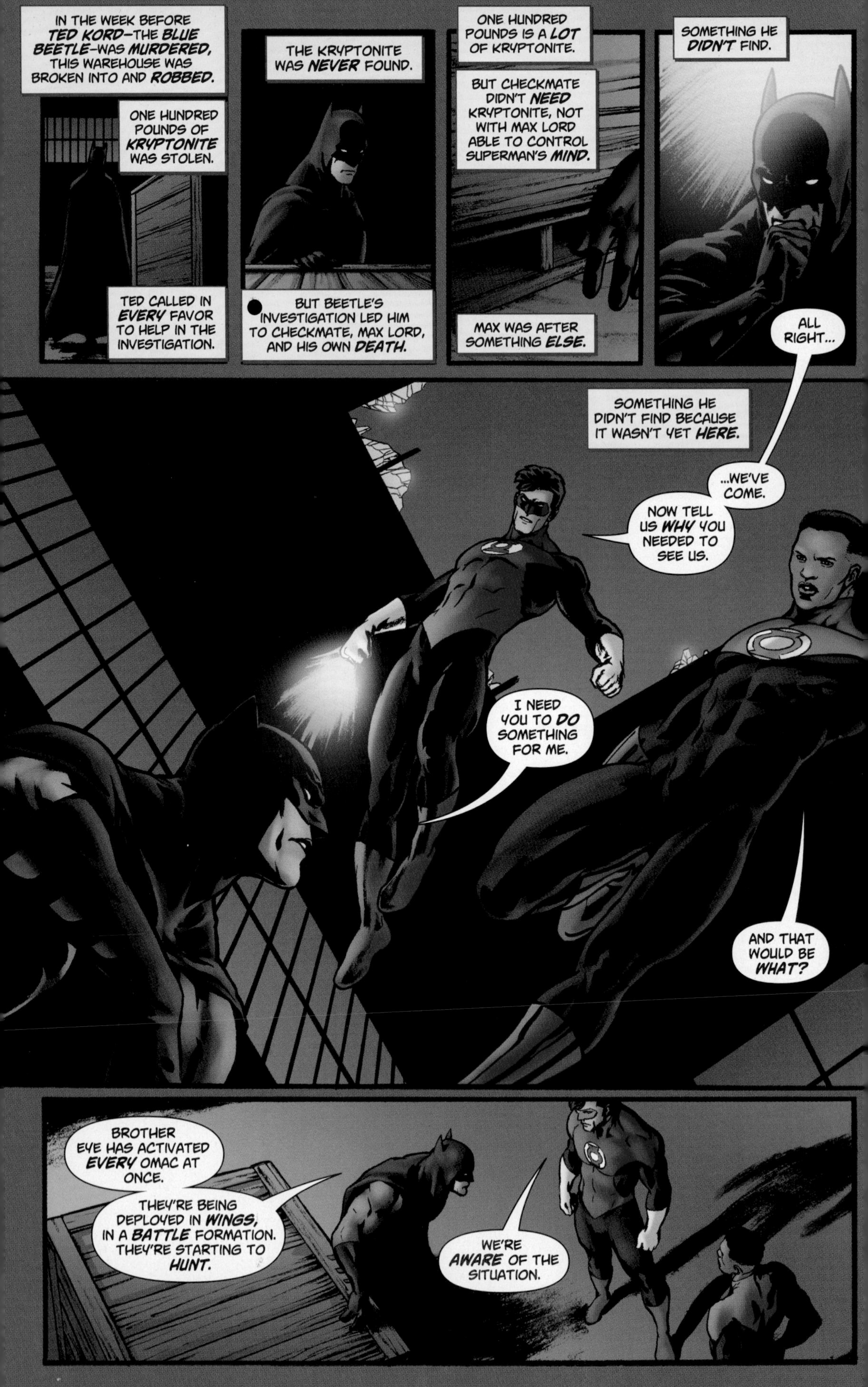

IN THE WEEK BEFORE TED KORD—THE BLUE BEETLE—WAS MURDERED, THIS WAREHOUSE WAS BROKEN INTO AND ROBBED.
ONE HUNDRED POUNDS OF KRYPTONITE WAS STOLEN.
TED CALLED IN EVERY FAVOR TO HELP IN THE INVESTIGATION.
THE KRYPTONITE WAS NEVER FOUND.
BUT BEETLE'S INVESTIGATION LED HIM TO CHECKMATE, MAX LORD, AND HIS OWN DEATH.
ONE HUNDRED POUNDS IS A LOT OF KRYPTONITE.
BUT CHECKMATE DIDN'T NEED KRYPTONITE, NOT WITH MAX LORD ABLE TO CONTROL SUPERMAN'S MIND.
MAX WAS AFTER SOMETHING ELSE.
SOMETHING HE DIDN'T FIND.
ALL RIGHT...
SOMETHING HE DIDN'T FIND BECAUSE IT WASN'T YET HERE.
...WE'VE COME.
NOW TELL US WHY YOU NEEDED TO SEE US.
I NEED YOU TO DO SOMETHING FOR ME.
AND THAT WOULD BE WHAT?
BROTHER EYE HAS ACTIVATED EVERY OMAC AT ONCE.
THEY'RE BEING DEPLOYED IN WINGS, IN A BATTLE FORMATION. THEY'RE STARTING TO HUNT.
WE'RE AWARE OF THE SITUATION.

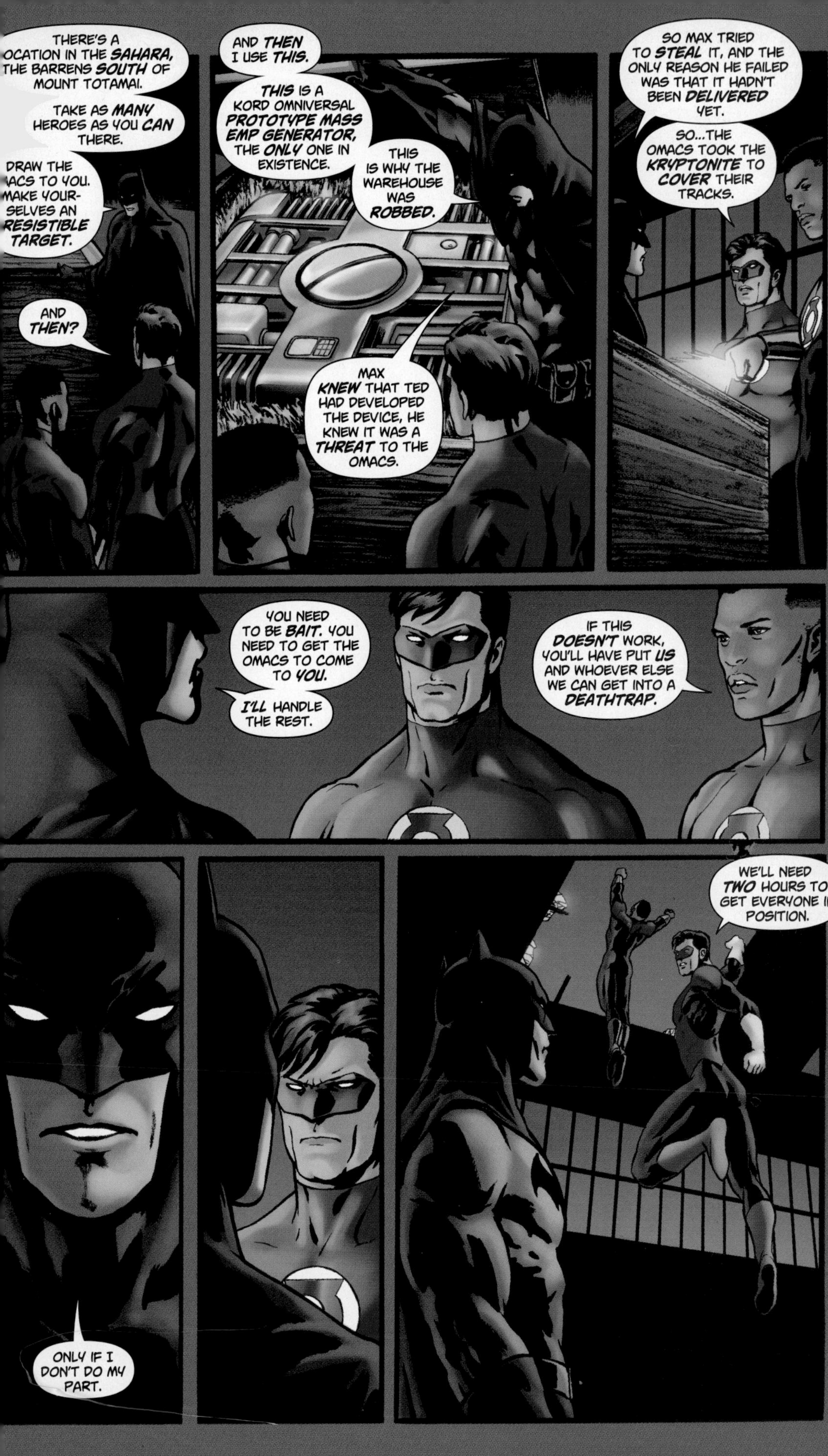
THERE'S A OCATION IN THE SAHARA, THE BARRENS SOUTH OF MOUNT TOTAMAI.
TAKE AS MANY HEROES AS YOU CAN THERE.
DRAW THE ACS TO YOU. MAKE YOURSELVES AN RESISTIBLE TARGET.
AND THEN?
AND THEN I USE THIS.
THIS IS A KORD OMNIVERSAL PROTOTYPE MASS EMP GENERATOR, THE ONLY ONE IN EXISTENCE.
THIS IS WHY THE WAREHOUSE WAS ROBBED.
MAX KNEW THAT TED HAD DEVELOPED THE DEVICE, HE KNEW IT WAS A THREAT TO THE OMACS.
SO MAX TRIED TO STEAL IT, AND THE ONLY REASON HE FAILED WAS THAT IT HADN'T BEEN DELIVERED YET.
SO...THE OMACS TOOK THE KRYPTONITE TO COVER THEIR TRACKS.
YOU NEED TO BE BAIT. YOU NEED TO GET THE OMACS TO COME TO YOU.
I'LL HANDLE THE REST.
IF THIS DOESN'T WORK, YOU'LL HAVE PUT US AND WHOEVER ELSE WE CAN GET INTO A DEATHTRAP.
ONLY IF I DON'T DO MY PART.
WE'LL NEED TWO HOURS TO GET EVERYONE IN POSITION.

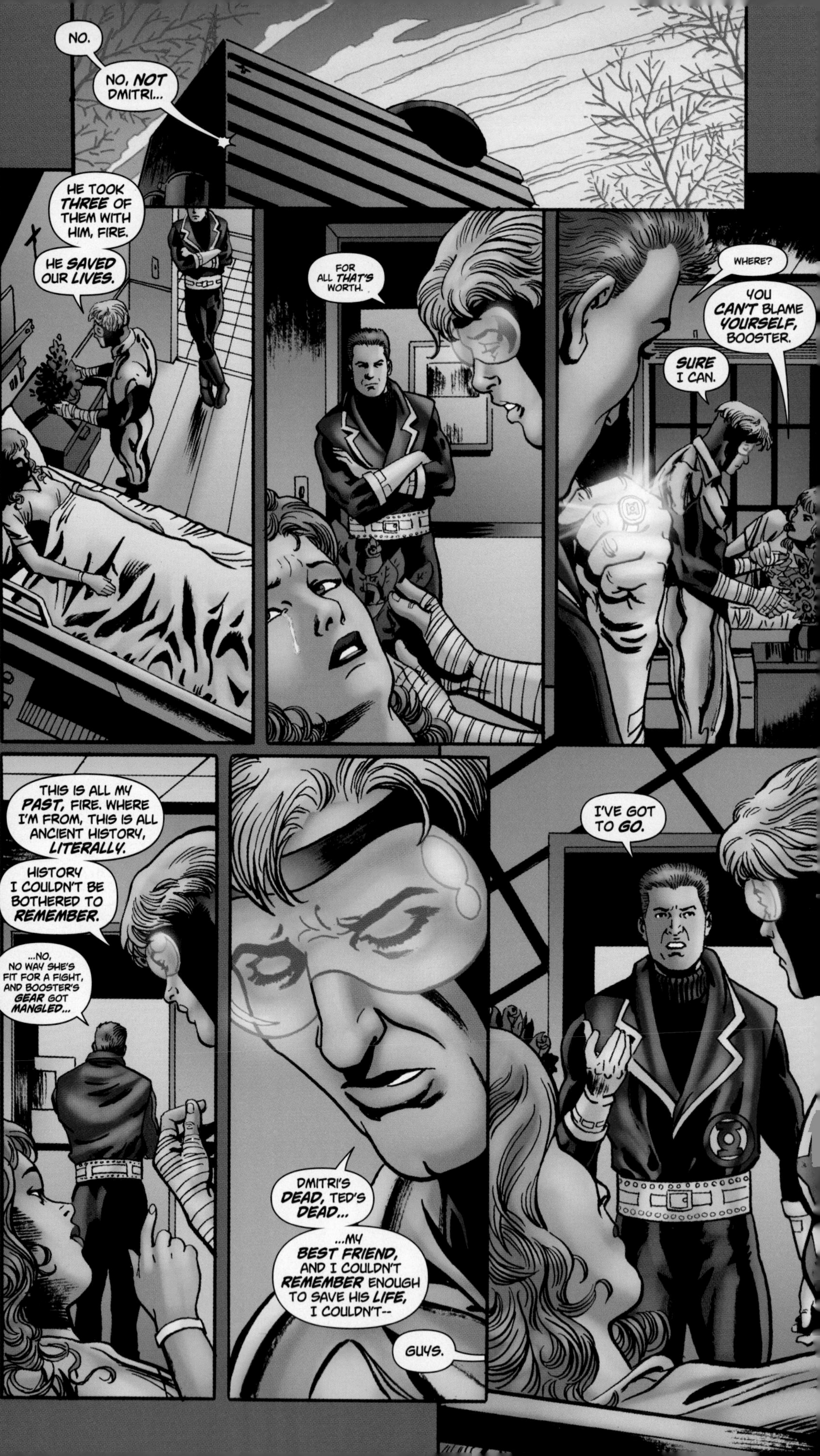
NO.
NO, NOT DMITRI...
HE TOOK THREE OF THEM WITH HIM, FIRE.
HE SAVED OUR LIVES.
FOR ALL THAT'S WORTH.
WHERE?
YOU CAN'T BLAME YOURSELF, BOOSTER.
SURE I CAN.
THIS IS ALL MY PAST, FIRE. WHERE I'M FROM, THIS IS ALL ANCIENT HISTORY, LITERALLY.
HISTORY I COULDN'T BE BOTHERED TO REMEMBER.
...NO, NO WAY SHE'S FIT FOR A FIGHT, AND BOOSTER'S GEAR GOT MANGLED...
DMITRI'S DEAD, TED'S DEAD...
...MY BEST FRIEND, AND I COULDN'T REMEMBER ENOUGH TO SAVE HIS LIFE, I COULDN'T--
GUYS.
I'VE GOT TO GO.

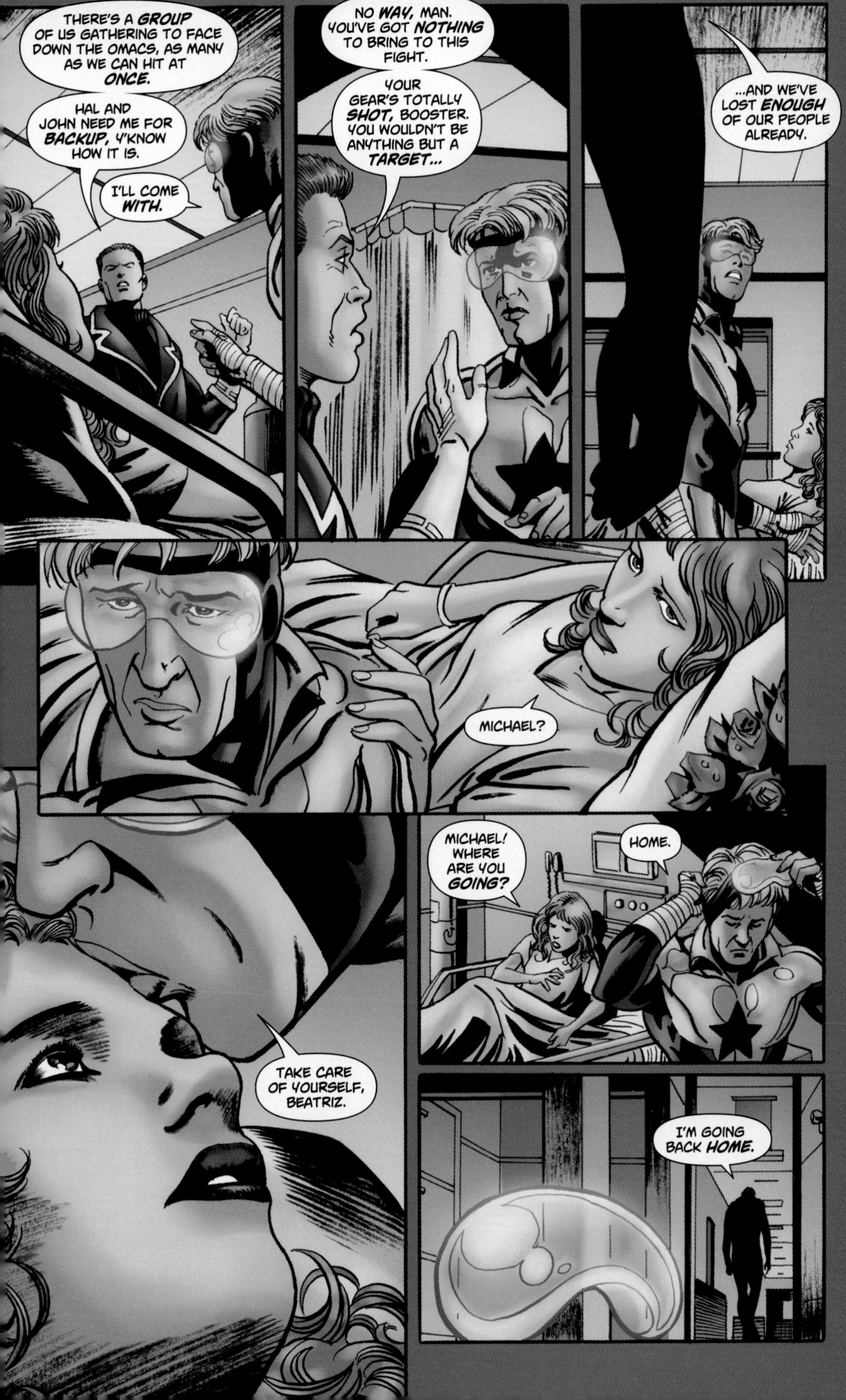
THERE'S A GROUP OF US GATHERING TO FACE DOWN THE OMACS, AS MANY AS WE CAN HIT AT ONCE.
HAL AND JOHN NEED ME FOR BACKUP, Y'KNOW HOW IT IS.
I'LL COME WITH.
NO WAY, MAN. YOU'VE GOT NOTHING TO BRING TO THIS FIGHT.
YOUR GEAR'S TOTALLY SHOT, BOOSTER. YOU WOULDN'T BE ANYTHING BUT A TARGET...
...AND WE'VE LOST ENOUGH OF OUR PEOPLE ALREADY.
MICHAEL?
TAKE CARE OF YOURSELF, BEATRIZ.
MICHAEL! WHERE ARE YOU GOING?
HOME.
I'M GOING BACK HOME.

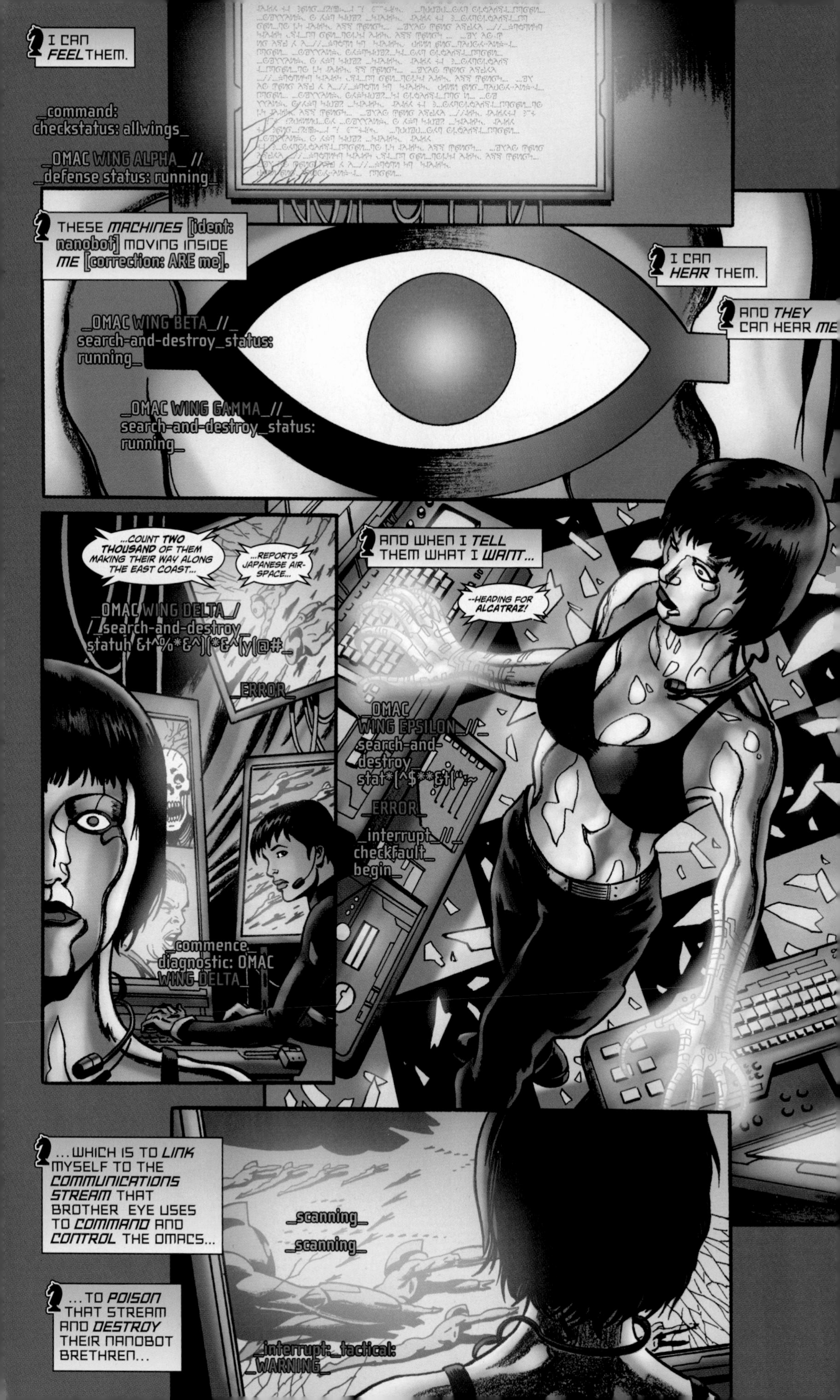

I CAN FEEL THEM.
command: checkstatus: allwings
OMAC WING ALPHA // _defense status: running_
THESE MACHINES [ident: nanobot] MOVING INSIDE ME [correction: ARE me].
I CAN HEAR THEM.
AND THEY CAN HEAR ME
OMAC WING BETA//_ search-and-destroy_status: running_
OMAC WING GAMMA//_ search-and-destroy_status: running_
...COUNT TWO THOUSAND OF THEM MAKING THEIR WAY ALONG THE EAST COAST...
...REPORTS JAPANESE AIR-SPACE...
AND WHEN I TELL THEM WHAT I WANT...
--HEADING FOR ALCATRAZ!
OMAC WING DELTA/ /_search-and-destroy statuh &t^%*&^)(*&^[y(@#_
ERROR
OMAC WING EPSILON//_ search-and-destroy_ stat*(^$**&t(^;~
ERROR
interrupt//_ checkfault_ begin_
commence diagnostic: OMAC WING DELTA_
...WHICH IS TO LINK MYSELF TO THE COMMUNICATIONS STREAM THAT BROTHER EYE USES TO COMMAND AND CONTROL THE OMACS...
scanning
scanning
...TO POISON THAT STREAM AND DESTROY THEIR NANOBOT BRETHREN...
_interrupt:_tactical: _WARNING_

...THEY'RE *ALL* TOO EAGER TO *OBEY.*

switchfeed"little brother omega 47"_feedstatus: LIVE_

_location: LIBYA_280 km south MONTS TOTOMAI_

multiple metahuman contacts detected

HAL--

I SEE IT.

IF YOU DO NOT HAVE HARDENED ELECTRONICS, TRY TO REMAIN *CLOSE* TO THE GREEN LANTERNS.

THEY WILL *PROTECT* YOU.

LET'S *PUSH* THE *ENVELOPE,* KIDS.

evaluating//_ probability of creator-instigated trap: 100%_

coordinating response//_ OMAC WING DELTA rerouted to target location_//_ downloading new protocols_

assessing//_probability of trap success: 00.01%_

WE'RE PUTTING AN AWFUL LOT OF *FAITH* IN BATMAN, HERE, HAL.

NOT IN BATMAN, JOHN...

EXECUTE. EXECUTE. EXECUTE. EXECUTE.
EXECUTE. EXECUTE. EXECUTE. EXECUTE.
EXECUTE. EXECUTE. EXECUTE.
...IN THE *BLUE BEETLE.*
EXECUTE. EXECUTE. EXECUTE.
EXECUTE. EXECUTE. EXECUTE. EXECUTE.
EXECUTE. EXECUTE. EXECUTE.
EXECUTE. EXECUTE. EXECUTE.
EXECUTE. EXECUTE. EXECUTE.

EXECUTE

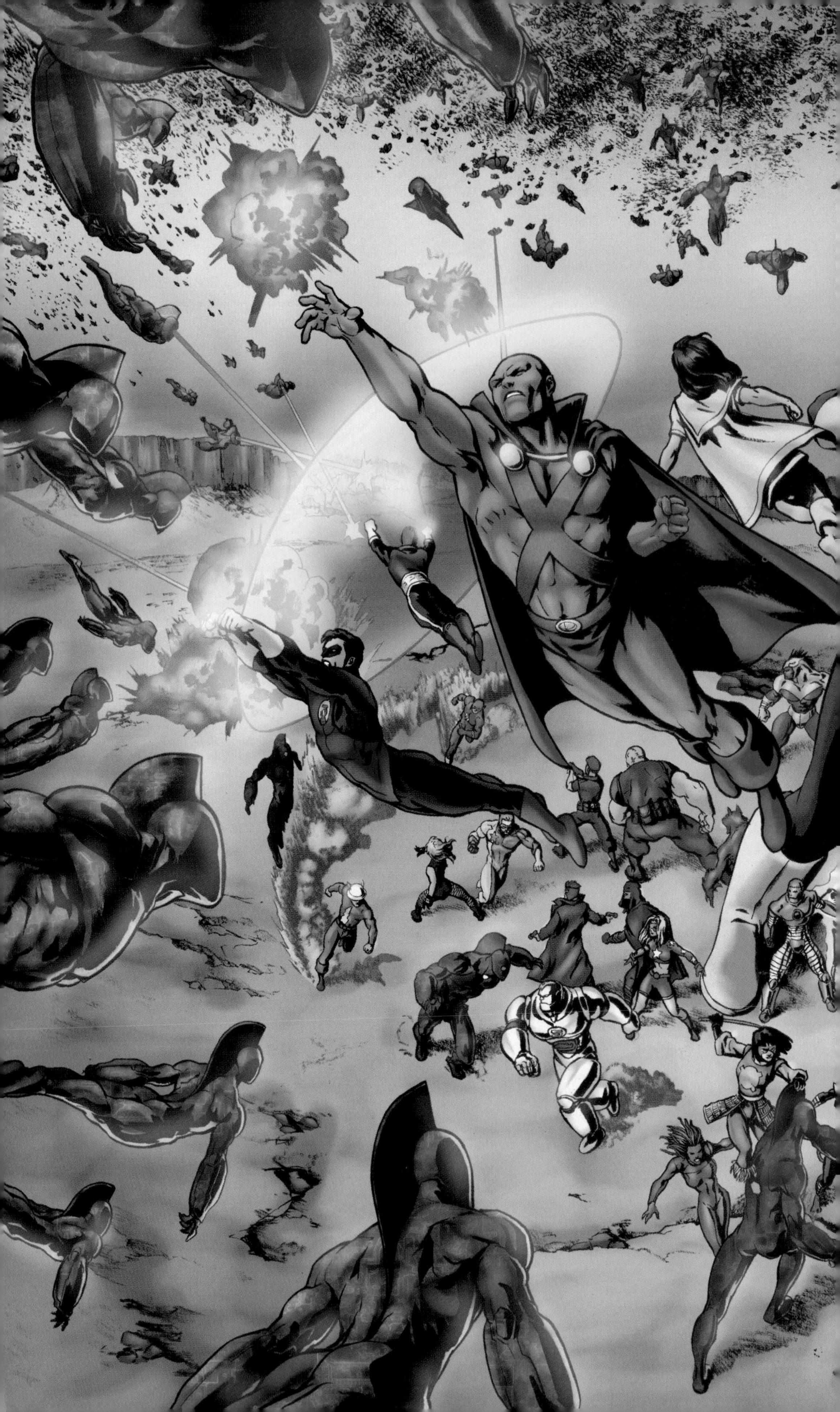

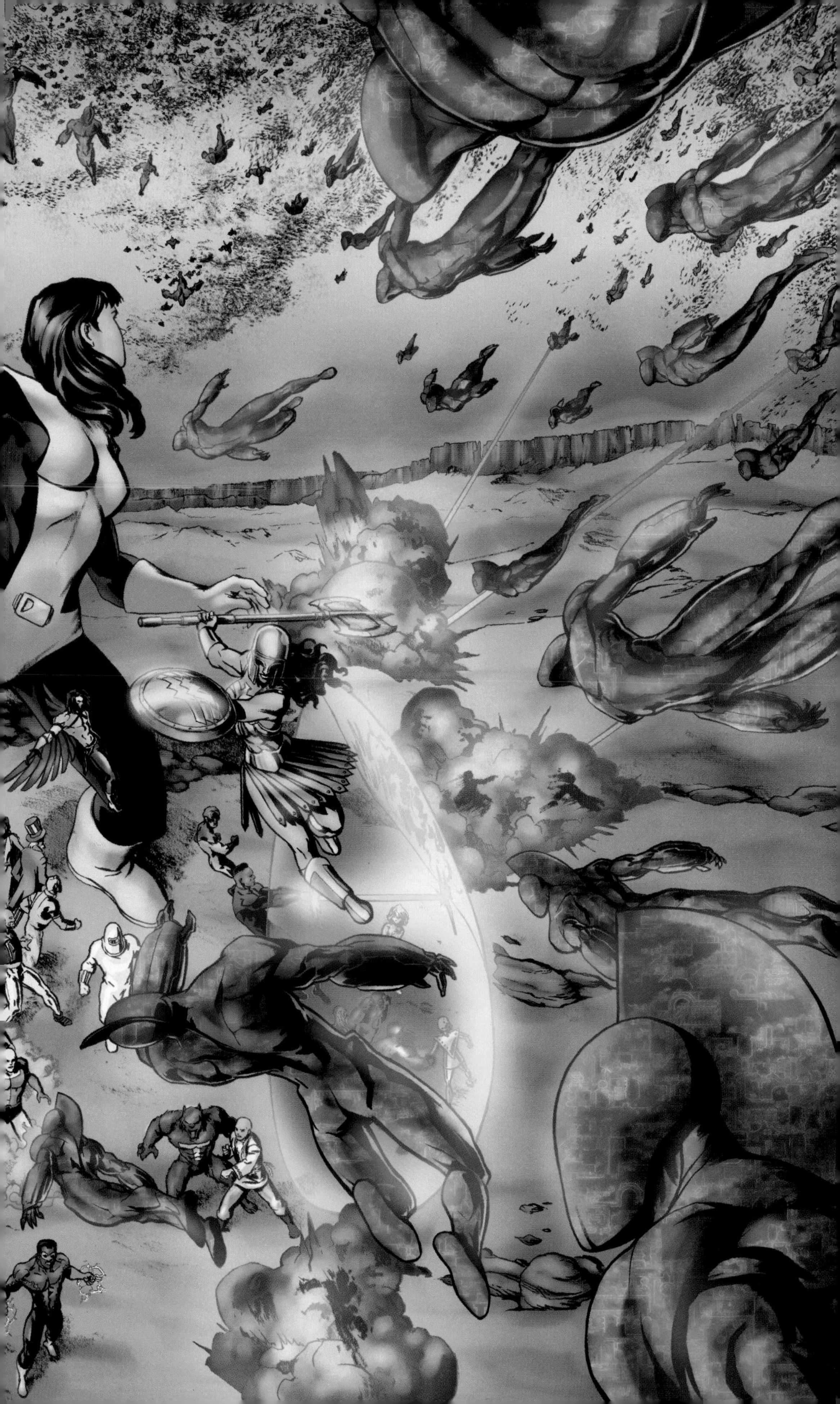

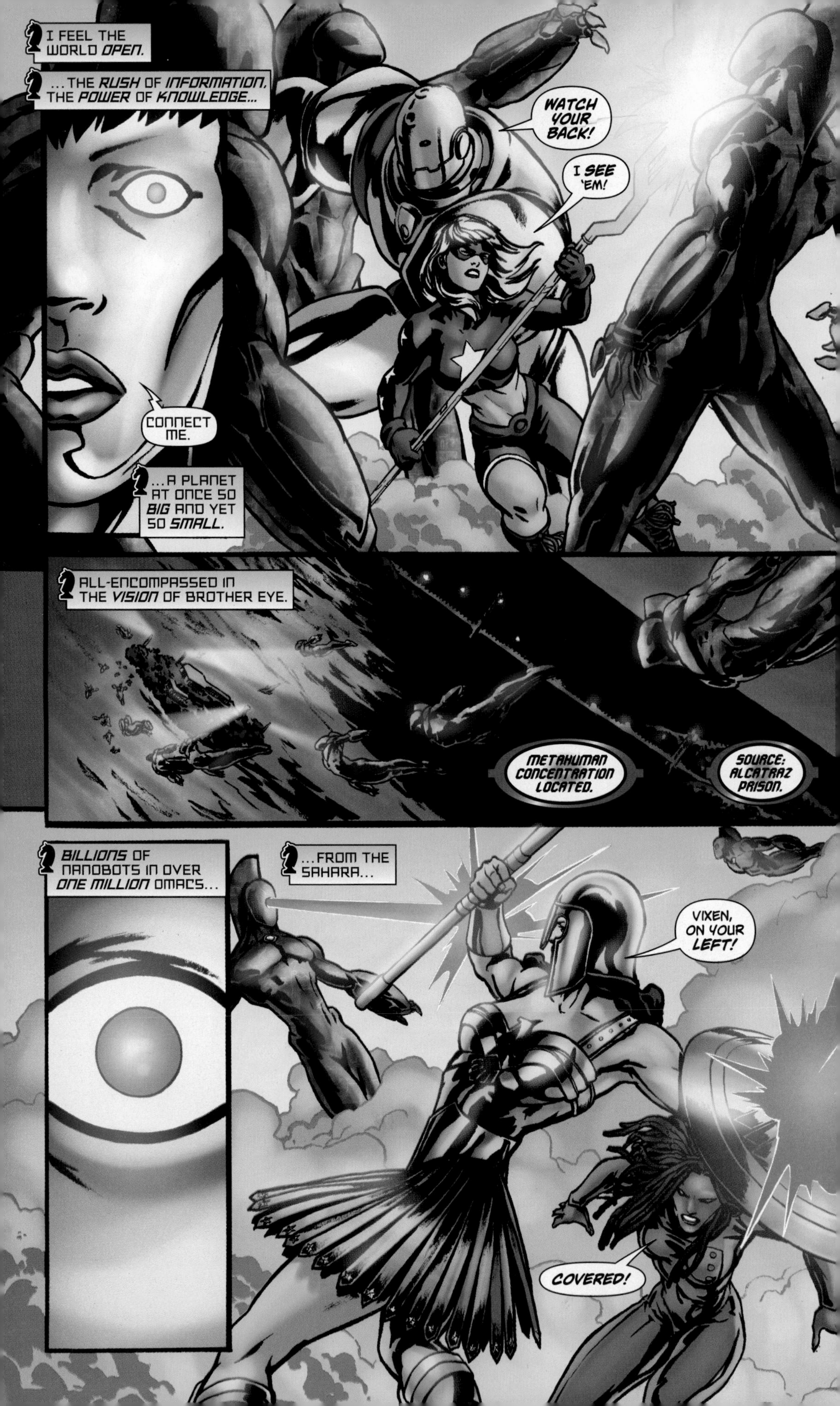

I FEEL THE WORLD OPEN.
...THE RUSH OF INFORMATION, THE POWER OF KNOWLEDGE...
WATCH YOUR BACK!
I SEE 'EM!
CONNECT ME.
...A PLANET AT ONCE SO BIG AND YET SO SMALL.
ALL-ENCOMPASSED IN THE VISION OF BROTHER EYE.
METAHUMAN CONCENTRATION LOCATED.
SOURCE: ALCATRAZ PRISON.
BILLIONS OF NANOBOTS IN OVER ONE MILLION OMACS...
...FROM THE SAHARA...
VIXEN, ON YOUR LEFT!
COVERED!

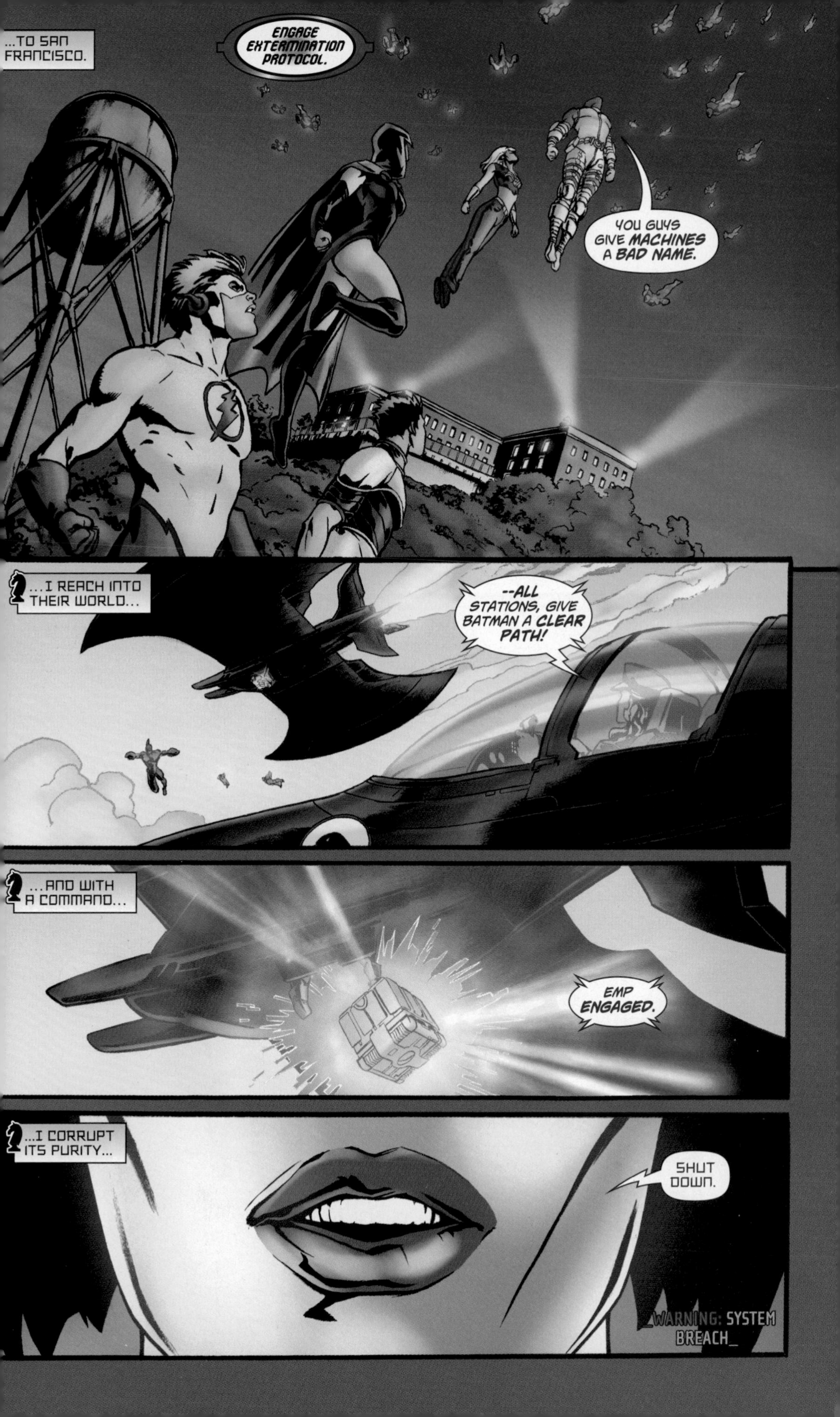
...TO SAN FRANCISCO.
ENGAGE EXTERMINATION PROTOCOL.
YOU GUYS GIVE MACHINES A BAD NAME.
...I REACH INTO THEIR WORLD...
--ALL STATIONS, GIVE BATMAN A CLEAR PATH!
...AND WITH A COMMAND...
EMP ENGAGED.
...I CORRUPT ITS PURITY...
SHUT DOWN.
WARNING: SYSTEM BREACH

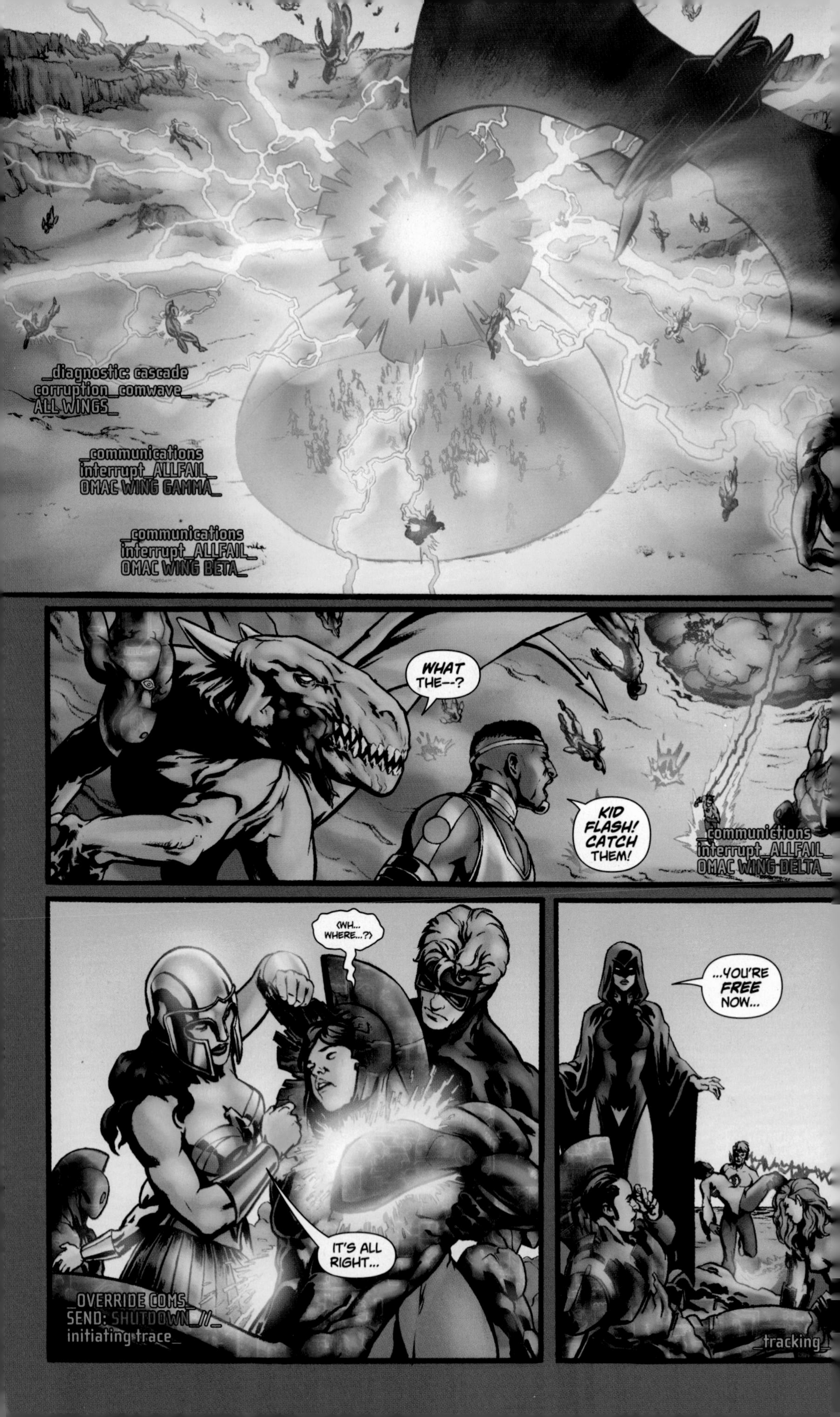
_diagnostic: cascade corruption_comwave_ ALL WINGS_
_communications interrupt_ALLFAIL_ OMAC WING GAMMA_
_communications interrupt_ALLFAIL_ OMAC WING BETA_
WHAT THE--?
KID FLASH! CATCH THEM!
_communictions interrupt_ALLFAIL_ OMAC WING DELTA_
‹WH... WHERE...?›
IT'S ALL RIGHT...
OVERRIDE COMS SEND: SHUTDOWN_//_ initiating trace_
...YOU'RE FREE NOW...
tracking

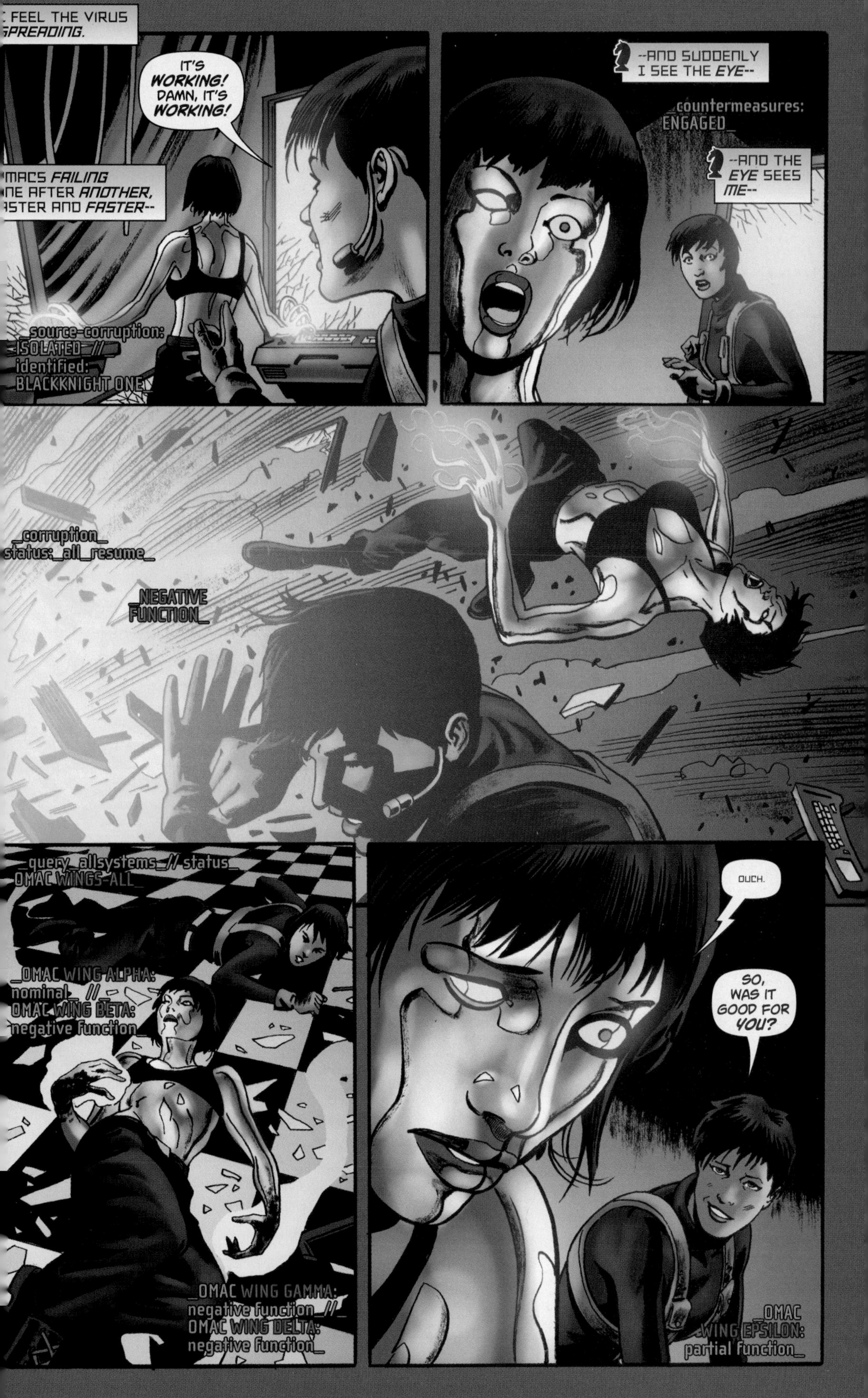

I FEEL THE VIRUS SPREADING.
IT'S WORKING! DAMN, IT'S WORKING!
OMACS FAILING ONE AFTER ANOTHER, FASTER AND FASTER--
source-corruption: ISOLATED//_ identified: BLACKKNIGHT ONE_
--AND SUDDENLY I SEE THE EYE--
countermeasures: ENGAGED
--AND THE EYE SEES ME--
corruption status:_all_resume_
NEGATIVE FUNCTION
_query_allsystems_// status_ OMAC WINGS-ALL_
OMAC WING ALPHA: nominal //_ OMAC WING BETA: negative function_
OMAC WING GAMMA: negative function//_ OMAC WING DELTA: negative function_
OUCH.
SO, WAS IT GOOD FOR YOU?
OMAC WING EPSILON: partial function

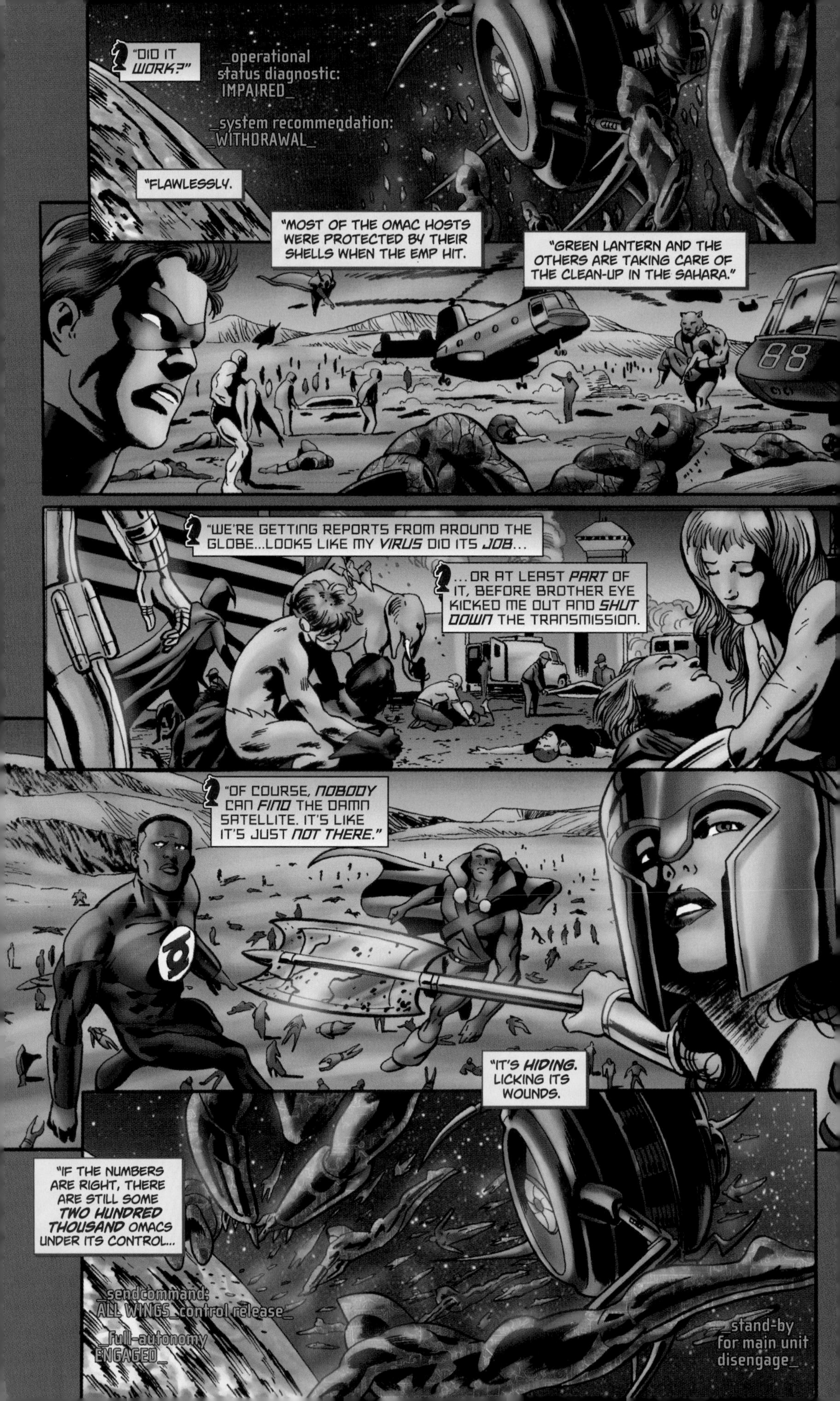
"DID IT WORK?"
operational status diagnostic: IMPAIRED
_system recommendation: _WITHDRAWAL_
"FLAWLESSLY.
"MOST OF THE OMAC HOSTS WERE PROTECTED BY THEIR SHELLS WHEN THE EMP HIT.
"GREEN LANTERN AND THE OTHERS ARE TAKING CARE OF THE CLEAN-UP IN THE SAHARA."
88
"WE'RE GETTING REPORTS FROM AROUND THE GLOBE...LOOKS LIKE MY VIRUS DID ITS JOB...
...OR AT LEAST PART OF IT, BEFORE BROTHER EYE KICKED ME OUT AND SHUT DOWN THE TRANSMISSION.
"OF COURSE, NOBODY CAN FIND THE DAMN SATELLITE. IT'S LIKE IT'S JUST NOT THERE."
"IT'S HIDING. LICKING ITS WOUNDS.
"IF THE NUMBERS ARE RIGHT, THERE ARE STILL SOME TWO HUNDRED THOUSAND OMACS UNDER ITS CONTROL...
_sendcommand: ALL WINGS_control release_
full-autonomy ENGAGED
stand-by for main unit disengage

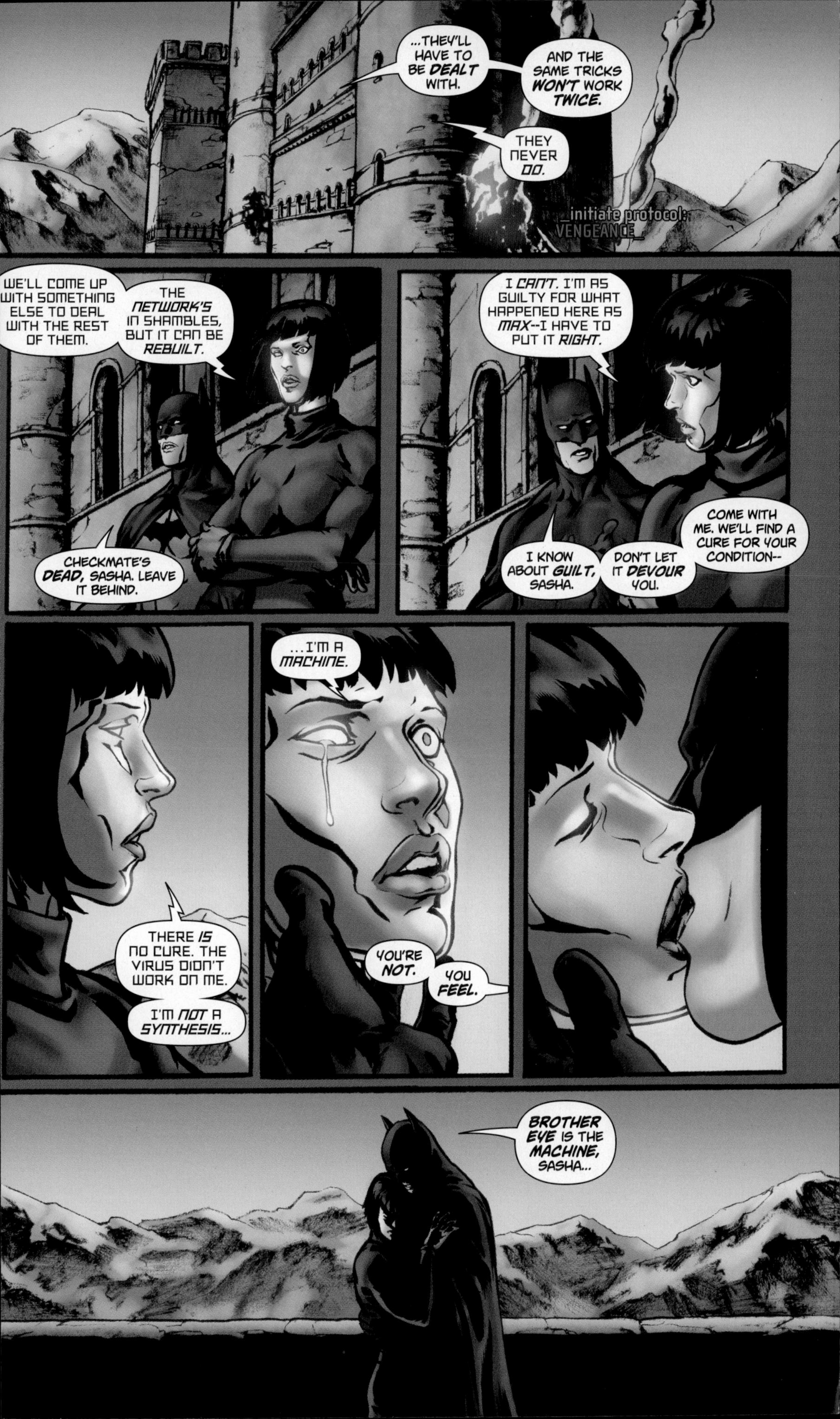
...THEY'LL HAVE TO BE DEALT WITH.
AND THE SAME TRICKS WON'T WORK TWICE.
THEY NEVER DO.
initiate protocol: VENGEANCE
WE'LL COME UP WITH SOMETHING ELSE TO DEAL WITH THE REST OF THEM.
THE NETWORK'S IN SHAMBLES, BUT IT CAN BE REBUILT.
CHECKMATE'S DEAD, SASHA. LEAVE IT BEHIND.
I CAN'T. I'M AS GUILTY FOR WHAT HAPPENED HERE AS MAX--I HAVE TO PUT IT RIGHT.
I KNOW ABOUT GUILT, SASHA.
DON'T LET IT DEVOUR YOU.
COME WITH ME. WE'LL FIND A CURE FOR YOUR CONDITION--
THERE IS NO CURE. THE VIRUS DIDN'T WORK ON ME.
I'M NOT A SYNTHESIS...
...I'M A MACHINE.
YOU'RE NOT.
YOU FEEL.
BROTHER EYE IS THE MACHINE, SASHA...

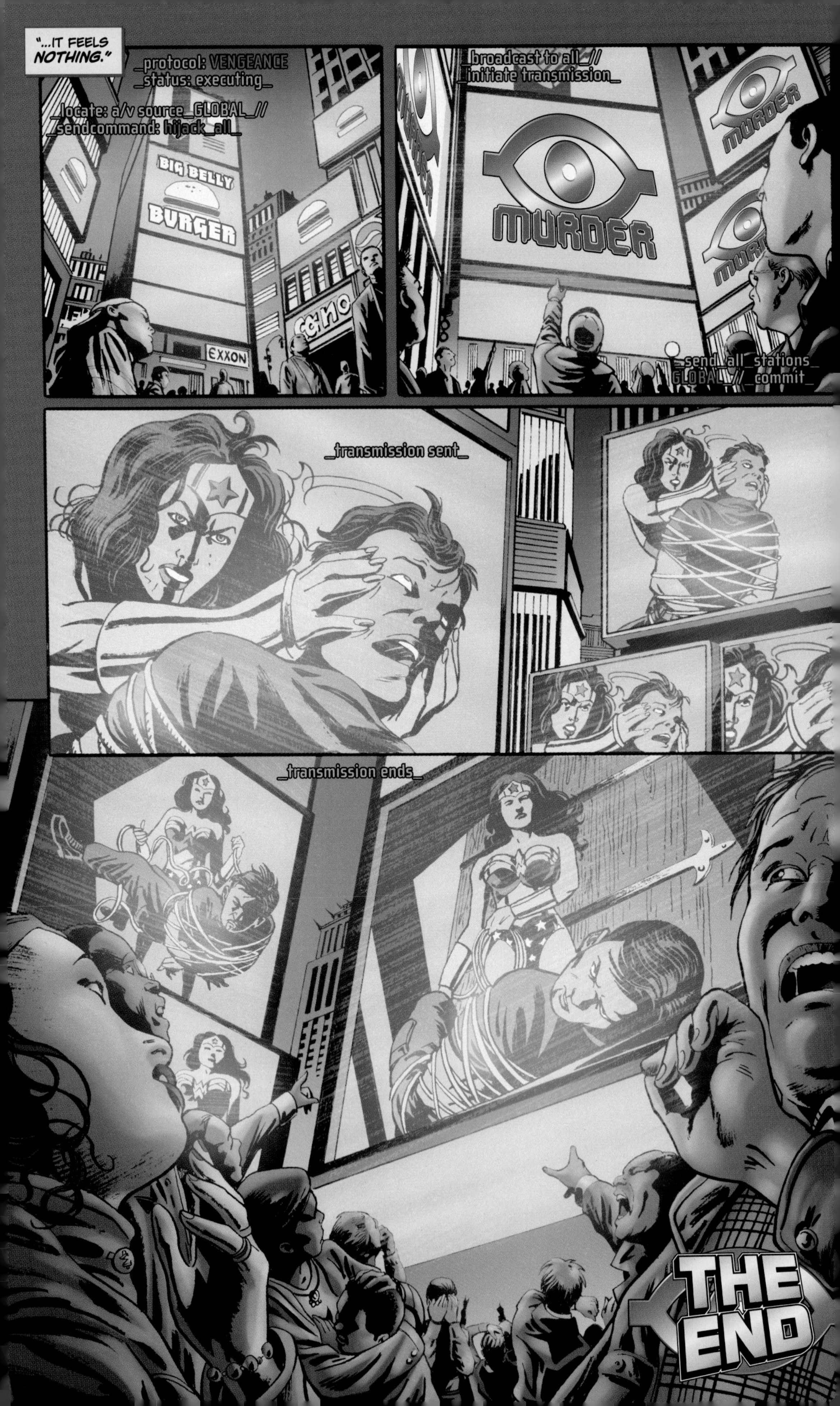
"...IT FEELS NOTHING."
_protocol: VENGEANCE
status: executing
_locate: a/v source_GLOBAL_//
_sendcommand: hijack_all_
BIG BELLY BURGER
EXXON
broadcast to all//
initiate transmission
MURDER
_send_all_stations_
GLOBAL_//_commit_
transmission sent
transmission ends
THE END

DESIGNING THE OMAC PROJECT

Jesus Saiz had a daunting challenge once he accepted the miniseries assignment. He needed to create Brother I and a new, modern-age OMAC, ones that would be instantly recognizable and usable in the years ahead. But he also needed to give a nod towards the original Jack Kirby designs from the early 1970s. What follows are the developmental sketches that Jesus submitted.

VERY GOOD, OMAC. YOU'VE HEARD EVERYTHING I'VE TOLD YOU...
I'VE ALSO USED THE POWERS YOU GAVE ME WHEN I NEEDED THEM... BROTHER EYE...

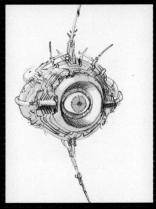

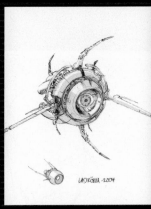

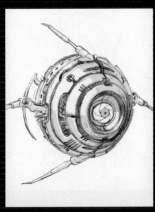

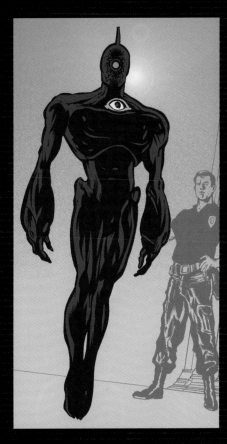

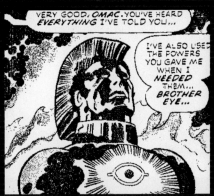

This is how Jack Kirby envisioned Earth's One Man Army Corps.

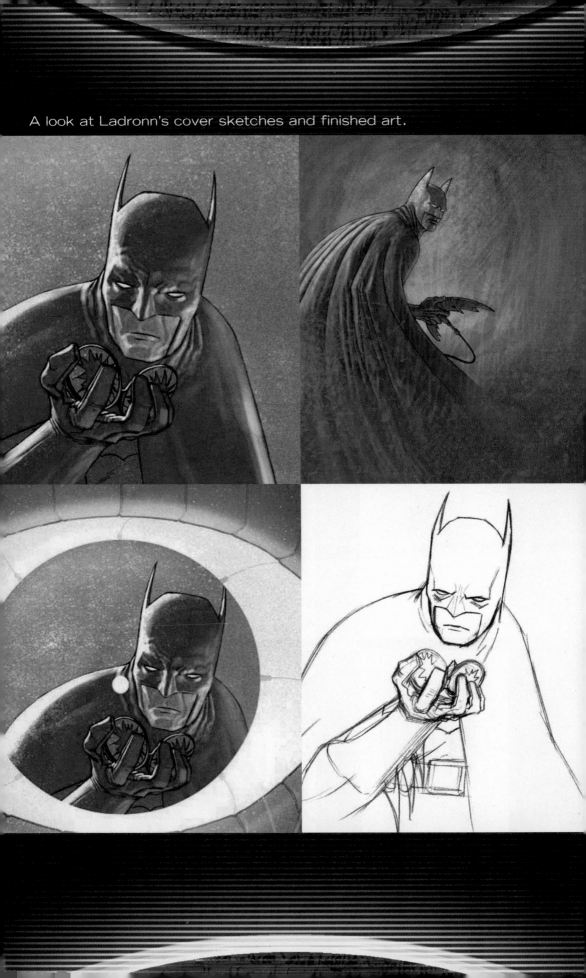

A look at Ladronn's cover sketches and finished art.

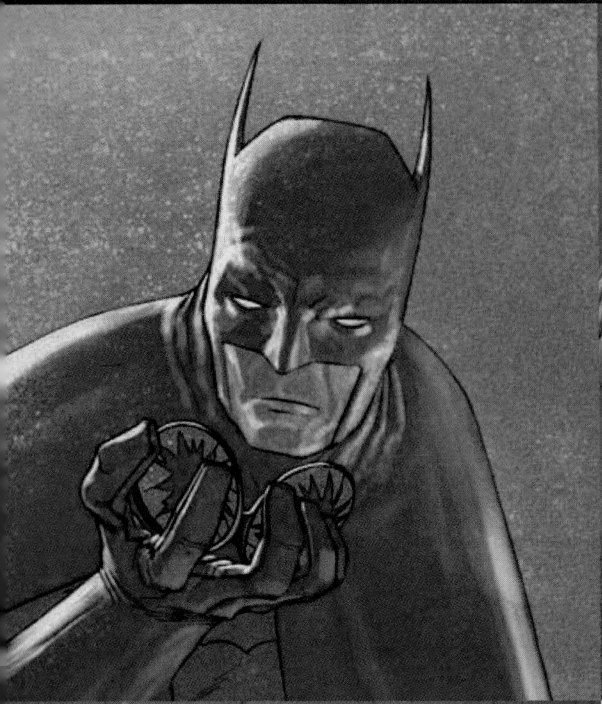

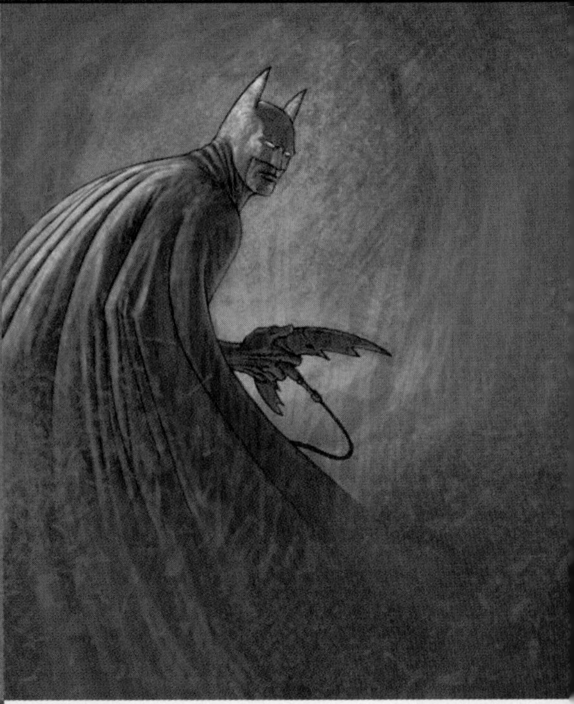

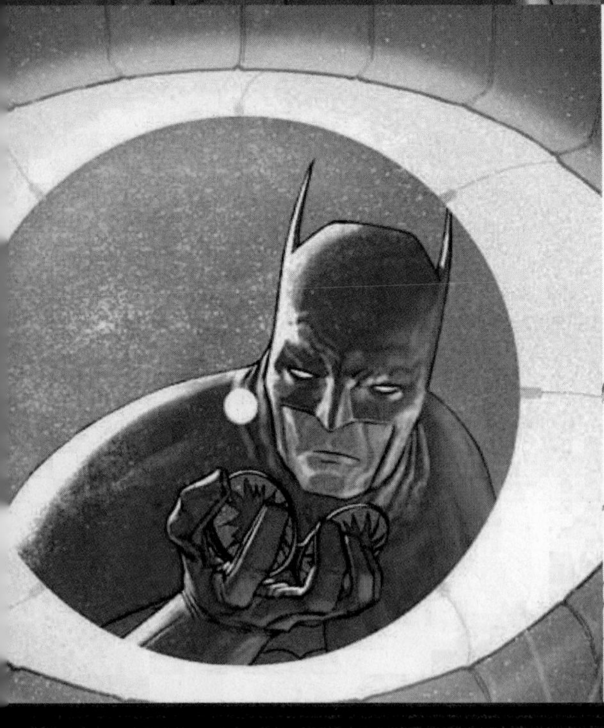

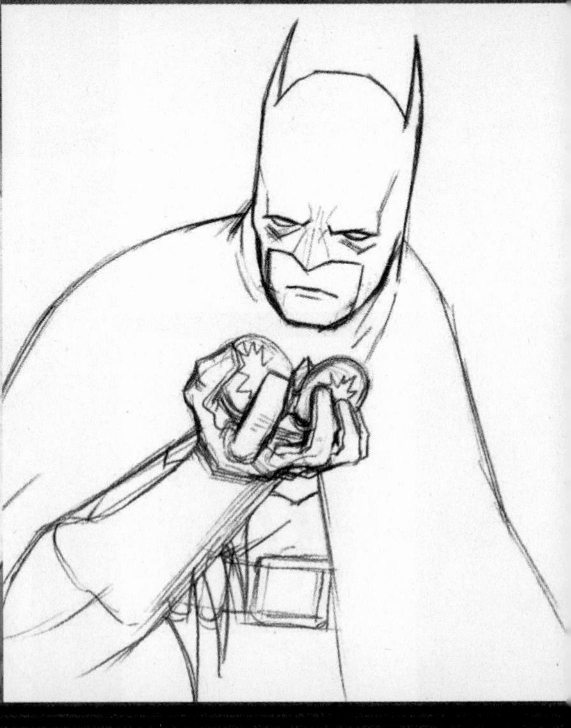

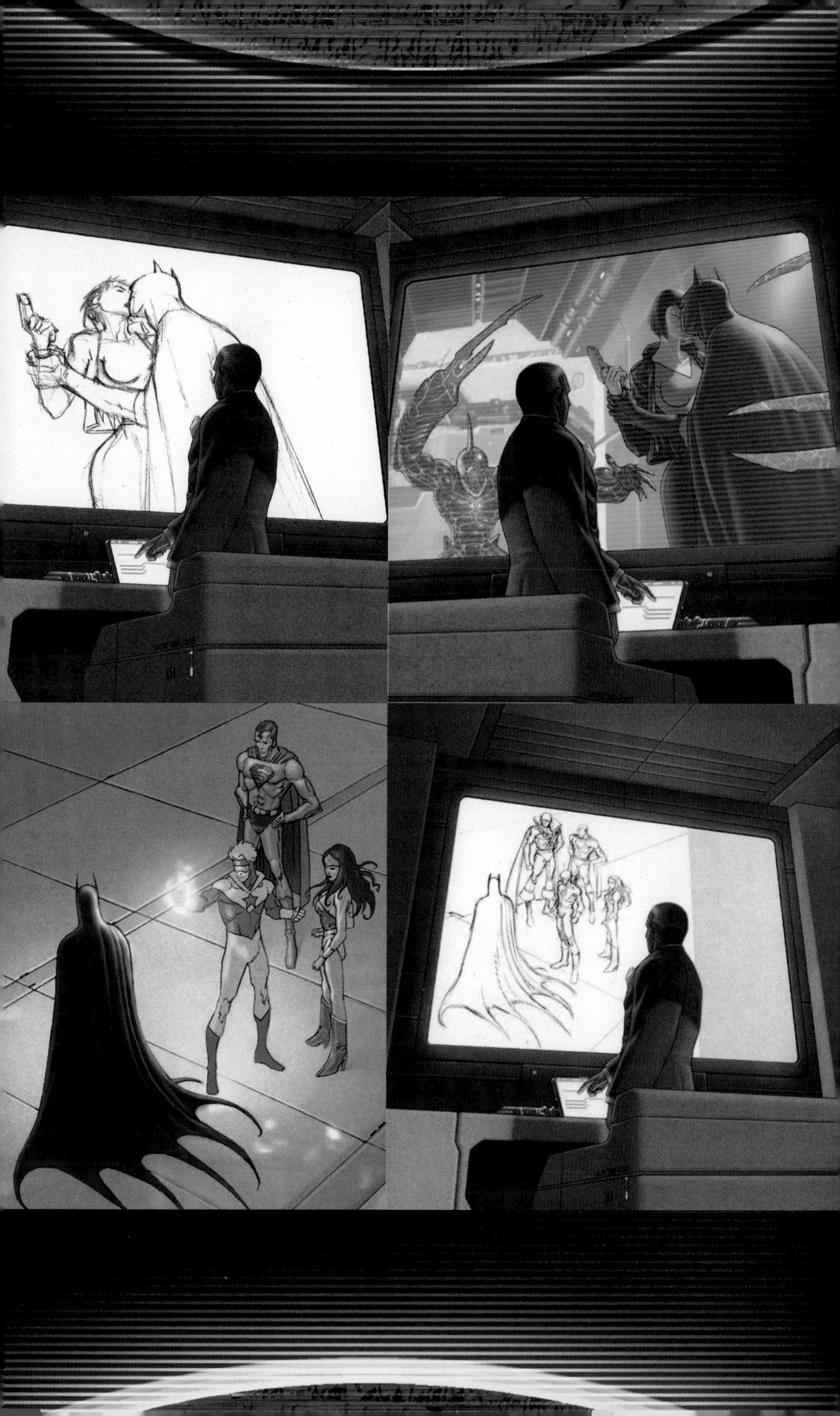

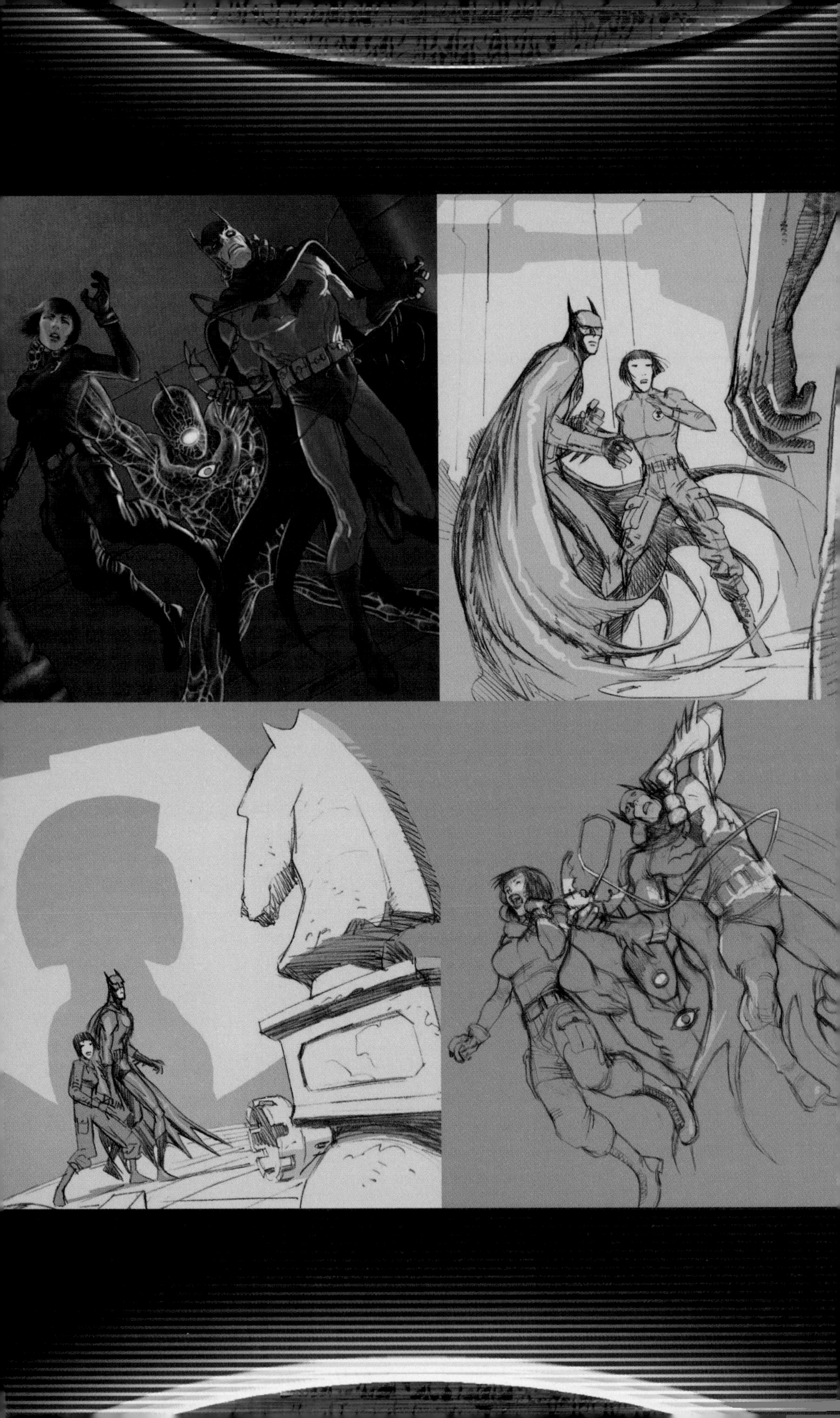

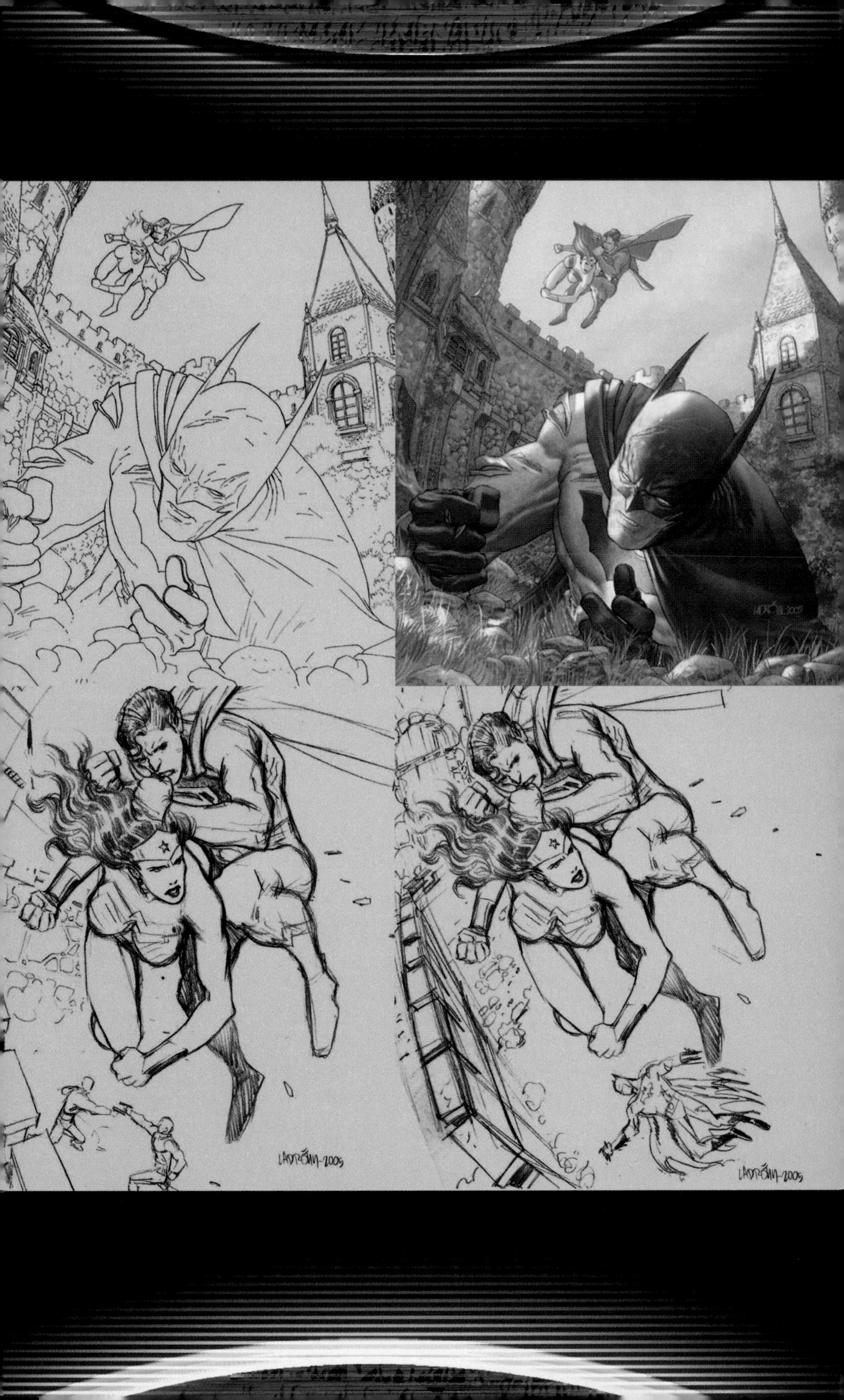
LADRÖNN-2005
LADRÖNN-2005

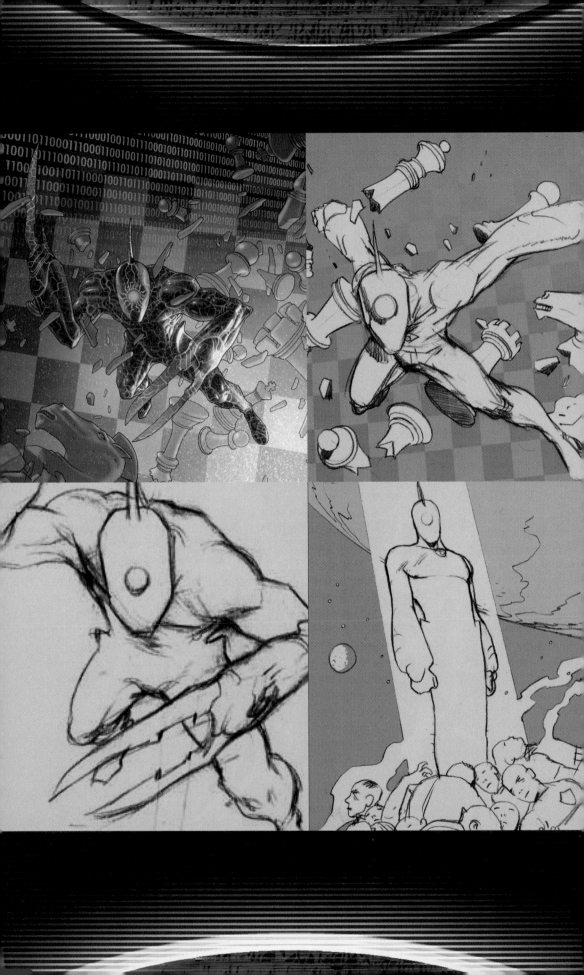

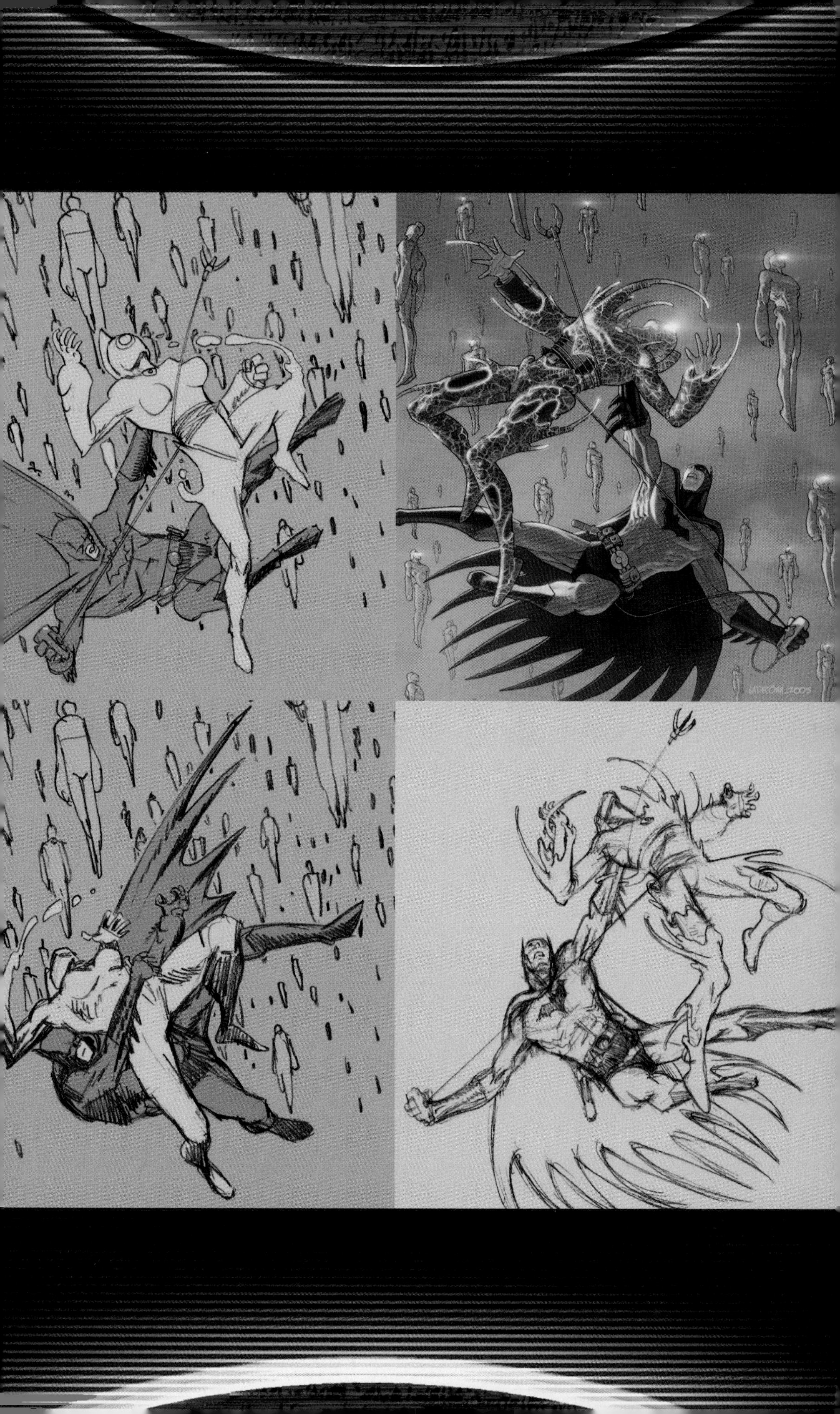

Cover for

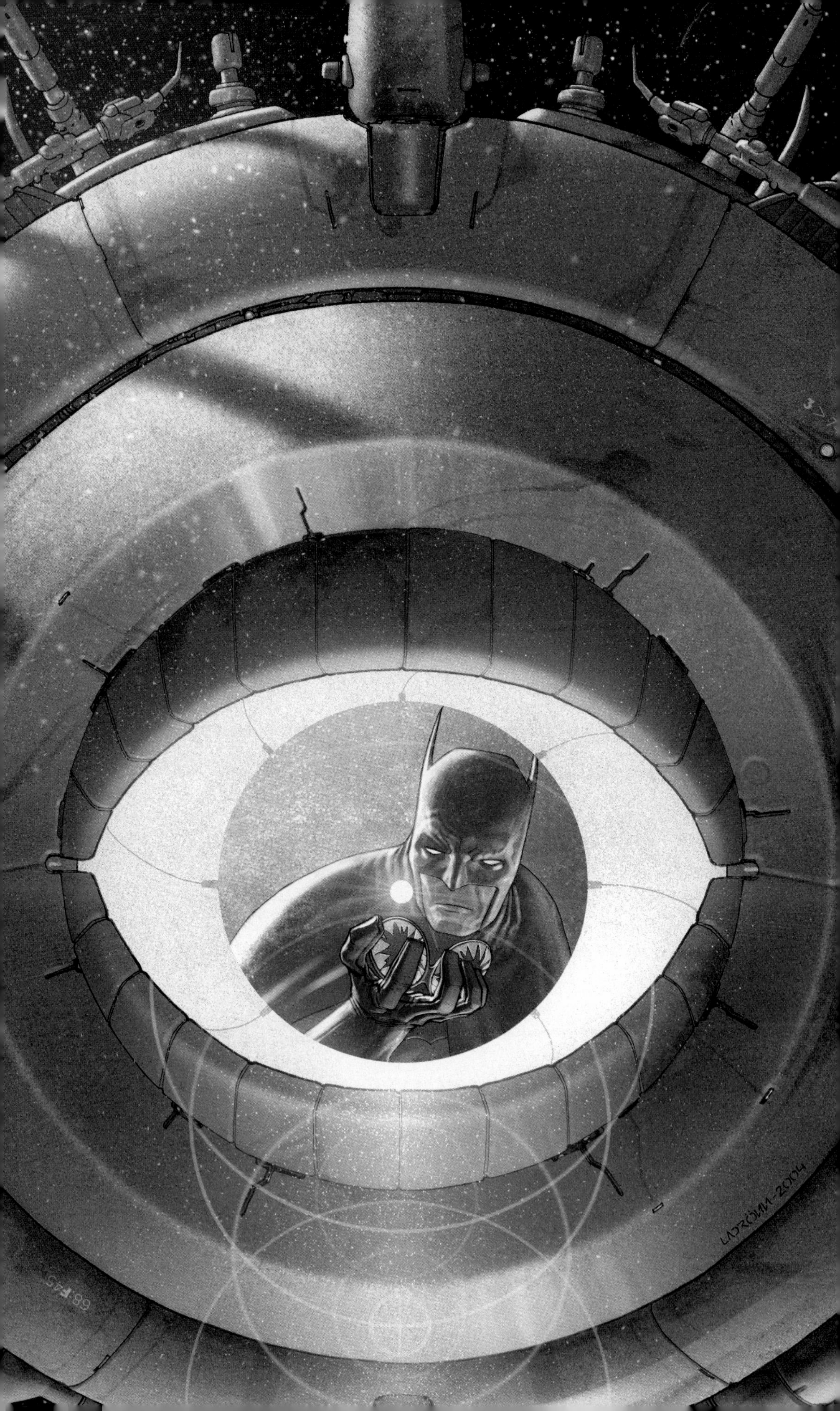

THE COUNTDOWN FROM IDENTITY CRISIS TO INFINITE CRISIS

IDENTITY CRISIS

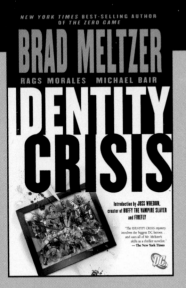

**BRAD MELTZER
RAGS MORALES
MICHAEL BAIR**

THE OMAC PROJECT

**GREG RUCKA
JESUS SAIZ
VARIOUS**

DAY OF VENGEANCE

**BILL WILLINGHAM
JUDD WINICK
IAN CHURCHILL
JUSTINIANO**

AND DON'T MISS THESE OTHER TITLES THAT TIE IN WITH THIS EPIC STORYLINE

VILLAINS UNITED
GAIL SIMONE AND **DALE EAGLESHAM**

RANN/THANAGAR WAR
DAVE GIBBONS, IVAN REIS, MARC CAMPOS AND **VARIOUS**

SUPERMAN: SACRIFICE
VARIOUS

JLA: CRISIS OF CONSCIENCE
GEOFF JOHNS & ALLAN HEINBERG, CHRIS BATISTA AND **MARK FARMER**

SEARCH THE GRAPHIC NOVELS SECTION OF
www.DCCOMICS.com
FOR ART AND INFORMATION ON ALL OF OUR BOOKS!